Design

of the 20th Century

Charlotte & Peter Fiell

KÖLN LONDON MADRID NEW YORK PARIS TOKYO

Front Cover: Alvar Aalto, *Savoy vase*, 1936
Spine: Eero Aarnio, *Ball* or *Globe chair*, 1963–1965

© 1999 Benedikt Taschen Verlag GmbH
Hohenzollernring 53, D–50672 Köln

© 1999 for the works by
Charles & Ray Eames: Eames Office, Venice, CA, www.eamesoffice.com
John Heartfield: The Heartfield Community of Heirs/VG Bild-Kunst, Bonn
Le Corbusier: FLC/VG Bild-Kunst, Bonn
Alphonse Mucha: Mucha Trust/VG Bild-Kunst, Bonn
Man Ray: Man Ray Trust, Paris/VG Bild-Kunst, Bonn

© 1999 for the works by Anni Albers, Josef Albers, André Arbus, Giacomo Balla,
Herbert Bayer, Peter Behrens, Lucian Bernhard, Max Bill, Adolphe Cassandre,
Luigi Castiglioni, Gunnar Cyrén, Raoul Dufy, Jean Dunand, Richard Hamilton,
Victor Horta, Johannes Itten, Wassily Kandinsky, René Lalique, Stig Lindberg, El
Lissitzky, Adolf Loos, Robert Mallet-Stevens, Mariscal, Ludwig Mies van der Rohe,
László Moholy-Nagy, Jean Nouvel, Jacobus Johannes Pieter Oud, Charlotte
Perriand, Jean Prouvé, Eric Ravilious, Richard Riemerschmid, Gerrit Rietveld,
Alexander Rodchenko, Raymond Savignac, Joost Schmidt, Frank Schreiner, Gunta
Stölzl, Nikolai Suetin, Vladimir Tatlin, Theo van Doesburg, Bart van der Leck,
Wilhelm Wagenfeld, Frank Lloyd Wright: VG Bild-Kunst, Bonn

Edited by Susanne Husemann, Cologne
Production: Ute Wachendorf, Cologne
Design: Claudia Frey, Cologne
Cover design: Angelika Taschen, Claudia Frey, Cologne

Printed in Germany
ISBN 3–8228–7039–0

Contents

Throughout the 20th century, design has existed as a major feature of culture and everyday life. Its compass is vast and includes three-dimensional objects, graphic communications and integrated systems from information technology to urban environments. Defined in its most global sense as the conception and planning of all man-made products, design can be seen fundamentally as an instrument for improving the quality of life.

To some extent, the origins of design can be traced to the Industrial Revolution and the birth of mechanized production. Prior to this, objects were craft-produced, meaning that the conception and realization of an object was most often undertaken by an individual creator. With the advent of new industrial manufacturing processes and the division of labour, design (conception and planning) was separated from making. At this time, however, design was viewed as just one of the many interrelated aspects of mechanized production. The forethought that went into design had no intellectual, theoretical or philosophic foundation and so had little positive impact on the nature of the industrial process or on society. Modern design can be seen to have evolved from 19th-century design reformers, and in particular from **William Morris**, who attempted to unite theory with practice. While this endeavour was largely unsuccessful due to the craft-based means of production used by Morris, his reforming ideas had a fundamental impact on the development of the **Modern Movement**. It was not until the early 20th century, when individuals such as **Walter Gropius** integrated design theory with practice through new industrial means of production, that modern design truly came into being. In an attempt to bridge the gulf between the social idealism and commercial reality that had existed up to the end of the First World War and to promote an appropriate response to the emerging technological culture, Gropius founded the **Bauhaus** in 1919. The goal of modern design, as pioneered and taught at the Bauhaus, was to produce work that unified intellectual, practical, commercial and aesthetic concerns through artistic endeavour and the exploitation of new technologies. While the Bauhaus advanced important new ways of thinking about design, it developed only some of the ideas necessary for the successful integration of design theory with the industrial process. The principles forged there were later developed at the New Bauhaus in Chicago, which was founded by **László Moholy-Nagy** in 1937, and at the **Hochschule für Gestaltung, Ulm**, which was founded in 1953. Both these teaching institutions made important contributions to new thinking about the unification of design theory and practice in relation to industrial methods of production.

Throughout the 20th century, the products, styles, theories and philosophies of design have become evermore diverse. This is due in large part to the growing complexity of the design process. Increasingly in design for industrial production, the relationship between conception, planning and making is fragmented and complicated by a series of interlinked specialized activities involving many different individuals, such as model makers, market researchers, materials specialists, engineers and production technicians. The products of design that result from this multi-faceted process are not the outcome of individual designers, but the outcome of teams of individuals, all of whom have their own ideas and attitudes about how things should be. The historic plurality of design in the 20th century, however, is also due to changing patterns of consumption, changing taste, the differing commercial and moral imperatives of inventors/designers/makers, technological progress, and varying national tendencies in design.

In the study of design history, it is important to remember that the products of design cannot be fully understood outside of the social, economic, political, cultural and technological contexts that gave rise to their conception and realization. At different times in the 20th century, for example, the economic cycles of Western economies have had a significant impact on the prevalence of objects that emphasize design over styling – and vice versa. While styling is often a complementary element of a design solution, design and styling are completely distinct disciplines. Styling is concerned with surface treatment and appearance – the expressive qualities of a product. Design, on the other hand, is primarily concerned with problem solving – it tends to be holistic in its scope and generally seeks simplification and essentiality. During economic downturns, **Functionalism** (design) tends to come to the fore while in periods of economic prosperity, anti-rationalism (styling) is apt to flourish.

Increasingly throughout the 20th century, the interests of businesses to create competitive products have driven the evolution and diversity of design as well as the careers of individual designers. While some designers work within corporate structures, others work in consultancies or independently. Many independent designers choose to operate outside of the constraints of the industrial process, preferring to produce work that is mainly concerned with self-expression. Design is not only a process linked to mechanized production, it is a means of conveying persuasive ideas, attitudes and values about how things could or should be according to individual, corporate, institutional or national objectives. As a channel of communication between people, design provides a particular insight into the character and thinking of the designer and his/her beliefs about what is important in the relationship between the object (design solution), the user/consumer, and the design process and society. To this extent, this book

"design … is a manifestation of the capacity of the human spirit to transcend its limitations."
George Nelson,
The Problems of Design, 1957

does not promote a single unifying theory of design or ideology. Rather, its aim is to highlight the pluralistic nature of design and the idea that, historically, design can be viewed as a debate between conflicting opinions about such issues as the role of technology and the industrial process, the primacy of utility, simplicity and affordability over luxury and exclusivity, and the role of function, aesthetics, ornament and symbolism in practical objects for use.

This survey of design in the 20th century features those concepts, styles, movements, designers, schools, companies and institutions that have shaped the course of design theory and practice, or have advanced the development of innovative forms, materials applications, technical means and processes, or have influenced taste, the history of style in the applied and decorative arts, and culture and society in general. The areas of activity covered include: furniture, product, textile, glass, ceramic, metalware and graphic design, with interior design and architecture receiving only occasional mention. While a certain amount of industrial design has also been included, a companion book, entitled *Industrial Design*, will be dedicated to this broad field of study, which will encompass among other things the realms of transport, military, medical, heavy industrial, sports and safety-equipment design.

The geographic area covered by this book has been limited to mainly Europe and North America, with a few outlying countries. While the scope of the book's subject demands selectivity, it is hoped that those entries chosen for inclusion will be seen as broadly representative of the many different currents in thinking and approaches to design over the last hundred years. The entries have been laid out alphabetically with cross-references appearing in the text in bold type so as to reveal the many illuminating interrelationships between designers, schools, manufacturers, movements and styles. A time-line at the back of the book also shows the historical overlapping of styles and movements. The book sets out to provide as much factual information as the constraints of space allow. In the occasional instances where opinions and unconscious displays of bias have invariably crept in, it is hoped that these will be recognized as such.

Through highlighting the diverse nature of design, a further aim of this book is to demonstrate that the attitudes, ideas and values communicated by designers and manufacturers are not absolute, but are conditional and fluctuate. Design solutions to even the most straightforward of problems are inherently ephemeral as the needs and concerns of designers, manufacturers and society change. Perhaps the most significant reason for diversity in design, however, is the general belief that, despite the authority and success of particular design solutions, there is always a better way of doing things.

Catalogue

Aalto to Zsolnay

Alvar Aalto · Eero Aarnio · AEG · Aesthetic Movement · Agitprop · Otl Aicher · Anni Alber
Josef Albers · Franco Albini · Don Albinson · Studio Alchimia · Alessi · Emilio Ambasz · An
Design · Ron Arad · Junichi Arai · André Arbus · Archizoom Associati · Art Deco · Art Nouvea
Artemide · Arts & Crafts Movement (GB & USA) · Charles Robert Ashbee · Erik Gunn
Asplund · Sergio Asti · Gae Aulenti · Avant-garde · Mackay Hugh Baillie Scott · Giacomo Ball
Ercole Barovier · Saul Bass · Helmut Bätzner · Bauhaus · Hans Theo Baumann · Herbert Bay
· BBPR · Aubrey Beardsley · Henry Beck · Peter Behrens · Mario Bellini · Ward Bennett · S.
Benson's · Hendrik Petrus Berlage · Lucian Bernhard · Harry Bertoia · Fulvio Bianconi · Max E
· Siegfried Bing · Biomorphism · Misha Black · Mariani Cini Boeri · Theodor Bogler · Osvald
Borsani · Mario Botta · Marianne Brandt · Andrea Branzi · Braun · Marcel Breuer · Neville Bro
· Carlo Bugatti · California New Wave · George Carwardine · A. M. Cassandre · Anna Caste
Ferrieri · Livio, Pier Giacomo & Achille Castiglioni · Wendell Castle · Don Chadwick · Pier
Chareau · Serge Ivan Chermayeff · Chermayeff & Geisman · Pietro Chiesa · Antonio Citterio
Clarice Cliff · Nigel Coates · Wells Coates · Luigi Colani · Gino Colombini · Joe Colombo
Compasso d'Oro · Terence Conran · Constructivism · Coop Himmelb(l)au · Hans Coper · Ha
Coray · Corporate Identity · Craft Revival · Cranbrook Academy of Art · Walter Crane · Riccard
Dalisi · Darmstädter Künstlerkolonie · Daum Frères · Lucienne Day · Robin Day · Georges
Feure · Michele De Lucchi · William De Morgan · De Pas, D'Urbino & Lomazzi · De Stij
Deconstructivism · Paolo Deganello · Christian Dell · Donald Deskey · Desny · Deutsch
Werkbund · Erich Dieckmann · Niels Diffrient · Nanna Ditzel · Tom Dixon · Dresden
Werkstätten für Handwerkskunst · Christopher Dresser · Henry Dreyfuss · Nathalie
Pasquier · Raoul Dufy · Charles & Ray Eames · Charles Eastlake · Tom Eckersley · Ot
Eckmann · École de Nancy · Egon Eiermann · Jan Eisenloeffel · Harvey Ellis · August Ende
Ergonomi Design Gruppen · L. M. Ericsson · Hartmut Esslinger · Willy Fleckhaus · Paul Follo
Piero Fornasetti · Norman Foster · Kaj Franck · Jean-Michel Frank · Josef Frank · Paul Theodo
Frankl · Marguerite Friedlaender-Wildenhain · Frogdesign · Adrian Frutiger · Richa
Buckminster Fuller · Functionalism · Futurism · Eugène Gaillard · Émile Gallé · Abram Games
Garouste & Bonetti · Malcolm Garrett · Antonio Gaudí y Cornet · Norman Bel Geddes · Fra
O. Gehry · Gesamtkunstwerk · Eric Gill · Ernest Gimson · Stefano Giovannoni · Alexand
Hayden Girard · Giorgetto Giugiaro · Milton Glaser · Glasgow School · Global Tools · Edwa
William Godwin · William Golden · Good Design · Kenneth Grange · Michael Graves · Eile
Gray · Green Design · Greene & Greene · Vittorio Gregotti · April Greiman · Walter Gropius
William H. Grueby · Gruppo Strum · Hans Gugelot · Guild of Handicraft · Hector Guimard
Werkstätten Hagenauer · Ambrose Heal · John Heartfield · Jean Heiberg · Poul Henningsen
Frederick Henri Kay Henrion · René Herbst · Herman Miller · High-Tech · Matthew Hilton
Hochschule für Gestaltung, Ulm · Josef Hoffmann · Hans Hollein · Victor Horta · Vilmo
Huszár · Independant Group · Institute of Design, Chicago · International Style · Massimo Ios
Ghini · Paul Iribe · Maija Isola · Arata Isozaki · Johannes Itten · Arne Jacobsen · Jacob Jacobsen
Pierre Jeanneret · Charles A. Jencks · Georg Jensen · Jakob Jensen · Philip Johnson · Jugendstil
Finn Juhl · Wilhelm Kåge · Kartell · Edward McKnight Kauffer · Frederick Kiesler · King-Mirand
· Rodney Kinsman · Toshiyuki Kita · Kitsch · Poul Kjaerholm · Kaare Klint · Knoll International

Hugo Alvar Hendrik Aalto studied architecture at the Helsingin Teknilien Korkeakoulu, Helsinki from 1916 to 1921. For the next two years, he worked as an exhibition designer and travelled extensively in central Europe, Italy and Scandinavia. In 1923, he established his own architectural office in Jyväskyla, which later moved to Turku (1927–1933) and then Helsinki (1933–1976). In 1924, he married the designer, Aino Marsio (1894–1949) and for five years they conducted experiments together into the bending of wood. This research led to Aalto's revolutionary chair designs of the 1930s. In 1929, he co-designed an exhibition to celebrate Turku's 700th anniversary – his first complete and Modern structure for Scandinavian public display. His most celebrated architectural projects were his own house in Turku (1927), which is generally regarded as one of the first expressions of Scandi-navian Modernism, the Viipuri Library (1927–1935), the Paimio Tuberculosis Sanatorium (1929–1933) and the Finnish Pavilion for the New York World's Fair (1939).

Having turned to laminated wood and plywood as his materials of choice in 1929, Aalto began investigating veneer bonding and the limits of moulding plywood with Otto Korhonen, the technical director of a furniture factory near Turku. These experiments resulted in Aalto's most technically innova-tive chairs, the *No. 41* (1931–1932) and the cantilevered *No. 31* (1932), both of

Alvar Aalto

1898 Kuortane, Finland
1976 Helsinki

◄◄ *Model No. 3031 Savoy* vase for Karhula (later manufactured by Iittala), 1936

◄ *Model No. 41 Paimio* chair for Huonekalu-ja Rakennustyötehdas (later manufactured by Artek), 1930–1931

▲ *Model No. 31* armchair for
Huonekalu-ja Rakennustyötehdas
(later manufactured by Artek),
1930–1931

▲ *Model No. 98* tea trolley for Artek, 1935–1936

which were designed contemporaneously with or as part of the Paimio Sanatorium scheme. These designs signalled to the international avant-garde a new trend in materials towards plywood and established Aalto as one of the pre-eminent designers this century. The sales success of his furniture designs, such as the *L-legged* stacking stools (1933), led Aalto and his wife to form the manufacturing company Artek in 1935.

Aalto believed that his most important contribution to furniture design was his solving of the age-old problem of connecting vertical and horizontal elements. His bentwood solution developed in conjunction with Korhonen, which Aalto dubbed "the little sister of the architectonic column", allowed legs to be attached directly to the underside of a seat without the need for any framework or additional support. This novel technique gave rise to his series of *L-leg* (1932–1933), *Y-leg* (1946–1947) and *fan-leg* (1954) furniture. Aalto's designs are notably characterized by the use of organic forms, for example, his famous *Savoy* vase of 1937. Originally entitled "Eskimoerindens skinnbuxa" (Eskimo woman's leather trousers) and manufactured by Iittala, the *Savoy* vase is said to have been inspired by the fjord shorelines of his native Finland. Aalto strongly believed that design should

▲ *Model No. 60* stools for Huonekalu-ja Rakennustyötehdas (later manufactured by Artek), 1933

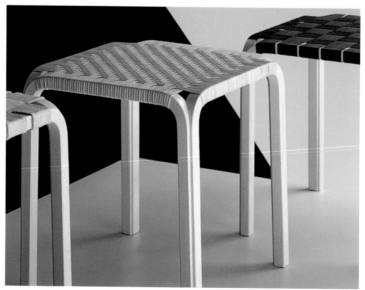

▶ *Y-leg* stools for Artek, 1946–1947

be humanizing and he rejected man-made materials such as tubular metal in furniture, because, for him, they were unsatisfactory to the human condition.

Aalto's work was very well received in Britain and America during the 1930s and 1940s and, as one of the founding fathers of **Organic Design**, his design philosophy was highly influential to post-war designers such as **Charles and Ray Eames**. As an early opponent of the **Modern Movement**'s alienating machine aesthetic and rigidly rationalist approach to design, Aalto stated: "The best standardization committee in the world is nature herself, but in nature standardization occurs mainly in connection with the smallest possible units, cells. The result is millions of flexible combinations in which one never encounters the stereotyped." (cited in Andrei Gozak, *Alvar Aalto vs. the Modern Movement*, Helsinki 1981, p. 78)

Aalto believed that design should not only acknowledge functional requirements but should also address the psychological needs of the user and that this was best achieved through the use of natural materials and especially wood, which he described as "the form inspiring, deeply human material" (Göran Schildt, *Alvar Aalto Sketches*, Cambridge, Mass. 1987, p. 77). Aalto's pioneering organic designs not only provided a new vocabulary of form, they also eloquently represented, to the general public, the acceptable face of Modernism.

▼ *Models No. X601 & X600 fan-leg stools for Artek, 1954*

In 1952, he married the architect Elissa Mäkiniemi, with whom he collaborated until his death. Aalto's life and work was celebrated by the **Museum of Modern Art, New York** through three exhibitions held in 1938, 1984 and 1997.

▲ *Ball* or *Globe* chair
for Asko, 1963–1965

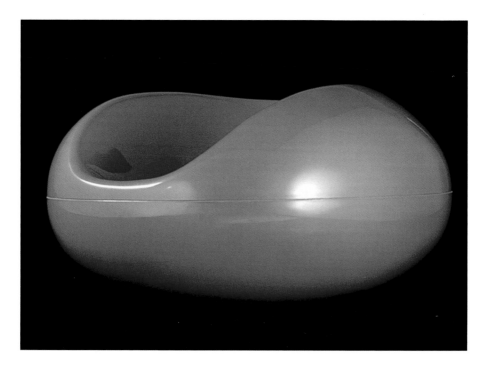

Eero Aarnio studied at the Institute of Industrial Arts, Helsinki, graduating in 1957. He established his own design office in 1962 and has since worked primarily as an interior and industrial designer, although he has also been active as a photographer and graphic designer. Initially, he designed furniture in natural materials, which employed handcraft techniques, as in his *Jattujakkare* wicker stool. During the 1960s, he began experimenting with fibreglass, which led to his best-known series of designs including the *Ball* or *Globe* chair (1963–1965) and the *Pastille* chair (1967–1968), for which he won an AID (Associazione per il Disegno Industriale) award in 1968. These bold iconoclastic seating solutions, which also included the perspex hanging *Bubble* chair (1968), captured the spirit of the 1960s with their visually exciting space-age forms. Aarnio did not, however, embrace Pop culture's ethos of ephemerality and disposability. His designs possess both an internationalism and an individualism while retaining a traditional Scandinavian concern for quality and durability. Aarnio looks forward optimistically to a time when "the personal approach of the past and the robot manufacture of the future clasp hands" (A. Lee Morgan, *Contemporary Designers*, London, 1985, p. 10).

Eero Aarnio
b. 1932 *Helsinki*

▲ *Pastille* chair for Asko, 1967–1968

AEG

Founded 1883
Berlin

After seeing Thomas Edison's light bulb at the "Exposition Internationale d'Electricité" in Paris in 1881, Emil Rathenau (1838–1915) acquired the patent licence and in 1883 founded the Deutsche Edison Gesellschaft (German Edison Company for Applied Electricity), known as DEG. The company was later renamed the Allgemeine Elektrizitäts Gesellschaft or AEG and the Jugendstil designer **Otto Eckmann** was employed to design its catalogue for the 1900 Paris "Exposition Universelle".

In 1907, AEG appointed the architect and designer **Peter Behrens** artistic director, with the task of creating the first wholly integrated corporate identity for the company. In achieving this, Behrens not only changed AEG's logo, but went on to design a unified range of electrical goods such as kettles, clocks and fans as well as the factory buildings required for the production of these products.

▲ **Peter Behrens,**
Design for the AEG turbine hall in Berlin, 1908

► **Peter Behrens,**
Light fixtures for AEG, c. 1908

AEG's production engineer Michael von Dolivo-Dobrowolsky realized that the key to the successful mass-production of high quality goods lay in the

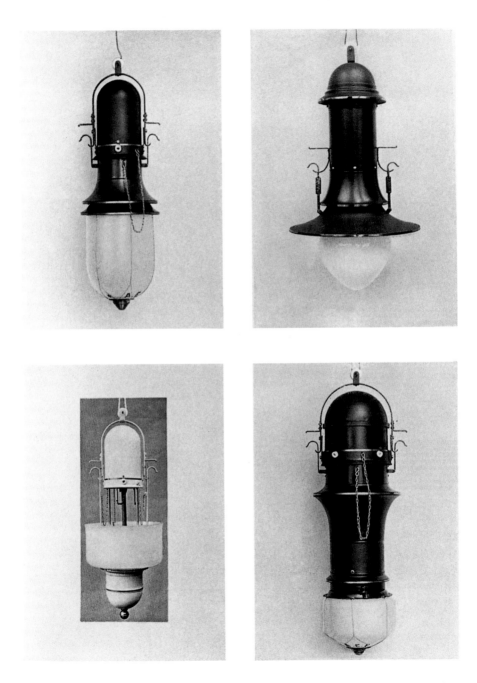

standardization of interchangeable components, which would allow them to be used for several products rather than just one. This type of product standardization and the modern methods of manufacture employed by AEG reflected the ideals of the **Deutscher Werkbund**, which Behrens had co-founded in 1907.

Today, AEG is a large design-oriented manufacturing company that is primarily known for its high quality white goods and electrical products.

Aesthetic Movement

Great Britain

▼ Thomas Jeckyll,
Sunflower and iron
for Barnard, Bishop
& Barnard, c. 1880

The Aesthetic Movement evolved out of a previous art movement in Britain, which had combined the Gothic and Queen Anne Revivals. These earlier styles were interwoven with Eastern influences, by Bruce Talbert (1838–1881) and Thomas Jeckyll (1827–1881) among others, so as to create a hybrid Anglo-Oriental style. Inspired by Japanese woodcuts as well as the Oriental and Middle Eastern wares imported by companies such as **Liberty & Co.**, Aesthetic Movement designers, including **E. W. Godwin** and **Christopher Dresser**, sought to reform design by adopting pure uncluttered lines. Aes-

theticism became a "life-style" choice for the progressive middle classes, such as those residing in Bedford Park in West London, and Liberty & Co. disseminated the style not only through their household furnishings but also through the marketing of loose and flowing Aesthetic clothes for women. James Abbot McNeill Whistler (1804–1903) and Thomas Jeckyll's "Peacock Room" for F. R. Leyland's London residence (1876–1877) – now in the Freer Gallery, Washington – shows the Aesthetic Movement at its most exotic. The greatest proponents of Aestheticism were undoubtedly Oscar Wilde (1854–1900) and **Aubrey Beardsley** who glorified the doctrine of "art for art's sake" in the heady *fin-de-siècle* era. The Aesthetic Movement, which was symbolized by the sunflower motif, also manifested itself in the United States, most notably in the work of the Herter Brothers and **Louis Comfort Tiffany**, and in France in the work of **François-Eugène Rousseau**. The Aesthetic Movement had some influence on two quite separate design movements: **Art Nouveau** through its use of motifs taken from nature and the Modern Movement through its adoption of abstracted Japanese forms.

▶ **Sergei Vasilievich Chekhonin**, Propaganda plate for the State Porcelain Factory in Petrograd, 1919

Agitprop

Russia

The term Agitprop derives from the Russian phrase *agitatsiya propaganda* – "agitation propaganda" – that was put forth by Vladimir I. Lenin as an as- pect of Communist doctrine in which the strategies of agitation and propa- ganda were blended to achieve political victory. Agitation was defined as the use of political slogans and half-truths to stir the masses into confronting their grievances, while propaganda was defined as the promotion of histor- ical and scientific arguments to politically sway the intelligentsia. Following the Russian revolution in 1917, the Communist Party set up the *Agitprobyuro* (Bureau of Agitation and Propaganda) for the development of state-spon- sored Soviet art and design, which subsequently became known as Agit- prop. Using pre-Revolution blanks, designers such as Sergei Vasilievich Chekhonin (1878–1936), **Kasimir Malevich**, Maria Vasilievna Lebedeva (1895–1942) and Nikolai Suetin decorated porcelain with slogans and motifs found on political posters and rally decorations. For the Revolution's first anniversary, Futurist Agitprop buildings and monuments were designed by Natan Altman (1889–1970) for St. Peterburg's Uritskii Square. A year later, in 1919, Vasilii Ermilov (1884–1968) took part in several Agitprop projects for posters, train decorations and interiors of clubs. Agitprop was intended to drum up popular support for the Revolution, and its grandiose schemes, such as **Vladimir Tatlin**'s famous Constructivist structure *Pamiatnik III emu Internatsionalu* (Monument to the Third International) of 1919–1920 in Pet- rograd, reflected the desire for a new world order.

Otl Aicher studied sculpture at the Akademie der Bildenden Künste, Munich from 1946 to 1947 before setting up his own graphics studio in 1948 in Ulm, which was moved to Munich in 1967 and Rotis, Allgäu in 1972. During the 1950s, working alongside **Hans Gugelot** and **Dieter Rams**, Aicher formulated a coherent and rational design aesthetic for Braun. From 1949 to 1954, he was involved in the founding and development of the **Hochschule für Gestaltung, Ulm** – the most influential post-war German design school. In 1952, he married a co-founder of the school, Inge Scholl, and from 1954 to 1965 he lectured in the visual communications department at Ulm and was a visiting lecturer at Yale University. He subsequently held the directorship of the Hochschule für Gestaltung from 1962 to 1964 and his teachings and writings on design theory were notable for their advancement of Utopian ideals and, ultimately, **Radical Design**. Although Aicher mainly worked as a designer of corporate identities, he is best known for his graphics for the 1972 Munich Olympic Games, which incorporated a system of universally recognizable pictograms.

Otl Aicher

1922 *Ulm, Germany*
1991 *Rotis, Germany*

▲ Pictograms designed for the Munich Olympic Games, 1972

Anni Albers

1899 Berlin
1994 Orange,
Connecticut

Anni Fleischmann studied design under Martin Brandenburg in Berlin from 1916 to 1919 and later at the Kunstgewerbeschule, Hamburg from 1919 to 1920. She enrolled at the Bauhaus and from 1922 trained as a textile designer under Georg Muche (1895–1987), **Gunta Stölzl** and Paul Klee (1879–1940). In 1929/1930, she started teaching in the textile workshops at the Bauhaus in Weimar and later in Dessau, and was the first textile designer to weave with cellophane. In 1925, she married the German artist and designer **Josef Albers** who became master of the Bauhaus' foundation course the same year. In 1933, the couple emigrated to the USA, and from 1933 to 1949 Anni Albers was an assistant professor of art at Black Mountain College, North Carolina. She also worked as an independent textile designer of both hand-woven and machine-made work. Albers believed that high quality manufacture and a rigorous organization of form would enable modern crafts to be aesthetically pleasing and to possess a timeless appeal. She designed ranges of abstracted geometric textiles that emphasized the material's textural qualities for **Knoll International** from 1959 and for Sunar from 1978. In 1961, Anni Albers was awarded a gold medal for craftsmanship by the American Institute of Architects.

 No. 175
wallhanging, 1925

Josef Albers initially trained as a primary school teacher and taught in Westphalia from 1905 to 1913. He later studied at the Königliche Kunstschule, Berlin from 1913 to 1915 and under Jan Thorn-Prikker at the Kunstgewerbeschule, Essen, where he stayed on as a teacher for three years. Albers subsequently attended the Akademie der Bildenden Künste, Munich from 1919 to 1920, and from 1920 to 1933 studied and taught at the **Bauhaus** in Weimar and Dessau. After completing the preliminary course on 1921, he helped to establish a glass-painting workshop at the school, which he directed from 1923. Albers also taught on the Bauhaus' preliminary course in form and in 1925 was the first student to become a master. That same year, Albers married the textile designer, Anni Fleischmann, and in 1928 became director of the carpentry workshop at the Bauhaus. When the Bauhaus was closed by the National Socialists in 1933, he emigrated to the USA, teaching at Black Mountain College, North Carolina for the next sixteen years. From 1950 to 1960, Albers was director of the design department at Yale University, New Haven and from 1953 to 1954, was also a visiting professor at the **Hochschule für Gestaltung, Ulm**. Although his work was eclectic at times, it was fundamentally characterized by simplified abstracted geometric forms and a minimal use of materials.

Josef Albers

1888 Bottrop, Germany
1976 New Haven,
Connecticut

▲ Tea glass by
Jenaer Glaswerke
Schott & Gen. and
Meissen porcelain
factory for the Bauhaus Dessau, 1926

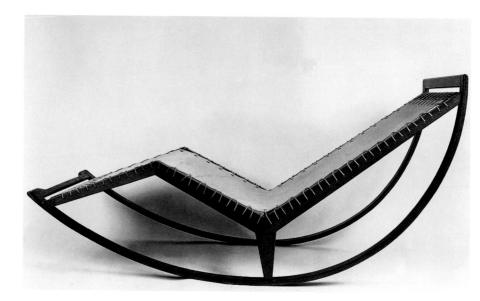

Franco Albini

1905 *Robbiate, Italy*
1977 *Milan*

Franco Albini studied architecture at the Politecnico di Milano, graduating in 1929. He worked in the studio of **Gio Ponti** until 1930, when he met the Rationalist, Edoardo Persico (1900–1936). In the same year, he established his own design and architectural practice and was subsequently joined by three partners: Franca Helg (b. 1920), Antonio Piva (b. 1936) and his son, Marco Albini (b. 1940) in 1952, 1962 and 1965 respectively. His influential suspension bookshelves of 1940, which epitomize Italian **Rationalism**, were innovative in that they also functioned as a room-divider. Albini was not only held in high regard for his interior schemes, but was also celebrated for his work as a town-planner, becoming one of the foremost Italian Rationalists. He edited *Casabella* from 1945 to 1946 and, from 1963 to 1977 taught architectural composition at the Politecnico di Milano. He received **Compasso d'Oro** awards in 1955, 1958 and 1964. Albini's designs have an underlying logic, both in terms of structure and in their methods of manufacture. His wicker and cane chairs, co-designed with Helg in the 1950s, also display a remarkable sensitivity to materials. In 1962 working with Helg and Bob Noorda (b. 1927), Albini redesigned the furniture and fittings for the Milan underground system.

▲ *Model No. PS16*
rocking chaise for
Carlo Poggi, 1956

Don Albinson studied in Sweden before attending **Cranbrook Academy of Art**, Michigan and Yale University, New Haven. At Cranbrook, he attended the industrial and product design classes taught by **Charles Eames**. In 1946, he entered the Eames Office and worked on the development of Charles and Ray Eameses' moulded plywood series of chairs. He was treated like a son by the Eameses and lived with them for six months in their apartment in Los Angeles. As a key member of staff at the Eames Office, Albinson was instrumental in the development of many of the furniture products created for **Herman Miller**, in particular the *Aluminium Group* chairs of 1958. Albinson's skills lay in his understanding of production processes and engineering, and many of the technical and design innovations in furniture developed by the Eameses can be accredited to him. Albinson left the Eames Office around 1959, and in 1964 was appointed director of design development for **Knoll International**. His first project for Knoll was the hugely successful die-cast aluminium and polypropylene *Albinson* chair of 1965.

Don Albinson
b. 1915 *Sparta, Michigan*

◄ *Model No. 1601 Albinson* stacking chairs for Knoll International, 1965

Studio Alchimia

Founded 1976
Milan

▲ *Olli* and *Soli*
collections, 1988

► Cupboard from
Mobile Infinito series
(handles by Ugo la
Pietra, feet by Denis
Santachiara, figures
by Andrea Branzi,
flags by Kazuko Sato
and magnetic deco-
rations by Francesco
Clemente, Sandro
Chia and Enzo
Cucchi, among
others), 1981

Studio Alchimia was founded in 1976 by the architect Alessandro Guerriero (b. 1943), initially as a gallery to display experimental work that was not constrained creatively by industrial production. The studio's allusion to alchemy intentionally mocked the scientific rationale behind Modernism. Alchimia subsequently grew into an influential design studio with contributions from **Ettore Sottsass**, **Alessandro Mendini**, **Andrea Branzi**, Paola Navone (b. 1950) and **Michele De Lucchi** among others. The ironically entitled *Bau.Haus 1* and *Bau.Haus 2* collections, of 1978 and 1979 respectively, drew inspiration and references from popular culture and ultimately **Kitsch**. During the 1980s, Mendini became the Studio's leading exponent and his redesigns of classic furniture, such as **Gio Ponti**'s *Superleggera* chair and **Marcel Breuer**'s *Wassily* chair, ridiculed the pretensions of **Good Design** and thereby good taste. Mendini's *Mobile Infinito* series of 1981 allowed the user to alter the position of the applied decorative elements, thus facilitating a creative interaction. Politically charged, elitist and self-consciously intellectual, Studio Alchimia's designs were fundamental to the second wave of Italian **Radical Design**, which culminated in the popularization of **Anti-Design** in the 1980s.

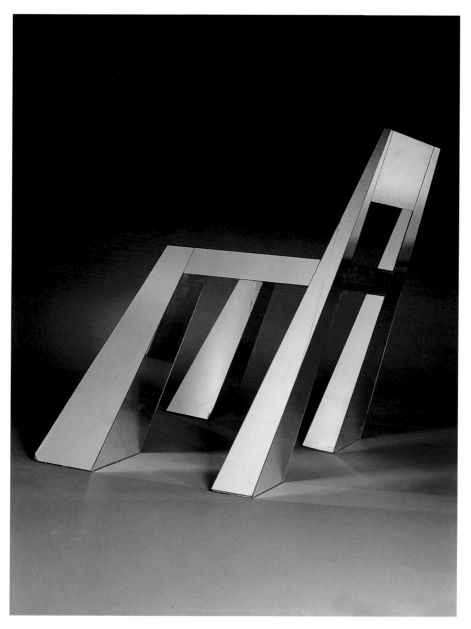

◄ **Alessandro Mendini & Giorgio Gregori,**
Manici vase made by Zabro for Alchimia, 1984

▲ **Alessandro Mendini,** *Scivolando* chair
made by Gavina for Alchimia, 1983

Alessi

Founded 1921
Omegna, Italy

FAO (Frattelli Alessi Omegna) was founded by Giovanni Alessi in Omegna, Italy in 1921. Around 1935, Alessi's son Carlo (b. 1916) became a designer for the firm and during this period the company moved away from its craft origins towards a more industrial modus operandi. In 1945, the year he designed his *Bombé* coffee set, Carlo Alessi was appointed general manager. Owing to the post-war shortage of nickel-silver and brass, Alessi began using pressed stainless steel and, so as to remain competitive, began commissioning work from well-known designers. In the late 1970s, with Carlo now president, the firm started to produce limited edition signed ranges by internationally celebrated designers and architects such as **Ettore Sottsass** and **Richard Sapper**. In 1983, a new trademark, Alessi Officina, was established for products of experimental design. Thus, in 1983, Carlo's son Alberto initiated the *Tea and Coffee Piazza* project in which eleven architects, including **Michael Graves**, **Robert Venturi**, **Aldo Rossi**, **Hans Hollein** and **Richard Meier**, designed limited edition services. This publicity-motivated "architecture in miniature" project brought Alessi international recognition and ensured the company's position as one of the leading exponents of 1980s **Post-Modernism**.

▲ **Michael Graves**,
Kettle, sugar bowl
and creamer for
Alessi, 1985

Emilio Ambasz studied architecture at Princeton University, receiving his MFA in 1966. In 1967 he began teaching there and, a year later, lectured at the **Hochschule für Gestaltung, Ulm** before returning to Princeton to take up a short professorship. In 1967, he co-founded the avant-garde Institute of Architecture and Urban Studies, New York. From 1970 to 1976, he was curator of design at the **Museum of Modern Art, New York**, and organized their groundbreaking exhibition "Italy: The New Domestic Landscape" in 1972. He subsequently established his own design studio, Emilio Ambasz & Associates in 1977 and the Emilio Ambasz Design Group in 1981 – both in New York. While Ambasz is widely celebrated for his design teaching and writing, he is also acclaimed for several notable seating and lighting designs, such as the highly successful *Vertebra* (1977) and *Dorsal* (1981) seating systems and the *Logotec* lighting range (1981). His architectural projects include the Center for Applied Computer Research and Programming, Las Promesas, Mexico (1975), the Grand Rapids Art Museum, Michigan (1975), the Museum of American Folk Art, New York (1980) and the San Antonio Botanical Garden Conservatory, Texas (1982).

Ambasz believes that design should not just fulfil functional requirements but should also take poetic form, so as to satisfy our metaphysical needs; a philosophy no doubt influenced by **Charles Rennie Mackintosh** among others.

In Ambasz' view, the inherent differences between European and American design are the result of contrasting historical outlooks: "Europe's eternal quest remains Utopia, the myth of the end. America's returning myth is Arcadia, the eternal beginning." (Ann Lee Morgan, *Contemporary Designers*, London 1985, p. 25). He maintains that designers must learn to reconcile the past and the future in their work and should give "poetic form to the pragmatic" (ibid).

Emilio Ambasz
b. 1943 *Resistencia, Argentina*

▼ **Emilio Ambasz & Giancarlo Piretti**, *Vertebra* office chair for Castelli and Krueg, 1977

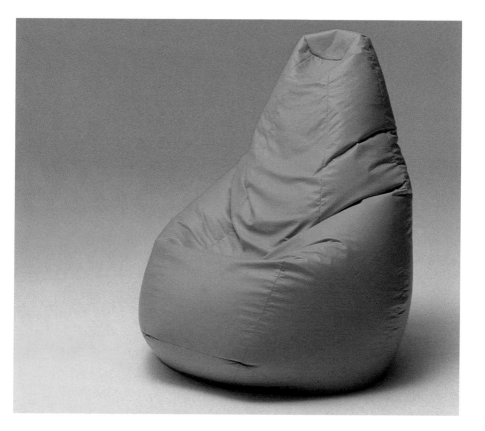

Rejecting the rational precepts of the **Modern Movement**, Anti-Design attempts to validate individual creative expression within design. Surrealism was one of the first conscious examples of Anti-Design and influenced the 1940s Turinese Baroque style of Anti-Rationalist designers such as **Carlo Mollino**. Anti-Design did not, however, become an **avant-garde** force until the late 1960s when several **Radical Design** groups were formed in Italy. These groups, such as **Archizoom**, **Superstudio**, UFO, **Gruppo Strum** and 9999, believed that Modernism was no longer attuned to the avant-garde and was no longer a cultural driving force, having been subverted by industrial interests into a blatantly consumerist marketing ploy.

Highly critical of advanced technology and consumerism, the Anti-Design movement propounded the "design of evasion" and sought to demonstrate through provocative projections, such as Superstudio's super structures and Archizoom's *No-Stop City*, that if rationalism was taken too far it be-

Anti-Design

▲ Piero Gatti, Cesare Paolini & Franco Teodoro, *Sacco*, 1968

◄ Guido Drocco & Franco Mello, *Cactus* coat rack for Gufram, 1972

came absurd. In 1974, **Global Tools**, a school of counter-architecture and design, was officially founded to explore simple non-industrial techniques in
an attempt to promote individual creativity. A year later, Global Tools was
disbanded, marking the end of the first Anti-Design phase of the 1970s. At
this time it seemed to many designers associated with the movement, such
as **Alessandro Mendini** and Ugo La Pietra (b. 1938), that there was no future
for radical counter-design. Within three years, however, the Anti-Design crusade was taken up again by others aligned to **Studio Alchimia**, who rejected
the prevailing conservatism of the mid-1970s and sought to bring spontaneity, creativity and meaning back into design.

At Studio Alchimia, the functional concerns of design were supplanted by
political content, ironic quotations from mass-culture and knowing references to past styles. Studio Alchimia claimed that "there is a need today for
distant, very distant objects to be situated among men and in the world as
signals of our vocation to the magic of thought, like lifebuoys in the stormy
sea of modernity. Paradoxical, unique, isolated, complete and self-defined
objects".

In the early 1980s, with the emergence of **Memphis** in Italy and with American critics of Modernism such as **Charles Jencks**, who called for "elements

which are hybrid rather than pure ... messy vitality over obvious unity" (M. Collins & A. Papadakis, *Post-Modern Design*, London 1989, p. 49), coming to the fore, Anti-Design, with its liberation of decoration for its own sake, evolved into a recognizable international style – **Post-Modernism**. During the boom years of the 1980s, Anti-Design made significant inroads into mainstream design, many consumers putting designer label cachet above all other considerations.

▶ **Alessandro Mendini**, *Zabro* chair/table for Zanotta, 1984

Ron Arad

b. 1951 *Tel Aviv*

Ron Arad attended the Jerusalem Academy of Art from 1971 to 1973 before moving to London to study at the Architectural Association under Peter Cook. After graduating in 1979, he briefly worked in an architectural practice before setting up his own architectural design office/showroom, One Off. Initially based in Covent Garden (later Chalk Farm, London), One Off acted as a forum for the exhibition of his own furniture designs as well as those of other avant-garde British designers, such as **Tom Dixon** and Danny Lane (b. 1955).

His early furniture, such as the *Rover* chair (1981), combined materials associated with the **High Tech** style, for example scaffolding poles, with *objets trouvés* to produce poetic Post-Industrialist "readymades". Arad's later mild steel designs of the late 1980s, such as the *Big Easy* Series (1988–1989), were less "rough and ready" in their constructions and employed labour intensive techniques, making them costly to produce. Consciously distanced from mass-produced furnishings, designs such as these functioned as "art furniture" and won Arad international recognition, bringing his work to the attention of established manufacturers.

▼ *Tom Vac* stacking chair (prototype), 1997

Although best known for his furniture, Arad has completed several important interior-design projects including the foyer of the Tel Aviv Opera House (1990). During the 1990s, Arad produced some of his most commercially successful designs including his *Bookworm* shelving (1997), 1,000 kilometres of which has been produced by **Kartell**. Other recent innovative designs include his *Tom Vac* vacuum-formed aluminium chair (1998) and his *Fantastic Plastic Elastic* chair (1998) for Kartell.

▲ *Little Heavy* chair
for One Off, 1989

◀ *Melted Off Contour* textile, 1958 (produced by Nuno Corporation from 1988)

Junichi Arai

b. 1932 *Kiryu/Gunma, Japan*

Junichi Arai developed some of the most technically interesting and experimental textiles of the 1980s and 1990s. Initially, Arai concentrated on highly textural woven fabrics, which incorporated a range of unusual media including celluloid, aluminium tape and metal filaments. Later, he turned his attention to more technologically inclined designs, employing a variety of state-of-the-art materials and processes, such as his *Nuno me Gara* (Woven Pattern) textile of 1983. Arai arranged and photocopied twisted cloth strips of differing weaves and then scanned the resulting textural pattern to produce this Jacquard-woven design. Other textiles, such *as Melted Off Contour*, designed in 1958 but not realized for another thirty years, are equally inventive. In this case, a patented process of vacuum-plating polyester film with aluminium was used. The aluminium coating is later dissolved in a weak alkali solution to produce a subtle contour pattern. Since closing his company Anthologie in 1987, Arai has worked as an independent designer, retailing his work from his own Tokyo-based shop, Nuno. Arai has also supplied textile designs to Issey Miyake and Comme des Garçons among others.

André Arbus initially studied at the École des Beaux-Arts, Toulouse and then trained in the cabinet-making workshop of his father and grandfather. From 1925, he became associated with the Société des Artistes Décorateurs and exhibited at their Salon as well as at the Salon d'Automne. He also exhibited at the 1925 Paris "Exposition Internationale des Arts Décoratifs et Industriels Modernes". In 1930, he set up his own showroom, Époque, in Paris, and two years later moved permanently to the city. His interior and furniture designs, like those of his contemporaries **Jacques-Émile Ruhlmann** and **Jules-Émile Leleu**, were in the **Art Deco** style and incorporated luxurious materials and exotic woods. While some of his designs were applied with painted motifs executed by Marc Saint-Saëns, Arbus' work relied less on the use of ornament than on purity of line. In 1926 Arbus designed a lounge for the ocean liner *Île-de-France* and around 1935 established an interior design department, known as Les Beaux Métiers, at the Palais de la Nouveauté. In 1937, he exhibited a **Moderne** style interior at the Paris "Exposition Internationale des Arts et Techniques dans la Vie Moderne". From the late 1930s, Arbus turned to architecture, his most notable commission being the Ministry of Agriculture, Paris (1937). He also designed interior schemes for three other ocean liners, the *Bretagne*, *Provence* and *France* as well as a bridge in Martigues in 1961.

André Arbus

1903 *Toulouse*
1969 *Paris*

▶ Music Room designed for the "Exposition des Arts et Techniques dans la Vie Moderne" in Paris, 1937

Archizoom Associati was founded by **Andrea Branzi, Paolo Deganello,** Gilberto Corretti (b. 1941) and Massimo Morozzi (b. 1941) in Florence in 1966, and took its name from the British architectural group Archigram and an issue of their journal *Zoom*. Archizoom created radical architectural projections such as *Wind City* (1969) and *No-Stop City* (1970) in an attempt to demonstrate, among other things, that if **Rationalism** was taken to an extreme it became illogical and thereby anti-rational. Archizoom stated that: "The ultimate aim of modern architecture is the elimination of architecture itself." (A. Branzi, *The Hot House; Italian New Wave Design*, London 1984, pp. 73–74). In 1966 and 1967, Archizoom organized two exhibitions of "Superarchitettura" with **Superstudio** in Pistoia and Modena. In 1968, Dario (b. 1943) and Lucia Bartolini (b. 1944) joined the group which, from 1971 to 1973, researched fashion design. They also produced several notable furniture designs including the *Dream Beds* series (1967), the *Safari* sectional seating unit (1968), the *Superonda* sofa (1966) and the *Mies* chair (1969), all of which drew references from popular culture and **Kitsch** while mocking the pretensions of **Good Design**. In 1972, Archizoom was included in the "Counterdesign as Postulation" section of the landmark exhibition "Italy: The New Domestic Landscape" held at the **Museum of Modern Art, New York.**

Archizoom Associati
1966–1974
Florence

◄ **Dario Bartolini,** *Sanremo* lamp produced by Poltronova for Archizoom Associati, 1968

▼ **Archizoom Associati,** *Safari* modular livingscape for Poltronova, 1968

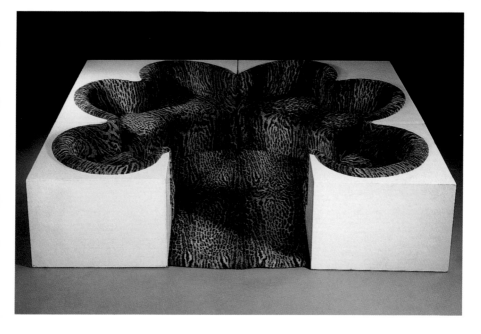

Art Deco was an international decorative style, rather than a design movement, which emerged in Paris during the 1920s. Prior to this, elements of the style had already appeared in the work of the **Wiener Werkstätte**, the Italian furniture designer **Carlo Bugatti** and the Russian Constructivists. Taking over from the turn-of-the-century **Art Nouveau**, which with its ahistorical bearing looked to natural forms, Art Deco drew its stylistic references from an eclectic range of sources including ancient Egyptian civilization, tribal art, Surrealism, Futurism, **Constructivism**, Neo-Classicism, geometric abstraction, popular culture and the **Modern Movement**. Leading exponents of the new style, such as **Jacques-Émile Ruhlmann**, espoused for the most part the ideal of superlative craftsmanship and incorporated exotic woods and luxury materials such as shagreen and mother-of-pearl in their designs. Its reliance on private patronage, most notably from the French couturiers, Paul Poiret and Jacques Doucet, and its incompatibility with industrialized production ensured that Art Deco was a relatively short-lived style, inevitably overtaken by more progressive approaches to design.

The "Exposition Internationale des Arts Décoratifs et Industriels Modernes", held in Paris in 1925, included **Le Corbusier**'s Pavillon de l'Esprit Nouveau as well as Ruhlmann's Hôtel du Collectionneur and exhibits by other well-known Art Deco designers such as Pierre-Émile Legrain. It was from the title of this landmark exhibition that the term Art Deco was eventually coined. From the beginning, the Art Deco style spanned the work of designers such as **René Lalique**, Jean Dunand (1877–1942), and Edgar-William Brandt (1880–1960) as well as the creations of modernists such as **Eileen Gray**, **Pierre Chareau** and **Robert Mallet-Stevens**. Indeed, even designers closely associated with the Modern Movement, such as Le

Art Deco
Founded c. 1925
Paris

◀ **Jacques-Émile Ruhlmann**, The Grand Salon, Hôtel du Collectionneur, 1925

▼ **Edgar-William Brandt**, *La Tentation* floor lamp, c. 1925 (base by E.-W. Brandt, shade by Daum Frères)

◄ **Emory Seidel**,
Candleholders for
Roman Bronze
Works of New York,
c. 1930

► **Ernest Boiceau**,
Pair of Torchères,
c. 1930

► **Edgar-William
Brandt**, *Le Paon*
wrought-iron
firescreen, 1926

Corbusier and **Jean Prouvé**, were at times inspired by the sumptuousness of Art Deco.

After 1925 the style was expressed in the work of many designers, not only in France and continental Europe but increasingly in Britain and the United States. It was particularly well received in America where designs such as **Paul Frankl**'s *Skyscraper* furniture and William van Alen's Chrysler Building (1928–1930) in New York – perhaps the ultimate expression of Art Deco architecture – were seen to encapsulate the aspirations of the nation. In Britain, the Art Deco style was more subdued than elsewhere and was subtly expressed in the architecture and product design of **Wells Coates**. The style was also frequently used in Britain for cinemas, especially those owned by Odeon, which projected, inside the silver-screen world of Art Deco, boudoirs and Hollywood-style chromed glamour. During the 1930s, the style became increasingly popular owing to its associations with this dreamlike Hollywood lifestyle and, as a result, was eventually fully embraced by mainstream manufacturers. Although Bakelite had been developed in America in 1907, it was not until the late 1920s that this thermoset plastic became a viable material for large-scale mass-production. The sculptural Art Deco style was eminently suited to the moulding requirements of this new medium and during the 1930s Art Deco radio casings, together with a plethora of other Bakelite objects, were mass produced. The Art Deco style, however, became increasingly debased with the production of kitsch objects that had little in common with the superior craftsmanship of earlier French Art Deco objects. Eventually, the style was curtailed by the advent of the Second World War when its essential reliance on decoration and its maximalist aesthetic could no longer be sustained.

In the 1960s, Art Deco began to enjoy a reappraisal both on the collectors' market and among young designers disillusioned with Modernism. During the 1980s, post-modern designers such as **Robert Venturi**, **Hans Hollein** and **Charles Jencks** paid homage to Art Deco through their own idiosyncratic work which, like that of their antecedents, revelled in excess and exuberance.

▼ Jean Dunand,
Snakevase, c. 1913

▲ **René Prou**, Desk,
c. 1929

▲ **Reuben Haley**,
Ruba Rombic vase
for Consolidated
Lamp & Glass,
c. 1928

Art Nouveau was an ahistorical style that emerged during the 1880s. It was inspired by the earlier British **Arts & Crafts Movement**, which was sometimes known as the "New Art". During the 1890s, **Charles Rennie Mackintosh** and designers associated with the **Vienna Secession**, such as **Josef Maria Olbrich**, introduced abstracted naturalistic forms to design that were curvilinear while others, such as **Hermann Obrist** and **August Endell**, pioneered the use of whiplash motifs.

One of the greatest exponents of Art Nouveau was the Belgian architect **Victor Horta**, whose Hotel Tassel (1892–1893) was one of the first expressions of the style in architecture. This residential project innovatively incorporated ironwork as both a structural and decorative device, and the designer's use of stem-like columns that branched into swirling tendrils led to the coining of the term "Horta Line". Similarly, in France, the style became known as "Style Guimard" in recognition of the writhing and intertwined forms employed by Hector Guimard – most, notably for his cast-iron entrances to the Paris Métro (c. 1900). There, the term "Le Style Moderne" was also used to

► **Émile Gallé**,
Cameo vase with
autumn crocus
decoration, 1899

identify Art Nouveau, while in Germany the name **Jugendstil** was adopted. In Spain, especially in Catalonia, the Art Nouveau style flourished through the work of **Antonio Gaudí y Cornet** and his followers. They generally referred to Art Nouveau as "Modernisme" while in Italy the term "Stile Liberty" was coined in recognition of the role played by the London department store **Liberty & Co.** in the promotion of the style.

Émile Gallé and other designers associated with the **École de Nancy** produced notable furniture and glassware in the Art Nouveau style. The sinuous lines

◄ **Eugène Gaillard**,
Pedestal for
J. P. Christophe,
c. 1901–1902

► **Victor Horta**,
Interior of the
Maison Tassel in
Brussels, 1893

and the elongation of floral forms, which readily identify Art Nouveau, were directly inspired by the natural world rather than past styles. Indeed, the abstracted and bulbous forms of **Louis Comfort Tiffany**'s Favrile vases capture the very essence of nature. The reason designers of the 1890s looked to nature for inspiration had much to do with earlier scientific research into the workings of the natural world such as Darwin's treatise *On the Origin of Species*, published in 1859, the botanical illustrations of Ernst Haeckel (1834–1919) and the exquisite photographic flower studies taken by Karl Blossfeldt (1865–1932) in the late 19th century.

With its outright rejection of historicism, Art Nouveau can be considered the first truly modern international style. It became inextricably linked to the decadence of the *fin-de-siècle*, however, owing to its reliance on ornamental motifs. As a result, it was overtaken stylistically in the early 20th century by the machine aesthetic and the avant-garde's preference for simple geometric forms better suited to industrial production.

▲ **Friedrich Adler,**
Coffee service for
Metallwarenfabrik
Orion, 1904

◄ **Paul Hankar,**
"New England"
shopfront in
Brussels, c. 1900

◄ **Émile Gallé,**
Dragonfly table,
c. 1900

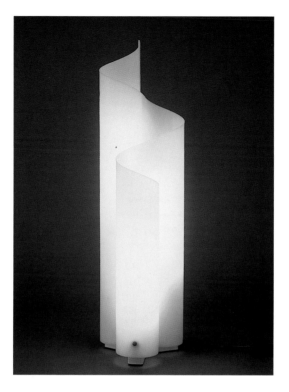

Ernesto Gismondi (b. 1931) founded Artemide in 1959 for the manufacture
of lighting and furniture products. Among Artemide's early successes were
Vico Magistretti's *Demetrio 45* table (1963), *Stadio* table (1966) and *Selene*
and *Gaudí* chairs (1969 & 1970), which were initially manufactured in reinforced plastic and later in injection-moulded ABS. High quality designs such
as these encouraged the general acceptance of plastics as noble materials
and helped to bring increasing international attention to Italian design.
Artemide also manufactured many landmark designs for lighting, most notably Gianfranco Frattini (b. 1926) and **Livio Castiglioni**'s snake-like *Boalum*
lamp (1969), Vico Magistretti's *Chimera* floor lamp (1966) and **Richard Sapper**'s *Tizio* task lamp (1972). Always at the forefront of progressive design,
Gismondi provided exhibition space in the Artemide showroom for the
launch of the **Memphis** Collection in 1981. Artemide has also produced lighting designs by **Michele De Lucchi**, **Enzo Mari**, **Ettore Sottsass** and Santiago
Calatrava (b. 1951), and their products are represented in over one hundred
museums worldwide.

Artemide
Founded 1959
Milan

The British Arts & Crafts Movement comprised a loose collaboration of progressive architects and designers whose aim was to reform design and ultimately society through a return to handcraft. Appalled by the social and environmental consequences of industrialization and by the plethora of overly decorated, poor quality machine-made products, designers in the mid-19th century such as **William Morris** led a crusade against the age in which they lived and advocated a simpler and more ethical approach to design and manufacture. Their distrust of industrial production, which had turned skilled craftsman into "wage slaves", led to efforts to re-invigorate the traditional crafts through the design and execution of high quality wares that were not only useful but also beautiful.

The first phase of the British Arts & Crafts Movement was influenced by the Pre-Raphaelite Brotherhood and the medieval escapism it popularized – the artists, Dante Gabriel Rossetti (1828–1882), Edward Burne-Jones (1833–1898) and Ford Madox Brown (1821–1893) all designed for Morris & Co. – and by late Gothic Revivalism, as practised by the architect George Edmund Street (1824–1881). Of greatest influence, however, were the reforming ideas of **Augustus Pugin** and John Ruskin (1819–1900), while William Morris was among the first to attempt to put many of their theories into practice when he established Morris, Marshall & Faulkner & Co. in 1861 (changed to Morris & Co. in 1874). Morris & Co.'s products did not embrace mechanized production methods but instead espoused the inherent simplicity of vernacularism and the honesty of handcraftsmanship. Rather than attempting to reform industrial production, which was driven by commerce, the early proponents of the Arts & Crafts Movement sought to promote democracy and social cohesion through craft. Working within a rampantly capitalist society, Morris was a committed socialist who had a utopian vision in which handcraft offered moral sal-

▼ **Walter Crane**, *The Orange Tree* textile for Jeffrey & Co., 1902 (reissued by Arthur Sanderson & Sons)

▲ **William De Morgan**, Lustre charger with galleon motif, c. 1880

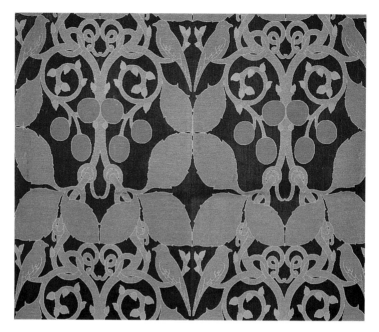

▶ Charles Voysey,
Woven textile, c. 1900

◀ Charles Voysey,
Tempus Fugit
aluminium and
copper clock, c. 1895

vation to both workers and consumers. He was most concerned by the
compartmentalization of the industrial process, for through the division of
labour, the worker's well-being and the arts as a whole were undermined.
Morris could only accept mechanization if it produced objects of quality and
reduced workers' burdens, rather than just increasing productivity. The para-
dox was that the handcrafted products of Morris & Co. and others were
costly to produce and could only be afforded by the wealthiest members of
society.

Inspired by both Morris and Ruskin's advocacy of morality in design and
their belief in the social importance of craft and community, the second
phase Arts & Crafts designers, William R. Lethaby (1857–1931), **Arthur Heygate Mackmurdo** and **Charles R. Ashbee**, founded organizations such as The
Century Guild (1882), the St George's Art Society (1883) and the Art Workers' Guild (1884) to produce objects of reformed design. The term "Arts &
Crafts" was not coined until 1888 when members of the Art Workers Guild
formed the Arts & Crafts Exhibition Society.

Though second phase Arts & Crafts designers increasingly embraced vernacularism, some such as **Charles Voysey** and Ashbee concluded that Morris' vision of widely available well-designed products was unattainable with-

out mechanization. Ashbee, who founded the **Guild of Handicraft** in 1888, even went so far as to accuse Morris, with his preoccupation with the past and near total rejection of machine production, of "intellectual Luddism". It was Ashbee, however, who came the closest to realizing the Movement's dream of a "rural ideal" when he moved his Guild of Handicraft to Chipping Campden in 1902. The Arts & Crafts Movement had by then close associations with the Cotswolds through **Ernest Gimson** and Sidney (1865–1926) and Ernest Barnsley's (1863–1926) working in Pinbury from the 1890s. From about 1910, **Gordon Russell** designed furniture in Broadway in the Arts & Crafts manner, yet by 1926 its production was largely mechanized in an ongoing attempt to reconcile high quality with affordability. Russell later oversaw the production of **Utility** furniture, and certainly the underlying morality of the Arts & Crafts Movement was central to the development of this state sponsored programme. Instrumental in the promotion of the Arts & Crafts style were **Liberty & Co.** and Heal & Sons, both of which had their own design studios and retailed Arts & Crafts furnishings and metalwork. Sometimes referred to as the "New Art", the second phase of the Arts & Crafts Movement can be seen to some extent as the British equivalent of the Continental **Art Nouveau** style and as such remained popular until the outbreak of war in 1914. The virtues of simplicity, utility and appropriateness that the Arts & Crafts Movement promoted, and its fundamental proposition that design could and should be used as a democratic tool for social change, were highly influential to the early pioneers of the **Modern Movement**. Throughout the 20th century, the Arts & Crafts idiom has survived through the work of designers allied to the **Craft Revival**.

▼ **Sidney Barnsley**, Wardrobe, c. 1911

◄ **Hugh Garden**, *Teco* vase for the Gates Pottery, c. 1900

Many American designers were inspired by the ideals of the British Arts & Crafts Movement and its demonstration in practice that a national style could be propagated through the espousal of traditional vernacular forms. **William Morris'** and **Charles R. Ashbee**'s advocacy of rural artistic communities appealed to American designers such as **Gustav Stickley**, Charles P. Limbert (1854–1923) and Elbert G. Hubbard (1856–1915) who were seeking refuge from the increasing industrialization of their country.

In 1898, Gustav Stickley visited Europe and while there met, among others, Charles R. Ashbee and **Charles Voysey**. On his return, Stickley established his own workshops in Syracuse, New York, and from 1901 began publishing his extremely influential magazine *The Craftsman*. While his rustic furniture designs looked back to the vernacular forms used in the pioneer days, he advocated honesty and simplicity in design believing that "decadence is the natural sequence of over refinement".

American Arts & Crafts designs were in general less complicated in construction and less decorated than their British counterparts, for it was the underlying social and democratic aspects of the Movement rather than its emphasis on superlative craftsmanship that appealed to designers in the United

States. The architect William L. Price (1861–1916), for instance, was so inspired by William Morris' utopian novel *News from Nowhere* (1889–1890) that he established the Rose Valley Community in Moylan, Philadelphia in 1901. This venture attempted to realize the Arts & Crafts ideal of a socially cohesive rural community in which members sought "joy through labour" and worked together to abolish social injustice. The social freedoms offered by the movement also attracted many women as it encouraged emancipation through its promotion of gender equality and female education. Many of the communities, however, were short lived due to the difficulties inherent in attempts at reconciling high quality handcraftsmanship with affordability.

Only the **Roycrofters** community, established by Elbert G. Hubbard in 1893, was notable for its commercial success. In 1906, the Roycrofters workshops employed over four hundred craftsmen and the community even boasted an inn for tourists and potential customers.

In California, architects and designers allied to the Arts & Crafts Movement were also inspired by the state's Spanish-Mexican heritage as well as Japanese Art and the Mission Style. Charles and Henry **Greene** eloquently fused these styles in their designs for wealthy clients' houses but their work differed significantly from Stickley's and Limbert's in that it incorporated exquisite detailing. Similarly, **Frank Lloyd Wright**, who was the greatest architect and designer to work within the Arts & Crafts idiom in the United States, synthesized Western and Eastern influences. His long and low Prairie School style of architecture combined with his skillful handling of natural materials enabled his buildings to blend in harmoniously with their surrounding environments. Wright's pioneering **Organic Design** bridged the Arts & Crafts Movement and the **Modern Movement** and in so doing greatly influenced later designers both in America and Europe.

THE CRAFTSMAN

VOL. V   JANUARY·1904   NO. 4

COPY 25 CENTS   PUBLISHED MONTHLY BY THE UNITED CRAFTS SYRACUSE·N·Y·-U·S·A·   YEAR 3 DOLLARS

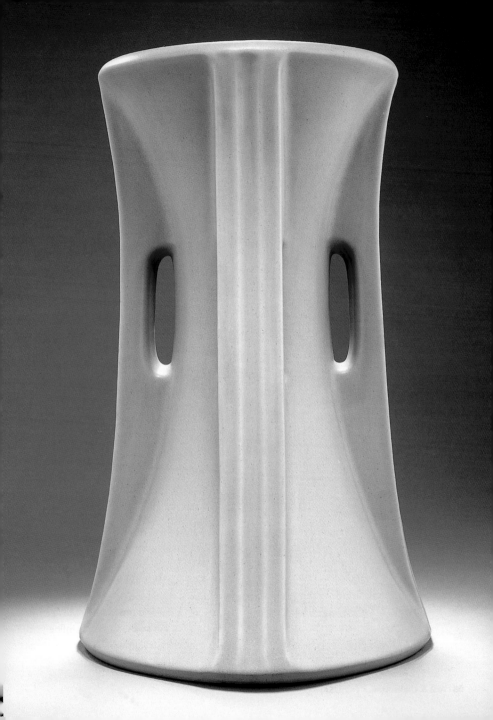

Charles R. Ashbee

1863 *Isleworth, London*
1942 *Godden Green/ Kent*

▲ Silver bowl with looped handles for the Guild of Handicraft, 1901

▶ Silver chalice with cover for the Guild of Handicraft, c. 1900

Having studied history at Cambridge University, Charles R. Ashbee later trained as an architect under G. F. Bodley (1827–1907). As a central figure of the British Arts & Crafts Movement, Ashbee was so influenced by John Ruskin (1819–1900) and **William Morris** that he founded the Guild and School of Handicraft in 1888 at Toynbee Hall in the East End of London, which two years later moved to Essex House, Mile End. In 1902 Ashbee attempted to realize the Arts & Crafts Movement's ideal of a rural community and so moved both the Guild and School to Chipping Campden in the Cotswolds. The distance from London, however, prevented the commercial success of this venture and it went into receivership in 1908. Previously, in 1898, Ashbee had founded the Essex House Press for the production of fine hand-printed books. In 1906, he published *A Book of Cottages and Little Houses* and in 1909 *Modern English Silverwork*. Ashbee remains, however, best known for his silverware with swirling organic decoration, which had a strong influence on **Liberty & Co**. and Vienna **Secession** metalwork and, ultimately, on **Art Nouveau**. Several buildings designed by Ashbee were built in Budapest, Sicily and London and he lectured in Britain and the United States. From 1915 to 1919, Ashbee was professor of English at Cairo University and for four years after that he worked on restoration projects in Jerusalem.

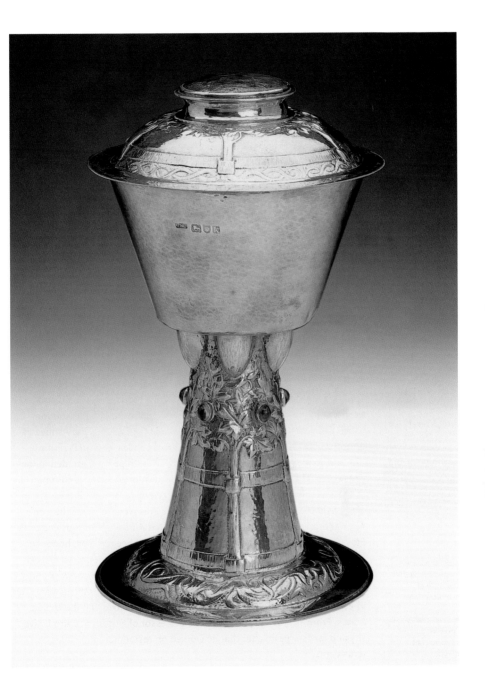

Erik Gunnar Asplund

1885 *Stockholm*
1940 *Stockholm*

Erik Gunnar Asplund studied at the Kungliga Konsthögskolan, Stockholm from 1905 to 1909 and initially pursued a career in painting. From 1909, he concentrated on architecture and opened his own office in Stockholm. In 1917, he became editor of the journal *Teknisk Tidskrift Arkitektur* and the same year received praise for his interiors exhibited in Stockholm at the Liljevalchs Art Gallery.

From 1911 to 1930, he designed neo-classically inspired architecture and furnishings, such as his *Senna* chair of 1925, designed for a public library. He was appointed chief architect for the 1930 Svenska Sljödföreningen's "Stockholmsutstäliningen" exhibition – an event that won international recognition, Asplund's "Paradiset" restaurant presenting the **International Style** in Sweden for the first time. In his designs, Asplund combined modernism with Scandinavian neo-classicism. From 1931 to 1940, he was professor of architecture at Kungliga Konsthögskolan, Stockholm.

▲ "Paradiset"
restaurant at the
"Stockholm-
sutstäliningen"
exhibition, 1930

Sergio Asti studied art and architecture at the Politecnico di Milano from 1947 to 1953. Having founded his own studio in Milan in 1953, he worked independently designing interiors, exhibitions, furniture, lighting, glassware, ceramics and electrical appliances for Brionvega, Poltronova, **Knoll International**, **Venini** and **Kartell** among others. In 1953, Asti began experimenting with plastics and in 1954 designed some highly sculptural and organic door handles, which were celebrated for their "plastic values". In 1956, the year he designed his famous soda siphon for Saccab, he became one of the founding members of the ADI (Associazione per il Disegno Industriale). From 1957 to 1958, he designed the first-ever acrylic-resin lamps for Kartell. Asti received **Compasso d'Oro** awards in 1955, 1956, 1959, 1962 and 1970 for his innovative consumer products and furnishings, which with their sleek lines were especially characteristic of post-war Italian design.

Sergio Asti
b. 1926 *Milan*

▶ *Ruota* glazed earthenware vase for Knoll International, 1972

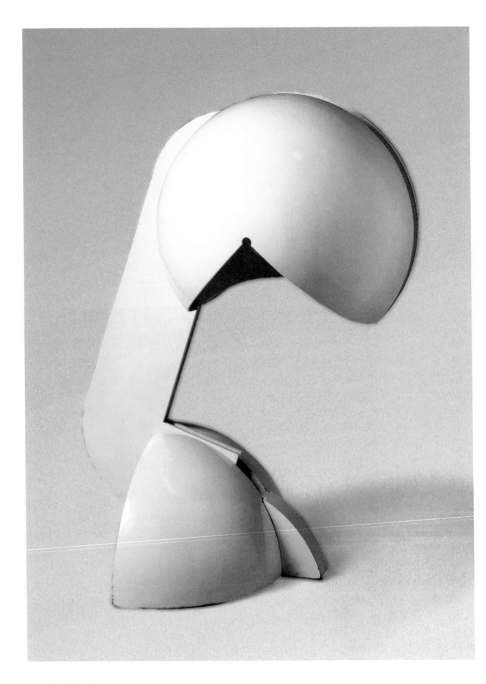

Gae Aulenti studied architecture at the Politecnico di Milano, graduating in 1954. Since then, she has operated from her own Milan practice, designing furniture and interiors for **Knoll International** and **Olivetti** and other companies. She has also designed lighting for Stilnovo and **Artemide**. In 1980, Aulenti created interiors for the Musée d'Orsay and worked on a project for the Musée d'Art Moderne at the Centre Georges Pompidou. Believing that space should be defined by an interior rather than by the objects in it, Aulenti's designs possess both originality and a quiet sophistication. While the underlying rhetoric of her designs for interiors and products is modern, Aulenti rejects sterile geometric formalism and instead promotes a humanized form of Modernism. Aulenti is one of the very few female designers of her generation to have achieved international recognition.

Gae Aulenti
b. 1927 *Palazzolo della Stella, Italy*

◄ *La Ruspa* lamp for Martinelli Luce, 1969

▼ Coffee table for Fontana Arte, 1980

The French term "avant-garde" refers to architects, designers, artists, writers and musicians, whose techniques and ideas are in advance of those generally known or accepted. Avant-garde design has traditionally made up only a small percentage of manufactured goods, yet its influence on the history of design has been enormous. Generally, such work has had an impact far beyond the circles of the minority audience for whom it was primarily intended, chiefly through media interest. For much of the 20th century, avant-garde designers have remained outside the industrial mainstream owing to the limited appeal of their work and it has taken sometimes many years for more widely held tastes and attitudes to catch up. **Marcel Breuer**'s pioneering tubular metal furniture from the late 1920s and early 1930s, for instance, was not nearly as widely accepted in its own day as it was in the 1960s and 70s. The avant-garde necessarily leads fashion, and styles are created in its wake. Post-war **Organic Design**, for example, stylistically influenced 1950s **Biomorphism**. The work of the avant-garde is frequently given the adjective "New" – New Art, **Art Nouveau**, New Wave – to describe its forward-looking agenda, and it is fair to say that the majority of the most important theoretical and practical innovations in 20th century design have been the direct result of avant-garde talent and vision.

▾ **Marcel Breuer**, *Model No. B27* table and *Model No. B46* chair for Thonet, 1928 and 1928–1929

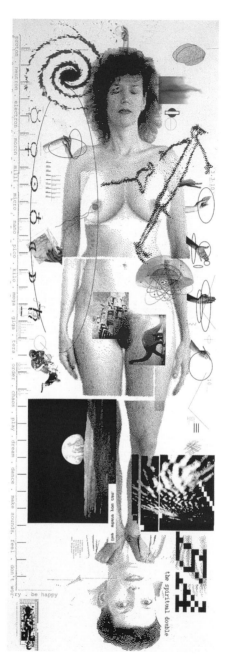

Mackay Hugh Baillie Scott came from a wealthy aristocratic Scottish family. He initially trained at Cirencester Agricultural College but in 1886 became articled to the Bath architect, Major Charles E. Davis. In 1889, he moved to the Isle of Man and studied at the School of Art in Douglas under **Archibald Knox**. He collaborated with Knox in the design of ironwork and stained glass, influenced by Celtic art. His earliest designs for houses were half timbered and in the Old English architectural style of the **Arts & Crafts Movement**, such as that practised by Norman Shaw (1831–1912), while his later work was influenced by the more vernacular style of **Charles Voysey**. Baillie Scott's Red House in Douglas (1892–1893) incorporated innovative folding screens between rooms, and in 1894 he wrote an article in *The Studio* outlining his ideal house, which would have "plain bricks and whitewash". He exhibited furniture, metalwork and wallpaper designs at the Arts & Crafts Society Exhibition in 1896 and in the same year designed the Manxman piano. He became one of the most influential exponents of the Arts & Crafts Move-

▼ Side chair,
probably for John P.
White, Pyghtle
Works, c. 1905

ment especially on the Continent, where he was commissioned by the Grand Duke Ernst-Ludwig of Hesse-Darmstadt to design the interiors and furnishings of his palace in Darmstadt. The resulting white-panelled interiors were startling in their simplicity while the specially designed functional yet beautifully inlaid furniture visually enriched the scheme. Baillie Scott subsequently received other German commissions and undertook the interior design of the Crown Princess of Romania's treehouse. After the First World War, Arts & Crafts vernacularism went out of fashion, so during the 1920s and 1930s Baillie Scott adopted a Neo-Georgian style. He did, however, continue to advocate handcraftsmanship over machine production.

Giacomo Balla studied at the Albertine Academy, Turin before teaching painting to pupils including Gino Severini (1883–1966). While staying in Paris from 1900 to 1901, he was strongly influenced by Divisionism. In 1910, he became a Futurist, putting his name to both the *Manifesto of Futurist Painters* and the *Technical Manifesto of Futurist Painting* and exhibiting with the group from 1912 onwards. He then went to Düsseldorf and designed the interior for the since destroyed Löwenstein House and, between 1913 and 1914, executed painted furniture for its interior. In 1913, he declared: "Balla is dead" and put all his paintings up for auction, turning his attention to design. In 1914, he designed clothing and wrote the *Futurist Manifesto on Menswear*, which argued for practical clothes that were "dynamic". Around 1918, he designed his Futurist House in Rome, which consciously distanced itself from the past with its brightly painted cut-out furniture. He also designed a Futurist interior for the Bal Tik-Tak dance hall in 1921. With fellow Futurists, Fortunato Depero (1892–1960) and Enrico Prampolini (1894–1956), Balla exhibited colourful wall-hangings at the 1925 Paris "Exposition Internationale des Arts Décoratifs et Industriels Modernes". In the late 1930s, Balla abandoned the Futurist style in favour of a more abstract approach to design.

Giacomo Balla

1871 *Turin*
1958 *Rome*

▲ Design for
Paravento screen,
1916–1920

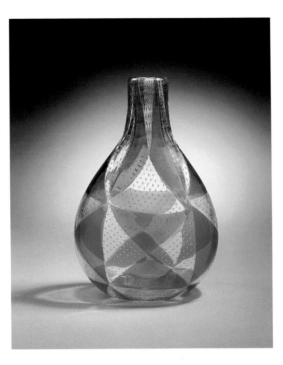

► *Vetro parabolico*
vase with air bubbles
for Barovier & Toso,
c. 1961

Ercole Barovier
1889 *Murano, Italy*
1974 *Venice*

The Barovier family have been glass makers since the 14th century. In
1878 Benvenuto Barovier (1855–1932) and his two brothers, Benedetto
(1857–1930) and Giuseppe (1863–1942), established a factory on the island
of Murano known as Fratelli Barovier and produced glassware that was inspired by 16th-century forms. Ercole Barovier, Benvenuto's son, founded his
own workshop, Artisti Barovier, in 1919 (later renamed Barovier e. C.). During the 1920s, he helped revive the art of glass making in Murano and produced over 25,000 designs for both decorative and functional glassware.
He experimented with different techniques and colours, which allowed him
to develop new types of surfaces including the stone-like "vetro gemmato",
the roughly textured "vetro barbarico" and his best known patchwork-like
"vetro parabolico". In the 1930s, he developed a type of glass in which small
air bubbles were trapped, known as "vetro rugiada". Later, he worked with
his son, Angelo who joined the firm in 1947 and together they produced
stripped vessels known as "vetro a fili" from coloured glass rods. In 1936,
Ercol took over the management of Fratelli Barovier, which later became
known as Barovier & Toso when Piero Toso succeeded him.

Saul Bass studied at the Art Students League in New York from 1936 to 1939. He subsequently worked as a graphic designer in Warner Brother's art department, which maintained the film industry's tradition of relying upon photographic/illustrative imagery to publicize movies. Their conservative graphic approach was pictorial and set out to depict elements of the films being promoted rather than reveal their essence. Disillusioned with this practice, Bass left Warner Brothers in 1946 and moved to Los Angeles. There he worked for various advertising agencies and in 1949 designed a magazine advertisement for the film "Champion" that broke all the established conventions for movie graphics – the ad being completely black with only a small half-tone logo and the film's title placed centrally on the page for maximum impact.

During the 1950s, Bass worked as a free-lance designer developing a simplified and symbolic language of design, which attempted to convey the essential qualities of films for promotional purposes. He designed visually effective and highly emblematic posters using paper cut-outs for two of Otto Preminger's films, "The Man with the Golden Arm" (1955) and "Anatomy of a Murder" (1959). Impressed by the strength of such images, Preminger asked Bass to create moving title sequences, which incorporated his powerful graphics and were accompanied by soundtracks. Through this, the new medium of animated graphics was created.

The visual impact of Bass' design work was immensely influential and captured the spirit of the time superbly. The abstraction found in his poster designs was continued in Bass' corporate design work dating from the 1970s.

Saul Bass
1920 *New York*
1996 *Los Angeles*

▼ Movie poster for "The Man with the Golden Arm", 1955

Helmut Bätzner
b. 1928 *Stuttgart*

Helmut Bätzner trained in carpentry before enrolling at the Technische Hochschule Stuttgart to study architecture. From 1962 to 1963, he studied in Rome and on his return became a lecturer at the Werkkunstschule in Krefeld, Germany, a position he held until 1966.

From 1964 to 1965, Bätzner developed the first mass-produced single-piece reinforced plastic chair, which was designed in conjunction with his planning work for the Badisches Staatstheater in Karlsruhe. Since their introduction in 1966, over 120,000 Bofinger chairs have been manufactured, thanks to their five minute production cycle and the minimal amount of finishing required. The *Bofinger* stacking chair, which was compression moulded by the "prepreg-process" in a heated ten ton double-shell press, was immensely influential to later plastic outdoor furniture.

Since 1964, Bätzner has worked as a freelance architect and designer and his projects include the Psychatrische Klinik Karlsruhe and the administration building for the Technische Hochschule Aachen.

▲ *Model No. BA 1171*
chair for Bofinger,
1964–1966

Although **Walter Gropius** was put forward for the directorship of the Kunstgewerbeschule at Weimar, which had been founded by **Henry van de Velde** in 1908, it closed before he could take up the position in 1915. Gropius maintained his contacts, however, at Weimar's other art school, the Hochschule für Bildende Kunst. As a soldier during the First World War, Gropius became anti-capitalist, his sympathies lying more with the craft ideals of the Helgar workshops than with the **Deutscher Werkbund** and its belief in industrial production. While at the front, Gropius formulated his "Proposals for the establishment of an educational institution to provide artistic advisory services to industry, trade and craft". In January 1916, his recommendations for the merging of the Kunstgewerbeschule and the Hochschule für Bildende Kunst into a single interdisciplinary school of craft and design were sent to the Großherzogliches Sächsisches Staatsministerium.

In April 1919, Gropius was duly appointed director of the new Staatliches Bauhaus in Weimar and that same year the Bauhaus Manifesto was published. The Bauhaus, which means "building house", sought to reform educational theory and, in so doing, bring unity to the arts. For Gropius, construction or "making" was an important social, symbolic and intellectual endeavour and this sentiment pervaded Bauhaus teaching. The curriculum included a one-year preliminary course where students were taught the basic principles of design and colour theory. After completing this foundation year, students entered the various workshops situated in two buildings and trained in at least one craft. These workshops were intended to be self-supporting, relying on private commissions. The tutors were known as "masters" and some of them were members of local guilds, while the students were referred to as "apprentices".

During the Bauhaus' first year, Gropius appointed three artists: **Johannes Itten**, who was responsible

Bauhaus
1919–1933
*Weimar,
Dessau & Berlin*

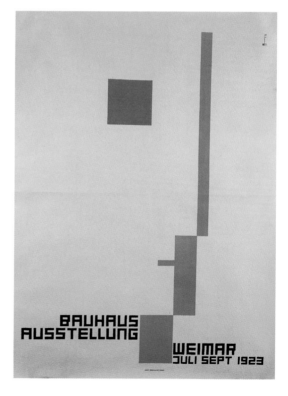

▼ **Fritz Schleifer,**
Poster for the
Bauhaus Exhibition
in Weimar, 1923

▶ **Gyula Pap**,
Candelabra made in
the metal workshop
in Weimar,
1922–1923

for the preliminary course, Lyonel Feininger (1871–1956) and **Gerhard Marcks**. These tutors were joined by other Expressionists – Georg Muche (1895–1987) at the end of 1919, Paul Klee (1879–1940) and Oskar Schlemmer (1888–1943) in 1921 and Wassily Kandinsky (1866–1944) in 1922. During the earliest period of the Bauhaus, it was the charismatic Itten who played the most important role.

Itten's classes, which often commenced with breathing exercises and gymnastics, were based on "intuition and method" or "subjective experience and objective recognition". He believed that materials should be studied so as to unveil their intrinsic qualities and encouraged his students to make inventive constructions from *objets trouvés*. Itten also taught theories of form, colour and contrast as well as the appreciation of art history. In accord with Gropius, Itten believed that natural laws existed for spatial composition just as they did for musical composition and students were taught the importance of elemental geometric forms such as the circle, square and cone. Like Kandinsky, Itten attempted to reintroduce the spiritual to art.

Both Itten and Muche were highly involved with the Mazdaznan sect and tried to introduce its teachings to the Bauhaus. Heads were shaved, loose monk-like garments worn, a vegetarian diet with vast amounts of purifying garlic and regular fastings adhered to, acupuncture and hot baths practised. However, this Mazdaznan adventure into meditation and ritual undermined Gropius' authority and turned students against him. Eventually, conflict arose between Gropius and Itten and the latter subsequently left in December 1922, marking the end of the Expressionist period at the Bauhaus. **Josef Albers** and **László Moholy-Nagy** were appointed as Itten's successors and although they followed the fundamental framework of his preliminary class, they rejected his ideologies for individual creative development and pursued a more industrial approach with students being taken on factory visits. Given Itten's bizarre teaching methods and the school's underlying socialist bearing, it is not surprising that, as a state institution, the Bauhaus attracted much political opposition in Weimar. The local authorities there, under

▶ **Lena Bergner**, Design for a bedroom carpet, 1928

pressure from local guilds who were concerned that work would be taken from their own members by Bauhaus students, demanded the staging of an exhibition so as to justify the State's continued support. The exhibition held in 1923 not only featured work from the Bauhaus but also included **De Stijl** designs such as **Gerrit Rietveld**'s *Red/Blue chair* of 1918–1923. The influence of De Stijl on the Bauhaus cannot be overstated, indeed **Theo van Doesburg** had lectured in Weimar. Another development seen at the 1923 exhibition was the new image that the Bauhaus forged for itself – the graphics from this period were self-consciously modern incorporating "New Typography", which was undoubtedly inspired by De Stijl and Russian **Constructivism**. Although this landmark exhibition received critical acclaim internationally, especially from the United States, it did not allay local fears. When Weimar became the first city in Germany to elect the National Socialist German Workers' Party, the school's grant was halved and in 1925 Gropius was forced to move the Bauhaus, which was by then regarded as a hotbed of communism and subversion.

The school was relocated to Dessau where the ruling Social Democrats and the liberal mayor were far more politically receptive to its continuation and

▲ **Walter Gropius**,
School complex for
the Bauhaus
Dessau, 1925–1926

◄ **Joost Schmidt**,
Poster for the
Bauhaus Exhibition
in Weimar, 1923

success. This industrial city, which was benefitting from the assistance loans from America made available by the Dawes Plan, offered the Bauhaus the financial support it so desperately needed. The aid was granted on the understanding that the school would part-fund itself through the production and retail of its designs. The amount of money offered meant that a new purpose-built school could be constructed and so, in 1926, the Staatliches Bauhaus moved into its newly completed Dessau headquarters, designed by Walter Gropius. In nearby woodland, a series of masters' houses of stark geometric design were constructed, which served as blueprints for future living. The Bauhaus Dessau building itself, with its highly rational pre-fabricated structure, marked an important turning point for the school from crafts towards industrial **Functionalism**. The masters were now referred to as professors and were no longer involved with the guilds while the school instituted the issuing of its own diplomas. By now, Gropius had become disillusioned with socialism and believed that Henry Ford's type of industrial capitalism could benefit workers and that in order to survive the Bauhaus needed to adopt an industrial approach to design.

▼ Marcel Breuer,
Lattenstuhl made
in the furniture
workshop in Weimar,
1922–1924

With the conviction that a better society could be created through the application of functionalism, Bauhaus designs were now conceived for industrial production and a machine aesthetic was consciously adopted. In November

1925, with the financial support of Adolf Sommerfeld, Gropius realized his long-held ambition of establishing a limited company to promote and retail the school's designs. Bauhaus GmbH duly produced a catalogue, designed by **Herbert Bayer**, which illustrated Bauhaus products. The sales of these items were far from overwhelming, however. For the most part, this was no doubt due to the severity of the products' aesthetic but there was a further problem: though they appeared to be machine-made, the majority of the products were in fact unsuitable for industrial production. A few licensing agreements were drawn up between the Bauhaus and outside manufacturers but these did not bring in the revenues Gropius had hoped for.

In 1928, Gropius tried to hand over the directorship of the Bauhaus to **Ludwig Mies van der Rohe** so that he could spend more of his time designing, but Mies refused. Eventually, the Swiss architect, Hannes Meyer (1889–1954), who had been appointed professor of the architecture department when it opened in April 1927, agreed to take over the position at the school, which by now was subtitled "Hochschule für Gestaltung" (Institute of Design).

Meyer, who was a Communist, held the directorship until July 1930. He believed that form had to be governed by function and cost so that products

▲ **Marcel Breuer**, *Model No. B3 Wassily* chair, Bauhaus Dessau, 1926 would be both practical and affordable for working-class consumers. He attempted to introduce lectures on economics, psychology, sociology, biology and Marxism to the curriculum and closed the theatre workshop and reorganized the other workshops in an effort rid the school of the costly "artiness" of previous years. During Meyer's tenure, the Bauhaus' approach to design became more scientific and the earlier Constructivist influence all but vanished. At this time, the Bauhaus also became more politicized with the school site being used as the focus for the political activities of a group of Marxist students. By 1930, there was a Communist cell of thirty-six students, which began to draw some unfavourable press. Upon the instigation of Gropius and Kandinsky, the city of Dessau authority fired Meyer when it was discovered he had provided funds for striking miners.

Under pressure to de-politicize the Bauhaus for its own survival, Mies van der Rohe took over the directorship. He promptly closed the school, replaced its existing statutes, then reopened it and forced the 170 students to re-apply. Five students who had been close to Meyer were expelled. A new curriculum was established with the preliminary course becoming non-compulsory. The study of architecture was given greater importance, which effectively turned the Bauhaus into a school of architecture. Although the applied

▼ **Karl Hermann Haupt**, Design for a covered box, 1923

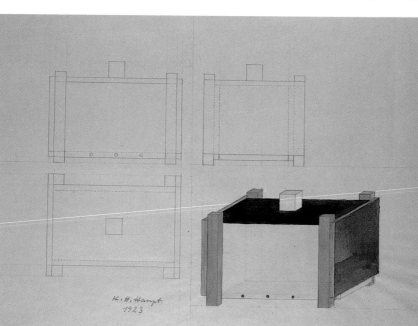

▶ Bauhaus wallpaper
book, 1930

art workshops continued, their remit was to supply only products that could
be industrially manufactured. With Mies, architectural theory triumphed for
a while over politics as he introduced, with his partner **Lily Reich**, the new
apolitical program of "Bau und Ausbau" (building and development). In October 1931, the National Socialists, who had been pushing for the closure of
the Bauhaus, swept to power in Dessau winning 19 out of 36 seats and, on
the 22nd August 1932, a motion was passed for the closure of the school.
The Bauhaus was subsequently re-established by Mies as a private school in
Berlin but its political past caught up with it when the National Socialists
eventually seized power in the city. The Gestapo raided the school's
premises looking for incriminating communist literature and sealed the
building, effectively closing it down. On the 19th July 1933, the masters gath-
ered together and voted to dissolve the Bauhaus – formally marking the end
of this truly remarkable institution.

Many of the masters, including Mies, **Marcel Breuer**, Walter Gropius, and
Josef Albers emigrated to the United States to escape persecution and in
1937 László Moholy-Nagy became the director of the short-lived New
Bauhaus in Chicago. A year later, a retrospective of Bauhaus design was
held at the **Museum of Modern Art, New York**, and the school's reputation

as the most important design institution of the 20th century grew. The Functionalist approach to design pioneered at the Bauhaus had a fundamental impact on subsequent industrial design practice and provided the philosophical bedrock from which the **Modern Movement** evolved. The Bauhaus also had a profound and widespread impact on the way in which design was subsequently taught and this was most especially felt at the **Hochschule für Gestaltung, Ulm**.

▼ **Wilhelm
Wagenfeld**, Tea set
for Jenaer Glaswerke
Schott & Gen.,
c. 1930

Hans Theo Baumann studied art and design in Dresden and Basel, before establishing his own studio in 1955. Since then he has specialized in the design of ceramics and glassware, using simple, unadorned geometric forms, which he softens by rounding off edges sculpturally. Baumann's designs combine the visual qualities of refinement and sturdiness. His clients have included, most notably, Rosenthal, Thomas, **Daum**, Arzberg, Süssmuth and Schönwald. His ceramic and glassware designs, such as the *Brasilia* dinner service of 1971 for Arzberg, brought him significant international recognition. Baumann has also designed textiles, furniture and lighting that express a similar, pared-down aesthetic. His work was presented in a one-man show at the Kunstgewerbemuseum in Cologne 1979–1980 and was included in the Philadelphia Museum of Art's "Design Since 1945" exhibition.

Hans Theo Baumann
b. 1924 *Basel*

▲ *Brasilia* dinner service for Arzberg, 1971

Herbert Bayer

1900 *Haag am Hausruch, Austria*
1985 *Montecito, California*

Herbert Bayer served a design apprenticeship from 1919 to 1920 in the Linz-based office of Georg Schmidthammer and produced his first typographical work there. In 1920, he worked in the studio of Emanuel Margold (1889–1962) in Darmstadt, before studying at the **Bauhaus** in Weimar from 1921 to 1923, where he was taught mural-painting by Oskar Schlemmer (1888–1943) and Wassily Kandinsky (1866–1944). In 1923/1924, he spent a period of time painting and took a trip to Berchtesgaden and Italy. On his return to Germany in April 1925, he became a teacher and a "young master" at the Bauhaus in Dessau. Until 1928, he headed the school's new workshop for printing and publicity, which later became known as the workshop for typography and advertisement design. In this position, Bayer was responsible for all the Bauhaus publicity material and also the layout of the Bauhaus series of books. Importantly, Bayer introduced lower-case sans-serif typography to Bauhaus graphics and encouraged the use of photographic images in advertising design. From 1928, Bayer headed the Berlin studio of the advertising agency Dorland, and was later responsible for the exhibition design of the German section at the 1930 Paris "Exposition de la Société des Artistes Décorateurs". In 1938, Bayer emigrated to the United States and that same year designed the catalogue for the "Bauhaus 1919–1928" exhibition held at the **Museum of Modern Art, New York**. He was a director of Dorland International until 1945, and from 1946 to 1956 was a consultant to the Container Corporation of America. From 1946, he was involved in the design of the Aspen Cultural Center, Colorado. Bayer also worked as a design consultant for many other American corporations including the Atlantic Richfield Company and the General Electric Company. In 1975 he moved to Montecito, California.

▼ Catalogue cover for "Staatliches Bauhaus in Weimar 1919–1923" exhibition, 1923

► Poster for the "50 Jahre Bauhaus" exhibition held in Stuttgart, 1968

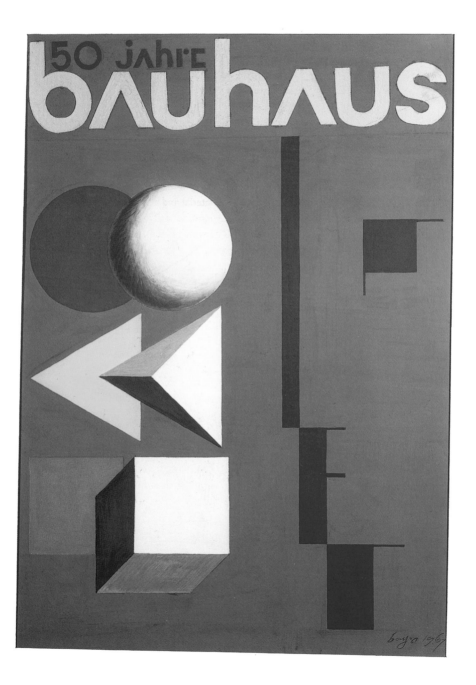

BBPR

Founded 1932
Milan

BBPR, founded in 1932 by Gianluigi Banfi (d. 1945), Lodovico Barbiano di Belgiojoso (b. 1909), Enrico Peressutti (1908–1976) and Ernesto Rogers (1909–1969), was one of the foremost Italian Rationalist architectural groups. In 1935, BBPR became a member of the CIAM (Congrès International d'Architecture Moderne) and in 1939 its partners opened a studio in Milan in the 16th-century cloister of Chiostri delle Benedettine di San Simpliciano. During the Second World War, Banfi died in a concentration camp and Rogers was interned in Switzerland, but after the war, the three surviving partners reformed BBPR and played an important role in the promotion of **Rationalism**. The practice worked in the areas of architecture, (most notably the Velasca Tower, Milan of 1950–1951, completed 1958), town planning, building restoration, exhibition design and product design. From 1954 to 1964, BBPR designed furniture for Arflex using state-of-the-art latex foam upholstery and designed the *Spazio* (1956) and *Arco* (1960) series of metal office furniture for **Olivetti**. BBPR was also an intellectual driving force, its members holding important teaching positions in Italy and abroad. From 1950 to 1962, Peressutti taught at the Architectural Association in London, at Massachusetts Institute of Technology, Princeton University and at Yale University, while Rogers held a professorship at the Politenico di Milano.

▲ *Urania* armchair
for Arflex, 1954

▲▶ *Elettra* chair for
Arflex, 1954

Although apparently having received only two months' formal artistic training, during his short career of just over six years Aubrey Beardsley created
hundreds of black and white illustrations in the **Art Nouveau** style. His work,
which was often highly risqué in nature, captured the decadence of the *fin-
de-siècle* period and brought him notoriety at an early age. In 1894, he was
appointed art director for *The Yellow Book* and his sinuous style of draughtsmanship for this publication was both exotic and erotic. Although his early
illustrations for *Morte d'Arthur* were influenced by the woodcuts of Edward
Burne-Jones (1833–1898), his style became more grotesque and sensual in
his designs for Oscar Wilde's *Salomé*. The later full-blown eroticism of his
images for *The Rape of Lock and Lysistrata* challenged prevailing notions of
acceptability and ensured his lasting fame. Beardsley's erotic illustrations
and graphics advertising theatre productions were intentionally shocking but
served their purpose in grabbing viewers' attention. Beardsley's exaggerated
and tortured forms not only exemplified the Art Nouveau style but, with their
bold outlines, were also highly influential to later graphic designers.

Aubrey Beardsley
1872 Brighton
1898 Mentone, France

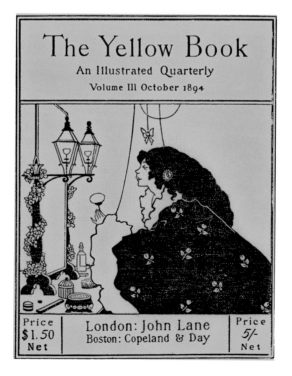

◄ Cover for *The
Yellow Book*, 1894

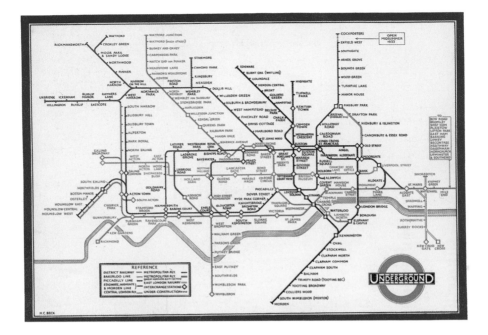

Henry Beck
1903–1974

From 1909, the commercial manager of London Underground, Frank Pick, was responsible for the commissioning of graphic design work. He commissioned designers such as Edward Johnson (1872–1944) and **Edward McKnight Kauffer**, but the most important graphic work produced for the company was designed by Henry Beck who had trained as an engineering draughtsman. The mapping of the London Underground system was becoming increasingly complicated and the maps of it from the 1920s were difficult to follow as they attempted to depict the actual geographic positions of the lines and stations. Beck re-designed the map in 1933 using a diagrammatic approach, which showed the spatial relationship of the stations to one another, rather than the geographical distances between them. This ingenious schematic map used colour symbolically and was worked up from an octagonal grid so that the lines and stations were placed together either at right angles or at 45 degrees, which provided great visual clarity. The inclusion of the River Thames also gave the map a strong and unmistakable London identity.

▲ London
Underground Map
for London
Transport, 1933

Between 1886 and 1889, Peter Behrens studied at the Kunstgewerbeschule in Hamburg, the Kunstschule in Karlsruhe and the Düsseldorfer Akademie. From 1890, he worked as a painter and graphic designer in Munich, where he came under the influence of the **Jugendstil** movement. During this period he produced colourful woodcuts, illustrations and bookbindings in the Jugendstil style and in 1893, became a founding member of the Münchner Sezession (Munich Secession), a progressive group of exhibiting artisans. In 1896, Behrens travelled to Italy and a year later joined **Hermann Obrist**, **August Endell**, **Bruno Paul**, **Richard Riemerschmid** and **Bernhard Pankok** in setting up the **Vereinigte Werkstätten für Kunst im Handwerk** (United Workshops) in Munich, for the production of handcrafted everyday objects. In 1898, Behrens worked on the journal *Pan* and designed his first pieces of furniture, which were exhibited at the Glaspalast in Munich the following year. From 1899 to 1903, he was an active member of the **Darmstädter Künstlerkolonie** (Darmstadt artists' colony), which had been initiated by Grand-Duke Ernst-Ludwig of Hesse-Darmstadt. In Darmstadt, Behrens designed his first building, the Behrens Haus. This project was conceived as a **Gesamtkunstwerk** with furniture and even glassware being specially designed for it. The house marked an important point of departure for Behrens away from Jugendstil and towards a more rational approach to design. Between 1902 and 1903, Behrens gave master classes at the Bayerisches Gewerbemuseum in Nuremberg and exhibited at the "Esposizione Internazionale d'Arte Decorativa Moderna" in Turin. From 1903 to 1907 he was director of the Kunstwerbeschule in Düsseldorf. The commercial sense of "Industrial Art" led the founder of **AEG**, Emil Rathenau – at the instigation of Paul Jordan (the director of the AEG factories) – to appoint Peter Behrens the company's artistic director in 1907. This was the first time a company had employed a designer to advise on all aspects of design. In this capacity, Behrens produced designs for workers' housing and factories, including the concrete, steel and glass AEG Turbine Factory

Peter Behrens
1868 *Hamburg*
1940 *Berlin*

▼ Stoneware jar for Reinhold Hanke, c. 1903

NORDFAÇADE DES HAUSES BEHRENS

(1908–1909), which, as one of the first true expressions of modern indus-trial architecture, was enormously influential. Beyond architecture, Behrens also undertook the design of electrical products such as kettles, fans and clocks, which incorporated in their constructions standardized components that were interchangeable between products so as to rationalize production methods. Behrens was also responsible for the graphics used by the com-pany and created a strong and highly unified corporate identity for it. Shortly after his appointment at AEG, Behrens, together with Peter Bruckmann (1865–1937), **Josef Maria Olbrich**, Fritz Schumacher (1869–1947), Richard Riemerschmid and Hermann Muthesius (1861–1927), founded the **Deut-scher Werkbund** in October 1907. The Deutscher Werkbund was inspired by the **Arts & Crafts Movement** in Britain and attempted to revive the status of craftsmanship and apply it to industrial production. As pioneers of the **Modern Movement**, Deutscher Werkbund members realized that standard-ization, and the rational approach to design this demanded, would have to be adopted if industrially produced goods were to achieve the high level of quality found in handcrafted products. In 1907, Behrens also established a major architectural and design office in Berlin and worked alongside **Walter**

▲ Goblets for Rhei-nische Glashütte AG (originally designed for the Behrens Haus), 1900–1901

◀ North façade of the Behrens Haus on the Mathilden-höhe, Darmstadt, 1901

Gropius from 1907 to 1910, **Ludwig Mies van der Rohe** from 1908 to 1911
and **Le Corbusier** from 1910 to 1911. This highly prolific practice undertook
numerous architectural commissions, including the German Embassy in St.
Petersburg (1911–1912), and much industrial design work over the following
years. After the First World War, Behrens' architectural style moved away
from "scraped classicism" and became influenced by Expressionism as can
be seen in his design for the Frankfurt office building of I. G. Farben Höchst
(1920–1925). In 1926, Behrens designed New Ways, a house in Northamp-
ton for the British industrialist Wynne Bassett-Lowke, which was the first
complete example of modern architecture in Britain. By the 1930s, Behrens
was working in the **International Style**, as his State Tobacco Administration
warehouse project in Linz (1930) demonstrates. Behrens also designed
porcelain for Franz Anton Mehlem, Bonn, and Gebrüder Bauscher, Weiden,
glassware for Rheinische Glashütten, Köln-Ehrenfeld and geometrically patterned linoleum for the Delmenhorster Linoleum Fabrik. From 1922 to 1936,
he was director of architecture at the Akademie der Bildenden Künste, Vienna where he gave master classes. In 1936, he became the director of the
architecture department at the Preußischen Akademie der Künste in Berlin,
a position he held until his death. As one of the very first industrial designers, Behrens was the most influential German practitioner of design in the
20th century. His simple, practical and rational design solutions were immensely influential to the formation and dissemination of Modernism.

Mario Bellini studied architecture at the Politecnico di Milano, graduating in 1959. From 1961 to 1963, he was design director at La Rinascente, the influential chain of Italian department stores. In 1963, he founded an architectural office with Marco Romano and later, in 1973, established Studio Bellini in Milan. Since 1963, he has held the position of chief design consultant for **Olivetti** and his designs for the company include the *Divisumma 18/28* calculators (1973) and the *Praxis 35* and *Praxis 45* typewriters (1981). From 1969 to 1971, he was the president of ADI (Associazione per il Disegno Industriale), and in 1972 showed a mobile micro-living environment entitled *Kar-a-Sutra* at the "Italy: The New Domestic Landscape" exhibition held at the **Museum of Modern Art, New York**. This led to his appointment as a research and design consultant for the car manufacturer Renault in 1978. During the 1970s, Bellini organized workshops to explore the complex relationships that exist between humans and their man-made environment – a theme that has informed all his work. From 1986 to 1991, Bellini was editor of *Domus* and since 1979 he has been a member of the Scientific Council for the Milan Triennale's design section. He held the positions of professor of design at the Istituto Superiore del Disegno Industriale, Venice from 1962 to 1965, professor of industrial design at the Hochschule für angewandte Kunst, Vienna from 1982 to 1983 and professor of industrial design at the Domus

Mario Bellini
b. 1935 *Milan*

▼ *Programma 1a* calculator for Olivetti, 1965

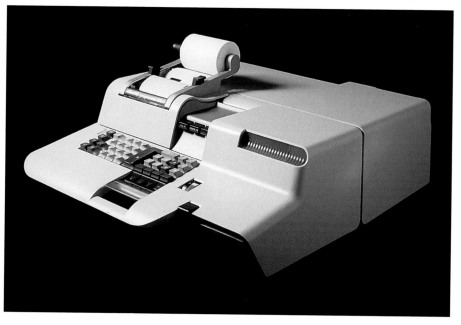

▲ *Cab* armchair and
Cab chair for Cassina,
1982 & 1976

Academy, Milan from 1986 to 1991. Bellini has also been a visiting lecturer to many other design colleges including the **Royal College of Art, London**. His most notable furniture designs include the *Le Bambole* seating system for B&B Italia (1972), the *Cab* seating for Cassina (1977) and the *Figura* office seating programme co-designed with Dieter Thiel for **Vitra** (1985). He has also designed lighting for Flos, **Artemide** and Erco and audio equipment for Yahama and BrionVega. Bellini has received numerous design accolades including seven **Compasso d'Oro** awards.

► Bachelor's apartment, with a living-dining room and a study, c. 1952

From the age of fourteen, Ward Bennett worked as a fashion sketcher for Saks Fifth Avenue and later for Joe Junior, before enrolling at the Porto Romano School of Art, Florence in 1937. From 1937 to 1938, he trained at the Académie de la Grande Chaumière, Paris while also working with the sculptor Constantin Brancusi (1876–1957). On his return to the United States, he moved to Los Angeles and then to San Francisco where he worked as a window dresser. Between 1940 and 1943, he served in the U. S. Army and afterwards studied painting under Hans Hoffmann (1880–1966) in New York. In 1947, he undertook the interior design of a penthouse for Harry Jason in New York, which established his reputation. From 1948 to 1950, he worked in **Le Corbusier**'s design practice in Paris, and on his return to New York in 1950 established his own interior design office. He subsequently undertook interior projects in America, Italy and Britain for corporate clients such as Chase Manhattan Bank and private clients such as the Rockefeller and Agnelli families. He is reputedly the inventor of the sunken "conversation pit" and the "U"-shaped sofa. Bennett's interior designs were also notable for his use of cabinet room dividers and Japanese screens to divide spaces. During his career, Bennett executed over one hundred furniture and textile designs for Brickel Associates, New York. He also designed china, glass and cutlery for Tiffany & Co., New York. From 1962 to 1963, he was a visiting professor at Yale University, and from 1969 to 1971 taught at the Pratt Institute, New York, where he became an associate professor. Bennett frequently used salvaged industrial materials, including telegraph poles, in his designs, and is generally regarded as one of the originators of the **High Tech** style.

Ward Bennett
b. 1917 *New York*

The advertising agency S. H. Benson's was established by Samuel Herbert Benson in 1893 on the advice of John Johnson, the owner of Bovril Ltd. Apart from Bovril, which was the agency's first client, S. H. Benson's also undertook graphics for Colman's, Rowntree and most notably Guinness. Using the talents of well-known artists and cartoonists such as **Abram Games**, **Tom Eckersley**, **Tom Purvis** (1888–1959), H. M. Bateman (1887–1970) and John Gilroy (1898–1985), S. H. Benson's was one of the first agencies to exploit the power of humour in advertising. From 1928 to 1969, John Gilroy designed posters for Guinness with the well-known catch phrases "My Goodness My Guinness", "Guinness for Strength" and "Guinness is Good for You", featuring humourous characters and creatures such as the Guinness Toucan, which became instantly recognizable to the British populace in the 1920s and 1930s. During the Second World War, S. H. Benson's posters incorporated light-hearted war-time themes. S. H. Benson's imagery was quintessentially British and was vital in establishing the identities of the products being advertised. The company's graphic designs demonstrated for the first time that an advertisement could do more than simply display a product – the viewer's attention could be held longer and a more powerful product association established if humour was used. The work of S. H. Benson's was enormously influential to later advertising design and product branding.

▼ John Gilroy, *My Goodness, My Guinness* poster for Guinness, 1936

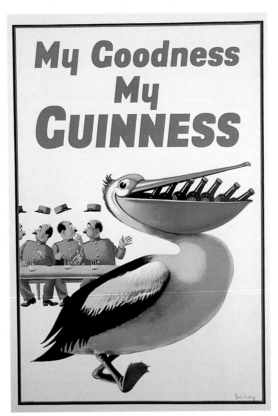

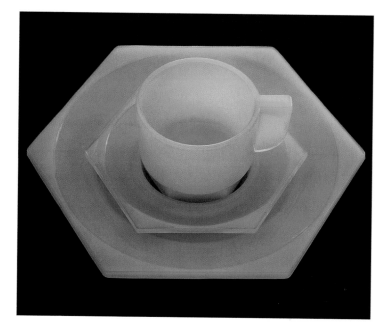

Hendrik Petrus Berlage trained at the Academy of Fine Art in Amsterdam before studying under Gottfried Semper (1803–1979) at the Bauschule, Eidgenössische Technische Hochschule, Zurich from 1875 to 1878. He subsequently worked for the Dutch Gothic Revivalist architect, Petrus Cuypers (1827–1921). In 1889, Berlage established his own architectural office in Amsterdam and abandoned historicism in favour of simplicity and honesty of construction. Although the detailing of his Amsterdam Exchange (1897–1903) was influenced by the Romanesque, its treatment was highly original and predicted Dutch Expressionism. During a trip to America in 1911, Berlage was influenced by **Frank Lloyd Wright** and Louis Sullivan (1856–1924) and on his return brought their work to the attention of both Swiss and Dutch architects. His rather heavy furniture designs were executed by the Het Binnenhuis workshop in Amsterdam. He moved to The Hague in 1911. From 1914 to 1919, he headed the construction department of W. H. Müller & Co. and later worked as a freelance architect. From 1924, he taught at Delft Polytechnic, and in 1928 attended the CIAM's (Congrès International d'Architecture Moderne) first congress. Although Berlage's designs were influential to **De Stijl**, they should be regarded as manifestations of Expressionism rather than of Modernism.

Hendrik Petrus Berlage
1856 *Amsterdam*
1934 *The Hague*

Lucian Bernhard

1883 *Stuttgart*
1972 *New York*

Lucian Bernhard studied at the Akademie der Kunst, Munich before moving to Berlin in 1901, where he began designing commercial posters using rounded serif typography, boldly outlined images and a reduced colour palette. These posters were influenced by the graphic work of the two British artists, William Nicholson (1872–1949) and James Pryde (1869–1941) who worked under the name of "Beggarstaffs" in England. One of Bernhard's first designs was executed for a competition to design an advertisement for Priester matches. His visually striking and prize-winning entry (1905), with its bold lettering and elimination of superfluous detailing, helped to establish his reputation. Bernhard was one of the leading exponents of the German Plakatstil, an approach in which simplified images were set against a plain background, accompanied by only a short copyline or company name. Bernhard was also a leading figure in the design of the Sachplakat (object poster), which boldly presented the advertised product with its brand name but without any advertising copy explaining its merits. In 1909, he helped found the magazine for collectors, *Das Plakat* (later known as *Gebrauchsgraphik*), which reproduced his poster designs and used the Bernhard Antiqua typeface that he had previously designed for Bauer, Frankfurt. In 1914,

▼ Lithographic
poster for Stiller
advertising shoes,
c. 1908

Bernhard designed his colourful and bold advertising posters and packaging for Bosch spark plugs. While living in Berlin he was one of a stable of graphic designers, including Hans Rudi Erdt (1883–1918) and Julius Gipkens (1883–1960s), who regularly submitted designs to the printers, Hollerbaum & Schmidt, well-known for their progressive Sachplakat advertising. In 1920, Bernhard was the first professor of poster design at the Akademie der Kunst Berlin. Three years later, he moved to New York and opened a design studio there, while continuing to run his office in Berlin. In the United States, he designed several fonts for American Type Founders (during his career he invented some thirty-six new typefaces) and many logos and posters as well as advertising, most notably for Amoco. In America, Bernhard also undertook stage design and interior design commissions. In 1928, together with fellow émigré designers Paul Poiret (1879–1944) and **Bruno Paul** and the American artist, Rockwell Kent (1882–1971), he established the interior design consultancy, Contempora.

▲ Lithographic poster for Bosch advertising sparkplugs, 1914

Harry Bertoia

1915 *San Lorenzo, Italy*
1978 *Bally, Pennsylvania*

Harry Bertoia emigrated with his family from Italy to the United States in 1930. In 1936, he graduated from the Cass Technical High School, Detroit and then studied at the Art School of the Detroit Society of Arts and Crafts until 1937. From 1937 to 1939, he trained on a scholarship at the **Cranbrook Academy of Art**, Michigan. Bertoia re-established the metalworking studio there, which had closed in 1933 and as head of that department taught from 1939 to 1943, when the workshop was closed due to wartime restrictions on materials. For a brief period, he worked in Cranbrook's graphic department. His father-in-law, William Valentiner, was director of the Detroit Institute of Arts and a champion of the abstract art movement. He undoubtedly influenced Bertoia's increasing move towards hard-edge abstraction and away from his earlier streamline style. Having moved to Venice, California in 1943, Bertoia worked with **Charles and Ray Eames** at the Evans Products Company, developing techniques for moulding plywood. After the Second World War, he was employed for a short period by the Eameses' Plyformed Products Company. However, after several disagreements over his contract,

▶ *Model No. 421LU Diamond* chair for Knoll International, 1950–1952

Bertoia left the company and began working for **Knoll**. In 1946, Bertoia became an American citizen and moved to Bally, Pennsylvania, so as to be close to the Knoll factory there. Within four years, he had established his own design and sculpting studio and was producing designs for Knoll. His innovative wire chairs, designed for Knoll in 1951, were such a commercial success, despite being almost entirely constructed by hand, that the royalties from them allowed him to concentrate solely on his sculpting career. As a sculptor, Bertoia is primarily remembered for his freestanding metal works, some of which resonated with sound when touched or had moving elements that chimed in the wind. Bertoia was awarded a gold medal by the Architectural League of New York for a screen commissioned by the Manufacturers Hanover Trust Co. (1954), and also received awards from the American Institute of Architects in 1973 and the American Academy of Letters in 1975. Bertoia's designs not only addressed functional requirements but, like his sculptures, were also studies in form and space.

▲ Coffee service (Prototype executed while at Cranbrook Academy), c. 1937–1943

Fulvio Bianconi moved to Venice with his family while still a child. During his youth, he worked in a glass studio in Madonna dell'Orto, and later studied at the Accademia di Belle Arti and the Liceo Scientifico in Venice. He first worked as a glass painter and earned a living painting portraits of guests staying in Venetian hotels. In 1935, he moved to Milan, where he designed perfume bottles for Visconti di Modrone. Then, in 1939, he worked for Motta and, after the Second World War, was employed by Gi Vi Emme, a perfume manufacturer, to design perfume bottles and graphics as well as a mural for the company's dining room. In 1948, Bianconi met **Paolo Venini** and began working for his glass studio. That same year, Venini exhibited Bianconi's playful glass Commedia dell'Arte figurines at the Venice Biennale. From 1948 to 1951, Bianconi designed more figurines for Venini as well as his famous and often copied handkerchief vase, or *Fazzoletto*. Other designs for Venini included his colourful patchwork and striped vessels known as *Pezzato* (pieced) and *A Spicchi* (sliced), which were exhibited at the 1951 Milan IX Triennale. From 1951, Bianconi worked as an independent designer, his glassware being produced by a number of manufacturers including Cenedese and Danese. For the next decade, he continued designing biomorphic vessels with motifs inspired by Abstract Expressionism and his tartan-like *Scozzese* vessels for Venini. During the 1960s, Bianconi also designed a vase with an internal spiral motif for Vistosi, which won an award at the 1964 Milan XIII Triennale, and a series of vases known as *Informali*. Gradually, through the 1970s, his work became increasingly sculptural. In more recent years, he has designed for the Swiss glass manufacturer, Hersgswil. During his long career, Bianconi also worked as a graphic designer for HMV, Pathé, Fiat and Pirelli as well as the publishing houses, Mondadori and Garzanti.

Fulvio Bianconi
1915 *Padua, Italy*
1996 *Milan*

◄ Striped bottle with stopper for Venini, c. 1950

▼ *Pezzato* vase for Venini, 1951

Max Bill

1908 Winterthur, Switzerland
1994 Berlin

Max Bill studied silversmithing at the Kunstgewerbeschule, Zurich from 1924 to 1927, during which period his designs were influenced by Cubism and Dada. He then studied art for two years at the Dessau **Bauhaus** and fully embraced the school's functionalist approach to design. On completion of his studies, Bill returned to Zurich and worked as a painter, architect and graphic designer. He became the leading exponent of **Constructivism** within the Swiss School of graphics and during the 1930s designed graphics for the Wohnbedarf store in Zurich. He had established his own architectural office by 1930 and, as a member of the SWB (Schweizerischer Werkbund), designed the Neubühl estate near Zurich (1930–1932) in the modern style. In 1931, he adopted **Theo van Doesburg**'s concept of "concrete art", which argued that universality could only be achieved through clarity. From 1932 onwards, he also worked as a sculptor and became a member of various art organizations including the Abstraction-Création group in Paris, the Allianz (Association of Modern Swiss Artists), the CIAM (Congrès International d'Architecture Moderne) and the UAM (Union des Artistes Modernes). In 1944, he turned his attention to industrial design and his subsequent aluminium wall clock (1957), manufactured by Junghans, and minimalist *Ulmer Hocker* stool (1954) are among his best-known products.

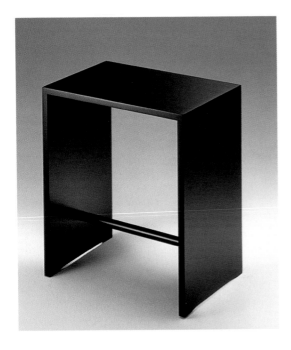

◄ *Ulmer Hocker*, 1954
(reissued by Zanotta)

▲ *Model No. 32/0389 wall clock, for Junghans, 1957*

Bill was responsible for setting up the German awards and exhibitions "Die Gute Industrieform", and co-founded the influential **Hochschule für Gestaltung, Ulm** in 1951, becoming the school's rector and head of its architectural and product design departments for the first five years. At Ulm, Bill championed Bauhaus-type geometric formalism, believing that products based on mathematical laws had an aesthetic purity and thereby a greater universality of appeal. This approach to design was continued by **Hans Gugelot** when he took over Ulm's product design department and was particularly influential to his pupil **Dieter Rams**. Upon leaving Ulm, Bill set up his own Zurich-based studio in 1957 and concentrated on sculpture and painting. He was the chief architect of the "Educating and Creating" pavilion at the Swiss National Exhibition of 1964 and the same year was made an honorary member of the AIA (American Institute of Architects). While the geometric formalism that Bill and many other exponents of the **Modern Movement** promoted was intended as a means of achieving greater universality, its severity and lack of humanizing qualities prevented its wide scale acceptance.

▲ Main entrance to Siegfried Bing's Pavillon de l'Art Nouveau for the 1900 Paris "Exposition Universelle" (painting by G. de Feure)

Siegfried Bing worked in a ceramics factory in Hamburg up to the outbreak of the Franco-Prussian War. In 1877, he opened an oriental warehouse in Paris – like Arthur Liberty in London two years before him – in response to the demand for eastern wares, and especially Japanese Art, made fashionable by the **Aesthetic Movement**. He became a friend of the designer **Louis Comfort Tiffany** and began retailing his glassware. In 1895, Bing opened his influential store, "L'Art Nouveau", at 22 Rue de Provence, retailing designs by **Émile Gallé** and **René Lalique** among others, alongside imported oriental art. The term **Art Nouveau** was coined after Bing's enterprise, which championed this ahistorical and international style that was inspired by organic growth (in Italy the style was known as "Stile Liberty" after Liberty & Co.). Through his firm, Bing also sold **Liberty & Co.** and Morris & Co. textiles as well as metalwork designed by W. A. S. Benson (1854–1924). Bing exhibited his Pavillon de l'Art Nouveau at the 1900 "Exposition Universelle et Internationale de Paris" to great acclaim. This pavilion consisted of six rooms designed by **Georges de Feure**, **Eugène Gaillard** and Edward Colonna (1862–1948). De Feure's two interiors were especially praised in *The Studio* and in 1903 Bing devoted an exhibition exclusively to his work. Bing also sold work by the artists Henri Toulouse-Lautrec (1864–1901) and Édouard Vuillard (1868–1940) and designers Alexandre Charpentier (1856–1909) and Auguste Delaherche (1857–1940) as well as stained-glass panels by Pierre Bonnard (1867–1947), which were manufactured by Tiffany. An American branch of the "Maison de L'Art Nouveau" was opened in 1887 in New York by John Getz, and by 1900 Siegfried Bing was retailing American designs, such as **Grueby** ceramics, in Europe. Bing's son Marcel took over the running of the shop in 1905, enabling Siegfried to turn his attention to antique dealing.

Siegfried Bing

1838 *Hamburg*
1905 *Vaucresson nr. Paris*

▼ Advertisement for Maison de l'Art Nouveau, c. 1900

L'ART NOUVEAU BING

PARIS
22, RUE DE PROVENCE

Installations Modernes

MEUBLES, TENTURES, TAPIS, OBJETS D'ART

A l'Exposition Universelle de 1900, modèles de Meubles vendus à tous les Musées d'Europe et hors d'Europe : Londres, Berlin, Crefeld, Hambourg, Kaiserslautern, Leipzig, Mulhouse, Nuremberg, Budapest, Gratz, Lemberg, Vienne, Copenhague, Naples, St-Pétersbourg, Helsingfors, Aarau, Berne, Drontheim, Tokio, Musée des Arts décoratifs de Paris, etc.

HORS CONCOURS, MEMBRE DU JURY

Unlike **Organic Design**, which is informed by nature and attempts to capture its abstract essence, Biomorphism copies and often distorts forms found in the natural world for purely decorative purposes. Biomorphism is not only characteristic of certain 20th-century styles, it can also be found in a number of much earlier period styles such as Baroque and Rococo. During the last quarter of the 19th century, significant advances in the understanding of the natural sciences were achieved and the natural world was seen by designers such as **William Morris** and **Christopher Dresser** as a lexicon of design. At the turn of the century, the general interest in botany was expressed through the biomorphic forms adopted by designers allied to **Art Nouveau**. These included swirling tendril-like motifs, elongated vegetal forms and a curious "melting" of naturalistic elements into one another. Once the Art Nouveau style had been superseded by **Art Deco** and Modernism, Biomorphism did not re-emerge in design until the 1940s, when the highly biomorphic furniture of the Italian designer **Carlo Mollino** and his followers, sometimes referred to as Turinese Baroque, pushed the expressive potential of wood to the limit. In contrast, contemporary **avant-garde** designers in America, such as **Charles and Ray Eames**, were developing a vocabulary of design that was inherently organic. The forms of their products, such as the *LCW* chair of 1945, were informed by a sound understanding of humanizing factors including ergonomics. Designs such as these were extremely influential and led many mainstream designers to adopt biomorphic forms, especially asymmetrical kidney shapes. Indeed, it is these frequently **Kitsch** biomorphic shapes that are most often generally associated with the look of the 1950s. In the 1990s, Organic design has re-emerged, together with its stylistic spin-off, biomorphism. This is particularly evident in automotive design, where the trend has been towards both progressive organic forms and retro-styled biomorphic forms, redolent of the 1950s.

► Deep sea vase manufactured by Amphora, c. 1900

▼ **Carlo Graffi & Franco Campo**, Armchair, c. 1955

Misha Black

1910 *Baku, Azerbaijan*
1977 *London*

Misha Black emigrated with his parents to Britain in 1912. He studied at the
Central School of Arts & Crafts, London, for a short while but was essentially
a self-taught designer and architect. He started off, in 1928, designing exhi-
bition stands, followed in 1929 by a series of coffee shops in London and
Manchester for Kardomah. By 1930, he had established Studio Z and, three
years later, began working with Milner Gray (b. 1899) at the Bassett-Gray
Group of Artists and Writers, which in 1935 became the Industrial Design
Partnership. This was the first inter-disciplinary design consultancy in
Britain and, most notably, designed television sets and radios for Ekco.
Black became a member of the Artists' International Association and ac-
tively supported the group's anti-war stance. In 1938, he was appointed secretary of MARS (Modern Architecture Research Group) and, from 1940 to
1945, he worked as an exhibition designer for the Ministry of Information.
Together with Milner Gray, Black co-founded the Design Research Unit in
1943 and, two years later, the Design Research Group. Black contributed
greatly to the 1946 "Britain Can Make It" exhibition, where his famous
"What Industrial Design Means" exhibit illustrated the design process
through the design of an egg cup. He was also involved in the design of the
1951 "Festival of Britain" and, throughout his career, tirelessly promoted
modern design. As professor of industrial design at the **Royal College of Art,
London** from 1959 to 1975, Black attempted to bring the teaching of design
and engineering together. In so doing, he helped advance the development
of design engineering as an important specialist discipline.

▲ **Misha Black &
Ronald Armstrong,**
Stainless steel
saucepan set for
Ernest Stevens, 1958

Cini Mariani Boeri studied architecture at the Politecnico di Milano, graduating in 1951. From 1952 to 1963, she worked in the design office of **Marco Zanuso**, before establishing her own studio in Milan. From the mid-1960s, she designed furniture for the Italian manufacturer, Arflex, including her block-like polyurethane foam *Bobo* seating (1967) and her sectional *Serpetone* sofa (1971) made of self-skinning polyurethane foam, which could be extended indefinitely with the addition of extra sections. In 1966, having begun experimenting with plastics, Boeri designed luggage for Franzi in injection-moulded ABS. Her *Lunario* tables, designed for Gavina in 1970, were later manufactured by **Knoll**. She also designed showrooms from 1972 to 1983 for Knoll, and in 1976 the company launched her *Brigadier* seating. She was awarded a **Compasso d'Oro** in 1979 for her *Strips* seating and bedding (1972), which utilized quilted covers and was co-designed with Laura Griziotti (b. 1942). From 1980 to 1983, Boeri taught at the Politecnico di Milano as well as the University of California, Berkeley. Then, in 1983, she was commissioned to design pre-fabricated housing for the Misawa Company, Tokyo. With Tomu Katayanagi, she co-designed the single-form glass *Ghost* chair for Fiam in 1987, and has also designed lighting for **Artemide**, Arteluce, Stilnovo and Venini.

Cini Mariani Boeri
b. 1924 *Milan*

▲ *Bobo* chair for Arflex, 1967

Theodor Bogler

1897 *Hofgeismar, Germany*
1968 *Maria Laach, Germany*

Theodor Bogler was among the first intake of students to the **Bauhaus** in 1919, and from 1920, he worked in the pottery workshop at Dornburg an der Saale, near Weimar, an annex of the school. His glazed earthenware teapots of 1923, which were made as prototypes in the workshop, were conceived for serial production and their elemental shaped components (handles, spouts and lids) could be differently positioned so as to create four variations. From 1923 to 1924, Bogler headed the workshop with **Otto Lindig** and advocated the practice of industrial design. In 1923, he designed a ceramic mocha machine for mass-production that could be easily disassembled, and was manufactured by the Aelteste Volkstedter Porzellanfabrik. Bogler also designed earthenware kitchen containers that were produced by the Steingutfabrik Velten-Vordam, where he became artistic director in 1925 and designed numerous products. Bogler's ceramics were included in the 1923 Bauhaus Exhibition and were illustrated in the publications, *Staatliches Bauhaus, Weimar, 1919–1923* (1923) and *Neue Arbeiten der Bauhaus Werkstätten* (1925). Although Bogler became a Benedictine monk in 1932, he produced some designs for the HB-Werkstätten of Hedwig Bollhagen, Marwitz from 1934 to 1938 and for the Staatliche Majolika-Manufaktur, Karlsruhe from 1936 to 1948.

▲ Earthenware teapot for the Bauhaus ceramics workshop at Dornburg, 1923

The son of the craftsman Gaetano Borsani, who won a silver medal at the first Monza Triennale in 1927, Osvaldo Borsani studied at the Politecnico di Milano, graduating in 1937. After his studies, he worked in his father's workshop, the Arredamento Borsani in Varedo, formerly known as the Atelier Varedo. In 1953, Osvaldo and his twin brother, Fulgenzio, founded the furniture manufacturing company Tecno. At first, Tecno produced only Osvaldo Borsani's designs, however, other designers' work was later manufactured by the company although Osvaldo remained its chief designer. The Tecno logo, comprising a large "T", was designed in collaboration with Robert Mango (b. 1920) and was used for the first time at the 1954 Milan Triennale. At this Triennale, Osvaldo built a small house in the park and furnished it with his lounge chair *P40*, which can be adjusted into 468 different positions, and his sofa *D70*, which can be turned into a divan bed (both 1954). Flexible designs such as these were intended to meet the need for space-saving furniture in post-war housing. Borsani's highly portable *S80* plywood folding chair of 1954 was similarly inventive. In 1956, Tecno opened its first shop on Via Montenapoleone in Milan to sell its integrated product line. As Osvaldo Borsani explained, "our products aren't the consequence of a sudden genial inspiration, but rather connected to one another; our collections have been progressively extended and integrated with no sudden fancies". Together with seven other designers, Borsani established the design journal *Ottagano* in 1966, with the aim of bringing Italian design to an international audience. Then, in 1968, with Eugenio Carli (b. 1923), Borsani co-designed the all-white Graphis office system, which redefined the look of the office environment. Two years later, Borsani established the Centro Progetti Tecno specifically for the design and development of contract furnishings.

Osvaldo Borsani
1911 *Milan*
1985 *Milan*

▾ *Model No. D70*
Sofa for Tecno, 1954

Mario Botta

b. 1943 *Mendrisio, Switzerland*

Mario Botta was apprenticed as a technical draughtsman in the architectural office of Tita Carloni and Luigi Camenischi from 1958 to 1961. He then studied at the Liceo Artistico, Milan from 1961 to 1964, and while there designed a house in Genestretta for the clergy that was strongly geometric in form. From 1964 to 1969, Botta studied architecture at the Istituto Universitario di Architettura, Venice, and worked for a while in 1965 in the Paris office of **Le Corbusier** and in the Venice studio of Jullian de la Fuente and José Oubrerie. He established his own design and architectural office in Lugano in 1969, the year he met Louis Kahn (1901–1974), and became involved in the design of the new Palazzo dei Congressi Laurea all'UIA in Venice. During the 1970s, Botta worked mainly on architectural projects, including the Staatsbank office building in Fribourg and numerous houses, such as his striped house in Ligornetto. Then, in the 1980s Botta turned his attention to furniture design. His *Seconda* chair of 1982 and his *Quinta* armchair of 1986, both manufactured by Alias, are quintessential examples of the short-lived "Matt Black" style. The very graphic, hard-edged lines of these designs, together with their well-resolved geometric structure reveal Botta's background in drafting and engineering. His totem-like *Shogun Terra* floor lamp of 1985 for **Artemide** with its bold geometric form, which is enhanced by its black and white striping, is an elegant affirmation of his belief that "Geometry is balance". Botta's work can be described as "Neo-High-Tech" and is notable for demonstrating a more sophisticated and rational aspect of **Post-Modernism**.

▼ *Seconda* chair for Alias, 1982

► *Shogun Terra* floor lamp for Artemide, 1985

◄ Brass and nickel plated ashtray for the metal workshop at the Bauhaus, Weimar, 1924

◄ *Kandem* table lamp for Körting & Mathiesen, 1928

Marianne Brandt enrolled at the Staatliches **Bauhaus**, Weimar in 1924. She served an apprenticeship in the metal workshop, which was then directed by **László Moholy-Nagy**. After taking her journeyman's exam, Brandt became deputy director of the workshop and organized projects in collaboration with the lighting manufacturers, Körting & Mathiesen AG (Kandem) in Leipzig and Schwintzer & Gräff, Berlin. At the Bauhaus, she worked alongside fellow metal-workers, **Christian Dell** and Hans Przyrembel (1900–1945), and co-designed the *Kandem* light with Hin Bredendieck (b. 1904) in 1928, as part of a class project. From 1928 to 1929, Brandt was the assistant master of the metal workshop at the Dessau Bauhaus. In 1929, she worked in the architectural office of **Walter Gropius** in Berlin and, over the next three years, developed new design concepts for the Metallwarenfabrik Ruppelwerk, Gotha. She then returned to Chemnitz, where she took up painting. During this period, she tried to license some of her products to the department store Wohnbedarf. Brandt taught at the Hochschule für Bildende Künste, Dresden from 1949 to 1951 and at the Institut für angewandte Kunst, East Berlin from 1951 to 1954, during which time she visited China and organized an industrial design exhibition there on behalf of the German government.

Marianne Brandt
1893 *Chemnitz, Germany*
1983 *Halle/Saale*

Andrea Branzi

b. 1938 *Florence*

▼ *Animali Domestici* chair for Zabro-Zanotta, 1985

Andrea Branzi studied architecture in his home city of Florence before co-founding the **Radical Design** group **Archizoom** with **Paolo Deganello**, Gilberto Corretti (b. 1941) and Massimo Morozzi (b.1941). Established in 1966, the group subsequently produced many **Anti-Design** furniture pieces that were extremely influential, such as the **Kitsch** *Safari* seating unit (1968) and the ironic *Mies* chair (1969). Branzi was also involved in Archizoom's architectural projections such as *No-Stop City*, and from 1972 to 1975 he contributed many theoretical writings to the magazine *Casabella*. Branzi set up his own design studio in Milan in 1973, and exhibited at the Venice Biennale in 1976, 1978 and 1980. Together with **Michele De Lucchi** and Paola Navone (b. 1950), he organized the landmark exhibition "Il Disegno Italiano degli anni 50" at Centrokappa in Naviglio, Milan in 1977, which re-assessed the contribution of post-war Italian design and in so doing had an enormous impact on Italian design throughout the 1980s. Branzi settled in Milan in 1979, exhibiting with **Studio Alchimia**. His designs of the 1980s include the *Century* sofa (1982) and the *Magnolia* bookcase (1985), as well as ceramics for **Memphis**, while in the 1990s he designed more rational furniture for Zanotta, such as his *Niccola* chair (1992). From 1982 to 1983, he was professor of industrial design at the Università di Palermo, and in 1983 was appointed educational director of the post-graduate design school, the Domus Academy, Milan. For the next four years, Branzi was the editor of *Modo* magazine and, for a brief period, was president of the design journal *Domus*. In 1985, Branzi designed his *Animali Domestici* series of furniture, and two years later published his book of the same title. In this publication, he argued that new relationships should be built between man and the environment and that it was valid to think of furnishings in the same terms as household pets. Branzi received the **Compasso D'Oro** speciale award in 1987, in recognition of his contribution to design. Since 1991, he has directed the Domus Design Agency in Tokyo and from 1991 to 1993, he took part in the Vitra Design Museum's "Citizen Office" project.

▲ Aluminium vases
from the *Amnesie
(Amnesia)* series for
the Design Gallery
Milano, 1991

Braun

Founded 1921
Frankfurt/Main

Max Braun (1890–1951), an engineer born in East Prussia, founded a manufacturing company in Frankfurt in 1921 to produce connectors for drive belts and scientific apparatus. In 1923, he began producing components for the newly emerging radio industry and, with the advent of plastic pellets in 1925, was among the first to manufacture components such as dials and knobs in this new material using home-made presses. In 1928, the company moved into a functional modern factory building on the Idsteiner Straße in Frankfurt, and a year later began producing their own radio sets, which were some of the first to incorporate the receiver and speaker in a single unit. The company expanded its product range in 1932, becoming one of the first manufacturers to introduce radio/phonograph combination sets. Braun developed its first battery-powered radio in 1936 and won an award at the 1937 Paris "Exposition Internationale des Arts et Techniques dans la Vie Moderne" for "exceptional achievements in phonographs". By 1947, the company was mass-producing radio sets and its *Manulux* flashlights, and

▼ Hans Gugelot &
Gerd Alfred Müller,
Sixtant SM 31 electric
shaver for Braun,
1962

in 1950 developed its first electric razor, the *S50*. This shaver incorporated an oscillating cutter-block screened by a thin steel shaver foil – a system that is still used today. In 1950, Braun also launched its first domestic appliance, the *Multimix*. After the death of the founder, Max Braun, in 1951, the firm was headed by his two sons, Artur (b. 1925) and Erwin (b. 1921), who decided to implement a rational and systematic design programme, and in 1952 the Braun trademark assumed its present day form. In 1953, Erwin identified a marketing opportunity for distinctive radios that were "honest, unobtrusive and practical devices" with a modern aesthetic. To this end, Professor **Wilhelm Wagenfeld** and designers, such as Fritz Eichler (1911–1991), associated with the **Hochschule für Gestaltung, Ulm**, were commissioned in 1954 to redesign the com-

pany's radios and phonographs. This new Braun line was introduced at the Düsseldorf Radio Fair in 1955 and won international acclaim. An in-house design department was established in 1956, headed by Eichler. In this capacity, Eichler developed a coherent house style for the company, based on geometric simplicity, utility and a functionalist approach to the design process. The Braun style was not only used in the design of products but was also applied to all areas of **corporate design** including packaging, logos and advertising. In addition, Eichler commissioned other designers associated with the Hochschule für Gestaltung, such as **Otl Aicher**, **Hans Gugelot** and **Dieter Rams**, to design sleek unornamented products. Notable designs from this period include Eichler and Artur Braun's line of radios and phonographs and Dieter Rams and Hans Gugelot's *Phonosuper SK4* (1955), which was nicknamed "Snow White's Coffin". Rams also designed the *Transistor 1* portable radio (1956), *T3-T4* pocket radio (1958) and the first component-

▲ **Gerd Alfred Müller**, *KM3* food mixer for Braun, 1957

based hi-fi system, the *Studio 2* (1959) – all of which helped establish Braun's international reputation. In 1955, the designer Gerd Alfred Müller (b. 1932) joined the Braun design team and was responsible for some of the company's best known designs from the late 1950s, including his *KM3* multipurpose kitchen mixer (1957), which embodied the austere rationalist aesthetic that became synonymous with German post-war design. Dieter Rams became head of the company's design department in 1961, and seven years later was appointed director of design. The **Museum of Modern Art, New York** opened a new design gallery with an exhibit of Braun's entire product line in 1964, and a year later, bolstered by its commercial success, the company began building a new headquarters in Kronberg/Taunus near Frankfurt. In the years that followed, Braun introduced a series of landmark designs including the *Permanent* lighter (1966) that incorporated an electromagnetic device rather than a traditional friction cylinder, the *ET22* elec-

▼ **Roland Ullmann,** *Flex Integral 6550 Ultra Speed* shaver for Braun, 1998

tronic pocket calculator (1976) and the first radio-controlled clock (1977). In 1967, the Gillette Company based in Boston acquired a controlling interest in Braun AG, and a year later the International Braun Awards for design in engineering were established. The company itself was awarded the first Corporate Design Award at the 1983 Hanover trade fair, for "exemplary conception of product design, information and presentation". Braun discontinued hi-fi production in 1990 so as to concentrate on the production of personal grooming products, such as the *Silk-épil EE1* depilator (1989), the highly successful *Flex Control* line of razors (1990) and the *Plak Control D5* electric toothbrush (1991) as well as a range of hair driers. During the 1990s, Braun also introduced innovative coffee machines, food processors, hand mixers, irons and alarm clocks. In 1996, Braun

launched the *Thermoscan* infrared thermometer, which marked the company's entry into the personal diagnostic appliance market. Certainly, Braun's success lies in the fact that their products are jointly developed by designers, engineers and marketing experts in accordance with basic design principles. The company uses design innovation to achieve technical and functional advances and has established a tradition of progressiveness within its design team. The strong aesthetic clarity of Braun products is the outcome of a logical ordering of elements and the quest for a harmonious and unobtrusive totality.

▲ **Dietrich Lubs**, *ABR 314 df time control* digital radio with clock for Braun, 1997

Marcel Breuer

1902 *Pécs, Hungary*
1981 *New York*

Marcel Lajos Breuer won a scholarship in 1920, which allowed him to study at the Akademie für Bildende Künste in Vienna. Dissatisfied with the institution, he remained there for only a brief period before finding work in a Viennese architectural office. From 1920 to 1923, he studied at the Staatliches **Bauhaus**, Weimar, completing the basic course, the carpentry apprenticeship and his journeyman's exam. During his tuition there, Breuer designed his *African chair* (1921) and his *Slatted chair* (1922–1924). After the completion of his studies, he went to Paris, where he worked in an architectural office. On his return the following year, Breuer became a "young master" and was appointed head of the carpentry workshop at the Bauhaus, which had by then moved to Dessau. Here, he designed his first tubular metal chair the *B3* (1925) – the innovative choice of material having been reputedly inspired by his recently purchased Adler bicycle. Breuer subsequently designed a whole range of tubular metal furniture including chairs, tables, stools and cupboards, which were manufactured and distributed by Standard-Möbel, Berlin. Tubular metal offered many benefits – affordability, hygiene and an inherent resiliency that provided comfort without the need for springing – and Breuer regarded his designs as essential equipment for modern living. At the Bauhaus, Breuer also designed the interiors and furnishings for the school's new complex and for the masters' houses. His *B3* or *Wassily* chair

▼ *Model No. ti 2* chair and *Model No. ti 13* stool for Bauhaus Dessau, 1924

was designed originally for **Wassily Kandinsky**'s accommodation. Breuer not only created standardized furnishings – in 1926 he also designed a small standardized metal house and, a year later, his *Bambos* house. That year he made a graphic about the evolution of seat furniture, which concluded with his dematerialist ideal of sitting on "springy columns of air". Breuer continued to teach at the Bauhaus until April 1928 and, for the next three years, directed his own architectural practice in Berlin, which employed the former Bauhaus student, Gustav Hassenpflug (1907–1977). During this period, Breuer continued to design furniture, interiors and department stores while his building projects remained unrealized. He was commissioned by the **Deutscher Werkbund** to design interiors for the German section at the 1930 "Société des Artistes Décoratifs Français" exhibition. In 1931, with little work available due to the economic downturn, Breuer closed his office in Berlin and travelled to the South of France, Spain, Greece and Morocco. The next year, he completed his first architectural commission, the Harnischmacher House, Wiesbaden and designed the Wohnbedarf furniture store, Zurich. Then, two years later, he joined Alfred (b. 1903) and Emil Roth (1893–1980) in designing the Doldertal Houses, a pair of experimental apartment blocks

▲ *Model No. B35* armchair for Gebrüder Thonet, 1928–1929

in Zurich, for Sigfried Giedion (1888–1968), the founder of the Wohnbedarf company. From 1932 to 1934, Breuer developed a range of pliant furniture using a patented method of construction that incorporated flat bands of steel and aluminium. This range of metal furniture was manufactured by Embru and retailed by Wohnbedarf. In 1933 and 1934, he visited Switzerland and worked in Budapest with Farkas Molnár and Josef Fischer on an unrealized architectural project. To escape Nazi persecution on account of his Hungarian-Jewish origins, Breuer emigrated to London in 1935, initially working in partnership with the architect, F. R. S. Yorke (1906–1962). Together, they completed several architectural commissions including houses in Sussex, Hampshire, Berkshire and Bristol and the Gane Pavilion in Bristol (1936), which combined wood and local stone (a far cry from the Bauhaus aesthetic of steel and glass). Breuer and Yorke also designed a "Civic Centre for the Future", which remained unrealized. Later, as controller of design at Jack Pritchard's company Isokon, Breuer produced five plywood furniture designs between 1935 and 1937, which were basically translations of his earlier metal designs. These Isokon designs reflected the popularity of **Alvar**

Aalto's earlier plywood furniture, which had been exhibited in Britain in 1933. While in London, three years later, Breuer also designed a group of plywood furniture for Heal & Sons. In 1937, Breuer moved to the United States of America, **Walter Gropius** having offered him a professorship at Harvard University's School of Design in Cambridge, Massachusetts. They also set up an architectural practice together in Massachusetts, designing the Pennsylvania Pavilion at the 1939 New York World's Fair and several private houses, including Gropius' own residence. In 1941, Gropius and Breuer dissolved their partnership and Breuer established his own architectural practice, which he moved to New York in 1946. During the late 1940s and 1950s, Breuer designed some seventy private houses, mainly in New England, and in 1947 built a home for himself in New Canaan, Connecticut. The **Museum of Modern Art, New York** initiated a touring exhibition of his work in 1947 and the following year invited him to build a low-cost house in the museum's grounds, which would suit the needs of an average American family. He furnished this project with affordable plywood cut-out furniture. In 1953, Breuer worked as part of a team on the new UNESCO building in Paris and also designed the Bijenkorff department store, Rotterdam. He founded Marcel Breuer and Associates in New York in 1956, and around that time, like **Le Corbusier**, made concrete his material of choice. He used this medium

▼ Armchair for
Isokon Furniture
Company, 1936

in a highly sculptural and innovative way for his design of the monumental Whitney Museum of American Art, New York (1966). Breuer was one of the foremost exponents of the **Modern Movement** and the enduring appeal of his highly democratic furniture designs, such as the iconic *B3* chair and the hugely successful *B32* or *Cesca* cantilevered chair (1928), testifies to his mastery of aesthetics and production methods.

Neville Brody

b. 1957 *London*

Neville Brody took a course in fine arts before studying graphic design at the London College of Printing from 1976 to 1979. He subsequently designed album covers for several independent labels including Stiff Records. In 1981, he was appointed art director of the youth-based music magazine, *The Face*. Brody developed a strong identity for the magazine by using experimental post-modern typefaces. He created a new and unconventional language of graphics that was visually noisy and full of youthful exuberance. His fonts deconstructed letter forms and had symbolic content.

From 1983 to 1987, Brody produced design work for the London listings magazine *City Limits* as well as the *New Socialist* and *Touch*. He left *The Face* in 1986 to work on its sister publication *Arena*. In 1988, a retrospective exhibition of his work was held at the **Victoria & Albert Museum**, London. Around 1986, Brody moved away from his earlier "rough and ready" style of graphics, which encapsulated the "New Romantic" style and which had become increasingly imitated, and instead began producing graphics on Apple Macintosh computers that were influenced by electronic media such as those he produced in the 1990s for *Fuse* magazine.

▶ Poster for "Fuse 94 Fuse Lab Conference and Exhibition" at the Royal College of Art, London, 1994

◀ Cover for *Fuse* magazine, 1994

FUSE

THE FORUM FOR EXPERIMENTAL TYPOGRAPHY

FUSE94:FUSELAB:CONFERENCE:EXHIBITION
NOVEMBER 1994 ROYAL COLLEGE OF ART KENSINGTON GORE LONDON SW7
FUSELAB 25 26 27 : CONFERENCE 26 27 : EXHIBITION AND STUDENT FUSE
EXHIBITION NOVEMBER 25 TO DECEMBER 7 : LIVE ON THE INTERNET

Carlo Bugatti

1855 *Milan*
1940 *Molsheim, France*

▼ *Cobra* chair designed for the *Snail* Room at the Turin Exhibition, 1902

Carlo Bugatti studied at the Accademia di Belle Arti di Brera, Milan and at the École des Beaux-Arts, Paris. His earliest known pieces of furniture were designed in 1880 for his sister, Luiga, on the occasion of her marriage to the artist Giovanni Segantini (1858–1899). Bugatti's designs of the 1880s were often assymetrical in form and covered in decorated parchment, and frequently displayed Japanese influences. In 1888, Bugatti established his own cabinet-making workshop and decorating business in Milan. Around 1900, he adopted a Moorish style, his furniture designs becoming highly embellished with tassels and metal inlays. He exhibited his work at the 1900 "Exposition Universelle" in Paris and was awarded a silver medal. In the same year, he also created furniture for the Khedive's palace in Istanbul, and designed a completely unified interior scheme in London for Cyril Flowers, the First Lord Battersea, which was notable as an early example of **Gesamtkunstwerk**. In 1902, he received a diploma of honour at the "Esposizione Internazionale d'Arte Decorativa Moderna", Turin for his design of four interiors, including

his remarkable *Snail* Room. This interior, which included his biomorphic *Cobra* chairs (1902), was more organic than his previous schemes and ensured Bugatti an international reputation as a highly eccentric and idiosyncratic designer. In 1904, he sold his decorating firm in Milan to De Vecchi and moved to Paris. There, he established his own cabinet-making workshop and his furniture designs were retailed by the Bon Marché department store. He also designed silverware, which was produced and first exhibited by A. A. Hébrard in 1907, and later shown at the "Salon des Artistes Décorateurs" exhibitions. While in Paris, Bugatti spent most of his free time painting. His sons were also highly successful in their chosen fields; Ettore (1881–1947) as an automobile designer and Rembrandt (1885–1916) as a sculptor of animal bronzes.

The term California New Wave refers to the highly influential post-modern style of graphics developed by designers working on the West Coast of America during the 1980s. Designers such as **April Greiman** and Lucille Tenazas created a layered style by combining modern fonts such as Garamond or Baskerville with collage-like images. Inspired by electronic media, California New Wave graphics produce the sense of messages being filtered through layers, which effects a strong three-dimensional quality or visual depth. Using Apple Macintosh software, California New Wave designers created a language of hybrid imagery with encoded messages, and the seemingly random placement of collage-like images provided their work with a refreshing vitality. The California New Wave style was also pioneered by graphic designers, Rudy VanderLans (b. 1955) and his wife Zuzana Licko (b. 1961), who together launched the large-format graphics magazine *Émigré* in 1982.

California New Wave

▲ **April Greiman**, Poster for Southern California Institute – Arc Admissions, 1993

George
Carwardine
1887–1948

▲ *Anglepoise* task
lamp for Herbert
Terry & Sons, 1932

George Carwardine, a director of Carwardine Associates, Bath, was an auto-motive engineer who specialized in the design of suspension systems. In 1932 he patented the design of his articulated table lamp, the *Anglepoise*. This innovative design, which allowed flexible re-positioning, was based on the constant-tension principle of human limbs, with the lamp's spring act-ing in much the same way as muscles. Produced in large numbers over fifty years by the English manufacturer Herbert Terry in Redditch, the patent for the lamp was acquired in 1937 by the Norwegian lighting designer, Jacob Jacobsen (b. 1901), who had been influenced by it when he designed his own highly successful *Luxo 1001* lamp the same year. Carwardine's *Angle-poise*, which was subsequently manufactured in Norway and retailed under a different name, was highly influential to later generations of task lighting.

Born Adolphe Jean Édouard-Marie Mouron, Cassandre studied painting under Lucien Simon (1861–1945) and René Menard (1862–1930) at the Académie Julian, Paris from 1918 to 1921. His first large poster design, which was for the Paris furniture shop Au Bûcheron, appeared in 1923. This dynamic image showing a muscular woodcutter at work, set against a background of bold geometric ray-like planes, is emphatically **Art Deco** in style. Cassandre was very much part of the **avant-garde** in the Paris of the 1920s,

A. M. Cassandre

1901 *Kharkov, Ukraine*
1968 *Paris*

▼ Poster for the
Chemin de Fer du
Nord, 1927

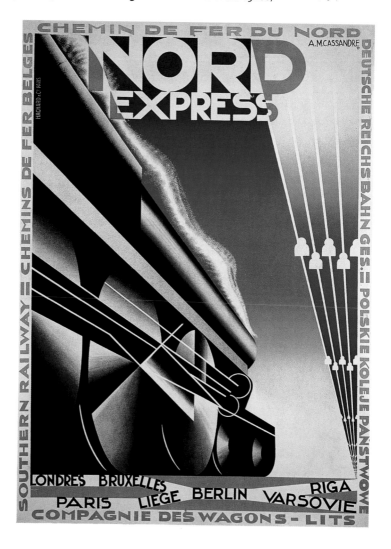

being a friend of the artists Robert Delaunay (1885–1941) and Fernand Léger (1881–1955), the poet Guillaume Apollinaire (1880–1918), and the composer Erik Satie (1866–1925). His work was influenced by Cubism and modern industrial design, and from 1923 he worked under the pseudonym A. M. Cassandre. His designs for railway posters for the Compagnie des Chemins de Fer du Nord, such as his *Étoile du Nord* advertisement of 1927, helped establish his reputation, and he subsequently joined Charles Loupot (1898–1962) and Maurice Moyrand in founding the advertising agency and design consultancy, Alliance Graphique Internationale, and in 1930 joined the UAM (Union des Artistes Modernes). During his career, Cassandre designed several hundred posters including ones advertising Pivolo aperitif (1924), *L'Intransigeant* newspaper (1925), Pernod (1934), Dubonnet (1934) and the ocean liner *Normandie* (1935). Using strong geometric forms in his designs, Cassandre's method of working always began with the text and choice of typography, which in turn inspired the more graphic elements of the posters. He believed that it was the poster designer's duty to dispatch messages rather than to draft them. Cassandre visited the United States on several occasions and, apart from graphics, also designed theatrical sets, which like his posters possessed a strong monumentality. Cassandre designed the highly stylized and quintessentially Art Deco typeface *Bifur*, which was issued by the type foundry Deberny & Peignot in 1929, as well as three other typefaces: *Acier Nord* (1930) and *Peignot* (1936), which were intended as text faces, and finally *Cassandre* (1968). Apart from teaching at the École des Arts Décoratifs from 1934–1935, Cassandre ran his own small design school, with names such as **Raymond Savignac**, Bernard Villemot (1911–1989) and André François (b. 1915) among its alumni. In 1963, he designed the famous YSL monogram for Yves Saint Laurent. Five years later Cassandre tragically took his own life.

▼ Poster for the French Line, c. 1930

Anna Ferrieri studied architecture at the Politecnico di Milano from 1938
to 1943 under **Franco Albini**, in whose studio she later worked for a brief
period. In 1943, she married the chemical engineer Giulio Castelli, who
in 1949 founded the plastics manufacturing company, **Kartell**. She was a
founding member of the Movimento Studi per l'Architettura in Milan, and
in 1946 established her own architectural practice there. The following year,
she acted as editor of the magazine *Casabella-Costruzioni,* and for five years
was Italian correspondent for the London-based journal, *Architectural
Design*. In 1952, she joined the Istituto Nazionale di Urbanistica, and four
years later became a founding member of ADI (Associazione per il Disegno
Industriale). Between 1959 and 1973, she was in architectural partnership with
Ignazio Gardella (b.1905), with whom she had co-designed a condominium
in Milan in 1951. In 1965, she turned her attention to industrial design and a
year later began working as a design consultant for Kartell, designing objects
in state-of-the-art plastics. Her highly influential 4953-54-55-56 system of injection-moulded ABS cylindrical containers (1969) could be stacked and combined in a variety of ways to provide flexible storage. For her 4830 stool (1979),
Castelli Ferrieri utilized a frame that combined tubular metal with ABS while
the seat was formed from rigid expanded polyurethane. Other notable designs include her collapsible 4300 table (1982) and her 4310 table (1983),
which are produced in an advanced technopolymer. As an accomplished designer and an expert in plastics technology, Anna Castelli Ferrieri was appointed design director of Kartell's in-house design studio, Centrokappa.

**Anna Castelli
Ferrieri**
b. 1920 *Milan*

▲ **Achille & Pier Giacomo Castiglioni**, *Luminator*
floor lamp for Gilardi and Arform, 1955

▶ **Achille Castiglioni**, *Gibigiana*
directional table lamp for Flos, 1980

The eldest of the Castiglioni brothers, Livio studied architecture at the Politecnico di Milano, graduating in 1936. In 1938, Livio and Pier Giacomo established a studio together with Luigi Caccia Dominioni (b. 1913), designing silver and aluminium cutlery. Their most notable design, the *Phonola* (1939), was the first Italian radio made in Bakelite and as such changed the future design of radios, which had hitherto mostly been cased in wooden boxes. The design was awarded a gold medal at the VII Milan Triennale of 1940, where the designers also curated a whole exhibition of radios. From 1940 to 1960, Livio worked as a design consultant, first for the company Phonola from 1939 to 1960 and later for Brionvega from 1960 to 1964. From 1959 to 1960, he was president of the ADI (Associazione per il Disegno Industriale). Livio also designed many audio-visual presentations and collaborated with his younger brothers on several lighting projects. His best-known design, the snake-like *Boalum* light (1970), was executed in conjunction with Gianfranco Frattini (b. 1926).

Livio, Pier Giacomo & Achille Castiglioni

Livio Castiglioni
1911 *Milan*
1979 *Milan*

Pier Giacomo and Achille Castiglioni graduated from the Politecnico di Milano, in 1937 and 1944 respectively. Achille joined his elder brothers' design studio in Piazza Castello and during the post-war years they undertook town-planning and architectural commissions as well as exhibition and product design. The brothers were extremely active and helped establish the Milan Triennale exhibitions, the **Compasso d'Oro** awards and the ADI. When Livio left the partnership in 1952, the two younger brothers continued to design together until Pier Giacomo's death in 1968. They designed the "Colori e forme nella casa d'oggi" exhibition at the Villa Olmo, Como, where, for the first time, they exhibited their "ready-made" designs of 1957 – the *Mezzadro* (Sharecropper's Stool), incorporating a tractor seat, and the *Sgabello per Telephono* (Telephone

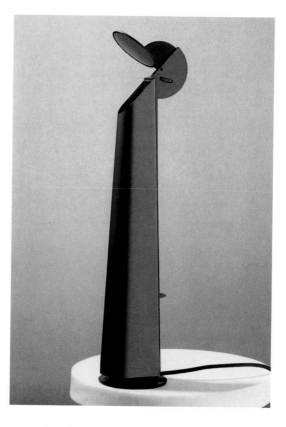

Pier Giacomo
Castiglioni

1913 *Milan*
1968 *Milan*

▼▶ **A. & P.G.
Castiglioni**, *Sella*
readymade stool, 1957
(Reissued by Zanotta)

▼ **A. & P.G.
Castiglioni**, *Mezzadro*
readymade stool, 1957
(reissued by Zanotta)

Stool), with a bicycle seat. The brothers also created less radical designs, such as the Neo-Liberty style *Sanluca* armchair (1959) for the furniture manufacturer, Dino Gavina, whose company offices in Milan they fitted out in 1963. Other notable creations of Pier Giacomo and Achille Castiglioni include the *Tubino* desk lamp (1951), the *Luminator* floor lamp (1955), the *Arco* floor lamp (1962) and the *Taccia* table lamp (1962). In 1966, they designed the *Allunaggio* seat, which was inspired by the first moon landing. Their long and prestigious client list included **Kartell**, Zanotta, Brionvega, Bernini, Siemens, **Knoll**, Poggi, Lancia, Ideal Standard and Bonacina.

After Pier Giacomo's death, Achille continued to work in industrial design, creating such well-known pieces as the *Lampadina* table lamp (1972) for Flos, his sleek cruet set (1980–1984) for Alessi and the *Gibigiana* directional table lamp (1980) for Flos. The brothers had much influence on the following generation of Italian designers, with Pier Giacomo teaching at the Politecnico di Milano from 1946 to 1968 and with Achille acting as professor of artistic industrial design from 1970 to 1977 and as professor of interior

▲ **Achille & Pier Giacomo Castiglioni**, Record player
with speakers for Brionvega, 1966

Achille Castiglioni
b. 1918 *Milan*

architecture and design from 1977 to 1980 at the Politecnico di Torino. Additionally, from 1981 to 1986, Achille Castiglioni was professor of interior design at the Politecnico di Milano and then became professor of industrial design there.

During his long career, which has spanned over half a century, Achille Castiglioni has been honoured with eight Compasso d'Oro awards as well as numerous other design prizes. While the language of design he and his brothers pioneered was grounded in **Rationalism**, it was tempered with ironic humour and sculptural form – an unusual approach to design that has been described as "rational expressionism". This, and the remarkably consistent quality of his designs, which are both structurally inventive and aesthetically pleasing, make Achille Castiglioni one of the most important figures in Italian design of the 20th century.

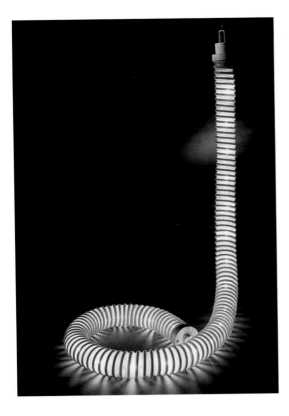

◀ **Livio Castiglioni &
Gianfranco Frattini,**
Boalum lamp for
Artemide, 1969

▲ **Achille Castiglioni,**
AC01 oil & vinegar
set for Alessi, 1980

Livio, Pier Giacomo & Achille Castiglioni · **153**

Wendell Castle
b. 1932 *Emporia, Kansas*

▲ *Molar* sofa for
Beylerian, 1969

Wendell Castle studied sculpture at the University of Kansas. Castle's brief experimentation with fibreglass in the 1960s gave rise to his highly sculptural and organic *Castle* and *Molar* series of seating (both 1969), the latter's form being inspired by the shape of back teeth. Around 1970, Castle dedicated himself to designing and crafting furniture from stack laminate blocks of wood, as in *Two-Seater love-seat* (1979). Since 1976, he has created sculptural and extraordinarily illusionistic furniture from solid wood using virtuoso *trompe-l'oeil* carving techniques, such as his *Coatrack with Trench Coat* and *Chair with Sports Coat* (both 1978). Castle founded a school for craftsmanship in wood, The Wendell Castle Workshop, in 1980, and over the next few years concentrated on designs inspired by the **Art Deco** style. Produced in exquisitely worked exotic materials, Castle's intention was to "pick up where **Jacques-Émile Ruhlmann**, the last of the great *ébénistes* left off". By the mid-1980s, Castle had adopted a more expressionistic approach to design. The surfaces of this later work, such as his *Dr. Caligari* desk and chair (1986), were painted or stained while their forms were less functional and more concerned with symbolism.

Don Chadwick studied industrial design at the University of California, Los Angeles, graduating in 1959. He subsequently worked in the architectural office of Victor Gruen & Associates. In 1964, Chadwick established his own design office in Los Angeles and his early work included designs for aerial photographic equipment and for the aerospace industry. In 1974, he designed his *Modular Seating* system for **Herman Miller**, which used a cold-cure polyurethane process. In 1977, Chadwick went into partnership with the former vice-president of design research at Herman Miller, **Bill Stumpf**, forming the design consultancy Chadwick, Stumpf & Associates in Winona, Minnesota. The office's most notable designs include state-of-the-art office desking and seating for Herman Miller, such as the *C-Forms* desk system (1979), the ergonomically based *Ergon* (1970–1976) and *Equa* (1984) seating programmes as well as the highly innovative *Aeron* (1992) office chair, which uses a breathable polyester mesh for the seat and back.

Don Chadwick
b. 1936 *Los Angeles*

Pierre Chareau

1883 *Bordeaux, France*
1950 *Easthampton,
Massachusetts*

Pierre Chareau worked from c. 1899 to 1914 in Paris as a draughtsman for the British furniture company, Waring & Gillow. In 1919, Chareau established his own design and architectural office and subsequently designed furniture, lighting and interiors, including a study and bedroom set for the Paris apartment of Annie Dalsace. These suites, together with their site-specific furniture were exhibited at the Salon d'Automne in 1919. Other furniture and interiors were shown at the 1920 Salon d'Automne and attracted critical acclaim. In 1922, he exhibited his work for the first time at the Salon des Artistes Décorateurs and, as a now solid member of the Parisian **avant-garde**, began collecting works of art by Modigliani, Braque, Klee, **Raoul Dufy**, Ernst and Mondrian among others. A year later, Chareau worked with Fernand Léger (1881–1955) and **Robert Mallet-Stevens** on the design of sets for Marcel L'Herbier's film *L'Inhumaine*. In 1924, Chareau opened his own shop, La Boutique, and began working with the metalworker, Louis Dalbert, their collaborative work being shown at that year's "Groupe des Cinq" exhibition. Chareau exhibited furniture and interiors at the 1925 "Exposition Internationale des Arts Décoratifs et Industriels Modernes" in Paris, where he met the Dutch architect, Bernard Bijvoët (1889–1979). Chareau subsequently collaborated with Bijvoët on several commissions, including the Clubhouse at Beauvallon (1926) for Emile Bernheim and the revolutionary steel and glass Maison de Verre,

▼ *Les Cigares* silk
textile, 1929–1930

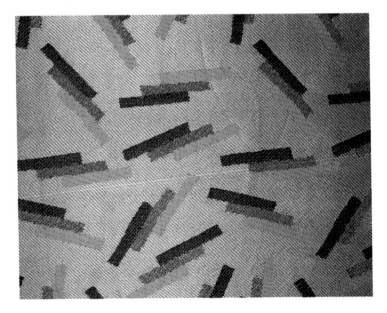

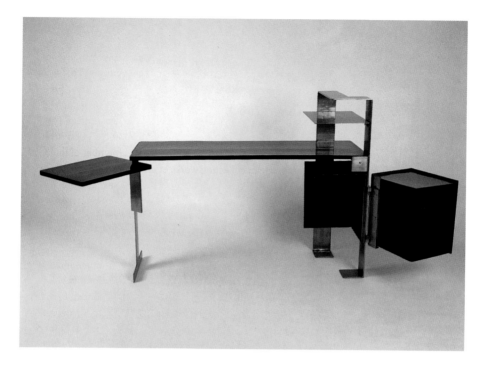

Paris (1928–1933), which he designed for Jean and Annie Dalsace. In 1925, Chareau designed furniture for **Le Corbusier**'s studio house for Jacques Lipchitz. By the late 1920s, his designs were no longer in the French *décorateur* tradition but had become patently modern. Undoubtedly influenced by Le Corbusier, Chareau's interiors and architecture were now conceived as "machines for living" and his furniture was designed to function as "equipment". In 1929, Chareau left the Société des Artistes Décorateurs and became a founding member of the UAM (Union des Artistes Modernes). During the depression in the 1930s, Chareau received few commissions. In 1936, however, he exhibited collapsible school furniture at the Salon d'Automne and, in 1939, his last French commission involved the design of furniture that could be made from packing crates for soldiers posted to the colonies. In the autumn of 1940, Chareau emigrated to America and was joined there by his wife, Louise, the following year. In New York, he worked for the French Cultural Attaché and organized exhibitions on Balzac and Daumier. One of Chareau's last projects involved the conversion of a Quonset hut into a weekend house for the artist Robert Motherwell (1915–1991) in East Hampton, Long Island.

▲ Model No. MB 744 office table, 1927

Serge Ivan Chermayeff

1900 *Grosny, Azerbaijan*
1996 *Wellfleets, Massachusetts*

Serge Ivan Chermayeff emigrated to Britain in 1910 and settled in London. From 1928 to 1931, he co-directed the Modern Art Studio of the furniture company Waring & Gillows with **Paul Follot**. Then, a year later, he qualified as an architect, and from 1931 to 1933 ran his own design and architectural practice. A subsequent three-year partnership with the architect Erich Mendelsohn (1887–1953) resulted in the De La Warr Pavilion, Bexhill-on-Sea (1933–1936), the Nimmo House, Chalfont-St-Giles (1934–1935) and the Levy House, London (1935–1936). In 1937, Chermayeff returned to independent practice and became a member of MARS (Modern Architectural Research Group). During the 1930s, Chermayeff was one of the foremost pioneers of the **International Style** in Britain, designing Bakelite radio casings for Ekco and tubular metal furniture for **PEL**. In 1939, he emigrated to the United States where he initially worked as a town-planner and architect before becoming director of the design department at the **Institute of Design, Chicago** in 1940. From 1942 to 1946, Chermayeff was head of the art department at Brooklyn College, New York, and in 1946, upon the death of **László Moholy-Nagy**, he returned to the Institute of Design in Chicago to become its president.

▲ Design for a study, 1928–1929

Ivan Chermayeff (b. 1932), the son of the architect and designer **Serge Ivan Chermayeff**, studied at Harvard University (1950–1952), the **Institute of Design, Chicago** (1952–1954) and the School of Art and Architecture at Yale University (1954–1955) where he met Thomas Geismar (b. 1932). In 1956, together with Robert Brownjohn (1925–1970), they founded a graphic design studio, Brownjohn, Chermayeff & Geismar. Two years later, they designed a display for the American Pavilion at the Brussels World Fair, which comprised images of fragments of the American environment, including traffic signs and a giant Pepsi-Cola logo. In 1960, Ivan Chermayeff and Thomas Geismar established the design office, Chermayeff & Geismar, and subsequently undertook a wide variety of graphic design assignments including over one hundred **corporate design** programmes for clients such as, Chase Manhattan Bank, Xerox, Mobil Oil and the **Museum of Modern Art, New York**. Their abstract logo for the Chase Manhattan Bank (1960) served as a prototype for other such commissions and paved the way for the wider use of abstraction in corporate logos. The firm also designed American displays at Expo '67 and Expo '70, and in 1987, the corporate logo of NBC, the famous rainbow-coloured peacock. The philosophy upon which the firm operates is based on problem-solving – understanding the points at issue and then tailoring a solution uniquely appropriate to the need. While the firm claims not to have a house style, their work has shown kinships with geometric abstraction, minimalism, dada and Pop art. Their designs are characteristically clear, direct, multi-layered, evocative and often surprising, while also being completely in tune with the times. This, together with the consistent quality of their highly innovative products, has made Chermayeff & Geismar perhaps the most influential firm of graphic designers in America, if not the world.

Chermayeff &
Geismar
Founded 1960
New York

▼ **Tom Geismar**,
Logo for Graphics
Arts USA, 1963

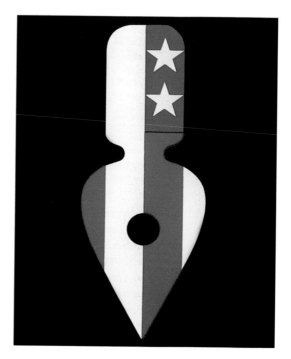

▼ *Luminator* floor
lamp for Fontana
Arte, 1936

Pietro Chiesa studied in Grenoble and Turin before serving an apprentice-ship in the studio of the furniture and interior designer, Gionvan Battista Gianotti. In 1921 Chiesa established his studio, the Botega di Pietro Chiesa, in Milan where he mainly produced designs that incorporated glass – his preferred material. Four years later, he exhibited his work at the "Exposition Internationale des Arts Décoratifs et Industriels Modernes" in Paris, and then collaborated with Gustavo Pulitzer on the design of glazing for the Italian naval vessels: *Saturnia, Vulcania, Conte Grande* and *Conte di Savoia*. In 1927, with **Gio Ponti**, Michele Marelli, Tomaso Buzzi, Emilio Lancia and **Paolo Venini**, Chiesa co-founded the association "Il Labirinto" for the manufacture of high-quality furniture in the **Novecento** style. The association, which aimed to broaden the impact of the decorative arts on domestic environments, presented its work at the III Biennale di Monza, where Chiesa's designs incorporated monochromatic geometric patterns and opalescent glass. In 1933, the Botega di Pietro Chiesa was merged into a newly established company, Fontana Arte, which had been founded by Gio Ponti and Luigi Fontana. Initially, Fontana Arte concentrated on the design and manufacture of furniture, basic utensils and glassware, although it became better known for its lighting designs in later years. As the company's artistic director, Chiesa designed some 1500 prototypes. Using glass as though it were a precious material, he employed grinding, moulding and cutting techniques in the production of his highly refined designs, such as the 2633 glass table of 1933. As one of the greatest exponents of Italian **Art Deco**, Chiesa's work was widely exhibited: at the Biennali di Monza (1923, 1925, 1927 and 1930) the Biennali di Venice (1924 and 1925), the "Exposición Internacional de Barcelona" (1929 and 1930) and at the decorative art exhibitions held in Paris (1935 and 1937), Berlin (1937) and Buenos Aires (1938). Though simple in concept, the forms he invented possessed a certain monumentality, as his *Luminator* floor lamp of 1936 demonstrates particularly well.

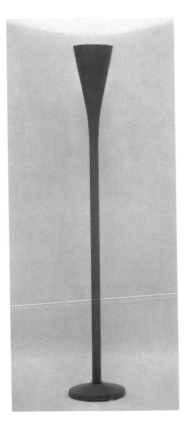

◄ Antonio Citterio &
Glen Oliver Löw,
Model No. AC1 from
the *Citterio Collection*
for Vitra, 1990

Antonio Citterio studied architecture at the Politecnico di Milano, graduating in 1972. In the same year, he set up a studio in Lissone, and in 1973 went into partnership with Paolo Nava – a collaboration that lasted until 1981. Citterio also worked with Gregotti Associati on the restoration of the Brera Art Gallery in Milan. In 1981, he established his own independent office, and from 1987 began working with his wife, the American architect Terry Dwan (b. 1957). Their design studio, Citterio-Dwan, has undertaken the partial restoration of the Pinacoteca di Brera, as well as the design of showrooms for B&B Italia, **Vitra** and shops for Esprit. Citterio-Dwan also developed an office furniture system for **Olivetti**. During his career, Citterio has designed lighting and furniture for **Artemide**, **Kartell**, B&B Italia, Flexform and Moroso among others. His most notable design is the office seating system, the *Citterio* Collection (1990), developed with Glen Oliver Löw for Vitra, which provides anatomical support without reducing freedom of movement. Citterio is a member of the ADI (Associazione per il Disegno Industriale) and has taught at the Domus Academy. He received **Compasso d'Oro** awards in 1979 and 1987.

Antonio Citterio
b. 1950 *Meda, Italy*

Clarice Cliff

1899 *Tunstall/
Staffordshire*
1972 *Newcastle-under-
Lyme*

Clarice Cliff began working at the age of thirteen in the studio of the potter Lingard Webster, where she learnt how to decorate earthenware ceramics with freehand painting. Prior to 1916, she also attended painting classes at the School of Art in Tunstall, and, for a while, worked for Hollinshead & Kirkham, Tunstall, learning lithographic techniques used for the decoration of ceramics. She worked for four years at the potteries of A. J. Wilkinson (Royal Staffordshire Pottery) situated in Stoke-on-Trent, a major centre of the pottery industry, where she met her future husband, Colley Shorter, the firm's managing director. For a year, she took evening classes in painting at the School of Art in Burslem and around 1926 set up her own ceramics decorating studio at A. J. Wilkinson, decorating old blanks from the adjoining Newport Pottery (a subsidiary of A. J. Wilkinson) with hand-painted and

▼ *Bizarre* vase for
Newport Pottery,
c. 1930

brightly coloured **Art Deco** patterns. From 1929 to 1935, Cliff worked at Newport Pottery, producing a range of colourful ceramic ware known as *Bizarre*. This was so commercially successful that other painters were recruited to execute designs in her idiosyncratic style, including her later *Fantasque* and *Biarritz* ranges. In 1934, she returned to Wilkinson's and as the firm's artistic director, oversaw the manufacture and decoration of *Bizarre* pottery designed by artists such as Paul Nash (1889–1946), Dame Laura Knight (1877–1970), Duncan Grant (1885–1978) and Vanessa Bell (1879–1961). At the height of *Bizarre* ware's popularity in the mid-1930s, the workshop was employing some 150 people. Cliff combined the traditions of studio ceramics with the contemporary Art Deco style to produce hybrid designs that were highly colourful and strongly geometric. Her work captured the spirit of 1930s Britain and appealed strongly to popular taste.

▶ *Tongue* chair for
SCP, 1989

Nigel Coates studied architecture at the Architectural Association, London from 1972 to 1974, and taught there himself from 1979 to 1989. In 1983, he co-founded NATO (Narrative Architecture Today) and edited their first magazine. Together with Doug Branson (b. 1951), he established Branson Coates Architects in 1985, and has since worked on numerous projects including shops for Jasper Conran (1986), Katherine Hamnett (1988) and Jigsaw (from 1993), as well as the Erotic Design Exhibition at the Design Museum, London (1997), Powerhouse UK exhibition, London (1998) and a new gallery at the Geffrye Museum, London (1998). Coates has also undertaken many architectural projects in Japan. Apart from his architectural and interior design projects, Coates has produced several notable furniture designs, including the *Genie* stool (1988), the *Noah* collection (1988), the *Tongue* chair (1989), and the *Gallo* collection (1989) for SCP and Poltronova, as well as vases for Alessi (1990) and a collection of mannequins launched by Stockman in 1994. His expressive designs are often sexually charged and have an urban quality that reflects Coates' celebration of the vitality and chaos found in city environments. In 1995, Coates was appointed professor of architectural design at the **Royal College of Art, London**.

Nigel Coates
b. 1949 *Malvern/ Worcestershire*

Wells Coates

1895 Tokyo
1958 Vancouver

Wells Coates was born in Tokyo, where his Canadian father worked as a missionary. Prior to this, his mother had been a pupil of the architects, Louis Sullivan (1856–1924) and **Frank Lloyd Wright** in Chicago. From 1913 to 1915, Wells Coates studied engineering at the University of British Columbia, Vancouver. However, his studies where curtailed by the outbreak of the First World War and he was drafted, first as an infantryman and later as a pilot. After the war, he returned to the University of British Columbia, graduating in 1921. He subsequently moved to Britain and, from 1922 to 1924, took a doctorate in engineering at the University of London. From 1923 to 1926, he worked as a journalist for the *Daily Express* and for a brief period was one of their correspondents in Paris. During this time he wrote from a humanist perspective, viewing design as a catalyst for social change. In London in 1928, he designed fabrics for the Crysede Textile Company and interiors for the firm's factory in Welwyn Garden City, incorporating plywood elements. From 1931, Coates was a consultant to Jack Pritchard's plywood products company, Isokon – a firm pioneering Modernism in Britain. Coates was also commissioned by Pritchard in 1931 to design the Lawn Road Flats, Hampstead, which are seminal examples of British **Modern Movement** architecture. In 1933, Coates co-founded MARS (Modern Architecture Research Group) and established design partnerships with Patrick Gwynne

▼ Desk for PEL, 1933

in 1932 and David Pleydell-Bouverie in 1933. From 1932, he designed a series of bakelite radios for Ekco, including his famous circular *Ekco AD65* (1934), which were conceived for industrial production and were among the first modern products available to British consumers. After the Second World War, Coates worked in Vancouver, designing aircraft interiors for De Havilland and BOAC, while in the 1950s he produced designs for television cabinets.

▼ *Ekco AD65* radio
for E.K. Cole, 1934

Luigi Colani
b. 1928 *Berlin*

▲ *Körperform* fibre-
glass chairs for Fritz
Hansen, 1971–1973

Luigi Colani studied sculpture and painting at the Hochschule der Bildenden Künste, Berlin in 1946. Then in 1948, he went to Paris to study aerodynamics and worked on concept vehicle studies for car and motorcycle
magazines. From 1952 to 1953, Colani undertook research for the California-
based aircraft manufacturer, Douglas on suitable materials for high-speed
conditions. On his return to Europe in 1954, he worked for numerous clients
including Alfa-Romeo, Lancia, Volkswagen, BMW, Thyssen, Boeing, Rosenthal, Villeroy & Boch and Rockwell (NASA). The organic form of his porcelain *Drop* tea service (1970) for Rosenthal arises from ergonomic and functional considerations, and his brightly coloured plastic, multi-purpose sitting
tools, the *Sitzgerät* (1971–1972) for adults and the *Zocker* (1972) for children,
are characteristic of his interest in materials and function. In 1973, the
Colani Design Centre was founded in Japan and a decade later he moved
there. In 1993, Colani designed computers for VOBIS and two years later
established a Colani Design Centre in Lünen, Germany. While the organic
forms of Colani's innovative designs are born from a deep understanding
of ergonomics and aerodynamics, the playfulness of his design rhetoric is
a feature rarely found in German design.

Gino Colombini worked in the architectural office of **Franco Albini** from 1933 to 1952, designing commercial and domestic buildings as well as furniture. In 1949, he was appointed technical director of **Kartell**, a recently formed plastics manufacturing company. Colombini designed many of the firm's first products, which were intended for everyday domestic use, including a carpet-beater (1957), a milking pail (1958), a lemon squeezer (1958), a children's lunch-box (1958), a washing tub (1957) and various buckets and dustpans (1956–1957). These innovative and highly functional designs were among the first to exploit the potential of plastics as materials suitable for high-volume mass-production. Colombini's designs for Kartell were extremely influential and he was awarded **Compasso d'Oro**'s for them in 1955, 1957, 1958, 1959 and 1960.

Gino Colombini
b. 1915 *Milan*

▲ Plastic lemon
squeezer for Kartell,
1958

Joe Colombo
1930 *Milan*
1971 *Milan*

▲ *Optic* clocks for
Alessi, 1970

▶ *Acrilica* table lamp
for O-Luce, 1962

Cesare "Joe" Colombo trained as a painter at the Accademia di Belle Arti
di Brera, Milan until 1949 and then studied architecture at the Politecnico
di Milano until 1954. In 1951, he joined the Movimento Nucleare (Nuclear
Painting Movement), which had just been founded by Sergio D'Angelo (b.
1931) and Enrico Baj (b. 1924). For the next four years, Colombo was active
as an abstract expressionist painter and sculptor, exhibiting his work with
other group members in Milan, Como, Brescia, Turin, Palermo, Verviers,
Venice and Brussels. Later in 1955, Colombo became a member of the Art
Concret Group, but around 1958 gave up painting to pursue a career in design. Prior to this, he had worked on an exhibition for the X Milan Triennale
of 1954, documenting the ceramic designs that resulted from the International Meetings held in Albisola. At this Triennale, Colombo also created
three outside seating areas, which were combined with a shrine-like display of television sets. After the death of his father in 1959, Colombo was left
to run the family business, which manufactured electrical equipment. During this time, he began experimenting with new materials, including reinforced plastics, as well as novel construction techniques and manufacturing
methods. In 1962, Colombo established his own design office in Milan, focusing on architectural and interior design projects, the majority of which
were for mountain hostels and ski-resort hotels. These early designs reveal
an interest in function born out of structures with strong sculptural qualities. In 1964, Colombo was awarded the IN-Arch prize for his interiors for
a hotel in Sardinia (1962–1964), which included ceiling fixtures made from

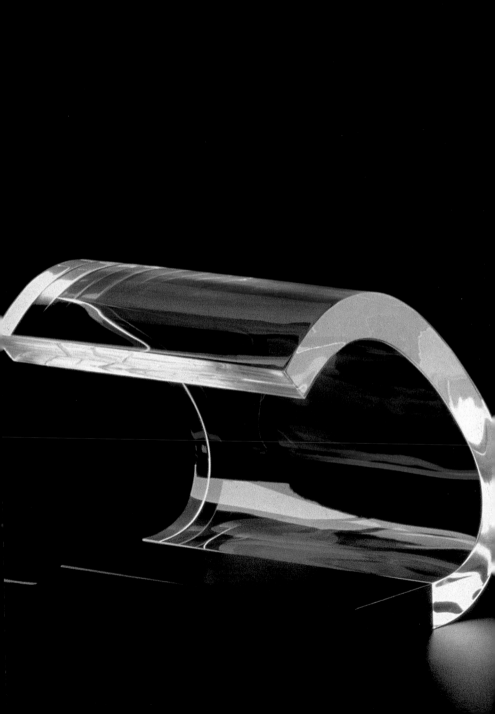

perspex prisms that diffracted the light. With his brother Gianni, Colombo developed this idea in his design for the *Acrilica* lamp (1962). His first design for **Kartell** was the *No. 4801* chair (1963–1964), which was constructed of three interlocking plywood elements. The fluidity of this chair's form anticipated his later designs in plastics, such as the *Universale No. 4860* chair (1965–1967), which was the first adult-sized chair to be manufactured in injection-moulded plastic (ABS). Colombo produced other innovative designs for furniture, lighting, glassware, door handles, pipes, alarm clocks and wristwatches. He also created a professional camera, the *Trisystem* (1969), an air-conditioning unit for Candy (1970), in-flight service trays for Alitalia (1970) and an ergonomically resolved motorized drafting table (1969). From the beginning of his career, Colombo was interested in domestic systems products, as his early Combi-Centre container unit (1963) demonstrates. This interest in systems furnishings gave rise to his *Additional Living System* (1967–1968), *Tube* chair (1969–1970) and *Multi* chair (1970), all of which could be assembled in a variety of ways so as to provide a wide assortment of flexible sitting positions, thus reflecting his primary goal in design – adaptability. His most forward-looking designs, however, were his integrated micro-

▶ *Central living block of the Wohnmodell 1969* shown at the Visiona I exhibition for Bayer, 1969

▲ *Elda* armchair for
Comfort, 1963

environments. These included his Visiona habitat of the future shown at Bayer's Visiona exhibition in 1969, which comprised a space-age "Barbarella-like" interior where furnishings transmuted into structural elements and vice versa. Traditional furniture items were replaced with functional units, such as the *Night-Cell* and *Central-Living blocks* and the *Kitchen-Box*, so as to create a dynamic and multi-functional living environment. For his own apartment, Colombo designed the *Roto-living* and *Cabriolet-Bed* units (both 1969), and these were followed by his *Total Furnishing Unit* (1971), which was a highly influential example of "Uniblock" design. Shown at the 1972 "Italy: The New Domestic Landscape" exhibition at the **Museum of Modern Art, New York**, the *Total Furnishing Unit* was proposed as a complete machine for living and comprised four different units: kitchen, cupboard, bathroom and bed/privacy – all within a twenty-eight square metre space. Colombo designed products for O-Luce, **Kartell**, Bieffe, **Alessi**, Flexform and Boffi, and received ADI (Associazione per il Disegno Industriale) awards in 1967 and 1968 as well as a Premio **Compasso d'Oro** in 1970. His remarkably prolific and illustrious career was cut tragically short in 1971 when he died, at the age of forty-one, from heart failure.

▼ *Spider* lamp for O-Luce, 1965

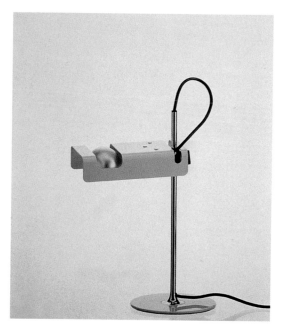

Compasso d'Oro

Established 1954
Milan

The Compasso d'Oro awards were founded by the La Rinascente department store owner, Aldo Borletti, in 1954. Borletti stated that the awards were "to encourage industrialists and craftsmen to raise their production standards both from a technological and aesthetic standpoint". Initially, the Compasso d'Oro prizes were only awarded for the design of objects retailed and distributed by La Rinascente. From 1959, the ADI (Associazione per Il Disegno Industriale) helped in the running of the awards and, in 1967, completely took over their administration. The ADI widened the range and types of products eligible for the awards and thus ensured international recognition of the Compasso d'Oro's status. Notable winners have included **Marcello Nizzoli** for the *Lettera 22* typewriter for Olivetti (won in 1954) and the *Mirella* sewing machine for Necchi (1957), **Marco Zanuso** & **Richard Sapper** for the *Doney 14* television for Brionvega (1962) and *Grillo* telephone for Siemens (1967), **Achille** & **Pier Giacomo Castiglioni** for their vacuum cleaner for R. E. M. (1957) and **Mario Bellini** for the *Totem* record player/radio for Brionvega (1979).

▲ Marco Zanuso &
Richard Sapper,
Grillo telephone for
Siemens, 1965

► Habitat store, early 1970s

Terence Conran studied textile design under Eduardo Paolozzi (b. 1924) at the Central School of Arts & Crafts, London from 1949 to 1950. He then designed textiles for a year at the Rayon Industry Design Centre, London, and from 1951 created interiors for the design and architectural office of Dennis Lennon & Associates, London. In 1952, he set himself up as an independent designer of furniture and textiles, under the name of Conran & Co., and produced designs for Edinburgh Weavers, the John Lewis Partnership and Simpsons of Piccadilly. A year later, together with Ian Storey, Conran opened a successful chain of budget "Soup Kitchen" restaurants. In 1956, he co-founded the Conran Design Group (later renamed Conran Associates) with John Stephenson. Then, after eight years, Conran branched out into design retailing, opening his first Habitat shop on Fulham Road, London. Attempting to provide well-designed modern domestic products at affordable prices, Conran developed the concept of "lifestyle" retailing. From 1982 to 1986, the Conran Foundation funded the Boilerhouse Project at the **Victoria & Albert Museum**, and in 1989 helped to establish the Design Museum, London. During the 1980s, Conran acquired several companies including Mothercare, British Home Stores and Heals, which together with Habitat and Next made up the massive Storehouse Group. He resigned from Storehouse in 1990 and two years later re-purchased the flagship Conran Shop. During the 1990s, Conran opened numerous restaurants and became London's foremost restaurateur.

Terence Conran
b. 1931 *London*

Constructivism

Russia

The term Constructivism refers to a movement primarily in Russian art, design and architecture. Prior to the First World War, the Russian **avant-garde**, like their European counterparts, were inspired by Cubism and **Futurism**. After the 1917 revolution, however, the Russian avant-garde sought new forms of expression that related to the Soviet desire to supplant the capitalist system with more democratic schemes for the production and distribution of goods. To this end, artists such as **Vladimir Tatlin**, **Kasimir Malevich**, **Alexander Rodchenko**, Wassily Kandinsky (1866–1944), Naum Gabo (1890–1977), Antoine Pevsner (1886–1962) and **El Lissitzky** began promoting an aesthetic and approach to design that was allied to industrial production. The publication of two manifestos in 1920, *The Programme of the Group of Constructivists* by Alexei Gan, **Varvara Stepanova** and Rodchenko and *A Realistic Manifesto* by Pevsner and Gabo, heralded the emergence of Constructivism. The Constructivists believed that the applied arts could bring about a new social order and so began creating utilitarian "production art" and architecture. The political and economic instability that followed the revolution, however, meant that few large-scale projects were undertaken and the Constructivist's output was mainly confined to the fields of exhibition design, ceramics and graphics. Constructivist ceramics were often decorated with Suprematist motifs – geometric forms set against plain white backgrounds – which produced a strong sense of dynamism and modernity.

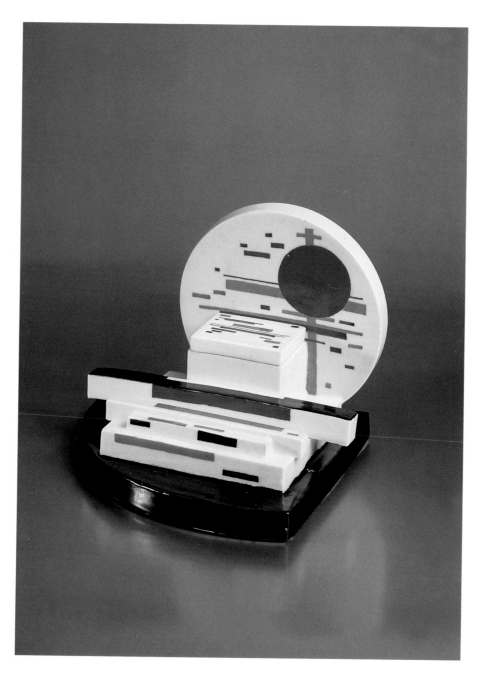

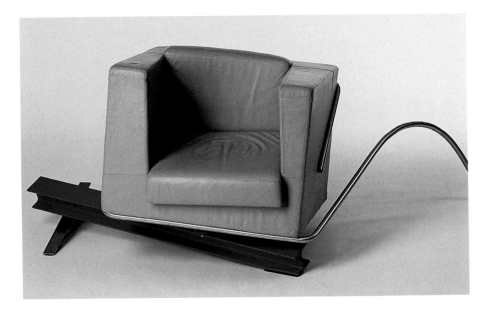

Coop Himmelb(l)au

Founded 1968
Austria

▲ *Vödöl* chair for
Vitra, 1989

Coop Himmelb(l)au was founded in 1968 by Wolf D. Prix (b. 1942) and Helmut Swiczinsky (b. 1944) in Vienna. Initially, influenced by **Hans Hollein** and Haus-Rucker-Co, the work of this Austrian architectural office explored the idea of pneumatic-space architecture. Coop Himmelb(l)au began designing "Open Structures" in 1975, which were mostly loft buildings that countered traditional building types with the use of slanting angular forms. The studio was awarded the Berliner Förderpreis für Baukunst for the Roter Engel Bar in Berlin that they designed in 1981. Throughout the 1980s, Coop Himmelb(l)au pioneered **Deconstructivism** – or "Open Architecture" as Prix and Swiczinsky referred to it – a post-modern approach to architecture and design that explodes traditional forms into splintered elements in a highly expressive and dynamic way. In 1988, Coop Himmelb(l)au took part in the "Deconstructive Architecture" exhibition at the **Museum of Modern Art**, **New York**. The office's first large-scale industrial commission was a chipboard manufacturing plant for Funder in Carinthia (1988–1989). Coop Himmelb(l)au's work, which could be described as gestural "action" architecture, was included in the "Architects Art" exhibition at the Gallery of Functional Art, Los Angeles in 1990. In the same year, Wolf D. Prix became professor of architecture at the Hochschule für angewandte Kunst, Vienna. Coop Himmelb(l)au's interest in subverting Modernism is clearly demonstrated by its *Vodöl* chair (1989), which is a reworking of **Le Corbusier**'s *Grand Confort* of 1928.

Hans Coper initially studied textile engineering and then, in 1939, emigrated from Germany to Britain. In 1946, he saw **Lucie Rie**'s studio ceramics at her Albion Mews pottery in London, and subsequently began collaborating with her. Coper's approach to studio pottery was inspired by Oriental production techniques and forms. His vessels were shown at the Berkeley Galleries, London from 1950 and at the Röhsska Konstslöjdmuseet, Gothenburg in 1955. Four years later Coper moved to Digswell, Hertfordshire, and began producing ceramic work that was influenced by primitive and Cycladic art. As an admirer of the sculpture of Henry Moore (1898–1986) and Constantin Brancusi (1876–1957), Coper's work possessed a similar sense of monumentality. From 1961 to 1969, he taught at Camberwell School of Arts & Crafts and in 1966 moved back to London. Between 1966 and 1975, he taught at the **Royal College of Art, London**. Coper's beautiful totem-like vessels narrowed the distinctions between art and design and, together with Lucie Rie, he inspired a revival of studio pottery.

Hans Coper

1920 *Chemnitz, Germany*
1981 *Somerset, England*

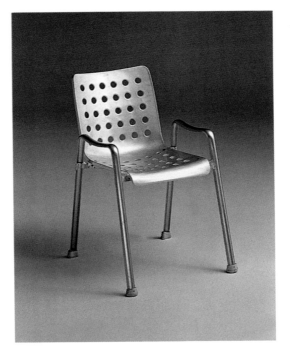

Landi stacking chair for P. & W. Blattmann, 1939 (reissued by Zanotta as the 2070 *Spartana*)

Hans Coray

1906 *Wald, Switzerland*
1991 *Zurich*

Hans Coray studied languages until 1929, and in 1931 became a secondary school teacher in Aarau and Zuoz. From 1932 until 1938, he continued his education, studying design, astrology, theology and graphology. During this period, Coray also began designing metalwork and creating models of chairs. In 1938, he designed the lightweight stamped aluminium *Landi* chair for the "Schweizerische Landesausstellung" (Swiss National Exhibition) held in Zurich the following year. The chair's perforations not only reduced its weight but also allowed water drainage, making it ideal for outdoor use. The *Landi* chair was initially manufactured by P. W. Blattmann from around 1939 and was then reissued by Zanotta in 1971 as the *2070 Spartana*. In 1941, Coray took a metalworking course in Zurich, and from 1945 worked as an independent designer, artist and art dealer. He designed several exhibitions for Swiss chemical companies during the Second World War and in the late 1940s created a range of furniture using aluminium, tubular metal and wood, which Wohnbedarf retailed. In the early 1950s, Coray designed a number of other chairs, some with upholstery, before devoting himself completely to fine art. Coray's sculptures, which were mostly in metal, were exhibited in Zurich from 1950 to 1985, Bern in 1951 and Cologne in 1981.

Corporate identity, which is strongly related to packaging design, is a means by which companies and/or brands can give their products or services a visually unified character that will differentiate them from others in the marketplace. Central to corporate identity is the company logo, which is normally used on all corporate projections from stationery to advertising. Some design-oriented companies or brands, such as **Braun**, approach corporate identity holistically and implement a rigorously managed design regime throughout their organizations, which influences not only the form of their products, but the design of their offices and factories as well. **Peter Behrens** was the first designer to put into action such a programme when he became the artistic adviser to **AEG** in 1907. He applied an integrated language of design, not only to the company's products and graphics, but to housing for its workers and a factory as well – all of which was instrumental in forging AEG's easily recognizable identity. Throughout the 20th century, especially with the progressive globalization of many markets today, commercial organizations have increasingly embraced the universal language of corporate design in an effort to compete more effectively.

Corporate
Identity

▲ **Raymond Loewy Associates**, Logos for Shell, 1967, and BP, 1938; **Landor Associates**, Logos for Alitalia, 1969, and Spar, 1970

The origins of the Craft Revival can be traced to the mid-19th century when design reformers such as John Ruskin (1819–1900) and **William Morris** urged for the preservation and revitalization of traditional crafts in the wake of unprecedented industrialization in Britain. The success of Morris & Co., which produced and retailed handcrafted vernacular-style products, inspired the following generation of designers aligned to the **Arts & Crafts Movement**, such as **Charles Voysey**, **Charles R. Ashbee** and **A. H. Mackmurdo**. During the 1880s, some members of the movement founded guilds, such as the Art Worker's Guild, the Century Guild and the **Guild of Handicraft**. Later designers affiliated with the movement based in the Cotswolds, such as **Ernest Gimson**, Sidney (1865–1926) and Edward Barnsley (1863–1926) and **Gordon Russell**, advocated a more austere form of vernacularism based on functional appropriateness. Arts & Crafts designers in America, such as **Gustav Stickley**, Elbert H. Hubbard (1856–1915) and **Frank Lloyd Wright** were also instigating a return to vernacularism in design and traditional craftsmanship through their promotion of the Mission style. From the mid-20th century, as industrial manufacturing processes

◄ **John Makepeace**, *Millenium 3* chair, 1988

▼ **Fred Baier**, *Megatron* whatnot, 1986

offered ever greater possibilities, design and production became increasingly divorced from one another and craft skills went into decline. To reverse this trend, **John Makepeace** and **Wendell Castle**, two of the most important protagonists of the Craft Revival today, have preserved craft skills through their work as designer-makers and through their schools for craftsmen in wood. During the 1980s, the Craft Revival was stylistically accomplished by **Post-Modernism**, and designers such as Fred Baier (b. 1949) combined technical virtuosity with bizarre forms to create objects that were the very antithesis of the "good citizen's furniture" that had been espoused by Morris and Ruskin.

Cranbrook Academy of Art

Founded 1927
Bloomfield Hills, Michigan

▼ Selection of objects by designers associated with the Cranbrook Academy of Art, 1940s & 1950s (Harry Bertoia, *Diamond* chair; Eero Saarinen, *Grasshopper* chair; Ray Eames, *Cross Patch* textile; Charles & Ray Eames, screen; Charles Eames & Eero Saarinen, storage unit and bench; Maija Grotell and Leza McVey, ceramics).

In 1904, George G. Booth, a wealthy newspaper baron, purchased an estate, which became known as Cranbrook, in the Michigan Township of Bloomfield – a suburb of Detroit. Inspired by the ideals of 19th-century design reformers, Booth founded the Detroit Arts & Crafts Society in 1906 and later established a community at Cranbrook. In 1922, the Bloomfield Hills School was opened for elementary students. The same year, Booth visited the American Academy in Rome, which inspired him to set up a similar institution in America. In 1924, Booth asked the Finnish architect **Eliel Saarinen** to undertake the further development of the Cranbrook Educational Community and two additional schools were subsequently opened. Three years later, Booth authorized the Cranbrook Foundation's trustees to establish a school of arts and crafts that would also function as a fine art academy, to be run on similar lines to European design schools where the decorative arts were taught alongside disciplines such as architecture, painting and sculpture. The Academy was officially founded in 1932, and Saarinen appointed its first president. As at the **Bauhaus**, the staff at Cranbrook actively promoted the exchange of ideas between different studios and workshops, while encouraging rational design practices. Visiting lecturers to the Academy during the 1930s included **Frank Lloyd Wright** and **Le Corbusier**, and among its permanent staff members were the sculptor Carl

Milles (1875–1955), the ceramicist Maija Grotell (1899–1973), and the textile designers, Loja Saarinen (1879–1968) and Marianne Strengell (b. 1909). Among Cranbrook's illustrious alumini were **Ray Eames**, Florence Knoll (b. 1917) and **Jack Lenor Larsen** as well as **Charles Eames** and **Harry Bertoia**, who together with **Eero Saarinen**, were also faculty members in the late 1930s. During the inter-war years, Cranbrook forged its reputation as the premier design school in America. Today, Booth's vision continues to flourish and Cranbrook, though small in size, remains an important centre of artistic and academic excellence.

► Double-handled
vase for Maw & Co.,
1892

Walter Crane, the son of a portrait painter, was initially apprenticed to a
woodcarver. Around 1863, he began designing and illustrating mainly children's books for the publisher Edmund Evans, which sold in large numbers.
During the 1870s, Crane's illustrative style was influenced by the work of
William Blake (1757–1827), the Pre-Raphaelites and by Japanese art. In 1867,
he began designing ceramic wares, which were manufactured by Wedgewood, and tiles for Maw & Co. and Pilkington's as well as wallpapers for Jef-
fery & Co. During this period, he also created embroideries for the Royal
School of Needlework and a tapestry for Morris & Co. Working as an interior
designer, Crane contributed to the decorative scheme of 1, Holland Park, the
London residence of the Greek collector A. A. Ionides, and in 1877 designed
the mosaic frieze for the Arab Hall at Leighton House, London. In 1884, he
became a founding member of the Art Worker's Guild and was its master
from 1888 to 1889. Crane also helped establish the Arts & Crafts Exhibition
Society in 1888 and was its president for several years. He was director of
design at Manchester School of Art from 1893 to 1896 before becoming
the principal of the **Royal College of Art**, **London** from 1897 to 1898. In the
1890s, he wrote a number of important books on the applied arts including
The Decorative Illustration of Books (1896) and *Line and Form* (1900). Ironically, Crane's Arts & Crafts designs had much influence on **Art Nouveau** designers, though he himself was a strong critic of the style.

Walter Crane
1845 *Liverpool*
1915 *Horsham/
Sussex*

Riccardo Dalisi

b. 1931 *Potenza, Italy*

Riccardo Dalisi studied architecture at the Università di Napoli, graduating
in 1957, and subsequently becoming professor of architecture there. During
the early 1970s, he was involved with the **Radical Design** movement in
Naples and undertook "tecnica povera" (poor technology) experimentations
by organizing groups of designers to work with young members of the public in the poorer areas of the city. Such "do-it-yourself" activities attempted
to revive personal creativity and individual expression in design. This research formed the basis of the **Anti-Design** debate and instigated the formation of the counter-design school **Global Tools** in 1973. As one of the founding members of Global Tools, Dalisi was among the most influential
exponents of Anti-Design during the late 1960s and 1970s and wrote several
books on the subject including *L'Architettura della Imprevedibilità* (Unfore-
seeable Architecture) in 1969 and *Architettura d'Animazione* (Animated Architecture) in 1974. With Filippo Alison (b. 1930), he organized Minimal Arts
and in 1979 published a book on **Antonio Cornet y Gaudí**, which celebrated
the expressive tendencies found in his architecture and designs. During the
1980s, Dalisi designed limited-edition furniture for Zanotta, including the
Pavone chair (1986), and the *Caffettiera Napoletana* coffee-maker
(1987–1988) for Alessi.

The Grand Duke Ernst Ludwig of Hesse was the last ruler of the formerly independent state of Hesse-Darmstadt, which became part of the new German Empire in 1871. During his rule from 1892 to 1918, and probably inspired by the founding of the **Vereinigte Werkstätte für Kunst im Handwerk** in Munich in c. 1897, he established an artists' colony in 1899 on the Mathildenhöhe in Darmstadt with the aim of bringing design reform and a renewal of artistic creativity to the Darmstadt-Hesse region. The colony's earliest members included the designers **Josef Maria Olbrich**, **Peter Behrens**, Hans Christiansen (1866–1945), Paul Bürck (1878–1947) and Patriz Huber (1878–1902). The colony initially comprised a central studio building and seven artists' houses including the Behrens Haus, which was conceived by Peter Behrens as a **Gesamtkunstwerk** with every element of its internal decoration, from furniture to drinking glasses, being specially designed for the project. Olbrich also designed similar residences for himself and Hans Christiansen. The colony exhibited its Darmstadt Room at the 1900 Paris "Exposition Universelle", and in 1901 presented the "Ein Dokument Deutscher Kunst" (A Document of German Art) exhibition at the Mathildenhöhe. For this latter event, several other buildings were specially constructed at the colony including an exhibition hall designed by Olbrich. Although this exhibition was for the most part critically acclaimed, it was not the commercial success that the Grand Duke Ernst Ludwig had hoped for. Between 1899 and 1914, a total of twenty-three artists were designing furniture, jewellery, glass, ceramics and silverware at the colony. Some of its best known designs, by Ernst Riegel

Darmstädter
Künstlerkolonie
1899–1914
Darmstadt, Germany

▼ Josef Maria
Olbrich, Poster for
the "Ein Dokument
Deutscher Kunst"
exhibition at the
Darmstadt artists'
colony, 1901

▲ Opening of the artists' colony exhibition, 15th May, 1901

(1871–1939) and Theodor Wende (1883–1968), were for silverware. Many of the colony's designs were featured in Alexander Koch's journals, *Innen-Dekoration* and *Deutsche Kunst und Dekoration* and through their publication, reached a wide audience. Behrens taught the annual four-week "Applied Art Master Course" at the Bayerische Gewerbemuseum in Nuremberg until his departure in 1903. Courses were subsequently undertaken by **Richard Riemerschmid**, Paul Haustein (1880–1944) and Friedrich Adler (1878–c. 1942). The colony established a ceramics factory in 1906 and a glass factory in 1908, which stimulated experimentation with industrial production techniques. The Darmstädter Künstlerkolonie directly influenced the formation of the **Wiener Werkstätte** in 1903 and was the most important centre of design innovation in Germany prior to the First World War.

Jean Daum (1825–1885), was born in Bischwiller on the Lower Rhine and later moved to Nancy, where he became involved with the Verrerie Sainte-Catherine glassworks when it opened in 1875. The business soon experienced serious financial difficulties, some of which Jean Daum was liable for and in an attempt to recoup his losses he bought the factory, renaming it Verrerie de Nancy. His sons, Auguste and Antonin, joined him in 1879 and 1887 respectively to administrate the financial and production activities of the firm. Initially, the glassware produced by the Verrerie de Nancy, which included watch glasses, tableware and plate glass, was little different from that of other manufacturers. The Daums, however, brought together a stable of artists, designers and craftsmen who began to create more innovative designs for them. During the 1890s, glassware in the **Art Nouveau** style was produced, which, although similar to the work of **Émile Gallé**, was less expressive and less technically refined. In 1891, a decorating studio was established, directed by Eugène Damman, which eventually employed fifty workers including, among others, Émile Wirtz, Alméric Walter, Jacques Gruber, Henri Bergé and Eugène Gall. The factory had a total workforce of three hun-

◄ Cameo glass
vases, c. 1900

▲ Cameo glass vases,
c. 1900

dred, and the two most successful areas were the production of engraved or cameo-etched vases and glass lamp shades, the latter being produced for their own lighting products as well as those of **Louis Majorelle** and later those of Edgar-William Brandt (1880–1960). In 1893, the firm exhibited their first acid-etched designs at the Chicago World's Fair but their decisive success came at the 1900 Paris "Exposition Universelle" where they won a Grand Prix and Antonin Daum was awarded a "Légion d'Honneur". In 1906, Alméric Walter established a workshop for "Paté-de-Verre", a technique in which finely crushed glass is bound, often using water, and heated to form a malleable medium that is modelled before it is allowed to cool. The resulting form is then placed in a mould and re-heated sufficiently to vitrify it. Much of the glassware produced with this technique was designed by Henri Bergé. The Daum brothers, together with Émile Gallé, also assisted in the founding of the **École de Nancy** and Antonin subsequently became its vice-president. In 1909, Paul Daum (Auguste's third son) joined the factory and his short tenure, before the outbreak of the First World War suspended production, was marked by a stylistic change in the firm's output towards a reduction of ornament. When production resumed in 1919, the Verrerie de Nancy designs were more in tune with the contemporaneous **Art Deco** style.

Lucienne Conradi studied at Croydon School of Art from 1934 to 1937 and then at the **Royal College of Art, London**, graduating in 1940. In 1942, she married the furniture designer, **Robin Day**, and began teaching at Beckenham School of Art, where she remained until 1947. In 1948, she and her husband set up a design office and began working collaboratively. One of Lucienne Day's earliest commissions was for her *Calyx* textile, designed for the 1951 Festival of Britain. This innovative design, which was awarded a gold medal at the Milan IX Triennale of 1951, was influenced by currents in contemporary fine art and introduced elemental abstraction to British textile design. *Calyx* and other designs by Lucienne Day, including textiles, carpets, table linen and wallpapers, were most influential, spawning a plethora of imitations during the 1950s. In 1952, she received the first Award of the American Institute of Decorators, who judged her textiles to be the best available in America. Her abstract and rhythmic designs were produced by several manufacturers including Wilton Royal Carpets, John Lewis, Alistair Morton's Edinburgh Weavers, Cavendish and most notably, Heal's, who retailed her designs for some twenty-five years. Between 1957 and 1959, Day also designed porcelain for Rosenthal. In the late 1970s, she turned to crafts and began producing "silk mosaics", which were one-off abstracted tapestry wall hangings. During this period, she and her husband also co-designed several stained-glass panels for domestic use. She received three awards from the Council of Industrial Design during the 1950s and 1960s and has written several books on design practice. Lucienne Day is not only one of the most notable textile designers of the 20th century, she is also one of the few women to have achieved international recognition for her design work.

Lucienne Day
b. 1917 *Coulsdon/Surrey*

▼ *Calyx* textile for Heal Fabrics, 1951

Robin Day

b. 1915 *High Wycombe/ Buckinghamshire*

Robin Day received a scholarship in 1935 to the **Royal College of Art, London**, and graduated in 1938. In 1942, he married the textile designer, Lucienne Conradi, and after opening a design office with her in 1948, began working as a freelance exhibition, graphic and industrial designer. The following year, Robin Day won first prize with Clive Latimer (b. 1915) for their design of wooden and tubular metal storage units for the "International Competition for Low-Cost Furniture Design" held at the **Museum of Modern Art, New York**. Shortly afterwards, he was commissioned by Hille International to design modern furniture for the 1949 "British Industry Fair". In 1950, Day was involved in the design of Hille's corporate identity and became the company's chief designer. In 1951, Day designed the "Homes and Gardens" pavilion at the Festival of Britain and was awarded a Gold Medal at the Milan Triennale. From 1962 to 1963, Day developed his injection-moulded *Polyprop* stacking chair, which was among the first pieces of furniture to fully exploit the mass-manufacturing potential of thermoplastics. Since production began in 1963, a staggering 14 million units have been sold in twenty-three countries, making it one of the most democratic modern designs of the 20th century.

Dutch-belgian-born Georges Joseph van Sluijters was the son of an architect. Initially, he became a craftsman in the Netherlands and for a while
worked at a bookbindery in The Hague. In 1891, he moved to Paris and became an illustrator for the newspapers *Le Courrier Français* and *Le Boulevard*.
During this period, he changed his name to Van Feuren and later to de
Feure. In 1894, a one-man show of his Symbolist drawings was held in Paris.
The same year, he also designed furniture in the **Art Nouveau** style for Maison Fleury. From 1900, de Feure headed the design department of **Siegfried
Bing**'s Maison de l'Art Nouveau. In this capacity, he designed furniture, ceramics and glassware as well as the shop's fixtures and fittings. He was also
responsible for two influential rooms in Bing's Pavillon de l'Art Nouveau at
the 1900 Paris "Exposition Universelle". With Theodor Cossmann, de Feure
established the Atelier De Feure for the production of his furniture designs,
and in 1903 his work was exhibited in a one-man show organized by Bing.
After the war, he was professor of decorative arts at the École Nationale
des Beaux-Arts, Paris and, for a while, he lived in London working as a stage
designer. In 1924, he designed extravagant interiors for the couturier
Madeleine Vionnet in Paris.

Georges de Feure
1868 *Paris*
1928 *Paris*

▲ Ladies' Sitting
Room exhibited in
Siegfried Bing's
Pavillon de l'Art
Nouveau, 1900

**Michele
De Lucchi**

b. 1951 *Ferrara, Italy*

Michele De Lucchi studied in Padua and later at the Università di Firenze under Adolfo Natalini (b. 1941), graduating in 1975. In 1973, together with Piero Brombin, Pier Paola Bortolami, Boris Pastrovecchio and Valerio Tridenti, he co-founded the design and architectural group Cavart, which promoted a **Radical Design** agenda through happenings, publications and seminars, the best known of which was entitled "Culturally Impossible Architecture" and was held in a Paduan marble quarry. From 1975 to 1977, De Lucchi taught architecture at the Università di Firenze, and in 1978 moved to Milan to work at Kartell's in-house design studio Centrokappa. He subsequently met **Ettore Sottsass** and assisted him with the planning of the first **Memphis** exhibition. In 1979, he designed several post-modern prototypes of domestic electrical appliances for **Studio Alchimia** and became a consultant to **Olivetti**. In 1981, he co-founded the co-operative Memphis and was responsible for the introduction of geometric motifs on the plastic laminates used by the enterprise. He founded Solid, a Milan-based design group in 1986, and also began teaching at the Domus Academy, Milan. In the early 1990s, he established the De Lucchi Group and has since worked widely in Japan and Germany, his designs becoming less experimental and more suited to industrial production.

◄ *Siner Pica* lamp by Belux for Studio Alchimia, 1979

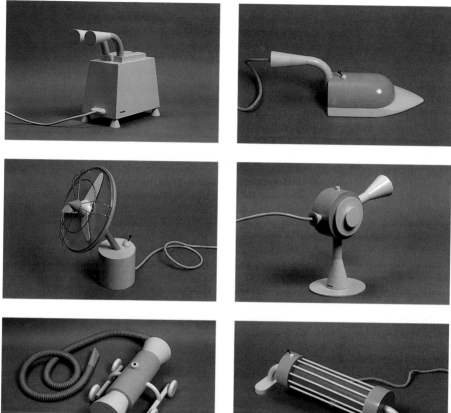

▲ Prototypes
(varnished wood) of
domestic appliances
for Girmi, first
exhibited at the
Milan Triennale in
1979 (never put into
production)

William De Morgan

1839 *London*
1917 *London*

The son of a mathematics professor and a suffragette campaigner, William De Morgan began studying art in 1855 at Cary's School in Bloomsbury, London. In 1859, he continued his training at the Royal Academy Schools, and in 1863 he was introduced by a fellow student, Henry Holiday (1839–1927), to **William Morris** and Edward Burne-Jones (1833–1898). During that year, he became closely associated with the Pre-Raphaelites and decided to abandon fine art in favour of the decorative arts. Between 1863 and 1872, he designed stained glass, tiles and painted furniture for Morris, Marshall, Faulkner & Co. In 1869, De Morgan discovered that if paint containing silver was used for stained glass, it created an iridescence. This discovery led him to experiment with glazes and firing techniques so as to produce a lustre finish for ceramic tiles. In 1873, he established the Orange House Pottery in Chelsea, which had a showroom attached for the retail of his ceramics, the majority of which were tiles. In 1879, he created tiles for the Arab Hall at Leighton House and supplied tiled panels for the Czar of Russia's yacht. De Morgan tiles were also retailed through Morris & Co., while his workshop manufactured tiles designed by Morris & Co. This close business collaboration was furthered when De Morgan moved his pottery to a site adjacent to William Morris' workshops at Merton Abbey. De Morgan's distinctive ceramics, which were decorated with strange animals, swirling flora or galleons in stormy seas, were stylistically influenced by Medieval and Persian antecedents. In 1888, he moved his workshop to the Sands End Pottery in Fulham and went

▼ *Snake* tile from Chelsea period, c. 1880

into partnership with the architect, Halsey Ricardo (1854–1928), whose Peacock House on Addison Road (1904) was decorated extensively internally and externally with de Morgan tiles. In 1906, De Morgan published his first novel, Joseph Vance, which was an instant success both in Britain and America, and a year later he gave up pottery so as to concentrate on his writing career, completing another six novels. His workshop, however, continued to operate until 1911 under the guidance of Charles and Fred Passenger and Frank Iles.

▲ *Pelican* charger
in Persian colours
from Fulham period,
c. 1888

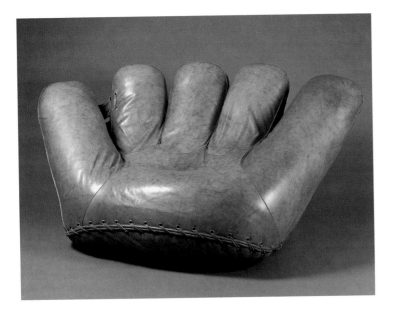

De Pas, D'Urbino & Lomazzi

De Pas
1932 *Milan*
1991 *Milan*

D'Urbino
b. 1935 *Milan*

Lomazzi
b. 1936 *Milan*

▲ *Joe* chair for
Poltronova, 1970

Gionatan De Pas, Donato D'Urbino and Paolo Lomazzi trained at the Politecnico di Milano and set up an architecture and design office together in 1966. Initially, they experimented with modular and inflatable PVC furniture designs. Their subsequent *Blow* chair (1967) was the first mass-produced piece of inflatable furniture and became an icon of 1960s' Pop culture.

In 1970, the office assisted in the design of the Italian Pavilion at the Osaka World Fair, and in 1972 participated in the "Italy: The New Domestic Landscape" exhibition held at the **Museum of Modern Art, New York**. Their *Joe* chair (1970), named after the American baseball legend Joe DiMaggio, was inspired by the oversized and out-of-context sculptures of Claes Oldenburg (b. 1929).

In 1979, De Pas, D'Urbino & Lomazzi were awarded a **Compasso d'Oro** at the Milan Triennale for their *Sciangai* coat rack (1974) and a year later, the office designed the "Italian Furniture Design 1950–1980" exhibition in Cologne. In 1987 an exhibition of the group's work was held in Kyoto. During the 1980s, they also made a television programme, entitled "Dal cucchiaio alla città: il design italiano dal 1950 al 1980" (From the Spoon to the City). For over three decades, De Pas, D'Urbino & Lomazzi have consistently produced well-executed designs for flexible, interchangeable and adaptable furniture and lighting, ranging from radical to more main-

stream solutions, which have been manufactured by Acerbis, **Artemide**, BBB, Bonacina, Cassina, Driade, Palina, Poltronova, Stilnovo and Zanotta among others.

▲ Zanotta advertisement for *Blow* chairs, c. 1968

De Stijl

Founded 1917
Netherlands

▲ **Gerrit Rietveld,**
Isometric drawing
of the interior of the
Rietveld-Schroeder
House in Utrecht,
1927

In October 1917, a small group of Dutch architects, designers and artists established an art journal entitled *De Stijl*. Led by **Theo van Doesburg**, the group initially included Piet Mondrian (1872–1944), Bart Anthony van der Leck (1876–1958), **Vilmos Huszár, Jacobus Johannes Pieter Oud**, Robert van 't Hoff (1887–1979), Jan Wils (1891–1972) and Georges Vantongerloo (1886–1965). The magazine became a forum for art and design debates and eventually the focus of a larger and wider ranging group of intellectuals. This loosely organized movement shared a common objective, that of absolute abstraction. The journal not only featured the latest developments in **avant-garde** Dutch art and design but also the work of the Russian Constructivists, the Dadaists and the Italian Futurists. The publication called for a purification of art and design through the adoption of a universal language of abstracted cubism or, as Piet Mondrian described it, Neo-Plasticism. De Stijl members believed that the search for honesty and beauty would ultimately bring harmony and enlightenment to humanity. Theo van Doesburg, who was editor-in-chief of the magazine, tirelessly promoted the De Stijl message on his numerous trips to Belgium, France, Italy and Germany. In 1921, he established contacts with staff at the Staatliches **Bauhaus** in Weimar, and a year later gave a De Stijl course of lectures in Weimar. Theo van Doesburg also developed links with Constructivists, such as **El Lissitzky** and **László Moholy-Nagy**. The De Stijl movement not only influenced developments in the fine arts, its members also designed extremely influential furniture, interiors, textiles, graphics and architecture. **Gerrit Rietveld**'s revolutionary *Red/Blue* chair of 1918–1823, which in its design encapsulated the philosophy of the De Stijl Movement, was exhibited at the Staatliche Bauhaus in 1923 and inspired **Marcel Breuer**'s later tubular metal *B3 Wassily* chair of 1925–1927. Like Rietveld's *Red/Blue* chair, De Stijl architecture and interior designs were characterized by the use of strong geometric forms and coloured block-like elements that delineated space. Partitions were used to divide internal areas, while utilitarian furnishings were kept to an absolute minimum. The strong lines incorporated in these interiors produced a dynamism, while a

▼ **Gerrit Rietveld**, Sideboard, 1919 (executed by G. van de Groenekan)

sense of lightness was achieved through the purging of ornament. This dematerialist approach to design was highly influential to the development of the **Modern Movement**, as was De Stijl's use of geometric formalism. Although the De Stijl group was never formally organized, its output was highly distinctive and shared a common visual language – that of geometric abstraction. The application of this new vocabulary of form and colour blurred the traditional distinctions between the fine and decorative arts, but sadly the group's intention of bringing a greater universality to the arts was never fully realized. The De Stijl movement's vision of Utopia was inspired by the vitality of the modern city, while its utilitarian approach to the design of objects for use was influenced by Dutch Puritanism. Though sharing many of the ideas propounded by Russian **Constructivism**, such as spatial dynamism, De Stijl is generally acknowledged as the first modern design movement, because it heralded a new aesthetic purity. The *De Stijl* magazine was published until Theo van Doesburg's death in 1931, after which the movement gradually lost its focus and was unable to maintain its former momentum.

▼ **Bart van der Leck**, Carpet for Metz & Co., 1918–1919

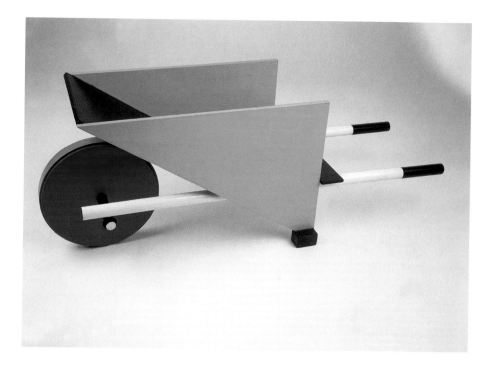

▲ **Gerrit Rietveld**, Child's wheelbarrow, 1923 (executed by G. van de Groenekan)

◄ **Jan Pieter Dirk van Gelder**, Doll's house furniture for Metz & Co., 1920s

Deconstructivism

Deconstruction is a method of analysis primarily associated with literary criticism that was first postulated in the 1960s by the French philosopher Jacques Derrida (b. 1930). Through his writings, he argued that by analysing or "deconstructing" the logic of Western metaphysics, its underlying biases could be uncovered. Deconstruction was also used to demonstrate that because a creative work is subject to different interpretations, its content is ultimately ambiguous, which in turn undermines its logic. By deconstructing the formal language of the **Modern Movement**, its multiplicity of meanings and biases were revealed, which resulted in the questioning of its philosophical foundations. During the 1970s, Derrida's ideas were translated and transformed into a style of architecture and design – Deconstructivism. The style is allied to **Post-Modernism**, as it counters the traditional premisses of Modernism. However, unlike Post-Modernism, it rejects historicism and ornamentation. Likewise, Deconstructivism often alludes to the deconstruction of meaning, whereas Post-Modernism playfully subverts meaning and double-codes it. Stylistically if not philosophically similar to Russian **Constructivism** of the 1920s, Deconstructivism also adopted fragmented and expressive forms. Its most notable practitioners in architecture and interior design are **Frank O. Gehry, Coop Himmelb(l)au**, Zaha Hadid (b. 1950), Peter Eisenman (b. 1932) and Bernard Tschumi (b. 1944). Being an essentially anti-rational style, Deconstructivism is linked to **Anti-Design** and has had little impact on product design, apart from a few examples such as **Daniel Weil**'s *Radio in a Bag* (1981–1883), which by revealing its constituent parts countered traditional forms and deconstructed conventional design logic.

▼ **Zaha Hadid**, Interior of Moonsoon Restaurant in Sapporo, Japan, 1990

◄ *Model No. 654 Torso* chair for Cassina, 1982

Paolo Deganello studied architecture at the Università di Firenze from 1961 to 1966. On graduating, he co-founded the **Radical Design** group **Archizoom Associati** in Florence, with **Andrea Branzi**, Gilberto Corretti (b. 1941) and Massimo Morozzi (b. 1941). Between 1963 and 1974, he assisted with the urban planning of Calenzano, Florence. He also taught: from 1966 at the Università di Firenze, from 1971 to 1974 at the Architectural Association, London, and in 1976 at the Università di Milano, finally being appointed professor of design at the ISIA (Istituto Statale di Disegno Industriale), Rome. In 1974, Archizoom was dissolved, and a year later Deganello joined Corretti, Franco Gatti and Roberto Querci in forming another design co-operative, the Collettivo Technici Progettisti (the Group of Technical Designers), to promote Radical furniture designs. From 1972, Deganello contributed articles to magazines such as *Domus, Rasegna, Lotus, Casabella, IN* and *Modo* and in 1975, with Ennio Chiggio, he published a series of essays in *Quaderni del Progetto* (Project Sketchbooks). In 1981, he established his own studio, designing furniture for Marcatré, Cassina, Driade and **Vitra** among others, as well as lighting for Venini and Ycami Collection. His collapsible *AEO* chair (1973) and multi-functional *Torso* chair (1982) were inspired by 1950s furniture and characterize his approach to design. In 1981, Deganello's work was exhibited at the Clocktower, New York, and in 1983 he designed interiors for the Schöner Wohnen Company, Zurich.

Paolo Deganello
1940 *Este, Italy*

Christian Dell

1893 Offenbach, Germany
1974 Wiesbaden, Germany

Christian Dell served an apprenticeship as a silversmith at the silver factory of Schleissner & Söhne, Hanau from 1907 to 1912, while studying at the Königliche Preussische Zeichenakademie. From 1912 to 1913, he worked as a silversmith in Dresden before training under **Henry van de Velde** at the Kunstgewerbeschule, Weimar. After military service in the First World War he worked as a journeyman from 1918 to 1920, and later as a master silversmith for Hestermann & Ernst in Munich. In 1920, he worked in the silver workshop of Emil Lettré (1876–1954) in Berlin, before returning to Hanau and re-enrolling at the Königliche Preussische Zeichenakademie. A year later, he established his own silver studio in Hanau and, from 1922 to 1925, was the "Werkmeister" of the metal workshop at the Staatliches **Bauhaus** in Weimar, where he worked closely with **László Moholy-Nagy**. Unlike most of his Bauhaus colleagues, Dell believed that designers should not completely reject historicism. From 1926 to 1933, he taught in the newly established metalwork department at the Frankfurter Kunstschule, designing silverware

that was produced in the school's workshop. During this period, Dell also designed innovative lighting, such as his *Rondella-Polo* table lamp (1926–1927) for industrial mass-production. His lighting designs were manufactured by Rondella and by Kaiser, who produced his *Idell* range that was later copied by Helo. In 1933, he was removed from the teaching staff at the Frankfurter Kunstschule by the Nazi regime and later, in 1939, he established his own jewellery business in Wiesbaden.

◄ Silverplated wine jug with ebony handle for metal workshop at the Weimar Bauhaus, 1922

During the mid-1920s, after a visit to the 1925 "Exposition Internationale des Arts Décoratifs et Industriels" in Paris, Donald Deskey took up three-dimensional and interior design. He created screens for Saks Fifth Avenue in 1926, and a year later designed window displays for this New York department store as well as for Franklin Simon. His modernist windows for Saks incorporated an influential combination of metal and cork. Deskey also designed painted screens for **Paul Frankl**'s gallery and undertook private interior design commissions for Adam Gimbel and the Rockefeller family, among others. In 1927, he went into partnership with Phillip Vollmer, producing exclusive one-off metal furniture and lighting designs, but this venture was dissolved in the early 1930s. He also developed a stained-wood laminate known as Weldtex in the late 1920s. In 1931, Deskey designed **Moderne** interiors and furnishings for the Radio City Music Hall – a prestigious and influential commission, which exemplified the American **Art Deco** style. During the 1930s, he executed a variety of designs for mass-production such as washing machines, vending machines, printers and even a rack for bowling balls, which were exhibited at the Metropolitan Museum of Art, New York in 1934. From the late 1930s until 1975, he was the principal of Donald Deskey Associates and designed graphics, packaging, interiors, lighting, office furniture and exhibitions. Deskey was one of the greatest proponents of Art Deco in America and was also an important pioneer of industrial design consulting.

Donald Deskey

1894 *Blue Earth, Minnesota*
1989 *Vero Beach, Florida*

Desny

1927–1933
Paris

Located at 122 Avenue des Champs-Elysées in Paris, La Maison Desny was a design-oriented firm that operated between 1927 and 1933. Although little is known about its founders, the designers Desnet and René Nauny, the firm's output of innovative chrome-plated lighting and Cubist-inspired silverware was highly influential. Among the company's staff members was the designer, Louis Poulain. Essentially a decorating firm, Desny produced a wide range of objects in the **Moderne** style, ranging from rugs with abstracted geometric motifs to aluminium furniture. The firm also executed painted murals and bathroom accessories. Although stylistically inspired by Modernism, Desny designs did not embrace the utilitarianism of the **Modern Movement**, and instead often used exotic woods and other costly materials in its work. The firm undertook the design of elegant and luxurious interiors for the residences of Pierre David-Weill, Georges-Henri Rivière and Mlle. Thurnauer among others. Desny incorporated in its interior schemes designs by the sculptors, Alberto (1901–1966) and Diego Giacometti (1902–1985) and the artist André Masson (1896–1987) as well as those by **avant-garde** designers such as **Jean-Michel Frank** and **Robert Mallet-Stevens**. In 1933, the company was closed owing to the death of Desnet, and René Nauny subsequently established a costume jewellery business known as Hippocampe. Although Desny was a relatively short-lived venture, its metalwork captured the dynamic spirit of the Art Deco style and for this reason, remains highly collectable today.

► Silverplated metal bowl for Desny, c. 1925

▼ Silverplated metal goblet for Desny, c. 1925

In 1906, the III Deutsche Kunstgewerbeausstellung (German Arts & Crafts Exhibition) held in Dresden revealed that the expressive **Jugendstil** style was being overtaken by a more formal language of design that emphasized function. Only those designs that were the result of a positive collaboration between designers associated with established workshops, such as the **Dresdener Werkstätten für Handwerkskunst** were shown. This work was more utilitarian than any previously exhibited in Dresden and reflected the realization of designers, such as **Richard Riemerschmid**, that the only way to produce large quantities of well-designed and executed products that were also affordable was through the manufacturing industry. In promoting this new direction, the exhibition highlighted a new aesthetic and social imperative in design and acted as a catalyst for the formation of the Deutscher Werkbund. Founded in October 1907, the Deutscher Werkbund attempted from its outset to reconcile artistic endeavour with industrial mass-production. Thus, its founding body was made up of a dozen designers, including Riemerschmid, **Bruno Paul**, **Peter Behrens** and **Josef Maria Olbrich**, and a dozen established manufacturers, including Peter Bruckmann & Söhne and Poeschel & Trepte, as well as design workshops, such as the **Wiener Werkstätte** and the Munich-based **Vereinigte Werkstätten für Kunst im Handwerk**. Peter Bruckmann (1865–1927) was appointed the association's first president, and within a year its membership had risen to around five hundred. From 1912, the Werkbund began publishing its own yearbooks, which included articles with illustrations on its members' designs, such as factories by **Walter Gropius** and Peter Behrens and cars by Ernst Naumann. The yearbooks also listed members' addresses and areas of

◄ **Fritz Hellmut Ehmke**, Poster for the Deutsche Werkbund Exhibition in Cologne, 1914

▼ Founder members of the Deutscher Werkbund

AUF Grund einer in München stattgefundenen Zusammenkunft von Angehörigen der Kunst und Industrie haben sich zur Gründung eines Deutschen Kunstgewerbebundes bereit erklärt:

PETER BEHRENS	DÜSSELDORF
THEODOR FISCHER	STUTTGART
JOSEF HOFFMANN	WIEN
WILHELM KREIS	DRESDEN
MAX LAUGER	KARLSRUHE
ADELBERT NIEMEYER	MÜNCHEN
JOSEF OLBRICH	DARMSTADT
BRUNO PAUL	BERLIN
RICHARD RIEMERSCHMID	MÜNCHEN
J. J. SCHARVOGEL	DARMSTADT
PAUL SCHULTZE-NAUMBURG	SAALECK
FRITZ SCHUHMACHER	DRESDEN
P. BRUCKMANN & SÖHNE	HEILBRONN
DEUTSCHE WERKSTÄTTEN FÜR HANDWERKSKUNST G. M. B. H.	DRESDEN
EUGEN DIEDERICHS	JENA
GEBRÜDER KLINGSPOR	OFFENBACH a. M.
KUNSTDRUCKEREI KÜNSTLER-BUND G. M. B. H.	KARLSRUHE
POESCHEL & TREPTE	LEIPZIG
SAALECKER WERKSTÄTTEN G. M. B. H.	SAALECK
VEREINIGTE WERKSTÄTTEN FÜR KUNST IM HANDWERK A.-G.	MÜNCHEN
WERKSTÄTTEN FÜR DEUTSCHEN HAUSRAT, THEOPHIL MÜLLER	DRESDEN
WIENER WERKSTÄTTE	WIEN
WILHELM & CO.	MÜNCHEN
GOTTLOB WUNDERLICH	ZSCHOPENTHAL

specialization, in an attempt to promote collaboration between art and industry. In 1914, the Werkbund organized a landmark exhibition in Cologne, entitled "Deutsche Werkbund-Ausstellung", which included Walter Gropius' steel and glass model factory, Bruno Taut's Glass Pavilion and **Henry van de Velde**'s Werkbund Theatre. A year later, the Werkbund's membership had swollen to almost two thousand. The increasing divergence between craftsmanship and industrial production, however, continued to fuel a debate within the Werkbund, with some members such as Hermann Muthesius (1861–1927) and Naumann arguing for standardization, while others such as van de Velde, Gropius and Taut argued for individualism. This conflict, known as the "Werkbundstreit" almost led to the disbanding of the association. The widespread need for consumer products after the devastation of the First World War, however, led Gropius to accept the necessity of standardization and industrial production, although other members such as Hans Poelzig (1869–1939) continued to resist change. From 1921 to 1926, Riemerschmid was president of the Deutscher Werkbund and during his tenure the Functionalists' approach to design was advanced. In 1924, the Werkbund published *Form ohne Ornament* (*Form without Ornament*), which presented industrially produced designs and expounded on the virtues of plain undecorated surfaces and ultimately, **Functionalism**. In 1927, the Werkbund staged a unique exhibition in Stuttgart, entitled "Die Wohnung" (The Dwelling), which was organized by **Ludwig Mies van der Rohe**. The focus of the exhibition was a housing estate project, the "Weissenhofsiedlung", for which the most progressive architects throughout Europe were invited to design buildings. The interiors of these specially commissioned houses were furnished with modern tubular metal furniture designed by Mies van der Rohe, **Mart Stam**, **Marcel Breuer** and **Le Corbusier** among others. Widely publicized, this exhibition led to a greater acceptance of Modernism. Although the Werkbund was eventually disbanded in 1934, it was re-established in 1947 but was by then a spent force. The Deutscher Werkbund bridged Jugendstil and the **Modern Movement** and, through its activities, had an enormous impact on the evolution of German industrial design.

▼ Yearbook with emblem of the Deutscher Werkbund, 1913

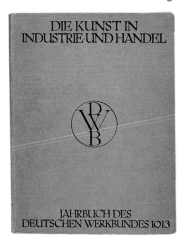

DIE KUNST IN
INDUSTRIE UND HANDEL

JAHRBUCH DES
DEUTSCHEN WERKBUNDES 1913

From 1918 to 1920, Erich Dieckmann studied architecture at the Technische Hochschule in Danzig. He then enrolled at the Staatliches **Bauhaus**, Weimar, and served an apprenticeship in the carpentry workshop, where he was employed briefly after his journeyman's exam in 1924. When the school was forced to move to Dessau, he remained in Weimar as master of the joinery workshop at the Bauhochschule Weimar until 1930. For the next three years, he taught furniture design in the carpentry workshop of the influential Kunstgewerbeschule Burg Giebichenstein, Halle. In 1933, the Nazis removed him from this teaching position and for the following three years he was unemployed and produced very few designs. From 1936 to 1939, Dieckmann was a member of the Nazi instigated "Amt der Schönheit der

Erich Dieckmann
1896 Kauernick/
West Prussia,
1944 Berlin

► Armchair for the furniture workshop at the Staatliche Bauhochschule in Weimar, c. 1926

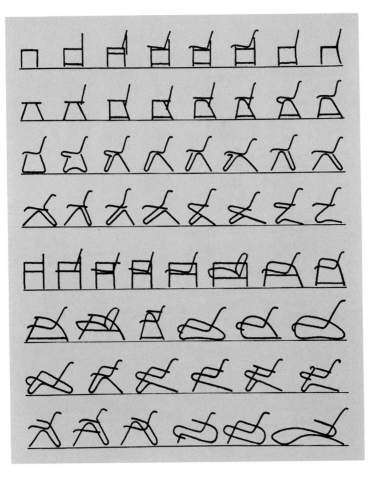

Arbeit" (Beauty of Labour Board) in Hanover, after which he was in charge of the "Deutsche Kunsthandwerk" (Germany Craftsmanship) department of the Chamber of Arts in Berlin until his death in 1944. Although Dieckmann experimented with the structural potential of tubular metal in many of his seating designs, he is best remembered for his standardized wooden furniture. Dieckmann elegantly synthesized craft with functionalism in these restrained designs, which are characterized by cubic forms and simple construction techniques. Through his use of woods, such as beech, cherry, oak and ash, he softened the geometric formalism associated with the **Modern Movement**. After **Marcel Breuer**, Erich Dieckmann is widely regarded as the most important Bauhaus-trained furniture designer.

Niels Diffrient studied aeronautical engineering at the Cass Technical High School, Detroit, graduating in 1946. During the late 1940s and early 1950s, he trained at the **Cranbrook Academy of Art**, Bloomfield Hills, Michigan and at Wayne State University, Detroit. From 1954 to 1955, he was in Italy on a Fulbright Fellowship in design and architecture and worked in the office of **Marco Zanuso** in Milan. Before that, he had already worked for five years as a designer and modeller in the office of **Eero Saarinen** and for two years at Walter B. Ford Associates, Detroit. In 1952, he entered the firm of the famous product designer, **Henry Dreyfuss**, becoming a partner in 1956. While at Henry Dreyfuss Associates, he assisted with the compiling of anthropometric data, which was eventually published in the three influential volumes entitled *Humanscale 1-2-3* (1974), *Humanscale 4-5-6* (1981) and *Humanscale 7-8-9* (1981). He also designed aircraft interiors for Hughes, Lockheed and Learjet as well as computers for Honeywell and X-ray equipment for Litton Industries. He remained at Henry Dreyfuss Associates until 1981, when he left to set up his own design office, Niels Diffrient Product Design, in Ridgefield, Connecticut. Since then, he has designed ergonomically conceived office systems furniture, such as the *Diffrient Operational* seating (1980) for **Knoll** and the *Helena* seating programme for Sunar-Hausmann (1984). His multifunctional reclining *Jefferson* armchair and ottoman (1983), which adjusts to fit all body types, introduced state-of-the-art seating technology and ergonomics to the domestic environment. With computer tablet and task-lighting options, the chair also provided an integrated micro work centre for home/office use. Diffrient's main interest lies in functional performance and with his mastery of ergonomics, he is able to promote a highly resolved physical interaction between object and user.

Niels Diffrient

b.1928 *Star, Mississippi*

▼ *Diffrient Advanced Management* office chair for Knoll International, 1979

Nanna Ditzel

b. 1923 *Copenhagen*

▼ *Sommerfugle* chair
for Frederica
Stolefabrik, 1990

Nanna Hauberg studied furniture design at the Kunsthandvaerkskolen, Copenhagen where she was taught by Orla Mølgård Nielsen (1907–1994) and Peter Hvidt (1916–1986). While there, she met her future husband, Jørgen Ditzel (1921–1961), who had earlier trained as an upholsterer. In 1944, they exhibited living room furniture together at the Cabinetmakers' Annual Exhibition in Copenhagen. These designs, which included a tea table with a removable tray designed for Louis G. Thiersen, received considerable attention. Two years later, the couple were married and established their own design studio in Hellerup. Initially, they concentrated their efforts on solutions for small living areas and Nanna explored the concept of using kitchen units as room dividers. In the early 1950s, she worked as a furniture designer in the architectural practice of Fritz Schlegel (1896–1965) while continuing to design and exhibit furniture with her husband. In 1952, they designed a range of children's plywood furniture for Knud Willadsen Møbelsnedkeri and collaborated with Gunnar Aagaard Andersen (1919–1982) on the design of a stand for the Cabinetmaker's Exhibition. During this period, Nanna also designed silver jewellery for **Georg Jensen**. In 1954, she and her husband published the book, *Danish Chairs* and in 1956 were jointly awarded the Lunning Prize. From 1957, they designed a range of wicker furniture for R. Wengler. However, their partnership ended with the untimely death of Jørgen in 1961. Driven by her "appetite for change", Nanna Ditzel went on to execute innovative craft-based designs for furniture, metalware, tableware, jewellery and textiles. Her work possesses a remarkable sense of lightness and texture and was the subject of a film produced by the Danish Ministry of Education in 1992.

▶ *Jack* light, 1996
with piled-up
Euroblocks, 1998

Tom Dixon studied at Chelsea School of Art, London, graduating in 1978.
From 1983, he began designing furniture from *objets trouvés* and a year later
was welding scrap metal on the stage of the Titanic nightclub in London as
"performance art". In 1987, he established his own manufacturing company,
Dixon PID, which later became known as Space, producing one-off and
limited edition furniture and lighting. His *Kitchen* chair (1987) and *S* chair
(1988), which were purposely distanced from the technical perfection of industrial production, are typical of his work from this period. In 1989, his furniture and lighting designs were exhibited at a one-man show at the Yves
Gastou Gallery in Paris and attracted considerable press attention. During
the 1990s, Dixon's work became less craft orientated and more sculptural
in form. Among his most notable designs are his upholstered furniture for
Cappellini and his highly successful plastic *Jack* light (1996) for another of
his own manufacturing ventures, known as Eurolounge. His work was exhibited at the British Council in Cologne and in Beirut during the mid-1990s,
and in 1998 Dixon was appointed head of design at Habitat.

Tom Dixon
b.1959 *Sfax, Tunisia*

Like the **Vereinigte Werkstätten für Kunst im Handwerk** (United Workshops), which had been founded in Munich a year earlier, the Dresdener Werkstätten für Handwerkskunst (Dresden Workshops for Handicraft Art) were established for the design and production of high quality products for everyday use. The formation of workshops such as these was inspired by the efforts of pioneering British design reformers, such as **William Morris**, but was also prompted by the desire to recapture the design retail market from the French *décorateurs*. Initially, the Dresdener Werkstätten für Handwerkskunst focused on traditional craft methods of manufacture and produced simple vernacular designs that reflected the influence of the British **Arts & Crafts Movement**. The model rooms designed by **Richard Riemerschmid** around 1905 were not only decorated with furniture, textiles and ceramics produced by the workshops but also with traditional china, art-prints and birdcages, which gave them a homely appeal. Such utterly unpretentious interiors were the very antithesis of contemporary high style and reflected the widespread desire for design reform in Germany. Although initially committed to handcraftsmanship, the Dresden Workshops soon sought to gear artistic endeavour to industrial production. To this end, Richard Riemerschmid designed a series of standardized furniture, the *Maschinenmöbelprogramm* from 1906. Known as "machine furniture", these designs were constructed of standardized elements that were visibly screwed together. From its inception, this revolutionary programme of furniture was wholly informed

▼ *Herrenzimmer
interior III, 1905*

by mechanized production considerations and was immensely influential to later progressive furniture design. Riemerschmid subsequently designed a factory building for the workshops in Hellerau, near Dresden (1908–1910), presumably to increase the production of such furniture. The products manufactured by the Dresden Workshops, most of which were designed by Riemerschmid, were more vernacular in style and less exclusive than those produced by the Vereinigte Werkstätten für Kunst im Handwerk in Munich and other German workshops. Although their adoption of ethical manufacturing practices did not allow the workshops to produce low-cost products, the Dresdener Werkstätten für Handwerkskunst's quest for inexpensive and honest design was highly influential, especially to the foundation of the **Deutscher Werkbund**.

▲ Richard Riemerschmid, *Herrenzimmer* desk, 1905

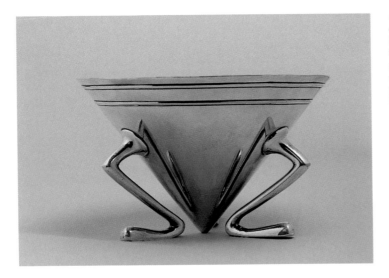

◄ *Model No. 247* electroplated sugar bowl for Elkington & Co., c. 1880

► *Model No. 2045 Crow's Foot* claret jug for Hulkin & Heath, 1878

Christopher Dresser

1834 Glasgow
1904 Mulhouse/Alsace, France

Christopher Dresser trained from 1847 to 1854 under the botanist John Lindley at the Government School of Design, London, where he then lectured for fourteen years. His advocacy of "Art Botany" – the stylized yet scientifically based depiction of nature – helped replace the overblown and false naturalism common to the High Victorian style with a more formalized type of ornamentation. In 1856, Dresser contributed a plate showing "Plants and Elevations of Flowers" to Owen Jones' seminal work, *The Grammar of Ornament*. In 1857, he was appointed professor of "Botany Applied to the Fine Arts" at the School of Design, South Kensington. He also published various articles in the *Art Journal* and three books, which helped establish his reputation and contributed to his receiving an honorary doctorate from the University of Jena. Having adopted the title "Doctor", Dresser applied for the Chair of Botany at the University of London in 1860. He was unsuccessful in winning this position and so instead embarked on a career in design. He established his own studio, which from the outset was enormously successful. Dresser supplied designs for metalware, ceramics, glass, tiles, textiles, wallpapers and cast-iron furnishings to at least thirty of the most eminent manufacturers in Britain. He was also highly influential as a design theorist and was one of the first to promote the special qualities of Japanese applied art. His forward-looking designs reflected his belief in industrial production and his pursuit of "Truth, Beauty, Power". Apart from his prominence as a design reformer, Dresser was also one of the first professional industrial designers.

Henry Dreyfuss

1904 *New York*
1972 *South Pasadena,
California*

Henry Dreyfuss studied at the Ethical Culture School in New York before
becoming apprenticed to the industrial designer **Norman Bel Geddes** in
1923. While working in Geddes' office, Dreyfuss mainly concentrated on
theatrical work and designed costumes, sets and lighting for the Strand
Theater, New York, and for the R. K. O. (Radio-Keith-Orpheum) chain of
Vaudeville theatres. For a while Dreyfuss worked as a consultant to Macy's
department store, before establishing his own New York-based industrial
design practice in 1929. His straightforward and business-like approach to
the design process contributed to the success of his office, which attracted a
large corporate clientele including Bell Telephone, AT&T, American Airlines,
Polaroid, Hoover and RCA. His designs such as the *Trimline* telephone of
1965 were characterized by the use of sweeping sculptural forms, and as
such exemplified **Streamlining** in American design. Like **Raymond Loewy**,
Norman Bel Geddes and **Walter Dorwin Teague**, Dreyfuss re-styled many
products for manufacturers to increase consumer demand, not so much
through technical innovation but by means of stylistic novelty. Some of his
designs bore a facsimile of his signature – an early example of designer la-
belling. Dreyfuss was a founder member of the Society of Industrial Design
and the first president of the Industrial Designers Society of America. He
also published two highly influential books on anthropometrics, *Designing
for People* (1955) and *The Measure of Man* (1960). Dreyfuss and his wife committed suicide in 1972.

Nathalie du Pasquier travelled extensively throughout Africa, Australia and India from 1975 to 1978. On her return to Bordeaux, she studied drawing and design for a year, and then moved to Italy, living first in Rome and then in Milan. A year later, she joined Studio Rainbow as a textile designer and from 1981 to 1988 produced bright and colourful post-modern upholstering textiles, laminates, furniture and ceramics for **Memphis**. From 1982, she also worked as an in-house designer for the clothing company, Fiorucci, which was then at the forefront of New Wave fashion. In 1984, du Pasquier and her husband **George Sowden** (a fellow Memphis designer) produced a range of lamps for Arc 74 entitled Objects for the Electronic Age, and in 1988 they collaborated again on their *Neos* series of brightly coloured clocks for Lorenz. When Memphis was dissolved in 1988, the couple set up their own Milan-based design office to undertake architectural projects as well as the design of textiles, carpets, ceramics and metalware. Du Pasquier's clients have included Elio Palmisano, Maison des Couteliers, Lorenz, Pink Dragon, Missoni, Esprit and NAS Oleari. In 1989, she temporarily abandoned design in favour of painting and was appointed curator of the Musée des Arts Décoratifs in Bordeaux. Du Pasquier's highly patterned and intensely coloured

Nathalie du Pasquier
b. 1957 *Bordeaux, France*

▼ *Gabon* textile for Rainbow, 1982

designs are inspired by various tribal cultures – African, Indian and Aboriginal – and by a diversity of styles – Cubism, **Art Deco** and **Futurism** – as well as aspects of popular culture – graffiti and sci-fi comics. The vibrancy and eclectism of her designs for textiles and laminates contributed much to the refreshing and youthful vitality of Memphis and helped to give the group's output a strong visual identity.

1877 *Le Havre*
1953 *Forcalquier, France*

While best known as a painter, Raoul Dufy is also celebrated as a designer of colourful textiles and ceramics. He studied at the École des Beaux-Arts, Paris, and initially painted in an Impressionist style. From around 1903, he became associated with the Fauves through his friendship with Albert Marquet (1875–1947) and Othon Friesz (1879–1949) and exhibited alongside Henri Matisse (1869–1954), André Derain (1880–1954) and Maurice de Vlaminck (1876–1958) from 1903 to 1909. During this period, he adopted a new style of painting that involved the use of simplified and abstracted forms and bright colours. After a brief flirtation with Cubism, he worked on folk-inspired designs he had seen in Munich in 1909 and at the Salon d'Automne in Paris in 1910. He then executed a series of simple woodcuts in a primitive style for Guillaume Apollinaire's *Bestiaire*. In 1911, he designed a letterhead for the couturier, Paul Poiret, who helped Dufy to establish his own studio-cum-workshop. Later, Dufy was commissioned by Poiret to create various textiles similar to those produced by the couturier's own Atelier Martine. From 1912 to 1930, Dufy designed dress and upholstery fabrics as

▼ *Feuilles (Leaves)*
textile for Bianchini-
Férier, c. 1920

well as textile panels for the Lyons-based manufacturer, Bianchini-Férier. From 1923 to 1930, he also created a tapestry screen and a seating panel for Beauvais as well as ceramics for Artigas. Dufy designed fourteen famous hangings for Paul Poiret's barge *Orgues*, moored on the Seine during the 1925 "Exposition Internationale des Arts Décoratifs et Industriels Modernes", and from 1930 to 1933 he designed silk textiles for Amalgamated Silk and Onandaga, New York. Like his paintings, Dufy's designs were vibrant and often incorporated strong calligraphic lines and white "shadows". His designs such as *Feuilles* of c. 1920, with their almost child-like spontaneity and rhythmic primitivism, have come to epitomize the **Art Deco** style.

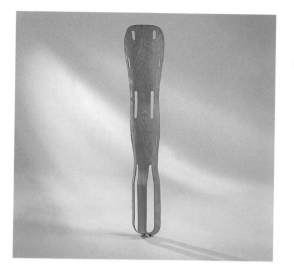

◄ Leg splint designed for U. S. Navy and made by Evans Products Company, 1943

Charles Eames initially studied architecture at Washington University, St Louis. During this period, from 1925 to 1928, he worked in his vacations as a draughtsman for the architectural practice of Trueblood & Graf and in 1929 travelled to Europe, where he was exposed for the first time to the work of **Modern Movement** architects such as **Le Corbusier**, **Ludwig Mies van der Rohe** and **Walter Gropius**. In 1930, Charles Eames and Charles Gray opened an architectural office in St. Louis, and were later joined by Walter Pauley. Although the firm executed a number of private residences, by 1934 no more commissions were forthcoming owing to the depression and so Eames left St Louis and briefly resided in Mexico. Returning to St Louis in 1935, he established a new architectural partnership with Robert Walsh, and a year later designed the Meyer House in Huntleigh Village. For this project, Eames sought the advice of the Finnish architect **Eliel Saarinen** and in 1937 met his son **Eero Saarinen**. In 1938, Eames was offered a fellowship at the **Cranbrook Academy of Art** by Eliel Saarinen and so began studying design and architecture there in the autumn of that year. In 1939, he was made an instructor of design and in 1940 was appointed head of Cranbrook's industrial design department. That autumn a new student arrived at Cranbrook, Ray Kaiser, who had previously studied painting in New York at Hans Hofmann's school – an important centre for the development of Abstract expressionism. She studied weaving under Marianne Strengel (b. 1909) and assisted Charles Eames and Eero Saarinen with their entries for the "Organic Design in Home Furnishings Competition", held at the **Museum of**

Charles Eames
1907 *St. Louis, Missouri*
1978 *St. Louis*

Ray Eames
1912 *Sacramento, California*
1988 *Los Angeles*

Modern Art, New York in 1940. Their revolutionary and prize-winning design proposals for seating incorporated two state-of-the-art manufacturing techniques – the moulding of plywood into complex curves and cycle-welding, an electronic bonding process developed by the Chrysler Corporation, which enabled wood and metal to be joined. A year later, having obtained a divorce from his first wife, Eames married Ray Kaiser in Chicago. The couple moved to California and Charles began working as a set designer for MGM. It was then that they started experimenting with moulding techniques for plywood in their apartment and developed the "Kazam! Machine" – a press for moulding plywood over two geometric planes into complex curves. In 1942, they were commissioned by the United States Navy to design plywood leg and arm splints as well as litters and they then established the Plyformed Wood Company to mass-produce the first trial run of 5000 splints. Due to financial difficulties, the Eameses were forced to sell this manufacturing company and so it became the Molded Plywood Products Division of the Detroit-based Evans Products Company. For a while, Charles acted as the division's director of research and development. In 1945, a series of com-

▲ Interior showing *LCW* chairs (1945), *LCM* chair (1945–1946), *CTW* table (1946) and *FSW* screen (1946) for Herman Miller

◄ Prototype of the *LCW* chair, c. 1945

pound-moulded plywood children's furniture designed by the Eameses was produced and distributed by the Evans Products Company. In 1946, the Museum of Modern Art staged a one-man show entitled "New Furniture by Charles Eames", which displayed prototypes of the couple's famous series of plywood chairs (1945–1946). These innovative chairs were born out of the Eameses' mission "to get the most of the best to the greatest number of people for the least". Initially, Evans produced the chairs and shortly into production, they were exclusively marketed and distributed by **Herman Miller**, who took over their manufacture in 1949. In 1948, Charles Eames won second prize at MoMA's "International Competition for Low-Cost Furniture Design" for the couple's innovative proposal for a series of moulded fibreglass chairs. This revolutionary seating programme was amongst the very first unlined plastic seat furniture to be mass-produced and its concept of a universal seat shell that could be used in conjunction with a variety of bases to provide numerous variations was extremely influential. Throughout the 1950s and 1960s, the Eameses worked closely with Herman Miller and created more highly innovative furniture, including their *Aluminium Group* seating (1958). Apart from their furniture designs, they also received much acclaim for their architectural projects, particularly Charles Eames and Eero Saarinen's Case Study Houses No. 8 and No. 9, completed in 1949. Both

▲ *PAC-1* armchairs, 1950–1953 with laminate-top dining tables for Herman Miller, c. 1958

◀ *DAR* chair for Zenith Plastics and later for Herman Miller, 1948–1950

were built in Pacific Palisades – No. 8 was designed for the Eameses own
use and became better known as the Eames House, while No. 9 was designed for John Entenza, the editor and publisher of *Arts & Architecture*
magazine, who sponsored the project. The interior of the Eames House was
remarkable for its lightness and sense of space and was decorated with an
eclectic and colourful mix of ephemera – toys, kites, eastern wares – that humanized the otherwise unforgiving modern aesthetic of the interior. During
their careers, the Eameses were also celebrated for their numerous short
films, including *A Communications Primer* (1953), *Tops* (1969) and *Powers of
Ten* (1977), some of which were made as accompaniments to their many exhibitions. They excelled in exhibition design for they were able to powerfully
yet playfully communicate often complex ideas to an audience through a variety of media, including beautifully designed time-lines. The Eameses were
also early pioneers of multi-media presentations and their landmark exhibitions such as *Mathematica* (1961), *Nehru: His Life and His India* (1965), *A
Computer Perspective* (1971), *Copernicus* (1972) and *The World of Franklin and
Jefferson* (1975–1977) were highly influential. Another significant contribution
by the Eameses to communication design, were their screen presentations,
such as *Glimpses of the USA* (1959), which visually communicated everyday

life in America to the Russians who could see the show at the American
National Exhibition in Moscow. With their designs, film-making and photography the Eameses created a new and exciting visual language that had
an enormous impact both in America and abroad. Through their work, they
communicated the values of appropriateness, social morality, egalitarian-
ism, optimism, informality and dematerialism, and while their message was
distinctly American in tone, it enjoyed worldwide approval as it offered an
acceptable face of Modernism. What made the Eameses' output so compelling was not just its underlying humanity but the way in which it balanced
the poetic with the pragmatic. While both were driven by the same moral
imperatives and shared a deep affinity for structure, Charles approached design from a technological, material and production point of view, while Ray
put more emphasis on formal, spatial and aesthetic considerations. This dynamic approach to problem solving helped them to make structural, functional, psychological, intellectual, and cultural connections across the broad
spectrum of their output. As the greatest exponents of **Organic Design** and
two of the most important designers of the 20th century, Charles and Ray
Eames demonstrated through practice how modern design can and should
be used to improve the quality of life, human perception, understanding and
knowledge.

Charles Locke Eastlake, nephew of the painter Sir Charles Locke Eastlake (1793–1865) who was a director of the National Gallery, London, initially studied architecture under Philip Hardwick (1792–1870) and then attended the Royal Academy Schools, London. He exhibited several architectural projects at the Royal Academy in 1855 and 1856 before turning his attention to art criticism. In 1864, he published the first of many articles on furniture and interior design entitled *The Fashion of Furniture*. He was appointed assistant secretary to the Royal Institute of British Architects (RIBA) in 1866 and five years later, secretary. In 1868, he published his seminal manual *Hints on Household Taste in Furniture, Upholstery and Other Details*, which was an amalgamation of several earlier articles he had written for the *Cornhill Magazine* and *The Queen*. *Hints* championed the Reformed Gothic style as practised by George Edmund Street (1824–1881), Richard Norman Shaw (1831–1912) and John Pollard Seddon (1827–1906), the hallmarks of which included honesty of construction and materials, rectilinear forms and geometric patterns and ornament. Eastlake's own furniture and wallpaper designs were included in this work as were designs for jewellery by Sir Matthew Digby Wyatt (1820–1877), metalwork by Beham & Froud, glassware by Salviati, geometric tiles by Maw and ceramics by Copeland. Such was the popularity of the publication that four editions were printed in England. It enjoyed even greater success in America, however, where six editions were printed in Boston between 1872 and 1879. *Hints* prompted many other similar works in America, in particular C. C. Cook's *The House Beautiful* (1877) and H. P. Spofford's *Art Decoration Applied to Furniture* (1878). Eastlake was more influential as a writer and arbiter of taste than as a designer. His greatest written work was *A History of the Gothic Revival* (1872).

Charles Eastlake

1836 *Plymouth/Devon*
1906 *London*

◄ Inlaid oak cabinet for Heaton, Butler & Bayne, c. 1867

▼ Frontispiece from *Hints on Household Taste*, published 1868

Tom Eckersley

b. 1914 *Newton-le-Willows/Lancashire*

Tom Eckersley studied at Salford School of Art from 1930 to 1934. There he met Eric Lombers and together they moved to London in 1934 and established a design partnership, which lasted until 1940. In the 1930s, the office produced graphics for London Transport, Shell-Mex, the General Post Office, British Petroleum (BP), the British Broadcasting Company (BBC) and Austin Reed, among others. This early work by Eckersley was inspired by the posters of **Edward McKnight Kauffer** and **A. M. Cassandre** as well as by Cubism and **Surrealism**. During the Second World War, Eckersley created public information posters for the Ministry of Information and the Royal Society for the Prevention of Accidents and also designed cartography and posters for the Royal Air Force (RAF). From 1937 to 1939, he taught at Westminster School of Art and after the war, worked as a freelance graphic designer. In 1949, he was awarded an OBE (Order of the British Empire) for his wartime design work and a year later was elected a member of the Alliance Graphique Internationale. From 1958 to 1978, he was head of the Design Department at the London College of Printing, during which time his graphic style became increasingly direct through the use of clear typography and simplified forms, while retaining that element of humour so characteristic of British graphic design from the 1930s. In 1976, he was commissioned to design a series of murals for the new station at Heathrow Airport.

▼ Advertising poster for Shell, c. 1938

Otto Eckmann studied at the Kunstgewerbeschule in Hamburg and Nuremberg and at the Akademie der Künste, Munich. Initially, he pursued a career
in fine art and from 1890 displayed his work at the Munich exhibitions. In
1894, he abandoned painting, auctioned off all his pictures in Frankfurt, and
began concentrating his efforts on graphic design and handicrafts, such as
embroidery. From 1895, he contributed illustrations that were influenced by
Japanese woodcuts to the *Pan* journal in Berlin, and a year later to *Jugend*
magazine in Munich. In 1897, he began teaching ornamental painting at the
Kunstgewerbeschule, Berlin, where he became professor of applied arts, and
in the same year, exhibited his designs at the International Art Exhibition,
Munich. From 1899 to 1900, he designed trademarks for **AEG** and in 1900
developed a new typeface, *Eckmannschrift*, for the Rudhard'sche Gießerei,
Offenbach. Eckmann also designed posters and bookplates in the **Jugendstil**
style for the Leipzig-based publisher, E. A. Seeman and ceramic tiles for
Villeroy & Boch, Mettlach. His most prestigious commission, however, was
the interior design of the Grand Duke Ernst Ludwig IV of Hesse-Darmstadt's
study at the Neues Palais (1898). Although Eckmann died at the early age
of thirty-seven, during his short career he created many designs for textiles,
furniture, carpets, wallpapers, metalware and ceramics and was one of the
most important proponents of the German Jugendstil.

Otto Eckmann
1865 Hamburg
1902 Badenweiler,
Germany

► **Louis Majorelle,**
Room in the Café de
Paris, Nancy, 1899

École de Nancy

Founded 1901
Nancy, France

Between 1871 and 1900, many skilled artisans fleeing from Prussia settled in Nancy, which was only twenty kilometres from the Franco-Prussian border. This influx of émigrés boosted the cultural and commercial life of Nancy, which became the most important city in Eastern France. Jean **Daum**, one such immigrant, established the Verrerie Sainte-Claire in 1878 and began producing glassware in the **Art Nouveau** style. Other Lorraine-based designers such as **Émile Gallé** and **Louis Majorelle** also produced Art Nouveau furniture and glassware, which received critical acclaim as well as being a financial success. In 1901, spurred on by the general enthusiasm for such work, a number of firms and workshops working within the Nancy area joined together to found the Alliance Provinciale des Industries d'Art. This Alliance, which became known as the École de Nancy, was initially led by Émile Gallé and included among it members Louis Majorelle, Victor Prouvé (1858–1943), Eugène Vallin (1856–1922) and the Daum Brothers (who led the organization after Émile Gallé's death in 1904). The Alliance's first group exhibition was held at the Salon de l'Union Centrale des Arts Décoratifs, Paris in 1903.

Egon Eiermann studied architecture from 1923 to 1927 at the Technische Hochschule, Berlin-Charlottenburg and while there, attended the master classes taught by Hans Poelzig (1869–1936). From 1931, he worked as a freelance architect, and under the Third Reich designed several industrial buildings. During the Second World War, he designed furniture for his own office, and after 1945 established an architectural partnership with Robert Hilgers and continued to design interiors. In 1949, he created a model home for the "Wie Wohnen" exhibition, showing that his affiliation with the Nazis had not damaged his professional reputation. Eiermann often designed furniture specifically for his architectural commissions, which was later mass-produced, for example his popular woven rattan tub chairs (1952) manufactured by Friedrich Herr and his series of moulded plywood chairs (1952) produced by Wilde & Spieth. From 1947, he taught at the Technische Hochschule in Karlsruhe, and in 1951 became a founding member of the Rat für Formgebung (Germany Design Council). In 1962, together with Paul Baumgarten and Sep Ruf, Eiermann sat on the planning commission for the new West German Parliament Building and Upper House in Bonn. Eiermann's most important architectural projects were the Ciba AG factory in Wehr/Baden, the German Pavilion for the Brussels World Fair (1958), the Kaiser-Wilhelm-Gedächtniskirche, Berlin (1957–1963) and a high-rise office building for members of the German Bundestag in Bonn (1965–1969). In addition to his architectural prowess, Eiermann enjoyed much success as a furniture designer, with innovative solutions such as the SE 18 folding chair (1952) manufactured by Wilde & Spieth, Esslingen, which incorporated a spring-mechanism that automatically folded the chair when not in use. Egon Eiermann, who was married to the noted interior designer, Charlotte Eiermann (b. 1912), was one of the most important post-war designers in Germany.

Egon Eiermann
1904 Neuendorf/Berlin
1970 Baden-Baden, Germany

▼ *Model No. SE18 folding chair for Wilde & Spieth, 1952*

Jan Eisenloeffel

1876 *Amsterdam*
1957 *Laren, Netherlands*

▲ Brass tea service
for De Woning,
c. 1903

Johannes (Jan) Eisenloeffel studied at the Rijks Normaalschool, Amsterdam from 1892 to 1896 where he trained as a teacher of draughtsmanship. Between 1893 and 1896, he also trained at the metalware factory of W. Hoecker & Zoon, Amsterdam, and in 1898 travelled to Russia, staying in Moscow and St Petersburg where he studied the engraving and enamelling techniques used by Peter Carl Fabergé (1846–1920). On his return to the Netherlands, he went back to W. Hoecker & Zoon and was appointed head of the metalwork studio at their newly founded company Amstelhoeck, Amsterdam. In 1902, Eisenloeffel established his own metalware company with J. C. Stoffels, and a year later assisted in the founding of the Amsterdam store, De Woning, through which he retailed his own designs. In 1903, he joined the Kunst ann het Volk (Art to the People) organization, which sought to improve the quality of everyday objects. From 1904 to 1907, Eisenloeffel produced metalware and flatware designs for C. J. Begeer, Utrecht, and then worked in Munich at the **Vereinigte Werkstätten für Kunst im Handwerk** (United Workshops). In 1908, Eisenloeffel returned to the Netherlands and established a workshop at the Laren Artists' Colony near Amsterdam.

Harvey Ellis attended West Point Military Academy but was dismissed and subsequently travelled to Venice. He returned to Albany, New York, studying art under Edwin White (1817–1877) and working for a while in the architectural practice of Arthur Gilman in Rochester. He later trained as a draughtsman in the Albany based architectural office of Henry Hobson Richardson (1838–1886), whose Reformed Gothic style influenced him greatly. From 1879 to 1884, he and his brother Charles ran their own architectural practice in Rochester. For the next decade, Ellis worked as a journeyman draughtsman throughout the Midwest, and during this period took up painting and designed posters for the *Rochester Herald* (1895) and *Harper's Magazine* (1898). Later, he returned to Rochester, and from 1903 designed furniture and textiles inspired by the British **Arts & Crafts Movement,** for **Gustav Stickley**'s United Crafts Workshop, and contributed various articles to Stickley's magazine *The Craftsman.* In keeping with the British and the American Arts & Crafts Movements, the majority of the designs produced by Ellis at this time were vernacular in style. His graceful oak side chair and armchair of 1904, however, owe more to the **Art Nouveau** style with their lighter, less rustic forms and their sinuous inlaid decoration.

Harvey Ellis
1852 Rochester, New York
1904 Syracuse, New Jersey

▼ Oak chair for the Craftsman Workshops, 1903–1904

August Endell

August Endell
1871 *Berlin*
1925 *Berlin*

August Endell, the son of an architect, studied philosophy in Tübingen before moving to Munich in 1892 to study the works of the philosopher Theodor Lipps (1851–1914). Influenced by **Hermann Obrist**, whom he met in 1896, Endell abandoned philosophy in order to concentrate on architecture and the applied arts. From 1897 to 1898, he designed the façade and interior decoration of the Photoatelier Elvira, Munich. For the former, he executed a swirling plaster composition that was inspired by Obrist's whiplash style. In 1898, he became involved with the Munich Vereinigte Werkstätten and designed the sanatorium on Föhr. During this period, he also produced illustrations for the art journals, *Jugend* and *Pan* (1897), and in 1898 published his first article on aesthetics entitled *Um die Schönheit*. A year later, he was exhibiting jewellery designs at the Munich Secession exhibition. He moved to Berlin in 1901 and decorated the Bunte Theater there in a more colourful and expressive style than he had previously used and began distancing himself from the swirling forms of **Jugendstil**. In 1903, he designed furniture with formalized foliate motifs that was manufactured by Theophil Müller at the Werkstätten für Deutschen Hausrat, Dresden. For the next ten years Endell ran a design school in Berlin and published many articles on design and architectural theory including *Die Schönheit der Großstadt* (The Beauty of the Big City). During this period, he also designed and built many town houses and villas in Potsdam and Berlin. At the outbreak of the First World War, his name was put forward as a possible successor to **Henry van de Velde** for the post of director at the Kunstgewerbeschule, Weimar but **Walter Gropius** was chosen instead. From 1918 until his death in 1925, he was director of the Akademie für Kunst und Kunstgewerbe in Breslau.

► Entrance gates to the Elvira Studio in Munich, 1896–1897

▼ Long-case clock, 1904

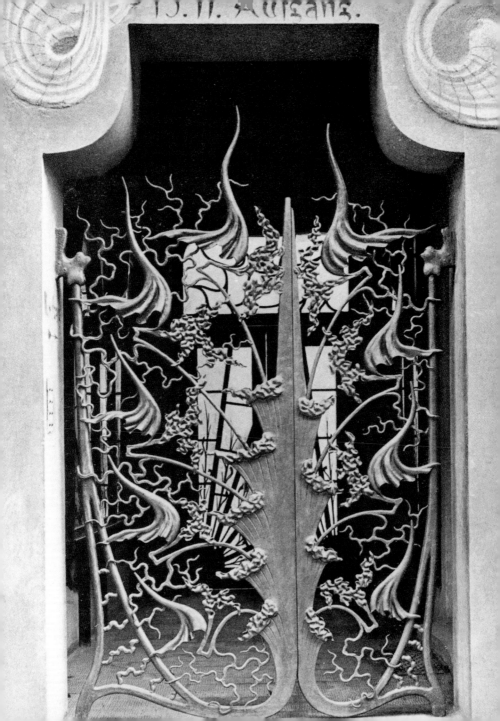

Ergonomi Design Gruppen

Founded 1979
Stockholm

▼ Maria Benktzon &
Sven-Eric Juhlin,
Eat/Drink cutlery for
RFSU Rehab, 1980

Two Swedish design groups founded in the late 1960s, the Designgruppen and Ergonomi Design, amalgamated in 1979 to form the 14-member Ergonomi Design Gruppen, based in Bromma. The group is dedicated to the research and development of safe, reliable and efficient designs based on ergonomic principles. It analyses user-system problems by, for instance, building full-scale models to evaluate designs in experimental situations. Many of the projects undertaken by the group have been part-sponsored by government bodies including the Swedish Work Environment Fund and the National Board for Occupational Health and Safety, as well as by manufacturers such as Gustavsberg. Its most notable designs include the Eat and Drink combination cutlery, drinking vessels and plates (1980), manufactured by RSFU Rehab for use by the disabled, and machinery for printing and welding that reduces the risk of accidents and repetitive strain injury. Founders of the group include Maria Benktzon (b. 1946) and Sven-Eric Juhlin (b. 1940), both alumni of the Konstfackskolan (School of Arts & Crafts), Stockholm. Before setting up the group, Benktzon had studied the design of clothing for the handicapped and Juhlin had worked as an in-house designer for Gustavsberg. Both subsequently undertook research in 1972 into muscular ability and its relationship to the actions of gripping and holding and have since then specialized in design for disability.

The L. M. Ericsson Company was founded in Stockholm in 1876 by Lars Magnus Ericsson (1846–1926), initially as a telegraph repair workshop. By 1878, however, the firm was manufacturing its own telephones based on an earlier prototype developed by Alexander Graham Bell (1847–1922). Within a short while, L. M. Ericsson was producing telephones of its own design and exporting them throughout Europe, their success leading to the opening of several factories including one in Mexico. In 1909, the L. M. Ericsson Company produced the first cradle telephone, which was enormously influential throughout Europe. Seeking to update this earlier design, in 1930 the company commissioned the artist **Jean Heiberg** (1884–1976) and the Norwegian engineer Johan Christian Bjerknes to design a telephone in Bakelite. Although not the first plastic telephone to be manufactured, this sculptural design was certainly the most notable and it inspired **Henry Dreyfuss**' later *Bell 300* model (1930–1933). From 1940 to 1954, Hugo Blomberg (b. 1897), Ralph Lysell (b. 1907) and Gösta Thames (b. 1917) developed the *Ericofon* – a telephone that integrated the earpiece, mouthpiece and dial into a single sculptural form. Exploiting the use of new lightweight materials such as plastic, rubber and nylon as well as component miniaturization, the forward-looking Ericofon remained the most popular one-piece telephone for over three decades. Today, L. M. Ericsson continues its commitment to innovation within the telecommunications industry and as a result, maintains a high-profile within this sector.

▼ *Ericofon* telephone, 1954

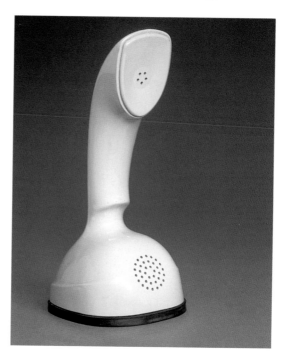

◄ *Concept 51K* hi-fi
system for Wega,
1975

**Hartmut
Esslinger**
b. 1945 *Altensteig,
Germany*

Hartmut Esslinger initially studied electrical engineering at the University
of Stuttgart, before training in industrial design at the Fachhochschule in
Schwäbisch Gmünd. In 1969, he won the German national award Gute
Form and established his own Altensteig-based design consultancy. His
first client was the electronics company, Wega Radio, which was purchased
by Sony in 1975, an acquisition that introduced Esslinger to the Japanese
consumer electronic market. His sleek designs, such as the *Concept 51K* hi-fi
system for Wega (1975), brought him international recognition and were influenced by the functionalist approach to design promoted by **Max Bill** and
Hans Gugelot at the **Hochschule für Gestaltung, Ulm**. In 1982, Esslinger
renamed his consultancy, **Frogdesign** (frog = Federal Republic of Germany)
and opened an office in Campbell, California to meet the design needs of
the burgeoning computer industry in Silicon Valley. In 1986, he also opened
an office in Tokyo. In 1984, the consultancy designed the off-white Mackintosh Classic for Apple Computer and in so doing, redefined the aesthetic
parameters of the personal computer. Frogdesign has also branched into
cameras, synthesizers, binoculars, communications equipment and office
seating for RCA, Eastman Kodak, Polaroid, Motorola, Seiko, Sony, Olympus,
AT&T, AEG, König und Neurath, Erco, Villeroy & Boch, Rosenthal and
Yamaha, among others. By incorporating sculptural forms or visual references in his designs, Esslinger attempts to humanize technology and create
more user-friendly products.

Willy Fleckhaus trained as a journalist but was more attracted to the design aspects of publishing than to writing itself. Initially, he was inspired by the design of American magazines and journals, such as those produced by Alexey Brodovitch (1898–1971), which were less formal in their graphic style than the ones of the **Swiss School**. In 1952 Fleckhaus began designing the trade unions' magazine *Aufwärts*, using full-bleed images and pages that combined photography and text. Through his work, the publication became one of the earliest lifestyle journals to be printed in Germany. Following the success of *Aufwärts*, Fleckhaus was appointed art director (1959–1976) of *Twen* – a new magazine that focused on popular interests ranging from films and contemporary music to current affairs and events. Influenced by his friend **Max Bill** and the directness of approach advocated by the **Hochschule für Gestaltung, Ulm**, Fleckhaus created a radically new "modish" type of layout for *Twen*. Although its symmetrical grid was influenced by the Swiss School, the layout, which used cropped images and bold typography that contrasted black and white areas, was totally innovative and had a startling immediacy. However, his art direction was at odds with the editorial input of the magazine and after six successive editors had left over a period of a dozen years, Fleckhaus' own contract was not renewed. In 1974, he became a professor at the Folkwangschule in Essen, and later, in 1980, took up a professorship at the Gesamthochschule Wuppertal. During the post-war period, Fleckhaus pioneered a new style of "Popular" graphics in Germany that countered the Bauhaus tradition and became enormously influential.

Willy Fleckhaus
1925 Velbert, Germany
1983 Castelfranco di Sobra, Italy

▼ Cover for *Twen*
No. 4, 1965

Paul Follot

1877 *Paris*
1941 *Sainte-Maxime, France*

Paul Follot's earliest designs, some of which were illustrated in *Art et Décoration*, were inspired by Gothic Revivalism. In 1901, he began working for La Maison Moderne, a shop that had been established in 1899 by Julius Meier-Graefe (1867–1935). Highly influenced by its director and manager, Maurice Dufrêne (1876–1955), who became a leading exponent of the **Art Deco** style, Follot began designing modern silverware, textiles, bronzes and jewellery for the store. That year he also became a founder of the art group, L'Art dans Tout and from then on strongly supported the French decorative tradition, the dominance of which was threatened by the ascendancy of German industrial design. In 1904, Follot began working as an independent designer and later exhibited an **Art Nouveau** interior at the Société des Artistes Décorateurs. For a while his work was characterized by the use of foliate motifs, however, around 1910 he began to seek "des architectures calmes" (tranquil architecture) and adopted a more restrained and classical style that was synonymous with the emerging Art Deco style. He was commissioned by Wedgewood to design ceramics in 1911, and throughout his career he also designed textiles for Cornille et Cie, carpets for Savonnerie and silverware for Orfèvrerie Christofle. Follot was appointed art director of the Au Bon Marché store in 1923, and five years later became the co-director of the Paris branch of the English furniture company, Waring & Gillow.

▲ Silver-plated brass teapot for Christofle, 1900

From an early age Piero Fornasetti showed remarkable talent for draughts-manship. He won a scholarship to study at the Accademia di Belle Arti di Brera, Milan from 1930 to 1932 but found the tuition too formal and was re-putedly expelled. In 1933, he exhibited his first paintings at the Università di Milano. These were self-consciously archaic and "Giotto-esque" in style and countered the overbearing "Coppedé" or **Art Deco** style, which was fashion-able in Milan at that time. Fornasetti was not only influenced by **Surrealism** and "Metaphysical" art, as practised by Giorgio de Chirico (1888–1978) and Alberto Savinio (1891–1952), but was also inspired by the tradition of illu-sionism found in Lombardy, which appealed to his ironic sense of humour. During the 1930s, he produced designs for Venini and exhibited printed silk scarves at the VII Milan Triennale (1940), where his work was seen by the architect and designer, **Gio Ponti**. Sharing a love of ornament and a deep respect for Italian heritage, the designers collaborated from the late 1940s onwards on many interior and furniture design projects. Throughout the 1930s and 1940s, Fornasetti also designed several posters and covers for *Domus* and *Graphis*. During the Second World War, Fornasetti was con-scripted into the Italian army. However, he spent most of the war painting the regimental barracks in Piazza S. Ambrogio, Milan, with *trompe-l'œil* and fruit motifs. Fornasetti fled to Switzerland for a while to avoid the final throes of the war, not returning to Milan until hostilities had ceased. Ponti

Piero Fornasetti
1913 *Milan*
1988 *Milan*

► *Architettura*
(architecture) desk,
c. 1951

and Fornasetti's many joint projects of the 1950s included the *Architettura* range of furniture first exhibited at the IX Milan Triennale (1951), interiors for the ocean liner *Andrea Doria* (1952) and the quirky interiors for the Casino at San Remo (1950). From then on, Fornasetti also independently designed a vast range of products from ceramics and waistcoats to screens and magazine racks, all of which bore his illusionistic and ironic silkscreen-printed motifs of musical instruments, roman coins and blazing suns. His extensive *Themes & Variations* series, featured the beautiful and enigmatic female face that virtually became his trademark. In 1970, Fornasetti established his own shop in Milan, close to the Accademia di Belle Arti di Brera, to retail the huge range of his individualistic and playful designs. After his death in 1988, his son Barnaba took over the business and during the 1990s, larger premises for the shop were found in Via Manzoni. Having been dismissed for decades by Modernists, Piero Fornasetti's work enjoyed a reappraisal and a revival in popularity with the ascendancy of **Post-Modernism** in the early 1980s.

► *Strumenti Musicali*
(musical instruments)
table, c. 1953

Norman Foster

b. 1935 *Manchester*

Norman Foster studied architecture and planning at the University of Manchester, graduating in 1961. He then continued his studies, on a Henry Fellowship, at Yale University, New Haven, Connecticut, where he graduated in 1963. While there, he trained with another scholarship student, Richard Rogers (b. 1933), under **Serge Chermayeff** and was influenced by the work of Louis Kahn (1901–1974), who had designed the Yale Art Gallery in which the architectural faculty was sited. On his return to Britain in 1963, Foster, together with Rogers, Georgie Wolton and Wendy Cheesman (whom he married in 1964), established the Team 4 partnership in London, which designed the notable Reliance Controls Limited factory in Swindon. After Team 4's dissolution in 1966, Foster founded Foster Associates in London. From 1968 to 1983, he worked on several projects with **Richard Buckminster Fuller** and received a number of architectural commissions from Fred Olsen Limited. In 1977, Foster won the Royal Institute of British Architects Award for his black-glass-clad office building for Willis Faber & Dumas in Ipswich (1973–1975) and has since then become internationally celebrated for numerous architectural projects, including the Hongkong & Shanghai Banking Corporation Headquarters, Hongkong (1981–1986), Stansted Airport, Essex (1991) and the new Reichstag (German Parliament) in Berlin (1995–1999). Like his buildings, Foster's **High-Tech** designs, such as his *Nomos* furniture system (1986–1988) for Tecno and his lighting system produced by Erco (1986), are highly engineered and have a strong sense of geometric order. Foster's elegant yet hard-edged architecture and design celebrates modernity through his application of state-of-the-art materials and his exploitation of cutting-edge construction technology.

◄ *Nomos* table for Tecno, 1986–1988

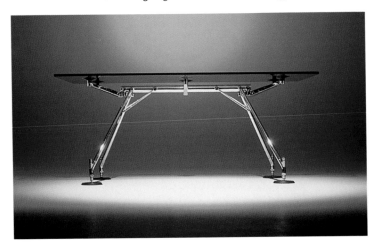

Kaj Franck studied furniture design under Arttu Brummer at the Taideteollinen Korkeakoulu, Helsinki, graduating in 1932. In 1938, he became a textile designer at the Hyvinkää United Wool Factory and a year later was conscripted into the military. During the war, he met many fellow countrymen from less privileged backgrounds and this experience profoundly influenced his views on society. In 1945, he began working for the Arabia ceramic factory and a year later, designed a range of utilitarian tableware for the Väestöliiton (Family Welfare Association). In 1950, he became art director of Arabia, and during the 1950s created ranges of everyday modern crockery and kitchenware that were designed for multi-purpose use. In 1955, Franck received an Asla grant to study design teaching in America and during his time in the USA he researched eating habits, which had a direct bearing on his subsequent design work. From 1954, until he left Arabia in 1973, Franck also designed limited-production wares, such as his *Lumipallo* (Snowball) series. Glassware designed by him was produced by Iittala (1946–1950) and Nuutajärvi-Notsjö (1950–1976). Franck's informal tableware and glassware designs not only addressed contemporary functional needs, but through their adoption of elemental forms also had an aesthetic purity.

Kaj Franck
1911 *Viipuri, Finland*
1989 *Santorini, Greece*

▲ *Kartio* glassware, 1958 with *Teema* ceramics, 1981

**Jean-Michel
Frank**
1895 *Paris*
1941 *New York*

Jean-Michel Frank worked as a cabinet-maker in the workshop of **Jacques-Émile Ruhlmann** after the First World War. In the 1920s, he met the Chilean society hostess, Eugenia Errazuriz and was inspired by her dematerialist approach to interior design. During this period, he probably created designs for **Desny** and became one of the first designers to use a white-leaded finish on wooden surfaces. In 1931, he joined the decorator Adolphe Chanaux in founding a workshop in La Ruche, and a year later they opened a retail outlet on the Rue du Faubourg St. Honoré, Paris. Frank's furniture and lighting designs of the 1920s were influenced by the geometric formalism of **Le Corbusier** and **Robert Mallet-Stevens**. Although his interiors, such as those at the Hotel Bischoffstein created for Vicomte Charles de Noailles, were sparsely decorated, Frank lavished much attention on their detailing and used luxury materials such as shagreen, bronze and vellum. By around 1935, however, Frank's designs had become more flamboyant and theatrical and he began to incorporate *trompe-l'œil* effects into his interiors. Having previously designed interiors and furnishings for Nelson Rockefeller's apartment in New York, Frank moved to the city in 1940, presumably to work for the interior design firm, McMillen. Shortly afterwards, suffering from depression, he committed suicide.

◄ Design for *Rox & Fix* textile for Svenskt Tenn, 1943–1944

Josef Frank was brought up in Vienna and trained as an architect. From 1925 to 1934, he ran an interior design co-operative with Oskar Wlach, known as "Haus und Garten". In 1934, he settled in Sweden and became chief designer of the Stockholm-based interior design firm, Svenskt Tenn. He designed textiles for the company, such as *Vegetable Tree* (1944), and furniture inspired by the 19th-century British **Arts & Crafts Movement** and by Viennese design from the turn of the century. Although he rejected Functionalist dogma, Frank's work was essentially modern and was characterized by a purity of form. His furniture was remarkable for its harmonious proportions and high quality craftsmanship as well as its practicality and comfort. In this area of activity, Frank became a virtual guru to the younger generation of Scandinavian furniture designers. From 1941 to 1943, he taught at the New School for Social Research in New York and as a design and architectural theorist, published several titles including *Architectur als Symbol* (1930) and *Accidentism* (1958). Like Carl Malmsten (1888–1972) and **Bruno Mathsson**, Josef Frank is generally regarded as one of the three "classicists" of Swedish design and, as an early proponent of Scandinavian Modernism, his contribution has been immense.

Josef Frank
1885 Baden, Austria
1967 Stockholm

Paul Theodore Frankl

1886 *Vienna*
1962 *Los Angeles*

Paul T. Frankl studied architecture in Paris, Berlin, Munich and Vienna. In 1914, he emigrated to the United States of America and subsequently designed several interior schemes for the cosmetician, Helena Rubinstein (1870–1965). From 1915 to 1916, he created stage sets for the Theatre Guild, New York, and from around 1925 began designing geometric furnishings, which he christened *Skyscraper* furniture. These **Art Deco** designs, which were inspired by the forms of 1920s high-rise architecture, were sold through his own New York gallery and were also shown at the "Art in Trade" exhibition held at Macy's department store in 1927. Frankl not only lectured on "The Skyscraper in Decoration", he also promoted his **Moderne** style of interior design through books that illustrated his work, including *New Dimensions: The Decorative Arts of Today* (1928), *Form and Re-Form* (1930) and *Space for Living: Creative Interior Decoration and Design* (1938). While the

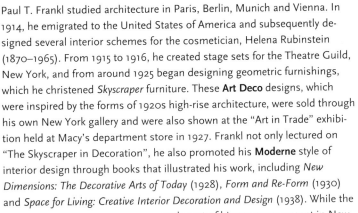

▼ *Skyscraper*
bookcase, c. 1928

early part of his career was spent in New York, where he produced lavish designs that were comparable to the Art Deco work of his French contemporaries, for the latter part of his life he lived in California. In 1928, he was the principal founder of the American Designers' Gallery and in 1930 he helped to form the AUDAC (American Union of Decorative Artists and Craftsmen). Frankl was perhaps the most important American exponent of Art Deco, his Modernist work being more influenced by the skyline of 1920s New York than by currents in contemporary European design. He believed that design should be informed by the culture surrounding it and resolved to give the decorative arts in America an appropriate and recognizable identity.

Marguerite Friedlaender studied at the Hochschule für angewandte Kunst in Berlin from 1917 to 1918, afterwards producing designs for the Rudolstadt Porzellanmanufaktur in Thuringia. From 1919 to 1925, she trained at the Staatliches **Bauhaus** in Weimar and, as the ceramicist Trude Petri (1906–1989), concentrated her efforts on the production of functional objects. Between 1925 and 1933, she taught in the ceramic workshop of the Kunstgewerbeschule Halle/Burg Giebichenstein, which she later directed. While there, she established close links with the Staatliche Porzellanmanufaktur (KPM) in Berlin, who manufactured her designs including the *Hallesche Form* tea service of 1930–1931. In 1926, she took her master's exam, followed by a study sabbatical in Höhr-Grenzhausen. In 1930, she married the ceramicist and fellow-Bauhaus alumnus, Franz Rudolf Wildenhain (1905–1981), and in 1933, when she was removed from her teaching position at Halle, they emigrated to the Netherlands. While in Holland, the couple established the Het Kruikje ceramics workshop in Putten, which they ran for seven years until Marguerite Friedlaender moved to America. For two years she headed the ceramics workshop at the College of Arts and Crafts in Oakland, California. Then, in 1942, her husband joined her and she established the Pond Farm artistic community at Guerneville, California. When this association was disbanded in 1949, she continued to run the ceramics studio at Pond Farm and held summer workshops there for young students. Friedländer's studio ceramics and her designs for mass-production were distinguished by the use of simplified elemental forms.

Marguerite Friedlaender-Wildenhain
1896 Lyons, France
1985 Guerneville, California

▼ Stoneware jar for the ceramics workshop at the Kunstgewerbeschule Burg Giebichenstein, Halle, 1926–1927

Frogdesign

Founded 1969
Altensteig, Germany

This international design consultancy was founded in Altensteig, Germany by the industrial designer **Hartmut Esslinger** in 1969. Leading designers of consumer products, the consultancy's clientele includes Sony, **AEG**, Zeiss, Olympus and Apple Computer. In 1982, the name Frogdesign (frog = Federal Republic of Germany) was adopted when the consultancy opened an office in Campbell, California, to cater to the design requirements of Silicon Valley. Four years later, another international office was opened in Tokyo to meet the demands of the burgeoning Japanese consumer electronics market. Employing a large staff of designers, which at one time included **Ross Lovegrove**, the consultancy developed a house-style that combined **Modern Movement** rationalism – as pioneered at the **Bauhaus** and later at the **Hochschule für Gestaltung, Ulm** – with organic forms. Frogdesign's output is characterized by a highly functional approach to design that is informed by ergonomics. This rationalism, however, is often tempered by the incorporation of visually expressive and sometimes whimsical references to the product's function – for instance, the *Personal Communicator* (1992) for AT&T, which has elements that resemble ears.

▲ *Z-Lite* lap-top computer for Zenith, 1992

▶ Binoculars for Zeiss, 1991

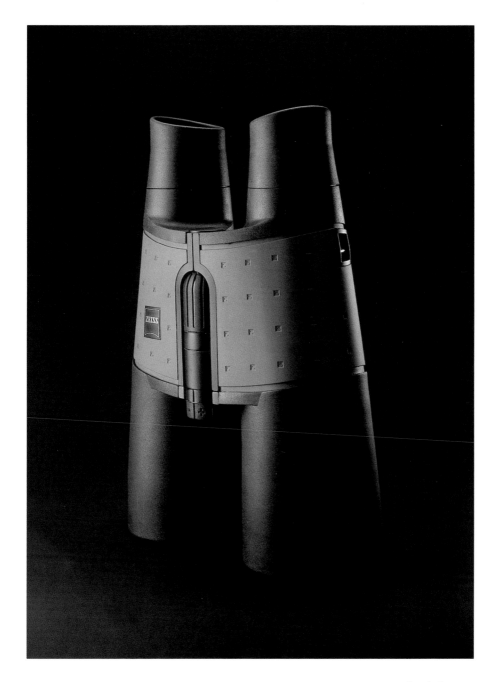

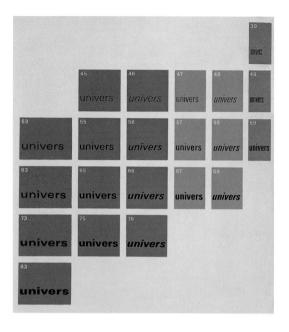

◄ Twenty-one
variations of the
Univers typeface for
Deberny & Peignot,
1954–1957

Adrian Frutiger

b. 1928 *Interlaken,
Switzerland*

Adrian Frutiger trained as a type compositor under Ernst Jordi and Walter Zerbe at Otto Schaefli AG in Interlaken. Between 1948 and 1951, he studied sculpture, illustration and engraving at the Kunstgewerbeschule, Zurich. He initially created typefaces for Deberny & Peignot foundry in Paris (1952) before working as a freelance typographer designing new fonts and corporate symbols for the Paris Metro, Orly Airport, Bauer, BP and Air France, among others. In 1962, Frutiger established his own Paris-based design studio with André Gürtler and Bruno Pfäffli, and from 1957 to 1967 was art director of the French publishing house, Editions Hermann. He also designed typewriter fonts for IBM from 1963 and several notable typefaces including *Univers* (1954–1955), which was created specifically for filmsetting, and *Frutiger* (1974–1976), which was initially conceived for signage at Charles De Gaulle Airport. Frutiger was one of the founders of the **Swiss School** of graphics and his sophisticated and rational approach to typography was highly influential, particularly in France where he spent most of his career. During the 1970s he improved computer typefaces, and his development of the easily readable *OCR-B* faces led to their international standardization in 1973. By harmoniously balancing the scientific and artistic aspects of typography, Frutiger created rational typefaces that were notable for their legibility and internationalism.

Richard Buckminster Fuller studied mathematics at Harvard University from 1913 to 1915 and two years later, enrolled at the US Naval Academy in Annapolis. While at the Academy, he began his "theoretical conceptioning", which included a proposal for "flying jet-stilts porpoise" transport that was eventually published in 1932. After leaving the military in 1922, he founded the Stockade Building System, which was a financial failure and led to his personal bankruptcy.

He set himself to finding universal solutions to social problems after the death of his four-year old-daughter in 1922, which he believed was due to inadequate housing. In 1927 he founded the 4-D Company in New York to develop his design concepts, which were driven by his ambition to evolve a "design science" that would bring about the best solutions with minimal consumption of energy and materials. He based this concept on the **Modern Movement** principle of getting the most with the least and named it "Dymaxion", which was derived from "dynamic" and "maximum efficiency". In 1929, he established the magazine *Shelter* and was its publisher and editor from 1930 to 1932. For the next six years he was director and chief engineer of the Dymaxion Corporation, which he set up to develop and manufacture three streamlined prototype cars that were based on his dymaxion principles and inspired by aircraft design. Fuller claimed that the Dymaxion car of 1934 could accelerate from 0 to 60 miles per hour in three seconds

Richard
Buckminster
Fuller
1895 *Milton,*
Massachusetts
1983 *Los Angeles*

▲ Geodesic Dome in
Seattle, 1958

and had a fuel consumption of 30 miles per gallon. The prototype car, however, was never produced owing to several serious design flaws. From 1927, Fuller also developed the Dymaxion House concept, and in 1945 he invented a pre-fabricated metal dwelling known as the Witchita House. Although the company he set up for its manufacture received an astonishing 38,000 orders after the press launch, he was not prepared to start production until its design had been perfected. His backers grew disheartened with all the delays and the project was shelved.

Fuller's most famous invention was the Geodesic Dome of 1949, which had a wide range of applications from industrial to military to exhibitions. Through his "more for less" approach, minimal amounts of materials were used in the construction of the domes making them highly transportable and easily assembled. This landmark design offered a means of producing ecologically efficient housing for the mass-market, and Geodesics Inc was set up in 1949 to develop the concept. As a mathematician, he discovered Synergetics – a vectorial system of geometry. He was also the first person to coin the expression "Spaceship Earth". Prolific communicator, humanist and polymath, Buckminster Fuller believed that the creative abilities of humanity were unlimited and that technology and design-led solutions could eliminate the physical and metaphysical barriers to humanity's expansion into a positive future.

▼ Dymaxion car, 1934

Functionalism is essentially an approach to architecture and design rather than a style, and is concerned with addressing practical problems as logically and efficiently as possible. The origins of Functionalism can be found in the theories of the first-century BC Roman architect, Vitruvius, which themselves were based on the Hellenistic tradition. The Classical or functional approach to architecture has since been revived many times: during the Renaissance in the 15th and 16th centuries, in the 18th century by Neo-Classical architects and in the 19th century by luminaries such as Gottfried Semper (1803–1879) and Eugène-Emmanuel Viollet-le-Duc (1814–1879). In the last half of the 19th century, design reformers in Britain such as **A. W. N. Pugin** and **William Morris** also advocated a functional approach to design, which led to the manufacture of utilitarian products. But it was the American architect Louis Sullivan (1856–1924) who coined the expression "Form Follows Function" in 1896 and who is therefore commonly credited with formulating 20th-century Functionalism. These early pioneers of Functionalism promoted a methodology that took into consideration the specific culture and environment of the region in which a design or building was created. During the early half of the 20th century, however, **Modern Movement** designers allied Functionalism with **Rationalism** and looked for universal design solutions rather than national ones. The teaching at the Staatliches **Bauhaus** in Dessau was founded on this quest and designers

Functionalism

▲ Stand selling products from the metal workshop of the Kunstgewerbe-schule, Burg Giebichenstein, Halle, c. 1927

such as **Ludwig Mies van der Rohe, Marcel Breuer, Le Corbusier** and **J. J. P. Oud** experimented with industrial materials such as tubular metal, steel and glass so as to create functional furniture and buildings. However, these new materials were chosen by many as much for their modern machine-aesthetic as for their functional potential. In the 1920s, the formal vocabulary of Functionalist design was evolved into a style, especially in France and Germany, by **avant-garde** designers who were concerned with promoting the appearance of modernity. By the 1930s, the Functionalist aesthetic had become widely accepted, and ushered in the **International Style**. During the 1960s, the social morality of Functionalism – which was seen by some as mainly style-led – was questioned by **Anti-Design** groups and this in turn gave rise to the emergence of **Post-Modernism**. Modernism in the 20th century has for the most part been affiliated with Functionalism and Rationalism – terms that are virtually indistinguishable since they both pro-pose a technologically driven logic of construction as the basis of design.

▲ Precursor of the *B5* chair, c. 1926 and *B3* chair for Standard-Möbel, later manufactured by Thonet, 1926–1927

◀ **Wilhelm Wagen-feld**, *Sintrax* coffee maker for Jenaer Glaswerke Schott & Gen., 1931

► **Fortunato Depero**,
Design for a visiting
card for the Depero
Typographic Works,
1927

Futurism
Italy

Futurism was founded in 1909 by the Italian writer Filippo Tommaso Marinetti (1876–1944). As its name suggests, the movement dissociated itself from the past by embracing technological progress. Marinetti's *Futurist Manifesto* of 1909 celebrated the inherent potential and dynamism of the machine and systems of communication. As the first cultural movement to distance itself from nature and to glorify the metropolis, Futurism was extremely influential to subsequent design movements. The energetic flux of modern city life was captured in the artistic works of Umberto Boccioni (1882–1916), Gino Severini (1883–1966), Carlo Carrà (1881–1966) and **Giacomo Balla** through the use of fragmented Cubist-like geometric elements that evoked the feeling of speed and acceleration. Within graphic design, Futurism was asserted through the use of typography that was laid out expressively rather than conventionally. This idea of expressive structure was also used in the composition of poetry. In 1910, the *Manifesto of Futurist Painting* was signed by Carrà, Balla, Boccioni, Severini and Luigi Russolo (1885–1947), and later Balla became the first to experiment with the practical application of Futurist theory to the decorative arts. These expressive forays into design were followed up by the artist and designer, Fortunato Depero

(1892–1960), who set up a craft workshop for Futurist art in Rovereto, which operated throughout the 1920s. Depero wrote the *Complessità plastica – gioco libero futurista – L'essere vivente-artificiale* (Plastic complexity – free futuristic play – the artificial-living being) in 1914 and at his House of Art in Rovereto he devised a neo-plastic language of design that was later promoted by the Italian Rationalists. The architect Antonio Sant'Elia (1888–1916) joined the movement in 1914 and exhibited his proposals for "The New City" in Milan. The sweeping dynamic forms of his architecture were left unornamented and, with their raw unfinished surfaces and violent colouring, verged on Brutalism. Although Sant'Elia died in 1916, his *Manifesto for Futurist Architecture* remained influential, especially to members of **De Stijl** who received it in 1917. Futurism attempted to subvert bourgeois culture and was in some ways a destructive force in that it necessarily expressed the aggressive aesthetic of urban life in the machine-age. Aligned to Fascism, the Futurists sought order through radicalism and in so doing can be seen as the first truly radical design movement.

▼ Fortunato Depero's craft workshop for Futurist art in Rovereto, 1920

Eugène Gaillard

1862 *Paris*
1933 *Paris*

▶ Chair, c. 1905

▼ Bedroom
designed for
Siegfried Bing's
Pavillon de l'Art
Nouveau, 1900

Eugène Gaillard was the brother of the jeweller Lucien Gaillard and initially practised law. After abandoning his legal career, Gaillard spent ten years working as a sculptor before becoming a leading **Art Nouveau** designer of interiors, furniture and textiles. His interiors were exhibited alongside those of **Georges de Feure** and Édouard Colonna (1862–1948) in **Siegfried Bing**'s pavilion at the 1900 "Exposition Universelle et Internationale de Paris". From 1900 to 1914, he designed elegant furniture, which incorporated decoration that was inspired by natural forms yet did not copy or imitate nature. He explained this approach in his essay *À Propos du Mobilier* of 1906, in which he set out his aim of putting: "an undeniable character into the most humble object, the ordinary piece of furniture". Gaillard was a founding member of the Société des Artistes Décorateurs and showed his designs at the organization's salon exhibitions. Although Gaillard's designs had a great sense of plasticity, they also possessed remarkably refined structures. Unlike the work of many other Art Nouveau designers, Gaillard's designs avoided artifice while remaining rhythmically organic.

Émile Gallé

1846 Nancy, France
1904 Nancy

▼ Carved mahogany
and marquetry
cabinet, c. 1900

Émile Gallé studied at the Lycée Impérial in Nancy and by the age of sixteen had learnt much about decorating ceramics and glass in the workshops of the St Clément pottery, which supplied wares to his father's shop. His father, Charles Gallé-Reinemer, later acquired part-ownership of the St Clément pottery and Émile worked for him decorating both faience and glassware. During this period, Gallé also studied botany under Professor Vaultrin, draughtsmanship with Professor Casse and landscape painting with Paul Pierre. From 1864 to 1866, Gallé was in Weimar studying botany, mineralogy and art history. After completing his formal education, Gallé returned to Lorraine and spent a year working for his father before taking up a three-year-apprentice-ship at Burgun, Schverer & Co, the glassworks and decorating studio in Meisenthal that supplied the Nancy-based family firm with undecorated wares. In 1870, he returned to France and shortly afterwards enlisted in the military for the Franco-Prussian war. A year later, Gallé represented the family firm in the "Art de France" section at the "First Annual Inter-national Exhibition" in London, and on his return to France per-suaded his father to re-site the family firm in Nancy, as St Clément was now under German occupation. In 1873, a new glassworks was founded in Nancy and four years later Gallé became director of the family firm. He developed many new techniques and his decorations became increas-ingly informed by the natural world. In 1878 Gallé achieved critical acclaim and was awarded four gold medals at the "Exposition Univer-selle" in Paris. Spurred on by this success, he built larger workshops so as to achieve greater production ca-pacity and in 1884, after a fruitless

search for suitable wooden bases for his **Art Nouveau** glassware, he acquired land for a new cabinet-making workshop. Gallé's subsequent furniture designs, the structure and decoration of which was inspired by plant forms, were first exhibited at the 1889 "Exposition Universelle", where he also received praise for his new glass designs that incorporated a wide range of techniques, including etching, wheel-carving and gilding. At this exhibition, he was awarded a Grand Prix and the highest of French accolades – the "Légion d'Honneur". In 1894, he opened a larger glassworks with an immense production capacity. In 1901, he became the first president of the "Alliance Provinciale des Industries d'Art" group, later known as the **École de Nancy**.

Abram Games

1914 *London*
1996 *London*

Abram Games briefly attended the "commercial art" course at St. Martin's School of Art, London, and afterwards took life-classes in the evenings while working in a commercial graphic studio. He disliked the contemporary practice followed by several designers of working on a "master" poster, which would then be used by various companies who could later add their own lettering. He preferred the posters from the 1920s and 1930s, created for specific clients by designers such as **A. M. Cassandre**, **Edward McKnight Kauffer** and Tom Purvis (1888–1959). In 1935, Games began to design graphics independently, often using chromolithographic processes. During the Second World War, he created nearly a hundred posters for the War Office, which appointed him as its official poster artist. For the war effort, he developed a direct graphic style in accordance with his belief that images should communicate "maximum meaning" with "minimum means". During the 1940s and 1950s, his clients included London Transport, the Post Office, Orient Line, The Financial Times, British Petroleum and Shell. His most notable commission, however, was for the graphic emblem of the 1951 "Festival of Britain." Games was one of the last designers of lithographic posters, which by the late 1950s were being superseded by those produced by photomechanical techniques.

Elizabeth Garouste (b. 1949) studied at the École Camondo, Paris, and also trained in theatre and costume design. She initially worked as a theatrical designer for Fernando Arrabel and as a stylist for Maire Berani. Garouste also collaborated with the painter Gérard Garouste (her husband) and the interior designer Andrée Putman (b. 1925). She commissioned Mattia Bonetti (b. 1953) to design window displays and graphics for her parents' shop. Bonetti had previously studied at the Centro Scolastico per l'Industria Artistica and worked as a photographer. Later in 1981 Garouste and Bonetti undertook their first design collaboration, the interior for the Restaurant le Privilège at the nightclub Le Palace. That same year, they exhibited their first collection of "objets primitifs" and "objets barbares" at Jansen. Their work was consciously distanced from industrial methods of production and re-vived the French *décorateur* tradition. Garouste and Bonetti subsequently researched glass techniques for the Centre de Recherche sur le Verre (CIVRA), Marseille and worked closely with La Manufacture Nationale de Sèvres, executing their Cabinet des Sèvres in 1988. From 1985, they exhibited their designs to inter-national acclaim at Galerie Néotù, Paris, and in 1987 designed Baroque-style interiors and furniture for Christian Lacroix's Paris fashion-house. Subsequently, they also did the offices interiors of the magazine publisher Hachette and the publish-ing house J. C. Lattes. During the 1990s, they designed packaging for Nina Ricci, glassware and ceramics for Daum, furnishings for Anthologie Quartett and interiors for the Bavarian castle of Princess Gloria von Thurn und Taxis. Inspired by tribalism and primi-tivism, Garouste and Bonetti's early designs were referred to as "New Caledonie Gothique" in style and earned their creators the title of "The New Barbarians".

Garouste & Bonetti

Founded 1981
Paris

▼ *Dawson* lamp for Néotù, 1990

Malcolm Garrett

b. 1956 *Northwich/
Cheshire*

Malcolm Garrett studied typography and graphic communication at Reading
University for one year before training in graphic design at Manchester
Polytechnic. While studying, he became involved in the Punk movement,
which had a significant influence in Manchester after the Sex Pistols' appearance there in 1976. His first published design was a Punk-style record
sleeve for the Buzzcocks' *Orgasm Addict* (1977) album. A year later, he established his own graphic studio, Assorted Images, and created album covers
for the independent music industry, which had emerged after the success
of the first Punk bands. His record sleeves for Duran Duran, Simple Minds,
Phil Collins and Culture Club attempted to develop the bands' visual identities for marketing purposes. During the 1980s, Garrett also designed graphics for emerging youth magazines and continued to develop new merchan-
dising materials for the music industry. In 1986, Garrett discovered the
graphic design potential of the Apple Mackintosh desktop computer, which
virtually eliminated the need for hard copy and allowed film or animation to
be used in conjunction with still images. By 1989, he had fully committed
himself to digital technology and his studio was one of the first to exchange
drawing tables for computer terminals. Garrett left Assorted Images in 1994,
and together with Alasdair Scott set up a new company, AMX, to design and
develop interactive multi-media, including CD-based titles and web sites.

Antonio Gaudí y Cornet studied natural sciences at the University of Barcelona from 1869 to 1874, and then architecture at the newly established Escola Provincial d'Arquitectura, Barcelona. In 1878, he was commissioned to design street lighting for the city of Barcelona and worked on the design of a workers' cooperative settlement in Mataró. From around 1882, he worked closely with the architect Joan Matorell who introduced him to Gothic Revival architecture, which was seen as an expression of Catalan autonomy. Intensely proud of his Catalonian roots, Gaudí went on pilgrimages with the "Centro Excursionista" to view Catalonian historical sites, from Gothic cathedrals to Moorish buildings, which stylistically influenced his own work. For his Casa Vicens (1883–1888), for instance, he combined the native Gothic style with Mudéjar features to produce a bizarre hybrid form of ornamentation. Gaudí believed that ornament was a key factor in providing a building or a design with character and for many of his highly integrated projects, such as Palau Güell (1886–1889), the Casa Calvet (1889–1900) and Casa Battló (1904–1906), he experimented with melting, oozing and distorted organic motifs. In 1883, he began designing his masterwork – the Sagrada Familia in Barcelona – a still unfinished cathedral project to which he devoted most of his working life– and which passionately expressed both his intense Catalan nationalism and the fervour of his Christian faith. Through his highly sculptural and idiosyncratic style, Gaudí pioneered – virtually single-handedly – a Spanish version of **Art Nouveau**.

Antonio Gaudí y Cornet

1852 Reus, Spain
1926 Barcelona

▼ Carved chair for the Casa Calvet, c. 1902

Norman Bel Geddes

1893 *Adrian, Michigan*
1958 *New York*

Norman Bel Geddes studied art at the Cleveland Institute of Art and later at the Art Institute of Chicago. In 1913, he worked as a draughtsman in the advertising industry in Detroit and shortly afterwards became an art director. He wrote a play in 1916 and subsequently worked as a theatrical designer for six productions staged in Los Angeles. Two years later, he became a set designer for the Metropolitan Opera Company, New York, and in 1925 moved to Hollywood and designed lavish film-sets for the producers, Cecil B. De Mille and D. W. Griffith. Influenced by his contact with **Frank Lloyd Wright**, whom he had worked with on a theatrical project for Aline Barnsdall in 1916, and his association with the German Expressionist architect Erich Mendelsohn (1887–1953), Geddes decided to turn his attention to architecture and product styling. In 1932, he published the book *Horizons*, which outlined his streamlined approach to industrial design and his belief in the supremacy of the tear-drop shape. Geddes became one of the greatest exponents of **Streamlining** and designed futuristic cars for the Graham Paige automobile company (1928), radios for Philco (1931), radio casings for RCA and metal bedroom furnishings for Simmons. One of his most notable achievements was his standardization of kitchen equipment, which included the modular *Oriole* stove (1931–1936). In 1939, he designed General Motor's "Futurama" display for the New York World's Fair, projecting his vision of the world in 1960, and predicting a freeway system for roads.

Frank O. Gehry studied architecture at the University of Southern California, Los Angeles up to 1954 and spent a year at the Harvard Graduate School of Design, Cambridge, Massachusetts. After his formal studies, Gehry worked as an architect and planner for a number of architectural practices in Los Angeles, Atlanta, Boston and Paris, and in 1962 he established his own architectural office, Frank O. Gehry & Associates Inc. in Los Angeles. Ten years later, he designed the remarkable *Easy Edges* series of fourteen cardboard furniture pieces. These designs, initially conceived as low-cost furniture, were immediately successful. However, Gehry withdrew them from production after only three months, fearing that his success as a popular furniture designer would detract from his reputation as an architect. During the late 1970s, Gehry designed a number of residences, including his own house in Santa Monica and the Spiller Residence in Venice, California, using industrial materials and deconstructed forms. He received international acclaim for his Deconstructivist architectural projects, such as the Loyola Law School (1981–1984), the California Aerospace Museum (1983–1984), the Fishdance Restaurant in Kobe, Japan (1987) and the **Vitra** Design Museum and Factory in Weil am Rhein (1989). In the 1980s, he returned to furniture design and created his *Experimental-Edges* cardboard furniture (1982), which functioned more as art-furniture than as practical furnishing solutions. From 1990 to 1992, Gehry developed a series of chairs for **Knoll International**, which were constructed of woven strips of plywood and required no additional structural support. Gehry also designed his series of *Fish Lamps* for the Formica Company, who were looking for innovative applications for their newly developed material, ColorCore. As one of the leading exponents of **Deconstructivism,** Gehry has received numerous awards including the Pritzker Prize in 1989. His greatest architectural achievement to date is the spectacular titanium-clad Guggenheim Museum in Bilbao, which was completed in 1997.

Frank O. Gehry
b. 1930 *Toronto, Canada*

▼ *Wiggle* chair and low table set from *Easy Edges* series for Jack Brogan, 1972 (reissued by Vitra)

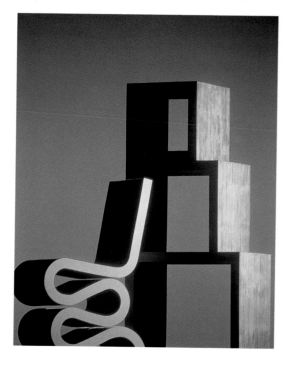

**Gesamt-
kunstwerk**

Gesamtkunstwerk is a German term, which literally means "complete-art-work". Its use dates from the 19th century and refers to an amalgamation of all the arts. Originally, the concept of Gesamtkunstwerk was associated with the operas of Richard Wagner (1813–1883), which blended music with drama. Later, it was related to the notion of wholly integrated design in architecture and interiors whereby every element involved in an artistic scheme was meticulously designed, usually by a single creator. This idea of design unification was taken up most famously by architects aligned to the **Arts & Crafts Movement** such as **Charles Rennie Mackintosh** and **Frank Lloyd Wright**. They took the idea of the total work of art one step further by ensuring that their buildings were in complete harmony with the surrounding environment and were functionally appropriate. They also designed the smallest of details for their buildings and interiors, down to cutlery and door fittings. In Austria and Germany, **Josef Hoffmann** and **Peter Behrens** were also prominent exponents of the concept of Gesamtkunstwerk. The idea of completely unified design, as expressed through Gesamtkunstwerk, later influenced the practice of "total design" in which the design, manufacture and marketing of products is approached holistically.

▲ **Frank Lloyd Wright**, Dining room of
Hollyhock House, Los Angeles, designed
for Aline Barnsdall, 1917–1920

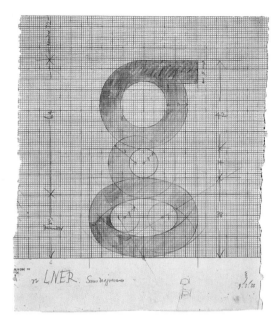

Eric Gill

1882 *Brighton*
1940 *Harefield/London*

Eric Gill studied at Chichester Art School before becoming articled to the architect, W. D. Caröe, in London from 1899 to 1903. During this period, he also studied letter-cutting under Edward Johnston (1872–1944) at the Central School of Arts and Crafts, London. He was first employed as a letter-cutter and designed several title pages for the Leipzig publishing house, Insel Verlag. Then, after moving to Ditchling, Sussex in 1907, he began to receive considerable acclaim for his stone carvings. In 1913, he converted to Roman Catholicism and for the next five years, was occupied in carving the Stations of the Cross at Westminster Cathedral. Around 1918, Gill assisted in the formation of the Guild of St Joseph and St Dominic – a quasi-religious craft community. He became a founder of the Society of Wood Engravers in 1920, and from 1924 began designing page layouts for books published by the Golden Cockerel Press, Berkshire. His page layouts were in the Arts and Crafts idiom, with stylistically integrated typography and illustrations. A year later, he began designing typefaces for the **Monotype Corporation,** including *Perpetua* (1927) and *Gill Sans* (1928). In 1928, Gill established his own printing works at Speen in Buckinghamshire and undertook commissions from various publishing houses, including the Cranach Press, Faber & Faber, J. M. Dent & Sons and the Limited Editions Club.

Ernest Gimson was the son of Joseph Gimson, an engineer and member of the Secularist Society. At the age of seventeen, he began his architectural training in the offices of a local architect, Isaac Barradale, while also studying part-time at Leicester School of Art. In 1884, he met **William Morris**, and on his advice moved to London to become articled to the Gothic Revivalist architect, John Dando Sedding (1838–1891). Following Morris' example, Gimson spent all his spare time mastering traditional crafts such as chair-making and decorative plasterwork. While working in Sedding's office, Gimson became friends with Ernest Barnsley (1863–1926) and his brother Sidney Barnsley (1865–1926), who was articled at the time to Richard Norman Shaw (1831–1912). In 1891, together with other members of Shaw's staff including Reginald Blomfield and William Lethaby (1857–1931), the friends founded the short-lived decorating firm Kenton & Co. in Bloomsbury, offering "good design and good workmanship". In 1892, Gimson and the Barnsleys moved to the Cotswolds and two years later set up a workshop in Pinbury. Having independent means, they were able to pursue the rural ideal of the **Arts & Crafts Movement** and produce exquisite, high-quality furniture that was not constrained by commercial concerns.

Ernest Gimson

1864 *Leicester*
1919 *Sapperton/*
Gloucestershire

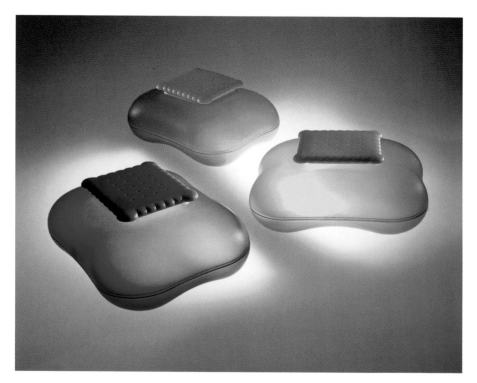

Stefano Giovannoni

b. 1954 *La Spézia, Italy*

▲ *Mary Biscuit*
container for Alessi,
1995

Stefano Giovannoni studied architecture at the University of Florence, where he lectured and undertook design research as a post-graduate until 1990, while also teaching at the Domus Academy, Milan and at the Institute of Design, Reggio Emilia. He was a founder member of the Bolidist movement, which advocated the use of **Streamlining** in product design, and founded a studio with Guido Venturini known as King-Kong Production to undertake research into architecture and the design of domestic products, interiors and fashion. From 1989, they co-designed the highly successful *Girotondo* range for **Alessi**, with its characterful "stick-man" motif. During the 1990s, Giovannoni also independently designed several post-modern products for Alessi, with intentionally humorous and playful designs, such as the *Fruit Mama* bowl (1993), the *Merdolina* toilet brush (1993) and the *Mary Biscuit* container (1995). In 1991, he designed the Italian pavilion for the "Les Capitales Européennes de Nouveau Design" exhibition held at the Centre George Pompidou Paris. Giovannoni has also worked for Cappellini, Arradaesse and Tisca France and his idiosyncratic designs have been widely exhibited both in Italy and abroad.

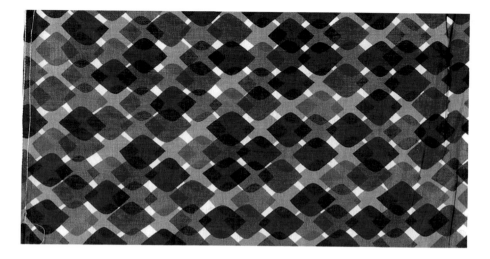

Alexander Hayden Girard spent much of his childhood in Florence and later studied at the Architectural Association, London. After graduating in 1929, he established his own Florence-based architectural practice and began designing furnishings and interiors. During this period, he also trained at the Royal School of Architecture, Rome, graduating in 1931. After completing his formal studies at New York University in 1935, Girard moved to Detroit and opened a design office there two years later. He designed office interiors for the Ford Motor Company in 1946, and in 1952 was appointed director of **Herman Miller**'s textile division, for which he produced boldly coloured and patterned upholstery fabrics. A year later, he moved his office to Santa Fe and undertook several other interior design projects, including the Irwin Miller residence in Columbus (co-designed with **Eero Saarinen** in 1955), Billy Wilder's Los Angeles home, the L'Etoile Restaurant, New York, and the La Fonda del Sol Restaurant, New York (1960). In 1957, Girard and **Charles Eames** made a documentary film together in Mexico, entitled "Day of the Dead", and his fascination with Mexican culture led to a deep appreciation of folk art. During his life, Girard collected 106,000 toys and folk art items which formed the basis of the Girard Foundation Collection, now housed at the Museum of International Folk Art, Santa Fe. Although he designed furniture, wallpapers and graphics, including a corporate identity for Braniff Airlines (1965), Girard is best remembered for his rhythmically structured and colour-saturated textiles.

Alexander Hayden Girard
1907 *New York*
1993 *Santa Fe, New Mexico*

▲ *Feathers* textile for Herman Miller, 1957

**Giorgetto
Giugiaro**

b. 1938 *Garessio, Italy*

Giorgetto Giugiaro began working at the age of seventeen in Fiat's design department after studying technical drawing and graphic design at the Accademia di Belle Arti in Turin. In 1959 he became head of the styling department at the Carrozzeria Bertone, Turin. Giugiaro left Bertone in 1965 to become the director of the Ghia studio, which was similarly concerned with automotive styling and while there he designed the Fiat *Dino* Coupé (1967). In 1968, he formed the design partnership ItalDesign with Aldo Mantovani and Luciano Bosio, innovatively offering car manufacturers not just a design service but also pre-production assistance including the carrying out of feasibility studies and the construction of prototypes. Although Giugaro was particularly noted for his stylish and sleek sports cars, such as the Alfa Romeo *Alfasud* (1971), the oil crisis in the early 1970s provoked the design of more utilitarian vehicles that were characterized by rectilinear forms, including the Volkswagen *Golf* (1974), the Fiat *Panda* (1980) and the Fiat *Uno* (1983). In 1981, he established Giugaro Design and designed the *Logica* sewing machine for Necchi (1982), the Nikon *F4* camera (1988) a chronograph watch for Seiko, crash helmets for Shoei and furniture for Tecno. During the 1980s, Giugiaro Design had around four hundred employees, and in 1987 Giugiaro SpA was founded for the design of men's clothing and accessories.

▼ *Logica* sewing machine for Necchi, 1982

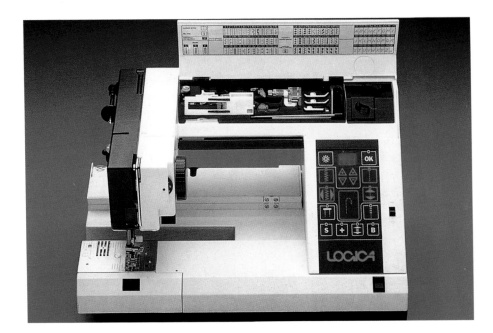

Milton Glaser trained at the High School of Music & Art, New York, before studying art at the Cooper Union, where he graduated in 1951. He was awarded a Fulbright Scholarship, which enabled him to study under Giorgio Morandi (1890–1964) at the Accademia delle Belle Arti e Lieco Artistico in Bologna, Italy. On his return to New York in 1954, Glaser joined Seymour Chwast (b. 1931), Reynold Ruffins and Edward Sorel in founding the Push Pin Studio. His subsequent poster designs inspired by psychedelic art, such as his famous *Dylan* (1967), *Rainbow Palette* (1966) and *From Poppy with Love* (1969) brought him widespread recognition during the 1960s – indeed, in 1969 he was pictured on the cover of *Time magazine*. The *Push Pin Graphic Magazine* was first issued in 1954 to promote the studio's "freer" approach to graphics, which was characterized by the use of quirky perspective, flattened planes, psychedelic colouring and the incorporation of past typographic styles and art historical quotations. The playfulness of this graphic style led to Glaser's being commissioned to illustrate several children's books and to design the Child Craft toy-shop in New York in 1970 and the Sesame Place Play Park in 1979. During the 1970s, Glaser redesigned the formats of several magazines including *Paris Match* (1973), *Village Voice* and *Esquire* (1977) and the Push Pin Studio became increasingly involved in the development of corporate identities. Glaser was president of the Push Pin Studio until 1970, and after its closure in 1974 he established his own graphic studio, Milton Glaser Inc., in New York. Glaser banished the austere formalism of the **Swiss School** from graphic design and replaced it with a vibrant and humourous vocabulary that was informed by both contemporary culture and historic styles.

Milton Glaser
b. 1929 *New York*

P. 286: Poster for the Winter Olympics in Sarajevo, 1984

▼ Poster for *Valentine* typewriter for Olivetti, c. 1970

VALENTINE   OLIVETTI

▶ **Ernest Archibald Taylor**, Secretaire for Wylie & Lockhead, c. 1906

The term Glasgow School refers to the group of turn-of-the-century design-ers associated with the Glasgow School of Art while it was under the pro-gressive directorship of Francis H. Newbery (1853–1946). Its most promi-nent members were **Charles Rennie Mackintosh**, Margaret Macdonald Mackintosh (1864–1933), Frances Macdonald MacNair (1873–1921) and Herbert MacNair (1868–1955), who exhibited Celtic-inspired designs to-gether from 1894 and became known as "The Four". Their sparsely fur-nished white interiors possessed an ethereal quality, while the content of much of their graphic work concentrated on the "other world". The work they produced was extremely well received by designers associated with the **Vienna Secession**. The emergence of the Glasgow School coincided with the ascendancy of The Glasgow Boys – a group of Post-Impressionist painters, including George Henry (1858–1943) and E. A. Hornel (1864–1933), who were similarly influenced by Japanese and Celtic themes. The poetic work of other Glasgow School designers, **George Walton**, Talwyn Morris (1865–1911), Jessie King (1875–1949), George Logan (1866–1939), Ann Macbeth (1875–1948) and E. A. Taylor (1874–1951) contributed to the emergence of **Art Nouveau**. Although the Glasgow School was affiliated with the British **Arts & Crafts Movement**, its output differed significantly from work pro-duced south of the border, being less inspired by vernacularism and having a greater sense of organicism.

Glasgow School
1890s–early 1900s
Glasgow

GLOBAL TOOLS — 12 GENNAIO 1973

▲ Members of
Global Tools on
Casabella cover, 1973

During the late 1960s, several **Radical Design** groups were established in Italy, including **Archizoom**, **Superstudio**, **Gruppo Strum**, UFO, 9999 and Zziggurrat, to investigate the concept of design and architecture as universal tools of communication. As part of the counter-design debate, **Riccardo Dalisi** also organized workshops for poor children in the Traiano district of Naples, where he undertook experiments with "tecnologia povera" (poor technology) in an attempt to bring personal creative expression and spontaneity back into design. These researches led members of the many Radical Design groups to assemble in the offices of *Casabella* in 1973, to discuss the formation of a "school" of counter-architecture and design, which became known as Global Tools. This educational co-operative was officially founded a year later in Florence, to "promote individual and collective creativity". It established several workshops, known as "laboratories", to develop a "do-it-yourself" approach to design and to explore the potential applications and characteristics of technical materials. With its left-wing political agenda of ten scientific and political "tesi" (theses), Global Tools sought to creatively connect ordinary people as well as designers with the design process. While in operation, the co-operative was the central forum for the Radical Design debate and its disbanding in 1975 marked the end of the first phase of the movement in Italy. During the late 1970s and 1980s, former members of Global Tools, including Dalisi and **Ettore Sottsass**, went on to become major exponents of **Post-Modernism**.

Global Tools
Founded 1973
Florence

▼ **Riccardo Dalisi**, Experiment with "poor technology", Naples, 1973

▼ Sideboard for
William Watt,
1867–1869

Edward William Godwin initially trained with William Armstrong, a Bristol-based civil engineer, surveyor and architect who was an acquaintance of the great British engineer, Isambard Kingdom Brunel (1806–1859). Godwin established his own office in Bristol in 1854, but receiving few commissions, moved to Ireland in 1857 to work with his brother, another engineer. There he worked on the design of a railway bridge and also received his first major architectural commission, the design of St Johnston's Church in County Donegal. In 1858, he met the Gothic Revival architect, William Burgess (1827–1881), and a year later returned to England. During the 1860s, Godwin undertook several architectural projects including North-hampton Town Hall (1861). After his exposure to Japanese Art at the 1862 "International Exhibition" in London, Godwin began collecting oriental arte-facts, which triggered the development of his Anglo-Japanese style. In 1865, he established his own London-based practice and subsequently designed wallpapers for Jeffrey & Co., textiles for Warner & Ramm, metalwork for Messenger & Co., tiles for Minton and furniture for the short-lived Art Furniture Company (1867–1868).

He also designed Anglo-Japanese furniture for William Watt's Artistic Furniture Warehouse as well as for Gillow's and Collinson & Lock. His architectural commissions in-cluded Dromore Castle, Limerick (1866–1873), J. McNeill Whistler's White House in Chelsea (1877–1878) and vernacular-style housing in Bedford Park, West London (1876). Through his liaison with the ac-tress, Ellen Terry (1847–1928), Godwin became interested in cos-tume design, and in 1884 was ap-pointed director of **Liberty & Co.**'s newly opened fashion department, which promoted reformed "artistic dress". Godwin was one of the lead-ing exponents of the **Aesthetic Movement**, and through his Anglo-Japanese style he introduced an in-fluential geometric vocabulary of form to design.

William Golden studied at the Vocational School for Boys, New York, where he was taught photo-engraving and graphic design. He began his working career in Los Angeles, first at a printing works and later at the *Los Angeles Examiner* as a designer. After this, he returned to New York to join the staff of *Journal American* and *House and Garden* magazine, and spent some time at Condé Nast working under Mehemed Fehmy Agha (1896–1978) who advocated the use of "white space". In 1937, he was employed by CBS (Columbia Broadcasting System) and was the network's art director for six years. Between 1941 and 1943, he worked in Washington for the Office of War Information and for the next three years, served as a captain in the United States army. While stationed in Europe, he was responsible for the layout and design of several army training manuals. In 1950, he designed the famous "eye" logo for CBS and a year later was appointed creative director of advertising and sales promotion for the network. Golden's main ambition was to raise design standards and he argued for integrity in design at the Aspen Design Conference of 1959. He warned people not to confuse art with design, declaring: "The obvious function of a designer is to design. His principle talent is to make simple order out of many elements." As the artistic director responsible for CBS's bold and visually integrated design programme, Golden was an early pioneer of the concept of **Corporate Identity**.

William Golden
1911 *New York*
1959 *Stony Point, New York*

◄ **Design Council**,
Kitemark, 1959

selected for the
DESIGN
CENTRE
LONDON

Good Design

Good Design is a concept based on a rational approach to the design process whereby products are created in accordance with the formal, technical and aesthetic principles generally associated with the **Modern Movement**. The **Museum of Modern Art, New York** staged the first Good Design exhibition in 1950, which was laid out by **Charles and Ray Eames**. The winning designs were selected by a three-man jury and were retailed through stores with an accompanying Good Design label. The premise of Good Design was also favourably received in Europe, especially in Germany. In 1952, **Max Bill** co-founded the **Hochschule für Gestaltung, Ulm** to promote the virtues of Good Design that had previously been extolled at the Bauhaus. Bill was also responsible for the establishment of the "Die Gute Industrieform" exhibitions in Germany. The concept of Good Design was most notably embraced at **Braun**, where **Dieter Rams** developed a functionalist house-style for electrical products. In Britain, Good Design was actively promoted by the Design Council (founded in 1960) through exhibitions and its journal *Design*. The Council implemented the use of its famous "kitemark" label as a seal of approval for worthy products. In the 1960s there was a reaction against the conservative conformity of Good Design and what was seen as the Establishment's dictation of "good taste". The popular reaction to Good Design ushered in **Post-Modernism**, which brought radicalism, emotion, spontaneity and character back into mainstream design.

Kenneth Grange studied at the Willesden School of Arts & Crafts, London, from 1944 to 1947. He trained as a technical illustrator with the Royal Engineers as part of his national service, and afterwards worked as an assistant for various London-based architectural and design practices, including Arcon Chartered Architects, Bronek Katz & Vaughan George Bower and Jack Howe & Partners. In 1958, he established his own office in London, specializing in product design, and fourteen years later formed a design partnership with Theo Crosby, Alan Fletcher, Mervyn Kurlansky and Colin Forbes known as **Pentagram**. Grange combined German **Functionalism**, as practised at **Braun**, with a British sensibility to appropriateness, creating designs that had a sculptural purity and a no-nonsense robustness. Among his many notable designs for industrial production are the Kenwood *Chef* food-mixer (1960), the Kodak *Pocket Instamatic* camera (1975), the *Parker 25* range of pens (1979) and the *Protector* razor for Wilkinson Sword (1992). He also designed the exterior body of British Rail's 125 Intercity high-speed train (1971–1973) and Adshel bus shelters for London Transport (1990). Grange has received numerous awards for his design work, including ten Design Council Awards as well as the Duke of Edinburgh's Prize for Elegant Design in 1963. From 1985 to 1987, he served as Master of the Faculty of Royal Designers for Industry and was then appointed president of the Chartered Society of Designers. Since the 1970s, Grange has also received many commissions from companies in Japan – sewing machines for Maruzen, bathroom fittings for Inax, cosmetic packaging for Shiseido – and his work has had much influence on product designers working there. As a leading British product designer, his work was the subject of a one-man show in 1983 at the Boilerhouse at the

Kenneth Grange
b. 1929 *London*

▼ *Pocket Instamatic* cameras for Kodak, 1975

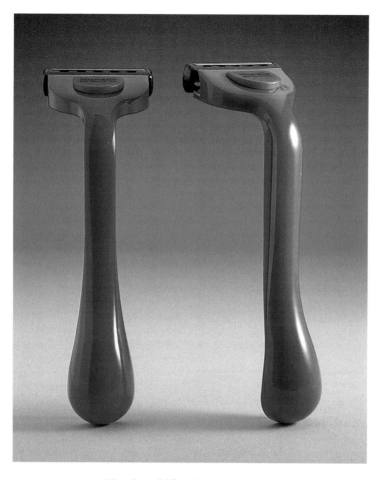

◄ *Protector* razors
for Wilkinson Sword,
1992

Victoria and Albert Museum. Grange views design not as aesthetic problem-solving but as an opportunity for innovation and believes that it should be an integral part of the manufacturing process. He has perpetuated the traditional attributes of British design – honesty and integrity – through his sleek, high-quality and meticulously detailed products.

Michael Graves took part in an architectural programme at the University of Cincinnati, which included practical experience in the offices of Carl A. Strauss & Associates. He later attended the Graduate School of Design at Harvard University and, after graduating in 1959, worked for **George Nelson** Associates. Around this time, Graves also worked as an artist, sharing a studio with **Richard Meier** in New York. A scholarship enabled him to study at the American Academy in Rome from 1960 to 1962, and on his return to the USA, he began teaching at Princeton University, New Jersey, where he became Schirmer Professor of Architecture in 1972. In 1964, he established his own architectural office in Princeton and designed the Hanselmann House in Fort Wayne, Indiana (1969). Graves' participation in a group exhibition with Peter Eisenman (b. 1932), Charles Gwathmey, John Hejduk and Richard Meier at the **Museum of Modern Art, New York** in 1969 brought him considerable recognition as a member of the "New York Five" as did the publication entitled *Five Architects*, which focused on the group. Shortly after this, Graves began to distance himself from the **Modern Movement** precepts to which he had previously subscribed and began designing colourful buildings and interiors, such as the Kalko House, New York and the presentations room for the Sunar Company, which incorporated elements from past historical styles, including gables and pillars. During the late 1970s, Graves became better known for his post-modern furniture designs for Sunar Hauserman (1979–1981), which were inspired by the Biedermeier and **Art Deco** styles. In the 1980s, he received much attention for his playful designs for **Memphis**, such as the Hollywood-style *Plaza* dressing table of 1981. But it was not until 1982, the year he completed his first large-scale public commission – the Public Services building in Portland, Oregon –that Graves came to prominence as an architect. Thereafter, he received numerous commissions including the San Juan Capistrano Library, Southern California (1983), the

Michael Graves

1934 *Indianapolis, Indiana*

▼ Pepper mill
for Alessi, 1988

▲ *Corinth* tableware
for Swid Powell,
1984

Humana Corporation Headquarters, Louisville, Kentucky (1982–1986), a
wing for the Newark Museum (1990), the Dolphin Hotel at Disney World
in Florida (1989), an addition to the Whitney Museum of Art, New York
(1989–1990), the Pegase di Domaine Clos winery in the Napa Valley,
California, and the New York Hotel at the Euro-Disney resort near Paris.
During the 1980s, Graves gained recognition for his work in the decorative
arts and designed jewellery for Cleo Munari (1985–1987), ceramics for Swid
Powell and a variety of objects for **Alessi** including his Tea & Coffee *Piazza*
service (1983). In 1993, Graves established his own shop in Princeton to retail his designs. His eclectic and historicising hybrid product designs from
the 1980s are iconic examples of **Post-Modernism**.

Eileen Gray studied at the Slade School of Fine Art, London from 1898 to 1902, while learning the art of lacquering at the Dean Street furniture workshop of D. Charles. She first visited Paris in 1900 and from 1902 to 1905 attended classes at the École Colarossi and the Académie Julian. In 1907, she settled in Paris and moved into an apartment at 21, Rue Bonaparte, which remained her home until her death in 1976. While in France, she was taught oriental techniques of lacquering by the Japanese craftsman, Seizo Sougawara. From around 1910, Gray began designing lacquered screens and panels with figurative motifs and in 1913 she exhibited her work at the Salon des Artistes Décorateurs where her designs caught the attention of the couturier and art collector, Jacques Doucet (1853–1929). He became her first major client and she executed several commissions for him, including the *Le Destin* four-panel screen (1914) and the *Lotus* table (1915), before her work was disrupted by the First World War. For a while, she worked as an ambulance driver in Paris under the aegis of the Duchess of Clermont-Tonnerre. However, in 1915 she left with Sougawara for London and resided there for two years. In 1917, she returned to Paris, receiving her first complete interior design commission in 1919 for the Rue de Lota apartment of Mme Mathieu Lévy – for which she designed her famous lacquered "block" screens. In 1922, having already executed many one-off **Art Deco** commissions for wealthy clients, Gray established her own shop, the Galerie Jean Désert. That same year, she exhibited her work in Amsterdam, where it came to the attention of the **De Stijl** architect Jan Wils (1891–1972). The Dutch **avant-garde** admired her design of a "Bedroom-boudoir for Monte Carlo", which was shown at the Salon des Artistes Décorateurs in 1923. This admiration was reciprocated when Gray attended an exhibition of Dutch design in Paris later that year. Her work subsequently became increasingly influenced by the pure geometric forms of De Stijl. In 1924, Gray and the architect Jean Badovici (1893–1956) took a study trip to view Modernist

Eileen Gray

1878 *Brownswood/*
Wexford, Ireland
1976 *Paris*

▼ *Transat* chair for
Galerie Jean Désert,
1925–1926

architecture and she was persuaded by him to become an architect. She consequently designed her own Modernist house at Roquebrune, the *E-1027* (1926–1929), for which she created some appropriately rational furniture including the *Transat* chair (1925–1930) and the *E-1027* tubular metal and glass table. From 1930 to 1931, she planned the interior of Badovici's apartment in Rue Chateaubriand, followed by another house for her own use, the Tempe a Pailla at Castellar, completed in 1934. After exhibiting her work at **Le Corbusier**'s Pavillon des Temps Nouveaux in 1937, and presenting an unrealized proposal for a Centre de Vacances, Gray faded into virtual obscurity until 1970, when an American collector, Robert Walker, began buying up her designs, initiating a significant revival of interest in her life and work.

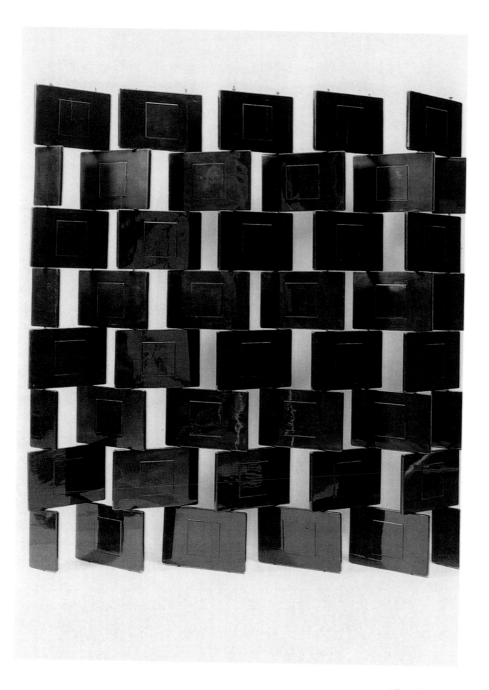

In the 1950s, **Richard Buckminster Fuller** promoted a minimal use of materials and energy in the design of products and coined the term "Spaceship Earth", which led people to think of the planet in a more holistic way. Vance Packard also criticized the consumerist culture in his influential book *The Waste Makers* (1961), and was particularly damning of the practice of built-in-obsolescence. This book was followed by Rachel Carson's *Silent Spring* (1962), which was the first bestseller to popularize the environmental debate and increase general awareness of green issues. Later, Victor Papanek related ecological awareness to the design process in *Design for a Real World* (1967) and urged for radical design solutions that were mindful of the environment. Such views were given greater currency during the early 1970s when the oil crisis increased concern about the finite aspect of the world's natural resources. After several man-made environmental disasters and the growing realization that industrialization was contributing to global warming, the term "Green Design" emerged in the 1980s to describe a holistic and environmentally responsible approach to design. Green Design is concerned with minimizing waste and the use of energy and materials and takes into consideration a product's complete life-cycle including: the extraction of raw materials and the impact of their processing; the energy required in the manufacturing processes together with any negative by-products; the energy required for and the effects of the distribution system; the durability of the product's service life; component recovery and the efficiency of recyclability; and the ultimate effects of disposal on the environment through, for instance, landfill or incineration. Although recycling can reduce energy consumption, it does not minimize it and in some ways it can be seen to actually perpetuate the throw-away culture. Increased product durability, on the other hand, minimizes waste and energy consumption – by doubling the lifespan of products their environmental impact can be halved.

▼ **Jane Atfield**, *RCP2* recycled high density polyethylene chair for Made of Waste, 1992

Charles Sumner Greene and Henry Mather Greene initially trained at the University of Washington's Manual Training School in St Louis, which was under the directorship of Calvin Milton Woodward who emphasized the dignity of craftsmanship. After that, both brothers studied architecture at the Massachusetts Institute of Technology, but worked separately in various architectural practices before establishing a joint office in 1893 in Pasadena, California. On their way to Pasadena, they stopped in Chicago to visit the "World's Columbian Exposition" and were inspired by the Japanese Section that included an oriental-style structure known as the Ho-o-den Temple, which had been designed by the young architect, **Frank Lloyd Wright**. Between 1893 and 1903, the majority of their designs were for private residences and their early furnishings were influenced by Will Bradley's designs published in his articles for the *Ladies Home Journal*. During this period, they became friendly with the Oriental dealer John Bentz and studied his personal collection, which inspired them to adopt less traditional forms. In 1903, they saw illustrations of Japanese homes and gardens and, stimulated by the inter-connectedness of such buildings to their surrounding environ-

ments, began developing their own holistic approach to design. They used projected beams and stained, roughly hewn timbers for the construction of their houses, while their rustic and homely interiors made use of natural materials. Working in the Arts & Crafts idiom, the Greene Brothers designed seven bungalows from 1907 to 1909 as completely integrated schemes or **Gesamtkunstwerke**. These homes, including the Blacker and Gamble Houses, did much to enhance their professional reputations but from 1910 onwards public taste began turning away from the **Arts and Crafts Movement**. It was not until the 1950s that Greene & Greene's approach to architecture and design – identifying what is necessary and giving it beautiful form – was reappraised and enjoyed a revival of interest.

▼ Interior of the Gamble House, 1908

Vittorio Gregotti
b. 1927 *Novara, Italy*

Vittorio Gregotti studied at the Politecnico di Milano, graduating in 1951. With Ernesto Rogers (1909–1969) and Giotto Stoppino (b. 1926) he designed a display entitled "Architettura, misura dell'uomo" for the IX Milan Triennale (1951), and a year later he established the partnership Architetti Associati with Giotto Stoppino and Lodovico Meneghetti in Navara. Together the trio developed several interesting chairs, a wall-supported shelving unit and a table – all of which used cut-out plywood elements. Around that time, they also designed their "Stanza per una ragazza" (Room for a girl), which incorporated an innovative shelving system. Later in the 1950s, they produced interiors and furniture in the Neo-Liberty style – notably the *Cavour* chair of 1959 – and in the early 1960s they experimented with woven rush seating. When the office moved to Milan in 1964, Gregotti took a teaching position at the Politecnico di Milano, which he held until 1978. He left the partnership in 1967 to found his own studio in Milan, and seven years later established the design consultancy Gregotti Associati with Pierluigi Cerri (b. 1939) and Hiromichi Matsui. Although mainly specializing in exhibition and interior design, he also worked as a product designer. Throughout his career, Gregotti has been associated in an editorial capacity with numerous design journals including *Casabella-Continuità* from 1952 to 1960, *Edilizia Moderna* from 1962 to 1964, *Il Verri* from 1963 to 1965 and,

▼ Door handles for
Fusital, 1981

during the 1980s, *La Rassegna Italiana* and *Lotus*. He has also published several books including *Il territorio dell'architettura* (1966) and *New Directions in Italian Architecture* (1969). Since 1978, Gregotti has been professor of architectural composition at the Istituto Universaritario di Architettura in Venice and a guest lecturer at numerous educational institutions in Buenos Aires, Lausanne, Sao Paolo and Toyko and at Berkeley University, California. The success of Vittorio Gregotti's Milan-based consultancy and his long-standing commitment to teaching and publishing has ensured his position as both a leading spokesman for Italian design and one of its most eminent practitioners.

April Greiman studied fine art at the Kansas City Art Institute, graduating in 1970. She then trained for a year under Wolfgang Weingart (b. 1941) and Armin Hofmann (b. 1920) at the Allgemeine Kunstgewerbeschule Basle. On her return to the United States, Greiman worked as a graphic designer in New York and Connecticut while teaching at the Philadelphia College of Art. In 1976, she settled in California and developed her own style of graphics that combined the **Post-Modernism** emerging from the West Coast with her **Swiss School** grounding. The resulting graphics used layered type and images to create a sense of three-dimensionality in which elements appeared to float. Many of the photographic images that she incorporated in her collage-like graphics were taken by Jayme Odgers. Greiman was one of the first graphic designers to fully exploit the design potential of the Apple Mackintosh computer in the 1980s. She became head of the design department at the California Institute of Arts in 1982 and throughout the 1980s was one of the leading exponents of the **California New Wave** graphics movement. In 1990, she published *Hybrid Imagery: The Fusion of Technology and Graphic Design,* which outlined her approach to visual communication. Greiman's work has been immensely influential especially on the design of graphics for electronic media.

April Greiman
b. 1948 *Rockville Center, New York*

Walter Gropius
1883 *Berlin*
1969 *Boston*

Walter Gropius studied architecture at the Technische Hochschule, Munich from 1903 to 1905 and then at the Technische Hochschule, Berlin from 1905 to 1907. His first building project in 1906, was for low-cost housing to accommodate farm-workers. From 1908 to 1910, Gropius worked in the Berlin-based office of **Peter Behrens**, designing offices and furniture for the Lehmann department store in Cologne. Then, in 1910, Gropius established an architectural partnership with Adolf Meyer (1881–1929) in Neubabelsberg and became a member of the **Deutscher Werkbund** (established 1907). As an active member of the Werkbund, Gropius initially opposed Hermann Muthesius' (1861–1927) urgings for standardization and sided with **Henry van de Velde**, who advocated individualism and personal creativity in design. Gropius' Fagus Factory (1911) innovatively incorporated a curtain wall that was suspended from the building's vertical elements and was featured in the Werkbund's *Jahrbücher* (Year-Books), which Gropius edited from 1912 to 1914. He also designed a model factory for the "Deutsche Werkbund-Ausstellung" held in Cologne in 1914, which with its steel and glass construction was a powerful expression of the **Modern Movement**. After the devastation of the First World War, Gropius accepted the need for **Standardization** in design and became the director of the Hochschule für angewandte

▼ Mahogany cabinet with bronze inlay designed for the salon of Dr. Karl Herzfeld in Hanover, 1913

Kunst, which he merged with the Kunstakademie in Weimar in 1919 to form the Staatliches **Bauhaus**. During his directorship of the school from 1919 to 1928, Gropius stressed unity of the arts and instigated a system of workshops headed by "masters". During this period, he undertook a number of private architectural commissions, including the Sommerfeld House (1921–1922), designed several pieces of white-painted furniture and developed a pre-fabricated house for the "Weissenhof-Siedlung" exhibition held in Stuttgart in 1927. When the Bauhaus moved to Dessau, the school embraced by necessity a new rationalism and in 1925, Gropius designed purpose-built premises for it that embodied this shift towards in-

dustrial modernity. In 1934, Gropius emigrated to Great Britain where he
worked in partnership with the architect E. Maxwell Fry (b. 1899) until 1937.
While in London, Gropius also worked for Jack Pritchard's company, Isokon,
where he was appointed controller of design in 1936. A year later, he emigrated to the United States and became professor of architecture at Harvard
University.

William
H. Grueby

1867 *Chelsea,
Massachusetts*
1925 *New York*

In 1893 William H. Grueby established the Boston-based company, Grueby
Faïence, to produce architectural wares and tiles inspired by the Italian
Renaissance ceramic plaques of Luca della Robbia (1400–1482) as well as
Chinese and Arabic ceramics. From around 1898, Grueby perfected the use
of dark green matt glazes and began to produce studio pottery that em-
ployed this technique. His matt glazed art pottery, which bore the Grueby
Pottery mark from 1899, had a marked influence on other American studio
potteries and was widely copied. While Grueby concentrated on the glazing
and firing aspects of this art pottery, the forms used were designed first by
George Prentiss Kendrick from 1897–1902 and later by Addison Le Boutiller.
Any decorative details, such as sprays of daffodils, were designed by female
art graduates. In 1908, the Grueby Pottery went into bankruptcy and was re-
opened as the Grueby Faïence & Tile Company, which produced art pottery
until c. 1911. As one of the leading Arts & Crafts ceramicists in America,
Grueby developed a truly national style of studio pottery that was remarkable
for its forward-looking decorative restraint.

Gruppo Strum was a **Radical Design** group founded in Turin in 1963 by
Giorgio Geretti, Pietro Derossi, Carla Giammarco, Riccardo Rosso and
Maurizio Vogliazzo. The group's name was an abbreviation of the members'
goal of creating "una architettura strumentale" (an instrumental architecture). Gruppo Strum most notably participated in the "Italy: The New
Domestic Landscape" exhibition held at the **Museum of Modern Art, New
York** in 1972, where its polyurethane foam *Pratone* (Big Meadow) of 1970
was shown. Inspired by the over-sized and out-of-context Pop Art sculptures
of Claes Oldenburg (b. 1929), *Pratone* was manufactured by Gufram and
was one of the few examples of **Anti-Design** that did not remain a prototype.
Members of the group were highly active in the promotion of Radical Design
in Italy during the late 1960s and early 1970s, organizing seminars and writing articles on the political agenda and design theories behind the movement. The group also developed a technique of using "picture stories" to explain the social and political contexts of contemporary architecture. Radical
Italian design groups such as Gruppo Strum laid the philosophical foundations of Anti-Design and in so doing paved the way for the emergence of
Post-Modernism in the early 1980s.

Gruppo Strum
Founded 1963
Turin

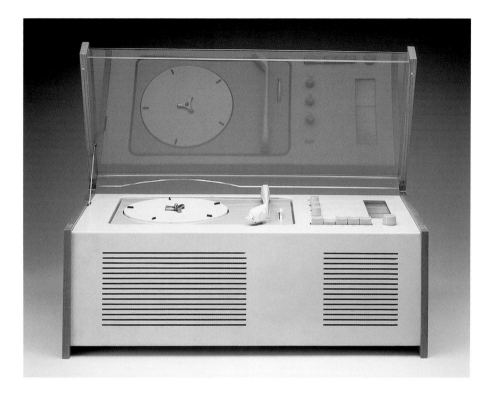

Hans Gugelot

1920 *Massakar, Indonesia*
1965 *Ulm, Germany*

▲ Hans Gugelot and
Dieter Rams,
Phonosuper
phonograph and
radio for Braun, 1956

Hans Gugelot was of Dutch and Swiss descent. From 1940 to 1942, he trained as an architect in Lausanne before studying at the Eidgenössische Technische Hochschule in Zurich. On completing his formal studies in 1946, Gugelot worked as a freelance architect with **Max Bill** for eight years, and during this time designed furniture for Horgen-Glarus. In 1954, after meeting Erwin Braun (b. 1921), Gugelot began designing sleek products for the consumer electronics company, **Braun**. He continued to work in Braun's design department until 1965, and while there helped to develop a house-style that had a strong visual identity, derived from the use of geometric forms, the elimination of ornament and the restricted use of colour. During this period, Gugelot ran his own design studio, the Gugelot Institute in Ulm and also directed the product design department of the **Hochschule für Gestaltung, Ulm,** where he rigorously promoted the **Modern Movement** dictum of "form following function". His advocacy of **Functionalism** strongly influenced subsequent consumer products designed by his colleague at Braun, **Dieter Rams**. One of his most notable products, the *Phonosuper*

(1956), was co-designed with Rams and was nicknamed "Snow White's Coffin" in view of its clear acrylic lid and hard-edged Functionalist aesthetic. Gugelot continued to practise architecture, specializing in the design of pre-fabricated housing, while also designing products for industrial manufacture, such as a sewing machine for Pfaff, the Kodak carousel slide projector (1964) and the first German programme of built-in furniture, which included his *M125* storage unit (1954) for Boffinger. Additionally, he worked as a consultant on the development of Hamburg's U-Bahn from 1959 to 1962 and in this capacity, developed railway carriages for over-ground use. Although Gugelot's design career was cut short by his premature death in 1965, his influence, especially on the development of German product design, was immense. The Institute of Product Development and Design Incorporated in Neu-Ulm, an independent organization that had emerged from the Development Group 2 at the Hochschule für Gestaltung, was renamed Gugelot Design after his death and promoted his rational approach to design until its closure in 1974.

► **Hans Gugelot and Reinhold Hocker,** *Carousel S-AV 1000* slide projector for Kodak, 1964

Having completed his studies at Cambridge, **Charles R. Ashbee** went to
work at Toynbee Hall – a philanthropic mission with an educational remit
that had been established by Canon Samuel Augustus Barnett in 1884 in
the East-End of London. There he organized readings of the works of John
Ruskin (1819–1900) and with students, undertook the decoration of the dining room at Toynbee Hall. In 1887, he founded the School of Handicraft at
Toynbee Hall and a year later, the Guild of Handicraft. The Guild was established with working capital of £50.00 and had three founding members,
including Ashbee who became its chief designer. Guild members designed
and executed silverware, metalwork, jewellery and furniture, and from 1889
showed their work annually at the Arts & Crafts Exhibition Society. The Guild
also became influential on the Continent through its furniture, designed
by **Hugo Mackay Baillie Scott,** for the palace of the Grand Duke Ernst
Ludwig of Hesse-Darmstadt and the exhibition of its designs at the VII
Vienna Secession Exhibition in 1900. The Guild was run as a co-operative
and was primarily known for its silverware and jewellery designs, especially
those of Ashbee, David Cameron, William Hardiman, J. K. Baily and W. A.
White that were enamelled and set with semi-precious cabochons and
mother-of-pearl. Objects such as these were inspired by Benvenuto Cellini's
(1500–1571) writings of the 1560s, in particular his *Trattato del'Oreficeria* and
Trattato della Scultura. These Renaissance treatises on goldsmithing and
sculpture were translated into English by Ashbee and published in 1898 as
a single volume, which he dedicated "to the metal workers of the Guild of
Handicraft". The book was published by the Guild's own Essex House Press,
the founding of which had been inspired by the earlier success of **William
Morris'** Kelmscott Press. Prior to this, in 1890 the Guild had leased a large
Georgian mansion, Essex House on Mile End Road, London, for its design,
manufacturing and printing activities, and had also opened a retail outlet
at 16a, Brook Street in the West-End of London. In 1901 Ashbee moved the
Guild of Handicraft, together with around a hundred and fifty people (artisans and their families), to Chipping Campden in the Gloucestershire Cotswolds hoping to realize William Morris' idyll of a self-sustaining rural community. The Guild ran summer schools for local people as well as students.
However, it came under increasing criticism for its preoccupation with social matters rather than artistic quality. Ultimately, the extra transportation
costs and the loss of a city profile led to its financial demise. In 1906, the
Essex House Press was closed and two years later the Guild of Handicraft
was forced into voluntary liquidation, having been unable to compete with
cheaper goods that imitated the Guild's designs.

▶ **Charles R. Ashbee,**
Silver mounted
decanter for the
Guild of Handicraft,
1901

Hector Guimard

1867 *Lyons*
1942 *New York*

Hector Guimard studied in Paris, from 1882 to 1885 under Eugène Train and Charles Génuys at the École Nationale des Arts Décoratifs and in 1889 under Gustave Gaulin at the École des Beaux-Arts. His first project was the interior design of the Au Grand Neptune Restaurant, Paris. This was followed by several commissions for private residences in and around the city including Charles Jassedé's villa (1893), which with its integrated interior and exterior scheme was conceived as a **Gesamtkunstwerk**.

He then became inspired by English Domestic Revival architecture and the swirling **Art Nouveau** designs of **Victor Horta**, and between 1894 and 1897 designed the Castel Béranger apartment building in Paris, which was especially influenced by the Gothic Revival and Henry II styles. Guimard was the main exponent of French Art Nouveau and his Castel Béranger can be viewed as a manifesto of the style, which in France was often referred to as "Style Guimard".

From 1899 to 1901, Guimard undertook many architectural commissions including the Maison Coilliot in Lille (1898–1900), the Castel Henriette in Sèvres (1899–1900) and the Humbert de Romans concert hall (1898–1900), for which he designed site-specific furniture and fittings that embodied a remarkable sense of organicism.

▲ Balcony railing for the Fonderies de Saint-Dizier, c. 1909

His most famous designs, however, were the cast-iron entrances to the

▲ Tea table, c. 1903

Paris Métro (1903), which exemplified the swirling exuberance of Art
Nouveau. In 1920, Guimard created his first pieces of standardized furniture
for serial production and a year later developed housing for workers and an
apartment building with standardized elements.

With the ascendancy of **Art Deco** in the 1920s, Guimard, like many other designers associated with Art Nouveau, fell out of fashion and faded into rela-
tive obscurity. In 1938, he emigrated to the United States and settled in New
York.

▲ Detail of a chair,
c. 1902

**Werkstätten
Hagenauer**
1898–1956
Vienna

Carl Hagenauer initially served a goldsmith's apprenticeship at Würbel &
Czokally in Vienna and later worked as a journeyman goldsmith for Bernauer
Samu in Pressberg (now Bratislava, Slovenia). Around the turn of the cen-
tury the demand for decorative metalwork escalated and by 1898 Vienna had
over two hundred and thirty workshops and factories producing metalware.
Against this background of prosperity, Carl Hagenauer founded his own
Viennese workshop, the Werkstätten Hagenauer, for the production of
metalwork, which he exported throughout the world. In 1919 his son Karl,
who had studied under **Josef Hoffmann** at the Kunstgewerbeschule in
Vienna, began designing objects for domestic use in a wide range of materials including, silver, copper, ivory, wood and enamel. Karl's designs were influenced by the work of the **Wiener Werkstätte** and were consciously distanced from **Jugendstil**. During the 1920s, Werkstätten Hagenauer's wares
became increasingly influenced by **Art Deco**, which was emerging in France
at the time. The workshop also produced metalware designed by Josef Hoffmann, **Otto Prutscher** and E. J. Meckel. On the death of Carl Hagenauer in
1928, his children, Karl, Franz and Grete, took over the running of the company and subsequently established a furniture workshop and retail shops in
Salzburg and Vienna. Four years later, the French designers, Jacques Adnet
(1900–1984) and René Coulon (b. 1907), designed furniture incorporating
tempered glass manufactured by Werkstätten Hagenauer, but the workshops eventually closed down in 1956.

▲ **Heal & Sons**,
Limed oak wall
clock, c. 1905

Heal & Sons was established on Tottenham Court Road, London in 1810, and subsequently became famous for their bedroom fittings and reproduction Queen Anne furniture. Ambrose Heal joined the family firm in 1893, after having studied at the Slade School of Fine Art and served a cabinet-making apprenticeship with Messrs Plucknett of Warwick. From 1886, he began designing furniture for Heal & Sons, which although in the Arts & Crafts style was more utilitarian than that produced by **Liberty & Co**. His first designs, illustrated in Heal & Co.'s *Plain Oak Furniture* catalogue from 1898, were simple and unpretentious and were highly praised by the editor of *The Studio*, Gleeson White. Like their main competitors, Liberty & Co., the company also began to retail "artistic textiles" and exhibited at the Arts & Crafts Exhibition Society (from 1899) and at the 1900 Paris "Exposition Universelle et Internationale". Ambrose Heal was an active member of the Art Workers' Guild and in 1913 became the chairman of Heal & Sons. Two years later, he assisted in the founding of the DIA (Design & Industries Association) – an organization that promoted collaboration between designers and manufacturers. His own furniture designs became increasingly rational and by the 1930s, exemplified British Modernism. In 1939, Heal stopped designing furniture owing to wartime restrictions and was appointed to the Faculty of Royal Designers for Industry.

Ambrose Heal
1872 *London*
1959 *Penn/Dorset*

► Cover for Kurt Tucholsky's *Deutschland über alles*, 1929

John Heartfield
1891
Schmargendorf/Berlin
1968 *Berlin*

Born Helmut Herzfeld, Heartfield studied at the Kunstgewerbeschule, Munich, from 1908 to 1911 and at the Kunst- und Handwerkerschule, Berlin, from 1913 to 1914. Two years later, Heartfield anglicized his name in protest to the anti-British campaign that was being waged in Germany. In 1917, together with his brother, he established a publishing house known as Malik-Verlag and designed graphics for their publications. He became a founding member of the Dada group in Berlin in 1918 and, being highly politicized, joined the German Communist Party in 1918, producing illustrations and writing articles for its magazine, *AIZ* (*Arbeiter-Illustrierte-Zeitung*) 1924–1933. For his work at both Malik-Verlag and *AIZ*, Heartfield adopted an experimental approach to typography and frequently used photomontages to create powerful visual statements, which during the 1930s were often highly critical of the Nazi party. As a result of his political sentiments, he was forced into exile, first to Prague in 1933 and then to England in 1939. While in England, Heartfield designed covers for Penguin Books and contributed to *Picture Post* as well as the pocket-sized magazine *Lilliput*. In 1950, he returned to Germany, settling in Leipzig, and later worked in East Berlin as a stage designer for the playwright Bertolt Brecht among others.

Jean Heiberg first studied painting in Munich and then, from 1908 to 1910 trained under Henri Matisse (1869–1954) in Paris. He stayed in Paris until 1929 and while there became a follower of the Fauves, receiving considerable recognition for his own paintings and sculptures. On his return to Oslo, he took up a professorship at the Statens Handverks-og Kunstindustiskole. Shortly afterwards, he was commissioned to model the casing of a newly developed bakelite telephone, which was intended to replace metal models. The internal layout of this early plastic telephone had been designed by the Norwegian engineer, Johan Christian Bjerknes, for a joint venture of the Norsk Elektrisk Bureau and the Swedish telephone manufacturing company, **L. M. Ericsson**. Heiberg's resulting housing for the *DHB 1001* bakelite telephone (1930) was more sculptural than earlier models and set the standard for telephone design up to the 1950s. The *DHB 1001* was produced from 1932 and was widely distributed throughout Scandinavia, Britain, Italy, Greece and Turkey. The telephone was also manufactured under licence by Siemens, in England, France and America. This landmark design inspired **Henry Dreyfuss'** moulded phenolic plastic telephone, which was developed in 1937 for Bell Laboratories.

Jean Heiberg
1884 *Oslo*
1976 *Oslo*

▼ *DHB 1001* bakelite telephone for Siemens, 1932

Poul Henningsen trained as an architect at the Tekniske Skole, Copenhagen, from 1911 to 1914 and at the Polyteknisk Laeranstalt from 1914 to 1917. After his formal studies, he took up journalism for eight years, first working as an art critic for the magazine *Klingen* and then writing for the newspapers, *Politiken* and *Extra Bladet*. From 1924, he began to design lighting for Louis Poulsen and the first lamp from his *PH* series was exhibited to great acclaim at the 1925 Paris "Exposition Internationale des Arts Décoratifs et Industriels Modernes". The *PH* lamps were the result of ten years scientific study and were designed to eliminate glare and produce soft warm light. From the mid-1920s until the outbreak of the Second World War, *PH* lamps were exported to Central Europe, North and South America, Africa and Asia. The *PH* lamps were especially popular in Germany and were featured in *Das Neue Frankfurt* magazine, which praised the technical excellence of their three-shade system. During this period, Henningsen also designed furniture for the Copenhagen-based firms, Zeiss and Goertz. From 1926 to 1928, he was editor of the magazine *Kritisk Revy*, after which he founded and edited his own short-lived review, *PH-Revy*. In 1929, he began writing for music hall revues and subsequently became a film writer. From 1935 to 1939, he also contributed to the anti-Nazi journal *Kulturkampen* and in 1941 undertook architectural projects in Tivoli. From 1943 to 1945, Henningsen lived as a political exile in Sweden, and on his return to Copenhagen after the Second World War worked as a correspondent and editor for a number of journals including the *Social-Demokraten*. Henningsen denounced the artistic pretensions of Scandinavian design and advocated a more utilitarian approach that would bring **Good Design** to the masses. Unlike the majority of **Modern Movement** designers, however, Henningsen regarded traditional forms and materials as eminently suitable for the manufacture of more democratic products. On his death in 1967, he left over one hundred lighting designs, some of which have been issued posthumously.

Poul Henningsen
1894 *Ordrup, Denmark*
1967 *Copenhagen*

◄ *PH Artichoke* hanging lamp for Louis Poulsen, 1957

▼ *PH4-3* table lamp for Louis Poulsen, 1966

Frederick Henri Kay Henrion

1914 *Nuremberg*
1990 *London*

▼ *Stub it Out* poster for The British Ministry of Information, 1943

Frederick Kay Henrion initially trained as a textile designer in Paris before studying graphic design at the École Paul Colin from 1934 to 1936. For the next three years he worked in London and Paris, assisting in the design of the Glasgow "British Empire Exhibition" (1938) and the New York World's Fair (1939–1940). From 1943 to 1945, he was design consultant to the Exhibition Division of the British Ministry of Information and was responsible for all Ministry of Agriculture exhibitions. He also designed visually bold wartime propaganda posters that were influenced by **Surrealism**. At the end of the war he was appointed consultant designer to the US Embassy in Britain and to the US Office of War Information. Henrion established his own design office, Henrion Design Associates, in 1951 and subsequently designed graphics, posters and corporate logos for his many corporate clients, including the General Post Office, BOAC, Council of Industrial Design, Blue Circle Cement, London Transport, KLM and BEA. Henrion also designed the Agriculture and Natural History pavilions for the 1951 "Festival of Britain". His work was the subject of a one-man show entitled "Designing Things and Symbols", held at the ICA (Institute of Contemporary Art), London, in 1961. He then became president of the SIA (Society of Industrial Arts) for two years and also participated in Expo '67 in Montreal. As a pioneer of **corporate identity** design, Henrion wrote a book with Alan Parkin entitled *Design Coordination and Corporate Image* (1969).

René Herbst trained as an architect in London and Frankfurt from 1908. He eventually settled in Paris and from 1919 started to practise as an architect there. Herbst adopted a Functionalist approach to design and became one of the leading French designers during the inter-war years. He designed exhibition stands for the 1925 Paris "Exposition Internationale des Arts Décoratifs et Industriels Modernes", and around this time designed Modernist interiors and furniture. From 1927 he began designing tubular metal seating, some of which incorporated elasticated strapping manufactured by his own firm, Établissements René Herbst. A catalogue showing these chairs was issued in 1933 and included Herbst's famous *Chaise Sandows* (1928–1929). This "elasticated" chair was first used in Herbst's interior scheme for M. Peissi's apartment (1929) and was subsequently widely exhibited, most notably at the 1934 Brussels "Exposition des Arts Décoratifs". From 1929 to 1932, Herbst contributed four articles on lighting to the magazine *Lux* in which he suggested that readers should seek the expertise of lighting engineers. At the same time, he designed several lights, which were retailed by Cottin, including a ceiling fixture that was displayed at the 1928 Salon d'Automne. In 1930 he became a founding member of the UAM (Union des Artistes Modernes), which was set up to counter the decorative excesses of the then popular **Art Deco** style. Herbst was responsible for the design of the UAM exhibitions, which were held from 1930 and after being appointed the Union's president in 1945, was highly involved in the organization of its design exhibition "Les Formes Utiles" that was staged in Paris from 1949 to 1950. As one of the most prominent French Modernists, Herbst described the members of the UAM, including himself, as "the puritans of art" and rejected ornamentation in favour of an industrial aesthetic.

René Herbst
1891 *Paris*
1982 *Paris*

▼ *Chaise Sandows* for Établissements Réne Herbst, 1928–1929

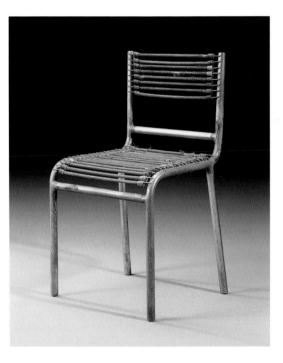

Herman Miller

Founded 1923
Zeeland, Michigan

▲ Page from the
Herman Miller
Collection catalogue,
1952 – showing
Charles & Ray
Eames' *ESU* range in
an office
environment

▶ **George Nelson**,
Action Office I for
Herman Miller,
1964–1965

The origins of the Herman Miller company can be traced back to 1847, when a group of Dutch immigrants settled in Zeeland, Michigan. The first enterprise they set up, a canning factory, was unsuccessful, and in 1905 it was decided that the premises should be used to make furniture for the community. D. J. De Pree, a recent high school graduate, was hired to perform general office duties for this new venture. In 1923 De Pree and his father-in-law, Herman Miller, acquired the majority holding in the furniture manufacturing company, which was first named the Michigan Star Furniture Company and subsequently rechristened the Herman Miller Furniture Company. During this period, the American furniture industry was largely made up of small family-run businesses clustered around Grand Rapids, Michigan; Rockford, Illinois; Jamestown, New York; Chicago and New York City. The reproduction furniture produced by these firms, including Herman Miller, was strongly dictated by large store buyers who were constantly attempting to predict the next trend in period styles. Neither the buyers nor the majority

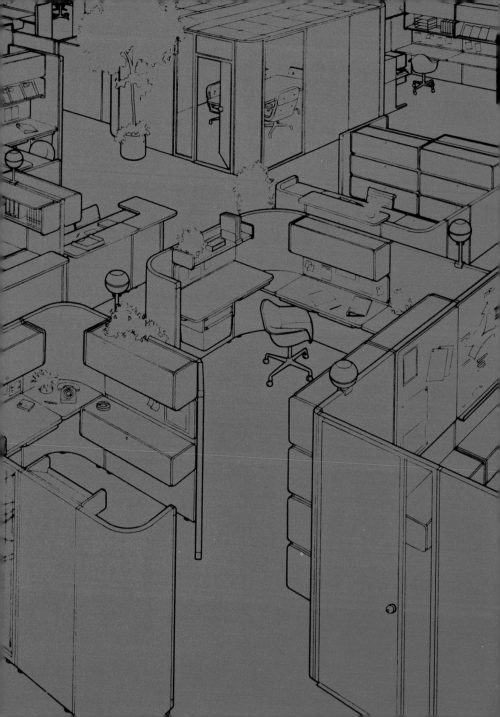

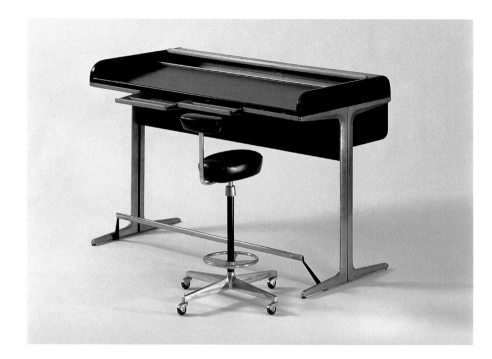

▲ George Nelson,
Action Office I
No. 6491 desk and
No. 64940 stool
for Herman Miller,
1964–1965

◄ Bill Stumpf,
Ethospace for
Herman Miller, 1984

of manufacturers were concerned with the way people lived, but only with what would sell. Against this background of fierce competition and the ever-changing demands of fashion, the stock market crashed in 1929 and Herman Miller faced financial crisis. A year later, De Pree met the designer **Gilbert Rohde,** who suggested producing a high quality range of modern furniture of the upmost simplicity, with all the value going into materials and construction rather than decorative surface treatment. This concept was a revelation to De Pree, who recognized not only the commercial potential but also the moral superiority of modern design. De Pree later identified three of Rhode's fundamental teachings that influenced the company's new direction: the designer's right to retain control of the production of his designs, the duty of the manufacturer to produce furniture "of the day" that would address and solve home furnishing problems by using the best available contemporary materials and, last but not least, truth to materials. The subsequent success of Rohde's range of modern furniture led Herman Miller to abandon the manufacture of reproduction furniture altogether in 1936, and by 1941 the company had opened a New York showroom to display its new

▼ **Robert Propst,**
Action Office II for
Herman Miller, 1968

designs. In 1946, two years after Rohde's death, in an effort to perpetuate the modern and moral ethos of the Herman Miller Furniture Company, De Pree appointed the architect, critic and inventor of the "storage-wall" concept, **George Nelson,** as design director. Nelson subsequently brought in other talented designers, including **Charles Eames**, **Isamu Noguchi** and **Alexander Girard**, to create modern furnishings for the company. Over the following years, Herman Miller led the furniture industry by producing designs that met De Pree's criteria for **Good Design** – "Durability, Unity, Integrity, Inevitability" – and revolutionized the way people lived and worked. These included Charles and Ray Eames' moulded plywood chairs (1945–1946) and plastic shell series of chairs (1948–1950) and George Nelson's *Comprehensive Storage System* (1959) and *Action Office I* (1964–1965). In 1968, **Robert Propst**'s *Action Office II* was launched and not only transformed the office landscape but, through its success, made Herman Miller the second largest furniture manufacturer in the world. The company has continued operating at the forefront of the contract furniture market and has produced a series of pioneering office chairs by **Bill Stumpf** and **Don Chadwick** – the *Ergon* (1976), the *Equa* (1984) and the *Aeron* (1992). Today, Herman Miller continues to flourish through its highly motivated workforce and its quest for design and manufacturing excellence.

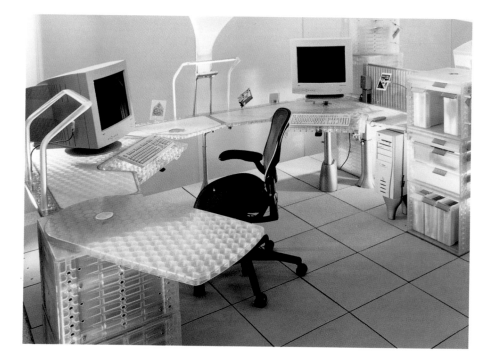

▲ **Ross Lovegrove &
Stephen Peart**,
Office system for
Herman Miller,
1995–1999

▶ Detail of the
office system

High-Tech

The High Tech style first emerged in architecture in the mid-1960s and was inspired by the geometric formalism of classical Modernism and the **Radical Design** proposals of **Buckminster Fuller**. The utilitarianism underlying the style countered the excesses of **Pop Design**. Pioneered by British architects such as **Norman Foster**, Richard Rogers (b. 1933) and Michael Hopkins (b. 1935), who incorporated unadorned industrial elements into their buildings, the High Tech style eventually found its way into mainstream interior design during the 1970s. Utilitarian equipment and fittings manufactured for factory and institutional use, such as trolleys, rubber flooring, clip-on lighting, galvanized zinc shelving and scaffolding poles were used in High Tech interiors, which often included primary colour schemes in homage to **De Stijl**. In America, exponents of High-Tech included Joseph Paul D'Urso and **Ward Bennett**, who worked with salvaged industrial materials. In 1978, Joan Kron and Susan Slesin published a book entitled *High-Tech – the industrial style and source book for the home*, but by this time the style was already waning and was superseded in the early 1980s by **Post-Modernism**. The promotion of industrial components through High Tech did, however, inspire British designers such as **Ron Arad** and **Tom Dixon** in the mid-1980s to create poetic "One-Off" designs from salvaged materials including scaffolding poles, car seats and manhole covers.

▲ **Michael Hopkins**, Hopkins House studio, 1979

Matthew Hilton studied furniture design at Kingston Polytechnic, London,
and subsequently worked for five years as an industrial designer for the
product design consultancy CAPA. In 1984, he established his own studio,
specializing in furniture and lighting. From 1986, he designed furniture for
SCP, London, including the *Antelope* table (1987) with polished aluminium
zoomorphic legs and the *Flipper* table (1988) with a base constructed of
three metal fins. In 1990, Hilton designed and produced a limited batch
edition of three cast aluminium tableware pieces with remarkably dynamic
lobster claw-like forms as well as the *Di-ordna* and *To-bor* bowls and the
Arclumis candle-holder. During the 1990s, he designed upholstered furniture
for SCP including the geometric *Club* chair (1991) and *Reading* chair (1995),
the softly curved and undulating *Balzac* chair (1991) and the *Orwell* sofa
(1996). Hilton's furniture and rugs have been produced by several European
manufacturers including Alterego, Nani Marquina, Mobles 114 and Santa &
Cole. His most important design to date is the *Wait* chair (1998) for
Authentics – a low-cost dining/desk chair with a single-form seat shell constructed of fully recyclable injection-moulded translucent polypropylene.

Matthew Hilton
1957 *Hastings/
East Sussex*

Hochschule für Gestaltung, Ulm

1953–1968
Ulm, Germany

The Hochschule für Gestaltung was founded in 1953 in Ulm, Germany, by **Otl Aicher** and Inge Scholl (b. 1917) with the aim of reviving the socially inspired teachings of the **Bauhaus**, which had been curtailed when the National Socialists came to power in the 1930s. The idea of establishing a new design school arose through a meeting with **Max Bill** in 1947, who drew up plans for the institution's buildings and became its first director. Aicher and Scholl married in 1952, and a year later the design courses began with a number of ex-Bauhaus staff members including **Ludwig Mies van der Rohe**, **Josef Albers** and **Johannes Itten** becoming visiting teachers. When **Hans Gugelot** became director of the product design department in 1954 he began advocating **Functionalism**. The new school buildings were opened in 1955 and the following year the Argentinian design theorist, Tomás Maldonado (b. 1922) took over the directorship from Bill. Although the school attempted to humanize design methodology by running courses on semiotics, anthropology, contextual study, games theory and psychology, it is best remembered for its development of a Functionalist and systematic approach to the design process that relied heavily on engineering. The resulting industrial aesthetic was highly influential to later German product design and was perhaps best expressed in the work of Hans Gugelot and **Dieter Rams** for **Braun**. In 1968, a year after Maldonado who called for "mass production, mass communication, mass participation" had left the HfG, the local authorities withdrew funding for the institution, declaring that its agenda had become too radical. Shortly afterwards, the teaching staff decided to close the school, which had often been referred to as "the new Bauhaus". While some staff members at the HfG had endeavoured to approach the design of products systematically and scientifically, others had ventured to free the design process from dogmatic Functionalism. It was this fundamental contradiction that had thwarted not only the success of the Hochschule für Gestaltung but also that of its spiritual antecedent, the Bauhaus.

▲ *Uppercase 5 edited by Theo Crosby, 1961 – a selection of essays by Tomás Maldonado outlining the Hochschule für Gestaltung's rational approach to design*

▲ *Exporter 2* portable radio for
Braun, 1956

Josef Hoffmann began his architecture studies in 1887 at the Höhere Staats-gewerbeschule in Brünn and continued his training under **Otto Wagner** and Carl von Hasenauer at the Akademie der Bildenden Künste in Vienna. After graduating in 1895, he became a founding member of the artistic group, Siebener-Club (Club of Seven) and travelled with **Josef Maria Olbrich** to Italy, having been awarded a Prix de Rome. In 1897, he worked in Otto Wagner's architectural practice and became a co-founder of the Wiener **Secession** – a reformist group of artists and architects that was established to counter the then prevalent **Art Nouveau** style. From 1899 to 1936, Hoffmann taught architecture and design at the Kunstgewerbeschule in Vienna. In 1900 he travelled to Britain, and while there met members of the British **Arts & Crafts Movement**, including **Charles Robert Ashbee** and **Charles Rennie Mackintosh** whom he invited to design installations for the VIII Secessionist Exhibition held in Vienna the same year. Hoffmann's work like that of other Secessionist designers was subsequently much influenced by the work of the **Glasgow School**, especially Mackintosh. In 1903, Hoffmann and **Koloman Moser** established the **Wiener Werkstätte** with the financial backing of the wealthy banker, Fritz Wärndorfer (1869–1939), who was the main

Josef Hoffmann
1870 *Pirnitz, Moravia*
1956 *Vienna*

▲ Brass fruit-cup for the Wiener Werkstätte, 1925

◄ Glass vase for Loetz Witwe, 1911–1912

patron of the Vienna Secession. Hoffmann was the artistic director and one of the most prolific designers of this co-operative workshop, which was inspired by Ashbee's **Guild of Handicraft**. Many of Hoffmann's metalwork designs for the Wiener Werkstätte were architectural in nature, while other more commercial and less expensive metalwares incorporated a grid-like pattern that became known as the Hoffmann-Quadratl. This type of pierced decoration was used on many of his chair designs, including the famous *Sitzmaschine* (c. 1908), which was manufactured by **Jacob & Josef Kohn**. Hoffmann also designed glassware for the J. L. Lobmeyr and **Loetz** Witwe glassworks, in which coloured overlays were cut and etched to reveal white underlays. Apart from his product design work, Hoffmann also ran a highly successful architectural office in Vienna and executed wholly integrated **Gesamtkunstwerk** schemes, such as the Purkersdorf Sanatorium (1904), the Palais Stoclet, Brussels (1905–1911) and the Cabaret Fledermaus (1907). In 1905, Hoffmann left the Vienna Secession and established the Kunstschau with the painter Gustav Klimt (1862–1918). Two years later, Hoffmann became a founding member of the **Deutscher Werkbund** and from 1912 to 1920 was chairman of the Österreichischer Werkbund. Hoffmann took part in many international exhibitions including the 1914 Cologne "Deutsche Werkbund-Ausstellung", the 1925 Paris "Exposition Internationale des Arts Décoratifs et Industriels Modernes" and the 1930 Stockholm "Stockholmsutstäliningen". While his approach to architecture and design was much influenced by the British Arts & Crafts Movement, Hoffmann's work was strongly anti-historicist. The characteristic and innovative pared-down rectilinear forms he evolved had a marked influence on the geometric vocabulary of form adopted by the **Modern Movement**.

▼ Bar room of the Cabaret Fledermaus in Vienna, 1907

▶ *Model No. 670 Sitzmaschine* for J.&J. Kohn, c. 1908

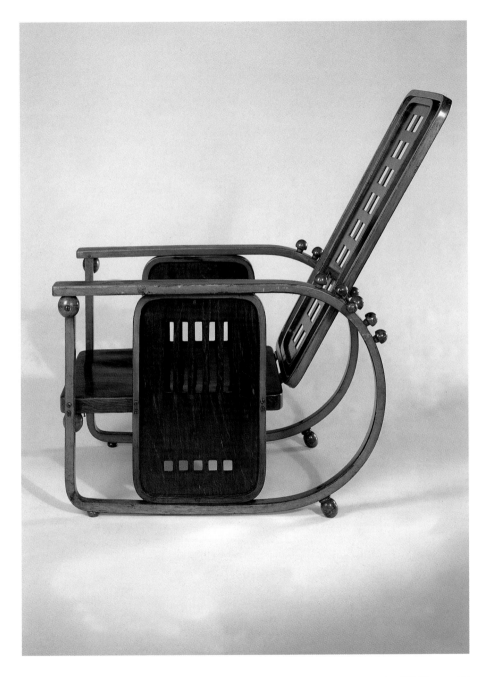

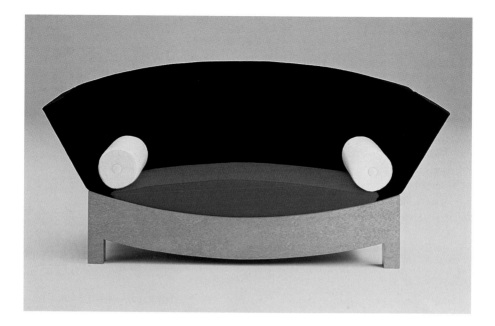

Hans Hollein
b. 1934 *Vienna*

▲ *Model No. D90 Mitzi* sofa for Poltronova, 1981

Hans Hollein studied at the Kunstgewerbeschule and the Akademie der Bildenden Künste, Vienna, graduating in 1956. He subsequently attended the Illinois Institute of Technology, Chicago, and the University of California, Berkeley, obtaining a masters degree in architecture in 1960. Hollein established his own practice in Vienna in 1964 and initially gained recognition for his exhibition designs and retail conversions, such as the Retti Candle Shop (1964–1965) and the Schullin Jeweller's Shop (1973–1974) in Vienna – the entrance to the latter being through an apparent crack in the façade. Hollein's practice of contrasting eye-catching façades with their surroundings, as in the Richard Feigen Gallery, New York (1967–1969), led to his being compared with earlier Viennese architects, such as **Josef Hoffmann**, **Otto Wagner**, Oswald Haerdtl (1899–1959) and **Adolf Loos**. Between 1967 and 1976, Hollein taught at the Staatliche Kunstakademie, Düsseldorf, and since 1976 has been a professor at the Akademie der Bildenden Künste, Vienna. He also planned interiors for Siemens' administration building in Munich (1972–1973) and the headquarters of the Vienna Tourist Office (1976–1978), which he embellished with post-modern elements including **Kitsch** golden palms and classical columns. In the 1980s, Hollein designed several pieces of post-modern furniture, including the *Marilyn* sofa (1981) as well as metalware and ceramics for **Alessi** and Swid Powell among others.

Victor Horta studied at the Académie des Beaux-Arts in Ghent and in Brussels, and in 1881 joined the office of the Neo-Classical architect, Alphonse Balat. He was much inspired by the French Gothic Revivalist architect and scholar, Eugène-Emmanuel Viollet-le-Duc (1814–1879), who advocated the totally integrated design of buildings and interiors. Horta embraced this approach and for many of his building projects designed every detail from doors to furniture to light fixtures. By 1892, Horta had rejected historicism, his work on the Hotel Tassel (1892–1893) being an exquisite illustration of this stylistic departure with its organic ironwork balustrading, swirling mosaic flooring and whiplash wall decoration. This residence in Brussels was one of the first buildings in the **Art Nouveau** style and was also the first private residence to incorporate ironwork for both structural and decorative purposes. Its remarkable visual lightness and interesting spatial qualities were achieved through innovative planning and the use of slender ironwork supports. These stem-like elements branched out into naturalistic tendrils and led to the coining of the term "Horta Line". Other similar projects followed, such as the Maison Autrique (1893), the Maison Winssinger (1895–1896), and the Hotel Solvay (1895–1900) – a **Gesamtkunstwerk** project designed for Baron van Eetvelde. Apart from private residences, Horta also designed the Belgian Socialist Party's headquarters, the Maison du Peuple (1896–1899), which incorporated the first steel and glass façade in Brussels and the city's À l'Innovation department store (1901). For his later work, Horta experimented with state-of-the-art materials and adopted a more austere style, as demonstrated by his reinforced concrete Palais des Beaux-Arts (1922–1928). Horta was one of the greatest exponents of Art Nouveau and although he only ever designed objects for his own integrated schemes, his work was immensely influential.

Victor Horta
1861 *Ghent*
1947 *Ixelles/Brussels*

▼ Dining Room of the Hotel Solvay, 1895–1900

Vilmos Huszár

*1884 Budapest
1960 Hierden,
Netherlands*

In 1917, Vilmos Huszár co-founded **De Stijl** and the same year his stained-glass designs were included in a published essay on new painting by **Theo van Doesburg**. Between 1917 and 1921, Huszár designed covers for the *De Stijl* magazine and contributed a series of articles entitled "Aestheticische Beschouwingen" (Aesthetic Considerations). In 1918, Huszár and Pieter Jan Christophel Klaarhamer (1874–1954) co-designed the "Boys' Bedroom" for Cornelius Bruynzeel's house in Voorburg. His colour scheme for this project and other designs has led to speculation that it was Huszár who advised **Gerrit Rietveld** on the coloration of his famous *Red/Blue* chair (1918–1923). From around 1918, he devoted his energies almost completely to the design of furniture, textiles, stained glass and complete interior schemes. He designed several pieces of furniture in conjunction with Piet Zwart (1885–1977) and in 1923, having left De Stijl, participated with Rietveld in a fringe show alongside the "Greater Berlin Art Exhibition". Huszár's use of bold colour and dynamic interior compositions, which contrasted separate elements while achieving a sense of unified or "total" space, were extremely influential to the De Stijl movement.

▲ Woven wool carpet, c. 1925

**Independent
Group**
Founded 1952
London

Formed in 1952, the Independent Group held regular meetings at the ICA (Institute of Contemporary Art) in London to examine the technical achievements of American industrial production and the emergence of popular consumerist culture. The group, which included Richard Hamilton (b. 1922), Eduardo Paolozzi (b. 1924), Reyner Banham (1922–1988) and **Peter and Alison Smithson**, rejected Modernist philosophy and drew inspiration from "low" rather than "high" art. As protagonists of popular culture, certain members of the Independent Group championed the idea of built-in obsolescence, which was naively seen as beneficial for the economic growth it offered through increased production. Significantly, in his collage of 1956 entitled *Just what is it that makes today's homes so different, so appealing?*, Hamilton incorporated an image of a lollypop bearing the word "POP". This was possibly the first time that a word used in a work of art became the label for a new art movement. Certainly, this landmark work heralded a new direction not only in art but also in design. Hamilton identified the characteristics of Pop as – "Popular (designed for a mass audience), Transient (short-term solution), Expendable (easily forgotten), Low Cost, Mass Produced, Young (aimed at youth), Witty, Sexy, Gimmicky, Glamorous, Big Business". By defining Pop and raising the status of popular culture to a subject of serious academic interest, the Independent Group laid the theoretical foundations upon which **Pop Design** was to flourish in the 1960s.

► Photograph of the New Bauhaus building in Chicago, 1937

In 1933, the Staatliches **Bauhaus** in Dessau was closed by the Nazi regime, who declared it a subversive institution, forcing many of its teaching staff to emigrate so as to escape persecution. Having first settled in London, **László Moholy-Nagy** moved to Chicago in 1937, on the invitation of the Association of Arts and Industries, to organize a new design school that would invigorate the cultural and economic life of that city. Based on the teaching principles of its German antecedent, the "New Bauhaus" as it was dubbed by Moholy-Nagy, attempted to promote a culture of "total education". The new school, however, was short-lived, the Association withdrawing its funding in the last few months of 1938, because they found its programme too experimental. The following year, Moholy-Nagy re-opened the institution with the private backing of Walter Papecke, the chairman of the Container Corporation of America, and it was rechristened the Chicago School of Design. In 1944 the school acquired its current title, the Institute of Design, and after the death of Moholy-Nagy in 1946 it became a department of the Armour Institute, which was itself renamed the Illinois Institute of Technology. That same year, the Russian émigré designer **Serge Chermayeff** succeeded Moholy-Nagy as director of the school. From its earliest beginnings, the Institute of Design approached design teaching from an experimental standpoint and the original curriculum included not only design studies but also courses in psychology and literature. Today, the Institute of Design remains dedicated to "pushing the boundaries of design" and specializes in the application of new technologies within the design process.

Institute
of Design,
Chicago

Founded 1944
Chicago

International
Style

The term International Style was first coined in 1931 by Alfred H. Barr Jr., the director of the **Museum of Modern Art, New York,** for the title of a catalogue, *International Style: Architecture Since 1922*, which accompanied Henry-Russell Hitchcock's and **Philip Johnson**'s landmark exhibition of 1932. In the work of Modernists such as **Le Corbusier, Jacobus Johannes Pieter Oud, Walter Gropius** and **Ludwig Mies van der Rohe,** Barr identified a universal style that transcended national borders – the like of which had not been seen in Western art and architecture since the Middle Ages, when the so-called International Gothic Style had flourished across Europe. The new 20th-century movement was named accordingly in tribute to this earlier precedent.

The term International Style referred specifically to the work of **Modern Movement** architects and designers, who married function and technology with a geometric vocabulary of form to produce a pared-down modern aesthetic. Although it is sometimes used to describe early Modernism (c. 1900 to 1933) and the work of designers such as **Adolf Loos** and J. J. P. Oud, it is now generally associated with the less utilitarian form of Modernism that emerged after the closure of the **Bauhaus** in 1933. The term also refers to the work of Le Corbusier and his followers, who during the late 1920s and 1930s promoted a more stylish and less austere version of Modernism. Perhaps the greatest exponents of the International Style, however, were Ludwig Mies van der Rohe and Walter Gropius, who having emigrated to the United States, tirelessly attempted to "internationalize" the Modern

◄ **Le Corbusier, Pierre Jeanneret and Charlotte Perriand,** Dining room exhibited at the Salon des Artistes Décorateurs in Paris, 1928

▲ Le Corbusier,
Pierre Jeanneret and
Charlotte Perriand,
*Model No. B301
Basculant* chair for
Thonet, c. 1928

▶ Le Corbusier,
Library in the Church
House at Ville
d'Avray, 1928–1929

Movement not only through their architectural commissions and exhibitions but through their high profile teaching positions in America during the post-war years. Many advocates of the International Style adopted the Functionalist aesthetic of the Modern Movement for purely stylistic reasons. Others, however, developed an aesthetic purity so as to promote a greater universalism in architecture and design. Later post-war designers – especially in America – such as Florence **Knoll**, **Charles Eames** and **George Nelson** married this modern and democratic approach to design with methods of industrial mass-production so as to create products that fulfilled all the criteria of **Good Design**.

During the 1920s and 1930s, International Style in architecture and interior design was characterized by geometric formalism, the use of industrial materials such as steel and glass and a widespread preference for white rendering. Later, some architects and designers, including **Eero Saarinen** and Charles Eames, sought to humanize the International Style through the adoption of sculptural forms and the contrasting of geometric and organic shapes, while Kenzo Tange (b. 1913) and others took International Style to its logical conclusion in the creation of Brutalism, an architectural style that employs dehumanizing materials and surfaces treatments such as exposed rough-cast concrete and rigid geometry.

◄ Jacobus Johannes Pieter Oud, *Giso 405* table lamp for Gispen, 1928

▼ Le Corbusier, Pierre Jeanneret and Charlotte Perriand, *Model No. B306* chaise longue for Thonet, 1928 (reissued by Cassina)

Although it appeared in the late 1970s and 1980s that the emergence of Post-Modernism had tolled the death knell of the International Style, by the late 1980s and 1990s architects such as **Norman Foster** and Richard Rogers (b. 1933) were winning acclaim for their highly engineered buildings, which bore the unmistakable characteristics of International Style – power, elegance and clarity.

In recent years, there has also been a return to a rational aesthetic within product and furniture design, as manufacturers seek global solutions that, like International Style, are trans-cultural. The term International Style can therefore refer to a very specific period and type of Modernism, while also alluding to the aesthetics resulting from a Functionalist approach to design, the ancestry of which can be traced back to the earliest beginnings of the Modern Movement.

Massimo Iosa Ghini trained in Florence before studying architecture at the Politecnico di Milano. In 1981, he became a member of the Zak-Art design group and started out creating "comic-like" illustrations for the *Per Lui* magazine and the music press in the United States. While working for Swatch, Solvay and Centro Moda Firenze, Ghini also became well-known for his illustrations for children's comics. From 1982, he began designing interiors for nightclubs and worked on various projects for videos and magazines. Two years later, he began to collaborate with the firm, AGO, and soon after became a consultant to the RAI television station, designing graphics and sets for television productions and art-house films. In 1986, Ghini's furniture designs were included in **Memphis'** *12 New* collection. He then designed his *Dinamic* furniture collection (1987) for Moroso and his *Juliette* chair (1987) and *Bertrand* sideboard (1987), which were less colourful and exuberant than work by other designers associated with the group. Designs such as these were inspired by American styling from the 1950s. In 1983 Iosa Ghini, together with other designers who shared his interest in **Streamlining**, including **Stefano Giovannoni** and Pierangelo Caramia (b. 1957), founded the Bolidismo movement. He also incorporated retro-1950s forms in his designs for the Bolidio discotheque (1988) in New York. In 1988, Iosa Ghini created a temporary installation for the square at the Georges Pompidou Centre. He has also produced designs for Fiam, BRF, Stilnovo and Bieffeplast among others.

Massimo Iosa Ghini
b. 1959 *Bologna*

▼ *Jo-Jo* tables from the *Tran Tran* Collection for BRF, 1993

Paul Iribe

1883 Angoulême, France
1935 Roquebrune/Cap
Martin, France

Born Paul Iribarne Garay, Iribe began his career as a caricaturist for magazines and journals such as *Le Rire*, *Le Cri de Paris* and *L'Assiette au beurre*. He founded his own journal, *Le Témoin (The Witness)*, in 1908 and also illustrated a limited-edition portfolio, *Les Robes de Paul Poiret*, for the couturier Paul Poiret, who was highly influential within Paris circles and revolutionized fashion illustration. Iribe subsequently established his own studio, and between 1908 and 1914 collaborated with the designer **Pierre Legrain**. While in Paris, Iribe designed exquisite textiles, wallpapers and jewellery, usually bearing his trademark, the floral motif that became known as the "rose Iribe" and was widely copied. He also designed **Art Deco** furniture and *objets d'art* that incorporated luxury materials such as shagreen, rosewood and ebony. His most important interior commission was for the apartment of the couturier Jacques Doucet at 46, Avenue du Bois, Paris, which he designed in a sumptuous and luxurious style with the assistance of Legrain. For this project, executed around 1912, Iribe designed a series of *fauteuils-gondole* and a mahogany, shagreen and ebony commode that was carved

▼ Sharkskin and
ebony cabinet,
c. 1913–1914

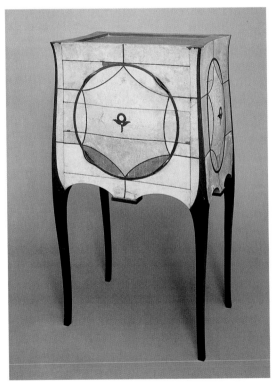

with neo-classical style garlands of flowers and inlaid with sprays of floral motifs. Working in the French *ébéniste-décorateur* tradition, Iribe's interior schemes verged on the theatrical and so it is not surprising that in 1914 he moved to the United States and settled in Hollywood. Here, he created lavish film sets for Cecil B. De Mille among others and, as a strong critic of industrialism, co-wrote an Anti-Modernist manifesto in 1926. He returned to France in 1930 and worked as an illustrator of books and periodicals. He also designed an emblem for the Lanvin fashion house and costume jewellery for Coco Chanel and in 1935, the year of his death, he established *Le Mot* magazine.

Maija Isola studied painting at the Taideteollinen Korkeakoulu (Central School of Industrial Arts) in Helsinki from 1946 to 1949. Then, for eleven years she was principal designer for the Finnish textile firm, Printex, which had been established by Vilho Ratio and was under the artistic directorship of Armi Ratia (1912–1979). Isola created numerous printed textiles for interior use that were produced by Printex. From 1951, she also did designs for Printex's sister company, Marimekko, which had been founded with the intention of promoting the use of Printex textiles in fashion and interior design. Her designs for dress and furnishing fabrics for this newly established company, as well as her textiles for Printex, were displayed at the Brussel's World Fair in 1958. Isola's earliest designs were inspired by African art and in the mid-1950s, she produced textiles decorated with botanical motifs. She also designed fabrics influenced by Slovakian folk art in the late 1950s and by traditional Karelian peasant motifs in the late 1960s and early 1970s. Many of her silk-screened textiles were translations of her artwork. In the mid-1960s, she produced her most famous range of printed cotton textiles, which incorporated large-scale geometric patterns that were printed in

Maija Isola
b. 1927 *Riihimäki, Finland*

▼ *Kaiva* textile for Marimekko, c. 1964

strong flat colours. These bold designs such as *Kaivo* (c. 1964), *Melooni* (1963) and *Cock and Hen* (1965) reflected contemporary artistic trends, most notably the influence of Colour Field painters in America. Isola's fabrics from this range had a strong graphic quality and came to epitomize not only Marimekko textiles but also a new direction in Finnish design. She received ID awards in 1965 and 1968, and until recently remained, together with Fujiwo Ishimoto (b. 1941), one of the few in-house designers working at Marimekko. Isola's colour saturated and elemental patterned fabrics have been exhibited widely in Europe, America and Australia and have had a powerful influence on contemporary textile design.

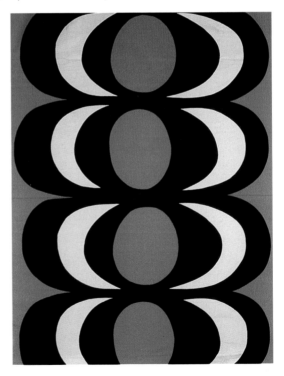

Arata Isozaki
b. 1931 *Kyushu, Japan*

Arata Isozaki studied under the Brutalist architect Kenzo Tange (b. 1913) at the University of Tokyo, graduating in 1954. For the next nine years he worked in Tange's architectural practice, before establishing his own office in 1963. Later, he collaborated with Tange on the architecture for Expo '70 in Osaka. Isozaki's other notable architectural projects include the Gunma Prefectural Museum of Modern Art, Takasaki (1971–1972), the Kitakyshu City Museum of Art (1972–1974), the Shukosha Building, Fukoa (1975), the Tokyo city hall (1986), the Museum of Contemporary Art, Los Angeles (1986) and the Guggenheim Museum in Soho, New York (1992). Like his architecture, Isozaki's product design work skillfully bridges Western and Eastern cultures. Inspired not only by Japanese art but also by post-modern classicism, his designs frequently make ironic reference to the **Modern Movement** and popular culture. These themes are often united in his furniture designs, such as the *Marilyn* chair for Sunar (1972) and the *Fuji* cabinets for Memphis (1981). For his wristwatch (1987) and jewellery (1985–1986) for Cleto Munari, Isozaki used bold geometric forms and quotations from past architectural styles, while the decoration of his *Streams* plate (1984) for Swid Powell incorporated traditional oriental motifs. In 1982 he designed furniture for Formica's "Surface and Ornament Design" competition, which was held for the purpose of exploring the potential of the company's newly developed material, Colorcore. For this project, Isozaki selected the colours of his materials randomly, by throwing dice and declared: "Anyone who complains about the combination of colours should protest against the God who presides over the chance of the thrown dice." Isozaki has been a visiting professor at numerous institutions, including the Rhode Island School of Design and Yale University and is author of the book *The Dismantling of Architecture*.

▼ *Fuji* cabinet for Memphis, 1981

Johannes Itten trained as a teacher near Bern from 1904 to 1908 and afterwards taught briefly at a primary school. From 1910 to 1912, he studied mathematics and natural sciences in Bern, and from 1913 trained as a painter under Adolf Hoelzel (1853–1934) at the Stuttgarter Akademie. In 1916, he had a one-man show at the gallery "Der Sturm" in Berlin and in the same year established his own school of art in Vienna. During this period, Itten became increasingly interested in Eastern philosophies – an enchantment that had much impact on his later teachings. Many of his Viennese students followed him when he moved to the Staatliches **Bauhaus** in Weimar to take up a teaching position there. In October 1919, he was appointed a master at the Weimar school and from October 1920, taught his own "Vorkurs" foundation course as well as several form theory classes. His teaching was highly influenced by his personal adoption of Mazdaznan beliefs. With his shaven head and flowing robes, Itten acted as part-teacher, part-mystic and converted many of the students to this extremist sect much to the dismay of other Bauhaus faculty members and the local German authorities. After 1921, he was given a less prominent role at the Bauhaus and was placed in charge of the metal, stained glass and mural paint workshops. His dominant influence remained however, and his alternative approach to art and design teaching prevailed during the school's final years in Weimar. His preoccupation with mysticism led to conflict with the school's director **Walter Gropius** and ultimately to his dismissal in 1923. He subsequently went to a Mazdaznan centre in Switzerland and in 1926 founded a private art school in Berlin, which became known as the "Itten School". Between 1932 and 1938, Itten directed a textile college in Krefeld and afterwards became director of the Zurich Arts & Crafts Museum and School. From 1950, he also helped to establish the Rietberg Museum of Non-European Art in Zurich, which he directed from 1952 to 1956. Itten's revolutionary theories on art and design teaching that were pioneered at the Bauhaus were highly influential and led to the widespread adoption of foundation courses.

Johannes Itten
1888 *Südern-Linden, Switzerland*
1967 *Zurich*

▼ **Johannes Itten & Friedl Dicker**, Text page from "Utopia, Dokument der Wirklichkeit", 1921

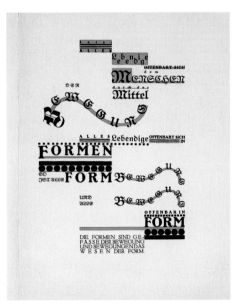

Arne Jacobsen

1902 *Copenhagen*
1971 *Copenhagen*

▲ *Model No. 3100*
Ant chairs for Fritz
Hansen, 1951–1952

Arne Jacobsen trained as a mason before studying at the Kongelige Danske Kunstakademi, Copenhagen, where he graduated in 1927. As a student, Jacobsen showed early promise, winning a silver medal for a chair that was exhibited at the 1925 Paris "Exposition Internationale des Arts Décoratifs". Between 1927 and 1929, Jacobsen worked in the architectural offices of Paul Holsøe, after which he established his own design office in Hellerup and began practising independently as an architect and interior designer. His early work was influenced by the achievements of **Le Corbusier** (whose "Pavillon de l'Esprit Nouveau" he had seen in Paris), **Gunnar Asplund** and other **Modern Movement** designers such as **Ludwig Mies van der Rohe**. Jacobsen was among the first to introduce Modernism to Danish design through his projects such as "House of the Future", which he co-designed with Flemming Lassen in 1929. His first important architectural commissions were for the Bella Vista housing project, Copenhagen (1930–1934) and the Functionalist Rothenborg House, Ordrup (1930), which was conceived as a **Gesamtkunstwerk**. For his best-known and most fully integrated works, the SAS Air Terminal and Royal Hotel, Copenhagen (1956–1960), Jacobsen designed every detail from textiles and sculptural furnishings, such as his

▲ *Model No. 3107 Series 7* chair
for Fritz Hansen, 1955

Swan and *Egg* chairs (1957–1958), to light fittings, ashtrays and cutlery. A decade earlier, Jacobsen had also worked as an industrial designer and achieved considerable success, most notably with his famous chair designs for the furniture manufacturer Fritz Hansen. His *Ant* chairs (1951–1952) and his *Series 7* chairs (1955) are still among the most commercially successful seating programmes ever produced. Jacobsen also designed lighting for Louis Poulsen, metalware for Stelton and Michelsen, textiles for August Millech, Grautex and C. Olesen, and bathroom fittings for I. P. Lunds. From 1956 until 1965, he was a professor emeritus at the Skolen for Brugskunst in Copenhagen. During the 1960s, Jacobsen's most important architectural scheme was St Catherine's College, Oxford, which, like his earlier work, was conceived as a wholly unified project and as such involved the design of site-specific furniture. Jacobsen combined sculptural and organic forms with the traditional attributes of Scandinavian design – material and structural integrity – to produce simple, elegant and functional designs that have a remarkable, timeless appeal.

Jacob Jacobsen

b. 1901 *Oslo*

Jacob Jacobsen was an engineer who initially trained in the textile manu-facturing industry in England and Switzerland. In 1937, he acquired the Scandinavian production rights to **George Carwardine**'s *Anglepoise* lamp (1934), which was manufactured in Britain by Terry & Son. That same year, Jacobsen designed a variation of this lamp, the *Luxo L-1*, which incorporated a similar auto-balancing system of springs. As a talented entrepreneur, Jacobsen successfully commercialized his re-designed lamp, which had a more refined connection between the shade and stand and a softer aes-thetic than Carwardine's. Within a few years, Jacobsen had also acquired the United States production rights to the *Angelpoise*'s constant tension prin-ciple and during the 1940s, had a virtual monopoly on the sale of task lamps in both Europe and America. His manufacturing company, Luxo continues to produce the classic *L-1* lamp, which is notable for the ease with which its arm and shade can be articulated. There are several variations of the design including one with an enlarged shade known as the Panoramic. The *Luxo L-1* has won numerous awards and is in the permanent collection of the **Museum of Modern Art, New York.** Although Jacobsen's lamp has been widely imi-tated over the years, its technical performance has rarely been equalled.

▼ *Luxo L-1* lamp
for Luxo, 1937

► **Pierre Jeanneret & Le Corbusier**, Living room in the Pavillon de l'Esprit Nouveau at the "Exposition Internationale des Arts Décoratifs" in Paris, 1925

Pierre Jeanneret, the cousin of Charles-Édouard Jeanneret, better known as **Le Corbusier**, trained as an architect in Geneva before moving to Paris in 1920. There he worked in the architectural practice of Perret Frères, which was well known for its bold use of concrete and functionalist forms. In 1922, he joined the studio of his cousin and subsequently co-designed a range of furniture with Le Corbusier and **Charlotte Perriand** including the *Basculant No. 301* chair (c. 1928), the *B306* chaise longue (1928) and the *Grand Confort LC2* club chair (1928). The trio also designed an apartment interior for the 1929 Paris Salon d'Automne, incorporating their own furniture. In the early 1920s, Jeanneret met the Purist artist Amédée Ozenfant (1886–1966) and subsequently produced many paintings that were influenced by Ozenfant's work. He became a member of the UAM (Union des Artistes Modernes) in 1930 and the furniture he co-designed with Le Corbusier and Charlotte Perriand was exhibited at the first UAM exhibition. His subsequent projects, such as the Villa Savoye, Poissy (1931), his Palace of the Soviets, Moscow (1932) and an urban planning scheme for Algiers, were shown at later UAM exhibitions. He patented the design of his birch *Scissor* chair (c. 1947), which incorporated an innovative steel bolt fitting and independently designed other pieces of furniture. During the post-war years, he worked with **Jean Prouvé** on the design of prefabricated housing and collaborated with Georges Blanchon on a town planning scheme for Puteaux. From 1952 onwards, Jeanneret assisted his famous cousin on several public architectural projects, including the Chandigarh government buildings in India.

Pierre Jeanneret
1896 *Geneva*
1967 *Geneva*

Charles A. Jencks

b. 1939 *Baltimore, Maryland*

Charles A. Jencks studied architecture and English literature at Harvard University and later continued his studies at London University, receiving a doctorate in architectural history in 1970. He taught at the Architectural Association, London from 1968 and at the University of California, Los Angeles from 1974. Jencks has also written several seminal books on Modernism and **Post-Modernism** in architecture including *Adhocism* (1972), *Modern Movements in Architecture* (1973), *The Language of Post-Modern Architecture* (1977) and *Post-Modern Classicism* (1980). A vehement critic of the **Modern Movement**, Jencks referred to the 1960s rectilinear high-rise buildings inspired by the architecture of **Le Corbusier** and **Ludwig Mies van der Rohe**, as "dumb boxes" and urged for a new architectural language that would counter the conservative banality of Modernism. He believed that buildings should be double-coded with symbolic references so as to appeal not only to the "interested minority who concern themselves with specific architectural problems" but also to the general public who were more concerned with "questions of comfort, traditional construction methods and their style of living". During the late 1970s and early 1980s, Jencks applied this post-modern approach to the design of objects such as his architectonic *Tea & Coffee Piazza* for Alessi (1983), which refers back to classical orders of architecture. In 1983, he designed furniture including the *Sun* chair for the Thematic House in London (1983), which was created in collaboration with the Terry Farrell Partnership.

▲ *Tea & Coffee Piazza* for Alessi, 1983

Georg Jensen was apprenticed to a gold and silversmith in Copenhagen, and from 1884 worked as a journeyman in that craft. From 1887 to 1892, he trained as a sculptor at the Kongelige Danske Kunstakademi. In 1898, Jensen started to produce sculptural ceramics for Mogens Ballin's workshop near Copenhagen and later, he worked at the Aluminia pottery and at the Bing & Grøndahl porcelain factory in Copenhagen before establishing his own silversmithing workshop in 1904. Jensen detested the prevalent taste for reproduction silver and so began designing Arts & Crafts style jewellery and silverware that was influenced by natural forms, such as berries, leaves and swirling tendrils. Jensen's most notable designs were the *Blossom* (c. 1904–1905) and *Grape* (c. 1918) ranges, which included a diversity of items from tableware to jewellery. In 1907, Jensen persuaded the artist, Johan Rohde (1856–1935) to produce designs for the workshop. When the company exhibited at the "Panama-Pacific International Exposition" held in San Francisco, the newspaper baron William Randolph Hearst was so impressed with the quality of the work on show that he purchased their complete inventory. The company subsequently became so commercially suc-

Georg Jensen

1866 *Raavad/Copenhagen*
1935 *Hellerup/Copenhagen*

▼ Silver fruit bowls from *Grape* range, 1918

▲ **Henning Koppel**, Covered silver fish
dish for Georg Jensen, 1954

cessful that in 1924 they opened a showroom on Fifth Avenue, New York. During the 1920s Jensen recruited other **avant-garde** designers, such as Harald Nielsen (1892–1977), Gundorph Albertus (1887–1970) and Sigvard Bernadotte (b. 1907) to produce designs for the firm. At the same time, Rohde introduced unornamented modern forms to the firm's line of silverware. Upon the death of Georg Jensen in 1935, the running of the company was taken over by his son Jørgen Jensen (1895–1966) who perpetuated their forward-looking ethos. After the Second World War, they began producing modern and supremely elegant handcrafted silverware designed by **Henning Koppel** and Tias Eckhoff (b. 1926), which exemplified the functional and aesthetic purity of Scandinavian Modernism. During the post-war years, the firm also began manufacturing stainless steel products, such as **Arne Jacobsen**'s flatware (1957) and glassware designed by **Finn Juhl**. Since the 1920s, the Georg Jensen name has been synonymous with Scandinavian Modernism and to this day, the company continues to produce beautiful metalware, jewellery and wristwatches of innovative forms and superlative craftsmanship, by designers such as **Nanna Ditzel**, Vivianna Torun Bülow-Hübe (b. 1927) and Jørgen Møller (b. 1920).

◄▼ Sigvard
Bernadotte,
Bernadotte silver
flatware, 1939

▼ Harald Nielsen,
Pyramid silver
flatware, 1926

▲ **Vivianna Torun Bülow-Hübe**, *Model
No. 326* stainless steel bangle
wristwatch for Georg Jensen, 1967

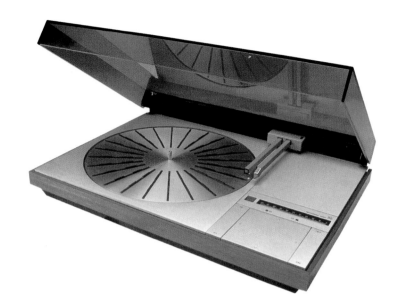

► *Beogram 4000*
record player for
Bang & Olufsen,
1972

On completing his training in industrial design at the Kunsthandvaerkerskolen (School of Arts & Crafts), Copenhagen in 1952, Jakob Jensen became
chief designer for the first Danish industrial design consultancy founded in
1949, Bernadotte & Bjørn. In 1959, he moved to the USA where he established a design office with Richard Latham (b. 1920) among others, and
taught at the University of Illinois, Chicago. On his return to Copenhagen
in 1961 Jensen founded his own industrial design office, and from 1964
began designing audio equipment for Bang & Olufsen. His sleek, high-
performance designs, such as the *Beogram 1200* hi-fi (1969), which was
awarded a Danish ID prize for its harmonious balance between "apparatus"
and "furniture", and the *Beogram 4000* record player (1972), which innovatively incorporated a tangential pick-up arm, set the aesthetic and technological standards for audio systems. Although best known for his pioneering
work for Bang & Olufsen, Jensen has also designed products for other
Danish manufacturers, including the *E76* pushbutton telephone (1972) for
Alcatel-Kirk, an office chair (1979) for Labofa, ultrasound scanning equipment (1982) for Bruel & Kjaer and a wristwatch (1983) for Max René. Jensen
has received numerous awards for his product designs including the
German Award "Die Gute Industrieform" and the IDSA prize.

Jakob Jensen
b. 1926 *Copenhagen*

Philip Johnson
b. 1906 *Cleveland, Ohio*

▼ **Philip Johnson &
Richard Kelly**, Floor
lamp for Edison
Price, c. 1953

Philip Johnson studied classics and philosophy at Harvard University, graduating in 1930. For two years, he directed the new department of architecture at the **Museum of Modern Art, New York**, during which time he curated the landmark 1932 exhibition "The **International Style**: Architecture since 1922" with Henry-Russell Hitchcock and wrote the accompanying catalogue. In 1940, Johnson returned to Harvard University to study architecture under **Marcel Breuer** and **Walter Gropius**, graduating in 1943. He then worked for four years as an independent architect before resuming his post at the Museum of Modern Art in 1946. In 1954, he left the museum to concentrate on his architectural career, becoming an associate architect on Mies van der Rohe's Seagram Building project in New York (1954–1958) and designing several residences in New Canaan, Connecticut, including the Glass House (1949), which was influenced by **Mies van der Rohe**'s Farnsworth House, the Hodgson House (1950) and the Wiley House (1953). The success of his Sculpture Garden at the Museum of Modern Art (1953) brought other public commissions including the Sheldon Memorial Art Gallery at the University of Nebraska (1963). Although he was a major proponent of the International Style, Johnson's projects revealed a strong Neo-Classical influence. During the late 1960s, his buildings became increasingly monumental, as the Kunsthalle, Bielefeld (1968) demonstrates, and in the 1970s he designed a series of glass skyscrapers including the IDS Center, Minneapolis (1973), Pennzoil Place, Houston (1970–1976) and the immensely influential AT&T Building, New York (1978–1983), with its post-modern broken pediment. Throughout his long and controversial career, from arch-modernist to post-modernist, Johnson's buildings and designs have been characterized by a strong sense of architectural identity and classical monumentality.

Jugendstil translates literally as "Youth Style" and refers to the branch of **Art Nouveau** that emerged in Germany during the 1890s. The term was derived from the title of the magazine *Jugend*, which was founded in Munich by Georg Hirth in 1896 and did much to popularize the new style. Inspired by the reforming ideas of John Ruskin (1819–1900) and **William Morris**, Jugendstil designers such as **Hermann Obrist**, **Richard Riemerschmid** and **August Endell** had more idealistic aims than other proponents of the Art Nouveau style in Europe. They not only sought to reform art but also advocated a return to a simpler and less commercial way of life. They possessed a youthful optimism and a reverence for nature that was expressed vigourously through their work. Like their contemporaries in Brussels and Paris, Jugendstil designers were inspired by the workings of the natural world as revealed through advances in scientific research and technology. The swirling vegetal motifs and whiplash forms employed by August Endell and Hermann Obrist, for example, were directly influenced by Karl Blossfeldt's (1865–1932) photographic studies of plant structures, which depicted remarkable spiral growth patterns, and by the botanical drawings of Ernst Haeckel (1834–1919). The new understanding of nature provided by detailed analyses such as these helped Jugendstil designers to capture a sense of dynamism and energetic organic growth in their work. In Germany, this new ahistorical style challenged the official imperial art policy emanating from Berlin, and regions wishing to express their sense of cultural autonomy, such as Dresden, Munich, Darmstadt, Weimar and Hagen, embraced Jugendstil wholeheartedly. Although this desire for artistic independence was a theme that united the emerging schools of Art Nouveau in other European cities such as Brussels, Nancy and even Glasgow, it was perhaps felt most strongly across Germany. Jugendstil designers came closer than any of their European contemporaries associated with Art Nouveau to bridging the

▼ **Otto Eckmann**,
Stoneware vase with
bronze mount,
c. 1900

gulf that existed between "artistic manufacture" and industrial production. Many workshops were established to produce their reformed designs, most notably the **Vereinigte Werkstätten für Kunst im Handwerk** (United Workshops for Artist Craftsmanship) in 1897 and the **Dresdener Werkstätten für Handwerkskunst** (Dresden Workshops for Artist Craftsmanship) in 1898. These ventures were set up with the objective of producing honest domestic wares through ethical manufacturing practices. The objects produced in Dresden were less elaborate and hence less expensive than those manufactured in Munich but were still beyond the means of the average householder. Richard Riemerschmid, chief designer at the Dresden workshop, adopted a simple vernacular style that was similar to the work of British Arts & Crafts designers such as **Charles Voysey**. Riemerschmid sought to reform design through standardization and his adoption of rational manufacturing practices at the Dresdener Werkstätten für Handwerkskunst was extremely influential, contributing to the founding of the **Deutscher Werkbund**. The Vereinigte Werkstätten für Kunst im Handwerk, which were founded in Munich by **Bruno Paul** and others, also played a key role in the promotion of Jugendstil. Paul designed boldly outlined cartoons and graphics for the journal *Simplicissimus,* which, like the magazine *Jugend*, popularized the new aesthetic. His linear style was shared by his fellow Munich designer

4. JAHRGANG · Nr. 12

JUGEND

MÜNCHNER
ILLUSTR.
WOCHENSCHRIFT
FÜR KUNST & LEBEN.

QUARTALPREIS 3 MARK.
PREIS DER NUMMER 30 PFG.

VERLAG VON G. HIRTH, MÜNCHEN.

Herausgeber: Georg Hirth. — Redakteur: Fritz v. Ostini. — Alle Rechte vorbehalten.

BEDRUCKTER BAUMWOLLENER SATIN
von SCHEURER LAUTH & Cᵒ in THANN ¹/Els.

Aus dem Hohenzollern - Kaufhaus
(H. HIRSCHWALD), BERLIN

Bernhard Pankok, whose Lange house in Tübingen (1902) was conceived as a **Gesamtkunstwerk**. The building was influenced by vernacularism, as were the Jugendstil interiors, which were startlingly modern in their simplicity. In Darmstadt, the Jugendstil cause was heavily patronized by Grand Duke Ernst Ludwig of Darmstadt-Hesse who instigated an exhibition entitled, "Ein Dokument Deutscher Kunst" (A Document of German Art) in 1901. The exhibition celebrated the artistic achievements of the **Darmstädter Künstlerkolonie** (Darmstadt Artists' Colony), which had been established with the Grand Duke's private funding in 1899. The Darmstädter Künstlerkolonie initially comprised eight buildings including **Josef Maria Olbrich**'s "House for Decorative Art" studio building and seven artists' residences built for members of the colony. The Darmstädter Künstlerkolonie was not only important for the new civic architectural style it promoted, which embraced Jugendstil, but also for its encouragement of the manufacture of art works. In Weimar, the promotion of Jugendstil was similarly prompted by both civic pride and economic necessity and also received ducal patronage.

▲ Covered bowl, c. 1900

◄ Printed sateen, Scheurer Lauth & Co., Thann

In 1860, the Grand Duke Karl Alexander of Saxony-Weimar privately funded the establishment of an art school in Weimar. He was succeeded by his grandson in 1901 who was persuaded by Count Harry Kessler to appoint the Belgian architect **Henry van de Velde** as art counsellor to his court. The belief that the local economy would be boosted through art education eventually led to van de Velde's being commissioned to design the Weimar Kunstgewerbeschule (School of Applied Arts) in 1904. He directed the institution until 1914, and during his tenure, produced many Jugendstil designs for silverware and ceramics that were remarkable for their simplicity of form. Jugendstil architecture and design often united structural innovation with abstracted naturalistic forms to produce an extraordinary combination of monumentality and visual lightness. The style reached its zenith around 1900 and was shortly afterwards superseded by the industrial rationalism of the Deutscher Werkbund, founded in 1907 by a group of designers and architects who had been affiliated with Jugendstil. Through its promotion of natural forms and "folk" types as a means of reforming design and ultimately society, Jugendstil had much in common with the British **Arts & Crafts Movement**, while its adoption of more industrialized methods of production paved the way for later developments in German design. The term 'Jugendstil' can also be used to refer to Scandinavian Art Nouveau.

▼ **Ferdinand Morawe**, Clock for the Vereinigte Werkstätten für Kunst im Handwerk, 1903

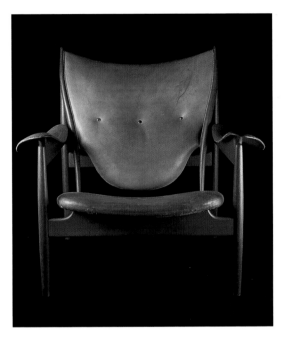

◄ *Chieftain* chair for
Niels Vodder, 1949

Finn Juhl studied architecture under Professor Kay Fisker (1893–1965) at the
Kongelige Danske Kunstakademi (Danish Academy of Fine Arts), Copenhagen, graduating in 1934. He first worked for ten years as an architect in the
office of Vilhelm Lauritzen, and during this period designed many pieces of
furniture in collaboration with the furniture maker, Niels Vodder. Juhl's furniture, such as the *Pelican* chair (1940) and the *No. 45* chair (1945), differed significantly from the modern re-workings of traditional furniture types advocated by **Kaare Klint** and his followers and heralded a new direction in Danish
design towards organic forms. In 1945, Juhl set up his own office and concentrated on designing sculptural, solid wood chairs, tables and sofas, which
brought him much acclaim – he was awarded six gold medals at Milan
Triennale exhibitions and fourteen prizes by the Copenhagen Cabinet-makers
Guild. His pieces, such as the *No. 48* chair (1948) and the *Chieftain* chair
(1949), were distinguished by a harmonious balancing of superlative craftsmanship and expressive, almost floating forms. Juhl developed numerous
constructional techniques for the use of teak, which led to the material's widespread use in Danish furniture. From 1945, Juhl was the senior instructor at
the School of Interior Design at Fredericksberg Technical School, and from
this position he played a key role in directing the course of Danish design.

Finn Juhl
1912 *Copenhagen*
1989 *Copenhagen*

Wilhelm Kåge

1889 *Stockholm*
1960 *Stockholm*

▼ *Terra Spirea*
stoneware vase for
Gustavsberg, c. 1955

Having studied painting at the Valand Art School in Gothenburg, then under Carl Wilhelmson (1866–1928) in Stockholm, and lastly under Johan Rohde at the Artists' Studio School, Copenhagen in 1912, Wilhelm Kåge finished his training by studying graphic design at the Plakatschule, Munich, where he became well known for his poster designs. Kåge was recruited by the Swedish ceramics firm, Gustavsberg, to update its product line in 1917, a period when Svenska Slöjdföreningen (Swedish Industrial Design Society) were actively campaigning for manufacturers, such as Gustavsberg, to employ artists to improve the quality of everyday objects. Kåge's *Liljebala* (Blue Lily) dinner service of 1917, with its folk art inspired decoration, did just that, and, being affordable for the working classes, became known as the "Workers' Service". Kåge was awarded a Grand Prix for his ceramics at the 1925 Paris "Exposition Internationale des Arts Décoratifs et Industriels Modernes". During the 1930s, he designed the oven-to-table *Pyro* service (1930) and the *Praktika* tableware (1933), which were both inexpensive and functional – their simple lines allowing the pieces to be stacked for easy storage. Interestingly, *Praktika* ware was the first service by Gustavsberg to be offered as open stock, whereby pieces could be sold individually rather than as a complete set. Apart from his designs for industrially produced ceramics, Kåge also made exquisite studio pieces, such as his *Terra Spirea* vase (c. 1955). His *Farsta* moulded stoneware designs, which were named after the island on which the Gustavsberg pottery was located, were inspired by Chinese and Mexican ceramics as well as by natural forms, while his *Surrea* range of studio pottery with its fragmented forms was influenced by Cubism and Surrealism. Wilhelm Kåge's functional ceramic designs for mass-production set standards for modern tableware, while his studio ceramics displayed his undoubted skill as a potter.

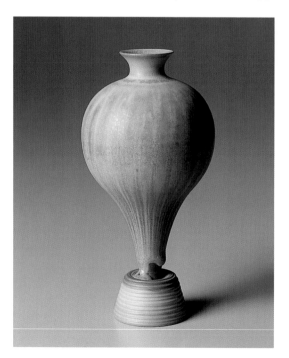

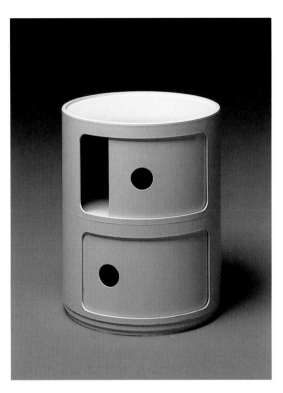

The plastics manufacturing company, Kartell was founded in 1949 by Giulio
Castelli (b. 1920), a chemical engineer and son of an early pioneer of plastics applications. Castelli had studied under Giulio Natta (1903–1979) – the
inventor of polypropylene – in 1954, and while training had made many contacts with **avant-garde** architects and artists who directly after the war were
urging for design to become an integral part of the manufacturing process
so as to assist the Italian reconstruction programme. Thus, the first product
launched by Kartell was a mundane ski-rack, designed by the architect and
industrial designer, Roberto Menghi (b. 1920). This was followed by a range
of household articles, many of which were designed by **Gino Colombini**.
From lemon squeezers and dustpans to washing-up bowls and buckets,
Kartell translated every-day objects into sleekly designed polyethylene products that were startlingly forward-looking. The company's design and
materials innovations were widely celebrated and Kartell received Premio
Compasso d'Oro awards in 1955, 1957, 1959, 1960 and 1964 as well as gold
and silver medals at Milan Triennale exhibitions. From the mid-1950s, the

Kartell
Founded 1949
Milan

company also produced furniture, including a metal and plastic sectional cupboard system (1956) designed by Gino Colombini and Leonardo Fiori, but it was not until the 1960s that they became widely known in this area, through their manufacturing of **Marco Zanuso** and **Richard Sapper**'s *No. 4999/5* stacking child's chair (1961–1964) and **Joe Colombo**'s revolutionary *Model No. 4860 Universale* (1965–1967), which was produced in ABS and was the first adult-sized fully injection-moulded plastic chair. The company also produced furniture by **Anna Castelli Ferrieri**, Alberto Rosselli (1921–1976), Giotto Stoppino (b. 1926), **Ettore Sottsass** and **Gae Aulenti**, much of which, like Castelli Ferrieri's injection moulded ABS *4953–54–55–56* stacking storage cylinders (1970), was modular. Kartell also produced lamps designed by **Sergio Asti**, **Marco Zanuso** and **Achille and Pier Giacomo Castiglioni**. During the 1980s, Kartell remained a high profile company through their production of furniture designed by **Philippe Starck** such as the characterful *Dr. Glob* chair (1988). In the 1990s, the company was awarded yet another Compasso d'Oro for **Antonio Citterio** and Glen Oliver Loew's translucent drawers units *Mobil* (1995) produced in injection moulded PMMA. They then began producing **Ron Arad**'s highly successful *Bookworm* shelving, also made out of an injection-moulded techno-polymer. Kartell's in-house design studio, Centrokappa, which is directed by Giulio Castelli's wife, Anna Castelli-Ferrieri, has also produced some notable designs including the *5300, 5312, 5320* system of childrens' furniture in playful primary colours. To this day Kartell continues to practise "an idea of design in which the quality of the relationships between materials, shapes and purpose is defined in relation to the industrial manufacturing process" while asserting their identity through innovative application of state-of-the-art plastics manufacturing technology.

▼ Marco Zanuso & Richard Sapper, *Model No. 4999/5* stacking child's chair for Kartell, 1961–1964

Edward Kauffer trained as a painter in the United States and was funded by Joseph E. McKnight to take a study trip to Paris in 1913. He subsequently adopted the name of his benefactor and settled in England in 1914. A year later, he received his first major design brief, a poster for the London Underground, from Frank Pick (1878–1941) who, as the railway company's publicity manager, was responsible for commissioning graphic designs. In 1920, Kauffer became a founding member of Group X, an artists' group led by the Vorticist painter, Percy Wyndham Lewis (1882–1957). The following year, however, Kauffer abandoned the fine arts so as to concentrate entirely on graphic design and commercial art. His list of corporate clients included London Transport, the Great Western Railway, Shell-Mex, British Petroleum, the Orient Line and the General Post Office, for whom he designed eye-catching posters that were initially inspired by Vorticism and later tended towards **Surrealism**. In 1929, Edward McKnight Kauffer and his wife, the textile designer Marion Dorn (1899–1964), exhibited handknotted rugs produced by the Royal Wilton Factory Company, incorporating Cubist and biomorphic patterns. During the 1930s, he also worked as a book illustrator, most notably on Miguel de Cervantes' *Don Quixote* (1930), T. S. Eliot's *Triumphal March* (1931) and Arnold Bennett's *Venus Rising from the Sea* (1931), and designed many book covers, including one for the *Studio Yearbook*. His posters were featured in a one-man show held at the **Museum of Modern Art, New York** in 1937, and the following year he became the first émigré to be made an Honorary Designer for Industry by the Royal Society of Arts, London. In 1940, he moved back to America with Marion Dorn for the duration of the war, but found few commissions there, although he did design posters for American Airlines until 1953.

Edward McKnight Kauffer
1890 *Great Falls, Montana*
1954 *New York*

▼ Hand-woven wool rug for The Wilton Royal Carpet Factory, c. 1935

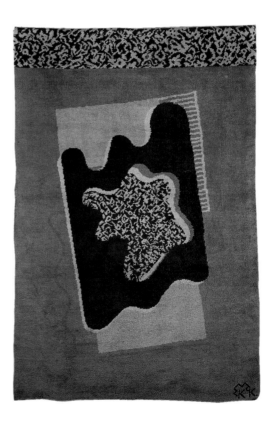

► Interior of Peggy Guggenheim's "Art of This Century Gallery" in New York showing Frederick Kiesler's *Multi-Use* chairs, 1942

Frederick Kiesler

1890 *Vienna*
1965 *New York*

Frederick Kiesler studied at the Akademie der Bildenden Künste and the Technische Hochschule, Vienna, from 1910 to 1914. Then, from around 1920, he worked briefly with **Adolf Loos** and began to design interiors and theatrical sets. In 1923, Kiesler became a member of **De Stijl** and devised his Endless House and Theatre, a modular building system that was based on an egg-shape, which was highly flexible in terms of configuration. The project was also energy efficient and considerably reduced the number of elements required for a building. During this period, Kiesler was associated with the G group that had been formed by **Ludwig Mies van der Rohe**, Hans Richter (1888–1976) and Werner Graeff (1901–1978). He designed the "International Exhibition of New Theatre Technique" at the Konzerthaus, Vienna in 1924 and, a year later, the Austrian pavilion at the Paris "Exposition Internationale des Arts Décoratifs et Industriels Modernes". In 1926, Kiesler emigrated to America and for two years worked in a New York architectural partnership with Harvey Wiley Corbett. He became a member of the AUDAC (American Union of Decorative Artists and Craftsmen), and from 1934 to 1937 was director of scenic design at the Julliard School of Music in New York. He also directed the laboratory for design correlation at Columbia University's School of Architecture from 1936 to 1942, and later worked in partnership with Armand Bartos in New York for six years. His sculptural furniture designs, such as the *Multi-Use* chairs (1942) and *Two-Part Nesting* tables (1935–38) were immensely influential, leading to the emergence of **Biomorphism** in the 1950s, while his artistic schemes for interiors were notable for their extraordinary spatial qualities.

The collaboration between the British designer Perry A. King (b. 1938) and Spanish designer Santiago Miranda (b. 1947) began in the mid-1970s. Since 1956 King had worked for **Olivetti**, designing office equipment such as the *Valentine* typewriter, which he co-designed with **Ettore Sottsass**, and from 1972 he oversaw the development of the company's **corporate identity** and designed a typeface (with Santiago Miranda) for use on dot-matrix printers. King also designed a corporate identity programme for C. Castelli, dictaphones for Süd-Atlas Werke and electrical equipment for Praxis during the 1970s, while Santiago Miranda (nine years King's junior) was studying at the Escuela de Artes Aplicadas y Oficios Artisticos in Seville. King – Miranda began their successful design partnership in 1975 in Milan, and subsequently designed graphics, furniture and lighting for Marcatré, Disform, Flos and Arteluce among others, while also developing computers and keyboards for

King – Miranda
Founded 1975
Milan

▼ *Donald* table lamp for Flos, 1978

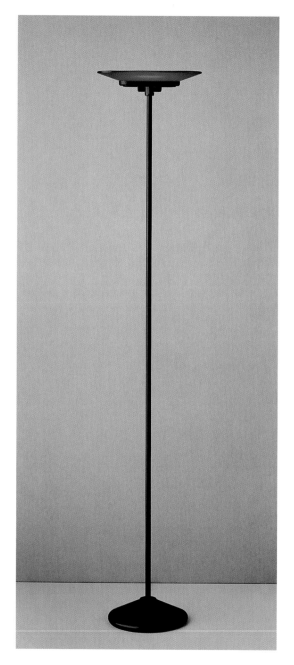

Olivetti. Further designs of theirs include Black & Decker power tools, Murano glassware and the *Lucerno* lighting system (1991) used for the public areas at Expo '92 in Seville. While King & Miranda's products are primarily informed by technology and industrial methods of production, they possess a poetic quality and at times even an element of humour, as their *Donald* lamp (1978) demonstrates. For them: "Design clearly must comprehend not only technology and economics, but sociology, too. This leads us to the conclusion that designers must have a political or philosophical model on which to base their work." (King – Miranda 1983 – *Design Since 1945* p. 217).

◄ *Jill* floor lamp for Flos, 1978

► *Omstak* chairs for Bieffeplast, 1971

Rodney Kinsman studied furniture design at the Central School of Art, London. In 1966, he established OMK Design with Jurek Olejnik and Bryan Morrison, and by 1967 the group was producing its own furniture, such as the vinyl-covered block foam *F Range* (1966), and supplying designs to **Terence Conran**'s Habitat stores. Since its formation, Kinsman has headed OMK and executed several notable designs, including the very successful *Omkstak* chair (1971), which epitomized the **High Tech** style of the 1970s. This highly rational design was conceived for large-scale mass-production and was licensed to the Italian manufacturer, Bieffeplast – a business partnership that remains to this day. Other furniture designs by Kinsman include the *Graffiti* display system (1981), the *Vienna* (1984) and *Tokyo* (1985) ranges – all of which share a similar rational aesthetic. Kinsman's first public seating system, the *Transit* range, designed in collaboration with Peter Glynn-Smith, was launched in 1981. This fire-proof all-metal system has a wave-like rhythmic form and was initially developed for Gatwick Airport. Kinsman was awarded a fellowship by the Society of Industrial Artists and Designers in 1983 and was made an Honorary Fellow of the **Royal College of Art** in 1988. His airport/station seating system for Trax came out in 1989, while perhaps his most original public seating solution, the *Seville* extruded aluminium bench (1991) was designed for Expo '92. Kinsman believes that design should not be influenced by fashion and he strives to create furniture that will have a longevity of appeal through sound technological reasoning.

Rodney Kinsman
b. 1943 *London*

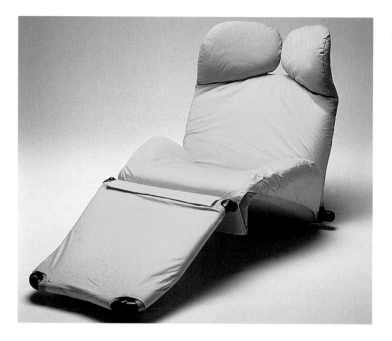

◄ *Wink* chair for
Cassina, 1980

Toshiyuki Kita
b. 1942 *Osaka*

Toshiyuki Kita studied industrial design at the Namiwa College, Osaka,
graduating in 1964, and establishing his own industrial and furniture design
studio in Osaka that same year. In 1969, he moved to Italy, initially working
in the design offices of **Mario Bellini** and Silvio Coppola (1920–1986),
though around this time he began designing furniture for Bernini and later
also for Cassina. His best-known design, the articulated and multi-functional *Wink* chair (1980), with its Mickey-Mouse shaped headrest, anticipated the early 1980s predilection for quirky forms. The design, which took
four years to develop, had removable covers to prolong its service life. In
1981, Kita received the Kitaro Kunii Industrial Design Award, and in 1987
took part in the "Les avant-gardes de la fin du XXème siècle" exhibition
held at the Centre Georges Pompidou, Paris. Together with the artist Keith
Haring (1958–1990), he co-designed the *On Taro* and *On Giro* tables for
Kreon in 1988, and was commissioned by Sony to design a multi-functional
hall for their Tokyo headquaters in 1989. With European clients, such as
Interflex, Sharp and Tribu, and Japanese clients, such as Koshudo, Johoku
Mokko and Yamagiwa, Toshiyuki Kita can truly be said to straddle both
cultures and, for this reason, he is regarded as one of the "most European"
of Japanese designers.

The term Kitsch derives from the German verb "verkitschen" (to cheapen) and is used to describe vulgarized designs that have a popular appeal. Kitsch has therefore come to be seen as the very antithesis of **Good Design**. The term was originally used to describe non-functional items such as souvenirs, knick-knacks and novelties. One of the first studies on the subject was by the German philosopher Fritz Karpfen in his publication of 1925, entitled *Der Kitsch*. However, it was not until the American art critic Clement Greenberg wrote *Kitsch and the Avantgarde* in 1939 that its meaning was widened to define elements of contemporary popular culture, such as commercial advertising and "trashy" literature. In the 1950s, Kitsch design reached its zenith with manufacturer's producing "knock-off" products that bore only a passing resemblance to the "high" design artefacts that had inspired them. During this period, a plethora of cheap and tacky products was produced, often in plastics, that relied on gimmickry and an element of humour for their appeal. This phenomenon was spurred on by popular consumerism and can be seen as a reaction against the state and institutional promotion of Good Design. During the 1960s, Kitsch continued to be used as a derogatory term, but by the 1970s, Kitsch objects were being used ironically in interiors and were knowingly appreciated for their self-conscious bad taste. With the emergence of **Post-Modernism** in the 1980s, Kitsch became lauded for its cultural honesty and its subversive tendencies. Through its mocking of "good taste", Kitsch had at last found fertile ground within the **avant-garde**.

▼ Selection of umbrella stands, late 1950s

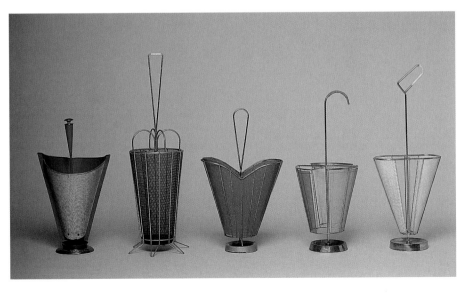

► *Model No. PK22*
chair for E. Kold
Christensen, 1955

Poul Kjaerholm

1929 *Oster Vra, Denmark*
1980 *Hillerod, Denmark*

Poul Kjaerholm trained as a carpenter before studying furniture design and cabinet-making at the Kunsthandvaerkerskolen (School of Arts & Crafts), Copenhagen. He later taught at the school for four years and at the Kongelige Danske Kunstakademi (Royal Academy of Arts), Copenhagen for twenty years, until 1976 when he became director. Throughout his career, Kjaerholm concentrated on the design of furniture for mass-production, and from 1955 worked mainly in conjunction with the furniture manufacturer, E. Kold Christensen, Hellerup. His elegant and rational designs, such as the *PK22* chair (1955) and the *Hammock PK24* chaise (1965), owe much to designers of the **Modern Movement**, especially **Le Corbusier**. The manufacture of his furniture for E. Kold Christensen was taken over by Fritz Hansen around 1970. Kjaerholm was awarded a Grand Prix at the 1957 and 1960 Milan Triennale exhibitions and also received the Lunning Prize in 1958. Of all the Scandinavian designers, Kjaerholm was perhaps the most influenced by the **International Style**. His sophisticated designs, which fused functionalist logic with Scandinavian sensibilities, possessed a very pure aesthetic, arising from his mastery of materials and technical construction. Kjaerholm was also celebrated for his exhibition layouts that were memorable for their over-riding sense of spatial organization.

After studying painting at Fredericksberg Polytechnic from 1903, Kaare Klint was apprenticed to his architect father, P. V. Jensen Klint, and later joined the Copenhagen architects, Kai Nielsen and Carl Petersen. From 1917 he began working as an independent furniture designer, and within three years had established his own design office, producing work for Fritz Hansen and Rud. Rasmussen among others. Klint's furniture designs, such as the *Model No. 4699* deck chair (1933), were largely reworkings of earlier types and were influenced by vernacularism, **Shaker** design, Regency furniture and oriental cabinet-making. He established the furniture department at the Kongelige Danske Kunstakademi (Royal Academy of Arts), Copenhagen in 1924, and together with his students undertook important pioneering research into anthropometrics. As an influential design theorist, Klint urged his pupils to combine the chief qualities of traditional craftsmanship, such as attention to detail and in-depth knowledge of materials, with rational design principles. In 1944, he became professor of architecture at the Kongelige Danske Kunstakademi (Royal Academy of Arts), Copenhagen, and the same year designed his *Fruit* lamp, which was constructed of folded paper. These inexpensive paper lamps were manufactured by Le Klint, a company that had evolved from a cottage industry established by his father who had also made and designed paper lamps. Klint believed that design should serve the public and that the best way of achieving this was through the adoption of rational design principles and the study of ergonomics. Klint's teachings laid the foundations for the renewal of Danish design after the Second World War.

Kaare Klint
1888 *Frederiksberg, Denmark*
1954 *Copenhagen*

▼ *Model No. 4699* deck chair for Rud. Rasmussen, 1933

▲ Florence Knoll,
Model No. 2080
conference table for
Knoll International,
1961

▶ Herbert Matter,
Advertisement
showing Harry
Bertoia's *Diamond*
chairs for Knoll
International, c. 1952

Hans Knoll (1914–1955) was the son of Walter Knoll, a German furniture maker. In 1937, he moved to New York and established the Hans G. Knoll Furniture Company, and around 1941 began producing a range of modern furniture designed by **Jens Risom**, which incorporated army surplus webbing. It was then that Hans Knoll met Florence Schust, an architect who had studied at the **Cranbrook Academy of Art**, at the Architectural Association, London, and under **Mies van der Rohe** at the Armoury Institute, Chicago, and who had also worked for the architects **Marcel Breuer** and **Walter Gropius**. Schust was taken on as an interior designer for Hans Knoll in 1943, and subsequently changed the direction of the company's product line from Scandinavian style to **International Style**. In 1946, Hans and Florence were married, and that same year they formed Knoll Associates. They began manufacturing modern sculptural furniture designed by **Eero Saarinen, Isamu Noguchi** and **Harry Bertoia** among others, which greatly raised the profile of the company, and in 1948 they acquired the production rights to Mies van de Rohe's furniture designs. During the 1950s, the distinctive Knoll look was pioneered by Florence Knoll who oversaw all aspects of corporate projection, from the design of showrooms and interiors, which were characterized

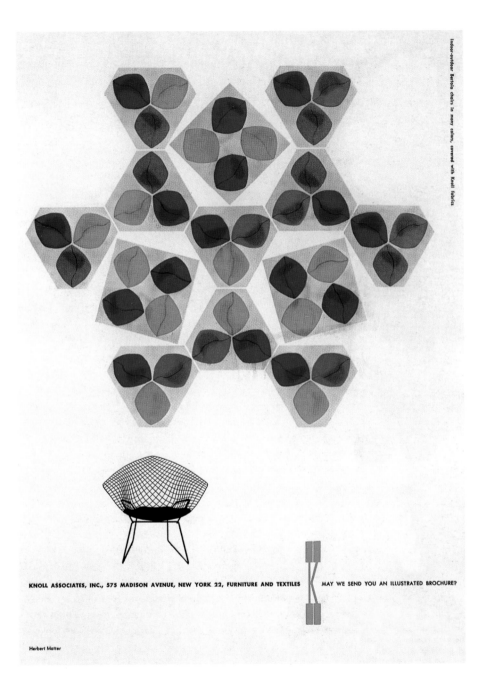

Indoor-outdoor Bertoia chairs in many colors, covered with Knoll fabrics

KNOLL ASSOCIATES, INC., 575 MADISON AVENUE, NEW YORK 22, FURNITURE AND TEXTILES   MAY WE SEND YOU AN ILLUSTRATED BROCHURE?

Herbert Matter

Knoll International

▲ **Massimo Vignelli**,
Poster for Knoll
International,
1967 (first poster
designed by Vignelli
for Knoll)

by a clarity of layout and meticulous attention to detail, down to the design of graphics. To this end, she recruited the Swiss designer, **Herbert Matter**, who during the 1950s, created a powerful series of posters advertising Knoll products and the large "K" logo. Matter's graphics had a similar clarity to Florence Knoll's furniture and interiors and he contributed much to the company's famous **corporate identity**. In 1955, Hans Knoll was tragically killed in a car accident, but under Florence Knoll's direction the company continued to flourish. Unlike many interior designers, she had such a remarkable knowledge of architectural form that her interiors always made full use of the space available while complementing the buildings in which they were sited. With her remarkable "eye", she was able to harmoniously unify form, colour and materials. From 1967, the Knoll identity was strengthened by **Massimo Vignelli**, who designed a programme of bold graphics that had a strong geometric uniformity. Increasingly, Knoll became associated with the production of contract furnishings and are today the third largest manufacturers of office furniture. They continue to produce highly innovative designs, such as Luke Pearson and Tom Lloyds' *Homer* range of movable workstations (1997).

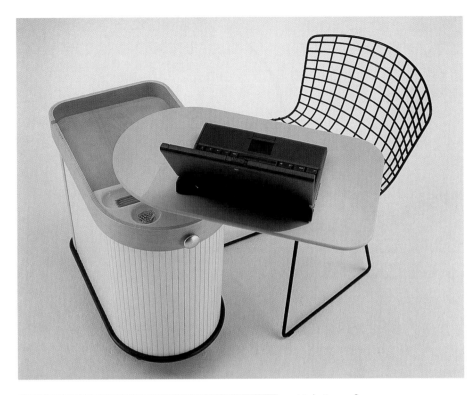

▲ **Luke Pearson & Tom Lloyd**, *Homer* mobile office for Knoll International, 1997 (with Harry Bertoia's *Model No. 420 C* wire chair)

◄ **Luke Pearson & Tom Lloyd**, *Homer* mobile office for Knoll International, 1997

▲ *Cymric* clock for Liberty & Co., 1903

Archibald Knox studied at the Douglas School of Art on the Isle of Man from 1878 to 1884 where he later taught. He worked with fellow Manx designer **Hugh Mackay Baillie Scott** before moving to London in 1897, from where he commuted to teach at Redhill School of Art. He also began to design textiles for the **Silver Studio** and metalware, with the assistance of **Christopher Dresser**, and between 1898 and 1912 produced metalware, textile and carpet designs for **Liberty & Co**. He was primarily responsible for the two highly influential Liberty metalware ranges, *Cymric* (from 1899), which comprised silverware and jewellery, and *Tudric* (from c. 1900), which included less expensive pewterwares. Knox's organic forms and swirling decoration were inspired by Celtic motifs, and his designs with their interlaced patterning and turquoise enamelling, were synomous with the "Liberty Style", which was immensely influential especially in Continental Europe. From

Archibald Knox
1864 *Isle of Man*
1933 *Isle of Man*

▼ *Cymric* silver and enamel coronation spoon for Liberty & Co., 1901

1900 and 1904, Knox lived on the Isle of Man before returning to mainland Britain. He taught at a number of art institutions, including Kingston School of Art, where his teaching methods were criticized by the official examiners. He subsequently resigned from his teaching position at Kingston in 1911, and with a group of his ex-students set up the Knox Guild of Craft and Design, which remained active until 1939. Knox ceased designing for Liberty & Co., which had by 1909 licensed a number of his metalwork designs to James Connell & Co., and in 1912 he went to the United States to design carpets for the Philadelphia-based manufacturer, Bromley & Co. A year later, he moved back to the Isle of Man and after the First World War took up painting and continued to teach. He also designed several Celtic Revival gravestones, including Arthur Lasenby Liberty's in 1917. Knox's highly refined silverware and his more utilitarian pewterware were characterized by exaggerated organic forms and abstracted floral motifs and thus eptimomized the second phase of the British **Arts & Crafts Movement**.

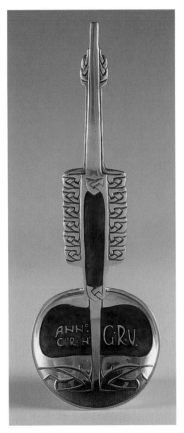

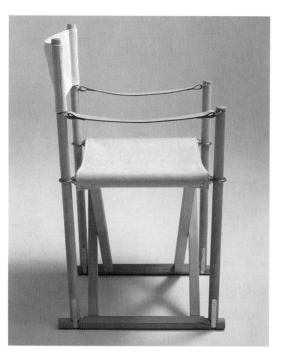

► *MK* folding chair
for Rud. Rasmussen,
1932

Mogens Koch

1898 *Copenhagen*
1993 *Copenhagen*

After completing his training as an architect at the Kongelige Danske
Kunstakademi (Royal Academy of Arts), Copenhagen in 1925, Mogens Koch
worked as an assistant to Carl Petersen and **Kaare Klint**. He designed his *MK
Safari* chair, which was manufactured by Interna and Rudolf Rasmussen in
1932, and later designed many other furniture pieces for these two manufacturers as well as for Danish CWS and N. C. Jensen Kjaer. Influenced by
Kaare Klint's evolutionary approach to design, Koch's furniture can be seen
essentially as modern reworkings of traditional types. Koch also designed
silverware, textiles and carpets in connection with Danish church restora-
tions. His work was regularly exhibited at the Milan Triennale exhibitions
and was included in the "Arts of Denmark" travelling exhibition that
toured America in 1960. He was a professor at the Kongelige Danske
Kunstakademi from 1950 to 1968 and a visiting lecturer at the Massachus-
setts Institute of Technology from 1956 and at the Industrial Art Institute,
Tokyo, from 1962. The designs he produced were extremely practical, being based on existing solutions that had been refined over many decades.
Koch's subtle yet fundamentally modern approach to problem solving was
highly characteristic of Danish design during the inter-war years.

The manufacturing company J.&J. Kohn was formed by Jakob Kohn and his son out of the family's lumber company in Holleschau, Moravia (Holesov, Czech Republic) in 1850. Ten years later, when **Michael Thonet**'s patents for the production of bentwood furniture expired, J.&J. Kohn built two factories in Wsetin and Litsch and began producing bentwood furniture. The firm grew rapidly and a further eight factories were built in what is now Poland and the Czech Republic, until in 1873 they were employing two thousand-eight hundred workers. Although there were some fifty other firms producing bentwood furniture around this period, it was J.&J. Kohn that became Gebrüder Thonet's most serious rival. By 1882, the firm had established branches in Hamburg, Berlin, Paris and London, and in 1904 it was offering four hundred and seven different models and manufacturing some five and a half thousand pieces of furniture a day. The company's award-winning stand at the 1900 Paris "Exposition Universelle et Internationale" comprised several partitioned interiors that displayed progressive bentwood furniture and fittings. These designs have been attributed to **Gustav Siegel** who, the previous year, had been appointed head of J.&J. Kohn's design department at the youthful age of nineteen. The Viennese architect, **Adolf Loos** also produced designs for the firm, most notably his *Café Museum* chair (c. 1898), as did **Otto Wagner**. Like Thonet, J.&J. Kohn pioneered the application of the "New Art" to industrial production through its mass-production of "artistic designs". Similarly, they also developed novel manufacturing techniques, which included a machine that made circular seat frames and a method of bending wood to an angle of nearly ninety degrees. The façade of the J.&J. Kohn building

Jakob & Josef Kohn
Founded 1850
Moravia

▼ J.&J. Kohn advertisement from the catalogue of the XV Vienna Secession exhibition, 1902

ERSTE ÖSTERR. ACTIEN-GESELL-SCHAFT ZUR ERZEUGUNG V. MÖBELN AUS GEBOGENEM HOLZE

JACOB & JOSEF KOHN
WIEN, I. BURGRING 3

GRAND PRIX   PARIS 1900

o SCHLAFZIMMER, SPEISEZIMMER o SALONMÖBEL IN MODERNEM STILE

in Vienna was designed by **Josef Hoffmann** and **Koloman Moser**, who also designed several pieces of furniture for the firm. Hoffmann's *Sitzmachine Model No. 670* (c. 1908) was manufactured by J.&J. Kohn and, with its pierced geometric motifs and flat planes, exemplified the Secessionist style that was so characteristic of the company's product range. The last J.&J. Kohn catalogue, published in 1916, two years after their merger with the furniture manufacturer Mundus, shows over one thousand models which were sold through the company's branches in Germany, Belgium, Poland, Switzerland and America. In 1922, the Kohn and Mundus partnership was absorbed into the Thonet company to form Thonet-Mundus-J.&J. Kohn, but by 1932 the name Kohn had been dropped from the company's title.

▶ **Koloman Moser**, Bentwood and glass vitrine for J.&J. Kohn, c. 1905

Jurriaan Jurriaan Kok studied architecture at Delft Polytechnic and sub-sequently worked in the Hague-based architectural office of D. P. van Ameijden van Duym, who periodically designed ceramics for the Rozenburg factory. Through his contact with van Ameijden van Duym, Kok was ap-pointed artistic adviser to the pottery around 1893, and a year later was nominated director of the Rozenburg porcelain factory in The Hague. Prior to Kok's appointment, Theodorus A. C. Colenbrander (1841–1930) had acted as Rozenburg's first design director and had introduced abstracted orna-mental patterns resembling Javanese batik work to the pottery. During Kok's tenure, the ceramic decoration at Rozenburg became more naturalistic, although the Indonesian influence remained. In 1899, Kok introduced the fine translucent "egg-shell" wares for which the factory became famous. Products such as these, with their attenuated **Art Nouveau** forms and styl-ized motifs of flora and fauna, were shown at the 1900 Paris "Exposition Universelle et Internationale" to much critical acclaim. In 1900, the N. V. Haagche Plateelbakkerrj Rozenburg, as the factory was officially known, was given a royal warrant and its name was changed to the Koninklijke Porselein-en-Aardewerkfabriek Rozenburg. Kok maintained his directorship of the company until 1913, when he became a public works commissioner for The Hague.

Jurriaan Jurriaan Kok
1861 *Rotterdam*
1919 *The Hague*

▲ "Egg-Shell" porcelain vases with polychrome decoration for Rozenburg, 1901–1903

Henning Koppel

1918 *Copenhagen*
1981 *Copenhagen*

► *Model No. 978*
silver wine pitcher
for Georg Jensen,
1948

▼ *Model No. 992*
silver pitcher for
Georg Jensen, 1952

Henning Koppel studied drawing under Bizzie Høyer in Copenhagen from 1935 to 1936 and sculpture under Anker Hoffmann at the Kongelige Danske Kunstakademi (Royal Danish Academy of Fine Arts), Copenhagen from 1936 to 1937. He then trained at the Académie Ranson, Paris for a year, where he was undoubtedly exposed to new currents in **avant-garde** sculpture. Koppel spent the Second World War in Stockholm, and while there produced designs for Orrefors and Svenskt Tenn and began designing gold and silver jewellery. He then returned to Denmark and began his long association with the **Georg Jensen** silversmithy, which lasted until his death in 1981. From 1961, Koppel produced sculptural ceramics such as the *Form 24* service (1962) for Bing & Grøndahl Porcelaensfabrik, and also designed clocks and lighting for Louis Poulsen, glassware for Orrefors and even Danish postage stamps. It was, however, his beautiful sculptural silverware designed for Georg Jensen that brought him the greatest international acclaim. Inspired by the abstract sculptures of Hans Arp (1887–1966) and Constantin Brancusi (1876–1957), Koppel created biomorphic silver jewellery, such as his bracelet *Model No. 89* (1946), which had a wonderful plasticity of form and was exceptionally forward-looking. Although he followed the traditions of craftsmanship for which Denmark was so renowned, Koppel's designs, such as the wine pitcher *Model No. 978* (1948) and fish dish (1954), expressed a universal language of organic form that was fundamentally modern. His ideas for designs were initially sketched in ink and then modelled in clay, which allowed him to perfect the lines from every side before they were translated into silver. His *Caravel* cutlery of 1957 introduced expressive form to the Georg Jensen flatware collection. Koppel was awarded three gold medals at the Milan Triennale exhibitions (1951, 1954 and 1957), and was awarded the Lunning Prize in 1953.

► *Karuselli* club chair
for Haimi, 1965

Yrjö Kukkapuro

b. 1933 *Yiipuri, Finland*

Yrjö Kukkapuro studied at the Institute of Industrial Arts, Helsinki, graduating as an interior designer in 1958. A year later, he established his own studio in Kauniainen and began designing functionalist furniture. His work was greatly influenced by his teacher at the Institute of Industrial Arts, Helsinki, Ilmari Tapiovaara (b. 1914), who was a pioneer of knock-down furniture. The ergonomic form of Kukkapuro's inventive *Karuselli* (Carousel) chair of 1965 was reputedly inspired by the imprint of the designer's body in deep snow. In 1978, he designed the more sober *Fysio* office chair, the form of which was dictated by anthropometric data. Kukkapuro was a professor at the Taideteollinin Korkeakoulu (Institute of Technology) in Helsinki from 1974 to 1980 and rector of that institution from 1978 to 1980. With the ascendancy of **Post-Modernism** in the 1980s, he began producing more expressive designs, such as in his *Experiment* chairs (1982–1983) and declared: "Post-Modernism has once again put us in touch with the vital element that the French call *joie de vivre*." Kukkapuro's designs were originally manufactured by Haimi, but in 1980 a new company, Avarte, was established specifically to produce his furniture.

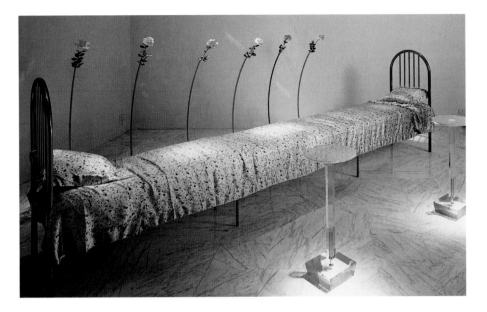

Shiro Kuramata studied architecture at the Tokyo Municipal Polytechnic High School until 1953 and then worked for the furniture manufacturer, Teikokukizai for a year. He also trained in the department of living design at the Kuwazawa Institute for Design, Tokyo, graduating in 1956. For the next seven years, Kuramata worked in the San-Ai design studio of the Maysuya department store in Tokyo, concentrating on retail design. In 1965, he founded his own Tokyo-based practice, the Kuramata Design Studio, and designed interiors for over three hundred bars and restaurants, including the Judd Club (1969), as well as furniture that tempered Japanese minimalism with a Western sense of irony. He received a Mainichi Design Award in 1972 and became a consultant to the Mainichi board in 1975. Kuramata's extraordinary *Drawers in an Irregular Form* (1977) was one of the first furniture designs to bring him international recognition. In the 1980s, he used unusual materials, such as steel expand-metal and acrylic resin, to create highly original and poetic furniture with remarkable spatial qualities such as his *How High The Moon* chair (1986) and *Miss Blanche* chair (1988). The titles of these illusory designs made reference to Western culture – namely, the title of Duke Ellington's jazz number and a character from Tennessee William's play *A Streetcar Named Desire*. In 1981, Kuramata was awarded the Japanese Cultural Prize for Design, and over the next six years designed several pieces for **Memphis**, including his cement and glass

Shiro Kuramata
1934 *Tokyo*
1991 *Tokyo*

▲ Interior at the "Il Dolce Stile Nuove – delle casa" exhibition held at the Palazzo Strozzi in Florence, 1991 – showing a *Laputa* bed, *Placebo* tables and *Ephemera* vases for Cappellini, 1991

Kyoto table (1983) and his metal and broken glass *Sally* table (1987), which were more refined and aesthetically reserved than designs normally associated with the Italian group. Throughout the 1980s, Kuramata designed minimalist furnishings and fittings for the Issey Miyake stores in Tokyo (1986), Paris (1984) and New York (1987) and created interiors for the Seibu store in Tokyo (1987). He purchased a house in Paris in 1988 that had originally been designed by **Robert Mallet-Stevens** for Jöel and Jan Martell and established his own design office on the Rue Royale, Paris. Kuramata's designs have been manufactured by many companies including **Vitra**, Cappellini, XO, Fijiko, Ishimaru, Mhoya Glass Shop, Aoshima Shoten and Kurosaki.

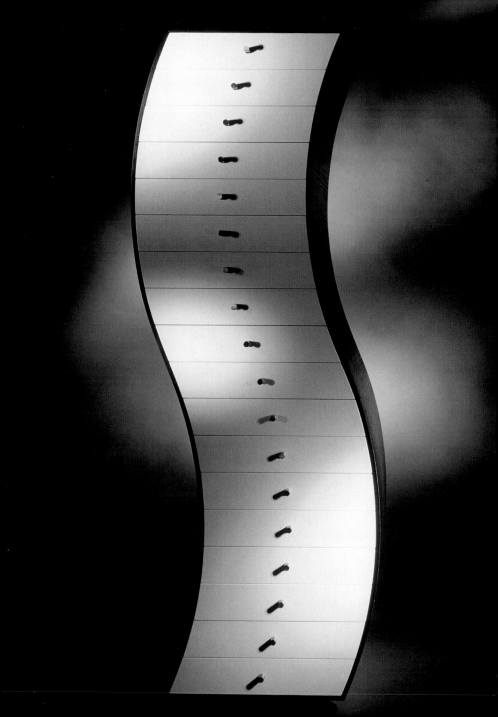

René Lalique
1860 *Ay, France*
1945 *Paris*

After leaving the Turgot School in 1876 at the age of sixteen, René Lalique became apprenticed to a leading Parisian goldsmith, Louis Aucoc, and attended classes at the École des Arts Décoratifs, Paris. He spent two years in England, completing his formal studies at Sydenham College, London, and on his return to Paris in 1880 worked briefly for the jewellers, Petit Fils, before setting up his own studio with a family friend known as M. Varenne. He independently created jewellery for Cartier, Boucheron, Destape and Aucoc, as well as designing wallpapers and textiles, and studying sculpture under Lequien. In 1886, a year after being appointed manager of Jules Destape's jewellery workshop, Lalique acquired the small manufacturing business for himself. This workshop, which supplied designs to other established jewellers, moved twice to larger premises, and by 1894 Lalique was exhibiting his work regularly at the Paris Salons. In stark contrast to the contemporary taste for precious and ostentatious gems set in unobtrusive mounts, Lalique's jewellery designs incorporated carved ivory, horn, semi-precious stones and enamelling and were conceived as *objets d'art*. During the 1890s, Lalique made several pieces for the actress Sarah Bernhardt (1844–1923) and displayed his jewellery in **Siegfried Bing**'s shop, Maison de l'Art Nouveau. He then began experimenting with clear and coloured engraved glass in jewellery, exhibiting the resulting work at the 1900 Paris "Exposition Universelle et Internationale" where it received much critical acclaim. Bolstered by this success, Lalique established a small glass workshop at Clairefontaine in 1902, and five years later was commissioned by François Coty to design perfume bottles, which were produced at the Legras & Cie glassworks. In 1909, Lalique purchased a glassworks, the Verrerie de

▼ *Pierrefonds* vase for René Lalique et Cie., 1926

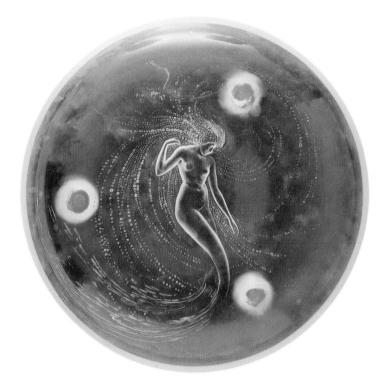

► *Sirène* opalescent dish for René Lalique et Cie., 1920

Combs-la-Ville, in Seine-et-Marne for the production of perfume bottles for his clients, including Worth and Roger & Gallet. This was followed by the acquisition of a second, much larger glassworks at Wingen-sur-Moder, Alsace, where he began to apply modern industrial production techniques to his designs. A stamping press was developed that enabled them to do high-relief moulding in addition to more traditional techniques such as *cire-perdue* casting and blow-moulding. Lalique produced a vast range of glass, which ranged stylistically from delicate and naturalistic **Art Nouveau** designs to chunky and highly stylized **Art Deco** items. Although he used many different colours of glass for his vessels, mascots, buttons, lighting etc., Lalique was particularly noted for his opalescent glass, which was widely copied but never matched in quality by other manufacturers. The glassworks was closed in 1937, but in 1945 the firm was re-established by René Lalique's son, Marc.

▶ *Tulpan (Tulip)* goblets for Orrefors, 1956

Nils Landberg
b. 1907 *Västra Vingaker, Sweden*

Nils Landberg studied at the Konstindustrieskolen in Götenborg from 1923 to 1925 and then trained at the newly established school of engraving at the Orrefors Glasbruk for two years, with his compatriot **Sven Palmqvist**. Landberg subsequently studied in Italy and France before returning to Sweden, where he began working under Edward Hald (1883–1980) as an assistant and engraver at Orrefors. Around 1935, he began creating his own designs for the company and became a member of its in-house design team. His engraved glassware from this period was shown at both the 1937 Paris "Exposition Internationale des Arts et Techniques dans la Vie Moderne" and the 1939 New York World's Fair. During the 1950s, Landberg experimented with abstracted and attenuated forms using either clear or delicately tinted glass. In these pieces, he pushed the medium's tensile strength to its limits, giving the designs a powerful inner tension. Landberg's famous *Tulpanglas* (1957) with its slender waist was blown as a single piece and received a gold medal at the Milan XI Triennale in 1957. He also designed tableware and lighting as well as decorative doors and windows. Landberg retired from Orrefors in 1972, and fourteen years later the Orrefors Museum held a retrospective exhibition of his work.

Gerd Lange studied at the Werkkunstschule in Offenbach/Main from 1952 to 1956, and for the next five years designed exhibitions and interiors while also working as an industrial designer. In 1964, he established his own workshop and studio in Kapsweyer, specializing in the design of contract furniture and lighting. Lange designed furniture for Thonet, most notably his *Flex 2000* multi-purpose chair (1973–1974) and his *Thonet-Cut* stacking chair (1985). From 1964, he exhibited his work annually at the exhibition "Die Gute Industrieform" in Hanover, and in 1969 he was awarded two Gute Form first prizes for his seating designs. In addition to pieces such as his knock-down *Farmer* range (1966), which comprised a chair, a table, a bed and a wardrobe, for Wilhelm Bofinger, Stuttgart, Lange also designed furniture for Drabert and Schlapp as well as lighting systems for Staff and **Kartell**. In 1970, a one-man show of his work was held by the Rat für Formgebung in Darmstadt. The success of Lange's work is very much due to his ability to combine technical inventiveness with simplicity of form.

Gerd Lange

b. 1931 *Wuppertal, Germany*

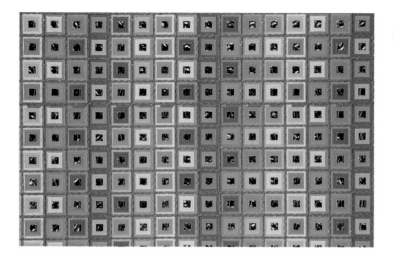

◄ *Magnum* textile for
Jack Lenor Larsen
Inc., 1970

**Jack Lenor
Larsen**
*1927 Seattle,
Washington*

Jack Lenor Larsen studied architecture and furniture design at the University of Washington, Seattle, and at the University of Southern California, Los Angeles, graduating in 1950. He also took weaving courses, and in 1949 established a weaving studio in Seattle. After studying for a year at the **Cranbrook Academy of Art**, Michigan, where he obtained a masters' degree in fine art, he settled in New York and in 1951 founded his own workshop. His first commission was for textile hangings for Skidmore, Owings and Merrill's Lever House, New York (1952). During this period, Larsen also began designing machine-woven textiles that appeared to have been hand-woven. These ingenious designs were highly influential and were also widely imitated. In 1953, he set up Jack Lenor Larsen Inc., and by 1956 was using power-looms to manufacture his textiles.Two years later, he established the Larsen Design Studio, which was headed by Win Anderson. Larsen also became a consultant to the United States State Department on the issue of grass-weaving in Vietnam and Taiwan. He opened branches of Jack Lenor Larsen Inc. in Paris, Zurich and Stuttgart in the late 1960s, acquired Thaibok Fabrics, Bangkok in 1972, founding a carpet division in 1973 and a furniture division in 1976. Over the last fifty years, Larsen has pioneered numerous innovations including printed-velvet upholstery fabrics, stretch upholstery fabrics and warp-knit Saran-monofilament casement textiles. He has also designed and mass-produced many textile collections that "maintain the great tradition of luxurious quality". Larsen's technical inventiveness and success as a manufacturer have made him one of the world's most influential textile designers.

Carl Larsson studied at the Academy of Art in Stockholm, where he subsequently took courses in classical art and life drawing. While still a student, Larsson contributed caricatures to the journal *Kasper* and graphics to the newspaper *Ny Illustread Tidning*. He moved to Paris in 1877, and in 1882 settled in Grez with a number of other Swedish painters, where he produced watercolours that had a poetic realism and a narrative quality. In 1879, he met the Swedish artist Karin Bergöö, whom he married in 1883. During the 1880s, Larsson joined the Swedish art group, Opponents, and worked as an illustrator. In 1888, Karin's father gave the growing Larsson family a small house, Lilla Hyttnäs in Sundborn, which they used as a summer residence until 1901 when they moved there permanently. From then on, the house became the centre of their lives. Karin decorated its interiors in a simple "folk" style – white-painted and built-in furniture, wooden floors, embroidered textiles – while Carl portrayed their daily life and their seven children in his watercolours. His brightly coloured stylized studies, which captured this idyllic, rural, self-sufficient and carefree lifestyle, were reproduced in an album *Ett Hem* (Our Home) in 1899 so as to "reform taste and family life". The Larssons' promotion of an integrated and simple lifestyle was highly influential in Scandinavia and Germany.

Carl Larsson
1853 *Stockholm*
1919 *Sundborn, Sweden*

▲ Watercolour of Carl Larsson's studio, illustrated in his book, *Ett Hem (Our Home)* published in 1899

Le Corbusier

1887 *La Chaux-de-Fonds,*
Switzerland
1965 *Cap Martin, France*

Charles-Édouard Jeanneret studied metal engraving at the School of Applied Arts at La Chaux-de-Fonds, Switzerland, where he was urged by his teacher, Charles L'Eplattenier, to take up architecture. He built his first house, the Fallett Villa, in 1905 for a member of the teaching staff at the school. After travelling around Italy and visiting Budapest and Vienna, he moved to Paris in 1908, where he worked in the architectural practice of Auguste Perret (1874–1954), who was noted for his pioneering use of concrete and reinforced steel. While there, he met Wolf Dohrn, the director of the **Dresdener Werkstätten für Handwerkskunst**, as well as the German design theorist, Hermann Muthesius (1861–1927) and the German architect and industrial designer, **Peter Behrens**. He worked in Behrens' office in Berlin for a year, gaining valuable experience and then, in 1911, returned to Switzerland for two years to teach at his alma mater. He also developed a concept for a serially produced reinforced concrete housing kit, the *Dom-ino-houses* (1914–1915) and designed and built the Schwab Villa, La Chaux-de-Fonds (1916). Jeanneret moved to Paris in 1917, and around 1920 adopted the pseudonym "Le Corbusier". In Paris, he developed a new approach to painting with the artist, Amédée Ozenfant (1886–1966), known as Purism and in 1918 they published a manifesto entitled *Après le cubisme, le purisme*. For the next two years, Le Corbusier edited the journal *L'Esprit Nouveau* to which he contributed many articles. His affection for Classical Greek architecture and his attraction to the concept of the machine was outlined in these highly influential articles, which were eventually republished under the title *Vers une Architecture* (1923). Wishing to transform the humble house into an industrialized product, he developed a system of building units known as the Citrohan Houses (1920–1922). He also executed plans for a large utopian city of standardized high-rise blocks known as "The Contemporary City for Three Million Inhabitants" (1922), which were exhibited at the 1922 Salon d'Automne. In the same year, Le Corbusier and his architect cousin, **Pierre Jeanneret**, established an architectural partnership in the Rue de Sèvres, Paris, and built a number of private residences and housing developments. Le Corbusier designed the Pavillon de l'Esprit Nouveau for the 1925 "Exposition Internationale des Arts Décoratifs et Industriels Modernes", which was a model building unit for a later apartment block. The pavilion attracted both acclaim and criticism – the latter eventually leading Le Corbusier and others to leave the conservative Société des Artistes Décorateurs and to form the UAM (Union des Artistes Modernes) in 1929. Le Corbusier's concept of the house as "a machine for living" included appropriately functional furniture or "équipment de l'habitation". Accordingly, he co-designed a range of systemized tubular steel furniture with Pierre Jeanneret and **Charlotte**

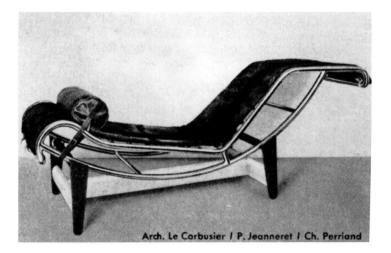

▲ Le Corbusier,
Pierre Jeanneret &
Charlotte Perriand,
Model No. B306
chaise longue for
Thonet and Embru,
1928

► Illustration from
Thonet catalogue
showing *Model No.
B306* chaise longue
in tilted position

Arch. Le Corbusier / P. Jeanneret / Ch. Perriand

▲ Le Corbusier,
**Pierre Jeanneret &
Charlotte Perriand**,
*Model No. LC2 Grand
Confort* club chair for
Thonet, 1928

Perriand, who entered the design and architectural partnership in 1927. Having first appeared in 1928, these seminal modern designs, which included the *Basculant No. B301* chair (c. 1928), the *No. B306* chaise-longue (1928) and the *Grand Confort No. LC2* club chair (1928), projected a new aesthetic purity and epitomized the **International Style**. During the late 1920s and 1930s, Le Corbusier concentrated on architectural commissions, including his famous Villa Savoye, Poissy (1928–1929), Cité du Refuge, Paris (1930–1933), the Pavillon Suisse, Cité Universitaire, Paris (1930–1931) and utopian architectural concepts such as the La Ville Radieuse city plan (1935). These relentlessly modern projects were extremely influential to the evolution of architecture, especially in the areas of high-density housing and office buildings. During the 1950s, Le Corbusier moved away from the formalism of the International Style towards a freer and more expressive idiom. He demonstrated his increasing interest in the sculptural potential of con-

▼ Le Corbusier, Pierre Jeanneret, Charlotte Perriand, *Model No. LC2* sofa, 1928 (reissued by Cassina)

▲ **Le Corbusier, Pierre Jeanneret, Charlotte Perriand,** *Model No. B301 Basculant* chair for Thonet, 1928 (reissued by Cassina)

crete with the roof of his Unité d'Habitation housing complex in Marseilles (1946–1952) and with his remarkable Notre Dame du Haut church at Ronchamp (1950–1955). Le Corbusier was one of the most influential architects, designers and design theorists of the 20th century and his promotion of geometric formalism had far-reaching consequences. Ironically, it was Le Corbusier-style public housing built in the 1960s – much of which was poorly constructed – that led to the discrediting of the **Modern Movement** when it appeared to have failed the very people it was intended to benefit.

▲ **Le Corbusier, Pierre Jeanneret, Charlotte Perriand,** Studio flat at the Salon d'Automne, Paris, 1929

Yonel Lébovici was a Paris-based designer who designed and manufactured his own highly distinctive lighting. His early *Satellite* table lamp (1965) was produced in a limited edition of twenty and reflected the 1960s infatuation with the Space Age. Although highly futuristic in form, this lamp was also reminiscent of the earlier acrylic resin and nylon sculptures of Naum Gabo (1890–1977). Its articulated discs of acrylic resin not only diffused the light from the central bulb to give a warm luminescence but owing to their thickness, glowed brightly around their edges. Though acrylic resin is now a common material with a huge application in commercial signage, Lébovici was one of the first to explore its potential in lighting design. His later *Soucoupe* hanging and standard lamps (1970) were, as their name suggests, inspired by flying saucers and functioned more as light sculptures than as practical lighting solutions. Lébovici also created several out-of-context and over-sized designs, including his *Safety Pin* light sculpture (1975), that were influenced by Pop Art. During the 1980s, he continued to experiment with unusual forms and materials. He contrasted, for example, a pyramidal stand constructed of exotic wood with discs of perforated nickel-plated metal for his *Phototaxie* standard lamp (1984). Many of Lébovici's light designs were included in the "Lumières" exhibition held at the Centre Georges Pompidou, Paris in 1985. He also designed lighting, glassware and furniture for Cardin, Club Med, Jansen and Lancel. Typically French in their sophistication and engaging subversiveness, Lébovici's offbeat, limited edition designs are highly collectable.

Yonel Lébovici

1937 *Paris*
1998 *Paris*

◄ *Satellite* table lamp, 1965

▼ *Soucoupe* floor lamp, 1970

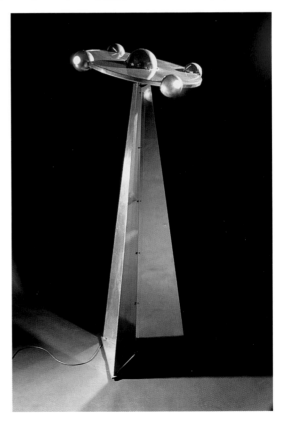

Pierre-Émile Legrain

1889 Levallois-Peret, France
1929 Paris

Pierre-Émile Legrain trained at the Collège Sainte-Croix de Neuilly before studying painting, sculpture and theatre design at the École des Arts Appliqués Germain-Croix, Paris. In 1908, he produced some cartoons for **Paul Iribe**'s satirical periodicals, *Le Mot*, *Le Témoin*, *La Baïonnette* and *L'Assiette au Beurre*. Legrain then entered Iribe's studio, where he remained until 1914, collaborating on a number of projects including the decoration of the couturier Jacques Doucet's apartment on the Avenue du Bois and studio on the Rue Saint-Jacques, Neuilly. Legrain and Iribe also co-designed jewellery for Robert Linzeler and dress designs for Paquin. Legrain particularly excelled in the design of book-bindings and covers, and in 1917 Doucet commissioned him to design bindings and wrappers for his recently acquired collection of new editions by contemporary authors such as André Gide, Francis Jammes, André Suarès and Paul Claudel. Doucet assisted Legrain in this project and the resulting books were exhibited at the 1919 Société des Artistes Salon. The same year, Legrain began working for René Kieffer's book bindery, producing exquisite bindings in exotic materials such as shagreen and mother-of-pearl with decorative geometric motifs. During this period, Legrain also worked as an interior designer and designed chairs, inspired by African art, which exemplified the **Art Deco** style. In 1925, he designed the interiors of Doucet's villa in Neuilly, which as a showcase for contemporary art and design, included furnishings by **Eileen Gray**, Paul Iribe, Marcel Coard (1889–1975) and André Groult (1884–1967) as well as fine art by Henri Matisse (1869–1954), Pablo Picasso (1881–1973) and Amedeo Modigliani (1884–1920). Legrain was a member of the Groupe des Cinq and joined the UAM (Union des Artistes Modernes) in 1929. By the time of his death, he had designed around 1,300 bookbindings and had almost single-handedly revived this ancient craft.

▼ *Tabouret Ashanti* stool, c. 1922

In 1901 Jules-Émile Leleu together with his brother, Marcel, took over the family painting firm and subsequently worked as an interior designer. Around 1918, Leleu founded his own design studio and furniture workshop in Paris, developing an **Art Deco** style similar to that of the Établissements Ruhlmann and Louis Süe and André Mare's Compagnie des Arts Français. His early designs were inspired by Neo-Classicism and had elegant yet monumental forms. By the mid-1920s, however, his furniture had become less bulky and frequently incorporated exotic woods, shagreen and ivory. He received many commissions for embassies, civic buildings and royal residences, mainly because his formal style of decoration was deemed highly appropriate for official interiors. During the 1930s, Leleu's furniture became less complicated in terms of line and construction. His Hotel Nord-Sud in Calvi, Corsica (1931) was included in the landmark exhibition "The **International Style**: Architecture since 1922" held in 1932 at the **Museum of Modern Art, New York**, and in 1937 he decorated the dining room of the Palais de l'Élysée with his first truly modern designs. For many of his decorating projects, Leleu collaborated with Edgar Brandt (1880–1960), Jean Dunand (1877–1942) and André Lurçat (1894–1970). He also designed interiors and furnishings for over twenty ocean-liners.

Jules-Émile Leleu
1883 *Boulogne-sur-Mer, France*
1961 *Paris*

▲ Dressing table and stool for Jules-Émile Leleu Workshops, 1929–1930

Liberty & Co.

Founded 1875
London

Arthur Lasenby Liberty (1843–1917) was apprenticed to John Weekes, the drapers in Baker Street, London, before working from 1862 at Farmer & Rogers' Great Shawl and Cloak Emporium on Regent Street. In 1864, Liberty was appointed manager of Farmer & Rogers' Oriental Warehouse, which retailed imported eastern wares and became a mecca for those associated with the **Aesthetic Movement**. After a decade of managing the hugely successful warehouse, Liberty was refused a partnership in the firm and so decided to establish his own shop. He acquired premises at 218, Regent Street and grandly named the new Tudor-style building, East India House. The shop opened in May 1875 with just three employees and initially sold only coloured silks from the East. Artists and designers such as **William Morris**, Lawrence Alma Tadema (1836–1912), Dante Gabriel Rossetti (1828–1882) and Edward Burne-Jones (1833–1898) frequented the shop and it soon began retailing buddahs, lacquerware, cloisonné, Satsuma ware and fans from Japan. By the 1880s, the Liberty store had diversified its imported range to include merchandise from China, India, Persia and Indonesia. Around this time, the company was also retailing its own textiles dyed in "Art Colours" and printed textiles that either copied old Indian patterns or were designed

▲ *Tulip* textile for
Liberty & Co.,
c. 1905

by contemporary designers such as **Charles Voysey**, and were block-printed by hand at the Liberty printworks at Merton Abbey. In 1883, Arthur Lasenby Liberty founded a clothing shop in Chesham House on Regent Street, which was managed by **E. W. Godwin**. He also established a new "Furnishing and Decoration Studio" that was headed by Leonard F. Wyburd, and which, through the 1880s and 90s, produced both Moorish style furnishings and vernacular-style Arts & Crafts furniture, including the *Althelstan* range. Liberty & Co. also became celebrated for their *Cymric* and *Tudric* metalware ranges designed by **Archibald Knox** and their carpets designed most notably by the **Silver Studio** and Voysey. Other designers who produced designs for Liberty included **Christopher Dresser**, **Charles Rennie Mackintosh** and **Hugh Mackay Baillie-Scott**. The Liberty & Co. range was distributed by **Siegfried Bing**'s "Maison de l'Art Nouveau" in Paris and by Metz & Co. in The Hague, and was so influential in the promotion of **Art Nouveau** on the Continent that "Liberty" became a generic term for the style. In Italy, for instance, the New Art movement became known as "Stile Liberty". Unlike many other exponents of the **Arts & Crafts Movement**, Arthur Lasenby Liberty believed that it was essential to embrace mechanized methods of production if well-designed goods were to be made affordable, and by putting this theory into practice Liberty & Co. enjoyed considerable commercial success.

▼ **George Walton** (attributed), Chair for Liberty & Co., c. 1905

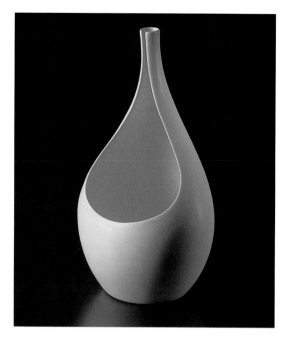

► *Pongo* vase for Gustavsberg, c. 1953

Stig Lindberg

1916 *Umeå, Sweden*
1982 *San Felice Circeo, Italy*

Frederick Stigurd (Stig) Lindberg studied in Jönköping and later at the Konstfackskolan, Stockholm. From 1937 to 1940, he worked under **Wilhelm Kåge** at the Gustavsberg ceramics factory, executing a number of geometric designs in the **Art Deco** style and at least one assymetrical design that anticipated his later organic approach to design. During this period, he also studied briefly in Denmark and at the Académie Colarossi, Paris – an experience which he later claimed had been crucial to his artistic training. Lindberg's ceramics were first shown publicly in Stockholm in 1941 and during the post-war years came to exemplify Scandinavian Modernism. From 1945 to 1947, Lindberg designed glassware for Maleras and textiles for Nordiska (from 1947) while also working as a book illustrator. He succeeded Wilhelm Kage as Gustavsberg's artistic director in 1949, introducing several new ranges including *Pongo* (1953). Lindberg also designed faïence wares painted with scenes inspired by the paintings of Marc Chagall (1887–1985), which were produced in the Gustavsberg Studio. In 1957, Lindberg left his directorship at Gustavsberg to teach at the Konstfackskolan (1957–1970), but continued to design glassware for both Holmegaard (1959–1960) and Kosta (1965). He later resumed his position at Gustavsberg from 1971 to 1980.

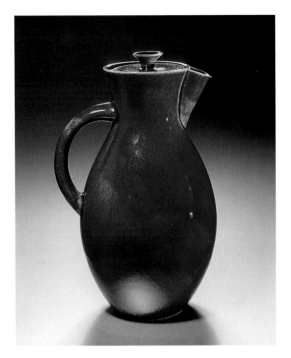

Otto Lindig attended sculpting and drawing classes in Lichte, Thuringia
and studied at the Großherzoglich Sächsische Kunstgewerbeschule, Weimar,
from 1913 to 1915, while working as an assistant sculptor at the Bechstein
Atelier, Ilmenau. From 1915 to 1918, he completed his training under Richard
Engelmann at the Großherzoglich Sächsische Hochschule für Bildende Kunst,
Weimar, established his own studio, and in 1919 enrolled at the **Bauhaus**
Weimar. He took the preliminary course and served an apprenticeship in
the ceramics workshop in Dornburg. Under his direction, the commercial
division of the Bauhaus' ceramic workshop began designing wares that
combined handcraft with mass-production techniques for the Aelteste
Volkstedter Porzellanfabik and the Staatliche Porzellanmanufaktur Berlin,
and in 1926 he became master of the ceramics workshop at the Staatliche Bauhochschule Weimar in Dornburg, where he produced semi-opaque
glazed ceramics that had undecorated elemental forms. Lindig continued
to operate independently from the Dornburg workshop after 1930, and
taught at the Hochschule für Bildende Künste, Hamburg from 1947 to 1960.

Otto Lindig

1895 *Pößneck, Germany*
1966 *Wiesbaden,*
Germany

Vicke Lindstrand

1904 Göteborg, Sweden
1983 Småland, Sweden

Viktor Emanuel (Vicke) Lindstrand studied graphic design at the Svenska Slöjdförenings Skola, Göteborg, and while studying contributed cartoons and illustrations to two local newspapers. In 1928, he began designing for Orrefors, his early glass being classically modern in form and engraved with figurative motifs. Designs such as these were exhibited at the 1930 "Stockholmsutstäliningen" to widespread acclaim. He later designed a window for the Swedish pavilion at the 1937 Paris "Exposition Internationale des Arts et Techniques dans la Vie Moderne" and a glass fountain for the 1939 New York World's Fair. Around this time, he began developing a softer and more fluid style and his engraved decoration became more rhythmic. Although he continued producing designs for Orrefors until 1941, Lindstrand also worked for the Kariskrona Porslinsfabrik and Upsala-Ekeby, acting as art director of the latter from 1943. He then ran his own studio in Arhus for twenty years and was design director of the Kosta Boda glass factory. There he produced some of his most sculptural vessels, which were influenced by the work of contemporary Venetian designers such as **Fulvio Bianconi**. Lindstrand's designs, however, were distinguished by less expressive organic forms and a restrained use of colour.

Lazar Markovich (El) Lissitzky trained as an architect at the Technische Hochschule, Darmstadt from 1909 to 1914 and then studied at the polytechnic in Riga. In 1919, he was invited by Marc Chagall to take up the professorship of graphic art and architecture at the newly reorganized art school in Vitebsk, where he became a member of **Kasimir Malevich**'s UNO-VIS group and developed his PROUN (Project for the Affirmation of the New) concept, which proposed the "interchange" of architecture and painting so as to create a more powerful means of expression. His prototype for a Speaker's Platform (1920) developed at Vitebsk used iron girders and glass and incorporated an elevator in its dynamic structure. In 1921, Lissitzky began teaching at the official Soviet design institute, **Vkhutemas**, and participated in the "Erste Russische Kunstausstellung" held in Berlin in 1922, while editing the Berlin-based multilingual magazine, *Veshch-Objet-Gegenstand*. Between 1922 and 1925, he taught in Switzerland and Germany and established important links between the Russian Constructivists, members of **De Stijl** and the **Bauhaus**. After designing his most radical architectural proposal, the *Wolkenbügel* (Skyhanger) office block (1924–1925), in collaboration with **Mart Stam**, he returned to teaching at the Vkhutemas and designed the abstract art section for the Staatliches Museum in Hanover in 1927. His armchairs for the "Pressa Ausstellung" in Cologne (1928) and for the "Hygiene Ausstellung" in Dresden (1930) both reflected the influence of the Bauhaus, De Stijl and Dada. Lissitzky also designed the Soviet Pavilion for the 1939 New York World's Fair. Throughout his career, Lissitzky experimented with photography, typography, book design, graphic design and interior design and produced many works that were of a propagandist nature. Lissitzky's greatest contribution, however, were the links he forged between Russian **Constructivism** and the West European **avant-garde**.

El Lissitzky
1890 *Smolensk, Russia*
1941 *Moscow*

▼ Cover for Alexander Tairoff's book *Das entfesselte Theater*, Potsdam, 1923

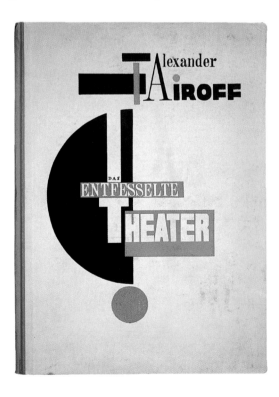

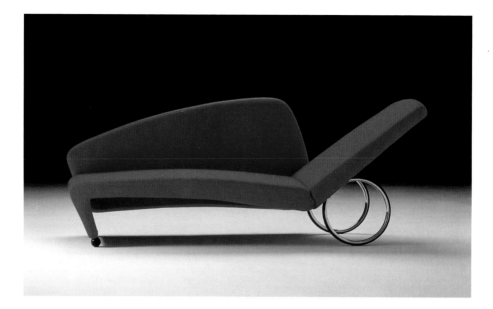

Josep Lluscà
b. 1948 *Barcelona*

Josep Lluscà studied industrial design at the Escuela de Diseño Eina, Barcelona and at the École des Arts et Métiers, Montreal. During the 1970s, he experimented in various areas of design before concentrating on furniture and lighting. Many of these early designs, which were inspired by contemporary sculpture, the architecture of **Antonio Gaudí** and 1950s **Organic Design**, were produced for Norma Europa. Between 1985 and 1987, Lluscà was vice president of the ADI-FAD (Industrial Designers' Association of Spain) and was a founding member of the ADP (Association of Professional Designers). His elegant cast-aluminium and plywood *Andrea* chair, which was launched by Andreu World in 1986, exemplifies the well-designed and executed furniture produced in Spain during the 1980s. In 1989 his *Lola* seating range was manufactured by Oken and his *Ketupa* lamp (1989), which was designed in collaboration with the silversmith Joaquín Berao, was issued by Metalarte. Lluscà is a member of the Design Council of the Catalonian government and has received many accolades including the 1990 National Design Award. His furniture pieces, such the *Faventia* chaise longue (1992) and the *BNC* chair (1988) for Oken, possess a strong sense of national identity and have been widely exhibited to much international acclaim.

▲ *Faventia* chaise longue for Oken, 1992

The glassworks at Klostermühle was founded in 1836 by Johann Baptist Eisner von Eisenstein. It was named Glasfabrik Johann Loetz Witwe by the third owner, whose grandson, Max Ritter von Spaun, took over the running of the company in 1879, with Eduard Prochaska as production manager. Von Spaun expanded the works and began producing a vast diversity of wares, often using newly developed techniques and metallic and lustre finishes that were patented by the firm. They launched their *Onyx* and *Octopus* glassware ranges in 1888, and were awarded a diploma at the Munich "German National Arts and Crafts Exhibition". In 1889, Loetz received a first prize at the "Exposition Universelle et Internationale de Paris", and a year later introduced their famous iridescent *Karneol* glassware. By 1890, the glassworks had around two hundred employees and distributors in Vienna, Berlin, Hamburg and Paris. The Loetz stand at the 1893 "World's Columbian Exposition" in Chicago won another first prize and displayed several new lines including *Columbia*, *Pavonia*, *Persica*, *Alpenrot*, *Alpengrün* and *Kamelienrot*. Von Spaun launched the *Papillon* and *Phenomenon* wares in 1899 and subsequently developed several other lines, winning a Grand Prix at the 1900 "Exposition Universelle et Internationale de Paris". **Koloman Moser** and his assistants designed wares for the company, as did the **Wiener Werkstätte** designers **Josef Hoffmann**, **Dagobert Peche**, **Otto Prutscher**, Hans Bolek (b. 1890), Leopold Bauer (1872–1938) and Carl Witzmann (1883–1952). Between 1903 and 1914, the Polish designer, Marie Kirschner, created over two hundred vessels for Loetz. Von Spaun's son took over the directorship of the glassworks in 1909 when Adolf Beckert was appointed its artistic director, and two years later the firm went into liquidation. However, it was revived and stayed in operation until its final closure shortly after the Second World War.

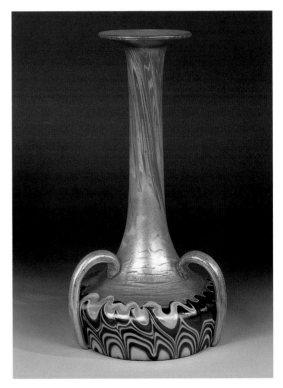

▼ Iridescent glass vase,
c. 1900

Raymond Loewy

1893 *Paris*
1986 *Monaco*

▼ Cover of *Time Magazine*, 31st October 1949

At the age of fifteen, Raymond Loewy designed, built and flew a toy model aeroplane that won the famous James Gordon Bennett Cup. He subsequently studied at the Université de Paris and later at the École de Laneau from where he obtained an engineering degree in 1918. During the First World War, he served in the French army as a second lieutenant and, after his demobilization in 1919, travelled to America. On his arrival in New York, Loewy was still wearing his French army uniform and had only fifty dollars in his pocket. He initially found employment as a window dresser for Macy's, Saks Fifth Avenue and Bonvit Teller, and then worked as a fashion illustrator for five years for *Vogue*, *Harper's Bazaar* and *Vanity Fair* among others. Loewy established his own industrial design office in New York in 1929 and designed a casing for Sigmund Gestetner's mimeograph machine using modelling clay to create a sleek form – a technique he later used for automotive designs. His *Hupmobile* car was already less box-like than existing automobiles, and his improved tapering model of the car with integrated headlamps from 1934 anticipated the streamlined forms for which he later became celebrated. He also designed the *Coldspot* refrigerator in 1934 for Sears Roebuck, which was the first domestic appliance to be marketed for its aesthetic appeal, and that same year the **Museum of Modern Art, New York**, displayed a mock-up of his office. From 1935, Loewy was commissioned to replan several large department stores, including Saks Fifth Avenue. Around this time, he was also designing aerodynamic locomotives, such as the *K4S* (1934), the *GG-1* (1934) and the *T-1* (1937), and in 1937 he published a book entitled *The New Vision Locomotive*. After remodelling coaches for Greyhound, he designed his innovative *Champion* car (1947) for Studebaker – a precursor of his European-styled *Avanti* car for that company. Loewy also became celebrated for his **corporate identity** work, in particular for his

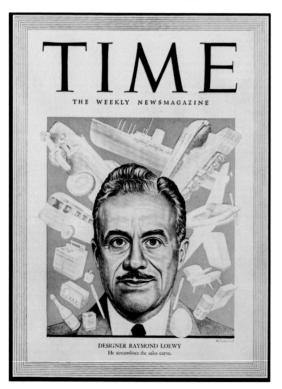

DESIGNER RAYMOND LOEWY
He streamlines the sales curve.

▲ Redesign of Lucky Strike cigarette packaging
for the American Tobacco Company, 1942

repackaging of Lucky Strike cigarettes (1942). Other clients of his included
Coca-Cola, Pepsodent, National Biscuit Company, British Petroleum,
Exxon and Shell. He founded a partnership with four other designers known
as Raymond Loewy Associates, which in 1949 was expanded to undertake
architectural projects and renamed the Raymond Loewy Corporation. That
year, Loewy became the first designer to feature on the cover of *Time* magazine. During the 1960s and 1970s, as a consultant to the United States
Government, he was responsible for the re-designing of Air Force One
for John F. Kennedy and for the interiors of NASA's Skylab (1969–1972).
Loewy's MAYA (most advance, yet acceptable) design philosophy was
crucial to the success of his products. Undoubtedly the greatest pioneer
of **Streamlining** in the 20th century, few design consultants have been as
influential or prolific as Raymond Loewy.

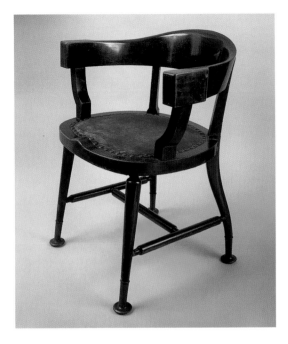

◄ *Manz* chair for
F. O. Schmidt, 1912

Adolf Loos studied building construction at the Gewerbeschule, Reichen-
berg, and architecture at the Technische Hochschule, Dresden, graduating
in 1893. He then travelled around America for three years, working as a mason and visiting the 1893 "World's Colombian Exhibition" in Chicago, where
he first encountered the Chicago School of architecture. On his return to
Europe, Loos settled in Vienna and worked in Carl Mayreder's architectural
office for two years. From 1897, he operated as an independent architect,
pioneering a more geometric and rational style than that associated with
the Vienna **Secession**, a style best illustrated by his Viennese Café Museum
(1899), which was subsequently nicknamed Café Nihilismus on account of
its stark interior scheme. He published numerous articles not only on art
and architecture but also on lifestyle and culture, and in 1903 established
the periodical *Das Andere*. In one highly influential essay, *Ornament und
Verbrechen* (Ornament and Crime) (1908), he argued that the excessive use
of decoration would lead to the debasing of society. Loos ran his own school
of architecture from 1912 to 1914 and was the chief municipal architect for
housing development in Vienna from 1920 to 1922. Linking morality with
functional, undecorated forms, Loos' teachings were immensely influential
to the early origins of the **Modern Movement**.

Adolf Loos

1870 *Brno, Slovakia*
1933 *Kalksburg, Austria*

Ross Lovegrove

b. 1958 *Cardiff/Wales*

Ross Lovegrove studied industrial design at Manchester Polytechnic, graduating in 1980. He subsequently trained at the **Royal College of Art, London**, receiving an MA in 1983, and then worked for the industrial design consultancy **Frogdesign** in Altensteig, where he was assigned to projects that included the design of Walkmans for Sony and computers for Apple. Lovegrove was associated with a number of companies in the mid-1980s. As an in-house designer for **Knoll International** in Paris he designed the successful Alessandri Office System, and as a co-member of the Atelier de Nîmes, France, with **Philippe Starck**, **Jean Nouvel**, Martine Bedin (b. 1957) and Gérard Barrau (b. 1945), he acted as a consultant designer to Louis Vuitton, Cacharel, Dupont and Hermès. In 1986, Lovegrove returned to Britain and set up an office with Julian Brown. However, this partnership was dissolved in 1990 when Lovegrove established his own London-based industrial design practice, Studio X. Since then, his clients have included British Airways, Parker Pens, **Kartell**, Ceccotti, Cappellini, Phillips, Moroso, Driade, Apple, Connolly Leather, Olympus, Luceplan, Tag Heuer, Fratelli

▼ *John II* stapler
for Acco, 1997

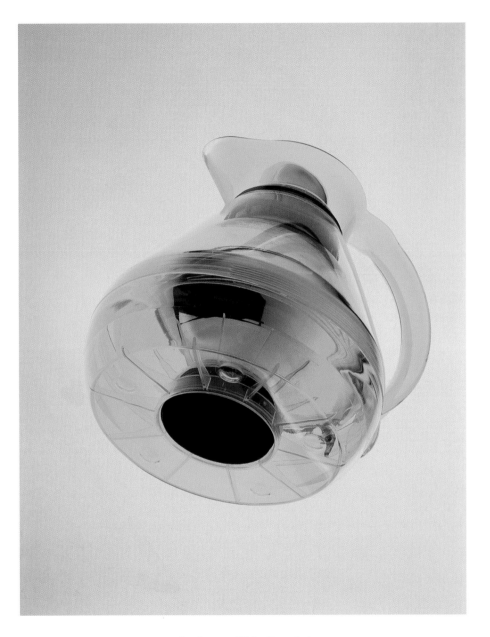

▲ **Ross Lovegrove & Julian Brown**, *Basic*
thermos flask for Alfi Zitzmann, 1990

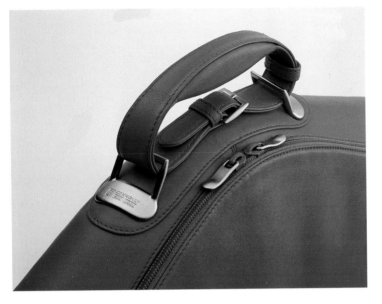

◄ Detail of suit
carrier for Connolly
Leather, 1994

Guzzini and **Herman Miller**. His visually seductive and technologically
persuasive designs – such as the *Organic* cutlery (1990) for Pottery Barn,
the *Basic* thermos flask (1990) for Alfi Zitzmann (co-designed with Julian
Brown), the *Crop* chair (1996) for Fasem, and the *Eye* digital camera (1996)
for Olympus – are inspired by the natural world and informed by his broad
understanding of ergonomics, state-of-the-art materials and cutting-edge
manufacturing techniques. Lovegrove curated the first permanent collection
at the Design Museum, London in 1993, and since 1997 has had solo exhibitions of his work in Copenhagen and Stockholm and Tokyo, the latter staged
by the Yamagiwa Corporation and Idée. Lovegrove is keenly aware of current
ecological and **Green Design** issues and many of his product designs, such
as his *Solar Bud* solar-powered garden lighting (1996–1997) for Luceplan directly address these concerns. He also worked on a proposal for lightweight
product architecture known as the *Solar Seed* that is similarly solar powered
and was inspired by the form of a cactus. Lovegrove's dematerialist, holistically derived and forward-looking products embody a new organic sensibility
and have set the stage for design in the 21st century.

◄ *Model No. ST14* chair for Desta, 1931

Hans Luckhardt studied at the Technische Hochschule, Karlsruhe, while his brother, Wassili Luckhardt attended the Technische Hochschule, Berlin. They were both signatories of the Architecture Programme drawn up by the Arbeitsrat für Kunst in 1919 and became involved with the artists' groups, Novembergruppe and Der Ring, as well as submitting many letters and drawings to Bruno Taut's (1880–1938) "Utopian Correspondence" project. They worked together in Berlin from 1921 onwards, and were joined by Alfons Anker in 1924. Their architecture was initially Expressionist in style, as the Hygienemuseum in Dresden (1921) and the Friedrichstraße office building project in Berlin (1922) demonstrate. However, from around 1925, the Luckhardts adopted a more rational approach to architecture and furniture design, as shown by the standardization in their *Model ST14* cantilevered chair (1931). They worked on numerous projects, mostly in Berlin, including terraced housing on the Schorlemer Allee (1927), business premises for the Hirsch and Telschow companies (1926–1928) and the replanning of Alexanderplatz (1929). In 1951, they designed the Berlin Pavilion for the "Constructa Exhibition", Hanover, and a year later Hans was appointed professor at the Hochschule für Bildende Künste, Berlin.

Wassili & Hans Luckhardt

Wassili Luckhardt
1889 *Berlin*
1972 *Berlin*

Hans Luckhardt
1890 *Berlin*
1954 *Bad Wiessee, Germany*

Charles Rennie Mackintosh

1868 *Glasgow*
1928 *London*

▲ Drawing room of
the Mackintoshes'
home – 6, Florentine
Terrace, Glasgow,
1906 (reconstruction
at the Hunterian Art
Gallery, Glasgow)

Charles Rennie Mackintosh served an apprenticeship in the architectural practice of John Hutchinson in Glasgow while taking evening classes in drawing and painting at the Glasgow School of Art. He went on a scholarship tour of Italy in 1891, returning via Paris, Brussels, Antwerp and London, and in 1892 was awarded the National Gold Medal at South Kensington, London. Seven years later he joined the newly established architectural practice of Honeyman & Keppie in Glasgow, where he remained until 1913. Mackintosh, Herbert MacNair (1868–1955), Francis Macdonald (1873–1921) and Margaret Macdonald (1864–1933) formed "The Four", later dubbed the "Spook School", exhibiting together for the first time in 1894, then at the Arts & Crafts Exhibition Society, London in 1896 and at the VIII Secessionist Exhibition in Vienna in 1900 to great acclaim. That same year, Mackintosh married Margaret Macdonald, with whom he collaborated on many of his decorative schemes. Mackintosh's white interiors had a profound influence on the subsequent designs of **Josef Maria Olbrich** and **Josef Hoffmann**, and one of the chairs he exhibited was actually purchased by **Koloman Moser**.

He was awarded a special prize at Alexander Koch's "Haus eines Kunst-
freundes" (House for an Art Lover) competition in 1901, and the following
year was commissioned by Fritz Wärndorfer (1869–1939), the main financial
backer of the Vienna **Secession** and later of the **Wiener Werkstätte**, to design
a music salon (1902–1903), which was described by the critic Ludwig Hevesi
as "a place of spiritual delight". Mackintosh designed several public buildings and private residences in Glasgow and its environs at the turn of the
century, including his masterwork, the Glasgow School of Art (1896–1909).
Some of his projects, such as Hill House (1902–1903), were conceived as
Gesamtkunstwerks and were thus provided with site-specific soft furnishings and furniture. Among his most important interiors, were the Glasgow
tea rooms that he decorated for Catherine Cranston; the two in Buchanan
Street (1896) and Argyle Street (1897) being designed in conjunction with
George Walton. Mackintosh's fa-

▼ High-backed chair
for the Luncheon
Room of the Argyle
Street Tea Rooms,
1897

mous elliptical high-backed chairs
adorned the Argyle Street tea rooms,
and the later rooms in Ingram Street
and Willow Street were decorated
entirely by him, down to the cutlery.
His holistic approach to architecture
and design included the use of symbolism and the balancing of oppos-
ites – modernity with tradition, light
with dark, the masculine with the
feminine. In 1914, he left Glasgow
and moved to London, where he designed colour-saturated and rhythmically patterned textiles for Foxton's
and Sefton's that anticipated **Art
Deco**. Unable to secure any architectural commissions in London, he
moved to Port Vendres, France in
1923 and dedicated himself entirely
to the painting of watercolours.
Mackintosh was the leading designer of the **Glasgow School** and both
his early organic style and his later
geometric style were enormously
influential to the Vienna Secession
and the Wiener Werkstätte.

Arthur Heygate Mackmurdo

1851 *London*
1942 *Wickham Bishops/Essex*

▼ Wallpaper produced by Jeffrey & Co. for the Century Guild, c. 1884

Arthur Heygate Mackmurdo was first apprenticed to the London architect, T. Chatfield Clarke (1829–1895) and later worked as an assistant for the Gothic Revivalist architect, James Brooks (1825–1901). On reading the works of John Ruskin (1819–1900), Mackmurdo was so impressed by the master's ideas that he enrolled at the School of Drawing where Ruskin was a professor. In 1874, he and Ruskin toured Italy together, and on their return Mackmurdo began teaching with his mentor at the Working Men's College, London. Mackmurdo then established his own London-based office, and two years later met **William Morris**, who inspired him to turn his attention to the crafts. He began teaching himself stone carving, embroidery, brass repoussé work and furniture-making, and in 1882 joined Selwyn Image (1849–1930), Herbert P. Horne (1864–1916), Clement Heaton (1861–1940) and Bernard Creswick in founding the artistic co-operative, the Century Guild, with the aim of rendering "all branches of art the sphere no longer of the tradesman, but of the artist". Other designers associated with the guild included **William de Morgan** and George Heywood Sumner (1853–1940).

Mackmurdo edited the first issue of *The Hobby Horse* journal, which was published quarterly by the Guild from April 1884. With his wide circle of friends, including Ford Madox Brown (1821–1893), James Abbott McNeill Whistler (1834–1903) and Frank Brangwyn (1867–1956), Mackmurdo bridged the reforming generation of Ruskin and Morris and the younger generation of Aesthetes. In 1883, he published *Wren's City Churches*, the title-page of which displayed a strong Japanese influence. After helping **Walter Crane** establish the National Association for the Advancement of Art in 1888, Mackmurdo concentrated on his theories for social reform, which were published in his books entitled *The Human Hive* (1926) and *A People's Charter* (1933).

Vico Magistretti studied at the Champ Universitaire Italien de Lausanne, and while there took a course on architecture and urban planning devised by Ernesto Rogers (1909–1969). As a strong advocate of Modernism, Rogers' influence on the younger generation of Italian designers, including Magistretti, was immense. Magistretti returned to Milan in 1945 to take his degree in architecture, and a year later designed a tubular metal bookcase and a simple deck chair for the RIMA (Riunione Italiana per le Mostre di Arredamento) exhibition. His nesting tables and a highly rational, ladder-like bookcase were exhibited alongside the works of **Marco Zanuso**, **Franco Albini**, Ignazio Gardella (b. 1905) and the **Castiglioni** brothers in an exhibition organized by Fede Cheti (1905–1978) in 1949. During the 1950s, Magistretti was mainly active as an architect, and his office block on the Corso Europa, Milan established his **avant-garde** credentials. His design of the Villa Arosio, which was presented at the CIAM (Congrès Internationaux d'Architecture Moderne) conference of 1959, created much discussion as Magistretti had attempted to humanize Modernism with the incorporation of Neo-Liberty elements. He used a similar tempered approach for the design of his clubhouse at the Carimate Golf Club in 1959. For this project,

Vico Magistretti
b. 1920 *Milan*

▶ *Telegono* table lamp for Artemide, 1968

Magistretti created a modern re-working of a traditional rush-seated chair that countered the industrial aesthetic of the **International Style**. The manufacturer Cesare Cassina, who had met Magistretti in 1960, began mass-producing the *Carimate* chair in 1962. During the 1960s, Magistretti started to design plastic furniture – his first success being the *Demetrio* tables of 1966, which married technical innovation with purity of form. Many of his later designs, such as the *Eclisse* table lamp (1965), the *Chimera* lamp (1966), the *Stadio* table, the single-piece *Selene* chair (1969), the *Gaudi* and *Vicario* armchairs (1970), also demonstrated the noble attributes of plastic through their high quality constructions and ingenious forms. Other famous designs of Magistretti's include the *Maralunga* sofa with adjustable headrest (1973), the *Nuvola Rossa* folding bookcase (1977), the *Atollo* lacquered metal lamp (1977), the *Sindbad* chair and sofa with blanket-like upholstery (1981), the adjustable *Veranda* chair and sofa (1983) and the multipurpose polypropylene and tubular aluminium *Silver* chair (1989). As one of the foremost industrial designers of the 20th century, Magistretti has been awarded numerous prizes, including a gold medal and a Grand Prix at the Milan Triennale exhibitions, two **Compasso d'Oro** and a SIAD (Society of Industrial Artists and Designers) gold medal. He has taught at the Domus Academy, Milan, and in 1983, was made an honorary fellow of the **Royal College of Art, London**, where he is a visiting professor. Throughout his career, whether working with traditional or state-of-the-art materials, Magistretti has harmoniously balanced technical ingenuity with sculptural elegance to create timeless modern designs that have a remarkable integrity. He regards design and styling as complimentary to one another and believes that usefulness and beauty are both essential to the creation of quality products. Throughout his career, Magistretti has consistently urged for long-lasting design solutions that do not perpetuate the "throw-away" culture.

▼ *Selene* chairs for Artemide, 1969

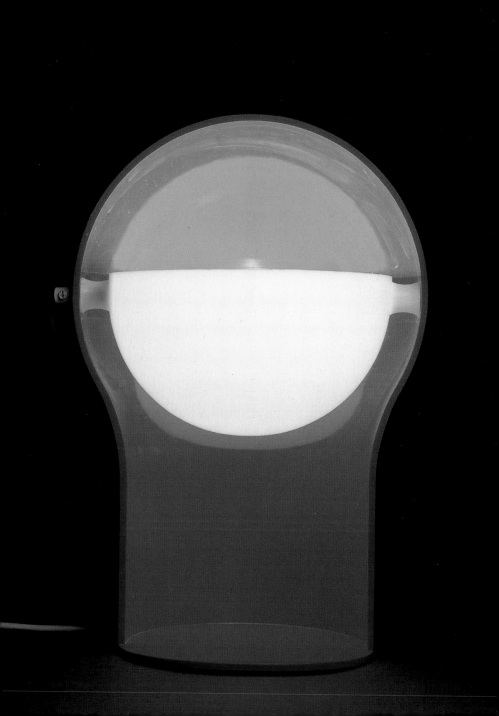

Louis Majorelle studied painting in Nancy and later at the École des Beaux Arts, Paris from 1877 to 1879. Upon the death of his father Auguste Majorelle in 1879, he took over the running of the family's furniture and ceramics firm in Nancy, which had been established in 1860. Initially, Majorelle designed furniture in the Rococo style, but in the 1890s he became increasingly influenced by the naturalism of **Émile Gallé**'s work and began producing **Art Nouveau** designs. His room display at the 1900 "Exposition Universelle et Internationale de Paris", for instance, had a water lily theme. His furniture became more structurally inventive than Gallé's, although it employed similar marquetry decoration. From 1900, Majorelle also designed metal stands and mounts for Auguste Daum's glassware and lamp shades, while **Daum Frères** produced glass elements for Majorelle's own range. Marjorelle was appointed vice-president of the newly established **École de Nancy** in 1901, and exhibited his flamboyant furniture and gilt-bronze lighting at the school's exhibition in Paris two years later. In 1916, the Majorelle factory in Nancy was badly damaged by fire and Louis Majorelle fled to Paris. After the First World War, he returned to Nancy and his factory recommenced production. During the 1920s, his work became more formal and less ornamented, reflecting the influence of the new **Art Deco** style. Assisted by his factory manager, Alfred Lévy, Majorelle designed a room for the Nancy Pavilion at the 1925 "Exposition Internationale des Arts Décoratifs et Industriels Modernes", while sitting on the exhibition jury. After Majorelle's death in 1926, the Nancy-based workshops of the Atelier Majorelle remained under the management of Lévy, who was joined by Paul Beucher around 1935. The company had showrooms in Nancy, Paris and Lyons, and produced not only very expensive and elaborate designs but also restrained and affordable products.

Louis Majorelle
1859 *Toul, France*
1926 *Nancy, France*

◄ Armchair, c. 1900

▼ Detail of a staircase balustrade for the Hôtel Bergeret in Nancy, 1904

John Makepeace
b. 1939 *Solihull/West Midlands*

▼ *Rhythm* chair for John Makepeace Furniture Studio, 1992

As a child, John Makepeace was interested in carpentry and visited the cabinet-making workshop of Hugh Burkett, a follower of the Arts & Crafts tradition. Makepeace subsequently served a cabinet-making apprenticeship with Keith Cooper in 1957 and later established his own workshop. He curated an exhibition at the Herbert Art Gallery, Coventry in 1962, displaying the work of a dozen designer-craftsmen including Ann Sutton, whom he married two years later. He then established a larger workshop at Farnborough Barn, and in 1972 travelled to America and discussed with **Wendell Castle** the possibility of setting up a New York-based school for craftsmen. On his return, Makepeace searched for an appropriate building for a similar institution in Britain, and in 1976 acquired Parnham House at Beaminster in Dorset. There he established his own studio/workshop as well as a school for craftsmen in wood, Parnham College. Through the superlative craftsmanship and unusual constructions of his own furniture, Makepeace promotes

the virtues of craftsmanship and is the leading British exponent of the **Craft Revival.** In 1987, Makepeace established the Hooke Park training centre to research and develop the use of sustainable resources. The German organic architect Otto Frei, and the structural engineer Edmund Happold, together with Richard Burton of the ABK design practice, oversaw the design of the training centre's buildings, which were innovatively constructed of thinnings from the surrounding woodland. These small-diameter trees, felled to allow more room for selected trees to grow to maturity, are normally used as firewood or pulped even though they have enormous structural potential both in architecture and furniture design. Through Makepeace's vision, this overlooked natural resource is now being used as an ecologically sustainable source of timber for the wooden furniture of the future.

Kasimir Malevich studied at the Drawing School in Kiev and at the Moscow Institute of Painting, Sculpture and Architecture. He was initially influenced by Neo-Primitivism, Cubism and **Futurism**, and in 1913 took part in the Futurist conference held at Uusikirkko, Finland. Between 1913 and 1915, Malevich developed his own hyper-orthodox form of Cubism known as Suprematism. His manifesto *From Cubism and Futurism to Suprematism: The New Painterly Realism,* published in 1915, explained "the supremacy of pure emotion" achieved through the placing of geometric elements on a white field or "void" and the elimination of objective representation. In 1918, Malevich became associated with the Izo NKP (the department of fine arts at Narkompros) and wrote his article *On New Systems in Art.* The same year, he succeeded Marc Chagall (1887–1985) as director of the Vitebsk art school, and in 1919 established the Posnovis group, which later became known as Unovis (Utverditeli novogo iskussetvo = Affirmers of the New Art). This artists' group was active until 1923 and included **Nikolai Suetin, El Lissitzky** and Ilia Chashnik among its members. During the 1920s, Malevich designed architectural models, graphics, clothes, textiles and ceramics. He moved to Petrograd with some of his students in 1922 and established a branch of Inkhuk (Institute of Artistic Culture) there. In 1927, he visited the **Bauhaus** in Dessau, which later published his book *The Non-Objective World.* Although best remembered as the artist who painted the ultimate abstract picture – a white square on a white ground (c. 1918) – Malevich's promotion of aesthetic purification was highly influential to the Bauhaus' adoption of pure geometric abstraction and thereby to the development of the **Modern Movement**.

Kasimir Malevich
1878 *Kiev*
1955 *Leningrad*

▲ **László Moholy-Nagy,** Cover for Kasimir Malevich's *Die Gegenstandslose Welt –* Bauhaus-bücher 11, 1927

Robert Mallet-Stevens
1886 *Paris*
1945 *Paris*

The son of an art-historian, Robert Mallet-Stevens studied at the École Spéciale d'Architecture, Paris from 1903 to 1906. He was much influenced by Cubism and the rectilinear work of **Charles Rennie Mackintosh** and **Josef Hoffmann**, who had designed the Palais Stoclet in Brussels for his uncle. Between 1911 and 1912, he wrote a number of articles that appeared in the magazines *Le Home, Tekhné, L'Art Ménager* and *Lux*. He exhibited his work at the Salons d'Automne from 1912 onwards, and in 1913 received much acclaim for his design of the colourful "Salon de Musique". With its geometric lines and rational furniture, this room introduced Modernism to French interior design, which up to then had been dominated by the *décorateur* tradition. His functional, unornamented work, such as the Alfa Romeo showroom in Paris (1925) and the Vicomte de Noailles' villa in Hyères (1923–1924), was extremely influential to French **avant-garde** design during the 1920s and 1930s. In 1922, Mallet-Stevens published an architectural portfolio, entitled *Une Cité Moderne*, with a preface written by Frantz Jourdain (1847–1935). From 1923, he was associated with the *L'Architecture Moderne* journal, as were **Theo van Doesburg** and **Ludwig Mies van der Rohe**. He designed many avant-garde film sets, metalware for **Desny** and several notable buildings with set pieces of furniture, mostly in tubular steel. In 1930, Mallet-Stevens co-founded the UAM (Union des Artistes Modernes) with **Charlotte Perriand**, **Jean Puiforcat**, **Pierre Chareau** and **Eileen Gray** among others, and became its first president.

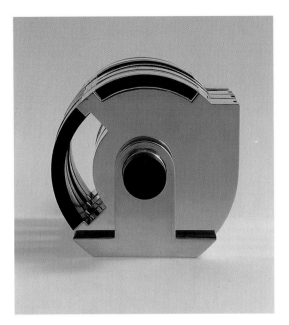

◄▼ Coffee and tea
service for Desny,
c. 1930

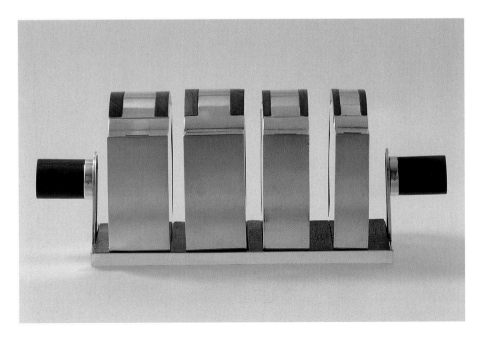

**Angelo
Mangiarotti**
b. 1921 *Milan*

Angelo Mangiarotti studied at the Politecnico di Milano until 1948. He subsequently established a design office in Ohio and became a visiting professor at the Institute of Design, Chicago. In 1955, he returned to Italy and
worked as a design consultant with Bruno Morassutti (b. 1920) until 1960,
producing designs for stackable shelving units, tables, a chewing gum dis-
penser (1958) and the well-known *Section* clock (1960). Mangiarotti became
a member of the ADI (Associazione per il Disegno Industriale) in 1960 and
from then on worked independently as an architect, industrial designer and
town-planner, experimenting with pre-fabricated constructions and reinforced concrete in the **International Style**. Mangiarotti's functionally based
yet sculptural product designs, such as the single-form self-skinning polyurethane *IN* chair (1969) for Zanotta and his glass vases and marble bowls
(1969 and 1970s) for **Knoll**, are notable for their high-quality finishes and
his skillful handling of materials. Mangiarotti has also collaborated with
the Japanese designer, Matomi Kawakami (b. 1940) and taught at various
institutions, including the University of Hawaii in 1970 and the faculties of
architecture at the Universities of Palermo and Florence from 1982 to 1984.

Gerhard Marcks taught himself to sculpt and then from 1908 to 1912 worked in the studio of the sculptor Richard Scheibe in Berlin. In 1914, he designed reliefs for the entrance hall of the factory designed by **Walter Gropius** at the "Deutsche Werkbund-Ausstellung" in Cologne, and in 1918 he joined the radical art association, Novembergruppe, which was founded in Berlin that year. After his military service, Marcks taught at the Kunstgewerbeschule (School of Applied Arts), Berlin for a year. He then became a member of the Arbeitsrat für Kunst (Working Council for Art) in Berlin and began teaching at the **Bauhaus** in Weimar. In 1920, Gropius appointed him the "Form-meister" (artistic director) of the Bauhaus' newly established ceramics work-shop at Dornburg, some thirty kilometres from Weimar. Marcks remained in this teaching position until 1924, and his ceramics from this period were relatively ornamental. In 1925, he became the director of the sculpture work-shop at the Kunstgewerbeschule Halle/Burg Giebichenstein and was ap-pointed the school's director in 1928, a position he held until 1933. His work became increasingly rational so as to be better suited for industrial manu-facture, as in the case of his highly rational *Sintrax* coffee maker for the Jenaer Glaswerke Schott & Gen., which was intended for large-scale mass-production. In 1933, he was dismissed from his post in Halle by the Nazis and subsequently moved to Niehagen. From 1937, he attemp-ted to work as a freelance artist in Berlin but was banned from exhibit-ing. Marcks suffered further perse-cution when his studio in Berlin-Nikolassee was destroyed in 1943. After the Second World War, he taught sculpture at the Landes-kunstschule, Hamburg for four years and then moved to Cologne in 1950, where he worked as an independent artist. In 1971, the Gerhard Marcks Foundation was established in Bremen, and in 1987 a retrospective of his work was held in Bremen, Cologne and Berlin.

Gerhard Marcks
1889 Berlin
1981 Burgbrohl, Germany

▼ *Sintrax* coffee maker for the Jenaer Glaswerke Schott & Gen., c. 1925

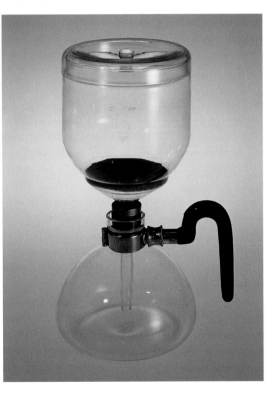

Enzo Mari

b. 1932 *Novara, Italy*

Enzo Mari studied at the Accademia di Belle Arte di Brera, Milan, from 1952 to 1956. He began working for Danese in 1957; one of his first projects for the company being an educational toy – a child's puzzle that was made up of a collection of stackable wooden animals (1957). In 1959, he began experimenting with plastics and these researches resulted in a number of high quality products that were also manufactured by Danese, including a PVC cylindrical umbrella stand (1962) and the *Pago-Pago* vase (1969) made of ABS. His sculptural marble *Paros* bowl (1964), modular system of exhibition equipment (1965) and plastic *Tortiglione* vases (1969) were also Danese products. Mari joined the radical Nuove Tendenze movement in 1963 and began teaching at the Scola Umanitaria, Milan. His radical theories were published in *Funzione della ricerca estetica,* and his "Proposta per un'auto-progettazione", which comprised a number of "tecnica povera" (poor technology) furniture pieces, was exhibited in 1974. Enzo Mari also collaborated with Elio Mari and has worked for ICF, Zanotta, Castelli, Artemide and **Olivetti** among others. As a leading design theorist, Mari was president of the ADI (Associazione per il Disegno Industriale) from 1976 to 1979, and has taught in Milan, Rome, Parma and Carrara.

▶ Bottle with
stopper, 1929

Maurice Marinot studied from 1889 at the École des Beaux-Arts, Paris under Fernand-Anne Piestre, who eventually fell out with his pupil over the latter's unorthodox approach to art. Marinot subsequently exhibited his paintings at the Salon d'Automne in 1905, alongside members of the Fauves group, including Henri Matisse (1869–1954) and André Derain (1880–1954). He then returned to his home town, Troyes, but continued to exhibit his work annually at the Salon d'Automne and the Salon des Indépendants until 1913. Marinot visited Eugène and Gabriel Viard's glassworks at Bar-sur-Seine in 1911 and was utterly entranced by the glass-making process, declaring that he had "a violent desire for this new game". He subsequently designed glassware with enamelled Fauvist-style embellishments, and in 1913 had the first major show of his glassware. When Marinot came to realize that the enamelling was masking the intrinsic beauties of his glass, he rejected surface decoration in favour of unusual techniques, such as sandwiching layers of metal oxides between clear glass. He also experimented with the use of "malfin" or imperfectly refined glass so as to create bubbles. His chunky glass vessels, which were sometimes engraved, were exhibited in New York and at the 1925 Paris "Exposition Internationale des Arts Décoratifs". After the closure of the Viard glassworks in 1937, Marinot returned to painting. Sadly many of his glass vessels were destroyed by bombing in 1944.

Maurice Marinot
1882 *Troyes, France*
1960 *Troyes*

Javier Mariscal studied philosophy at the University of Valencia and graphic design at the Elisava School, Barcelona up to 1971. Three years later, with a group of friends, he began publishing Spain's first underground comic, *El Rollo Enmascarado*. His first one-man show, held in Barcelona in 1977, featured drawings, glass paintings, sculptures and videos. Mariscal designed the "BAR-CEL-ONA" logotype in 1979 and, with the technical assistance of Pepe Cortés (b. 1945), produced his earliest piece of furniture, the *Duplex* bar stool, in 1980. The following year, prototypes of his idiosyncratic post-modern furniture were shown at an exhibition entitled "Muebles Amorales" in Barcelona. After being invited by **Ettore Sottsass** to participate in the "**Memphis**, an International Style" exhibition in 1981 in Milan, Mariscal showed several of his later "form follows fun" designs with Memphis, including his backward slanting *Hilton* tea trolley (1981). He also designed ceramics for Viçon, Barcelona (1985) and Axis, Paris (1986) and a range of textiles for Seibu, Japan (1986–1987). The humour, bold colouring and ebullience of these designs reflect the vibrancy and optimism of Post-Franco Spain and the country's growing eco-

Javier Mariscal
b. 1950 *Valencia, Spain*

◄ Official poster for the XXV Olympic Games in Barcelona, 1992 (showing Cobi)

▼ *Garriri* chair, 1988

nomic prosperity. In 1988, Mariscal created *Cobi*, the mascot selected for the 1992 Barcelona Olympics, which later featured in the television cartoon series "The Cobi Troupe" (1990) and, together with his compatriot Alfredo Arribas (b.1954), designed the El Gambrinus restaurant on Barcelona's waterfront, which had a huge shrimp-like cartoon character with a crooked smile looming over its wave-like roof. By 1992, the year of the Barcelona Olympics, Mariscal's work had become internationally celebrated and the subject of two publications and a Japanese travelling exhibition. Although Mariscal dismisses history and tradition, his work has a distinct Catalonian identity and reflects the exuberant nature of Barcelona's design and architectural heritage.

◄ Writing desk for
Nordiska, 1930

► *Pythagoras* textile
for Nordiska, 1952

Sven Markelius
1889 *Stockholm*
1972 *Stockholm*

Sven Markelius studied at the Kungliga Tekniska Högskolan (Royal Institute
of Technology), Stockholm and at the Kungliga Akademien för de fria
Konstrena (Royal Acadamy of Art), graduating in 1915. He later served an
apprenticeship in Ragnar Östberg's architectural office, where he assisted
on the design of the façade of Stockholm's town hall. His architecture
was initially inspired by Romanticism and later by Neo-Classicism. On en-
countering **Le Corbusier**'s architecture and the ideas emanating from the
Bauhaus, Markelius began to embrace Modernism. For the 1930 Stockholm
exhibition, he designed whole buildings as well as an interior that included
his writing desk manufactured by Nordiska Kompaniet. In 1932, he designed
the concert hall in Hälsingborg which included site-specific, functional,
modern stacking chairs. He also designed the Swedish pavilion for the 1939
New York World's Fair, which brought him international recognition. After
the Second World War, Markelius was elected to the United Nations building planning board and sat on the UNESCO Arts and Building Committees.
From 1944 to 1954, he headed the Stockholm Planning Office and developed
a scheme for expanding the city, which included suburban communities referred to as "town sections". During the 1950s, Markelius designed a range
of printed textiles with Astrid Sampe (b. 1909) for Nordiska, which were
marketed by **Knoll**.

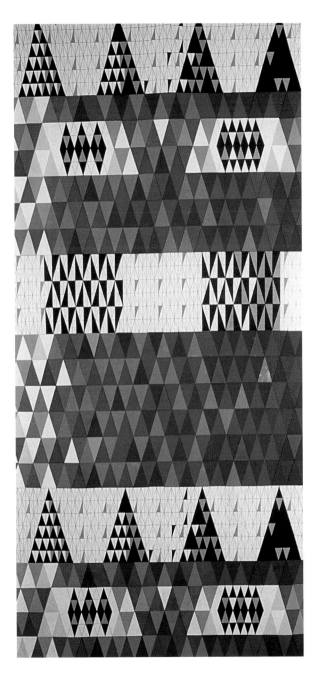

► *Model No. 5358*
vase for Aureliano
Toso, 1954

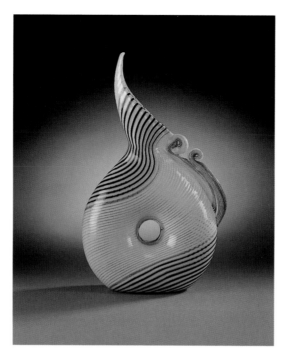

Dino Martens

1894 *Venice*
1970 *Venice*

Dino Martens studied painting at the Academia di Belle Arti, Venice. From 1925 to 1935, he worked as a painter in Murano, producing designs for several glassworks including SALIR, Salviati & C. and Cooperativa Mosaicisti Veneziani. He exhibited his paintings at the Venice Biennales from 1924 to 1930, and his glassware from 1932. In 1939, he became artistic director of Aureliano Toso and subsequently developed his well-known *Oriente* range, the designs of which comprised a bright patch-work of multicoloured "latticinio" pieces. For Aureliano Toso, Martens also designed his *Zanfirico* range, which used asymmetrical forms and twisted rods of coloured glass that were incorporated into clear glass bodies. Both of these ranges were widely copied during the 1950s and were highly influential to later American studio glass. His glassware designs, displayed at the IX Milan Triennale in 1951, were subsequently included in exhibitions at the Kunstgewerbemuseum, Zurich in 1954 and at the Corning Museum of Glass, New York in 1959 as well as in Verona in 1960 and Venice in 1981 and 1982. Martens' beautiful, expressive and highly collectable vessels exemplify the experimental approach of the Murano glassworks during the 1950s.

Bruno Mathsson trained in his father Karl's cabinet-making workshop, and from 1933 designed furniture primarily for the family business. His highly organic *Eva* chair (1934) and *Pernilla* chaise longue (c. 1934), with bent laminated wood frames, woven hemp webbing and solid beech seat frames, were less utilitarian but more ergonomically resolved than **Alvar Aalto**'s similar *Model No. 43* chaise longue (1936) and *Model No. 406* chair (1936–1939). In 1936, Mathsson was given a one-man show at the Röhsska Art Museum, Gothenburg, and a year later he participated in the 1937 "Exposition Internationale des Arts et Techniques dans la vie moderne" in Paris. Mathsson concentrated mainly on architecture from 1945 to 1957, designing several simple structures in glass, wood and concrete for use as summer houses and school rooms. He then took over the management of Firma Karl Mathsson, and from 1958 began developing furniture in collaboration with the mathematician Piet Hein (b. 1905), including the *Superellipse* table (1964), which was later manufactured by Fritz Hansen. He was awarded the Gregor Paulsson Medal in Stockholm in 1955 and his furniture was exhibited in Stockholm, Oslo, Dresden and New York in 1963, 1976, 1976 and 1982 respectively.

Bruno Mathsson
1907 Värnamo, Sweden
1988 Värnamo

▲ *Pernilla* lounge chairs and chaise longue for Karl Mathsson, c. 1934

Herbert Matter

1907 Engelberg, Switzerland
1984 Southampton, New York

Herbert Matter studied painting at the École des Beaux-Arts, Geneva from 1925 to 1927, and completed his training at the Académie de l'Art Moderne, Paris. Between 1929 and 1932, he designed typography and worked as a photographer for the Paris-based type foundry, Deberny & Peignot. He also collaborated on the design of posters with **A. M. Cassandre** and worked with **Le Corbusier** on displays and buildings. Like **Jan Tschichold**, Matter used his understanding of photography and knowledge of industrial printing techniques to pioneer a method of over-printing, which not only gave more visual depth to his posters but also created a dynamism between the photographic image and the typography. By combining powerful images with bold typography, Matter's posters, such as those for the Swiss Tourist Board, appeared extremely modern and had a remarkable directness. Matter emigrated to New York in 1936, where he worked as a photographer for the magazines *Vogue* and *Harper's Bazaar*. During the Second World War, he was commissioned by the US Government to design propaganda posters including his "America Calling" poster (1941), which featured a photographic image of an

▼ Travel poster for the Swiss Tourist Board, 1935

American eagle in flight. From 1943 to 1946, Matter worked as a graphic designer in the Eames Office in Venice, California. He then began to design colourful, humourous and eye-catching advertisements and posters for **Knoll** and also developed the company's distinctive "K" trademark. His art-direction of the Knoll advertisement (1959) for Eero Saarinen's *Tulip* chair was remarkable in that the images, which were displayed on sequential pages – one showing the chair wrapped in brown paper and the other showing it unwrapped – carried the message so powerfully, there was no need for copy. Matter's graphics, that combined the visual clarity of the **Swiss School** with American popular culture, defined the "look" of **avant-garde** graphics in the United States during the post-war years.

◄ Ingo Mauer &
Team, *One from the
Heart* lamp for Ingo
Mauer GmbH, 1989

Ingo Mauer trained as a typographer in Konstanz in southern Germany, before studying graphic design in Germany and Switzerland from 1954 to 1958.
He emigrated to the United States in 1960 and worked as a designer for
IBM and Kayser Aluminium. Three years later, Mauer returned to Europe
and became active as a graphic designer. He established his own lighting
design company, Design M in Munich in 1966, which became renowned for
its unusual and often humourous products. Some of Mauer's lighting designs, such as *Light Structure* (1969–1970) with its five fluorescent lighting
tubes and the *Ilios* standard lamp (1983) with its rocking frame and suspended halogen bulb, have a modern dematerialist aesthetic. However, he has
also designed pieces in the Pop and post-modern styles, such as his *Bulb-
Bulb* lamp (1980) in the form of a gigantic light bulb, his bird-like *Bibibibi*
lamp (1982) and his double-heart shaped *One from the Heart* lamp (1989).
Mauer has designed lighting suspension systems too, such as *Baka-Rù*
(1986) and *Yayaho* (1984), and during the late 1980s, he invented miniature
low-level lights with metal extensions, which allowed them to be moved
safely along uninsulated wires. In 1985, Mauer's work was included in the
"Lumières" exhibition held at the Centre Georges Pompidou, Paris.

Ingo Maurer
b. 1932 *Insel Reichenau,
Germany*

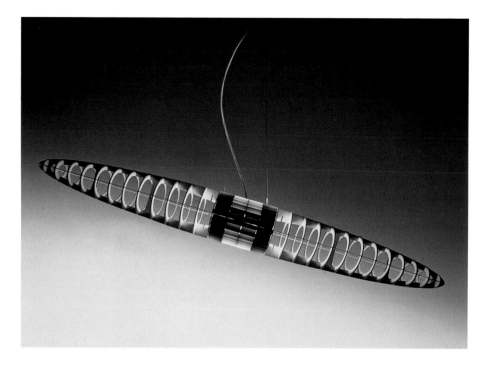

Alberto Meda

b. 1945 *Lenno Tremezzina, Italy*

▲ **Alberto Meda &
Paolo Rizzato,**
Titania lamp for
Luceplan, 1989

Alberto Meda studied mechanical engineering at the Politecnico di Milano, graduating in 1969. He subsequently worked for Magneti Marelli, and in 1973 was appointed technical director and head of planning for the design-oriented plastics manufacturer, **Kartell**. He went independent in 1979, working as a designer and engineer, and acting as a design engineering consultant to Alfa Romeo and Italtel Telematica among others. In 1983, Meda began teaching industrial technology at the Domus Academy. Four years later he created his *Light Light* chair using state-of-the-art materials – a piece which, with its Nomex-honeycomb core and matrix of carbon-fibre, achieved remarkable strength and lightness. His lighting for Luceplan, such as the *Titania* lamp (1989) with its polycarbonate filters, is likewise technically innovative. The range of cast-aluminium seating, including the *Armframe* chair and *Longframe* lounger (1996), designed by Meda for Alias in the 1990s, combined structural soundness with visual coherence, testifying to his engineering background. Other clients of his include Gaggia, Lucifero, Cinelli, Anslado, Mondedison, Carlo Erba, Fontana Arte and Mandarina Duck. Meda has received many international accolades, including a **Compasso d'Oro** and a Design Plus award.

458 · Alberto Meda

► *Tea & Coffee Piazza* for Alessi, 1979–1983

Richard Meier studied architecture at Cornell University in Ithaca, graduating in 1957. He subsequently worked in the New York architectural offices of Davis, Brody & Wisniewski in 1959 and Skidmore, Owings & Merrill in 1960. He then joined **Marcel Breuer**'s office for two years before establishing Richard Meier & Partners in 1963. He designed a studio and apartment in 1965 for the artist, Frank Stella (b. 1935), whose belief that "Light is Life" influenced his Purist approach to architecture. In 1969, Meier participated in the "New York Five" exhibition at the **Museum of Modern Art, New York**, and in later years he continued to adhere to the group's promotion of the **International Style**. The geometric plans of his buildings are often based on the circle and square. Like **Le Corbusier**'s architecture, they are usually clad in white rendering, however their detailing – enamelled panels and railings – is reminiscent of 1920s ocean liners. Meier's volumetric buildings have an instantly recognizable style – white, light, space – which borrows references from the past while remaining very much part of the present. Meier became a visiting professor of architecture at Yale University in 1975. During the 1980s, he continued to design "Neo-Moderne" buildings and products such as his *Tea & Coffee Piazza* for Alessi (1979–1983).

Richard Meier
b. 1934 *Newark, New Jersey*

▶ *Pride* cutlery for
Walker & Hall, 1951
(reissued by David
Mellor)

David Mellor

b. 1930 *Sheffield/*
Yorkshire

David Mellor trained at Sheffield College of Art, the **Royal College of Art**,
London and the British School in Rome, graduating in 1954. His student
designs received much praise – a silver coffee set, for example, being
awarded a national prize in 1950. In 1954, the year his elegant *Pride* flatware
(1951) was put into production by the Sheffield manufacturers, Walker &
Hall, Mellor established his own design office/workshop in Sheffield, a city
that has historic connections with the cutlery industry. His later cutlery
designs, the elegant *Embassy* (1963) and *Thrift* (1965) ranges, were widely
used in British Embassies and government institutions. Mellor has also
acted as a design consultant to British Rail, the Post Office and the Department of the Environment. He began manufacturing his own cookware in
1969 and established his first shop in Sloane Square, London to retail his
products. During the early 1970s, Mellor began producing his cutlery at
Broom Hall, Sheffield, but in 1990, his design and manufacturing facility
was moved to an historic building in Haversage, re-designed by Michael
Hopkins (b.1935), which subsequently won a BBC Design Award. Mellor
is an active member of the Design Council of Great Britain, and in 1983
was appointed chairman of the Crafts Council.

Memphis was founded in Milan in 1981 with the aim of re-invigorating
the **Radical Design** movement. During the late 1970s, **avant-garde** Italian
designers such as **Ettore Sottsass**, **Andrea Branzi** and **Alessandro Mendini**,
and other members of **Studio Alchimia**, experimented with alternative artistic and intellectual approaches to design. Mendini's promotion of "re-design"
and "banal design" became central to the output of Studio Alchimia, and
Sottsass, who found these approaches too creatively restricting, eventually
left the group. On the 11th of December 1980, Sottsass hosted a gathering
at his house of designers such as Barbara Radice (b. 1943), **Michele De
Lucchi**, **Marco Zanini**, Aldo Cibic (b. 1955), **Matteo Thun** and Martine Bedin
(b. 1957) to discuss the need for a new creative approach to design. They
decided to form a design collaborative, and that very night it was christened
Memphis, after a Bob Dylan song entitled "Stuck Inside of Mobile with the
Memphis Blues Again", which had been played repeatedly throughout the
evening. The name, Memphis, also made reference to the ancient Egyptian
capital of culture and the Tennessee birthplace of Elvis Presley and was
therefore suitably "double-coded". The group, now including **Nathalie du
Pasquier** and **George Sowden**, convened again in February 1981, by which

Memphis
Founded 1981
Italy

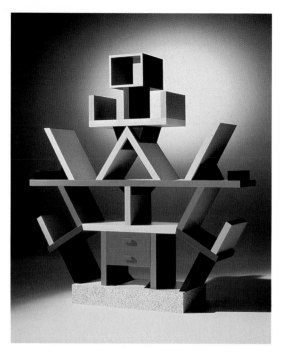

► **Ettore Sottsass,**
Carlton bookcase for
Memphis, 1981

time its members had executed over a hundred drawings of bold and colourful designs, drawing inspiration from either futuristic themes or past decorative styles including **Art Deco** and 1950s **Kitsch,** and intentionally mocking
the pretensions of **Good Design**. They threw themselves into the project:
finding furniture and ceramics manufacturers willing to batch produce their
designs; convincing Abet to make new laminates printed with extraordinarily
vibrant patterns inspired by Pop Art, Op Art and electronic imagery; designing and producing promotional material and so on. The head of Artemide,
Ernesto Gismondi, subsequently became the president of Memphis, and on
the 18th of September 1981 the group showed its work for the first time at
the Arc '74 showroom in Milan. The furniture, lighting, clocks and ceramics
exhibited by Memphis had been designed by an international array of architects and designers including **Hans Hollein, Shiro Kuramata, Peter Shire,
Javier Mariscal, Massanori Umeda** and **Michael Graves.** The group's products caused an immediate sensation, not least owing to their blatant **Anti-
Design** agenda, and the same year, the book *Memphis, The New International
Style* was published as a means of promoting their work. Artemide, which
produced Memphis' 1982 designs, gave the group space to display their

◄ Broadsheet for
"Memphis Milano
in London"
exhibition held at
The Boilerhouse,
Victoria & Albert
Museum, 1982

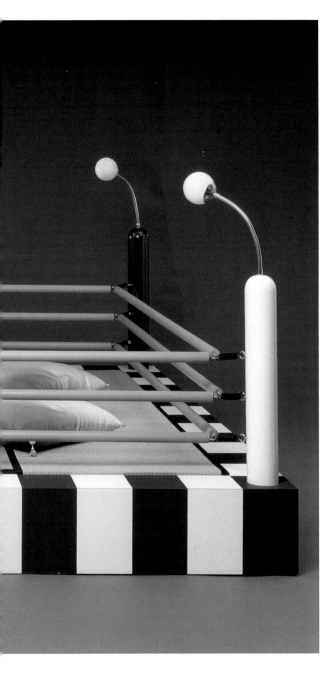

◄ **Masanori Umeda**,
Tawaraya boxing
ring conversation pit
for Memphis, 1981

▶ **Ettore Sottsass,**
Mizar vase for
Memphis, 1982

products at the company's showroom on Corso Europa, Milan. From 1981 to 1988, Barbara Radice was art director of Memphis and organized exhibitions in London, Chicago, Düsseldorf, Edinburgh, Geneva, Hanover, Jerusalem, Los Angeles, Montreal, New York, Paris, Stockholm and Tokyo. Many of Memphis' monumental designs used colourful plastic laminates, a material favoured for its "lack of culture". The vibrancy, eccentricity and ornamentation of Memphis' output evolved from a knowledge of Modernism and then an utter rejection of it. The hybrid themes and oblique quotations of past styles used by Memphis produced a new post-modern vocabulary of design. The group always acknowledged that Memphis was a "fad", tied to the ephemerality of fashion, and in 1988, when its popularity began to wane, Sottsass disbanded it. Although a short-lived phenomena, Memphis, with its youthful vitality and humour, was central to the internationalization of **Post-Modernism**.

► Re-designed
Wassily chair for
Studio Alchimia,
1978

Alessandro Mendini studied architecture at the Politecnico di Milano, receiving a doctorate in 1959. He subsequently became a partner of the industrial
design practice, Nizzoli Associati, where he remained until 1970. While there,
he worked on a project for experimental accommodation – the Italsider – in
Taranto. From 1970 to 1976, Mendini was editor-in-chief of *Casabella*, after
which he founded the journal *Modo* that he edited until 1981. He was a
founding member of **Global Tools**, a school of counter-architecture and design established in 1973, and in the late 1970s was closely associated with
the design collective **Studio Alchimia**, becoming its leading propagandist. In
1978, Mendini produced his first examples of "re-design" – **Joe Colombo**'s
Universale chair with a faux marble finish, **Marcel Breuer**'s *Wassily* chair with
applied motifs and **Gio Ponti**'s *Superleggera* chair to which ensigns were
attached. The point of "re-design" was to convey, in a humorous way, the
idea that truly innovative design was no longer possible in respect of what
had gone before. Re-design also sought to strip away the pretensions of
Modernism while showing that the meaning and value of a design could be

Alessandro
Mendini
b. 1931 *Milan, Italy*

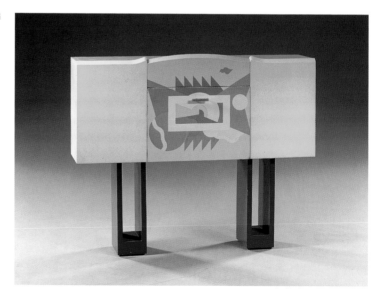

communicated solely through applied decoration. As a design theorist, Mendini also promoted the idea of "banal design", which attempted to address the intellectual and cultural void that was perceived to exist in the mass-design of industrialized society. The banality of existing objects was emphasized by applying bright colours and quirky ornamentation to them, as in Mendini's famous *Proust* armchair (1978). With the same purpose in mind, Mendini organized "L'oggetto banale" (The Banal Object) exhibition at the Venice Biennale in 1980. The **Anti-Design** activities of Mendini heralded the end of Modernism's "prohibitionism" and the rebirth of a symbolic language in design. His *Kandissi* sofa (1978), which was introduced in 1980 as part of Studio Alchimia's ironically named *BauHaus I* collection, mocked the distinctions between fine art and design with its brightly coloured applied wooden cut-outs that were inspired by the work of Wassily Kandinsky. Between 1980 and 1985, Mendini was chief editor of the design journal *Domus,* and from 1983 he taught design at the Hochschule für angewandte

▼ *Manici (Handles)* vases produced by Zabro-Zanotta for Studio Alchimia, 1984

Kunst, Vienna. In 1981, he was invited by the furniture manufacturer, Cassina, to participate in the company's Bracciodiferro project. For this he developed his *Mobile Infinito* series that included decorative magnetic cutouts, allowing the user a degree of creative interaction. Mendini also acted as design and communications director for **Alessi** and took part in the company's *Tea & Coffee Piazza* project in 1983. Alessi then commissioned Mendini together with **Achille Castiglioni** and **Aldo Rossi** to design the Casa della Felicità (1983–1988), after which Mendini designed the Groninger Museum, Groningen, The Netherlands (1988–1993). He has received several awards including a **Compasso d'Oro** in 1979. As a prolific designer and a leading design theorist, Mendini has contributed much to the Anti-Design debate and the propagation of **Post-Modernism**.

◄ Branding
programme
for Boehringer
Ingelheim, 1997

MetaDesign
Founded 1979
Berlin

MetaDesign was established in Berlin by Erik Spiekermann in 1979. Spiekermann had previously studied history of art at the Freie Universität in Berlin
and, in the 1970s, had worked as a typographer in London and taught at
the London College of Printing. He subsequently acted as a consultant to
Henrion Design Associates and Wolff Olins – design consultancies known
primarily for their **corporate identity** work. Having returned to Germany with
experience in both typography and corporate design, Spiekermann founded
the MetaDesign office. One of its first commissions was from the Deutsche
Bundespost to redesign their postal service literature. The studio forged
strong links with the Berthold type foundry and became a member of EDEN
(European Designers' Network), formed in 1991. MetaDesign went on to establish a worldwide reputation for its innovative typographic work and corporate identity programmes and today employs a staff of one hundred and
seventy in its Berlin office and has additional branches in London and San
Francisco. Spiekermann outlined his approach to typography in his 1987
publication, *Ursache & Wirkung: Ein Typografischer Roman* (Rhyme & Reason:
A Typographer's Novel). MetaDesign is generally recognized as Germany's
premier graphic design practice and Spiekermann's belief in integrated systems of corporate communication is borne out by the firm's motto, "You
cannot *not* communicate".

Ludwig Mies, as he was originally known, trained first as a builder, and from 1900 to 1904 worked as a draughtsman of stucco ornaments for a local architectural firm in Aachen. He moved to Berlin in 1905 and worked for **Bruno Paul** until 1907 – the year he designed his first building. In 1908, Mies joined **Peter Behrens'** design practice, where he assisted with designs for **AEG** and for the German Embassy in St Petersburg. In this office, he worked alongside **Walter Gropius**, Hannes Meyer (1889–1954) and **Le Corbusier**, and, like Behrens, was inspired by the Neo-Classical architecture of Karl Friedrich Schinkel (1781–1841). Mies left Behrens' practice in 1911, and the following year established his own Berlin-based studio. He added his mother's maiden name, van der Rohe, to his surname in 1913, and between 1914 and 1918 undertook military service. In 1922, he became actively involved in the revolutionary Novembergruppe, organizing the group's exhibitions for the next three years. His architectural proposals for offices, houses and tower-blocks were "ideal" plans that promoted a modernist agenda. He became vice-president of the **Deutscher Werkbund** in 1926, and in 1927 organized the Werkbund's "Die Wohnung" (The Home) exhibition held at the Weissenhofsiedlung, Stuttgart. Inspired by **Mart Stam**'s drawing of a cantilevered chair constructed of welded gas pipes (1926), Mies designed his

Ludwig Mies van der Rohe

1886 *Aachen, Germany*
1969 *Chicago*

▲ Interior of the German Pavilion at the "Exposición Internacional de Barcelona", 1929

▲ *Model No. MR20* armchair
for Berliner Metallgewerbe
Joseph Müller, 1927

own versions in 1927 – the *MR10* chair and *MR20* armchair – which were made of resilient tubular metal and were first exhibited at the Weissenhof exhibition. The German Pavilion for the 1929 "Exposición Internacional de Barcelona" was furnished with a number of his designs, including his famous *Barcelona* chair which was used as a "throne" for King Alfonso XIII at the exhibition's opening ceremonies. The interiors of this pavilion, with its marble partitions, were quintessentially of the **International Style** and were blatantly distanced from the utilitarianism normally associated with the **Modern Movement**. Between 1928 and 1930, Mies designed the Tugendhat House in Brno, Czechoslovakia, for which he also created site-specific furniture. The majority of his architectural designs of the 1920s, such as his proposals for towering glass and steel structures, were speculative and relatively experimental. His furniture designs, however, were put into production by Berliner Metallgewerbe Josef Müller (1927–1931) and by the Bamberger Metallwerkstätten (from 1931). He exhibited his designs at the German Building Exhibition in 1931 and signed a contract with Thonet-Mundus granting them the exclusive marketing rights for fifteen models of

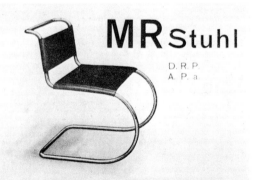

▼ Advertisement for *Model No. MR10 chair, c. 1928*

his chairs, some of which had been designed in collaboration with **Lilly Reich**. In 1930, Mies became the last director of the **Bauhaus**, where he taught architecture. He was responsible for the school's move from Dessau to Berlin and eventually oversaw its closure in 1933. From 1933, he worked as a freelance architect in Berlin, and in 1937 emigrated to the United States. He subsequently established a large architectural office in Chicago and acted as director of the architectural department at the Armour Institute (later to become the Illinois Institute of Technology) in Chicago. One of his students in Chicago was Florence Schust – who later married Hans **Knoll** – and in 1947, Knoll Associates re-issued Mies van der Rohe's furniture. Mies acquired American citizenship in 1944, and

MR Stuhl

D. R. P.
A. P. a

Entwurf: **Mies van der Rohe**

Ausführung: Stahlrohr vernickelt, verchromt, lackiert, mit Rindleder oder Korbgeflecht.

Prospekt und Preisliste durch

Berliner Metallgewerbe Jos. Müller

Neukölln, Lichtenraderstrasse **32**

Telefon Nr. 1122

until his death in 1969 worked on architectural projects including the Farnsworth House, Plano, Illinois (1946–1950), the Mannheim Opera House (1953) and his masterwork, the famous Seagram Building, New York (1954–1958), which was designed with assistance from **Philip Johnson**. Johnson also wrote the catalogue to the "Ludwig Mies van der Rohe" retrospective held at the **Museum of Modern Art, New York** in 1948. Mies van der Rohe was a leading exponent of the Modern Movement and one of the most influential architects and designers of the 20th century.

▶ *Model No. MR50 Brno* chair for Berliner Metallgewerbe Josef Müller, 1929–1930

▲ *Model No. MR90*
Barcelona chair for
Berliner Metall-
gewerbe Josef
Müller, 1929

Modern Movement

The Modern Movement in design was driven by a progressive and socially motivated ideology, the origins of which can be traced to the mid-19th century and the moral crusade of design reformers such as **A. W. N. Pugin**, John Ruskin (1819–1900) and **William Morris**. These early pioneers recognized that the prevailing High Victorian style was the product of a society corrupted by greed, decadency and oppression, and strove to reform society through a new approach to design. Although forsaking industrial production in favour of handcraftsmanship, Morris was amongst the first to put theory into practice by producing holistically conceived, well-designed and executed objects for everyday use. His reforming ideas – the supremacy of utility, simplicity and appropriateness over luxury; the moral responsibility of designers and manufacturers to produce objects of quality, and the proposition that design could and should be used as a democratic tool for social change – had a fundamental impact on the development of the Modern Movement. His ideas stimulated the foundation of craft-based guilds and workshops in Britain, Germany and America that were more receptive to machine production. Increasingly, it was seen that the machine offered a means to an end and that the industrial process would have to be embraced wholeheartedly if

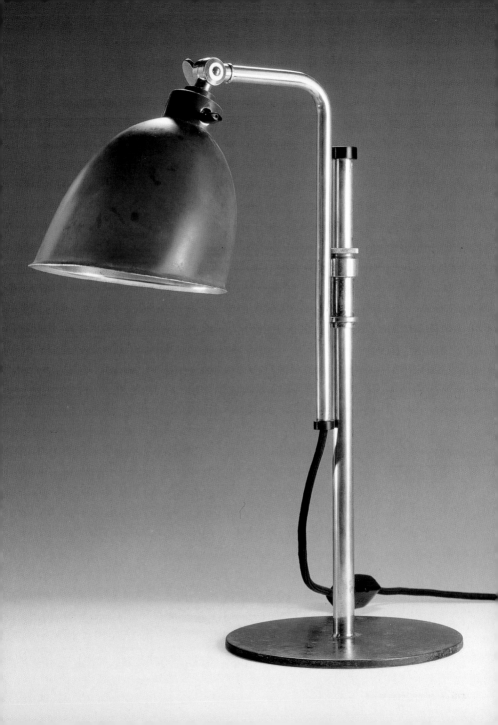

reform was to be widespread. The founding of the **Deutscher Werkbund** in 1907 marked the point in time when reforming ideology met industrial production. Members of the Deutscher Werkbund developed a new and highly rational approach to design that eliminated ornament and stressed **functionalism**. By eradicating superfluous surface decoration, elements were simplified and better **standardization** was achieved, which in turn promoted greater efficiency in terms of production and materials. The "saving" this

▼ Marcel Breuer,
Model No. B33
chair for Thonet,
1927–1928

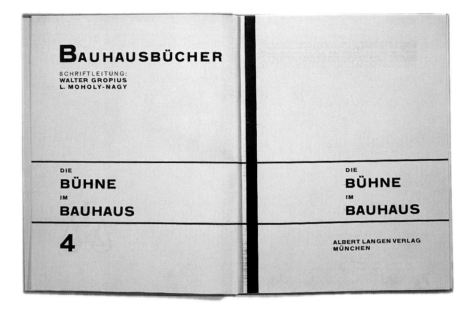

approach offered benefited both the user and manufacturer as more value could go into the quality of construction and materials. The aesthetic purification that resulted from the modern approach to design provided a universal language of design that was intended to be impervious to fashion. **Adolf Loos'** famous publication, *Ornament und Verbrechen* (*Ornament and Crime*) of 1908, linked excessive decoration to the debasing of society, while a later Werkbund publication of 1924 entitled *Form ohne Ornament* (*Form without Ornament*) illustrated and expressed the virtues of plain and rationally based designs for industrial production. This purging of ornament was also promoted by **De Stijl**, while **Constructivism** and **Futurism** celebrated the machine and the concept of "production art". After the devastation of the First World War, designers such as **Walter Gropius** recognized the moral imperative of Modernism. Gropius became the first director of the **Bauhaus**, which was established in 1919 to bring unity to the arts and to put the reforming ideals of the early pioneers of Modernism into practice. As the single most important design institution of the 20th century, the Bauhaus had an enormous impact on the development of the Modern Movement through its promotion of functionalism, industrial methods of production and state-of-the-art materials, such as tubular metal. The functional efficiency of Bauhaus interiors, furniture, metalware, ceramics and graphics led to a co-

▲ **László Moholy-Nagy**, Title pages for Walter Gropius and László Moholy-Nagy's "Die Bühne im Bauhaus" – Bauhausbuch 4, 1925

▲ Alvar Aalto,
Discussion and
lecture hall at the
Viipuri City Library,
1930–1935

herent vocabulary of design that became synonymous with Modernism.
The German term, Sachlichkeit (Objectivity) described this new rational approach to design. However, by 1927, when the "Werkbund-Ausstellung" was
held in Stuttgart, a clearly identifiable **International Style** of Modernism had
emerged that was distinguished by minimalism, industrialism and rectilinearism. **Le Corbusier** played a key role in promoting this reductivist machine
aesthetic, although his designs were significantly less utilitarian than those
produced at the Bauhaus. In the 1930s, the International Style became driven by fashion and was thought by some to have perverted the social objectives of Modernism. Exponents of the International Style took geometric abstraction to extremes and employed industrial materials and a severe formal
vocabulary for stylistic purposes. Modernism appeared to have lost its
moral bearings until it was taken up by Scandinavian designers, most notably **Alvar Aalto**, who pioneered a humanizing form of Modernism through
Organic Design. Aalto's work was especially well received in Britain and
America and inspired a new generation of Modern Movement designers,
such as **Charles and Ray Eames**, to perpetuate a holistic and organic approach to design that embraced state-of-the-art technologies and materials.
Although the achievements and future relevance of Modernism have been
debated for decades, its fundamental moral democratic premiss cannot be
refuted.

► Alvar Aalto,
High-back chair
for Huonekalu-ja
Rakennustyötehdas,
early 1930s

▲ **Walter Dorwin Teague,**
Interior of the Ford Pavilion at
the New York World's Fair, 1939

The French term Moderne refers to a form of **Art Deco** that was stylistically influenced by the **Modern Movement**. Although the Moderne style became popular in Europe during the 1920s and 1930s, it was in the United States that it really flourished. During this period, American promoters of the style, such as **Walter Dorwin Teague** and **Raymond Loewy**, used **Streamlining** and gleaming chromium and aluminium surface finishes on their product designs to give them an alluring modernistic appearance. The luxurious Moderne style was also frequently distinguished by heavy geometric forms that were inspired by the **Wiener Werkstätte**. The sumptuous interiors and furniture designed by **Donald Deskey** exemplified the style and were mostly commissioned by corporate and wealthy private clients. Deskey's interior and furnishings for the Radio City Music Hall (1932–1933) also reflected the Moderne style's association with silverscreen glamour. But more than anything else, it was the extravagant glass and chrome sets of Hollywood films that internationally popularized the Moderne style. The opulence and inherent optimism of the style offered an illusory respite from the ravages of the Great Depression and came to symbolize the American Dream. The enormous impact of Moderne in the United States was responsible for many of the differences that still exist between American and European automotive and product styling. Many of the decorative aspects of the style were revived through **Post-Modernism** and late 20th-century retro design.

▶ **Warren McArthur (attributed),** Table, early 1930s

Børge Mogensen

1914 *Aalborg, Denmark*
1972 *Copenhagen*

▲ *Asserbo* chairs for
Karl Andersson &
Söner, 1964

Børge Mogensen studied at the Kunsthandvaerkerskolan, Copenhagen from 1936 to 1938 and trained under **Kaare Klint** at the furniture school of the Kongelige Danske Kunstakademi, Copenhagen from 1938 to 1941, working as Klint's assistant there for two years after the war. He exhibited his work annually from 1939 at the Copenhagen Furnituremakers' Guild and headed the furniture design section of the Association of Danish Cooperatives from 1942 to 1950. He then established his own studio and subsequently designed furniture for Søborg Møbelfabrik, Frederica Stolefabrik and Karl Andersson & Söner. Like his mentor, Mogensen's approach to furniture design involved the reworking of traditional types, as his *No. 1789* sofa (1945), *Spanish* chair (1959) and *Asserbo* chair (1964) most notably demonstrate. Mogensen also followed Klint's example in undertaking ergonomic research, which resulted in his *Øresund* furniture system, designed in collaboration with Grethe Meyer. From 1953, he co-designed several furnishing textiles for C. Olesen with Lis Ahlmann (1894–1979). Mogensen's well designed and executed furniture epitomizes Danish design – the use of natural materials, high quality construction and the re-interpretation of historically successful forms.

László Moholy-Nagy studied law in Budapest. After military service, he became associated with the revolutionary art group, Ma (Tomorrow) and his work was illustrated in its journal. His artistic activities were originally confined to painting, but in 1920, when he settled in Berlin after a short stay in Vienna, he began experimenting with photography. His work, which was exhibited at the gallery Der Sturm, reflected the influence of both Dada and **Constructivism** and he subsequently participated in the 1922 Dadaist-Constructivist Congress in Weimar. The director of the **Bauhaus**, **Walter Gropius** invited Moholy-Nagy to become a member of the school's teaching staff, and in 1923 he and **Josef Albers** were appointed co-directors of the "Vorkurs". Although they retained the basic structure of this preliminary course as developed by **Johannes Itten**, they distanced themselves from his Mazdaznan beliefs. They promoted an industrial approach to design and to this end, Moholy-Nagy taught a "materials and space" class. He succeeded Paul Klee (1879–1940) as the "Master of Form" of the metal workshop, where his students included **Marianne Brandt** and **Wilhelm Wagenfeld**. Moholy-Nagy also practised film-making, typography and photography. He edited the *Bauhausbücher* series of titles and wrote several books, including *The New Vision: From Material to Architecture* (1928). In 1928, he left the Bauhaus and settled in Berlin where he ran a graphic design studio and designed exhibitions and theatre sets. He moved to Amsterdam in 1934, and from 1935 to 1937 resided in London where he designed posters for London Transport and devised special visual effects for the film-director Alexander Korda. He emigrated to America in 1937 and directed the short-lived New Bauhaus in Chicago. After its closure in 1938, Moholy-Nagy founded the **School of Design, Chicago** and continued to perpetuate the Bauhaus' functionalist design credo in America.

László
Moholy-Nagy
1895 *Bácsborsod,
Hungary*
1946 *Chicago*

▼ Herbert Bayer,
placard for
"Experiment in
Totality: Moholy-
Nagy", 1950

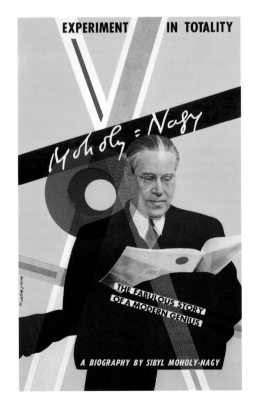

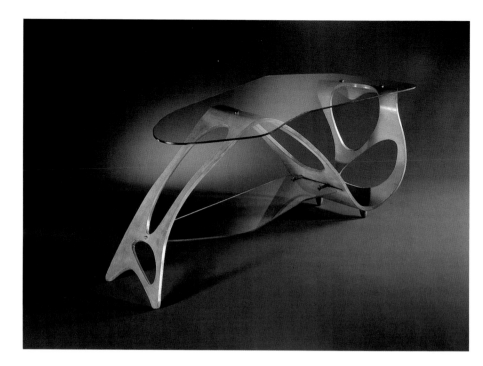

Carlo Mollino
1905 *Turin*
1973 *Turin*

▲ *Arabesque* table for Apelli & Varesio, 1950

► Combination radio and phonograph, 1949

Carlo Mollino was the son of Turin's most prominent architect and engineer, Eugenio Mollino. He studied engineering and art history prior to enrolling at the School of Architecture, University of Turin, from where he graduated in 1931. He subsequently worked in his father's practice, and in 1933 won first prize in the competition for the Federazione Agricoltori headquarters in Cuneo. The same year, he designed the interior of his own home, the Casa Miller, which he used as a photographic studio for his erotic female studies. In 1937, he designed the Società Ippica in Turin – home of the Turin riding club that is generally considered his architectural masterwork but has since been destroyed. Mollino designed site-specific furniture, which was very often biomorphic in form, for his interior design projects. His highly express-ive approach to design, which was inspired by **Futurism** and **Surrealism**, be-came known as the "Turinese Baroque" style and countered the **Rationalism** emanating from Milan. Between 1952 and 1968, Mollino also taught a course on the history of architecture at the Faculty of Architecture, Turin. He was an esteemed designer of racing cars – his *Osca 1100* was the winner of its class in the 1954 Le Man 24-hour race. The exuberant form of **Biomorphism** pion-eered by Mollino had a powerful influence on post-war Italian styling.

ABCDEFGHIJKLMN OPQRSTUVWXYZ abcdefghijklmnopqrst uvwxyz 1234567890 &.,:;'''""-!?()—

**Monotype
Corporation**
*1897–1992
Salfords/Surrey*

The American inventor, Tolbert Lanston, developed an innovative typesetting machine that he patented in 1885. Two years later, he founded the Lanston Monotype Corporation to commercialize his invention but was unable to secure the necessary financial backing in America. Eventually, in 1897, a sister company was established in Britain and a factory was set up in 1902 in Salfords, Surrey. Monotype differed significantly from its rival, Linotype, in that the machine produced individual characters of type rather than setting whole lines. Although typesetting with a Monotype machine was slower than with a Linotype, the monotype process was better suited for more complex copy, especially when this was not set as a solid block of text. In 1912, the Lanston Monotype Corporation issued the *Imprint* type. This was the first type to be developed for mechanical composition and its typographic clarity finally enabled the company to match the quality of traditional type foundries. In 1922, Stanley Morison (1889–1967) was appointed typographic adviser. He subsequently re-designed the *Garamond* (1922), *Baskerville* (1923) and *Fournier* (1924) typefaces and commissioned **Eric Gill** to design new faces, one of which was *Gill Sans* (1928). In 1931, the firm became known as the Monotype Corporation Limited and Morison was commissioned by *The Times* of London to create a new typeface for them. First issued by Monotype in 1932, *Times New Roman* went on to become one of the most widely used typefaces of the 20th century.

▲ **Stanley Morison**,
Times New Roman
typeface, 1931

William Morris studied theology at Exeter College, Oxford, and later trained
briefly as an architect with George Edmund Street (1824–1881). He was inspired by the social and artistic reforming ideas of John Ruskin (1819–1900)
and by the Romantic escapism of the Pre-Raphaelites. Upon the insistence
of Dante Gabriel Rossetti (1828–1881), Morris took up painting, which he
quickly abandoned in favour of the decorative arts. His first large-scale decorating project was on his own home, the Red House in Bexleyheath, that
had been designed in 1859 by Philip Webb (1831–1915). It was furnished by
Morris and his circle of friends with Pre-Raphaelite-style embroideries, murals, stained glass and painted furniture – a collaborative exercise that led to
the formation of Morris, Marshall, Faulkner & Co. in 1861. With this enterprise, Morris sought to put reformist theory into practice. In the 1860s,
Morris forged a "look" that promoted the virtues of simplicity, utility and
beauty. The company not only designed complete interior schemes but also
retailed a wide range of items including furniture, stained glass, wallpapers,
metalware, ceramics, tiles, embroideries, carpets and textiles. While Morris
wished to bring good design to the masses, he refused to embrace mechan-

William Morris
1834 *Walthamstow*
1896 *London*

▲ **Morris, Marshall, Faulkner & Co.,** *The Green Dining Room* at the South Kensington Museum (now the Victoria & Albert Museum), 1866–1867

ization, because he believed that the division of labour disconnected the worker from his work and, ultimately, from society. Paradoxically, this rejection of industrialized production meant that Morris' designs were expensive and could only be afforded by the wealthy. He nevertheless revitalized many handcrafts through his activities at Morris & Co. and was an early pioneer of ethical manufacturing practices. Apart from being the greatest proponent of the **Arts & Crafts Movement**, a prolific designer and a successful design manager, Morris was a highly celebrated poet and author whose writings reflected his yearning for a social utopia. He was also a leading Socialist who laid some of the foundations of the British Labour Movement. Morris' reforming ideas – the supremacy of utility, simplicity and appropriateness over luxury; the morality of producing objects of quality, and the use of design as a democratic tool for social change – had a fundamental impact on the early origins of the **Modern Movement**.

Jasper Morrison studied in London, at Kingston School of Art and Design and at the **Royal College of Art**, graduating in 1985. He also won a scholarship to the Academy of Arts in Berlin in 1984. In the early 1980s, Morrison became well-known for his experimental furniture, such as the *Flowerpot* table (1983) and the *Wing-Nut* chair (1984). He established his own London-based studio, Office for Design, in 1986, and the same year exhibited his work at the Shiseido store in Tokyo, Galerie Néotù in Paris and at the "British Design" exhibition in Vienna. The following year, he designed an installation for Reuter's news agency at the "Documenta 8" exhibition in Kassel, and in 1988 participated in "Design Werkstadt", presenting an installation entitled "Some New Items for the House I" at the DAAD gallery in Berlin. His celebrated indoor/outdoor *Thinking Man's* chair (1987) for Cappellini was followed by his *Ply*-chair (1989) for **Vitra**, which anticipated the de-materialistic approach to design characteristic of his later work. In 1992, together with James Irvine (b. 1958), Morrison organized the *Progetto Oggetto* for Cappellini – a collection of household items created by a group of young designers including **Stefano Giovannoni**, Konstantin Grcic (b. 1965) and Axel Kufus (b. 1958). The same year, Morrison published a book entitled *A World Without Words* and received a Bundespreis für Produktdesign award for his door handle range designed for FSB. He designed an installation in 1993 for the Österreichisches Museum für angewandte Kunst, Vienna, and two years later a one-man show of his work was held at the Arc en Rêve Centre d'architecture, Bordeaux. His most important commission to date is the design of the new Hanover Tram for Expo 2000, which was awarded the IF Transportation Design Prize and the Ecology Award. Morrison's aesthetically pure and highly functional work exemplifies the "new simplicity" in design.

Jasper Morrison
b. 1959 *London*

▼ *Three* Sofa for Cappellini, 1992

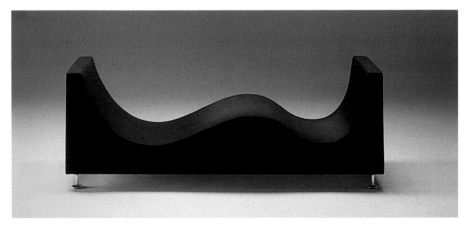

Koloman Moser

1868 *Vienna*
1918 *Vienna*

▼ Sherry decanter
with silver-plated
metal mount for
E. Bakalowits &
Söhne, 1901

Koloman Moser studied design and painting at the Akademie der Bildenden Künste, Vienna from 1885 to 1892, as well as attending classes given by Professor Franz Rumpler (1848–1922) at the Allgemeine Malerschule, Vienna in 1886. While still a student, Moser contributed graphic work to the magazines *Wiener Mode* and *Meggendorfers Humoristische Blätter*. From 1893 to 1895, he trained as a graphic designer at the Kunstgewerbeschule, Vienna, and taught drawing to Archduke Karl Ludwig's children. He became associated with many progressive artists including Gustav Klimt (1862–1918), and in 1894 co-founded the Siebener Club (Club of Seven) with **Josef Hoffmann** and **Josef Maria Olbrich**. Moser worked as an independent graphic designer from 1895 onwards, and participated with other artists and the publisher Martin Gerlach in the issuing of a series of folio volumes entitled *Allegorien, Neue Folge* (1895). He was a founding member of the **Vienna Secession** and in 1898 became editor of the group's journal, *Ver Sacrum*, for which he produced numerous illustrations. He started to teach painting at the Kunstgewerbeschule, Vienna, in 1899, obtaining a professorship in 1900. The same year, Moser exhibited his furniture and other forward-looking de-

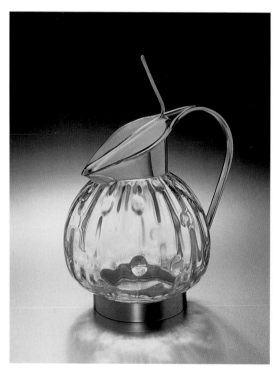

signs, including a series of liqueur glasses that were later distributed by Bakalowits & Söhne, at the VIII Secessionist Exhibition in Vienna and at the Paris "Exposition Universelle et Internationale". He co-founded the Wiener Kunst im Haus group in 1901, and two years later joined Josef Hoffmann and Fritz Wärndorfer (1869–1939) in establishing the **Wiener Werkstätte**. As an artistic director of this progressive manufacturing venture, Moser contributed furniture, silverware, metalwork, textile, jewellery and graphic designs. He also designed costumes and stage sets for the Cabaret Fledermaus – a theatre established by Hoffmann that was conceived as a Wiener Werkstätte **Gesamtkunstwerk**. From around 1901, Moser substituted Secessionist-style abstracted

▶ **School of Koloman Moser**, Glass and silver-plated metal jar for E. Bakalowits & Söhne, 1902

◀ Wooden box for the Wiener Werkstätte, c. 1905

▲ Clock for the
Wiener Werkstätte,
c. 1906

and naturalistic motifs for geometric patterning, including his characteristic black and white square grids that were inspired by Egyptian and Assyrian art. The severe geometry of these later designs anticipated the geometric formalism promoted by the **Bauhaus** in the 1920s. Apart from his work for the Wiener Werkstätte, Moser also designed glassware for Loetz, textiles for Johann Backhausen & Söhne and furniture for **J. & J. Kohn**. In addition, he worked as a book designer for various publishing houses including H. Bruckmann, and between 1904 and 1906 designed the stained glass windows for **Otto Wagner**'s Am Steinhof church. After quarrelling with Fritz Wärndorfer, Moser left the Wiener Werkstätte in 1908 and concentrated on painting. However, he went on to produce a number of stage sets for the State Opera. His paintings were exhibited in Düsseldorf, Dresden, Budapest, Rome and Berlin between 1909 and 1916. Moser was a prolific and multi-talented designer whose work made the stylistic transition from a naturalistic to a geometric manner, and in so doing bridged the 19th and 20th centuries.

Serge Mouille worked in the studio of the sculptor and silversmith, Gilbert Lacroix in 1937, prior to training as a silversmith at the École des Arts Appliqués, Paris. He completed his formal studies in 1941 and four years later, while teaching at his alma mater, established his own studio. He designed his first prototype lamp in 1953 for the architect and decorator Jacques Adnet (1900–1984), who was then director of Süe and Mare's Compagnie des Arts Français. This early floor lamp had three lights on arms that centrally pivoted on a three-legged stand. Mouille's characteristic *tétine* (teat) metal shades were the optimum shape for the reflection of light and could be angled in virtually any position. In 1953, he participated in an exhibition at the Musée des Arts Décoratifs, Paris, and two years later became a member of both the Société des Artistes Décorateurs and the Société Nationale des Beaux-Arts. Mouille collaborated with Louis Sognot (1892–1970) on lighting solutions and was one of a group of **avant-garde** designers, including **Jean Prouvé**, whose modern designs were shown at the Steph Simon gallery when it opened in 1956. Mouille's elegant lamps from the 1950s, such as *Oeil, Cocotte, Antony, Tuyau, Saturne, Agrafée* and *Secrétaire*, had adjustable black or white enamelled metal shades that were supported on slender metal rod stands. In 1958, Mouille launched two new lamps at the "Exposition Universelle et Internationale" in Brussels – a large wall-lamp with three arms and a hanging lamp with six arms. His later lighting designs, such as those for the Université d'Anthony and the Cathédrale de Bizerte, were weightier and more architectural in form. In 1961, Mouille established the Société de Création de Modèles for the encouragement of young designers, and in 1963 he was awarded a gold medal from the Société d'Encouragement à l'Art et à l'Industrie.

Serge Mouille
1922 *Paris*
1988 *Monthiers, France*

▼ Standard lamp, 1953

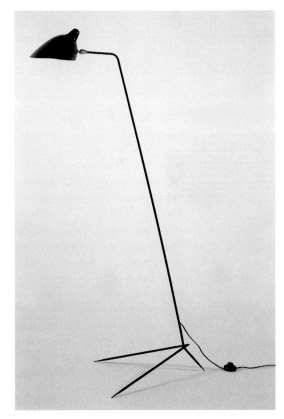

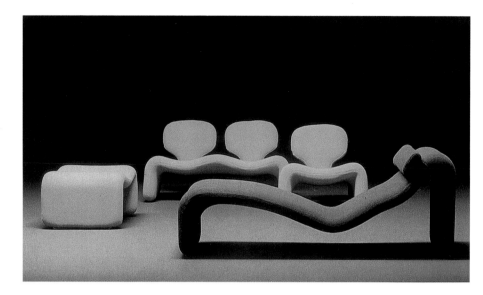

Olivier Mourgue
b. 1939 *Paris*

Olivier Mourgue began his training in interior design in 1954 at the École Boulle, Paris, and from 1958 to 1961 studied partly at the École Nationale Supérieure des Arts Décoratifs, Paris and partly in Sweden and Finland. After working as an interior designer for the Agence d'Architecture Intérieure Gautier-Delaye, Paris and designing furniture for Airborne (1963–1966), he established a Parisian studio, from which he produced furniture designs for Mobilier National (from 1966) and Prisunic (1969) as well as automobile interiors for Renault (1977). His highly sculptural and anthropomorphic *Djinn* seating range (1965), which was the first furniture to use urethane foam upholstery over tubular steel frames, was so futuristic in appearance that it was used in Stanley Kubrick's epic film *2001: A Space Odyssey* (1968). Mourgue also designed the interiors of the French pavilions at both Expo '67 in Montreal and Expo '70 in Osaka and received an ADI (Associazione per il Disegno Industriale) award and a Eurodomus award in 1968. Like **Verner Panton** and **Joe Colombo**, Mourgue became interested in the concept of living environments, space and mobility, designing a mobile wheeled studio for himself and an all-soft-surface plastic bathroom suite in 1970, and exhibiting an experimental system of modular room dividers in an installation at the 1971 "Visiona 3" exhibition held by Bayer in Germany. In 1976, he established a studio at Kéralio in Brittany and became professor of the Institut de Géo-Architecture at the École des Beaux-Arts, Brest. Mourgue's younger brother, Pascal (b. 1943), is also a well-known furniture designer.

▲ *Djinn* seating range for Airborne International, 1965

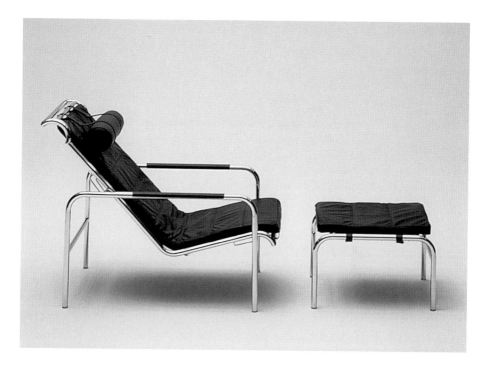

Gabriele Mucchi was the son of the painter Anton Maria Mucchi. He trained in Turin, Rome, Catania and Corregio, and later studied engineering in Bologna, receiving his doctorate in 1923. Mucchi regarded himself as a "discoverer of forms for objects of daily use" – the term "industrial designer" had yet to be coined. His work was included in the 1926 "Italian 20th Century" exhibition held in Milan, and from 1931 to 1933 he exhibited privately at the Galérie Bonaparte. In 1934, he moved into a house in Milan that became a focal point for a group of artists and anti-fascists who later organized themselves into the Corrente group. Although an active member of this anti-fascist group, Mucchi was also paradoxically part of the Rationalist movement in architecture and design that for a while was favoured by the Fascists. From 1934 to 1945, Mucchi designed seat furniture for the Milanese manufacturer, Crespi, Emilio Pino including his chromed tubular metal and leather *Genni* chair (c. 1935), which was later reissued by Zanotta in 1982. His designs were exhibited in Milan in 1949 and in Prague, Berlin and Dresden in 1955. He was awarded an honorary doctorate from the Humboldt-Universität in Leipzig in 1984. Mucchi's furniture designs epitomized Italian **Rationalism**, the proponents of which considered themselves to be champions of the Modern Age.

Gabriele Mucchi
b. 1899 *Turin, Italy*

▲ *Genni* armchair and stool for Crespi, Emilio Pina, c. 1935 (reissued by Zanotta)

Alphonse Mucha

1860 *Ivancice, Moravia*
1939 *Prague*

▶ Advertising poster
for Job cigarette
papers, 1896

▼ Zodiac for the
magazine *La Plume*,
1896–1897

Alphonse Mucha was employed from 1879 as a theatrical painter in Vienna, where he became influenced by the work of the artist Hans Makart (1840–1884). In 1883, Mucha worked on a decorative scheme for Schloß Emmahof, near Grussbach, that was owned by Count Khuen-Belassi. He also designed a three-panelled screen for the count who subsequently financed Mucha's fine art studies in Munich from 1884 to 1887 and then in Paris. Shortly after his arrival in Paris, Mucha began working as a designer, illustrator and graphic artist. In 1889 he executed his first designs for postage stamps, and in 1892 produced his first poster. After the printing of his famous poster of Sarah Bernhardt as Gismonda, the actress contracted him for six years to produce posters of her productions. Mucha also designed jewellery for Bernhardt, which was manufactured by the goldsmith George Fouquet (1862–1957), and created several interiors with his characteristic swirling motifs, including that of Fouquet's shop on the Rue Royale, Paris, for which he designed every detail including door handles, furnishings, stained glass and lighting. An exhibition was held of Mucha's work in Paris in 1897 and a special issue of *La Plume* magazine was dedicated to his oeuvre. The show later travelled to Prague, Munich, Brussels, London and New York and helped to establish his international reputation. Mucha designed the award-winning Bosnia-Herzegovina pavilion at the 1900 Paris "Exposition Universelle et Internationale" and published two books on his work in 1902 and 1905. He travelled to America in 1903, where he designed jewellery in collaboration with **Louis C. Tiffany**. His advertising posters for Waverley Cycles (1898), Job cigarette papers (1898) and Moët & Chandon champagne (1899) helped popularize his work, and in 1907 a soap was launched bearing his name on its packaging. Mucha's book illustrations, textile designs, advertising posters, publicity material, postcards and series of decorative lithographic prints, such as *Les Saisons* (1896), *Les Fleurs* (1897) and *Les Arts* (1898), are quintessential expressions of **Art Nouveau**.

► *Model No. 5000*
Singer chair, 1945
(reissued by
Zanotta)

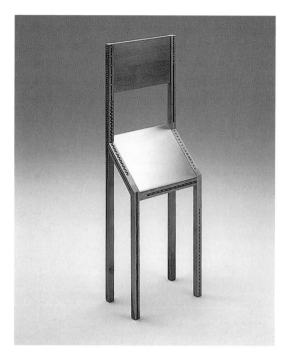

Bruno Munari

1907 *Milan*
1998 *Milan*

Bruno Munari studied at the Technical Institute in Naples in 1924 and worked as a painter and sculptor in Milan and Rome from 1927. He was associated with the Futurists and showed his work at the 1927 "Secondo Futurismo" exhibition and the 1929 "Trentate Futuristi" exhibition as well as the 1929 Venice Biennale. In 1932, he turned his attention to photography, and a year later began working as a graphic designer and produced his *Macchine Inutili* (Useless Machines) kinetic structures. He started to design books in 1945 and published a large number of children's books from 1949 onwards. Munari became a founding member of the Movimento Arte Concreta in 1948, and two years later began experimenting with colour inter-action using positive and negative images. He also designed products and furniture from 1945, including a toy monkey for Pigomma (1954) that was awarded a **Compasso d'Oro**. He has been a design consultant to IBM, **Olivetti**, Cinzano, Danese, La Rinascente, Pirelli and Mondadori among others. In the early 1970s, he lectured in basic design and advanced visual communications at Harvard University and held a professorship at the Scuola Politecnica, Milan. Munari's *Singer* chair (1945) reflects his belief in the unity of fine art and design.

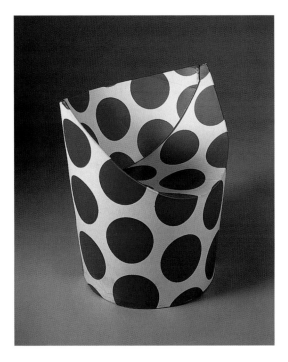

◄ *Spotty* cardboard child's chair for International Paper, 1963

Peter Murdoch trained at the **Royal College of Art**, London, graduating in 1963. While studying at the college, Murdoch designed his polka-dotted cardboard child's chair, *Spotty* (1963), which rapidly became an icon of the Pop era. The low production costs and inherent disposability of this **Pop Design** product were ideally suited to the demands of the mass-consumer market of the 1960s. The chair was produced in America by International Paper and sold in flat-pack form. It was assembled origami-style by the purchaser and was surprisingly resilient owing to its five-layer lamination of three different paper types. In 1967, Murdoch designed the similarly constructed *Those Things* chair, table and stool that were manufactured by his own company, Perspective Designs. This children's furniture, printed with a black and white alphabet motif inspired by Op art, received a Council of Industrial Design Award. In 1968, he established his own design office in London, which became known primarily for its work in graphics, signage and **corporate identity**. The same year, in collaboration with Lance Wyman, Murdoch designed the graphics for the Olympic Games in Mexico City. He has also acted as a design consultant to the British furniture manufacturer, Hille International.

Peter Murdoch
b. 1940 *Birmingham*

Keith Murray

1892 *Auckland,*
New Zealand
1981

Keith Murray studied at the Architectural Association, London, after military service in the First World War. In 1925, he travelled to Paris where he saw Scandinavian and other **avant-garde** Continental European glassware at the "Exposition Internationale des Arts Décoratifs et Industriels Modernes", which surpassed anything being produced by British manufacturers at the time. On his return to Britain, Murray worked for James Powell's Whitefriars Glassworks, designing simple glass vessels with engraved and shallow cut decoration that "did not destroy the clarity of the glass". Following the influential "Exhibition of Swedish Industrial Arts" held in London in 1931, the ceramics and glass manufacturers, Stevens & Williams were seeking a designer to work in the modern idiom and, at the suggestion of **Gordon Russell**, retained Murray to design part-time for their Brierley Hill Glassworks. The company subsequently held an exhibition of his work at their London showroom in 1932. Murray began designing bold geometric ceramics for Josiah Wedgewood & Sons from 1933, and went on to design silverware for Mappin & Webb. In 1936, he established an architectural office with C. S. White, and drew up plans for the new Wedgewood Factory at Barlaston (1938–1940). Later, in 1945, with fellow New Zealander, Basil Ward (1902–1976), he set up the architectural partnership Murray, Ward & Partners. Murray's ceramics for Wedgewood, with their simple yet monumental volumetric forms, epitomize British Modernism of the 1930s.

▲ Pottery vases and jug for Josiah Wedgwood & Sons, c. 1934

The Museum of Modern Art, New York, was officially opened just a few days after the Wall Street Crash of 1929. Its remit was to promote a "sanitized" version of Modernism that was ideologically removed from the left-wing politics of the European **Modern Movement**. Alfred Hamilton Barr (1902–1981) was the museum's first director and during his tenure from 1929 to 1943, he introduced **avant-garde** European art, architecture and design to America through important exhibitions such as "The **International Style**: Architecture Since 1922" (1932) and "Machine Art" (1932), which were both curated by **Philip Johnson**. Crucially, Barr was able to attract wealthy and high-profile patrons to the post-modernist cause, whose funding helped popularize the movement with the general public. When the curatorial department was split in 1940, **Eliot Fette Noyes**, the first director of the new industrial design department, curated the landmark competition and exhibition entitled "Organic Design in Home Furnishings", which introduced the pioneering work of **Charles Eames** and **Eero Saarinen** among others. Later, Edgar Kaufmann Jr. (1917–1989) became director of design and set up the **Good Design** exhibitions, which were held annually from 1950 to 1955. Through these shows and the museum's publications, Kaufmann attempted to change consumers' and manufacturers' attitudes towards the nature of manufactured goods, particularly in terms of quality. The museum hosted **Robert Venturi**'s series of lectures during the 1960s, and in 1972 held the famous exhibition "Italy: The New Domestic Landscape", which was largely a celebration of **Radical Design**. Throughout the 1980s and 1990s the museum staged important retrospectives and landmark exhibitions such as "Mutant Materials in Contemporary Design" (1995). The Museum of Modern Art is housed in a building that was designed in 1939 by Philip Goodwin and Edward Durell Stone, and later extended by Philip Johnson. In 1984, a west wing and condominium tower were completed that effectively doubled the museum's available space.

Museum of Modern Art

Founded 1929
New York

▼ Installation view of "Good Design" exhibition organized by the Museum of Modern Art, November 1950 – January 1951

George Nakashima

1905 *Spokane, Washington*
1990 *New Hope, Pennsylvania*

George Nakashima trained at the École Américaine des Beaux-Arts, Fontainbleu in 1928 and studied architecture at the University of Washington, Seattle in 1929, and the Massachusetts Institute of Technology in 1930. Nakashima was first employed by the Long Island State Park Commission and the New York State Government. Then, from 1933 to 1936, he travelled to Europe and also visited India and China on his way to Japan. There he worked in the Tokyo-based architectural office of Antonin Raymond (1890–1976) for two years and was also briefly employed by Kunio Maekawa (b. 1905). Soon after his return to Seattle in 1940, he established a furniture workshop with a priest, Father Tibesar. He was interned in Idaho from 1942 to 1943, on account of his Japanese ancestry, and during this period he began learning traditional Japanese carpentry from a nisei woodworker. After Raymond had arranged his release, Nakashima established a small furniture-making business on the architect's farm in New Hope, Pennsylvania. Although most of his exquisitely crafted furniture was specially made to commission, Nakashima also designed lines of furniture for **Knoll** (1946) and Widdicomb-Mueller (1957). He received the Craftsmanship Medal from the American Institute of Architects in 1952 and a National Gold Medal in 1962. Apart from his furniture that combined Western forms with Eastern craftsmanship, Nakashima also designed the interiors of several notable buildings including the Monastery of Christ in the Desert, Abiquiu, New Mexico (1970) and the Nelson Rockefeller residence in Tarrytown, New York (1973–1974).

▲ Walnut desk and *New* chair, 1971

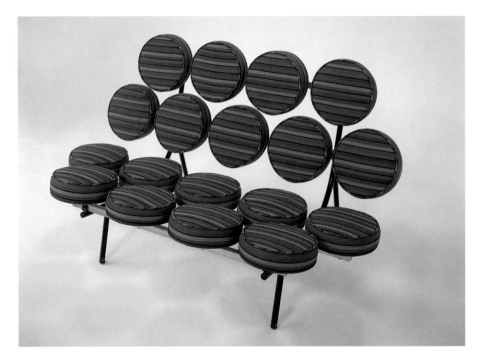

George Nelson studied architecture at Yale University until 1931, and then attended the Catholic University in Washington for a year and the American Academy in Rome from 1932–1934, having won a Rome Prize. In 1935, he became an associate editor of the magazines *Architectural Forum* and *Fortune*, and then wrote profiles of important architects for the journal, *Pencil Points*, which promoted the modernist cause. Between 1936 and 1941, Nelson and William Hamby ran an architectural partnership in New York, after which Nelson joined the faculty of architecture at Yale University and developed numerous innovative architectural and planning concepts, including the pedestrianized shopping mall in his "Grass on Main Street" proposal of 1942. He also pioneered the concept of built-in storage with his Storagewall of 1944. From 1941 to 1944, he taught at the School of Architecture at Columbia University, New York, and in 1946, became a consultant on interior design at the Parsons School of design, New York. The same year, Nelson succeeded **Gilbert Rohde** as director of design at **Herman Miller** – a position that he held until 1972. During his tenure there, Nelson brought in other talented designers including **Charles Eames**, **Alexander Girard** and **Isamu Noguchi** to design modern furnishings for the company. Nelson also

George Nelson
1907 *Hartford, Connecticut*
1986 *New York*

▲ *Marshmallow* sofa for Herman Miller, 1956 (upholstered in *Jacob's Coat* textile designed by Alexander Girard)

developed his own furniture designs, including a system of modular storage
units that rested on slatted platform benches (1945), a home-office desk
(1946), a moulded plywood tray table (1949), the *Comprehensive* Storage
System (1957), the *Marshmallow* sofa (1956), the *Swaged-Leg* Group of chairs,
tables and desks (1958), the *Catenary* chair and table (1962), the *Sling* Sofa
(1963) and, most importantly, the *Action Office I* system (1964–1965). In
1947, he established his own office, George Nelson & Co. in New York,
which, when he went into partnership with Gordon Chadwick in 1953, became known as George Nelson & Associates. As an industrial designer,
Nelson created the Prolon melamine line of dinnerware for the Pro-Phy-Lac-
Tic Brush Co. (1952–55), several wall and table clocks for the Howard Miller
Clock Company (late 1940s and early 1950s), the *Bubble* lamps made of self-
webbing plastic (1947–52) and the *Omni* extruded aluminium pole system
for Dunlap. Nelson was also interested in the concept of product architecture, and in 1957 he designed the modular plastic domed Experiment House.
He mooted the futuristic concept of the "hidden city" in which buildings are
constructed underground so as to create a more "humane environment". As

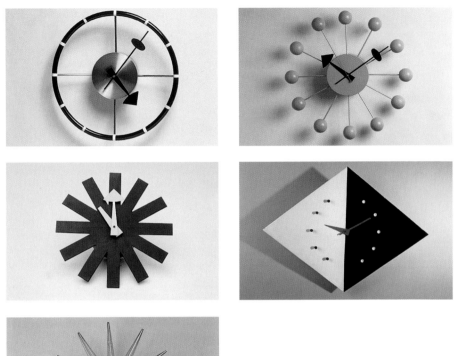

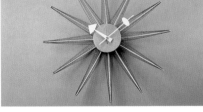

▲ *Model No. 4756* wall clock for the Howard Miller Clock Company, 1947

▲ *Model No. 2213A* Asterisk wall clock for the Howard Miller Clock Company, 1950

▲ *Model No. 2214S* Spider Web wall clock for the Howard Miller Clock Company, 1954

▲ *Model No. 4755* Ball wall clock for the Howard Miller Clock Company, 1947

▲ *Model No. 2201K* Kite wall clock for the Howard Miller Clock Company, 1953

► *MAA* chair from
the *Swaged-Leg*
group for Herman
Miller, 1958

a prolific writer and design critic, Nelson's ideas were extremely influential and forward-looking. He predicted in 1978, for example, that advances in computer technology would result in greater "miniaturization, ephemeralization, dematerialization" in the future. He was a close friend of **Buckminster Fuller** and, like him, promoted the still highly relevant notion of "doing much more with much less", implying that the ultimate goal of technology should be to do "everything with nothing". Nelson was not only an extremely talented and innovative designer, he was also an early environmentalist and a powerful communicator of ideas through his writings and teaching.

▼ *Platform* bench for
Herman Miller, 1946

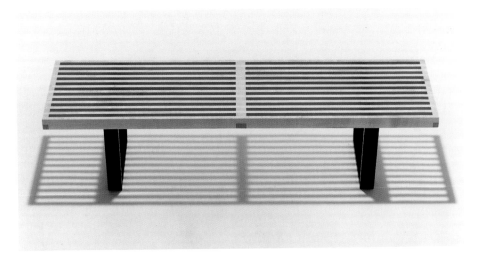

Richard Neutra

1892 *Vienna, Austria*
1970 *Wuppertal,
Germany*

Richard Neutra trained at the Technische Hochschule, Vienna from 1911 to
1917, and after the First World War worked as a landscape gardener in Zurich.
In 1921, he began working for the Municipal Construction Office in Lucken-
walde where he came into contact with Erich Mendelsohn (1887–1953).
Neutra subsequently moved to Berlin where he worked as an assistant in
Mendelsohn's office. He emigrated to America in 1923, working first for
William Holabird & Martin Roche in Chicago, then for **Frank Lloyd Wright**
in Spring Green, Wisconsin, and finally for the architect Rudolf Schindler
(1887–1953) in Los Angeles, where he was involved in various projects
including the Palace of Nations, Geneva (1927). In 1926, Neutra estab-
lished his own architectural practice, designing the reinforced concrete
Jardinette Apartment House, Los Angeles (1926–1927) and the Lovell House
(1927–1929), which had a skeletal steel structure that could be erected
within forty hours. He also developed pre-fabricated housing known as
"One plus Two" and a future city plan entitled "Rush City Reformed".
Between 1928 and 1929, Neutra founded the Academy of Modern Art, Los
Angeles, where he lectured on architecture. Throughout the 1930s, he experimented with various new materials and construction techniques for his
buildings, including his own home,
the Van der Leeuw Research House
(1931–1933), and after the Second
World War he designed a number
of private residences and apartment
buildings in the **International Style**.
By using large amounts of glazing
and cantilevered roofs, Neutra was
able to unite internal and external
space, while his site-specific furniture, which was frequently either
built-in or constructed of chromed
tubular metal, heightened the sense
of design unity. From 1949 to
1959, he collaborated with Robert
Alexander on larger public commissions including the Miramar
Chapel, La Jolla (1957). Neutra's elegant designs were influenced by
the informality of the Californian
lifestyle and projected a more re-
laxed form of Modernism.

▼ Side chair, 1947
(reissued by
Prospettive)

▶ *Bucky* chairs designed for the Cartier Contemporary Art Foundation, 1995

Bucky chairs designed for the Cartier Contemporary Art Foundation, 1995

Marc Newson studied jewellery design and sculpture at Sydney College of Art, graduating in 1984. Two years later he founded the POD design studio, specializing in furniture and clocks, and showed his furniture designs for the first time at the Roslyn Oxley Gallery in Sydney. In 1987, he worked in Japan, designing seating and lighting for Tentuo Kurosaki's company, Idée, which began limited production of his well-known fibreglass and rivetted aluminium *Lockheed Lounge* chaise (1985–1986). A year later, a one-man show of Newson's sculptural designs was held in Tokyo and his pieces were also exhibited at the Il Milione gallery in Milan in 1989 and at the VIA gallery in Paris in 1991. By the early 1990s, Newson had become internationally acclaimed: he was commissioned to provide furnishings for stores in Frankfurt and Berlin, he was selected Designer of the Year by the Paris Furniture Salon, and he took part in the "13 nach Memphis" exhibition at the Museum für Kunsthandwerk, Frankfurt in 1995. Newson was commissioned by the Cartier Contemporary Art Foundation in Paris in 1995 to create an interactive installation, which included his brightly coloured and amorphously shaped *Bucky* chairs, and he also designed the Swatch Watch Tower for the 1996 Atlanta Olympic Games, while continuing to work as an interior designer in London and Tokyo. Newson's playful and characterful work is strongly influenced by the **Biomorphism** and streamlined forms of 1950s American design.

Marc Newson
b. 1962 *Sydney, Australia*

◄ *Lettera 22*
typewriter for
Olivetti, 1950

Marcello Nizzoli

1887 Boretto, Italy
1969 Camogli, Italy

Marcello Nizzoli studied art, architecture and graphic design at the Scuola di Belle Arti, Parma from 1910 to 1913, and subsequently worked as a painter, exhibiting in 1914 with the Futurist group Nuove Tendenze (New Tendencies) in Milan. Nizzoli also designed textiles and posters, most notably for Campari and OM. In 1918, he founded his own design office in Milan, and during the 1920s became associated with the Rationalists. From 1934 to 1936, Nizzoli worked in partnership with the architect, Edoardo Persico (1900–1936) with whom he designed two Parker Pen stores (1934) and the Hall of Gold Medals for the 1934 "Aeronautical Exhibition" in Milan. Nizzoli also undertook a number of joint projects with **Giuseppe Terragni** between 1931 and 1936. At the same time, he was employed as a freelance graphic designer by **Olivetti**, and around 1938 became the company's chief product design consultant. His *Lexicon 80* and *Lettera 22* typewriters (1948 and 1950) were remarkable for their sculptural forms, and his designs for offices and workers' housing for Olivetti underlined the company's commitment to total design. Nizzoli produced sculptural designs for other manufacturers, including sewing machines and a kitchen mixer for Necchi, furniture for Arflex, lighters for Ronson and petrol pumps for Agip.

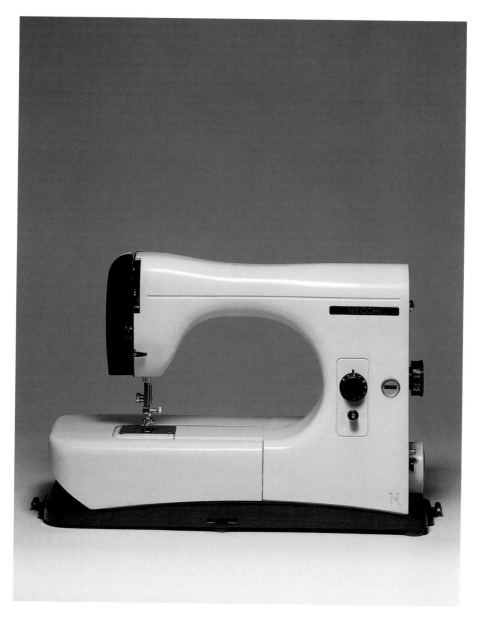

▲ *Mirella* sewing
machine for Necchi,
1957

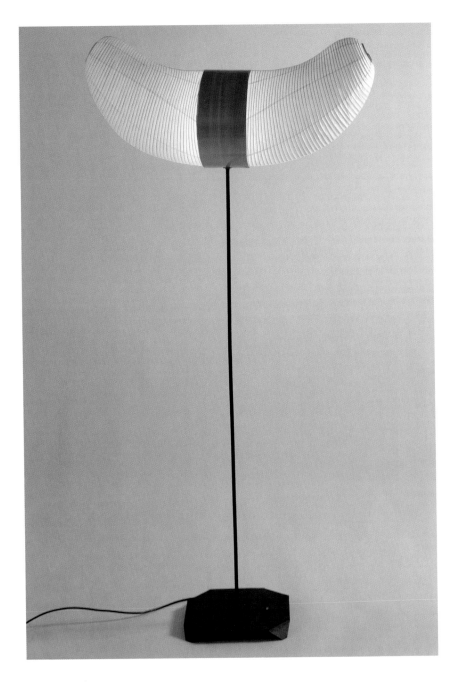

Isamu Noguchi, the son of a Japanese poet with an American writer mother, trained as a cabinet-maker in Japan in 1917. From 1923, he studied premedicine at Columbia University, New York, but wished to become a sculptor and so attended evening classes at the Leonardo da Vinci School, New York. Eventually, he abandoned his medical training altogether and became an assistant to the director of the art school. In 1927, Noguchi won a Guggenheim Fellowship that allowed him to travel to Paris where he worked for two years as an assistant to the sculptor Constantin Brancusi (1876–1957). Around 1930, Noguchi spent several months in Peking and also went to Japan where he discovered Zen gardens. On his return to New York in 1932 he concentrated on sculpture. He designed the Bakelite *Radio-Nurse* nursery monitor for the Zenith Radio Co. (1937), the form of which was reminiscent of a Japanese warrior's mask, and two years later designed a highly sculptural free-form dining table for the president of the **Museum of Modern Art, New York**, A. Congers Goodyear. Noguchi also designed glassware for Steuben and several pieces of furniture for **Herman Miller** and **Knoll** including the *IN50* coffee table (1944), *IN70* sofa (1946) and the *IN22* rudder tables, stools and rocking stool (1954). In the early 1940s, he created his paper *Lunar* light sculptures, and from 1952 designed a large number of *Akari* lamps, which revitalized the ancient Japanese craft of mulberrybark papermaking. As one of the most distinguished sculptors of the 20th century, Noguchi sought to involve some of the qualities of his sculpture more closely in the common experience of living and this he achieved through his industrially produced, visually seductive organic designs.

Isamu Noguchi
1904 *Los Angeles*
1988 *New York*

◄ *Horn Akari*-lamp for Ozeki & Co., 1960

▼ *Radio-Nurse* nursery monitor for Zenith Radio Corporation, 1937

Jean Nouvel
b. 1945 *Fumel, France*

Jean Nouvel studied at the École Nationale Supérieure, Paris from 1966 to 1971, establishing a partnership with François Seigueur in 1970, and thereafter undertaking several architectural commissions including the renovation of the Gaieté Lyrique theatre (1977) in Paris, the renovation and extension of the Centre Médico-Chirurgical clinic in Bezons (1978) and the Anne Frank College (1979). His entry to the competition for the new Ministère des Finances in 1982 was commended and his submissions for the competitions for the development of Parc de la Villette and the Centre d'Art Contemporain et la Médiathèque in 1983 and 1984 both won second prizes. In 1985, he founded his own office, Jean Nouvel & Associates, and subsequently worked on several theatre projects with the scenographer, Jacques Le Marquet, including the Théâtre de Jean-Marie Serreau, the Cartoucherie de Vincennes, the Opera house in Lyons and part of the Théâtre de Belfort. Nouvel also received widespread acclaim for his Institut du Monde Arabe in Paris, the Centre Culturel in Combs-la-Ville and the Nemausus 1 housing project at Nîmes, and was awarded the Équerre d'Argent and the Grand Prix d'Architecture in 1987. During the late 1980s, he also produced a number of elegant furniture designs that, while reminiscent of Louis Cuny's furniture of the 1920s, had the same functionalist aesthetic as his buildings. He was awarded "Carte Blanche" by VIA in 1987 to create a range of aluminium furniture, which included the *BAO* coffer, the *IAC* table and a system of extendable shelving. Nouvel has also designed furniture for **Knoll** and Ligne Roset as well as lighting for Luceplan.

▲ Canapé for Ligne Roset, 1988

◀ **Gio Ponti**, Vase for Richard-Ginori, c.1925

The Italian Novecento Movement was founded in 1926 with the aim of countering both the "fake antique" and the "ugly modern" in architecture and design. Its original members included **Gio Ponti** and Emilio Lancia, who were later joined by Giovanni Muzio (1893–1982) and Tomasso Buzzi. The movement, which was inspired by French **Art Deco** and the **Wiener Werkstätte**, opposed the **Rationalism** promoted by designers such as **Franco Albini**, and as a classicizing Italian derivative of Art Deco, it made few inroads into industrial design, apart from a couple of notable exceptions such as Alfonso and Renato Bialetti's *Moka Express* coffee-maker of 1930. As illustrated by Gio Ponti's neo-classically inspired ceramic designs for Richard Ginori, the influence of the movement was greater in the decorative arts and in architecture. Proponents of the Novecento Movement and Rationalism both sought to achieve stylistic hegemony in Italy during the 1930s. While the Fascists initially embraced Rationalism, they eventually adopted the neo-classical Novecento style, which looked back to the glories of Italy's imperial past, considering it better suited to the Fascist Party's grand statements of authority. Italian graphics were also influenced by the Novecento Movement in the 1930s.

Novecento
Italy

► *Selectric 1* golf-ball electric typewriter for IBM, 1961

► *Selectric 1* golf-ball electric typewriter for IBM, 1961

Eliot Fette Noyes

1910 *Boston*
1977 *New Canaan, Connecticut*

Eliot Fette Noyes studied architecture at Harvard University from 1928 to 1932 and at the Harvard Graduate School of Design until 1938. He first worked in the Boston office of Coolidge, Shepley, Bulfinch & Abbot and then in 1939 joined **Walter Gropius** and **Marcel Breuer**'s architectural practice in Cambridge, Massachusetts. Gropius subsequently recommended Noyes for the newly created position of director of industrial design at the **Museum of Modern Art, New York**. In this position, which he held from 1940 to 1942 and for one year after the war, he curated the famous competition and exhibition "**Organic Design** in Home Furnishings" in 1940. Noyes then worked for a year as design director of **Norman Bel Geddes**' industrial design practice, which advised IBM, and in 1947 founded his own office in New Canaan, Connecticut. From 1956 to 1977, as corporate design director of IBM, he was responsible for several revolutionary products, most notably the *Selectric 1* typewriter (1961) with its innovative moving "golfball" typing head and static carriage. He vigorously opposed the Harley Earl (1893–1969) school of styling: refusing to bow to marketing demands for annual changes to the IBM product-line. Noyes established instead a strong **corporate identity** for the company through the integrity of his own product designs and through the commissioning of graphics from **Paul Rand** and the design of buildings from architects such as Breuer. Noyes was a design consultant to many other companies including Westinghouse, Mobil, Xerox and Pan Am. He was one of the most influential advocates of **Good Design**, a man who re-shaped entire corporations and set new standards for design in America.

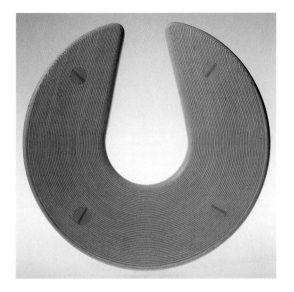

Antii Nurmesniemi initially worked in a metal workshop and an aircraft factory. He was inspired by the modern designs shown at the **New York Museum of Modern Art**'s 1945 touring exhibition "America Builds" in Helsinki, and in 1947 enrolled at the Central School of Applied Arts, Helsinki, where the "Nordic Line" approach to design concentrated on social and technical issues. Assisting the stage designer Kyllikki Halme in 1948, instilled in him a life-long love of film-making. After graduating in 1950, Nurmesniemi travelled to Stockholm and Copenhagen where he met the furniture designers, **Finn Juhl** and **Hans J. Wegner**. On his return to Finland, he joined the Helsinki office of Viljo Revell and Keijo Petäjä, who were pioneering a new rationalist approach to architecture in Finland. From 1951 to 1956, Nurmesniemi designed interiors and furniture for their projects, including his horse-shoe shaped *Sauna* stool for the Palace Hotel (1951–1952). In 1954, he worked for six months in Giovanni Romano's architectural practice in Milan where he was exposed to the functional yet stylish products of designers such as **Franco Albini**, **Marco Zanuso** and Roberto Sambonet (b. 1924). He married the textile designer, Vuokko Eskolin (b. 1930) in 1953, and founded his own Helsinki-based design office in 1956. Three years later he was awarded a Lunning Prize for his refined designs that combined modern European forms with Scandinavian craftsmanship. Like his compatriot **Alvar Aalto**, Nurmesniemi promoted a humanist approach to Modernism that revealed itself in the practical beauty of his products.

Antii
Nurmesniemi
b. 1927 *Hämeenlinna, Finland*

Hermann Obrist

1862 *Kilchberg nr. Zurich*
1927 *Munich*

Hermann Obrist moved from his native Switzerland to Germany in 1876 and subsequently studied natural sciences at the University of Heidelberg. From 1888, he trained at the Kunstgewerbeschule, Karlsruhe, and later designed ceramics for the Großherzog von Sachsen-Weimar-Eisenach's factory in Bürgel. He went to Paris to study sculpture, and in 1892 established an embroidery workshop with Berthe Ruchet in Florence. This enterprise was moved to Munich in 1894, and the following year his embroideries were illustrated in the magazine *Pan*. His vigorous and bizarre whiplash patterns inspired other **Jugendstil** designers, especially **August Endell**, to adopt abstracted naturalistic motifs. Forms such as these grew out of his scientific researches into plant morphology, cell structure and root formation and, in particular, spiral growth patterns. In 1897, Obrist displayed his textiles at the "VII International Art Exhibition" held at the Glaspalast, Munich, and became a key founding member of Munich's **Vereinigte Werkstätten für Kunst im Handwerk**. Apart from his wall-hangings and ceramics, Obrist designed furniture, ironwork and several monuments and fountains. He designed his own house that was furnished by **Bernhard Pankok**, and in 1902 joined Wilhelm von Debschitz in founding a design school in Munich. The sculptural decorations for **Henry van de Velde**'s theatre at the 1914 "Deutsche Werkbund-Ausstellung" in Cologne were also produced by Obrist, who became a leading advocate of design reform and was shortlisted for the directorship of the Kunstgewerbeschule Weimar in 1915. Obrist's sinuous and writhing designs were not only inspired by his study of the natural sciences, they were also the result of "visions" he experienced, and reflected his own inner turmoil.

▼ Detail of *Großer Blütentraum* wall hanging , 1895

George Edgar Ohr was apprenticed to the ceramist Joseph Fortune Meyer in New Orleans from 1879 to 1881, after which he established a pottery in his home town of Biloxi, Mississippi, and began producing earthenware vessels on a hand-built potter's wheel. He used local clays from the Tchouticabouffe and Pascagoula Rivers and his son Leo assisted in their preparation. Ohr pinched his almost paper-thin pottery into distorted naturalistic forms and decorated it with various glazes, which gave the objects a mottled appearance. Known as the "Mad Potter of Biloxi", Ohr was a highly idiosyncratic character and skilled showman who promoted the uniqueness of his wares with the claim, "No Two Alike". He exhibited over six hundred objects at the 1884 "World's Industrial and Cotton Centennial Exhibition" in New Orleans and also displayed his work at the 1900 Buffalo "Arts & Crafts Exhibition". In 1904, he received an award for the originality of his designs at the "Louisiana Purchase Exposition" in St Louis. However, around 1909 he closed his ceramics studio. He retained over six thousand examples of his work with a view to selling them to a national collection, but these pieces remained in the possession of his family until the early 1970s. Although Ohr's style of ceramics was unique in America, similar wares were produced in Britain, most notably by **Christopher Dresser**.

George Edgar Ohr

1857 *Biloxi, Mississippi*
1918 *Biloxi, Mississippi*

▲ Earthenware vases, c. 1900

Josef Maria Olbrich

1867 *Troppau, Silesia*
1908 *Düsseldorf*

▶ Pewter candlestick
for Eduard Hueck,
c. 1902

▼ Drinking glass for
E. Bakalowits &
Söhne, c. 1901

Josef Maria Olbrich studied architecture under Camillo Sitte (1843–1903) and Julius Deininger at the Staatsgewerbeschule (State School of Arts & Crafts), Vienna, from 1882 to 1886, and then worked for four years as an architect and engineer for the building contractor, August Bartel in Troppau. He continued his architectural studies in 1890 under Carl von Hasenauer at the Akademie der Bildenden Künste, Vienna, and on graduating in 1893 was awarded a Rome Prize and worked briefly as an assistant to **Otto Wagner** before travelling to Italy and Tunisia. In 1894, he returned to Vienna and resumed his position at Wagner's office, where he was involved in the planning of the Viennese Stadtbahn (railway), and where he met and befriended **Josef Hoffmann**. In 1897, Olbrich became a founding member of the Vienna **Secession**, and a year later contributed illustrations to the group's journal, *Ver Sacrum*. He planned the layout of the first Secession exhibition and planned the famous Secession Building (1897–1898) on Karlsplatz, Vienna. This simple geometric exhibition hall, topped with an ornate gilded ironwork globe of stylized laurel leaves, was decorated with floral motifs inspired by

the British **Arts & Crafts Movement**. Olbrich designed interiors in the **Art Nouveau** style for the Villa Friedmann in 1898, and the following year created colourful interiors for the Villa Stift and for David Beil's apartment, which included site-specific furnishings. In August 1899, he moved to the **Darmstädter Künstlerkolonie**, which had been founded a month earlier by the Grand Duke Ernst Ludwig of Hesse-Darmstadt at the Mathildenhöhe, Darmstadt to promote the arts and crafts of the region. From 1899 to 1907, Olbrich acted as artistic director and construction manager of the colony and designed seven buildings on the complex, including his own house, the Glückert house, the Wedding Tower, an adjoining exhibition hall, the Preacher's House and semi-detached housing for workers. Olbrich also designed a

bookcase for the colony's Hessian Room at the 1902 "Esposizione Internazionale d'Arte Decorativa Moderna" in Turin as well as silverware for
Bruckmann und Söhne, pewterware for Eduard Hueck, jewellery for Theodor
Fahrner and several light fixtures. The style of his architecture and design
was much influenced by the work of **Charles Rennie Mackintosh**, in particular his abstracted flora motifs and rectilinear forms. Olbrich became a
founding member of the **Deutscher Werkbund** in 1907 and moved to
Düsseldorf in 1908, while continuing to run an office in Darmstadt. His last
significant project was the Tietz Department Store (1908) in Düsseldorf for
which he adopted a neo-classical monumentality. Like fellow Secessionist,
Josef Hoffmann, Olbrich introduced the "New Art" of the **Glasgow School**
and the British Arts & Crafts Movement to the Continent and through his
functional yet beautiful work, paved the way for the development of the
Wiener Werkstätte, the Deutscher Werkbund and ultimately the **Modern
Movement**.

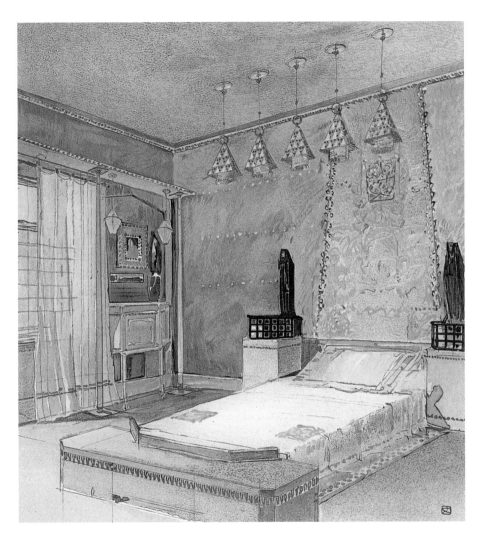

▲ Drawing showing
the main bedroom
of the Olbrich
House at the
Darmstadt Artists'
Colony, 1901

amarico

cirillico

greco

olivetti

STUDIO 42

TASTIERE PER TUTTE LE LINGUE E CARATTERI DI OGNI STILE

Camillo Olivetti (1868–1943) established Italy's first typewriter factory in Ivrea in 1908, after returning to Italy from a trip to the United States. Three years later, Ing. C. Olivetti & C. launched their first typewriter, the *M1*, which was described by a contemporary critic as, "robust and elegant" and was praised for faster carriage and smoother key movements. The company grew rapidly between the 1920s and 1940s, having established subsidiaries across Europe and further abroad, and Camillo Olivetti's son, Adriano, who was appointed managing director in 1933, raised the profile of the firm by developing a strong **corporate identity** through product design, architecture, exhibition design, advertising and graphics. As an "intelligence coordinator", Adriano Olivetti commissioned leading designers to create state-of-the-art products such as the sculptural *Lettera 22* typewriter designed by **Marcello Nizzoli** in 1950, and also engaged leading graphic designers, including **Xanti Schawinsky** and Giovanni Pintori (b. 1912) to produce eye-catching posters and advertisements for the firm. Olivetti introduced Italy's first electronic computer in 1959, but a series of financial difficulties forced the company to sell its Electronics Division after the death of Adriano Olivetti in 1960. However, they continued their research into electronic com-

Olivetti
Founded 1908
Ivrea, Italy

◄ **Xanti Schawinsky**, Poster advertising the *Studio 42* typewriter (designed by Xanti Schawinsky, Luigi Figini & Gino Pollini) for Olivetti, 1935

▼ **Ettore Sottsass & Perry King**, *Valentine* portable typewriter for Olivetti, 1969

munication systems, and in 1965 launched the *P101* programmable desktop computer – an innovative forerunner of the personal computer. During the late 1960s and early 1970s, the company launched other notable products including the *Editor* typewriter designed by **Ettore Sottsass** and Hans von Klier (1964–1969) and the *Divisumma 18* calculator designed by **Mario Bellini** (1973). In 1969, Olivetti also introduced the bright red *Valentine* portable typewriter designed by Ettore Sottsass and **Perry A. King** that transformed the humble typewriter into a must-have fashion accessory. Despite renewed financial problems in the 1970s, Olivetti developed a number of key products including the company's first electronic typewriter in 1978 and its first personal computer in 1982. In the 1980s, they expanded their operations in the IT (Information Technology) field and during the 1990s, the firm concentrated on telecommunications activities. Today, the Olivetti Group is made up of twelve different companies that operate either in information technology or telecommunications.

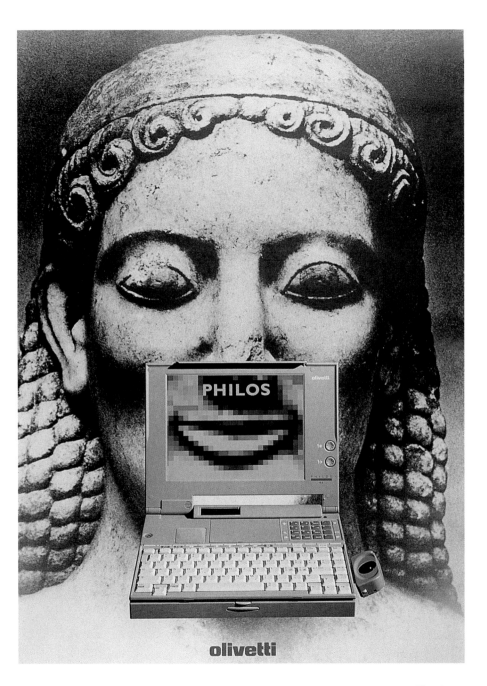

PHILOS

olivetti

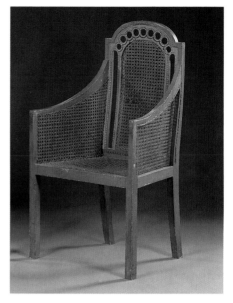

Omega
Workshops
1913–1921
London

▲ Exhibiton
invitation for Omega
Workshops

▶▲ Roger Fry
(attributed),
Chair for Omega
Workshops, c. 1913

The Omega Workshops were established in 1913 in the heart of Bloomsbury, London and were directed by the artist Roger Fry (1866–1934). Fry had been the curator of paintings at the Metropolitan Museum of Art, New York, and had also organized the 1910 landmark exhibition of Post Impressionist paintings at the Grafton Galleries, London. The concept for the workshops was born out of Fry's attempt to revive the art of mural painting and to bring employment to his friends in the Bloomsbury Group. In 1912, Fry, Vanessa Bell (1879–1961) and Duncan Grant (1885–1978) painted frescoes at his house in Guildford, and in 1913 the friends exhibited furniture they had decorated at the Alpine Club Gallery, London. Other members of the Omega workshops included the Vorticist painters, Percy Wyndham Lewis (1882–1957), David Bomberg (1890–1957) and Paul Nash (1889–1946) as well as the designer **Edward McKnight Kauffer**. In 1914, the workshops designed the interior of the Cadena Café in Westbourne Grove and produced a complete decorative scheme for Henry Harris' house in Bedford Square. The workshops also brought artistic endeavour to the design of pottery, textiles, stained glass, graphics and decorated furniture, some of which was painted with floral or figurative motifs in the Vorticist style or with abstract geometric patterns. The workshops finally closed in 1921. While the technical quality of their work was often amateurish, the Omega style, which also embraced Fauvism and Cubism, was remarkably advanced for England at the time.

Organic Design is a holistic and humanizing approach to design that was first pioneered in architecture in the late 19th century by **Charles Rennie Mackintosh** and **Frank Lloyd Wright.** Their method of working involved developing totally integrated **Gesamtkunstwerk** solutions whereby the whole of an architectural scheme was brought together in such a way that the complete effect was greater than the sum of its parts. Thus it was hoped that the whole work would capture something of the spirit of nature. Crucial to this organic approach was the consideration of how individual elements, such as objects and furniture, connected visually and functionally with the context of their interior setting and the building as a whole. Equally critical was how interiors connected visually and functionally with the whole of the scheme and how the building itself connected with its surrounding environment through the harmony of its proportions, use of materials and colour. While the interconnectedness and spirit of nature was at the heart of organic architecture, the use of organic forms was rare. It was not until the late 1920s and early 1930s that **Alvar Aalto**, one of the greatest advocates of Organic Design, pioneered a humanizing and modern organic vocabulary of form. The soft flowing curves of his revolutionary moulded plywood and laminated wood seat

Organic Design

▲ **Alvar Aalto**, *Model No. 43* chaise longue for Artek, 1936

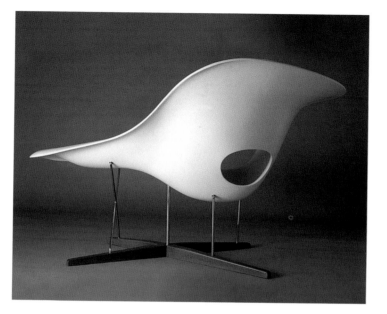

◄ **Charles Eames & Eero Saarinen**, Prototype armchair designed for the Museum of Modern Art's "Organic Design in Home Furnishings" competition, 1940 (made by Haskelite Corporation & the Heywood-Wakefield Company)

► **Charles & Ray Eames**, *La Chaise* designed for the Museum of Modern Art's "International Competition for Low-Cost Furniture Design", 1948 (reissued by Vitra)

furniture countered the ridged geometric formalism of the **International Style**. Like earlier organic architecture, Aalto's designs were holistically conceived but his core concern was not so much with spiritual transcendence as with the functional, intellectual and emotional connections his furniture made with individual users. He believed that wood was "the form-inspiring, deeply human material" and rejected alienating industrial materials such as tubular metal, then the materials of choice of the European **avant-garde**. So widespread was the success of Aalto's furniture and the dissemination of his ideas, particularly in the United States, that he virtually single-handedly changed the course of design towards organic Modernism. In 1940, **Eliot Fette Noyes** organized the landmark competition "Organic Design in Home Furnishings" held at the **Museum of Modern Art, New York**, to promote this new and more mindful approach to design. In the accompanying catalogue, Noyes defined Organic Design as "an harmonious organization of the parts within the whole, according to structure, material, and purpose. Within this definition there can be no vain ornamentation or superfluity, but the part of beauty is none the less great – in ideal choice of material, in visual refinement, and in the rational elegance of things intended for use." [*Organic Design in Home Furnishings* catalogue, Museum of Modern Art, New York, 1941] The prize-winning entries for the "Seating for a Living Room" category, jointly submitted by **Eero Saarinen** and **Charles Eames**, were among the most important furniture designs of the 20th century. Their armchairs were revolutionary not only in the state-of-the-art technology they deployed in the construction of the chairs' single-form compound-moulded plywood seat shells but also for the concept of continuous contact and support advanced through the shells' ergonomically refined organic forms. These immensely influential designs heralded a totally new direction in furniture – encouraging attempts to achieve the ideal of structural, material and functional organic unity of design – and led directly to such seminal designs as Charles and **Ray Eames**' moulded plywood chairs (1945–1946) the amorphous *La Chaise* prototype (1948) and *Plastic Shell* series of chairs (1948–1950) as well as Eero Saarinen's *Womb* chair (1947–1948) and *Pedestal Group* of chairs and tables (1955–1956). The practical application of Organic Design also had a significant impact on Saarinen's architecture during the 1950's and in particular on his masterwork, the remarkably organic TWA Terminal (1956–1962) at Kennedy Airport – one of the most extraordinary buildings of the 20th century. While the success of Organic Design during the post-war years stylistically influenced the rise of **Biomorphism** in mainstream design, it continued to inspire designers working in the 1960s and the 1970s, such as Maurice Calka (b. 1921), **Pierre Paulin** and **Olivier Mourgue**, to create highly sculptural forms in the organic idiom. By the early 1990s, fuelled by

▼ **Maurice Calka**, *Boomerang* desk for Leleu-Deshays, 1970

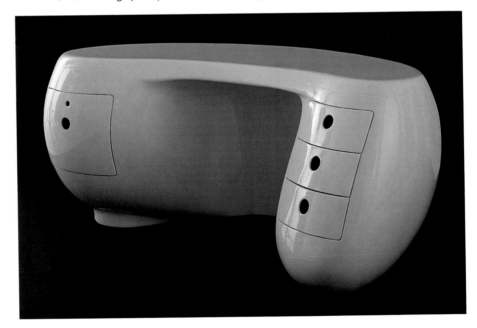

► **Ross Lovegrove**,
Lovegrove Landscape Collection for Frighetto, 1998

◄ **Ross Lovegrove**,
Surf Collection computer accessories for Knoll International, 1992

► **Ross Lovegrove**, *Pod* hanging lamp for Luceplan, 1996–1997

better ergonomic/anthropometric data and by advances in computer-aided design and manufacture, Organic Design re-emerged stronger than ever. Like Eames and Saarinen before them, industrial designers at the cutting-edge today, such as **Ross Lovegrove**, seek to evolve dematerialist organic designs through innovative applications of state-of-the-art materials and in-dustrial techniques. While Organic Design is often associated with natural materials, it is, ironically, plastics – the ultimate in synthetic materials – that are best suited to expressing the abstract essence of nature and to maximiz-ing functional connections by achieving the organic forms that most closely conform to our human morphology. Organic Design is at its most powerful, however, when its sensual and emotionally persuasive formal vocabulary connects with us subliminally by appealing directly to our primeval sense of natural beauty.

► Chair designs for Metz & Co., 1934

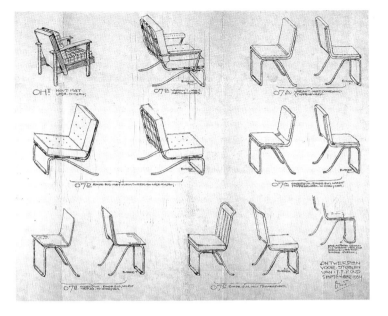

J. J. P. Oud studied at the Quellinus School of Applied Arts in Amsterdam from 1904 to 1907, and went on to work as an assistant in the architectural practice of P. J. H. Cuipers (1827–1921) and Jan Stuit in Amsterdam. He worked in the Munich-based office of Theodor Fischer in 1911, and subsequently practised as a freelance architect in Purmerend from 1912 to 1913 and in Leiden from 1913 to 1916. During this period, his buildings were influenced by the work of **Hendrik Petrus Berlage.** Oud's meeting with **Theo van Doesburg** in 1916 led directly to their collaboration on the De Geus House and their founding, with Jan Wils (1891–1972), of the De Sphinx artists' club. A year later, Oud became a co-founder of **De Stijl** and was one of the few members of the group who successfully put theory into practice. Through his contacts with Berlage, Oud was appointed chief architect of Rotterdam (1918–1933). In 1920, he founded the Opbouw (Reconstruction) group and refused to sign the manifestos of the De Stijl group, which he left the following year. In 1921, he travelled to Weimar and met **Walter Gropius** and **László Moholy-Nagy**, and his book *Dutch Architecture* was subsequently published in two volumes by the **Bauhaus** (1926 and 1929). During the 1930s, he designed a number of tubular metal chairs for the Metz & Co department store. Oud was the most important Dutch exponent of the **International Style** in both architecture and design.

Jacobus Johannes Pieter Oud
1890 Purmerend, Netherlands
1963 Wassenaar/ The Hague

Giuseppe Pagano

1896 *Parenzo, Italy*
1945 *Mauthausen,
Austria*

▼ **Giuseppe Pagano
& Gino Levi-
Montalcini**, *Chichibio*
telephone table,
1932 (reissued by
Zanotta)

Born Guiseppe Pogatschnig, Pagano adopted his Italian surname when he enlisted in the Italian army in 1915. Following military service, Pagano became a member of the Italian Fascist Party in 1920 and studied architecture at the Politecnico di Milano until 1924. He worked closely with Gino Levi-Montalcini (1902–1974) and together they designed the Gualino Office Building (1928–1930) and a number of rationalist buildings for the 1928 "Esposizione di Torino". With other young architects who had taken part in the Turin exhibition, including Levi-Montalcini, Edoardo Persico (1900–1936), Alberto Sartoris and Lavinia Perona, Pagano became a founding member of the Group of Six, which was inspired by the earlier Gruppo Sette (Group Seven), formed in 1926 by young Rationalist architects including **Giuseppe Terragni**. Pagano's use of tubular metal for his furniture designs was a distinguishing feature of Italian **Rationalism** – the design idiom favoured by the Fascists in the early 1930s. From 1931, Pagano acted as a consultant to the journal *Architettura e Arti Decorative*, and between 1930 and 1943 worked on the editorial staff of *Casabella* magazine, becoming chief editor from 1933. Pagano also designed the Institute of Physics, Rome

(1932) and the Università Bocconi, Milan (1938–1941), for which he created rational site-specific furniture with laminated wood frames. As a leading Rationalist, Pagano was an influential design theorist and his articles, including one in the *La Tecnica Fascista* (1939), which praised the Fascist regime's adoption of Modernism, were widely published. However, in 1942 Pagano left the Fascist Party and joined the Resistance. A year later he was arrested and interned at Mauthausen where he died in 1945.

Sven Palmqvist trained from 1928 at the glass engraving school at the Orrefors glassworks. He then studied at the Konstfackskolan and the Tekniska Skolan, Stockholm from 1931 to 1933 and attended the Kungliga Konsthögskolan, Stockholm from 1934 to 1936. During these years, he also studied under Paul Cornet and Aristide Maillol (1861–1944) at the Académie Ranson, Paris, as well as in Germany, Czechoslovakia, Italy and America. In 1936, Palmqvist returned to the Orrefors glassworks where he developed the *Kraka* technique, in which a grid-like pattern of white or coloured glass was sandwiched between layers of clear glass. Later, in 1954, he invented a method of centrifugally spinning molten glass in a mould so as to eliminate the need for hand finishing, and he was awarded a gold medal and a Grand Prix at the 1957 Triennale di Milano for his designs using this innovative technique. During the late 1940s and early 1950s, he developed his *Ravenna* glassware in which coloured geometric glass segments were surrounded with sand-sprinkled air channels to produce a mosaic-like effect. He used this technique for a free-standing glass wall entitled "Light and Dark", which was designed for the Union Internationale des Télécommunications, Geneva, and comprised two hundred blocks of *Ravenna* glass. Palmqvist remained at Orrefors until 1972, creating exquisite "industrial studio glass", and later worked as a freelance designer for the glassworks.

Sven Palmqvist
1906 *Lenhovda, Sweden*
1984 *Orrefors, Sweden*

▲ *Ravenna* bowl for Orrefors Glasbruk, c. 1954

◄ Flyleaf of the German section catalogue for the "Exposition Universelle et Internationale" in Paris, 1900

Bernhard Pankok

1872 *Münster, Germany*
1943 *Baierbrunn, Germany*

The son of a cabinet-maker, Bernhard Pankok was apprenticed to a decorator and restorer in Münster. He later studied at the Kunstakademie, Düsseldorf from 1889 to 1891 and in Berlin from 1891 to 1892. He established his own studio in Munich in 1892, and from 1896 contributed designs to the magazines, *Jugend* and *Pan*. A year later, he participated in the Glaspalast Exhibition and co-founded the **Vereinigte Werkstätten für Kunst im Handwerk** with **Hermann Obrist, Richard Riemerschmid** and **Bruno Paul**. He also participated in the Munich Secession exhibition in 1899, and designed furniture for Obrist's house in the Bavarian capital. His **Jugendstil** designs were notable for their carved naturalistic decoration and quirky forms. He designed his Alcove Room – a wooden panelled smoking room – for the Werkstätten's display at the 1900 Paris "Exposition Universelle et Internationale", which Obrist described as a combination of Rococo scrolls and Viking ship elements. In 1900, Pankok was commissioned by the art historian Konrad Lange to design a house in Tübingen. While the resulting building with its gabled roof was in the Black Forest tradition, the simplicity of the interiors was astonishingly modern. Pankok's most famous interior, however, was for a music room, which was exhibited at the 1904 "St. Louis

World Exhibition" and later at the Landesgewerbeanstalt in Stuttgart. More extravagant than the Lange interiors, this room exuded a sense of luxury with its plethora of detail and graceful curving lines and exemplified Munich Jugendstil. In 1908, Pankok became a member of the **Deutscher Werkbund**, and in 1913 was appointed director of the Königliche Lehr- und Versuchs-werkstätte, Stuttgart, which he merged with the Kunstgewerbeschule the same year. Although noted for his furniture and interiors inspired by natural forms, Pankok was also highly regarded as a portraitist and as a stage and costume designer.

▲ The Lange House in Tübingen, 1901–1902

Verner Panton

*1926 Gamtofte,
Denmark*
1998 Copenhagen

Verner Panton trained at the Odense Tekniske Skole and later studied archi-tecture at the Kongelige Danske Kunstakademi, Copenhagen, graduating in 1951. Between 1950 and 1952, he worked as an associate of **Arne Jacobsen**, and together they collaborated on a number of experimental furniture designs including Jacobsen's well-known *Ant* chair (1951–1952). In 1955, Panton established his own design and architectural office and became well known for his innovative architectural proposals, including a collapsible house (1955), the Cardboard House (1957) and the Plastic House (1960). He received greater recognition, however, for his numerous seating, light-ing, textiles and carpet designs and exhibition installations. In 1958, Baron Schilden Holsten commissioned Panton to rebuild and expand his Komigen Inn (Come Again Inn), sited in a forest on the Danish island of Funen. For this inn, Panton designed an all-red interior and his famous *Cone* chair (1958). This unusual seating solution and the slightly later *Heart* chair (1959) were subsequently manufactured by Percy von Halling-Koch's newly estab-lished firm, Plus-Linje. In 1959, a Panton exhibit at the Købestaevnet trade fair literally turned the world upside down – the ceiling was carpeted and all the furniture and lighting was inverted. Panton produced a equally uncon-ventional installation at the 1960 Cologne Furniture Fair with a ceiling

▼ *Panton* chairs
for Herman Miller,
1959–1960 (reissued
by Vitra)

▲ *Mira-Spectrum*
textile for Mira-X,
c. 1969

covered in silver foil, and that same year a commission to redesign the
Astoria Restaurant in Trondheim resulted in an interior that was shocking
not only for the unusual forms adopted but also on account of the bright-
ness of the colours used. In 1955, Panton designed the single-form cantilevered plywood *S*-chair, which was developed in co-operation with Thonet,
and for several years afterwards, he attempted to translate this design into
plastic. Eventually, he achieved his goal with the revolutionary *Panton* chair
(1959–1960), and in 1962 offered the production rights to **Herman Miller**.
Panton left Denmark in 1962 and stayed briefly in Paris before establishing a
design office in Cannes. He subsequently moved to Basel, however, to assist
Willy Fehlbaum (the Basel-based Herman Miller licensee and founder of
Vitra) with the five-year-long production development of the *Panton* chair,
which eventually became the first single-material, single-form chair to be
injection-moulded. Having established a design office in Basel, Panton

cultivated a wide-ranging clientele including A. Sommer, Kaufeld, Haiges, Schöner Wohnen, Nordlys, Kill, Wega Radio, Thonet, **Knoll International**, Lüber and Bayer. Panton also designed psychedelic "spacescape" installations for Bayer at the 1968 "Visiona O" and 1970 "Visiona II" exhibitions in Cologne, which combined fantastic sculptural shapes with pure saturated colour. From 1969 to 1985, he produced geometrically patterned textiles for Mira-X, using his characteristically bright rainbow palette. During the late 1960s and early 1970s, Panton designed a range of seating for Fritz Hansen and a system of storage units as well as floor and desk lamps with chromed wire constructions for Lüber. These designs were inspired by Op Art and were developed from his earlier wire seat furniture of 1959 to 1960. In 1973, he designed the *1-2-3* seating system for Fritz Hansen, which comprised twenty different models, and two years later designed a colourful block-system toy, the *Pantonaef,* for Naef, Switzerland. During the 1970s, Louis Poulsen produced several lights designed by Panton, including the spherical *VP-Globe* and *Panto* lamps (1975), while in the next decade Panton created his *Art Chairs-Chair Art* series (1981) of sixteen plywood single-form chairs

▼ Chair, *Cone* chair and *Heart* chair for Plus-Linje, 1960, 1958 & 1959

with unusual amorphous cut-out shapes, and experimented with pure geometric forms – cubes, spheres, cones – for a proposed seating range (1985). Unlike many other Danish designers, Panton took a revolutionary rather

than evolutionary approach to design. Throughout his career, he produced highly innovative, bold and playful designs that often utilized state-of-the-art technology and reflected his optimistic belief in the future.

▲ Room installation for Bayer's "Visiona II" exhibition in Cologne, 1970

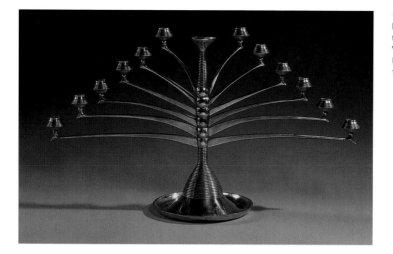

Bruno Paul

1874 *Seifhennersdorf/
Lausitz, Germany*
1968 *Berlin*

Bruno Paul studied at the Kunstgewerbeschule, Dresden, from 1886. Then, after moving to Munich in 1892, he trained under Paul Höcker and Wilhelm von Diez at the Akademie der Bildenden Künste, Munich. In 1897, Paul became a founder member of the **Vereinigte Werkstätten für Kunst im Handwerk** together with **Hermann Obrist**, **Richard Riemerschmid** and **Bernhard Pankok**. His furniture designs were strongly influenced by those of **Henry van de Velde**, while his metalwork was typified by simple geometric forms. He also contributed nearly five hundred humourous cartoons to the magazines *Simplicissimus* and *Jugend*. His design for a huntsman's room – a highly rustic Bavarian-style interior reflecting his interest in vernacularism – won a Grand Prix at the 1900 "Exposition Universelle et Internationale de Paris". He also designed a dining room for the 1902 "Esposizione Internazionale d'Arte Decorativa Moderna" in Turin, the parliamentary president's office in Bayreuth (1904) and a waiting room for Nuremberg's central station (1905). From c. 1905 to 1907, **Ludwig Mies van der Rohe** joined his architectural practice, and between 1907 and 1933 Paul directed the Kunstgewerbeschule, Berlin. He was a founding member of the **Deutscher Werkbund** in 1907 and designed the restaurant, beer hall and other public buildings for the 1914 "Werkbund-Austellung" in Cologne. He became an architectural consultant to the Maharaja of Mysore Colombo in 1932, and from 1933 worked as an independent architect in Berlin, Hanau, Frankfurt and Düsseldorf. Paul's **Jugendstil** designs were less ornamented than those of Pankok and Obrist and anticipated the linearity of later **Modern Movement** designs.

Pierre Paulin studied stone-carving and clay modelling at the École
Camondo, Paris. From 1954, he designed furniture for Thonet, and four
years later began working for the Dutch furniture manufacturer, Artifort, who
produced the majority of his designs including his first plastic chair, the 157
(1953). Between 1958 and 1959, Paulin worked in Holland, Germany, Japan
and the USA, and founded his own Paris-based industrial design office in
the mid-1960s. He then developed a series of chairs with foam upholstery
and polyester seats for Mobilier Nationale, including a modular sofa that
could be connected into an endless serpentine form. In 1968, Paulin was
commissioned to design visitor seating for the Louvre, and the following
year received an ADI (Associazione per il Disegno Industriale) award for his
582 Ribbon chair (1965). The design of this chair and his *577 Tongue* chaise
(1967) reflected the increasingly casual lifestyle of the 1960s, their foam-up-
holstered sculptural forms providing extraordinary comfort. In 1970, he designed seating for Expo '70 in Osaka, and was then commissioned to re-
design the French President's private apartment at the Élysée Palace. In
1975, Paulin founded ADSA + Partners and was joined by **Roger Tallon** and
Michel Schreiber in 1984. During the 1980s, Paulin created furniture for the
presidential office at the Élysée Palace (1983) and a range of handcrafted furniture for Mobilier Nationale. Apart from his innovative furniture, Paulin has
also designed car interiors for Simca, packaging for Christian Dior, signage
for the Musée d'Orsay and telephones for L. M. Ericsson.

Pierre Paulin
b. 1927 *Paris*

Dagobert Peche

1887 *St. Michael im Lungau, Austria*
1923 *Mödling, Austria*

▲ Silver bowl for the
Wiener Werkstätte,
c. 1915

► Silver jewellery
casket for the
Wiener Werkstätte,
1920

Dagobert Peche studied engineering at the Technische Hochschule, Vienna and architecture at the Akademie der Bildenden Künste, Vienna, from 1908 to 1911. Following his studies, he began designing carpets and ceramics inspired by Rococo and Baroque ornamentation for serial production. Peche participated in the 1914 "Deutsche Werkbund-Ausstellung" in Cologne, and in 1915 became a member of the **Wiener Werkstätte**. After two years, he was appointed the co-operative's co-director and was one of its most active and prolific members. Between 1917 and 1919, Peche resided in Zurich where he established and directed a shop for the Wiener Werkstätte. He adopted increasingly classical forms although his work remained highly decorated, usually with floral or animal motifs, until his style of ornamentation became influenced by contemporary trends in the fine arts. As one of the leading representatives of the Wiener Werkstätte, Peche produced some three thousand designs for the co-operative, for furniture, ceramics, commercial graphics, book bindings, textiles, toys, clothes and stage sets as well as painted Easter eggs and Christmas tree decorations. Despite his liberal use of ornament, which was in stark contrast to the geometric style of **Josef Hoffmann** and **Koloman Moser**, Peche had a strong influence on the design of Wiener Werkstätte products until his death in 1923.

PEL

Founded 1931
Oldbury/Birmingham

During the First World War, when the demand for tubular metal rose significantly in Great Britain, several manufacturers, including Accles and Pollock,
decided to join together to form a company, Tube Investments. In 1927 this
firm established a new entity, Tube Products, to exploit the manufacturing
potential offered by the newly developed arc-welding process. They supplied
tubular metal to many furniture manufacturers and also produced their
own furniture on a limited scale. In 1931, Practical Equipment Limited was
founded in an attempt to increase sales for the tubular metal manufacturing
company. Inspired by the success of standardized tubular metal furniture
manufactured by German companies such as Thonet, Practical Equipment
Limited (or PEL as it was renamed in 1932) commissioned designers such
as **Wells Coates** and **Serge Chermayeff** to design a range of highly rational
furniture including chairs, tables and beds. One of the most successful PEL
products was a nesting chair designed by Chermayeff in 1932 that was suitable for outside use and could be efficiently stowed – one hundred chairs
could be stored in an area measuring only twenty square feet. Like Thonet,
PEL promoted the furniture it produced as high-quality and suitable for a
modern lifestyle. Their customers included many well-known modernist designers such as **Edward McKnight Kauffer**, Marion Dorn (1899–1964) and
Betty Joel (b. 1896). PEL also manufactured Thonet furniture under license,
including some designs by **Marcel Breuer**, and during the Second World
War they produced tubular metal stretchers. Throughout 1930s, PEL's inexpensive and functional furniture helped to popularize Modernism in Great
Britain.

Jorge Pensi studied architecture in Buenos Aires. In 1977, he joined Alberto Liévore (b. 1948), Oriol Pibernat and Norberto Chaves in founding the design consultancy Grupo Berenguer, and that same year, having acquired Spanish citizenship, established another design office with Liévore in Barcelona. The studio subsequently designed exhibition stands for Perobell and the SIDI group in 1984. During the 1980s, Pensi contributed to the Spanish design journal, *On Diseño*, and specialized in the design of lighting and furniture. His elegant cast-aluminium *Toledo* chair (1986–1988), won numerous prizes including the first Award Selection from SIDI (1988), two silver Delta awards from the Associazione del Diesegno Industriale and a Design-Auswahl 90 Award from the Stuttgart Design Centre, and other remarkably fluid and elegant designs, such as the *Orfilia* chair (1989) for Thonet and the *Olympia* hanging lamp (1988) for B. Lux came to exemplify Spanish design in the 1980s. In 1994, Pensi designed the exhibition, "Salón Internacionale de Diseño para el Habitát". He is one of Spain's leading designers and has worked as a design consultant in Italy, Finland, Germany, Singapore, South America and the United States of America.

Jorge Pensi
b. 1949 *Buenos Aires*

▼ *Olympia* ceiling light for B. Lux, 1988

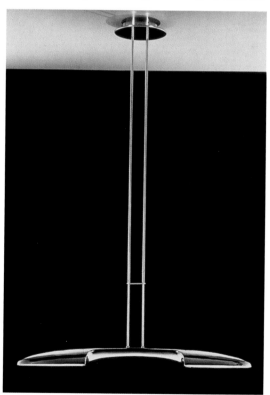

Pentagram, which was founded as a multi-disciplinary design consultancy in 1972, differed from other international design offices in that it was structured "federally" and had up to fifty designers associated with it, either individually or in groups. It evolved from an earlier graphic design office established in 1962 by Alan Fletcher (b. 1931), Colin Forbes (b. 1928) and Robert Gill (b. 1931), who were joined in 1965 by the architect Theo Crosby to form Crosby, Fletcher, Forbes. The industrial designer **Kenneth Grange** and the graphic designer Mervyn Kurlansky (b. 1936) became affiliated with the consultancy in 1972 when it was renamed Pentagram. Finally, during the 1970s and early 1980s, John McConnell, David Hillman, Peter Harrison and David Pelham also became partners. Pentagram became noted for its bold and direct **corporate identity** design for British Petroleum, Reuters, Faber & Faber, Watneys, Victoria & Albert Museum, the Tate Gallery, the Guardian and Prestel among others. They also developed typography for many large clients including Xerox, IBM and Nissan. The Pentagram "house-style" was perpetuated through its product design, most of which was undertaken by Grange, who also designed the *125 High Speed Train* for British Rail in 1976 and developed kitchen appliances for Kenwood, lighters for Ronson, writing

▼ **Daniel Weil**,
Interior of the
Swatch Timeship
in New York, mid-
1990s

equipment for Parker Pens and razors for Wilkinson Sword. Under the direction of Crosby, Pentagram also undertook the design of a number of exhibitions, including the British Industry Pavilion at Expo '67 in Montreal, and *The Environment Game* (1973) and *British Genius* (1977) in London. Central to all the group's activities is the belief that design should permeate all areas of life, an idea that was promoted through the publication of several books, including *Pentagram: The Work of Five Designers* (1972) and *Living by Design* (1977). The consultancy also issued a series of pamphlets, known as the *Pentagram Papers,* that highlight "curious, entertaining, stimulating, provocative and occasionally controversial points of view". It is, however, the group's retail designs that perhaps best reveal the consultancy's promotion of "design as lifestyle". Through the success of its graphics, which are occasionally tinged with irony, and its consumer products, which have a utilitarian directness that is tempered with subtle styling, Pentagram became a leading international design consultancy. In 1978, they founded a New York office and in 1986, established another branch in San Francisco. To this day, Pentagram is a highly prestigious organization that is led by designers rather than by administrators and accountants, thus ensuring the firm's continued commitment to creativity and innovation.

◄▲▲ **David Hillman,** Corporate identity for the Tate Gallery, 1989–1990

▲▲ **John McConnell,** Corporate identity for Faber & Faber, 1981

◄▲ **David Hillman,** Newspaper design for *The Guardian,* 1988

▲ **Alan Fletcher,** Corporate identity for the Victoria & Albert Museum, 1988

Charlotte Perriand

1903 *Paris*
1999 *Paris*

▼ Design for a
dining room interior,
c. 1929

Charlotte Perriand trained under Henri Rapin and Maurice Dufrène (1876–1955) at the École de l'Union Centrale des Arts Décoratifs, Paris from 1920 to 1925. She first showed her work at the Société des Artistes Décorateurs, and in 1927 designed a roof-top bar for the Salon d'Automne that included her first anodized aluminium and chromed steel furniture. This display attracted the attention of **Le Corbusier** and she subsequently collaborated with him and his cousin, **Pierre Jeanneret**, for ten years. Perriand was responsible for most of the furniture designs issuing from the Le Corbusier studio during this period, including the first tubular steel designs for systematized furnishings known as "Équipement de l'habitation" (1928–1929), which were first shown at the 1929 Salon d'Automne to much critical acclaim. This revolutionary collection of furniture, with its hard-edged modern aesthetic and functionalist aspect, reflected Perriand's belief in moral and physical fitness. In 1929, Perriand, Le Corbusier and Jeanneret

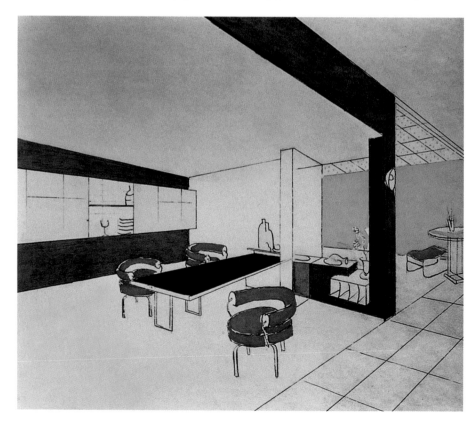

resigned from the Société des Artistes Décorateurs when its jury would not allow them sufficient exhibition space and founded the rival UAM (Union des Artistes Modernes). The following year, Perriand met the painter, Fernand Léger (1881–1955) who became a long-standing friend, and in 1931 she began exhibiting at the UAM exhibitions under her own name. In 1937, she and Jeanneret exhibited an aluminium mountain shelter at the "Exposition Internationale des Arts et Techniques dans la Vie Moderne" in Paris, and in 1940 they established an architectural office for the design of prefabricated aluminium buildings, together with **Jean Prouvé** and Georges Blanchon. From 1940 to 1942, Perriand was an adviser on arts and crafts to the Japanese ministry of commerce. On her return to France, after three years in Indochina, she resumed designing buildings, interiors and furniture, either independently or with Jeanneret and Blanchon. Her most notable projects from this period include furnishings for holiday chalets at Méribel-les-Allues (1946–1949), a prototype kitchen for Le Corbusier's Unité d'Habitation, Marseilles (1950), furniture for the Steph Simon gallery in Paris (1955–74), Air France's London office (1957) and conference rooms for the United Nations in Geneva (1959–1970). During the 1980s, Perriand briefly headed the jury for the "International Competition for New Office Furniture" that was sponsored by the French Ministry of Culture and worked as a consultant to the furniture manufacturer Cassina, which reissued the furniture she had designed with Jeanerret and Le Corbusier. Several major retrospective exhibitions have been held on Charlotte Perriand's work, most notably in Japan (1955), Paris (1965 and 1985) and London (1998). Although, Perriand is best remembered for her elegant **International Style** tubular steel furniture of the 1920s and 1930s, she also produced a number of craft-based designs, such as her diminutive *Synthèse des Arts*, chair (1955), that was a remarkable synthesis of elements of Western and Eastern cultures.

▼ *Synthèse des Arts* chair probably for Takashimaya, 1955

Gaetano Pesce
b. 1939 *La Spézia, Italy*

Gaetano Pesce studied architecture and industrial design at the University of Venice, graduating in 1965. Between 1959 and 1967, he worked as an independent film-maker and artist in Padua, experimenting with both serial and kinetic art forms, and during this period became a founding member of Group N – a group of artists who explored the concept of programmed art. Pesce also worked as a designer in Padua from 1962 to 1967 and in Venice from 1968, producing furniture and interior designs for C&B Italia, Cassina, Bernini, Venini and Bracciodiferro among others. His furniture designs were highly innovative, both in the materials they employed and the methods of their production. The polyureathane foam *Up Series* (1969), for example, was compressed and vacuum-packed into PVC envelopes, which when opened allowed the colourful seating to literally mutate into life. As a "contesting" designer, Pesce participated in the exhibition "Italy: The New Domestic Landscape" held at the **Museum of Modern Art, New York** in 1972. For this key event, celebrating **Radical Design**, he designed a curious installation that comprised a series of "archeological" documents relating to a fictional settlement from the "Great Contaminations" age. In 1973, Pesce formulated

▼ *Up 3* chair for
C&B Italia, 1969

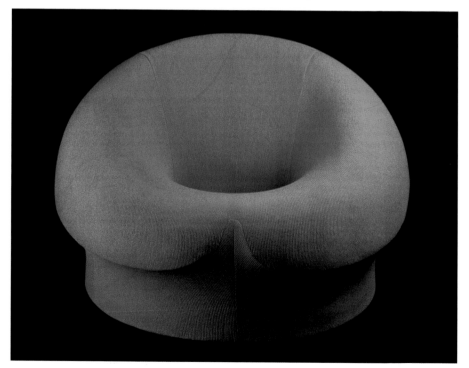

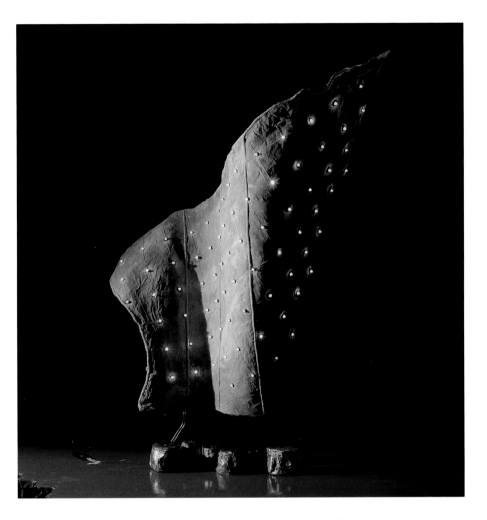

the theory that architecture and design should be a "representation of real-ity" and a "document of the times", while his search for liberation of expres-sion led him to explore the idea of "performance design" in many of his pro-jects. In the *Golgotha Suite* (1972–1973), with its coffin-shaped table and shroud-like chairs, Pesce experimented for the first time with the idea of a "diversified series". This concept was also employed in his *Sit Down* chairs and sofa (1975) for Cassina – each example, though similar, being slightly different owing to the variability of the materials used in the manufacturing process. Similarly, his *Airport* lamp (1986) was constructed from randomly

▲ *Golgotha Suite,*
1972–1973

coloured urethane and its form could be manipulated into innumerable positions. Now resident in New York, Pesce continues to explore the expressive potential of new materials and production techniques while often imbuing his designs with humour, as in his folding *Umbrella* chair (1992–1995) for Zerodisegno and his translucent epoxy-resin *543 Broadway* chair (1993) for Bernini that rocks and rolls on its spring-mounted feet. He is a professor at the Institut d'Architecture et d'Etudes Urbaines, Strasbourg, and has for many years taught at the Cooper Union school of architecture and art, New York. Throughout his career, Pesce's unconventional and highly innovative work counters the **Modern Movement**'s precepts of standardization and design uniformity, since for Pesce, architecture and design are multi-disciplinary activities that should allow the creator unrestrained freedom of expression.

Giancarlo Piretti studied at the Istituto Statale d'Arte, Bologna, graduating in 1960. After completing his formal studies, he worked as an in-house designer for Anonima Castelli and produced designs for both domestic and contract furniture. He was subsequently appointed director of research and design at Anonima Castelli, a position he held until 1972. During this period, Piretti designed the folding aluminum and perspex *Plia* chair (1969), his first design in plastic for which he received several major awards including a Smau prize (1971), a gold medal at the "Bio 4", Ljubljana (1971) and the German "Gute Form" award (1973). Piretti also designed the similarly constructed *Plona* armchair (1970) and *Platone* table (1971). Between 1963 and 1970, he taught at the Istituto Statale d'Arte, Bologna, and from the late 1970s onwards he collaborated with **Emilio Ambasz** on the design of ergonomically conceived seating, including the *Vertebra* (1977) and *Dorsal* (1981) systems, which greatly increased the support offered by office tasking chairs. These designs won a **Compasso d'Oro** and an Industrial Design Excellence Award respectively, and were produced by Open Ark in the United States as well as being manufactured under license in Europe by Castelli. Piretti and Ambasz also designed the *Logotec* (1980) and *Oseris* (1984) lighting ranges for Erco. In 1984, Piretti began designing for Castilia, and four years later Krueger launched the *Piretti* Collection, which comprised fifty different seating models. Piretti's innovative designs are conceived for large-scale mass-production and are characterized by sleek yet functional forms.

Giancarlo Piretti
b. 1940 *Bologna*

▼ *Plia* folding chair for Castelli, 1969

Flavio Poli

1900 *Chioggia, Italy*
1984 *Venice*

Although famed as a glass designer, Flavio Poli's artistic training was in the field of ceramics. In 1929, he began his collaboration with Libero Vitali's I. V. A. M. glassworks, where he worked as a glass sculptor using both solid and blown glass. He worked for the Seguso-Barovier-Ferro glassworks from 1934, where he designed his famous opalescent glass *Zodiaco* panel. The Murano-based firm changed its name to Seguso Vetri d'Arte in 1937 and continued to produce Poli's designs, including his *vetro traliccio* (lattice-work) chandeliers and his futuristic *vetro astrale* ornamental wares. During the 1950s, Poli designed a series of blown vessels using "cased" glass, for which he was awarded a **Compasso d'Oro** in 1954. These heavy and monumental designs were characterized by simple and undecorated forms and the use of contrasting colours of glass. In 1963, Poli abandoned his position as artistic director of the Seguso glassworks, and the following year started his artistic collaboration with the Società Veneziana di Conterie e Cristallerie. He abandoned this venture in 1966, however, for health reasons. Between 1950 and 1960, Poli won four Grand Prix at the Milan Triennale exhibitions for his beautiful glassware, which combined traditional craftsmanship with visually seductive contemporary forms.

▼ *Valva Siderale* vase
for Seguso Vetri
d'Arte, c. 1954

► Cased glass vase,
Model No.11902 for
Seguso Vetri d'Arte,
1955

Gio Ponti

1891 *Milan*
1979 *Milan*

▼ *Model No.699*
Superleggera chair
for Cassina, 1957

Giovanni (Gio) Ponti studied architecture at the Politecnico di Milano, graduating in 1921. He subsequently worked in the architectural office of Emilio Lancia and Mino Fiocchi, and from 1923 to 1930 was art director of the Richard Ginori ceramics factories in Milan and Florence. His porcelain designs for Richard Ginori, many of which were decorated with neo-classical motifs in the **Novecento** style, won a Grand Prix at the 1925 Paris "Exposition Internationale des Arts Décoratifs et Industriels Modernes". Around this period, Ponti also designed low-cost furniture for the La Rinascente department store as well as other more luxurious pieces. From 1925 to 1979, he was the director of the Monza Biennale exhibitions where he showed his own work along with that of other progressive designers. Ponti designed his first building – his own neo-classical style house on the Via Randaccio in Milan – in 1925, and a year later established an architectural partnership with Emilio Lancia in Milan, which continued until 1933. In 1928, at the suggestion of the journalist Ugo Ojetti, Ponti launched the prestigious design

journal, *Domus* that was published by Gianni Mazzocchi. *Domus* was initially established to promote the **Novecento** Movement, which sought to counter both "the fake antique" and "the ugly modern" in architecture and design. Between 1933 and 1945, Ponti worked in partnership with the engineers Antonio Fornaroli and Eugenio Soncini in Milan, and during this period undertook many architectural commissions for both private and public buildings, including the School of Mathematics for the University of Rome (1934), and the first Montecatini Building (1936) and the "Domuses"(typical houses) apartment buildings in Milan (1931–1936). Ponti was also commissioned by the Italian Cultural Institute in 1936 to re-design the interiors of the Fürstenberg Palace in Vienna, which he executed in a Neo-Secessionist style. From 1930, he designed lighting and furniture for the Fontana company, and in 1933 was made artistic co-director, with **Pietro Chiesa**, of its subsidiary Fontana Arte. During the 1940s, Ponti contributed extensively to *Stile* magazine (1941–1947), produced sets and costumes for La Scala opera house (1947), created multi-coloured glass bottles, glasses and a chandelier for Venini (1946–1950) and designed his famous coffee machine for La Pavoni (1948). He collaborated with **Piero Fornasetti** on several furniture designs and interiors schemes in the late 1940s and 1950s, including those

▲ **Gio Ponti & Piero Fornasetti**, Bedroom designed for the IX Milan Triennale, 1951

for the Casino at San Remo (1950). Apart from several prestigious building commissions, such as the second Montecatini Building, Milan (1951) and the Pirelli Tower, Milan (1956), Ponti also designed flatware for Krupp Italiana (1951) and Christofle (1955), sanitary fixtures for Ideal Standard (1953) and the legendary *Superleggera* chair (1957) for Cassina, which possessed the timeless classicism that was so characteristic of his work. During the 1960s and 1970s, Ponti's architecture, such as the Denver Art Museum (1971), and his design work became increasingly expressive and began to incorporate strong geometric forms. Beyond his remarkably productive career as a designer and architect, Ponti also taught at the Politecnico di Milano from 1936 to 1961, and, as a regular contributor to both *Domus* and *Casabella*, contributed much to the post-war revival of Italian design.

▲ Murano glass
chandelier for
Venini, 1946

The term Pop was coined in the 1950s and referred to the emergence of popular culture during that decade. In 1952, the **Independent Group** was founded in London and its members, including the artist Richard Hamilton (b. 1922), the sculptor Eduardo Paolozzi (b. 1924), the design critic Reyner Banham (1920–1988) and the architects, **Peter and Alison Smithson**, were among the first to explore and celebrate the growth of popular consumer culture in America. In the 1960s, American artists too, such as Andy Warhol (1928–1987), Roy Lichtenstein (1923–1998) and Claes Oldenburg (b. 1929) began drawing inspiration from the "low art" aspects of contemporary life such as advertising, packaging, comics and television. Not surprisingly, Pop also began to manifest itself in the design of objects for everyday use, as designers sought a more youth-based and less serious approach than had been offered by the **Good Design** of the 1950s. The ascendancy of product styling in the 1950s, in the name of productivity-increasing built-in obsolescence, provided fertile ground for the "use-it-today, sling-it-tomorrow" ethos that permeated industrial production during the 1960s. **Peter Murdoch**'s polka-dotted cardboard *Spotty* child's chair (1963) and **De Pas, D'Urbino and Lomazzi**'s PVC *Blow* chair (1967) were eminently disposable and epitomized the widespread culture of ephemerality. So too did the plethora of

Pop Design

▲ Gaetano Pesce,
Up Series for C&B
Italia, 1969

short-lived gimmicks such as paper dresses, which were lauded for their novelty in the large number of colour supplements and glossy magazines that became increasingly dependent on featuring such items. For many designers working within the Pop idiom, plastics became their materials of choice. By the 1960s, many new types of plastics and aligned processes, such as injection-moulding, became available and relatively inexpensive to use. The bright rainbow colours and bold forms associated with Pop Design swept away the last vestiges of post-war austerity and reflected the widespread optimism of the 1960s, which was bolstered by unprecedented economic prosperity and sexual liberation. Since Pop Design was aimed at the youth-market, products had to be cheap and were therefore often of poor quality. The expendability of such products, however, became part of their appeal as they represented the antithesis of the "timeless" modern classics that had been promoted in the 1950s. Pop Design with its **Anti-Design** associations countered the **Modern Movement**'s sober dictum "Less is More" and led directly to the **Radical Design** of the 1970s. It drew inspiration from a wide range of sources – **Art Nouveau**, **Art Deco**, **Futurism**, **Surrealism**, Op Art, Psychedelia, Eastern Mysticism, **Kitsch** and the Space-Age – and was spurred on by the growth of the global mass-media. The oil crisis of the early 1970s, however, necessitated a more rational approach to design and Pop Design was replaced by the **Craft Revival** on the one hand and **High Tech** on the other. By questioning the precepts of Good Design, and thereby Modernism, the influence of Pop Design was far-reaching and laid some of the foundations on which **Post-Modernism** was to grow.

◄ **Gunnar Cyrén**, *Pop* goblets for Orrefors Glasbruk, 1965–1966

▼ *Nivico 3240 GM television for JVC, (Yokohama Plant Victor Co. of Japan), 1970*

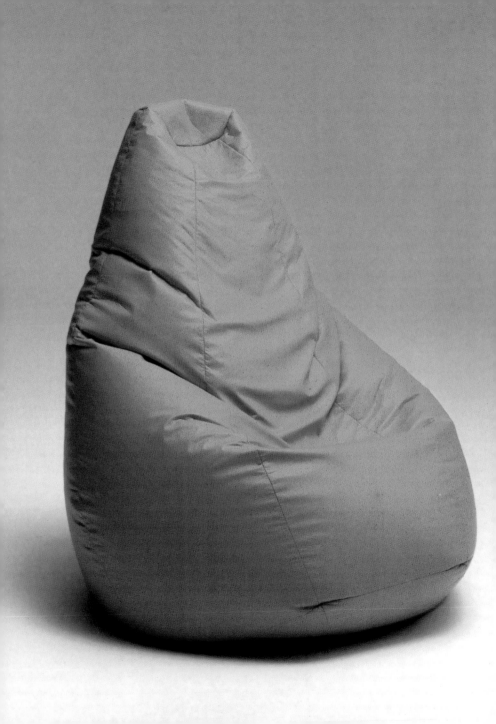

◄ **Piero Gatti, Cesare Paolini & Franco Teodoro**, *Sacco* bean-bag for Zanotta, 1968

► **Olive Sullivan**, Interior, c. 1965

◄ **Martin Sharp**, Cover of Cream's "Disraeli Gears" album for Polygram Int., 1967 (incorporating a photograph by Bob Whitaker)

Ferdinand Alexander "Butzi" Porsche is the son of the famous automobile designer, Ferdinand "Ferry" Porsche (b. 1909) and grandson of Professor Ferdinand Porsche (1875–1951) who founded the Porsche company in 1949. Ferdinand Alexander Porsche served an apprenticeship as an engineer at Bosch, Stuttgart, and from 1957 studied at the **Hochschule für Gestaltung, Ulm**. The following year, he began working under Erwin Komeda (1904–1966) in the design department of Porsche AG, which he headed from 1961 to 1972. In this position, he developed several cars including the *904 Carrera* (1963) and the *911* (1964). In 1972, he established the Porsche Design Studio, and from the mid-1970s concentrated on the design of "lifestyle" products. The experience he gained in automotive design proved useful in this pursuit. His sleek and highly engineered products, balancing function, technology and styling and thus epitomizing German product design, include the *Contax* camera for Yashica (1974), the *Cobra* motorcycle for Steyr-Puch (1976), sunglasses for Carrera (1977), a telephone for NEC (1981), the *Monolith* television for Grundig (1989), the *Antropus* chair for Poltrona Frau (1983) the *Jazz* light for Italiana Luce (1989) and wristwatches for IWC (1976 and 1993).

▼ *Jazz* lamps for
Italiana Luce, 1989

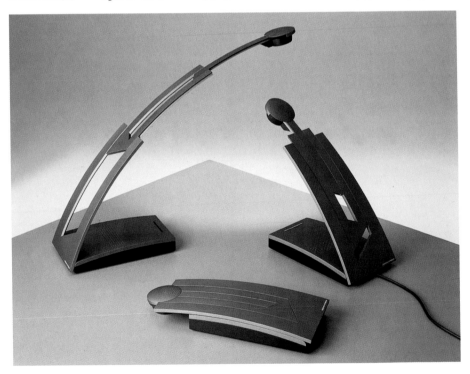

► **Ron Arad,** *Concrete Stereo* for One-Off, 1984

Post-Industrialism is a term that mainly refers to a post-modern approach to design whereby designed objects are produced outside the industrial mainstream. From the 1910s to the 1960s, the mass-production methods of Fordism dominated the design and manufacture of products, but during the late 1970s and 1980s, as Western economies became less reliant on manufacturing industry and more service-based, many designers began creating "one-off" or limited edition designs. This type of work not only reflected the post-industrial nature of the period but also allowed designers to explore their individual creativity more freely, because it was no longer subject to the constraints of the industrial process. Designers such as **Ron Arad** and **Tom Dixon** constructed "rough-and-ready" artefacts that were consciously distanced from the precision of standardized industrially manufactured products. Arad's *Concrete* Stereo (1984), for instance, opposed the "good forms" associated with audio-equipment produced by companies such as Bang & Olufsen and communicated a post-modern design rhetoric full of ironic content. Post-Industrialism heralded the notion of "usable artwork" and as such, gave rise to a new area of design practice that was both experimental and poetic.

Post-Industrialism

Post-Modernism   The ancestry of Post-Modernism can be traced to the 1960s and the emergence of Pop and **Anti-Design**. During that decade, the status quo was disputed in all areas of life, including the field of modern design. The first questioning of Modernism appeared most notably in Jane Jacobs, *The Death and Life of Great American Cities* (1961), which focused on the break up of social cohesion brought about in cities by the **Modern Movement**'s utopian building and planning schemes and **Robert Venturi**'s *Complexity and Contradiction in Architecture* (1966), which argued that modern architecture was fundamentally meaningless, for it lacked the complexity and irony that enriched historical buildings. In 1972, Venturi, Denise Scott Brown (b. 1932) and Steven Izenour published the seminal book *Learning from Las Vegas*, which lauded the cultural honesty of the commercialism found in the signage and buildings of this desert city. That same year, the translation of Roland Barthes' *Mythologies* (1957) into English led to the widespread dissemination of his theories on **Semiotics** – the study of signs and symbols as a means of cultural communication. The understanding then was that if

▼ Norbert Berghof,
Michael Landes &
Wolfgang Rang,
Frankfurter FIII chair
for Draenert,
1985–1986

buildings and objects were imbued with symbolism, viewers and users would be more likely to relate to them on a psychological level. The early proponents of Post-Modernism argued that the Modern Movement's espousal of geometric abstraction, which denied ornament and thereby symbolism, rendered architecture and design dehumanizing and ultimately alienating. From the mid-1970s, American architects, such as **Michael Graves**, began to introduce into their designs decorative motifs that frequently made reference to past decorative styles and were often ironic in content. Designers aligned to **Studio Alchimia**, such as **Alessandro Mendini** and **Ettore Sottsass**, began producing work within the post-modern idiom that made ironic comments on Modernism through the application

of applied decoration. Later, **Memphis** produced monumental and colourful "Neo-Pop" designs that, when exhibited for the first time in 1981, caused an international sensation. Memphis' output was influenced by an eclectic range of sources and intentionally mocked the notion of "good taste" through its use of boldly patterned plastic laminates and quirky forms. Significantly, Memphis helped to popularize Anti-Design and in so doing contributed significantly to the acceptance of Post-Modernism as an international style during the 1980s. Post-modern designs embraced the cultural pluralism of contemporary global society and used a language of shared

▲ **Michael Graves**, *Tea & Coffee Piazza* for Alessi, 1983

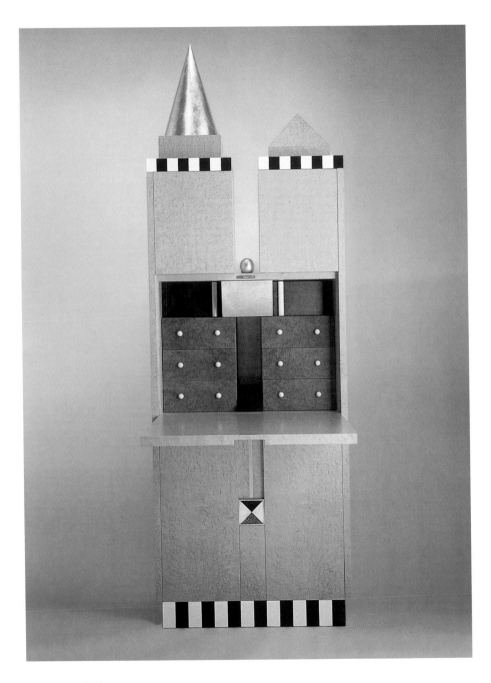

symbolism so as to transcend national boundaries. The forms and motifs found in such "symbolic objects" were not only drawn from past decorative styles, such as Classicism, **Art Deco**, **Constructivism** and **De Stijl** but at times also made reference to **Surrealism**, **Kitsch** and computer imagery. Among the most notable Post-Modern designers (apart from those already mentioned) were **Mario Botta**, **Andrea Branzi**, **Michele de Lucchi**, **Nathalie du Pasquier**, **Hans Hollein**, **Arata Isozaki**, **Shiro Kuramata**, **Richard Meier**, **Aldo Rossi**, **Peter Shire**, **George Sowden**, **Matteo Thun** and **Masanori Umeda**. Their bold designs for ceramics, textiles, jewellery, watches, silverware, furniture and lighting were produced on a limited-scale by companies such as **Alessi**, Artemide, Alias, Cassina, Formica, Cleto Munari, Poltronova, Sunar, Swid Powell and Draenert Studio. As Hans Hollein noted, Post-Modernism's rejection of the industrial process meant that products in this style were invariably "an affair of the élite", and as such represented capitalism's triumph over the social ideology that was the basis of the Modern Movement. The eclectic nature of Post-Modernism reflected not only the ascendancy of individualism but also the increasingly fragmented nature of society during the 1980s. The credit-fuelled boom of this decade allowed the anti-rationalism of the Post-Modern style to flourish and by the late 1980s, Post-Modernism had become even more stylistically diverse, encompassing Matt Black, **Deconstructivism** and **Post-Industrialism**. The global recession of the

▲ **Aldo Rossi,**
Il Conico kettle for
Alessi, 1988

early 1990s, however, motivated designers to seek less expressive and more rational approaches to design and the appeal of Post-Modernism began to wane. Although the bold statements of 1980s Anti-Design have been replaced with the muted purity of 1990s minimalism, the influence of Post-Modernism endures in that its questioning of the Modern Movement has led to an important and ongoing reassessment of what is essential in design.

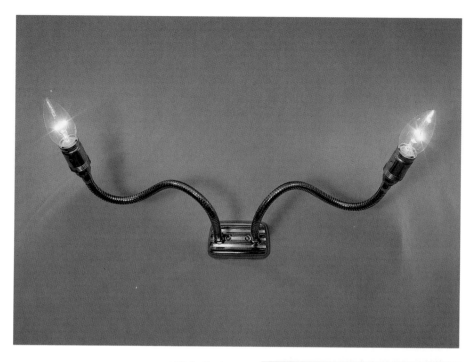

▲ **Stiletto (Frank Schreiner)**, *Suzuki* ready-made lamp for Stiletto Studios, 1988

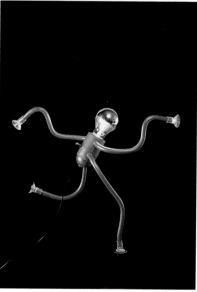

▶ **Marco Ferreri & Carlo Bellini**, *Eddy* lamp for Luxo Italiana, 1986

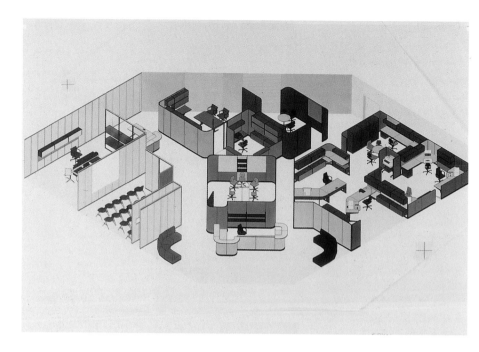

Robert Propst

b. 1921 *Marino,
California*

Robert Propst attended the University of Denver until 1943 and subsequently directed the art department at Tarleton College in Dublin, Texas, from 1946 to 1948. He continued his studies at the University of Colorado, graduating in 1950, and that same year founded his own firm, the Propst Company. He produced a wide range of designs: from playground and institutional equipment to ecclesiastical interiors and architectural sculptures; from furniture systems for hospitals to a harvester machine for timber. During the 1950s, he also undertook design research for **Herman Miller** and eventually in 1960, his own firm was absorbed into the furniture manufacturer's newly established research subsidiary in Ann Arbor, Michigan. In 1964, Propst assisted **George Nelson** in the technical development of the *Action Office I* system, for which he also designed the complementary *Perch* drafting stool. Propst became president and research director of Herman Miller Research in 1968, the year he designed the better performing and more flexible *Action Office II*. This revolutionary system of modules and partitions could be easily configured to provide workspace for individuals or groups of workers. It quite literally redefined the office landscape and through its massive sales success, established Herman Miller as the second largest furniture manufacturer in the world.

▲ *Action Office II* for
Herman Miller, 1968

Jean Prouvé was the son of the painter, Victor Prouvé (1858–1943) who had co-founded the **École de Nancy** in 1901. He was apprenticed to the art metalworker Émile Robert from 1916 to 1919, and then continued his metalwork training with Szabo in Paris. Following military service, Prouvé established himself as a *ferronier d'art* (art metalworker) and opened his own workshop in 1923 on the Rue du Général Custine, Nancy. Initially, he received commissions for doors, grilles and railings, but by 1924 he was designing thin sheet metal furniture, which was manufactured using the newly developed technique of electronic welding. The strong industrial aesthetic of his furniture attracted the attention of **avant-garde** architects such as **Pierre Jeanneret, Le Corbusier** and **Robert Mallet-Stevens**, all of whom commissioned work from him. In 1924, Prouvé developed the *tube aplati* technique for the structure of his chair designs, which involved flattening tubular metal in the areas of greatest stress so as to provide greater stability. He was awarded a Diplôme d'Honneur at the 1925 Paris "Exposition Internationale des Arts Décoratifs" for his utilitarian and often adjustable designs that used advanced production techniques. In 1929, he became a co-founder of the UAM (Union des Artistes Modernes) and showed a number of his designs, including three adjustable chairs, at the Union's first exhibition in 1930. The next year, Prouvé established a private limited company, Société des Ateliers Jean Prouvé, with his brother-in-law, the engineer A. Schotte, and opened a larger workshop on the Rue des Jardiniers, Nancy, investing in state-of-the-art stamping and folding machinery. Much of the furniture produced there, such as his metal desks for the Compagnie Parisienne d'Électricité of 1935 and his extensive range of school furniture of the 1930s and 1940s was intended for institutional use. Following the liberation of France in 1944, Prouvé was elected Mayor of Nancy, and in 1947 he founded Les Ateliers Jean Prouvé – a large factory on a 20,000 square

Jean Prouvé

1901 *Paris*
1984 *Nancy, France*

▼ Aluminium panel used as a wall element for Les Ateliers Jean Prouvé, 1948

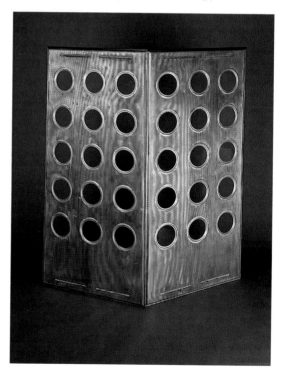

▲ *Antony* chair for
Les Ateliers Jean
Prouvé, 1950

metre site in Maxéville. Run more like an engineering works than a workshop, this operation attracted many young architects, and by 1950 it was employing some two hundred and fifty workers. Prouvé was made a Chevalier of the Légion d' Honneur in 1950 and was awarded a Grand Prix by the Cercle d'Etudes Architecturales (CEA) in 1952 for his design of façades and curtain walls for the Fédération du Bâtiment building. The aluminium company, Pechiney, that had previously been a minority shareholder of Les Ateliers Jean Prouvé, acquired the majority shareholding of the operation in 1953 and initiated a programme of organizational restructuring. Prouvé subsequently resigned as director of the factory, and in 1954 he established a design studio in Paris. From 1955 to 1956, he co-founded another company with Michel Bataille, which he named Les Constructions Jean Prouvé, and despite their being taken over in 1957 by the Compagnie Industrielle de Matériel de Transport (CIMT), he continued working for this venture until 1966. Both Prouvé's choice of materials and his methods of production derived from the aircraft industry, and many of his designs with their roughly welded constructions had more in common with "Art Brut" than with the highly refined aesthetic of the **International Style.**

▲ **Jean Prouvé & Charlotte Perriand**, Shelves/Room divider designed for the Maison du Mexique in Paris, 1953 (colour scheme devised by Sonia Delaunay)

Otto Prutscher

1880 *Vienna*
1949 *Vienna*

▼ Silver mantel clock
for Nikolaus Stadler,
c. 1906

Otto Prutscher trained in Vienna at the Fachschule für Holzindustrie (a woodworking college), prior to studying under **Josef Hoffmann** from 1897 to 1901 at the Kunstgewerbeschule. He then worked for two years as an independent architect in Vienna, designing several interiors and exhibiting his designs at the 1900 Paris "Exposition Universelle et Internationale" and at the 1902 Turin "Esposizione Internazionale d'Arte Decorativa Moderna". Prutscher also taught at the Graphische Lehr- und Versuchsanstalt (the Graphics Institute), Vienna from 1903 to 1909, and was then appointed professor of free-drawing at the Kunstgewerbeschule. From 1907, he produced numerous designs for the **Wiener Werkstätte** for glassware, textiles, furniture, bookbindings, metalware, silverware and jewellery. He submitted designs to the Deutsche Werkstätten and to many firms, including E. Bakalowits, **Loetz**, Ludwig, J. J. Hermann, Chwala, Lobmeyr and **Thonet**, while continuing to work as an architect and to design store interiors. Eventually, he became involved in Vienna's municipal building programme, and in 1919 became one of the city's educational inspectors for vocational training. He was dismissed from his teaching post at the Kunstgewerbeschule by the National Socialists in 1939, but was reinstated after the war as head of free-drawing. Prutscher's designs were stylistically influenced by Hoffmann's work and were similarly distinguished by simple geometric forms and square motifs.

◄ *Waste Not, Want Not* plate for Mintons, 1849

Augustus Welby Northmore Pugin was the son of the Gothic designer, Augustus Charles Pugin (c. 1769–1832). He was educated at Christ's Hospital School, London, and accompanied pupils of his father's school of architectural draughtsmanship on various field trips. In 1827, he designed Gothic furnishings for Windsor Castle and worked for the royal goldsmiths, Rundell & Bridge. He met the Scottish architect James Gillespie Graham (1776–1855) in 1829 and contributed to some of his commissions. In 1829, Pugin established his own furniture manufacturing business but the venture failed in 1831 and so he became a self-taught Gothic Revivalist architect. He converted to Catholicism in 1835, and that year published his first book, *Gothic Furniture,* and drafted Charles Barry's (1795–1860) winning entry for the competition for the new Houses of Parliament in London. In his controversial work *Contrasts*, published in 1836, he unfavourably compared 19th-century architecture to that of the Middle Ages. From the late 1830s to the early 1840s, Pugin executed many Roman Catholic Churches for which he designed interiors and fittings that were encrusted with Gothic style ornamentation. In 1841, he published *The True Principles of Pointed or Christian Architecture* in which he argued that the Gothic was the only true Christian style, whereas Classicism was deemed by him to be pagan. As one of the earliest advocates of truth to materials, revealed construction and appropriateness in architecture and design, Pugin was a far-reaching and highly influential design reformer.

A. W. N. Pugin
1812 *London*
1852 *Ramsgate*

Jean-Émile Puiforcat

1897 *Paris*
1945 *Paris*

▲ Silver-plated
bronze and marble
clock made by Hour-
Lavigne for Puiforcat
Orfèvre, c. 1930

Jean-Émile Puiforcat first worked for the silversmithing firm founded by his grandfather in 1820. After the First World War, while apprenticed to his father, he pursued his passion for sculpture by attending courses given by the sculptor Louis-Aimé Lejeune, who encouraged him to eliminate superfluous ornament. Puiforcat carefully considered the functional aspects of his silverware designs and, influenced by Pythagorean geometry, used simple geometric shapes – spheres, cones, cylinders – to attain more rational forms. However, his **Art Deco** designs conveyed a sense of luxury that was born out of his masterful handling of materials. His work was exhibited at the 1921 "Salon des Artistes Décorateurs" and at the 1925 "Exposition Internationale des Arts Décoratifs et Industriels Modernes". Around 1926, he became a founder member of the Groupe de Cinq and joined the UAM (Union des Artistes Modernes)in 1930. During the late 1920s, his brother-in-law Luis Estevez designed a modern residence for him near Saint-Jean-de-Luz, where he continued to design silverware, now influenced by the research of the mathematician Matila Ghyka into the "Golden Section" theory. Although Puiforcat worked in the Art Deco style, he was one of the first silversmith's to abandon surface decoration in favour of pure volumetric forms.

► Silver and glass
tea and coffee
service for Puiforcat
Orfèvre, 1925

▼ Silver and gilt
silver tea and coffee
service for Puiforcat
Orfèvre, c. 1933

The Vietnamese designer Nguyen Manhkhan'n (known as "Quasar") studied engineering at the École Nationale des Ponts et Chaussées (the National
School for Bridges and Roads) from 1955 to 1958. He then worked on the
Estrées viaduct project for two years and on the Manicouagan dam project
in Québec from 1960 to 1963. He designed a prototype for a small urban
car in 1964 that was essentially a clear acrylic cuboid with wheels, and three
years later his *Quasar Unipower* cars were produced in small numbers. Along
with other French designers, including Ronald-Cecil Sportes (b. 1943) and
Bernard Quentin (b. 1923), he then began to explore the potential of inflatable structures, which were promoted by the "Les Structures Gonflables"
exhibition staged at ARC in 1967, designing a series of inflatable furniture
pieces in 1966 and a small circular inflatable dwelling in 1968. During the
late 1960s, Quasar sponsored **Philippe Starck** to design several more inflatable structures. Nguyen Manhkhan'n established the manufacturing company Quasar-France in 1969 to produce foam-rubber seating as well as his
inflatable designs, such as the
Apollo, *Satellite* and *Venus* chairs
and the *Relax* and *Chesterfield* sofas.
Ever versatile, he designed a line of
menswear for Bidermann in 1970,
and more recently worked on the
design of a watercraft, the *Hydrair
KX1*. Quasar's inflatable designs
were, as one commentator put it,
"less furniture and more a way of
life", and as such they reflected the
rise of the counter-culture in Paris
during the late 1960s.

▼ Quasar, his wife
Emanuelle and their
children, Othello
and Atlantique
in an inflatable
environment, 1968

Jens H. Quistgaard was the son of the sculptor, Harald Quistgaard, who was a professor at the Kongelige Danske Kunstakademi (Royal Academy of Arts), Copenhagen. He trained as a sculptor, carpenter, ceramicist and draughtsman prior to his apprenticeship with the **Georg Jensen** silversmithy. Following the Second World War, Quistgaard became an independent designer and produced a range of product designs including a stoneware teapot with a brass and cane handle (1949). In 1954, Quistgaard was awarded a Lunning Prize and founded a manufacturing company, Dansk International Designs, with the American entrepreneur Ted Nierenberg. Quistgaard ran the firm with Nierenberg until 1984, and during their thirty-year partnership was responsible for the majority of designs produced by the company. Quistgaard's products were characterized by subtle organic lines and superlative handling of materials. His work, such as the enamelled steel *Kobenstyle* cookware (1954) or the teak and steel *Fjord* cutlery (1954), allowed the materials he used to reveal their inherent qualities. The sculptural form of Quistgaard's teak ice bucket (1960) was inspired by his study of the wooden hulls of Viking ships, while its bridge-like handle recalls those found on earlier Japanese ceramic vessels. Since 1984, Quistgaard has continued to run a studio in Copenhagen while designing buildings, furniture and jewellery for both European and American companies. His well-designed and executed objects typify the Danish Modern Style.

Jens Quistgaard
b. 1919 *Copenhagen*

▼ Teak ice-bucket for Dansk International Designs, 1960

Ernest Race

1913 *Newcastle-upon-Tyne*
1964 *London*

▲ *Antelope* chair
and table for Race
Furniture, 1950

Ernest Race studied interior design at the Bartlett School of Architecture, London from 1932 to 1935, and subsequently worked as a draughtsman for the lighting company, Troughton & Young. In 1937, he travelled to Madras, India to visit his missionary aunt who ran a weaving centre there, and on his return to Britain he opened a shop in London to sell his aunt's textiles that had been woven to his designs. In 1945, with the engineer J. W. Noel Jordan, he founded Ernest Race Ltd. with the aim of mass-producing low-cost contemporary furniture using materials allowed under the **Utility** Scheme, and from 1945 to 1964 they manufactured over 250,000 of his *BA* chairs (1945) from 850 tons of resmelted aluminium wartime scrap. This highly rational design was first exhibited at the 1946 "Britain Can Make It" exhibition and was later awarded a gold medal at the IX Milan Triennale of 1951. Race similarly complied with the Utility Scheme's restrictions when he designed the *Antelope* chair, bench and table (1950) and the *Springbok* chair (c. 1951) for use on the Royal Festival Hall's outdoor terraces during the 1951 "Festival of Britain". These designs with their spindly legs terminating on ball feet echoed the contemporary interest in molecular chemistry and nuclear physics.

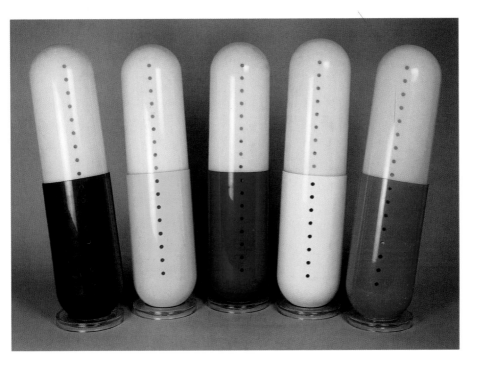

Radical Design emerged in Italy during the late 1960s as a reaction to **Good Design**. While similar to **Anti-Design**, Radical Design was more theoretical, politicized and experimental, and attempted to alter the general perception of Modernism through utopian proposals and projections. The primary exponents of Radical Design were the design and architectural groups **Superstudio**, **Archizoom**, UFO(founded 1967, Florence), **Gruppo Strum**, Gruppo 9999 (founded 1967, Florence), Cavart (founded 1973, Padua) and Libidarch (founded 1971, Turin). These groups attacked notions of what constituted "good taste" and staged subversive happenings and installations that questioned the validity of rationalism, advanced technology and, above all, consumerism. Radical architectural projections, such as Superstudio's *Il Monumento Continuo* (Continuous Monument) of 1969 and Archizoom's *Wind City* of 1969, speculated on the idea of "architecture as a political instrument", while radical designs such as UFO's *Doric Temple* (1972) and Archizoom's *Superonda* (1966) were often characterized by their potential for user-interaction. At once poetic and irrational, designs such as these epitomized the counter-culture of the late 1960s and sought to destroy the hegemony of the visual language of Modernism. In 1973, members of the

▲ **Cesare Casati & Emanuele Ponzio**, *Pillola* lamps for Ponteur, 1968

various Radical Design groups convened at the offices of *Casabella* magazine where **Alessandro Mendini** was director. The meeting led to the formation of **Global Tools** in 1974, but a year later this school of radical architecture and design was disbanded and the Radical Design debate briefly lost its impetus. By questioning long established precepts of the purpose of design, radical designers, such as **Andrea Branzi**, **Riccardo Dalisi** and Lapo Binazzi (b. 1943), laid the theoretical foundations from which **Post-Modernism** evolved in the late 1970s and early 1980s.

◄ UFO Group (Lapo Binazzi), *Doric Temple* prototype, 1971

From an early age, Dieter Rams was exposed to construction techniques in his grandfather's carpentry workshop. He studied architecture and interior design at the Werkkunstschule, Wiesbaden from 1947 to 1948, served a three-year carpentry apprenticeship in Kelkheim to gain practical experience and then resumed his training at the Werkkunstschule, graduating in 1953. Between 1953 and 1955, he worked in Otto Apel's architectural office in Frankfurt, which was affiliated to the American practice, Skidmore, Owings & Merrill. In 1955, Rams joined the staff of **Braun** as an architect and interior designer, and the following year began working as a product designer for the company, most notably co-designing with **Hans Gugelot** the *Phonosuper SK4* hi-fi system of 1956. Rams also designed other audio equipment for Braun including the portable *Transistor 1* radio (1956) and the combination phonograph and pocket radio (1959), which embodied the practical and or-dered approach to design promoted by the **Bauhaus** and the **Hochschule für Gestaltung, Ulm**. In 1961, Rams was appointed head of the company's de-sign department and during the 1960s, he designed the *KM 2* kitchen appli-ances, the *M140* hand mixer, the *Sixtant* electric razor and a cylindrical table lighter. Modern designs such as these were characterized by the pared-down

Dieter Rams
b. 1932 *Wiesbaden, Germany*

▲ *Audio 1* record player for Braun, 1962

▶ **Dieter Rams &
Dietrich Lubs,**
Control ET22
calculator for Braun,
1977

aesthetic of **Functionalism** and exemplified the attributes of **Good Design**.
During the 1960s, Rams also designed the *606* shelving system and *620*
and *601/601* modular seating ranges for the furniture manufacturer Vitsoe
that shared the rational purity of his product designs for Braun. In 1968,
Rams became director of design at Braun, and the same year was elected an
Honorary Designer for Industry by the Royal Society of Arts, London. In the
late 1960s, the idea of "product aesthetics" came under increasing attack
as it was seen by many as a promotion sales tool. Rams, however, remained
unswayed by such criticism and continued to promote a modern industrial
dematerialist aesthetic through well-designed products, executed using
state-of-the-art technology. Rams believes that the central responsibility
of designers is to instil order in contemporary life. He is among the most influential and pre-eminent product designers of the second half of the 20th
century.

▲ *TP2* combination radio/record
player for Braun, 1958–1960

Omar Ramsden

1873 *Sheffield*
1939 *London*

▲ **Omar Ramsden &
Alwyn Carr**, Silver
and enamel box for
the Ramsden-Carr
Workshop, 1902

Omar Ramsden was apprenticed to a silversmith in Sheffield and also attended evening classes at Sheffield School of Art, where he met Alwyn Charles Ellison Carr (1872–1940). In 1898, following a tour of Europe, Ramsden and Carr established their own silver workshop in London, and a year later completed their first commission, a ceremonial mace for the city of Sheffield. The workshop, which employed a team of assistants, produced silverware in the Arts & Crafts style as well as base-metal wares. During the First World War, Ramsden ran the business – Carr having enlisted in the army – and subsequently produced many war memorials. In 1919, the partnership was dissolved but Ramsden and his many assistants continued to produce relatively large quantities of silverware in various revivalist styles including Tudor, Queen Anne and Georgian, some of which were mass-produced using spinning techniques. To give the impression that these objects were individually handcrafted, many of them were inscribed "Omar Ramsden me fecit". Ramsden's designs were more commercial than those normally associated with the **Arts & Crafts Movement** and the scrolling and swirling motifs he frequently used were in many ways more typical of Continental **Art Nouveau**.

Paul Rand studied art in New York, at the Pratt Institute, the Parson's School of Design, and the Art Students League, where he trained under the German Expressionist painter, George Grosz (1893–1959), graduating in 1934. Rand's graphics, which were much influenced by the ideas in **László Moholy-Nagy**'s book *The New Vision* (1932), were among the first in America to utilize the European **avant-garde** approach to modern graphic design. In the process, he rejected traditional narrative illustration and symmetrical layout and, instead, dynamically combined typography and imagery to produce work that was powerful, expressive and often humorous. Between 1936 and 1941, Rand was the art director of the magazines *Esquire* and *Apparel Arts*, and from 1938 to 1945 designed covers for the bi-monthly magazine *Direction* that were notable for their incorporation of photomontage and historical quotations. From 1941 to 1954, he was creative director of the New York advertising agency William H. Weintraub, where he collaborated with the copywriter Bill Bernbach.

Together, they established new standards for advertising by harmoniously integrating copy and design. In *Thoughts on Design*, published in 1946, Rand detailed his ideas on the communicative strength of symbols. From 1956, he mainly concentrated on trademark and **corporate identity** design and acted as a consultant to many large companies including United Parcel Services, American Broadcasting Company, Westinghouse Electric Corporation, Cummins Engine Company and IBM. Rand's programme of corporate communications for IBM, with its use of "coded" symbols and restrained typography, was especially influential. From 1956, Rand was a professor of graphic design at Yale University, New Haven, and in 1972 he was elected to the Hall of Fame of the New York Art Directors Club.

Paul Rand
1914 *New York*
1996 *Norwalk, Connecticut*

▼ Poster for IBM, 1981

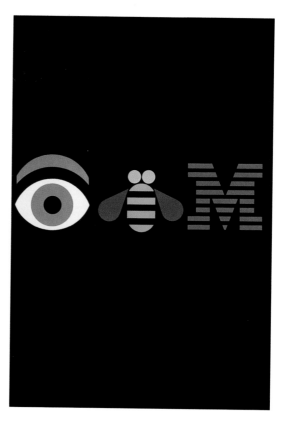

► *Sitzgeiststuhl*
(The Spirit of Sitting
Chair), 1927

Heinz & Bodo Rasch

Heinz Rasch
b. 1902 *Berlin*

Bodo Rasch
b. 1903 *Berlin*

Heinz Rasch trained at the Kunstgewerbeschule, Bromberg in 1916 and at the Technischen Hochschulen in Hanover and Stuttgart from 1920 to 1923. Then, in 1922, with his younger brother Bodo, he established a factory in Stuttgart for the production of household furnishings. Heinz the architect and Bodo the cabinet-maker, worked together to produce a range of moulded plywood designs that were technically advanced, including their first cantilevered chair (1924), which weighed little more than two kilos, and a folding chair (1924) for L. C. Arnold. In 1925, Heinz joined the editorial staff at the journal *Baugilde* and met both **Ludwig Mies van der Rohe** and **Mart Stam**. The Rasch brothers later exhibited tables, case furniture and chairs in the display houses designed by **Peter Behrens** and Mies van der Rohe for the exhibition "Die Wohnung" (The Dwelling) organized by the **Deutscher Werkbund** in Stuttgart in 1927. These designs included the cantilevered *Sitzgeiststuhl* (The spirit-of-sitting chair), the title of which was taken from a poem by Christian Morgenstern. A year later, Heinz Rasch edited the book *The Chair* (Der Stuhl), and during the 1980s helped to set up the Stuhlmuseum (Chair Museum), Burg Beverungen.

The term Rationalism refers in general to a logical approach to architecture and design but also denotes a form of Modernism pioneered by architects and designers in Italy during the late 1920s and 1930s. Inspired by both the social and aesthetic aspects of earlier modern work by architects such as **Walter Gropius** and **Le Corbusier**, the Gruppo Sette (Group of Seven) published a four-part manifesto in the magazine *Rassegna* in 1926 that effectively launched the Italian Rationalist movement. The group's members, which included **Giuseppe Terragni**, Gino Pollini (b. 1903), Luigi Figini (b. 1903), Adalberto Libera (1903–1963), Carlo Enrico Rava, Sebastiano Larco and Guido Frette, strongly opposed **Futurism** and instead sought to reconcile the **Functionalism** of the European **avant-garde** with Italy's Classical tradition. The first notable expressions of Italian Rationalism in architecture were Luciano Baldessari (1896–1982), Luigi Figini, Gino Pollini's Bar Craja in Milan (1930) and Giuseppe Terragni's Casa del Fascio in Como (1933). The Rationalists celebrated modern progress through a severe geometric formal vocabulary and the use of state-of-the-art materials such as chromed tubular metal. Rationalism was embraced by the Fascists, who regarded themselves as champions of a new world order, but eventually adopted the conservative **Novecento** style. After the Second World War, designers such as **Franco Albini** continued to perpetuate the Rationalist style.

Rationalism
Italy

▲ Conference Room of the Casa del Fascio (later renamed Casa del Popolo) in Como, 1933

Eric Ravilious

1903 *Acton/London*
1942 *Iceland*

▲ *Travel* tea service
for Josiah
Wedgwood & Sons,
1937

Eric W. Ravilious studied at Eastbourne School of Art from 1919 to 1922 and at the **Royal College of Art, London** from 1922 to 1925. He was noted for his wood-engravings for book illustrations, such as those for Walter de la Mare's *The Elm Angel* (1930), William Shakespeare's *Twelfth Night* (1932) and Gilbert White's *The Natural History of Selborne* (1937), and also designed printers' ornaments for Curwen, publications for London Transport, advertisements for Austin Reed and decorations for the BBC. Between 1928 and 1929, he collaborated with Edward Bawden (b. 1903) on the design of mural decorations at Morley College. For the next nine years, Ravilious taught at the Royal College of Art. Around 1935, he was introduced to Thomas Wedgewood by Lady Sempill of Dunbar Hay, a furniture manufacturing company for which he had previously produced designs. He subsequently designed many transfer-printed decorations for Wedgwood, which were applied to standard earthenware blanks and coloured with enamels. He designed glassware for Stuart Crystal in 1935 and created wall decorations for the British pavilion at the 1937 Paris "Exposition Universelle et Internationale". In 1940, he became an official war artist, and in 1942 disappeared while on a mission off the coast of Iceland.

Lilly Reich worked under **Josef Hoffmann** at the **Wiener Werkstätte** from 1908. Then, in 1911 she returned to Berlin and became associated with the design theorist, Hermann Muthesius (1861–1927), and collaborated with Else Oppler-Legband. She became a member of the **Deutscher Werkbund** in 1912, and was the first female to be elected to the Werkbund's board of directors. From 1924 to 1926, she produced designs for the Atelier für Ausstellungsgestaltung und Mode, Frankfurt, after which she began her long professional collaboration with **Ludwig Mies van der Rohe**, assisting him with the organization of the 1927 Stuttgart "Die Wohnung" exhibition. Together they designed many pieces of furniture, mainly in tubular metal which were frequently credited to Mies alone. They also co-directed the "Deutsche Bauausstellung" exhibition (1931) and co-designed stands at exhibitions in Berlin in 1927, 1931 and 1943. From 1932 to 1933, Reich headed the interior design workshop at the **Bauhaus** in Berlin, and in 1939 she briefly joined Mies in Chicago. From 1945 to 1946, Reich taught at the Hochschule für Bildende Künste, Berlin.

Lilly Reich
1885 *Berlin*
1947 *Berlin*

▲ **Lilly Reich & Ludwig Mies van der Rohe**, Wardrobe and closet, c. 1930

▶ Stoneware bowl with sgraffito decoration, c. 1965

Lucie Rie
b. 1902 *Vienna*

Lucie Rie studied under Michael Powolny (1871–1954) at the Kunstgewerbe-schule, Vienna from 1922 to 1926. After graduating, she set up her own pottery studio in Vienna, which she ran for twelve years. In 1938, Rie emigrated to Britain, and a year later established another pottery and workshop in Albion Mews, London, producing handmade ceramic buttons. Although her activities had to be suspended during the war, the venture reopened in the mid-1940s. In 1946, the German émigré **Hans Coper** visited the Albion Mews Pottery and subsequently began collaborating with Rie. Although both studio potters favoured stoneware, Coper's vessels were characterized by sculptural forms whereas Rie's were less expressive but beautifully precise and extremely delicate. During the mid to late 1950s, Rie became noted for her tea and coffee services, the production of which became an economic mainstay for many studio potters at the time. The forms and glazes used by Rie were often inspired by earlier Chinese and Japanese wares. She frequently used a raw-glaze technique in which the clay body interacts with oxides during a single firing to produce ceramics with interesting and unusual surfaces, and during the late 1940s she introduced incised *sgraffito* decoration into her stoneware designs. From the 1960s to 1971, Rie taught alongside Coper at Camberwell School of Arts & Crafts, London.

Richard Riemerschmid studied fine art at the Akademie der Bildenden Künste, Munich, from 1888 to 1890, after which he worked as a painter in Munich, and in 1895 designed his own house and furnishings. He designed a poster for the 1896 Nuremberg Bavarian Exhibition, and in 1897 exhibited a wall-hanging, a sideboard and stained glass at the Munich Glaspalast Exhibition. The same year, he joined **Hermann Obrist**, **Bernhard Pankok** and **Bruno Paul** in founding the **Vereinigte Werkstätten für Kunst im Handwerk** (United Workshops for Artist Craftsmanship), Munich, for the production of innovative and well-executed designs.

From 1898, Riemerschmid designed furniture for the workshop, such as his oak chair for a music room, which was first exhibited at the 1899 Dresden exhibition, and thereafter designed furniture for Hermann Obrist, collaborating with him on the room for an art collector displayed at the 1900 "Exposition Universelle et Internationale" in Paris. Between 1900 and 1901, Riemerschmid worked on the interior design of the new theatre in Munich, and from 1903 to 1905 directed the Kunstgewerblicher Meisterkurs at the Bayerisches Gewerbemuseum in Nuremberg.

He also began producing designs for the **Dresdener Werkstätten für Handwerkskunst** in 1902, and from 1905 adopted methods of **standardization** for a range of furniture for the Dresden Workshops, which was conceived for

Richard Riemerschmid
1868 *Munich*
1957 *Munich*

◄▼ Stoneware and pewter tankard for Villeroy & Boch Mettlach, c. 1901

▼ Stoneware jug for Reinhold Merkelbach, c. 1909

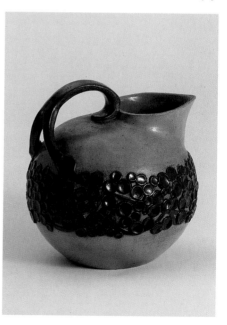

▶ Oak and brass longcase clock for the Dresdener Werkstätten für Handwerkskunst, 1903

▶▶ Chair designed for a music room for the Vereinigte Werkstätten für Kunst im Handwerk, Munich, 1898–1899

serial production. Known as *Maschinenmöbel*, this revolutionary furniture was the result of research he had previously undertaken with his brother-in-law, the cabinetmaker Karl Schmidt (1873–1948), into manufacturing processes suitable for low-cost furnishings. Riemerschmid was a founder of the **Deutscher Werkbund** in 1907 and subsequently became one of the Werkbund's most active members, exhibiting at the 1914 "Deutsche Werkbundausstellung" held in Cologne. Between 1907 and 1913, he also undertook the planning of Germany's first garden city, Hellerau, where he built a number of artists' studios. From 1913 to 1924, Riemerschmid was director of the Kunstgewerbeschule, Munich, which held a major exhibition of his architectural projects in 1913, and from 1918 to 1919 he was a member of the Künstlerrat der Stadt (Artists' Council) in Munich. He was chairman of the Deutscher Werkbund from 1921 to 1926, and principal of the Kölner Werkschulen (Cologne School of Applied Arts) from 1926 to 1931.

On his return to Munich in 1931, he established himself as an independent painter and architect, working in the Neo-Classical style. Riemerschmid's designs for industrial production, which were distinguished by rational yet elegant forms, were enormously

influential. His approach to design involved reconciling the artistic endeavour of the **Arts & Crafts Movement** with the industrial standardization of the **Modern Movement** so as to produce high-quality yet affordable products.

▼ Wardrobe for
the Dresdener
Werkstätten für
Handwerkskunst,
1905

▶ *Red/Blue* chair,
1918–1923

The son of a cabinet-maker, Gerrit Rietveld worked in his father's workshop from the age of twelve until he was fifteen. Between 1904 and 1913, he trained as a draughtsman at the C. J. A. Begeer goldsmith workshops, and in 1906 he attended evening classes in architectural drawing given by P. J. C. Klaarhamer and met Bart van der Leck (1876–1958). From 1911 to 1912, Rietveld was an active member of the Kunstliefde art group, and in 1917 he established his own furniture workshop in Utrecht. Shortly after designing the unpainted prototype of his famous *Red/Blue* chair (1918), he met **Theo van Doesburg** and **Jacobus Johannes Pieter Oud** who were exploring similar geometric forms. Rietveld became one of the first members of **De Stijl** in 1919, and designed a sideboard based on the doctrine of Neo-Plasticism

Gerrit Thomas Rietveld

1888 *Utrecht, Netherlands*
1964 *Utrecht*

that was promoted by the movement. In 1923, he produced his first painted version of the *Red/Blue* chair, which was first published in *De Stijl* magazine and was included in an exhibition held at the Weimar **Bauhaus** in the same year. Two years after having established himself as an independent architect in Utrecht, Rietveld started collaborating from 1921 with Mrs Truus Schröder-Schräder, for whom he designed the Schröder house (1924–1925). He kept a studio at the house until 1932 and resided there from 1958. Their joint architectural projects included a terrace of houses in Erasmuslaan (1934) and the Vreeburg Cinema, Utrecht (1936). He also collaborated with fellow De Stijl designer, **Vilmos Huszár** on a design for the Juryfreie Kunstschau Berlin of 1923. Rietveld's work was exhibited alongside other De Stijl designs in 1923 at Léonce Rosenberg's Galerie l'Effort Moderne in Paris. In 1928, Rietveld became a member of the Congrès Internationaux d'Architecture Moderne (CIAM), and from around this period his work became more international in outlook and he undertook numerous architectural projects both in the Netherlands and abroad. From around 1944, he also taught at a number of universities and designed the Netherlands pavilion for the 1954 Venice Biennale. It was Rietveld's furniture, however, rather than his

► *Crate* chair for
Metz & Co., 1934

architecture that was of greatest influence. The geometric formal vocabulary of his *Red/Blue* chair, for instance, inspired **Marcel Breuer**'s seminal tubular metal furniture designed at the Bauhaus in the late 1920s, which in turn briefly influenced Rietveld's choice of materials, as demonstrated by his *Beugelstoel* (1927). His *Zig-Zag* chair (1932–1934) and *Crate* chair (1934) reveal his return to elemental constructions in wood and can be seen as a response to the economic slump of the 1930s. During the 1940s and 1950s, Rietveld's work achieved much international recognition, and in 1958 he designed a fully upholstered armchair for the UNESCO building in Paris. Rietveld was one of the most innovative furniture and interior designers of the 20th century and was a key pioneer of the **Modern Movement**.

Jens Risom attended the University of Copenhagen and later studied furniture and interior design under **Kaare Klint** from 1935 to 1938 at the city's Kunstandvaerkerskolan. He also worked in Ernst Kuhn's architectural office in Copenhagen from 1937 to 1939, designing furniture and interiors. He then emigrated to the United States and became design director of Dan Cooper, New York, from 1939 to 1941, designing a range of textiles for them. In 1941, Risom designed the first chair to be manufactured by **Knoll**, which was followed by several variations that similarly incorporated army surplus webbing and were described by Risom as "very basic, very simple, inexpensive, easy to make". Apart from seating, Risom also designed tables, cabinets, chest-of-drawers and bookcases for Hans Knoll (1914–1955), and together they collaborated on the design of several interiors, including two that were displayed at the 1939 New York World's Fair. Between 1941 and 1943, Risom worked as a freelance designer most notably for **Georg Jensen**. He ran his own firm, Jens Risom Design in New York, from 1946 to 1973, which was acquired by Dictaphone in 1970. For the next six years, Risom acted as a trustee of the Rhode Island School of Design, and in 1973 he became chief executive of a new design consultancy, Design Control, based in New Canaan, Connecticut. Risom's simple yet well-constructed furniture reflected the tempered Scandinavian approach to Modernism.

▶ *Model No. 666 WSP* chair for Hans G. Knoll Furniture Company (later Knoll Associates), 1942 (redesigned 1946)

Alexander Rodchenko

1891 St. Petersburg
1956 Moscow

Alexander Rodchenko trained under Nikolai Feshin and Georgii Medvedev at the Art School in Kazan from 1911 to 1914 and studied graphic design at the Stroganov School of Applied Art, Moscow. Inspired by **Futurism**, Rodchenko executed both abstract and Cubist-style paintings and after meeting **Kasimir Malevich** in 1915 and **Vladimir Tatlin** a year later, he became a leading protagonist of **Constructivism**. As a convert to Malevich's ideas on Suprematism, Rodchenko executed a series of works in 1917 entitled "Movement of coloured plains with one projected on to the other", and the same year designed lighting for the Café Pittoresk in Moscow, which comprised intersecting elements that were similarly dynamic. From 1918, he co-directed the department of applied art at Narkompros (The People's Commissariat for Enlightenment) with Olga Rozanova, as well as teaching at the Moscow Proletcult School from 1918 to 1926. In 1920, together with his wife **Varvara Stepanova** and Alexei Gan, Rodchenko published *The Programme of the Group of Constructivists* and became both a member of Inkhuk and a professor at the Soviet-funded, **Vkhutemas** (Higher State Artistic and Technical Workshops). During the 1920s, he worked primarily as a graphic designer for the journals *LEF* and *Novyi LEF,* and produced numerous posters, many of which were photomontages exploiting the expressive potential of typography.

▼ Poster for Inga
(Theatre of the
Revolution), 1929

Gilbert Rohde initially worked as a reporter and political cartoonist for the *Bronx News*, but in 1927 he began designing furniture. The same year, he travelled to Paris where he was inspired by the work of the French **avant-garde**. He established his own New York office in 1929 and designed furniture for Heywood-Wakefield and Thonet among others. In 1930, Rohde suggested to D. J. De Pree that his company, **Herman Miller**, manufacture a modern line of furniture. Rohde subsequently produced designs for the company with simple yet well constructed forms, promoting a modern lifestyle and including storage units, a sectional sofa and the *Living-Dining Group*. Also for Herman Miller, he designed the *Executive Office Group*, which comprised 15 components that could be assembled in 400 different ways. Rohde displayed his "Design for Living House" at the 1933 "Century of Progress" exhibition in Chicago and designed interiors for the 1934 "Machine Art" exhibition held at the **Museum of Modern Art, New York**. Between 1939 and 1943, he headed the industrial design department of the School of Architecture at New York University. Rohde's approach to Modern design changed the philosophical orientation of Herman Miller and influenced the American furniture industry as a whole.

Gilbert Rohde
1894 *New York*
1944 *New York*

▲ Case furniture for Herman Miller, 1933 – first exhibited in Gilbert Rohde's "Design for Living" house at the "International Exposition – A Century of Progress" held in Chicago, 1933

► Copper & oak
plant stand, 1903

Charles Rohlfs

1853 *New York*
1936 *Buffalo, New York*

Around 1890, Charles Rohlfs established a small workshop in Buffalo for the production of Arts & Crafts furniture. His early pieces of carved and pierced oak furniture were commissioned mostly by friends in Buffalo. However, he soon had clients based in New York, Philadelphia, London, Paris and Bremen, his work being retailed by the Chicago department store, Marshall Field. Inspired by Norwegian, Moorish, medieval and **Art Nouveau** styles, Rohlfs' designs differed from mainstream American Arts & Crafts furniture through their unusual proportions and ornate carving. However, the more intricate work was undertaken by George Thiele. Around 1898, Rohlfs moved his workshop into larger premises in Buffalo, and in 1902 exhibited his work at the "Esposizione Internazionale d'Arte Decorativa Moderna" in Turin. He later became a member of the Royal Society of Arts, London, and was commissioned to design a set of chairs for Buckingham Palace. Rohlfs also lectured at the **Roycrofters** craft community in East Aurora and became one of the leading figures of the American **Arts & Crafts Movement**.

Aldo Rossi studied architecture at the Politecnico di Milano, graduating in 1959. During this period, he assisted in the offices of Ignazio Gardella and **Marco Zanuso**, and also worked for the magazines, *Il Contemporano* and *Casabella-Continuità*, which he edited from 1961 to 1964. During the 1960s, Rossi's architectural work included designs for the redevelopment of the Via Sarini district of Milan and for a Turin shopping centre – both projects that reveal a reductivist approach to architecture. In 1963, he assisted Lodovico Quaroni at the Scuola Urbanista, Arezzo and Carlo Aymonino at the University of Venice. Rossi co-planned the XIII Milan Triennale in 1964 with Luca Meda, and two years later published *L'Architettura della Città*. He became a professor at the Politecnico di Milano in 1969 and two years later collaborated with Gianni Braghieri on the winning design for the San Cataldo Cemetery, Modena (1971). He then taught at the Eidgenössische Technische Hochschule, Zurich for three years. As a leading post-modern architect, Rossi participated in **Alessi**'s *Tea & Coffee Piazza* project in 1980, going on to design other products for Alessi, including the famous *La Conica* (1984) and *La Cupola* (1989) coffee makers as well as carpets for ARP Studio and furniture for Molteni, Up & Up and Unifor.

Aldo Rossi
1931 *Milan*
1997 *Milan*

◀▲ *La Conica* expresso coffee makers for Alessi, 1984

▲ Design of *La Cupola* cafetièra for Alessi, 1989

François-Eugène Rousseau

1827 Paris
1891 Paris

François-Eugène Rousseau inherited a workshop on the Rue Coquillère, Paris, which manufactured porcelain and faïence. In 1866, he designed an earthenware dinner service based on drawings by Félix Bracquemond (1833–1914), who himself had been inspired by Japanese woodcuts such as those of Hokusai. Initially, Rousseau worked with Louis Salon before founding a partnership with Ernest-Baptiste Léveillé in 1869. They established a shop, Rousseau-Léveillé, retailing their own designs for glassware that were inspired by the forms and decorative motifs of Far and Middle Eastern art as well as by similar work executed by glass designers such as Philippe-Joseph Brocard (active 1867–1890). Rousseau became noted for his reintroduction of cased glass and crackled glass: the former being an 18th-century Chinese technique in which opaque glass was engraved to expose an underlay of translucent glass, and the latter, a 16th-century technique from Venice in which the glass is plunged into cold water between firings. Rousseau was one of the primary exponents of the **Aesthetic Movement** in Continental Europe and his glass designs, which were decorated by Eugène Michel and Alphonse-Georges Reyen among others, not only revitalized interest in decorative glassware but were also highly influential to the later **Art Nouveau** style.

▲ Faience plates,
1866 – decoration
based on drawings by
Félix Bracquemond

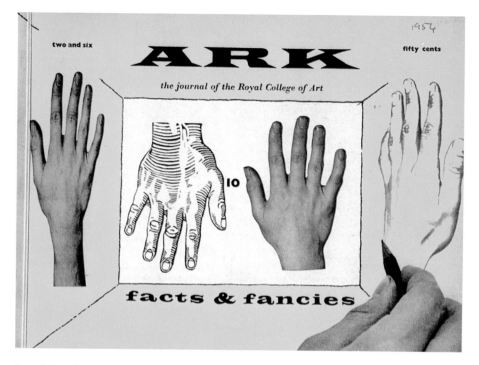

Founded as the Government School of Design in 1837, the college was initially concerned with the teaching of the "grammar of ornament" and drawing from nature was discouraged. The teaching structure devised by Sir Henry Cole (1808–1882) focused primarily on the training of students as "ornamentalists" for the manufacturing industries. Although a department of practical art was set up in 1852, it was not until the 1890s that more emphasis was placed on practical instruction. In 1896, the Royal College of Art adopted its present name and a new programme of teaching was implemented, which included classes in history, philosophy and architectural drawing for all first year students. Following this preliminary course, students selected one of four specialized areas of study – decorative painting, sculpture, architecture or design. Design reforms that germinated at the Royal college in the 1890s were later propagated at the **Bauhaus** and thereby had a direct bearing on the evolution of the **Modern Movement**. Until the 1950s, however, craft training rather than design teaching permeated the curriculum. In 1959, the Design Research Department and School of Industrial Design were opened, heralding a new professionalism at the college, which since then has been at the forefront of design practice.

Royal College of Art
Founded 1837
London

▲ **Len Deighton**,
Cover for *Ark*
journal, issue 10,
Spring 1954

► Leaded glass and copper table lamp for Roycrofters Workshop, c. 1910

Roycrofters Workshop
1895–1938
East Aurora, New York

Elbert G. Hubbard (1856–1915) became a leading figure of the American **Arts & Crafts Movement** even though he was not a designer, but a self-educated travelling salesman, working for the soap company he ran with his brother-in-law. Eventually, he sold his share of this venture and around 1893 moved to East Aurora, near Buffalo. In 1894, he travelled to Britain, where he met John Ruskin (1819–1900) and **William Morris** and was so inspired by Morris' Kelmscott Press that in 1895 he founded his own printing company. The Roycroft Press was named after the 17th-century British bookbinders, Samuel and Thomas Roycroft. Unlike the Kelmscott Press, however, Hubbard's Roycroft Press was blatantly commercial and he was described by **Charles Ashbee**'s wife, Janet, as an "Anarkist with a K". Slightly later, "Fra Hubbard" established a bindery and leather workshop in East Aurora and so the Roycroft craft community came into being. In 1896, a furniture workshop was founded to produce mission-style furniture as well as souvenirs for visitors staying at the Roycroft Inn. By 1906, over four hundred people were working at the community and in 1909, a metalwork studio was opened. After the sinking of the Lusitania in 1915, on which Hubbard and his wife perished, their son Bert oversaw the community until its closure in 1938.

From 1907, Jacques-Émile Ruhlmann headed his family's decorating business, which enjoyed the patronage of the architect Charles Plumet and the
couturier Jacques Doucet among others. The latter encouraged Ruhlmann
to publicly exhibit his work for the first time in 1911, and two years later
Ruhlmann's luxurious and elegant furniture designs appeared at the 1913
Salon d'Automne. In 1919, Ruhlmann co-founded, the Établissements
Ruhlmann et Laurent with Pierre Laurent, for which he designed carpets,
textiles, lighting and furniture that incorporated exotic woods such as am-
boyna and macassar ebony as well as inlays of ivory or tortoiseshell. These
designs appeared in many publications, most notably in an article in the
magazine *Art et Decoration* in 1920. The interiors of Ruhlmann's Hôtel du

Jacques-Émile
Ruhlmann
1879 *Paris*
1933 *Paris*

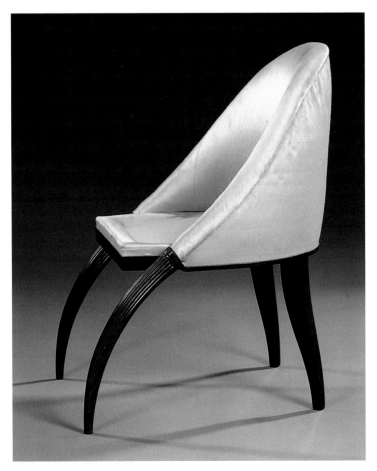

▶ *Défenses* chair for
the Établissements
Ruhlmann et
Laurent, c. 1920

Collectionneur, which included not only his own designs but also those of **Jean-Émile Puiforcat**, **Pierre-Émile Legrain**, Edgar-William Brandt (1880–1960) and Jean Dunand (1877–1942), caused a sensation at the 1925 "Exposition Internationale des Arts Décoratifs et Industriels Modernes" in Paris. Over the 1920s, Ruhlmann's furniture became more monumental, and in 1929 he exhibited his elegant *Study Bedroom for a Crown Prince* at the "Salon des Artistes Décorateurs". Then during the 1930s, his furniture began to incorporate chromium-plated metal and silver while the forms he adopted became increasingly modernistic. Ruhlmann undertook many commissions including the decoration of the tea-rooms of the *Île de France* oceanliner, various interiors for the Palais de l'Élysée, Paris, and the design of furniture for the Maharaja of Indore's palace. Throughout his career, Ruhlmann designed furniture and interiors that exuded a sense of luxury, not through the use of ornament but through his exquisite handling of materials. His high-quality work followed the French *décorateur* tradition and exemplified the sumptuousness and elegance of French **Art Deco**.

Gordon Russell spent his childhood at his father's hotel, the Lygon Arms, Broadway, in the Cotswolds. The **Arts & Crafts Movement** had strong associations with the Cotswolds, and in 1911 Russell began designing objects and furniture for the hotel in this idiom. Russell was better at drafting than actual crafting and so produced beautifully detailed drawings to enable others to execute his work. This clear-cut division between designing and producing enabled him to make a smooth transition from craft to industrial production. During the First World War, Russell saw action in many key battles and these experiences had much impact on his later social and political outlook. He continued designing Arts & Crafts furniture throughout the 1920s, and was awarded a gold medal at the 1925 Paris "Exposition Internationale des Arts Décoratifs et Industriels Modernes". In the 1930s, however, Russell's work entered the vanguard of British Modernism, and in 1935 he opened a new furniture factory in Park Royal, London, which by the late 1930s had a workforce of 800. In 1941 he joined the design panel of the **Utility** Furniture Committee, and from 1947 to 1959, he directed the Council of Industrial Design and in 1956 opened a permanent exhibition centre in the Haymarket, London. Russell's belief in public service through design, which stemmed from his Arts & Crafts origins, became a central tenet of modern British design during the 1940s and 1950s.

Gordon Russell
1892 *Cricklewood/ London*
1980 *Kingcombe/ Chipping Campden*

▲ Bedroom furniture for Russell & Sons, early 1920s

Eero Saarinen

1910 *Kirkkonummi, Finland*
1961 *Ann Arbor, Michigan*

Eero Saarinen was the son of the celebrated Finnish architect, **Eliel Saarinen** – the first president of the **Cranbrook Academy of Art**, Bloomfield Hills, Michigan. Born in Finland, Eero emigrated with his family to the United States in 1923. He initially studied sculpture at the Académie de la Grande Chaumière, Paris from 1929 to 1930 and later trained as an architect at Yale University, New Haven, graduating in 1934. He then received a scholarship from Yale, enabling him to travel to Europe for a year. On his return, he took up a teaching position at the Cranbrook Academy, and in 1937 began collaborating with **Charles Eames** – a fellow staff member at Cranbrook – which culminated in a series of highly progressive and prize-winning furniture designs for the 1940 "Organic Design in Home Furnishings" competition held at the **Museum of Modern Art, New York**. Their competition entries included a highly rational modular system of storage case furniture and a revolutionary group of chairs with single-form compound-moulded plywood seat shells that advanced the notion of continuous contact and support. The chairs were among the most important furniture designs of the 20th century and heralded a totally new direction in furniture design. They led directly to Saarinen's later highly successful furniture designs for **Knoll**, including the *No. 70 Womb* chair (1947–1948), the *Saarinen Collection* of office seating

◄ *Model No. 150 Tulip* chair (Pedestal Group) for Knoll Associates, 1955–1956

▶ Trans World Airline Terminal at John F. Kennedy Airport, New York, 1956–1962

▼ Interior design of the Trans World Airline Terminal at John F. Kennedy Airport, New York, 1956–1962

(1951) and the *Pedestal Group* of chairs and tables (1955–1956). With the *Pedestal Group*, Saarinen's stated objective was to clean up "the slum of legs" in domestic interiors. His quest for total material, structural and functional organic unity of design, however, remained unrealized due to the limitations of materials technology. Saarinen also worked in his father's practice in Ann Arbor and went into partnership with J. Robert Swanson in 1941. After Eliel Saarinen's death in 1950, he opened his own office, Eero Saarinen & Associates in Birmingham, Michigan. Like his design work, Saarinen's architecture was characterized by the use of expressive and sculptural organic forms. His most notable projects included the Jefferson National Expansion Memorial, St Louis (1947), the David S. Ingalls Ice Hockey Hall at Yale University (1953–1959), his masterwork: the extraordinary TWA Terminal at Kennedy Airport, New York (1956–1962), and Dulles International Airport, Washington DC (1958–1963). Like Charles Eames, Eero Saarinen promoted a humanized form of Modernism, and in so doing was one of the most important pioneers of **Organic Design**.

Gottlieb Eliel Saarinen studied fine art at the University of Helsinki and architecture at the Helsinki Polytechnic, graduating in 1897. His style of architecture was influenced by the **Glasgow School** and the Vienna **Seccession** as the bold massing of elements in his Helsinki railway station (1904) reveals. He became a leading exponent of the National Romantic movement in Finland, and in 1912 joined the **Deutscher Werkbund**. After winning second prize in the 1922 Chicago Tribune Tower competition, he emigrated with his wife Loja to the United States. He initially resided in Evanston, Illinois, before settling in Ann Arbor where he became a visiting professor of architecture at the University of Michigan. In 1923, Saarinen met the wealthy newspaper baron and philanthropist, George C. Booth, who asked him to draw up plans for the development of the Cranbrook Educational Community. Two years later, Saarinen moved to Bloomfield Hills and in 1932, the **Cranbrook Academy of Art** was officially founded with Saarinen as its first president. Under his directorship the Academy became the premier design institution in America and produced many of the country's most talented designers.

Eliel Saarinen

1873 *Rantasalmi, Finland*
1950 *Bloomfield Hills, Michigan*

Lino Sabattini
b. 1925 *Correggio, Italy*

Lino Sabattini first worked in a brassware shop, where he met the potter Rolando Hettner who impressed him deeply. He taught himself about design by avidly reading the influential journal *Domus*. One of his earliest designs was for a teapot that was produced by the German manufacturer, W. Wolf. In 1955, he established his own Milan-based metalworking studio and met the architect and designer, **Gio Ponti**. As the editor of *Domus* at the time, Ponti featured Sabattini's metalware designs in the journal in 1956 and organized an exhibition of his work in Paris the same year. Between 1956 and 1963, Sabattini also worked as design director of Christofle Orfèvrerie, Paris. While there, he produced a number of metal designs, characterized by sleek and abstracted free-form shapes, such as his *Como* tea and coffee service (1957), and over the same period designed metalware, glassware and ceramics for Rosenthal, Nava and Zani & Zani. In 1964, he established a studio and small workshop, known as Argenteria Sabattini, in Bregnano to produce his designs on a limited scale.

▲ *Como* tea and coffee service for Christofle Orfèvrerie, 1955–1956

Among his most notable products were, the *Estro* sauceboat (1977), the *Instrumenta* range of stainless steel cutlery (1978), the *Pale* silver servers (1973), the *Insect Legs* titanium cutlery (1986) and the *Connato* silver-plated

vase. Sabattini was a member of the ADI (Associazione per il Disegno
Industriale) and his designs were regularly exhibited at the Milan Triennale
exhibitions. He won numerous awards, including a gold medal at the 1971
"Mostra Internazionale dell'Arredamento" exhibition in Monza and a
Compasso d'Oro in 1979 for his silver-plated cylindrical *Eskimo* ice-bucket
(1978). Sabattini's innovative designs, combining traditional craftsmanship
with modern form, exude a sense of superlative quality.

▲ *Instrumenta*
stainless-steel
cutlery for Sabattini
Argenteria, 1978

Richard Sapper
b. 1932 *Munich*

Richard Sapper studied mechanical engineering and economics from 1952 to 1954 at the University of Munich. From 1956 to 1957, he worked in the car styling department of Mercedes Benz in Stuttgart, and then moved to Italy to work in the Milan studio of Alberto Rosselli (1921–1976) and **Gio Ponti**, where he stayed until 1959. That year he designed his *Static* table clock for Lorenz, which was awarded a **Compasso d'Oro**, and became a designer for the in-house design department of the La Rinascente stores, working there and in the studio of **Marco Zanuso** for the next two years. In 1970, Sapper established his own design office in Stuttgart and acted as a design consultant to Fiat and Pirelli among others. He continued collaborating with Zanuso until 1975 and together they produced an impressive series of landmark designs: the *Lambda* chair for Gavina (1963), the injection-moulded polyethylene *No. 4999/5* stacking child's chair for **Kartell** (1961–1964), the *Doney 14* television (1962), the *TS 502* radio (1965), the *Algol* and *Black Box* portable televisions for Brionvega (1965 and 1969) and the *Grillo* folding telephone for Siemens (1965).

In 1972, Sapper independently designed the highly successful *Tizio* task lamp for Artemide, which with its blatantly **High-Tech** design rhetoric became a cult object in the 1980s. The same year, together with **Gae Aulenti**, he established the Urban Transport Systems Study Group; their research

▶ *Bollitore* kettle for Alessi, 1983

◄ *Tizio* lamps for
Artemide, 1972

culminating in an exhibition held at the XVIII Milan Triennale in 1979.
Sapper has been a product design consultant to IBM since 1980, and during
the 1980s he combined his earlier High-Tech style with **Post-Modernism**
to create a number of notable designs for **Alessi**, including the *Cafetière*
coffee maker (1979), the *Bollitore* whistling kettle (1983) and the *Uri Uri*
watch (1988). He has also designed furniture for **Knoll**, Unifor, Molteni and
Castelli, and in 1981 became a member of ADI (Associazione per il Disegno
Industriale).

Timo Sarpaneva studied in the graphic department of the Taideteollinen Korkeakoulu (Central School of Applied Arts), Helsinki from 1941 to 1948, and two years later he became a product designer and head of the exhibition section at the Karhula-Iittala glassworks. One of his first technical innovations at Iittala was a steam blowing method, which was used for his early sculptural vessels, such as *Kajakki* (1953), *Maailmankaunein* (1954) and *Linnunsilmä* (1953), as well as for his delicately colour tinted thin glass plates known as Aquarelles. During the mid-1950s, Sarpaneva introduced his *I-Glass* range, which attempted to bridge the gap between expensive art glass and utility glassware. This industrially manufactured product line comprised seventeen items, which were available in several colours, including lilac-grey, blue-grey, smoke-grey and green-grey, which could be combined to produce different effects. He also developed other glass techniques for his *Ambiente* range (1964), *Archipelago* range (1978) and his *Claritas* range (1984). Many of Sarpaneva's designs, such as his *Claritas* vases (1984) for Iittala and his cast-iron cooking pot with a wooden handle for Rosenlew (1960), used closed "round-square" forms that relate to the smooth pebbles of the Indian Tantric cult, while others, like his large *Lasiaika* glass sculptures, have more open and expressive forms. Sarpaneva taught at the College of Applied Arts, Helsinki from the mid-1950s, and was awarded a Grand Prix at the 1951 and 1957 Milan Triennale exhibitions. He was made an Honorary Royal Designer for Industry in London in 1963 and received an honorary doctorate from the **Royal College of Art, London** in 1967. Apart from his exquisite glassware, Sarpaneva has also designed ceramics, metalware, textiles, books and theatre sets.

Timo Sarpaneva
b. 1926 *Helsinki*

◄ *Claritas* vase for Iittala, 1984

▼ *Orkidea* vase for Iittala, 1953

Timo Sarpaneva · **629**

Raymond Savignac worked as a tracer and sketcher from 1922 at the Compagnie des Transports Parisiens. In 1924, he was employed by the advertising agency, Lortac as an "ideas-man", and while there worked as an assistant to **A.M. Cassandre**. During the 1930s, Savignac began producing posters that were painted in the manner of Cassandre. His designs, however, were less pictorial and were executed in a cartoon-like style. Savignac was opposed to the modern approach of juxtaposing graphic elements and instead had as his motto: "A single image for a single idea." His posters held the viewer's attention through humorous content, often inspired by the antics played out in Charlie Chaplin and Buster Keaton films, and surreal elements, which he described as a "visual scandal". The strength of his images meant that little or no copy was needed to explain the item being advertised. His *Monsavon* poster of 1949 established his reputation as one of the leading French *affichistes* (poster designers). He subsequently designed

▼ Poster for
Monsavon soap,
1948

posters for companies including Bic, Perrier, Verigoud, Frigéco, Maggi and Citroën as well as for French public ventures such as Air France, SNCF and RATP. Savignac won the Martini prize in 1964 for his *Vite Aspro* poster advertising aspirin, and in 1969 he designed sets and costumes for "L'Avare" at the Comédie-Française. He published two books about his work: an autobiography in 1975 and *Savignac de A à Z* in 1987. While Savignac's graphic style is distinctively French, the direct humour of his surreal images can be universally decoded.

► Poster for Air
France, 1956

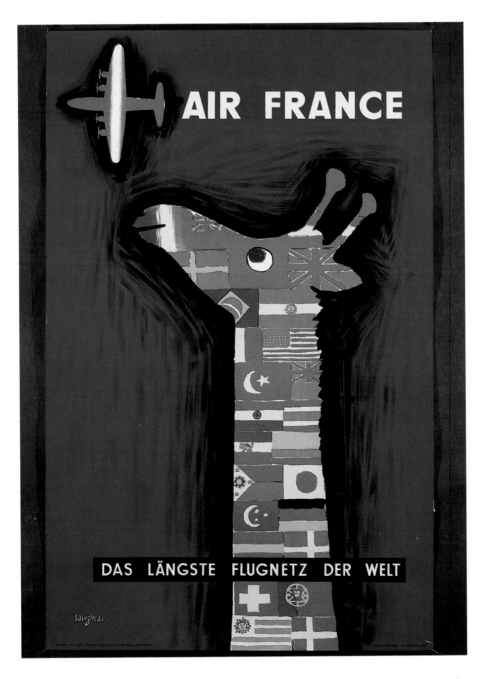

AIR FRANCE

DAS LÄNGSTE FLUGNETZ DER WELT

◄ *Model No. 3901*
vase for Venini & C.,
1938

◄ *Model No. 783*
chair for Bernini,
1977

Carlo Scarpa studied architecture at the Accademia di Belle Arti, Venice, graduating in 1926 and establishing his own practice in Venice a year later. His architectural work was influenced by Venetian architecture (a fusion of the Byzantine and Gothic styles), the Vienna **Secession**, **De Stijl** and **Frank Lloyd Wright**. Scarpa was particularly adept at the restoration and remodelling of historic buildings and also undertook the design of many exhibitions and interior schemes, including ones for the Ferruccio Asta House, Venice (1931). He was especially noted for his museum renovations, owing to his ability to masterfully combine historic elements with modern features while skillfully controlling natural light and delineating internal spaces. These public projects included the Accademia, Venice (1952), the Galleria Nazionale della Sicilia at the Palazzo Abatellis in Palermo (1953–1954) and the Castelvecchio Museum, Verona (1956–1964). In collaboration with G. D'Agaro and C. Maschietto, Scarpa designed the **Olivetti** showroom in Venice (1957–1958), which similarly combined the old with the new. Scarpa also designed furniture for Gavina and was a design consultant to the Murano glassworks, M.V.M. Cappellin & C. from 1926 to 1930 and Venini & C. from 1932 to 1947.

Carlo Scarpa
1906 *Venice*
1978 *Sendai, Japan*

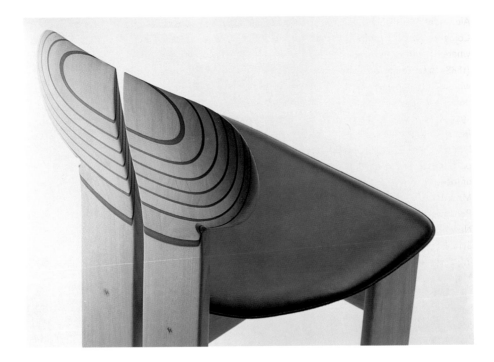

Tobia & Afra Scarpa

Tobia Scarpa
b.1935 *Venice*

Afra Scarpa
b. 1937 *Montebelluna, Italy*

▲ *Africa* chair for B&B Italia, 1975

Tobia Scarpa, son of the architect **Carlo Scarpa**, and Afra Bianchin both studied at the Istituto Universitario di Architettura in Venice. They married, and from 1957 to 1961 Tobia worked as a glass designer at the Murano glassworks of Venini & C., periodically collaborating with Afra. In 1960 the Scarpas began designing furniture for Gavina, most notably, the *Bastiano* sofa and chair (1961) and the *Vanessa* bed (1962). Like Carlo Scarpa, their designs for furniture, such as the *925* chair (1965), were informed by a deep understanding of materials and an empathy for traditional Italian craftsmanship. In 1960, they established their own office in Afra's home-town of Montebelluna and also designed furniture for B&B Italia, **Knoll**, Stildomus, Company of the Philippines, Maxalto and Molteni & C. among others, as well as lighting for Flos and cutlery for San Lorenzo. In 1962, they drew up a **corporate identity** programme for Benetton and in 1964, designed a factory for the company. They also designed the interior of the Cassina showroom in Meda (c.1966), the B&B Italia factory in Novedrate (1967) and the Villa Benetton residence near Treviso (1966) – all of which were characterized by a sense of modesty and a highly refined use of space. In the 1980s, the Scarpas restored the plazas in Veneto and Emilia.

Alexander "Xanti" Schawinsky studied painting and architecture in Zurich, Cologne and Berlin before becoming a student at the Weimar **Bauhaus**, where he worked in the theatre department with Oskar Schlemmer (1888–1943). When the school moved to Dessau in 1925, Schawinsky went with it. The year after that, he was engaged as a theatre designer in Zwickau before moving to Magdeburg where he worked as a graphic designer from 1929 to 1931. In 1933, Schawinsky moved to Milan and designed graphics incorporating photomontage, most notably for **Olivetti** and Motta. He collaborated with Luigi Fugini and Gino Pollini on the design of the *Studio 42* portable typewriter for Olivetti in 1936, and that same year, on the invitation of **Josef Albers**, he emigrated to America, subsequently teaching at Black Mountain College, North Carolina, and designing the interior for the Pennsylvania pavilion at the 1939 New York World's Fair. In 1950, Schawinsky concentrated on painting and set up a studio near Lake Maggiore, Italy, and from then until his death in 1979 divided his time between that base and New York. Schawinsky's bold photomontaged display advertisements incorporated little if any advertising copy, allowing the images to speak for themselves.

Xanti
Schawinsky
1904 Basel
1979 Locarno, Switzerland

▶ Poster advertising
MP1 typewriter for
Olivetti, 1935

▶ **Josef Maria Olbrich**, Poster for the II Secessionist exhibition in Vienna, 1889 – showing Olbrich's Vienna Secession building

► **Max Klinger**,
Sculpture of Ludwig
van Beethoven in the
Vienna Secession
building at the XIV
Secessionist
exhibition, 1902

In 1897, the Vereinigung bildender Künstler Österreichs-Secession (Association of Austrian Artists) was founded by the artists Gustav Klimt (1862–1918),
Carl Moll (1861–1945) and Josef Engelhart (1864–1941) and the architects
Josef Maria Olbrich, **Koloman Moser** and **Josef Hoffmann** as a breakaway
group opposed to the staid Academic tradition of the conservative Künstler-
haus. In 1897, Olbrich designed his famous Secession Building with its
large gilded dome of laurel leaves – a suitably imperial motif for Vienna.
Completed in 1898, the building, situated on Karlsplatz, provided a perma-
nent exhibition centre for the group. It has stained-glass panels and interiors
designed by Moser and above its entrance an inscription by the art critic
Ludwig Hevesi, which reads: "Der Zeit ihre Kunst, der Kunst ihre Freiheit"
(To the age its art, to art its freedom), encapsulates the *fin-de-siècle* spirit of
Vienna – by then the fourth largest city in Europe. Although it was not ready
in time for the first Secession exhibition, which was held instead at the
Horticultural Hall in Vienna, Olbrich's building was the venue for the second Wiener Sezession exhibition and subsequent displays of the group's
work. To further promote their cause, the Secession also published their
own journal, *Ver Sacrum* (Sacred Spring) from 1898. Though the Secession's
early work was essentially within the **Art Nouveau** style, their output became
increasingly rectilinear after the landmark VIII Wiener Sezession exhibition
of 1900, which was dedicated solely to the decorative arts. This exhibition
included installations by **Charles Rennie Mackintosh, Charles Robert
Ashbee** and **Henry van de Velde**. Josef Hoffmann's Purkersdorf Sanatorium

Secession
Vienna

▲ Josef Hoffmann,
Main hall of the
Purkersdorf
Sanatorium, 1904

(1904–1906) with its unrelenting geometry, which was echoed in Koloman
Moser's black and white cubic armchair designed specifically for the project,
exemplified the post-1900 Secessionist style and anticipated the geometric
abstraction of the **Modern Movement**. Inspired by Charles Ashbee's **Guild of
Handicraft**, Hoffmann and Moser, together with the banker Fritz Waerndorfer
(1869–1939), founded the **Wiener Werkstätte** in 1903 to produce and retail
"New Art" designs by members of the Vienna Secession. There were, however, growing tensions within the Secession, and when in 1905 the artist
Carl Moll was attacked by other members Klimt and his followers – known
as the "stylists" – left the group as did Hoffmann. The Secession nevertheless continued to operate, and from 1919 to 1920 Franz Messner was
its president. Although often associated with Art Nouveau, the Vienna
Secession was influenced by Classicism to a greater extent than other re-

▶ Koloman Moser,
Armchair designed
for the Purkersdorf
Sanatorium, 1902

forming artists' groups on the Continent. Its promotion of a geometric vocabulary of form had a profound impact on the evolution of modern design.

First introduced into philosophical debate by the 17th-century English politician and philosopher, John Locke (1632–1704), semiotics refers to the study of signs and symbols, which although most commonly applied to linguistics can be relevant to visual language. Throughout the history of design, buildings, interiors and objects have been decorated with symbols to convey meanings and values or to impart character. Many designers associated with the **Arts & Crafts Movement**, for example, such as **Charles F. A. Voysey** and **Charles Rennie Mackintosh**, produced designs as much for the mind as to fulfil functional needs and sought to infuse their work with spiritual meaning through the use of motifs such as pierced hearts, circles and squares, which symbolized love, the body and the spirit. The Swiss psychologist and psychiatrist, Carl Jung (1875–1961) undertook much research into symbols, especially alchemic ones, which he believed to be codes of the unconscious. The study of semiotics (or semiology as it is sometimes called) was also taken up in the early 20th century by the Austrian-born English philosopher, Ludwig Wittgenstein (1889–1951), who evolved his "picture theory" in the 1920s, suggesting that signs are pictures of reality; by the Swiss linguist Ferdinand de Saussure (1857–1913) who proposed that the language of signs is a social phenomenon, and by the American philosopher, Charles Sanders Peirce (1839–1914) who argued that semiotics was a logical and "formal doctrine of signs". These analytical researches into semiotics did not so much attempt to reveal the meaning of signs as to expose their underlying bias – for example, towards gender, class or race.

In 1938, the American behavioural semanticist, Charles Morris, divided semiotics into three branches of study: pragmatics (the way in which signs are used), semantics (the meaning of signs) and syntax (the arrangement of signs). Later, semiotics was seen as a tool with which to analyse the visual world and the Italian writer and semiotician, Umberto Eco, who published *A Theory of Semiotics* (1976) and *Semiotics and the Philosophy of Language* (1984), was the first to apply this area of study to architecture. Later, Roland Barthes (1915–1980) contributed much to the debate surrounding semiotics with a series of literary works including his famous book *Mythologies* (1957), which was translated into English in 1972 and became highly influential to the evolution of **Anti-Design**.

By the 1970s, it was widely believed that the **Modern Movement**'s aesthetic, founded on pure geometric abstraction, was ultimately alienating, because its lack of ornament – signs and symbols – denied a basic means of cultural communication. Post-Modernists, such as **Charles Jencks** urged for a return to symbolism in architecture and design, and during the 1980s semiotics

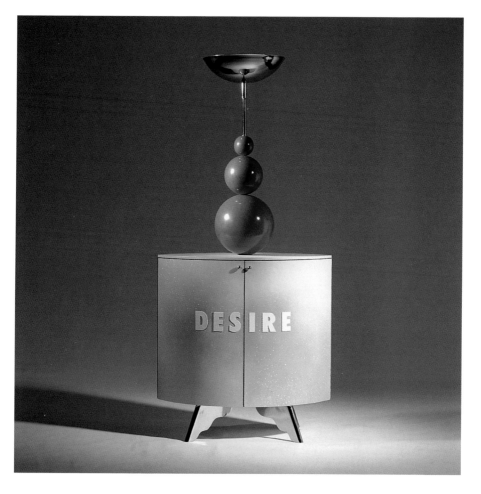

gained much ground through **Post-Modernism**. Today, many designers regard visual communication as an important aspect of design practice and seek to imbue their work with meaning or character through the application of semiotic theory.

▲ Dan Friedman,
Desire cabinet for
Néotu, 1990

**Gustave
Serrurier-Bovy**
1858 Liège, Belgium
1910 Antwerp

The son of a cabinet-maker, Gustave Serrurier-Bovy studied architecture at the Académie des Beaux-Arts, Liège. By 1883, he was working as an architect in Liège, his output influenced by the British **Arts & Crafts Movement** and the French architect, Eugène-Emmanuel Viollet-le-Duc (1814–1879). In 1884, he visited Britain, and on his return established a large store in Liège to retail furniture, textiles and wallpapers supplied by **Liberty & Co**. as well as Persian, Japanese and Indian items. Around 1890, Serrurier-Bovy produced his first catalogue, which included Arts & Crafts style furnishings. He established a shop in Brussels in 1896 and in the same year showed his designs at the Arts & Crafts Exhibition Society, London. In 1899, he established a large factory in Liège, and with the architect René Dulong opened another branch of his retail business in Paris, known as L'Art dans l'Habitation. He subsequently opened shops in The Hague in 1904 and Nice in 1906. Although he had abandoned the Arts & Crafts style in favour of **Art Nouveau** in 1902, Serrurier-Bovy's last designs from around 1910 were notable for their increasingly rectilinear forms.

▲ Oak hall stand,
c. 1898

▶ Mahogany, brass
and coloured glass
mantel clock, c. 1905

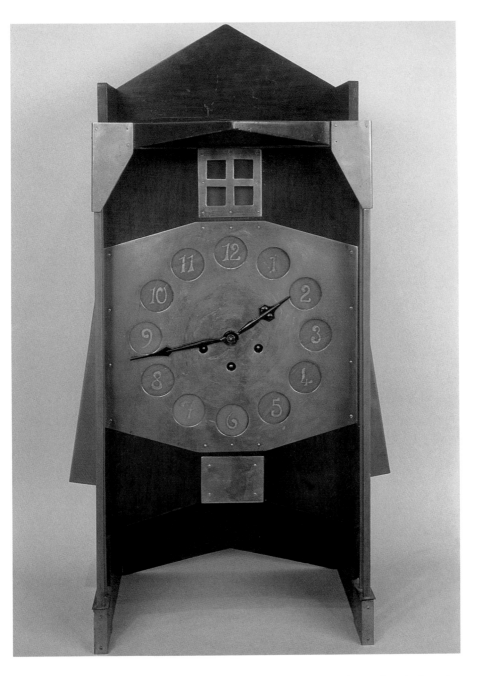

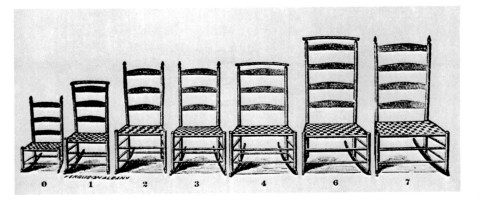

Founded in Northern England in 1747, the United Society of Believers in Christ's Second Appearance was a sect whose religious worship included communal dancing, hence the nickname "Shaking Quakers" or "Shakers". Fleeing persecution, "Mother" Ann Lee (1736–1884), the sect's spiritual leader, emigrated to America in 1774 and was later joined by followers from New England and New York State. In 1785, the first Shaker community was established at New Lebanon (renamed Mount Lebanon in 1861) in New York State and over the succeeding decades, another eighteen communities were founded in eight states. The religion stressed separation from "the World" and promoted the ideas of common property and celibacy. The Shaker communities sought complete self-sufficiency and physical labour was an important element of the sisters' and brothers' spiritual lives. The Shaker motto, "Hands to Work and Hearts to God", guided the Believers' daily chores, which included the crafting of practical yet well-made objects for everyday use. These utilitarian designs reflected the sect's overriding belief in the morality of "plain and simple" living. During the 19th century, the Shakers' much needed income from agriculture decreased and so the communities were compelled to produce furniture and other items for sale. In 1871, a factory was founded by the Shakers at Mount Lebanon for the manufacture of chairs. These mass-produced designs, which lacked the quality of the earlier furniture, were marketed through specially produced catalogues. Although Shaker designs became highly appreciated for their simplicity and honest craftsmanship during the 1860s and 1870s, the sect's membership continued to dwindle. By the late 19th and early 20th centuries, many of the communities had been forced to close. By the time the last community was shut down in 1947, Shaker designs had become highly collectable – much to the dismay of the few remaining Believers.

Shaker
USA

▲ Page from Shaker catalogue showing chair variations, 1874

◄ Stained maple rocking chair for the Shaker factory in New Lebanon, c. 1880

Peter Shire
b. 1947 *Los Angeles*

Having trained as a ceramicist at the Chouinard Institute of Art, Los Angeles, Peter Shire established his own studio in 1972 and had his first one-man show at a Hollywood gallery in 1975. His sculptural and brightly coloured ceramics and furniture designs can be seen as representative of the "Funk" aesthetic, which emerged in California during the late 1960s. Funk was an **Anti-Design** movement that was associated with the use of "hot" colours and quirky non-functional forms. Shire's work caught the attention of **Ettore Sottsass** who subsequently invited him to join the **Memphis** group. Shire's furniture, such as the *Bel Air* chair (1982) and *Brazil* table (1981) for Memphis, with characteristic boldly coloured asymmetrical sculptural elements, attempted to occupy a grey area between fine art and design, while his ceramics, such as his bizarre and impractical teapots, were admired by Sottsass for their inventive "slab" constructions. With their brash "sun-kissed" colours and expressive forms, Shire's designs exemplified Californian **Post-Modernism**.

▲ *Brazil* table for
Memphis, 1981

Gustav Siegel undertook a three-year cabinet-making apprenticeship in Vienna prior to studying at the Kunstgewerbeschule in Vienna from 1897 to 1901. While there, he qualified for admission to the architectural classes given by **Josef Hoffmann**, and in 1899 he was appointed by the president of **J.&J. Kohn**, Felix Kohn, to head the company's design department even though he was only nineteen years old. The following year, Siegel designed a bedroom for the company, which was displayed at the "Exposition Universelle et Internationale" in Paris. This interior with its bentwood wall decoration and bentwood furniture had a controlled organic rhythm that was typical of the Viennese **Art Nouveau** style. Siegel's designs for J.&J. Kohn after 1900 are difficult to identify, as both **Otto Wagner** and Hoffmann produced designs for the company in a similar style. It would, however, be safe to assume that Siegel was responsible for the majority of the bentwood furniture produced by J.&J. Kohn from 1900 to 1914. Several of the company's well-known designs, such as the *Model No. 728* suite (1905–1906), that have been traditionally attributed to Hoffmann, may well have been executed by Siegel. Among the designs positively identified as Siegel's are the *No. 415* suite of furniture, which was featured in *The Studio* in 1908 and a plant-stand that was displayed at the 1901/1902 Winterausstellung held at the Österreichisches Museum für Kunst und Industrie, Vienna. Siegel was also responsible for several of the company's posters and various graphics as well as advertisements that appeared in the Vienna **Secession** exhibition catalogues of 1904 and 1908. As head of the J.&J. Kohn design department, Siegel played a key role in the development of bentwood furniture and the promotion of the Secessionist style.

Gustav Siegel
1880 *Vienna*
1970 *Vienna*

▼ Room display designed for Jacob & Josef Kohn's stand at the "Exposition Universelle et Internationale de Paris", 1900

Jutta Sika

1877 Linz, Austria
1964 Vienna

Jutta Sika trained in Vienna, at the Graphische Lehr- und Versuchsanstalt from 1895 to 1897 and under **Koloman Moser** at the Kunstgewerbeschule from 1897 to 1902. She was a member of the Österreichischer Werkbund (Austrian Werkbund), the Wiener Kunst im Hause and the Vereinigung bildender Künstlerinnen Österreichs, and exhibited her work at many exhibitions including the 1900 Paris "Exposition Universelle et Internationale", the 1904 St. Louis "Louisana Purchase Exhibition" and the 1925 Paris "Exposition Internationale des Arts Décoratifs et Industriels Modernes". Apart from designing ceramics and postcards for the **Wiener Werkstätte**, Sika also designed glassware for E. Bakalowits, christmas tree decorations for the Hofkonditorei Demel, clothing for the salon Flöge, metal utensils for Argentor and porcelain for the Wiener Porzellan-Manufaktur Josef Böck, some of which was decorated with floral motifs devised by Antoinette Krasnik. Her tea and coffee service (1901–1902) for Böck was remarkably forward-looking both in its form and decoration and featured in many publications. From 1911 to 1933, Sika also taught at the Gewerbliche Fortbildungsschule, Vienna.

▲ Tea and coffee
service for the Wiener
Porzellan-Manufaktur
Josef Böck,
c. 1901–1902

Arthur Silver (1853–1896) trained at Reading School of Art, and in 1873 became an assistant to the **Aesthetic Movement** furniture designer, Henry W. Batley. In 1880, he established the Silver Studio in West London, which apart from producing designs for wallpaper and textile manufacturers also provided a complete interior design service. During the 1880s and 1890s, the majority of Silver Studio wallpaper designs were similar in style to those of Morris & Co. However, they were machine printed rather than hand-blocked making them less expensive. Arthur Silver also designed wallpapers that were in the Neo-Adam and Anglo-Japanese styles. In the early 1890s, the designers Harry Napper and John Illingworth Kay joined the studio, and later **Archibald Knox** and **Charles F. A. Voysey** also produced designs for the firm. From 1895 to the early 1900s, most of the Silver Studio designs were in the **Art Nouveau** style and often appeared in illustrated journals abroad, most notably *Der Moderne Stil*. In 1901, Arthur Silver's sons Harry and Rex took over the running of the studio in Brook Green, London. They produced colourful modernist designs in the 1930s and eventually closed in 1963.

▼ **Arthur Silver (attributed)**, *Poppy* wallpaper for Silver Studio, c. 1895

Bořek Šípek
b. 1949 *Prague*

Bořek Šípek studied furniture design at the School of Applied Arts, Prague,
graduating in 1968. Later, he studied architecture at the Hochschule für
Bildende Künste, Hamburg, and philosophy at the University of Stuttgart,
and continued his training as an architect at the Technische Hogeschool
in Delft. Between 1977 to 1979, he worked as a technical assistant in the
Institute of Industrial Design at the University of Hanover, and for the next
four years lectured in design theory at the University of Essen. After that, he
moved to the Netherlands, and in 1984 joined David Palterer (b. 1949) in
founding a design company, Alterego, based in Amsterdam. During the
1980s, he became celebrated for furniture designs such as his *Bambi* chair
(1988) that incorporated quirky forms and unusual combinations of materials and for his hand-blown glassware produced in Murano for Sawaya &
Moroni and in Novy Bor in his native country, the Czech Republic. He has
since designed furniture for Néotu, Driade, Sawaya & Moroni and **Vitra**,
glassware for Quartett and ceramics for Sèvres. Šípek works within the post-
modern idiom and rejects the rationalist industrial approach to design, believing that it "ignores function and disregards human individuality" in its
pursuit of technological prowess. For Šípek, design should be an expression
or interpretation of the culture in which it is created and should be more
about art than engineering.

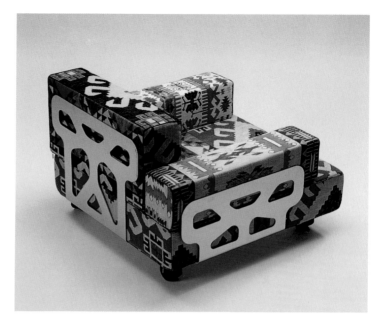

► *Model No. NF3400 Trundling Turk* chair for Tecta, originally designed 1954 – redesigned 1994

Peter and Alison Smithson both studied architecture at the University of Durham in Newcastle-upon-Tyne from 1944 to 1949. In 1950, they moved to London, and a year later became members of Team X – a breakaway group of ten young architects from the CIAM (Congrès Internationaux d'Architecture Moderne). During the 1950s, the Smithsons became internationally celebrated for their housing and town-planning proposals, including the urban study "Hauptstadt in Berlin" (1957–1958), the Golden Lane municipal building project in London and the Cluster Cities project. The latter proposal was particularly influential through its promotion of the idea of non-self-contained communities linked by a network of motorways. Their architecture during the 1950s and 1960s, which included Coventry Cathedral (1951) and the British Embassy in Brasilia (1964), was highly influential to the later emergence of Brutalism. They were also active members of the **Independent Group**, which was formed in 1952 to examine the emergence of American popular culture, and exhibited with other members at the 1954 "This is Tomorrow" exhibition at the Whitechapel Art Gallery, London. They designed the block-like *Trundling Turk* chair in 1954 and the minimalist tubular metal and acrylic *Pogo* dining chair in 1955. The following year, they designed the plastic *Egg* chair for their "House of Tomorrow". The Smithsons also wrote several publications on design and architectural theory.

Peter & Alison Smithson

Peter Smithson
b. 1923 *Stocton-on-Tees/Cleveland*

Alison Smithson
1928 *Sheffield*
1993 *London*

Ettore Sottsass

b. 1917 *Innsbruck, Austria*

▲ *Basilico* ceramic
teapot, 1969

Ettore Sottsass studied architecture at Turin Polytechnic from 1935 to 1939, and while still a student wrote articles on art and interior design in association with the Turin designer Luigi Spazzanpan. From 1942 to 1945, he served in the Italian Army, and after the war worked for the **Giuseppe Pagano** group of architects before establishing his own Milan-based office, The Studio, in 1947. He went to America in 1956 and briefly worked in the design office of **George Nelson**, assisting with *The Experimental House* – a system of product architecture. On his return to Italy in 1957, he was appointed artistic director of Poltronova and was involved in the design and production of contemporary furniture and lighting – including the *Mobili Grigi* fibreglass table and chairs (1970). He began working in 1958 as a design consultant to **Olivetti** and designed a number of well-known products for them including the *Logos 27* calculator (1963), the *Tekne 3* typewriter (1964), the *Praxis 48* typewriter (1964), the *Valentine typewriter* (with Perry **King**, 1969), the *Synthesis* office system (1973) and the *Lexicon 90* electric typewriter (1975). His most remarkable project for Olivetti, however, was the design of the *Elea 9003* main-frame computer (1959) for which he was awarded a **Compasso d'Oro** in 1959. In 1956, he began designing ceramics for the New York dealer William Hunter, and in 1961 he travelled to India, designing several series of ceramics that were inspired by Eastern forms and transcendentalism on his return. These included *Cemamiche della Tenebre* (1963), the *Offerta a Shiva* series (1964), *Yantra* (1968), *Tantra* (1969), and the gigantic totem-like *Indian Memories* (1972). In 1967, *Domus* published a series of photographs by Sottsass under the title *Memoires di panna montana* (Whipped cream memoirs), which visually documented "Swinging London". Following a prolonged lecture tour of universities in Britain, Sottsass was awarded an honorary degree by the **Royal College of Art, London** in 1968. He created a "House Environment" for the 1972 "Italy; The New Domestic Landscape" exhibition held at the **Museum of Modern Art, New York**, which included a prototype system of grey fibreglass "containers" comprising cooker/oven; sink/dishwasher; shower; toilet; shelves/storage; seat/bed and wardrobe modules. As a prominent member of the **Radical Design** move-ment, Sottsass became a founding member of **Global Tools** in 1973, and in 1976 was invited by the Cooper Hewitt Museum of Design, New York to exhibit a series of his photographs of buildings in desert or mountain loca-tions reflecting his ideas on architecture and design. During the same year,

▼ *Mobili Grigi* for Poltronova, 1970

the International Design Centre in Berlin organized a major retrospective
exhibition of his work, which was subsequently shown in Venice, Paris,
Barcelona, Jerusalem and Sydney. He was asked by the City of Berlin in 1978
to submit proposals for the re-building of the city's Museum of Modern Art,
and in 1979 participated in **Studio Alchimia**'s *BauHaus I* collection, designing furniture that incorporated plastic laminates. In 1981, in an attempt to
revive Radical Design, Sottsass established the **Memphis** design group with
Renzo Brugola, Mario and Brunella Godani, Ernesto Gismondi (b. 1931) and
Fausto Celati. As a long-time advocate of **Anti-Design** and skillful publicist,
Sottsass was the guiding light of Memphis, which was primarily made up of
young, recently graduated designers. The first Memphis exhibition, which
was held at the Arc '74 showroom in Milan in 1981, comprised several
monumental and colourful designs by Sottsass, including the *Casablanca*
(1981) and the *Carlton* (1981) case/shelf pieces. In 1981, together with fellow

▼ *Synthesis 45* office
chair for Olivetti,
1973

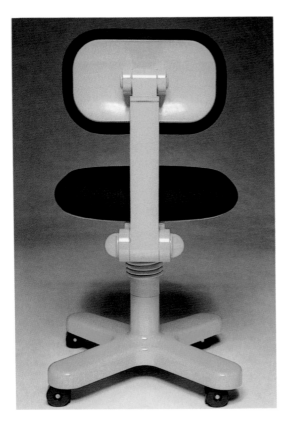

Memphis collaborators, Aldo Cibic
(b. 1955), **Matteo Thun** and **Marco
Zanini**, he co-founded the design
consultancy Sottsass Associati in
Milan. During the 1980s, the office
worked on the interior design of
Fiorucci stores, in close collaboration with **Michele De Lucchi** who
had previously assisted in the planning of the first Memphis exhibition. Sottsass Associati also
undertook several architectural
commissions, including Maison
Wolf in Ridgeway, Colorado
(1987–1988), the Esprit House in
Wels, Austria (1987–1988), the Bar
Zibibbo in Fukuoka, Japan (1988)
and Maison Cei in Florence, Italy
(1989–1992). Sottsass continued
designing furniture, metalware and
glassware for Memphis until 1985
and eventually disbanded the group
in 1988. During the 1980s, Sottsass
also produced designs for other
companies, including jewellery for
Cleto Munari, metalware for **Alessi**,

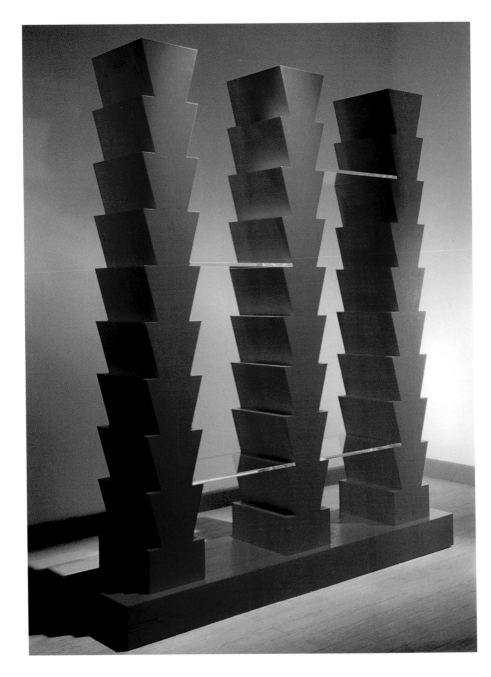

◄ *Adesso Perro*
lacquered wood and
glass shelves from
the *Rovine Collection*
for Design Gallery
Milano, 1992

◄ *Senza Spieganzioni*
ceramic vase from
the *Rovine Collection*
for Design Gallery
Milano, 1992

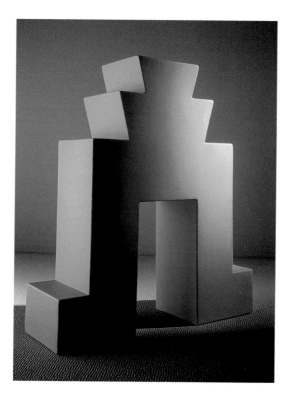

furniture, glass and ceramics for Design Gallery Milano and dinnerware
for Swid Powell. Described by his partner, the design critic Barbara Radice
(b. 1943), as a "cultural nomad", Sottsass has taken throughout his career
an almost "anthropological" approach to design – drawing references from
popular culture and other cultures as well as inspiration from his own
personal experiences. Sottsass was a leading figure of the Radical Design
movement in the 1970s and became the most important exponent of **Post-
Modernism** in design in the 1980s. Reflecting the compelling character of its
creator, Sottsass' work ranges from the poetic to the exuberantly colourful.
It is always questioning and could never be accused of being dull or bland.
In 1994, the Centre Georges Pompidou held a major retrospective of
Sottsass' work covering his remarkable and controversial career, which
has spanned over forty years.

George Sowden
b. 1942 *Leeds/ West Yorkshire*

George James Sowden studied architecture at Gloucester College of Art, graduating in 1968. He moved to Milan in 1970 and began working as a consultant in the **Olivetti** Studio designing calculators and computers in collaboration with **Ettore Sottsass** who headed the company's in-house design department. In 1980, Sowden set up a Milan-based design studio with his wife **Nathalie du Pasquier**, and in 1981 he became one of the founding members of **Memphis**. He contributed a great deal to the group – from early designs that incorporated boldly patterned laminates and brightly coloured textiles (often designed by Nathalie du Pasquier) such as the *Antibes* cabinet (1981), *Luxor* cupboard (1982), *Metropole* clock (1982), *Mamounia* chair (1985) and *Pierre* table (1981) to later more restrained wooden designs within the **Craft Revival** idiom, such as the *Liverpool* chair (1986) and *Gloucester* chair (1986). Sowden also designed textiles for Memphis, such as *Quadro* (1983) and *Triangolo* (1983). After the disbanding of the group in 1988, he worked both independently and in collaboration with du Pasquier, designing wallpapers for Rasch, ceramics for Swid Powell and metalware for **Alessi**. Other clients of Studio Sowden Design Associates' have included Olivetti, Italtel and Shiznoka of Japan. In 1990, Sowden's work was featured in a travelling exhibition organized by the Musées des Arts Décoratifs in Bordeaux, Marseilles and Lyons. In 1997, Alessi launched Sowden's brightly coloured *Dauphine* calculator designed specifically for use in kitchens, which with its organic form marked a completely new direction in his work. Sowden has won both a Smau prize and a **Compasso d'Oro**.

▼ *D'Antibes* vitrine for Memphis, 1981

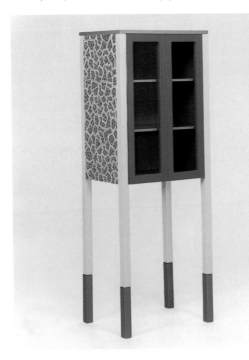

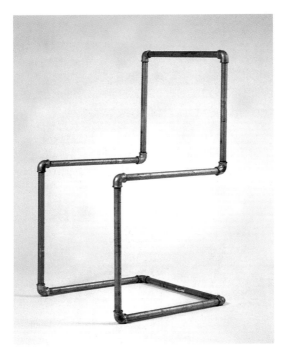

► Welded gas pipe
cantilever chair,
1926 (reconstructed
by Tecta)

Martinus Adrianus Stam studied drawing in Amsterdam from 1917 to 1919
and subsequently worked as a draughtsman for a Rotterdam architectural
practice until 1922. He then moved to Berlin where he met several leading
avant-garde architects including Hans Poelzig (1869–1936), Bruno Taut
(1880–1938) and **El Lissitzky**. In 1925, he returned to Amsterdam via Paris,
and a year later constructed a prototype of his revolutionary cantilevered
chair from welded gas pipes. At the 1926 meeting of architects held in
Stuttgart to discuss the organization of the Weissenhof Exhibition planned
for the following year, Stam showed drawings of this prototype, which inspired **Ludwig Mies van der Rohe** to design his own versions – the *MR10*
and *MR20* chairs (1927) – and **Marcel Breuer** and **Heinz** and **Bodo Rasch**
to follow suit. In 1927, together with his compatriots **Gerrit Rietveld** and
Hendrik Petrus Berlage, Stam became a founding member of the Congrès
Internationaux d'Architecture (CIAM). From 1931 to 1932, he worked in
Russia as a town planner and, in accordance with his socialist ideology, continued to design functionalist furniture. The cantilevered chair, invented by
Stam and perfected by Mies and Breuer, revolutionized structural form and
was one of the greatest achievements in 20th-century design.

Mart Stam

1899 *Purmerend,*
Netherlands
1986 *Goldbach,*
Switzerland

◀▼ Pages from Standard Möbel GmbH's "Das Neue Möbel" catalogue showing standardized furniture by Marcel Breuer, 1928

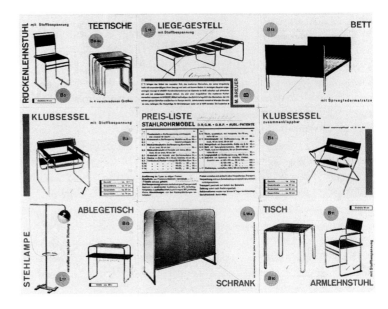

► Cover page from Thonet-Mundus' catalogue showing standardized furniture by Marcel Breuer, 1931

STAHLMÖBEL
Thonet
1 9 3 1
SYSTEM ARCHITEKT MARCEL BREUER

Standardization is a crucial aspect of industrial mass-production, for through its implementation, standard components can be fitted together with little or no adjustment and can be interchanged between products. The benefits of standardization are clear – it increases efficiency and productivity and allows manufacturers to effectively "clone" products, thus achieving a higher level of quality control. Certain members of the **Deutscher Werkbund**, such as Hermann Muthesius (1861–1927), advocated standardization and saw it as a powerful tool for the democratization of design. One of the first companies to implement a coherent system of standardization was **AEG**, and its integrated product-line designed by **Peter Behrens** reflected a deep understanding of modern manufacturing techniques. Later, the Dessau **Bauhaus** stressed the importance of standardization, and associated designers such as **Marcel Breuer**, **Gerhard Marcks** and **Wilhelm Wagenfeld** produced standardized designs intended for large-scale industrial production. Similarly in France, **Le Corbusier** designed a standardized housing unit (1925) and a range of systemized furniture (1928), which included standardized modular storage units. During the post-war years, standardization was fully embraced by industrial designers, because it offered the optimum means of manufacture and allowed the design of cost-effective product systems. **Charles and Ray Eames'** plastic shell group of chairs (1948–1950) and **Robin Day**'s *Polyprop* series (1962–1963), for instance, both employed single standardized seat shells that could be attached to a variety of bases to create different options.

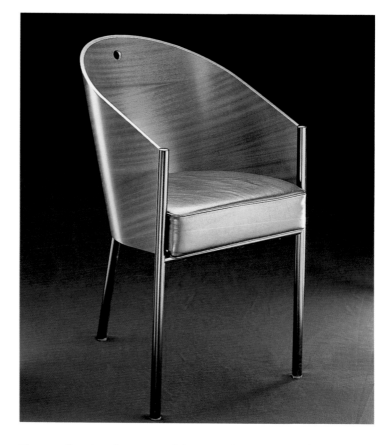

► *Costes* chair for Driade, 1984

Philippe Starck
b. 1949 *Paris*

► *Le paravent de l'autre* screen for Driade, 1992

The son of an aircraft engineer, Philippe Starck studied at the École Nissin de Camondo. In 1965, he won the La Vilette furniture competition and in 1968, was commissioned by L.Venturi and later **Quasar** to design inflatable furniture. The same year he founded his own company to produce this type of furniture. In 1969, Starck was appointed art director of the Pierre Cardin studio where he produced sixty-five furniture designs. During the 1970s, he worked as an independent designer and most notably created interiors for the nightclubs, La Main Bleue, Montreuil (1976) and Les Bains Douches, Paris (1978). After an around-the-world trip, Starck returned to Paris, founding his own manufacturing and distributing company, Starck Products, in 1980 to commercialize his earlier designs such as the *Francesa Spanish* chair (1970), *Easy Light* (1977) and the *Dr. Von Vogelsang* sofa (1978). In 1982, he received a prestigious commission to oversee the refurbishment of the

▲ *Dr. Glob* chairs and table for Kartell, 1990

President's private apartments at the Élysée Palace together with four other designers, and in 1984 he designed the interior of the Café Costes, Paris – both projects doing much to establish his international reputation. During the 1980s, Starck became the leading "superstar of design" and worked prolifically on numerous projects. He designed elegant and sumptuous interiors for hotels, most notably the Royalton Hotel, New York (1988) and Paramount Hotel, New York (1990) that were in the great French *décorateur* tradition. He also planned interiors for numerous nightclubs, shops (Kansäi, Yamamoto, Bocage, Creeks and Hugo Boss) and restaurants that incorporated his own designs for furniture, lighting, door handles, vases and other objects. He became celebrated for his numerous furniture designs – from the three-legged *Café Costes* chair (1984) and the injection-moulded plastic *Dr. Glob* chair (1990) to the elegant *Lord Yo* tub chair (1994) and collapsible *Miss Trip* chair (1996) – for manufacturers such as **Vitra**, Disform, Driade, Baleri, XO and Idée. Like his furniture, Starck's lighting and product designs were also given characterful names and sensual, appealing forms. Amongst the most commercially successful of these were the *Ara* table lamp for Flos (1988), and the *Juicy Salif* lemon squeezer (1990–1991), the *Max le Chinois*

◀ *Ara* lamp for Flos, 1988

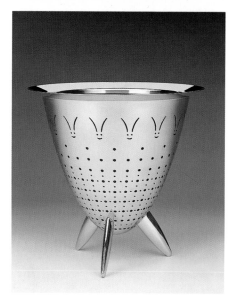

colander (1990–1991) and the *Hot Bertaa* kettle (1990–1991) for Alessi.
Apart from his product design work, Starck has also worked internationally
as an architect. His public buildings include the golden-horned Asahi Beer
Hall in Tokyo (1990), the sculptural Nani Nani building in Tokyo (1989), the
Le Baron Vert building in Osaka (1992) and the Groningen Museum (1993).
He has also designed several private residences, including Le Moult House
in Paris (1985–1987), Formentera House in the Balearics (1995), Placido
Arango Jr. House in Madrid (1996) and lastly, the wooden Starck House
(1994), the plans and construction information for which were retailed by
3 Suisses. During the 1990s, Starck designed consumer electronics for
Thomson, Saba and Telefunken that attempted to humanize technology.
His *Jim Nature* television (1994) for Saba, for instance, innovatively incorp-
orates high-density chip-board rather than plastic for its casing. He also
designed the *Moto 6,5* motorcycle (1995) as well as a prototype scooter for
Aprilia. Today, Starck acknowledges that much of the design produced during the 1980s and early 1990s, including some of his own, was narcissistic
"over-design" driven by novelty and fashion. He now promotes product
durability or longevity and has stated that this is the central issue of design
today, and that it can only be achieved if morality, honesty and objectivity
become an integral part of the design process. He has also argued that the
role of the designer is to create more "happiness" with less.

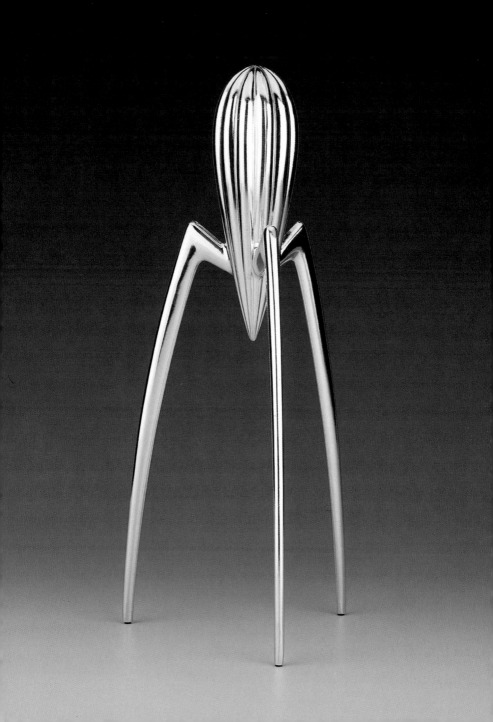

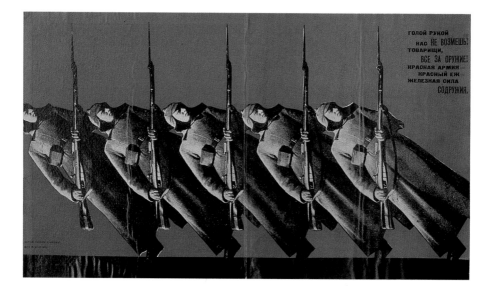

ГОЛОЙ РУКОЙ
НАС НЕ ВОЗМЕШЬ!
ТОВАРИЩИ,
ВСЕ ЗА ОРУЖИЕ!
КРАСНАЯ АРМИЯ —
КРАСНЫЙ ЕЖ —
ЖЕЛЕЗНАЯ СИЛА
СОДРУЖИЯ.

Varvara Stepanova

1894 *Kowno, Lithuania*
1958 *Moscow*

Varvara Stepanova initially studied at the Kazan Art School from 1910 to 1911 and after moving to Moscow in 1912, trained at the Stroganov Art School from 1913 to 1914. She also attended the Izo NKP (the department of fine art at Narkompros) from 1918. In Moscow, Stepanova was an active member of the **avant-garde** and worked as a painter and book illustrator. In 1922, she created costumes for the play, "Tarelkin's Death" that exemplified her functional approach to clothing design. Like her husband, **Alexander Rodchenko**, Stepanova was a leading figure of the Constructivist movement and also designed textiles from 1923 to 1924 for the Pervaya Gosudarstvennaya Sittenabivnaya Fabrika (First State Textile Factory) located near Moscow. During this period, she designed one hundred and fifty boldly geometric textiles, of which twenty-five or so were actually put into production. From 1924 to 1925, Stepanova was professor of textile design at the **Vkhutemas** (Higher State Artistic and Technical Workshops), and between 1923 and 1928 she also worked for the journals, *LEF* and *Novyi LEF*. From around 1925, Stepanova concentrated on graphics and collaborated with Rodchenko on the design of posters, books, magazines and typography. Together they pioneered the use of photomontage techniques to create striking propagandist images. During the 1930s, Stepanova produced designs for the journal *USSR in Construction* and continued to create dynamic photomontages that powerfully conveyed political messages.

▲ Endpaper for Vladimir Majakov-skij's book, "Groznij smech", 1932

Gustav Stickley trained with his father as a stonemason from 1869. He moved to Pennsylvania in 1875 where he worked in his uncle's factory, which specialized in the production of chairs with caned seats. In 1884, together with two of his brothers, Albert (1862–1928) and Charles (c. 1865–1928), he established the Stickley Brothers Company in Binghampton, New York, and was joined in 1888 by another two younger brothers, Leopold (1869–1957) and John George (1871–1921). This early business mainly produced reproduction furniture. Gustav, however, became interested in the reforming ideas of John Ruskin (1819–1900) and **William Morris**, and in 1898 visited Europe where he met **Charles F. A. Voysey** and was exposed to the work of other designers associated with the British **Arts & Crafts Movement**. On his return, he independently established the Gustav Stickley Company in Syracuse near Eastwood, New York, and expanding the company to form United Crafts in 1901. This venture, which was inspired by Morris' ideal of a self-sufficient community of craftspeople, was initially intended to be run as a profit-sharing guild with its workshops being supplied with timber from its own mill in the Adirondacks. As the enterprise grew, however, the craftsmen no longer received company stock and eventually the company was re-structured and re-named the Craftsman Workshops. The firm became widely

Gustav Stickley

1857 Osceola, Wisconsin
1942 Syracuse, New York

▼ Oak sideboard
for Craftsman
Workshops,
c. 1902–1903

◄ Wrought-iron and hammered copper chandelier for Craftsman Workshops, c. 1905

known for its well-crafted, solidly constructed and simple oak furniture in the mission style, and in 1901 Stickley launched *The Craftsman* magazine to promote this type of work as well as the socialist and artistic ideals of the Arts & Crafts Movement. In 1902, a metal workshop was established, which produced fittings for their furniture as well as chandeliers, vases, plaques and jardinères. In 1903, Harvey Ellis (1852–1904) joined the workshops, producing designs that often incorporated metal inlays and were more refined than Stickley's. The workshops' products were sold through mail-order catalogues and a twelve-storey New York showroom was opened in 1913. This over-ambitious expansion forced the company into bankruptcy in 1915 and it was subsequently absorbed into the L. J. G. Stickley company.

Adelgunde "Gunta" Stölzl studied at the Kunstgewerbeschule, Munich from 1913 to 1917. Between 1917 and 1918, she worked in a field hospital, and after the First World War resumed her studies at the Staatliches **Bauhaus**, Weimar. She initially trained under Paul Klee (1879–1940) and attended **Johannes Itten**'s Vorkurs classes. She also studied in the weaving workshop where she produced a woven seat and back for a chair designed by **Marcel Breuer** (1921) and designed textiles for **Walter Gropius**' Sommerfeld House (1921–1922).

Gunta Stölzl

1897 *Munich*
1983 *Küssnacht, Switzerland*

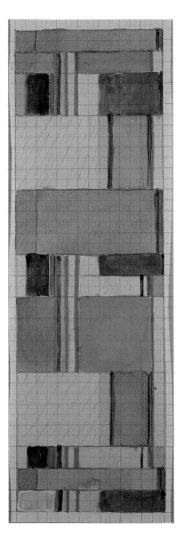

Around 1923, she passed her journeyman's examination, and in 1924 took courses in dyeing and production methods at the Fachschule für Textil-Industrie, Krefeld. During 1924, Stölzl established the Ontos weaving workshops in Herrliberg, near Zurich, which she ran for nine months. In 1925, she returned to the Bauhaus and became a master in the weaving workshop, which she subsequently headed from 1927. During her tenure, Stölzl established contacts with outside firms to produce and retail Bauhaus textiles. She left the Bauhaus in 1931, and with her former students, Gertrud Preiswerk and Heinrich Otto Hürlimann, founded S-P-H-Stoffe in Zurich. This studio and weaving workshop produced carpets and upholstering fabrics for Wohnbedarf and other companies. From 1937, she ran the workshop by herself, and in 1939 exhibited at the Swiss National Exhibition. During the 1950s, she produced gobelin tapestries, and in 1967 closed her studio. Stölzl was the single most important textile designer at the Bauhaus, and during her career made the crucial transition from craft to industrial-production.

◄ Watercolour design for a textile, c. 1925–1926

Marianne Straub

b. 1909 *Amriswil, Switzerland*

Marianne Straub began weaving as a child and later trained under Heinrich Otto Hürlimann (a former pupil of **Gunta Stölzl**) from 1928 to 1931 at the Kunstgewerbeschule, Zurich. Interested in industrial rather than craft methods of textile manufacture, Straub moved to England and studied at Bradford Technical College, where from 1932 to 1933 she learnt power loom manufacturing techniques. However, she also worked briefly at Ethel Mairet's (1872–1952) Gospels workshop, Ditchling, which was noted for its hand-woven textiles and use of natural dyes. From 1934 to 1937, Straub acted as a design consultant to the Rural Industries Board, which looked after the interests of the Welsh woollen mills. Straub was able to revitalize the flagging weaving industry there through her technical knowledge and modern designs, which included upholstery textiles used by **Gordon Russell**. In 1937, she was appointed chief designer of the Bolton-based textile company,

▼ *Surrey* curtain fabric for Warner & Sons, 1951

Helios – a subsidiary of Barlow & Jones. She designed a modern range of printed and woven textiles for the company and, despite wartime restrictions, made innovative use of different yarns. In 1947, she became managing director of Helios, which was taken over by Warner & Sons in 1950. She was invited as a representative of Warner's to participate in the Festival Pattern Group, which was established for the Festival of Britain by the director of the Council of Industrial Design, Mark Hartland Thomas. The biomorphic patterning of her rayon and wool *Surrey* curtain fabric (1951), specifically designed for the exhibition, was inspired by the dye lines of certain crystals and reflected the prevalent interest in crystallography and molecular chemistry. Straub also designed textiles for Heals and Tamesa Fabrics and taught at the **Royal College of Art** and the Central School of Arts & Crafts, London.

► *Jumo* Bakelite
streamlined lamp for
Jumo Brevete, Paris,
1945

Streamlining – the application of rounded, smoothly finished, often tear-drop shaped forms – was first used in early 20th-century transportation technologies, such as shipping, aircraft and automobiles, to improve hydro-dynamic and aerodynamic performance when moving at high speeds. By the 1930s, however, streamlined forms were being used not for functional rea-sons but to make household products look sleeker and more appealing to the consumer. In America, the Wall Street Crash of 1929 and the ensuing depression together with the implementation of the price-fixing National Recovery Act in 1932, meant that manufacturers were having to operate within a fiercely competitive market. Rather than investing in the develop-ment of new products, many manufacturers employed designers to re-style or "streamline" existing products to make them look new. Streamlining also assisted manufacturers in differentiating their products from those of their competitors, while annual restyling programmes helped accelerate the aes-

thetic life-cycle of products and, thereby, increase sales. Interestingly, many of the American designers who became noted for their streamlined designs, such as **Raymond Loewy, Norman Bel Geddes, Henry Dreyfuss** and **Walter Dorwin Teague,** had previously worked as fashion illustrators, stage designers and commercial artists. By using clay models, designers such as these were able to create sleek modern-looking forms for a whole range of consumer goods including refrigerators, vacuum cleaners, radios, cameras and telephones. Many of the casings for these products were made of Bakelite, a thermoset plastic eminently suited to the moulding of streamlined forms. In 1934, Loewy's *Coldspot* streamlined refrigerator for Sears was the first domestic appliance to be marketed on its looks rather than its performance. By the 1940s, the use of streamlining was widespread and its practitioners became highly celebrated. In 1949, Loewy was the first designer to be featured on the cover of *Time* magazine and his picture was accompanied with the telling copy-line, "He streamlines the sales curve". By "adding value" to products and boosting sales, streamlining helped American manufacturing industries regain strength and profitability.

◄ **Bill Stumpf &
Don Chadwick**, *Equa*
office chair for
Herman Miller, 1984

Bill Stumpf trained in industrial design at the University of Illinois and studied environmental design at the University of Wisconsin, graduating in 1968. He was subsequently commissioned by **Herman Miller** to design a comfortable and affordable office chair to be sold alongside **Robert Propst**'s *Action Office II* workstations. The resulting design, *Ergon* (1970), was one of the first office chairs – as its name suggests – to be designed ergonomically. Between 1970 and 1973, Stumpf was vice-president of research at Herman Miller, and in 1973 he established his own design consultancy in Winona, Minnesota. In 1977, he founded a partnership with **Don Chadwick**, and together they designed the next generation of office chairs for Herman Miller, the *Equa* range (1984). The same year, Stumpf also designed the *Etho*space open-plan office system, and in 1992 he and Chadwick co-designed the revolutionary *Aeron* chair, which, owing to its breathable Pellicle mesh, does away with the need for time-consuming upholstery and has a production cycle of only one minute. Like his predecessors at Herman Miller, **George Nelson** and Robert Propst, Stumpf is a skillful innovator whose work has had a significant impact not only on the company's product range but on office environments in general.

Bill Stumpf
b. 1936 *St. Louis, Missouri*

► Plate (pre-revolutionary blank) decorated with Suprematist motif for State Porcelain Factory in Petrograd, 1923

► Plate (pre-revolutionary blank) decorated with Suprematist motif for State Porcelain Factory in Petrograd, 1923

Nikolai Suetin

1897 *Kaluzhshaya Gubenia, Russia*
1954 *Leningrad*

Nikolai Mikhailovich Suetin studied under **Kasimir Malevich** at the Vitebsk art school from 1918 to 1922. He became a founding member of Malevich's art group, Posnovis (later Unovis) in 1920, and moved to Petrograd in 1922 with a number of other designers including Malevich and Ilya Chashnik (1902–1929), and a year later began designing for the State Porcelain Factory there. During this period, Suetin and Malevich co-designed several Suprematist architectural constructions known as "arkhitektony" and "planity". Between 1923 and 1926, Suetin also headed the department of general ideology at the Inkhuk (State Institute of Artistic Culture) in Petrograd. In 1925, he participated in the "Exposition Internationale des Arts Décoratifs et Industriels Modernes", and from 1927 to 1930 worked in the experimental laboratories of the Art History Institute, Leningrad, producing numerous designs for furniture and architecture. Between 1932 and 1954, Suetin was the artistic director of the Lomonosov State Porcelain Factory, initially designing Suprematist ceramics and later executing folk style designs. As a leading member of the Russian **avant-garde**, Suetin also designed the Soviet pavilions for the 1937 Paris "Exposition Internationale des Arts et Techniques dans la Vie Moderne" and the 1939 New York World's Fair.

◄ Bent plywood
armchair for Makers
of Simple Furniture,
1933–1934

Gerald Summers studied carpentry as part of the curriculum at Eltham College, and after leaving school in 1915, at the age of sixteen, he began a year-long apprenticeship with the engineering firm, Ruston, Proctor & Co. in Lincolnshire. In 1916, he enlisted in the military, and while in France began thinking about "dealing with wood and doing things with wood". After 1918, Summers became a manager at the Field and Air Division of Marconi's Wireless Telegraph Co. Ltd. While there, he met his future wife and colleague, Majorie Amy Butcher, and her desire to refurnish her accommodation led Summers to design a dressing table and wardrobe. This project fuelled the idea of opening a furniture manufacturing business, and around 1932 the couple established Makers of Simple Furniture in Fitzroy Street, London. The company produced modern furniture from bent plywood, the production of which was helped considerably by the owner of Isokon, Jack Pritchard, who shared his technical expertise with Summers. In 1933, Summers began experimenting with thin and flexible aeroplane ply, which allowed him to produce highly innovative and more organic constructions, such as his single-form Armchair (1933–1934). However, the company was forced to close in 1940 due to wartime restrictions on raw materials.

Gerald Summers
1899 *Alexandria, Egypt*
1967 *Barnet/London*

▶ *Quaderna* table for Zanotta, 1971 – evolved from the group's earlier "Istogrammi d'architettura" project of 1969 that employed grid-patterned plastic laminates by Abet

Superstudio
Founded 1966
Florence

Superstudio was founded in December 1966 in Florence by Adolfo Natalini (b. 1941) and Cristano Toraldo di Francia (b. 1941), initially to conduct theoretical research into urban planning and systems design. The year of its formation coincided with the worst flooding of the River Arno in living memory, and in some ways both events symbolized the destruction of traditional culture. Superstudio questioned the validity of **rationalism** in design and sought to replace the city as a system of social hierarchy with "a new free egalitarian state". Its provocative projections of "super structures" such as "Il momento continuo" (1969), pointed to a dream-like world without consumer products, where architecture would be either unfunctional and auto-destructing or symbolic. The group took part in the two "Superarchitettura" exhibitions held in Pistoia and Módena in 1966 and 1967 respectively, and in 1970 collaborated with Gruppo 9999 in the establishment of the Separate School for Expanded Conceptual Architecture (Sine Space School). During the early 1970s, Alessandro Magris (b. 1935), Roberto Magris, Gian Pietro Frassisinelli and Alessandro Poli joined the group. In 1972, Superstudio contributed to the "Counterdesign as Postulation" section at the "Italy: The New Domestic Landscape" exhibition held at the **Museum of Modern Art, New York**. Superstudio's work, which often incorporated grid-like patterns symbolizing infinity, was central to the evolution of **Radical Design**.

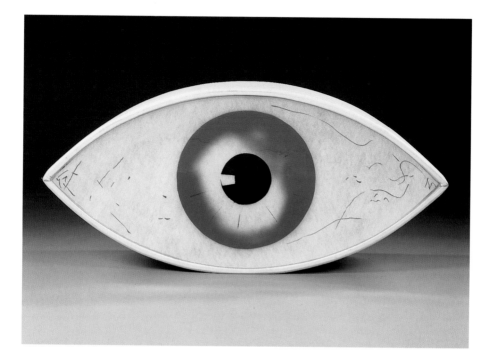

Surrealism was directly inspired by the researches into the subconscious and the analysis of dreams undertaken by Sigmund Freud (1856–1939). As an artistic movement, it can also be seen to have evolved from Symbolism and Dada, which it replaced. The poet, Guillaume Apollinaire (1880–1918) is thought to have first coined the term in 1917, while the poet André Breton (1896–1966) wrote the *Manifeste du Surréalisme* in 1924. In this publication, he defined Surrealism as "pure psychic automatism, by which it is intended to express ... the real process of thought. It is the dictation of thought, free from any control by the reason and of any aesthetic or moral pre-occupation." During the 1920s, proponents of Surrealism such as Salvador Dalí (1904–1989) and Man Ray (1890–1976) created assemblages that sought to combine objectivity with subjectivity, reason with nonsense and the conscious with the subconscious. During the 1930s, the Surrealist movement became increasingly politicized and many of its members became actively involved with the Communist Party. Its anti-rational stance countered preconceived notions of what art or design could be and blurred the distinctions between them – Salvador Dalí's *Mae West* sofa of c. 1936, for instance, can be considered a functional work of art.

Surrealism

▲ **Man Ray**, *Le Témoin (The Witness)* chair for Gavina, 1971

The term, Swiss School refers to a typographic style developed in Zurich and Basel prior to and during the Second World War. As Switzerland remained politically neutral during the war, Swiss designers were able to develop the typographic theories that had been advanced earlier at the **Bauhaus**. Ernst Keller (1891–1968), who taught at the Kunstgewerbeschule in Zurich from 1918, had previously established a national reputation for typographic excellence and innovative graphic design. His student, Theo Ballmer (1902–1965), who trained at the Bauhaus, combined a rational approach with spatial principles inspired by **De Stijl** to create a grid system for layouts. The Swiss School's graphics of the 1920s were typified by the use of photomontage and new typefaces (ie. sans-serif typography). During the 1930s, **Max Bill**, who had also trained at the Bauhaus, introduced a form of asymmetrical layout to the Swiss School that was influenced by **Constructivism**. Sometimes referred to as the "International Graphic Style", in the 1930s and 1940s the Swiss School was characterized by the use of sans-serif type,

▼ Karl Gerstner,
auch du bist liberal
(You too are liberal)
poster, 1959

auch Du bist liberal

"white space" and "objective photography" (ie. realistic images). The resulting reductivist aesthetic was precise, direct and clinical. The Swiss School's graphics were displayed at the 1939 "Swiss National Exhibition", and during the 1950s its influence was spread internationally through the journal *New Graphic Design*, which was launched in 1959. The success of Swiss School typefaces, such as *Univers* 1954 designed by **Adrian Frutiger** and *Helvetica* redesigned in 1957 by Max Mieddinger (1910–1980), also contributed much to the Swiss School's international standing. During the 1960s, Karl Gerstner (b. 1930) and Wolfgang Weingart (b. 1941) began experimenting with more expressive compositions while continuing to follow the modern approach of the Swiss School.

◀◀ *Pi* pedestal table for Néotu, 1984

◀ *Perrier* drinking glass for Perrier, 1996

◀◀ Biscuit porcelain table centrepiece from the *Collection Satragno* for CRAFT (Centre de Recherche sur les Arts du Feu et de la Terre) of Limoges, 1994

◀ *Message* briefcase for Maroquinerie Delvaux, 1992

Martin Székély studied at the École Estienne and later at the École Boulle in Paris. In 1979, twenty-five pieces of furniture he had designed for Souvagnat were displayed at the Salon du Meuble in Paris. He subsequently designed his *Pi* chaise-longue for VIA in 1983, and two years later his *Pi* Collection was launched by Néotu. These early designs possessed very graphic qualities and epitomized the sleek Matt Black style. By the late 1980s, Székély's furniture, such as his *Marie-France* chair for Néotu (1989), became more sculptural and colourful. He also designed several interiors for the Musée de Picardie in Amiens (1986–1992), the Boutique Régina Rubens in Paris (1992) and the Commissariat de Police in La Courneuve (1992) that incorporated bold elemental forms. He designed the podium for the 1992 Winter Olympic Games in Albertville and pews for **Mario Botta**'s Cathédral d'Evry in 1994. During the 1990's, Szekley also produced notable industrial designs including a range of street equipment for JC Decaux comprising; street lighting, a telephone kiosk, public information stands, benches, bollards and sign posts.

Martin Székély
b. 1956 *Paris*

Kazuhide Takahama

b. 1930 *Mijasaki, Japan*

Kazuhide Takahama studied architecture at the Industrial University of Tokyo, graduating in 1953. He adopted the **Modern Movement**'s functionalist approach to design yet retained a characteristic Japanese sensitivity to materials and aesthetics. At the X Milan Triennale exhibition in 1954 he met the furniture manufacturer, Dino Gavina, who subsequently invited Takahama to work for him in Italy. Takahama's first design for Gavina was the geometrically severe *Naeko* sofa-bed (1957). His later *Dadà* modular storage unit (1965) was also highly rational and comprised either stackable wooden or injection-moulded plastic cubes. In 1965, Takahama produced the sculptural *Suzanne, Raymond* and *Marcel* seating ranges – named in tribute to Marcel Duchamp (1887–1968) and his siblings – that were constructed of blocks of polyurethane foam. Three years later, he designed the *ESA* system (1968) of hexagonal polyurethane foam blocks that could be assembled into either beds, sofas or chairs. He also designed furniture that was constructed of simple geometric plywood elements with traditional lacquered finishes such as his *Kazuhide* chair (1968), *Antella* drop-leaf table (1978) and *Bramante* cupboard (1973). He produced several innovative lamps for Gavina, including the *Saori* range (1973), which paid homage to the artist Lucio Fontana (1899–1968). Takahama's very pure designs achieved a strong internationalism through his skilful blending of elements of Eastern and Western cultures.

▲ *Suzanne* seating for Gavina and Knoll International, 1965

Roger Tallon studied electrical engineering in Paris from 1947 to 1949 and then worked as a designer at Studio Avas from 1951 to 1953. He met the industrial designer and theoretician Jacques Viénot (1893–1959) in 1953, and subsequently joined the design consultancy Technès, where he became manager of research in 1960. While there, Tallon designed numerous innovative products, including cameras for SEM (1957 & 1961), a typewriter for Japy (1960), a portable television for Téléavia (1963), the *Module 400* furniture range (1964) and a polished aluminium modular spiral staircase for Lacloche (1966), drinking glasses for Daum (1970) and the *Chronograph X* watch for LIP (1973). He also worked as a consultant designing Frigidaire refrigerators for General Motors from 1957 to 1964. He began teaching at ENSAD (École Nationale Supérieure des Arts Décoratifs) in 1963 and established the multi-disciplinary design consultancy, Design Programmes SA in 1973. During the late 1960s and 1970s, Tallon acquired an international reputation for his transportation design, which included work for Mexico City's underground system (1969) and the *Corail* locomotive (1977) for SNCF. In

Roger Tallon
b. 1929 *Paris*

▼ *Module 400* chairs for Éditions Lacloche, 1964

1983, he co-founded the design partnership, ASDA+Partners with **Pierre Paulin** and Michel Schreiber (b. 1950), and continued designing trains including the high-speed *TGV-Atlantique* (1988) for SNCF and the *Trans-Euro-Star* shuttle for Euro-Tunnel (1987). In 1973, he was elected an Honorary Royal Designer for Industry in London, and in 1985 was awarded the French National Grand Prix for industrial design. Tallon is one of France's foremost industrial designers and his highly engineered designs are both materially and structurally innovative.

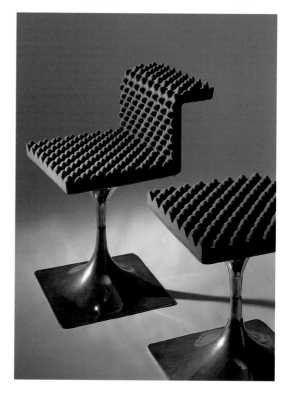

Vladimir Tatlin

1885 *Moscow*
1953 *Novodevitchi, Russia*

▼ Model of the
*Monument to the
Third International,*
1919–1920

Vladimir Tatlin studied at the Moscow Institute of Painting, Sculpture & Architecture and the Penza Art School. He initially worked as a painter, and in 1911 became associated with **Kasimir Malevich**. He met Pablo Picasso (1881–1973) in 1913, and was so inspired by his collages that he began creating relief constructions himself made from sheet metal, glass, wire and *objets trouvés*. In the 1910s, Tatlin became closely associated with the Russian Futurists – a literary group who viewed political and artistic revolution as interdependent. As a prominent member of the Russian **avant-garde**, he collaborated with **Alexander Rodchenko** and G. Yakulow (1884–1928) on the design of Constructivist furnishings for the Café Pittoresk (1917). Following the 1917 Revolution, he was put in charge of implementing Lenin's Plan for Monumental Propaganda. To this end, he designed a Monument to the Third International (1919–1920), a model of which was exhibited in Moscow and Petrograd. This unrealized and possibly unrealizable spiralling structure was to have been constructed from iron girders and to have had revolving halls suspended from it. The monument was inspired by other structures such as the Eiffel Tower, and through its dynamic modern construction symbolized the revolutionary desire for

a new world order. Its sense of tension and dynamism also exemplified Russian **Constructivism**. In 1918, Tatlin was made head of the Izo NKP (The department of fine arts at Narkompros) in Moscow, and from 1919 to 1920 he also directed the painting department at the Svomas (later known as **Vkhutemas**). In 1921, he established a studio at Petrograd to concentrate on "volume, material and construction". His designs included a cantilevered tubular metal chair (1927–1928) and the *Letatlin* glider (1932). He established a "production art" department at the Petrograd Museum of Artistic Culture in 1921 and taught industrial design at the Vkhutemas from 1927. Tatlin's fascination with the "culture of materials" inspired both his teachings and his work.

► *Model No. 114*
Executive desk lamp
for the Polaroid
Corporation, 1939

Walter Dorwin Teague attended evening classes at the Art Students League, New York from 1903 to 1907, and subsequently worked as an illustrator for a mail-order catalogue and for Hampton Advertising Agency, New York. In 1912, he established his own studio and worked as a freelance typographer and graphic designer. He took a trip to Paris in 1926, and while there was influenced by the work of **Le Corbusier**. On his return to New York, he founded an industrial design consultancy – one of the first of its kind – and began designing cameras for Eastman Kodak, including the *Bantam Special* (1936) that was more user-friendly and compact than earlier models. In 1930, assisted by his son, Teague designed the body of the *Marmon Model 16* car, which with its streamlined form produced less air resistance than other contemporary automobiles. He also designed other streamlined products –glassware for Corning Glass Works and its Steuben division, kitchenware for Pyrex, pens and lighters for Scripto, lamps for Polaroid, mimeo-

Walter Dorwin
Teague
1883 *Decatur, Indiana*
1960 *Flemington, New
Jersey*

graphs for A. B. Dick, radios for Sparton and the Centennial piano for Steinway. Apart from consumer products, Teague also designed a plastic truck body for UPS, supermarkets for Colonial Stores, interiors for the Boeing 707 airliner, United States pavilions at various international trade fairs, exhibition interiors for Ford, service stations for Texaco and a number of exhibits at the 1939 New York World's Fair, including his gigantic cash register for the National Cash Register Company. He also published his influential book, *Design This Day – The Technique of Order in the Machine Age* (1940), which celebrated the potential of machines and the "new and thrilling style" of the Machine Age. Teague's innovative and functional designs arose from his interest in proportion and symmetry and his espousal of mechanized methods of production.

◄ *Bluebird* radio for
Sparton
Corporation,
1934–1936

Giuseppe Terragni trained at the technical school in Como and later studied architecture at the Politecnico di Milano, graduating in 1926. The same year, he became a founder of the Gruppo Sette – a Milanese association of young rationalist architects. In 1927, he founded an office with his brother, Attilio, in Como, and subsequently designed the controversial five-storey Novocomum apartment block in Como (1927–1928). He was one of the foremost Italian Rationalists and participated in the first exhibition of "National Architecture" held in Rome in 1928. He designed the Fascist party headquarters in Como – the Casa del Fascio (1932–1936). For this box-like building, he designed site-specific furniture, including his *Sant'Elia* chromed tubular steel and leather cantilevered chair (1936) and the *Follia* chair (1934–1936). Other projects of his, included the Asilo Sant'Elia kindergarten, Como (1936), the Casa Bianca, Seveso (1936–1937), the Casa del Fascio, Lissone (1938–1939) and the Casa Giuliani Frigerio, Como (1939–1940). At the outbreak of the Second World War, he enlisted in the army, and in 1943 returned to Italy from the Russian front having suffered a nervous breakdown, and died a few days later. Terragni's refined designs exemplified the hard-edged and highly formalized style of Italian **Rationalism**.

Giuseppe Terragni
1904 *Meda, Italy*
1943 *Como, Italy*

► Page from
Gebrüder Thonet's
catalogue, 1904

► *Model No. 14*
armchair for
Gebrüder Thonet,
c. 1859

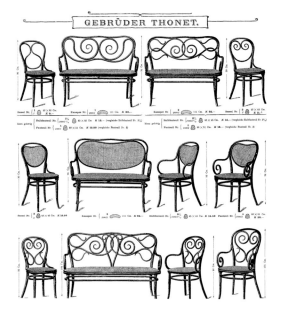

Michael Thonet

1796 Boppard, Germany
1871 Vienna

Michael Thonet established a furniture workshop in his home town of Boppard am Rhein in 1819, and from around 1830 he began experimenting with laminated wood and produced a number of innovative chairs in the Biedermeier style. He showed these at the 1841 Koblenz and 1842 Mainz exhibitions and their success led the chancellor of Austria, Count Metternich, to invite him to Vienna. The Austrian court granted Thonet a patent for his new process for bending wood laminates, and he began working with the Viennese cabinet-maker, Carl Leistler on seat furniture for the Palais Liechtenstein. With the backing of Prinz Liechtenstein and the British architect, P. H. Desvignes (1804–1883), Thonet and his sons, Franz, Michael, August and Joseph, set up their own furniture workshop in 1849. This enterprise was based in Gumpendorf – a suburb of Vienna – and for the next two years the Thonet family concentrated on developing techniques for mass-producing furniture, including the steam bending of solid wood. The Thonet's exhibited their new furniture designs at the 1851 Great Exhibition in London and won a bronze medal. By 1853, Gebrüder Thonet, as the company was now known, had moved into larger premises and were fully mass-producing their chair designs, the forms of which, while influenced by the contemporary Rococo

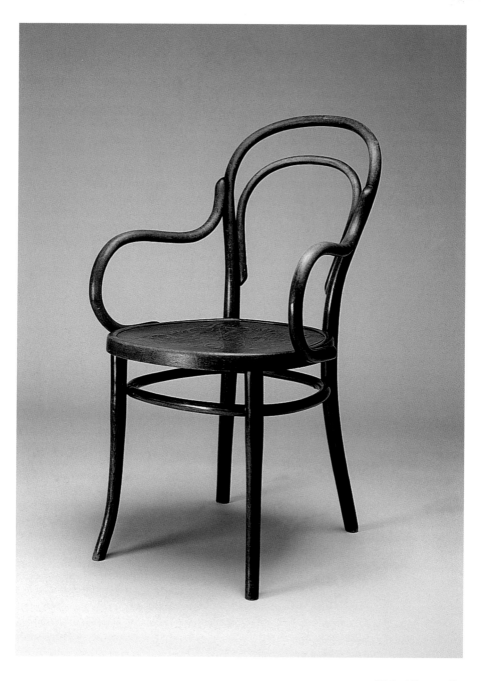

THONET

▲ Gebrüder Thonet advertisement showing Marcel Breuer's *Model B32* chair, 1933

Revival fashion for curvilinear lines, were distinguished by a reduction of elements and the elimination of extraneous ornament. They opened their first factory in 1857 in Koritschan and expanded rapidly over the following years. The remarkable success of the company stemmed from their adherence to mechanized methods of production, which allowed them to sell their products at very competitive prices. In 1860, for example, the firm's best-known model, the *No. 14* chair, cost less than a bottle of wine, and by 1891 a staggering 7,300,000 of these ubiquitous café chairs had been sold. By the early 1900s, several leading Viennese architects, including **Josef Hoffmann**, had begun designing furniture for Gebrüder Thonet in the Secessionist style. In 1929, a French subsidiary of the firm was established, Thonet Frères, that produced progressive tubular metal furniture designed by **Marcel Breuer**, **Ludwig Mies van der Rohe** and **Le Corbusier** among others. The production of this furniture was later moved to Frankenberg, but Thonet continue to operate and manufacture re-issues of their earlier seating as well as contemporary designs.

Matteo Thun studied architecture at the Università di Firenze, graduating in 1975, then trained as a sculptor at the Academy of Oskar Kokoschka, Salzburg, and also studied at the University of California, Los Angeles. On the recommendation of **Marco Zanini,** Thun was invited to join **Ettore Sottsass's** design studio, Sottsass Associati, and he subsequently became a founding member of **Memphis**, designing several ceramics for the group's first collection including the *Nefertiti* teaset and the *Tuja* stem vase with bold geometric forms and grey and red patterning. In 1982, he designed an extensive range of white porcelain wares for Memphis, which were more refined than his earlier ceramics and incorporated bizarre forms including cloud-like elements. These designs were partly-decorated with a mottled screen-printed motif and included the *Manitoba* porcelain tray, the *Titicaca* vase, the *Kariba* fruit bowl, the *Garda* amphora, the *Chad* teapot, the *Onega* cup and the *Ladoga* vase. Four Thun teapots from 1982 also incorporated unusual wave-like, geometric and zig-zag forms that completely countered all notions of functional **Good Design**. Thun began teaching at the Kunstgewerbeschule in Vienna in 1982, where his students assisted him with his project "In the Spirit of the USA" – a limited-edition ceramics commission from Villeroy & Boch. In 1983, he designed his pure white *Volga* and *Danube* stem vases and three ceiling lamps. Thun left Sottsass Associati in 1984, and a year later published a manifesto entitled *The Baroque Bauhaus*, which urged designers to integrate historical decorative styles in their work. He also designed the *Settimana* metal chest (1985) and the *Stillight* lighting range (mid-1980s) for Bieffeplast, the *Via Col Vento* vase for Lobmeyr (1986) and rugs for Vorwerk's *Dialog* collection (1988).

Matteo Thun
b. 1952 *Bolzano, Italy*

▼ *Danubio* and *Volga* vases manufactured by Porcellane d'Arte San Marco for Memphis, 1983

Louis Comfort Tiffany was the son of Charles Lewis Tiffany (1812–1902), who in 1853 established the well-known New York firm of silversmiths and jewellers, Tiffany & Co.. Louis Comfort studied painting in 1986 under George Inness (1825–1894), and the following year exhibited his work at the National Academy of Design, New York. He began experimenting with glass in 1873, and in 1879 established a professional decorating business, with Candace Wheeler, Lockwood de Forest and Samuel Colman, known as Louis C. Tiffany & Associated Artists, which received many commissions including interiors for Mark Twain's house (1880–1981) and several rooms for President Chester A. Arthur at the White House (1882–1883). The decorating firm was disbanded in 1883, and replaced by a new enterprise, the Tiffany Glass Company. This became the Tiffany Glass & Decorating company in 1892, when Tiffany established a glass furnace at Corona, Long Island. A year later, they began producing iridescent *Favrile* glassware and Tiffany displayed his "Byzantine" chapel – a dazzling array of leaded windows, glass mosaics, pressed glass electric lamps and glass chandeliers – at the "World's Columbian Exposition" in Chicago. The *Favrile* vases, conceived as "art glass", were quite unlike any glass being produced elsewhere in America at the time. **Siegfried Bing** exhibited Tiffany's glassware and leaded panels at his Maison L'Art Nouveau gallery in Paris from 1895 to 1899. Tiffany also exhibited at the 1900 Paris "Exposition Universelle", and the same year changed the name of his company to Tiffany Studios. On the death of his father in 1902, he became design director of Tiffany & Co. for whom he designed jewellery. Tiffany Studios continued to produce his exquisite **Art Nouveau** designs until the closure of the Corona glass furnaces in 1924.

Louis Comfort Tiffany
1848 *New York*
1933 *New York*

◄ *Pond Lily* lamp for Tiffany Studios, c. 1900

▼ *Jack-in-the-Pulpit* vase for Tiffany Studios, 1907

Total Design

Founded 1963
Netherlands

▲ Signage
programme for
Schiphol Airport in
Amsterdam, 1967

Total Design was founded in Amsterdam in 1963 by the typographer Wim Crouwel (b. 1928) and four colleagues, including the furniture designer Friso Kramer (b. 1922) and the graphic designer Benno Wissing (b. 1923). The word "total" in the consultancy's name refers to the multi-disciplinary nature of their operations. One of their first commissions was to develop a new **corporate identity** for the oil company PAM (1964), which involved not only the design of logos but also the restyling of petrol pumps and service stations. In 1965, Total Design was asked to submit proposals for a new "routing system" for Schiphol Airport, Amsterdam. Wissing directed the resulting scheme (1967), which was one of the earliest programmes of comprehensive signage. The visual clarity of this specially developed system, with its sans-serif lettering and bold symbols, was extremely influential to later public transport signage throughout the world. Total Design subsequently grew into a large organization that was divided up into creative teams. The consultancy notably developed a standardized layout grid system and single typeface for the Stedelijk Museum's catalogues, and later created a strong corporate identity for the Dutch post office, PTT (1978–1979). Total Design's bold and simplified graphics and typography were influenced by **Swiss School** minimalism and reintroduced rectilinearity to Dutch graphic design.

The son of a sign painter, Jan Tschichold studied graphic design at the Akademie für Graphische Künste und Buchgewerbe in Leipzig from 1919 to 1921. In 1923, he visited the **Bauhaus** exhibition in Weimar and was highly influenced by **László Moholy-Nagy**'s graphics and the school's promotion of "New Typography". He subsequently became a leading exponent of this new approach to typography, which was characterized by the use of geometric and ahistorical sans-serif lettering and simplified asymmetrical layouts. His manifesto entitled *elementare typographie*, published in 1925, set out his ten "elementary" principles, which stressed the functional, social and communicative aspects of typography. He also advocated the use of photography to produce powerful graphic imagery, as in his film posters for the Phoebus-Palast cinemas. From 1926, he taught at the Hochschule in Munich, and in 1928 published his seminal book, *Die neue Typographie*. In 1933, to escape Nazi persecution, he emigrated to Switzerland where he explored "classical" typographic forms. He later worked for Penguin Books in England from 1946 to 1949 devising standardized layouts. One of the most influential proponents of modern typography, Tschichold was also an important contributor to the **Swiss School**.

Jan Tschichold
1902 *Leipzig, Germany*
1974 *Locarno, Switzerland*

▲ Poster for the exhibition "der berufsphotograph, sein werkzeug – seine arbeiten" (The professional photographer, his work – his tools) held in Basel, 1938

▶ Nickel-plated
brass teamaker
for Metallwerkstatt
Wolfgang Tümpel,
1927

**Wolfgang
Tümpel**
1903 *Bielefeld,
Germany*
1978 *Herdecke,
Germany*

Wolfgang Tümpel served an apprenticeship as a gold and silversmith in the August Schlüter workshop and attended classes at the Kunstgewerbeschule in Bielefeld from 1921 to 1922. For the next three years, he trained at the Weimar **Bauhaus**, taking both the preliminary course and a silversmith apprenticeship, and then studied metalwork under Karl Müller (1888–1972), completing his journeyman's exam at the Kunstgewerbeschule Burg Giebichenstein in Halle in 1926. He became a member of the Gesellschaft für Goldschmiedekunst in 1927 and established the Werkstatt für Gefäße-Schmuck-Beleuchtung (workshop for dishes, jewellery and lamps) in Halle. There he executed standardized designs for industrial production, including his cylindrical lamps for Goldschmidt und Schwabe and his nickel-plated brass tea maker (1927), the forms of which were based on volumetric shapes. He moved to Cologne in 1929 and designed metalware for WMF and silverware for Bruckmann & Söhne. He also ran his own workshop in Bielefeld from 1934 to 1950, taught at the Landeskunstschule in Hamburg from 1951 to 1968 and established a workshop in Hamburg-Ahrensburg in 1968. Tümpel's elegant and functional designs combined the geometric formal vocabulary of the Bauhaus with the **standardization** principles of Halle.

Oscar Tusquets Blanca studied painting, architecture and design at the Escuela de Artes y Oficios de la Llotja, Barcelona from 1954 to 1960, and trained under Oriol Bohigas (b. 1925) and Frederico Correa at the Esculela Técnica Superior de Arquitectura, Barcelona from 1958 to 1965, while working in the architectural office of Correa and Alfonso Milá. In 1964, he banded together with fellow graduate architects Pep Bonet (b. 1941), Cristain Cirici (b. 1941) and Lluís Clotet (b. 1941) to form Studio PER, which became noted for its idiosyncratic approach to architecture and the meticulous detailing of its buildings, interiors and furniture. The group established its own manufacturing company, B. D. Ediciones de Diseño in 1972, which produced many of Tusquets' furniture and product designs. The same year, Tusquets published a Spanish edition of **Robert Venturi**'s *Learning from Las Vegas*, and together with Clotet designed the Belvedere Regás building, which was one of the earliest architectural statements of **Post-Modernism**. During the 1980s, he participated in **Alessi**'s *Tea & Coffee Piazza* project (1983) and produced numerous furniture designs such as the *Gaulino* chair (1987), which evoked the gaunt silhouette of Cervantes' Don Quixote. Tusquets has lectured extensively and is one of Spain's leading designers.

**Oscar Tusquets
Blanca**
b. 1941 *Barcelona*

Masanori Umeda

b. 1941 *Kanagawa, Japan*

▲ *Tawaraya* boxing-ring for Memphis, 1981 (showing from left to right: Aldo Cibic, Andrea Branzi, Michele De Lucchi, Marco Zanini, Nathalie du Pasquier, George Sowden, Martine Bedin, Matteo Thun and Ettore Sottsass)

► *Getsuen* chair for Edra, 1990

Masanori Umeda studied at the Kuwasawa Design School, receiving his diploma in 1962. Between 1967 and 1969, he worked in the design studio of **Achille and Pier Giacomo Castiglioni** in Milan, and from 1970 to 1979 acted as a design consultant to **Olivetti**, where he established close links with **Ettore Sottsass**. He was later invited by Sottsass to participate in **Memphis'** first collection in 1981. For this, he designed his famous *Tawaraya* boxing-ring (1981) that symbolized the contesting nature of **Post-Modernism**. Umeda also designed other furniture pieces for Memphis, intended as ironic comments on contemporary Japanese society, such as the *Ginza* bookcase (1982) with its robot-like form. He designed ceramics for Memphis too, including the *Orinoco* vase (1983) and *Parana* fruit dish (1983), and in 1986 established his own design studio, U-Meta Design, in Tokyo. Since then, he has designed a range of furniture, including the *Anthurium* side table (1990), the *Getsuen* chair (1990), the *Rose* chair (1991) and the *Orchid* chair (1991) manufactured by Edra, which can be seen as wry comments on the tension between the traditional and contemporary cultures of Japan. Umeda believes that through the wanton pursuit of commercialism Japan has destroyed its own natural beauty. By adopting floral forms, he hopes to rediscover the roots of Japanese culture. Umeda's other notable designs include ergonomic male and female bathroom products for Xspace (1989) and several post-modern interiors including the Yamato kimono shop in Yokohama (1986) and the Tomato Bank in Kurashiki City (1989).

Josef Urban

1872 Vienna
1933 New York

▼ Walnut armchair,
c. 1901

Josef Urban studied under Karl von Hasenauer at the Akademie der Bildenden Künste, Vienna from 1890 to 1993, and later trained at the Polytechnicum, Vienna. Together with his brother-in-law, Heinrich Lefler (1863–1919), he designed an interior for the 1897 winter exhibition held at the Österreichisches Museum für Kunst und Industrie that incorporated Secessionist-style motifs. In 1900, he became a founding member of the Viennese artisans' group, Hagenbund and acted as their president from 1906 to 1908. Urban and Lefler collaborated in 1902 on alterations to and decoration of the Hagenbund building, a former market-hall office, known as the Zedlitzhalle. Two years later, his craft-orientated work was displayed in the Austrian pavilion at the "Louisiana Purchase Exhibition" held in St. Louis. He emigrated to the United States in 1911 and established his own studio, specializing in the design of theatre and film sets. Then in 1927, he designed a theatre for the revue producer Florenz Ziegfeld and created lavish sets for his famous "Follies" productions. Urban also became the first art director to design **Moderne** film sets. He designed twenty-five sets that anticipated **Art Deco** for William Randolf Hearst's Cosmopolitan film productions. Between 1918 and 1933, Urban was also the chief stage designer for the Metropolitan Opera and worked on fifty-five productions. In 1921, he visited Vienna and came into contact with the **Wiener Werkstätte**. On his return to New York, he established the "Artists Fund", which sent financial aid to Wiener Werkstätte designers who were virtually destitute owing to the post-war economic recession in Europe. The same year, Urban also founded Wiener Werkstätte of America Inc., for which he designed a sumptuous showroom on Fifth Avenue. This venture, however, was a financial failure, and he withdrew from it around 1924. Urban later designed the first **International Style** building in America – the New School for Social Research (1929–1930) in New York.

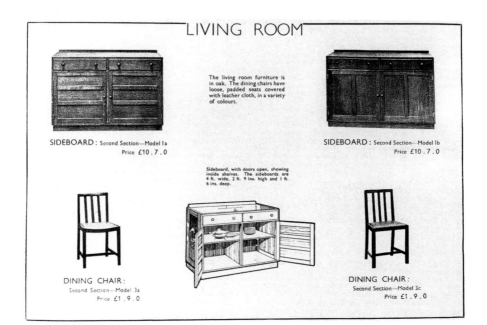

LIVING ROOM

The living room furniture is in oak. The dining chairs have loose, padded seats covered with leather cloth, in a variety of colours.

SIDEBOARD : Second Section—Model 1a
Price £10 . 7 . 0

SIDEBOARD : Second Section—Model 1b
Price £10 . 7 . 0

Sideboard, with doors open, showing inside shelves. The sideboards are 4 ft. wide, 2 ft. 9 ins. high and 1 ft. 6 ins. deep.

DINING CHAIR :
Second Section—Model 3a
Price £1 . 9 . 0

DINING CHAIR :
Second Section—Model 3c
Price £1 . 9 . 0

In Britain between 1941 and 1951, the manufacture of goods – from furniture to clothing – was subject to the Utility Scheme. The war-effort necessitated the re-direction of raw materials from civilian to military use and strict regulations were imposed on manufacturers by the British Board of Trade. Utility was as much a means of ensuring the rationing of materials as it was an ideology arising from the Government's social policy. In February 1941, the "Standard Emergency Furniture" programme was launched to provide furniture to "bombed out" families. Four months later, manufacturers were prohibited from producing any furniture except for that which complied with the Government's twenty models of "standard pattern furniture". The following year, the Utility Furniture Advisory Committee was established, with designers such as **Gordon Russell** on the board, to oversee the development of the first Utility range designed by H. J. Cutler and Edwin Clinch. Influenced by the values of appropriateness and honesty in design that were promoted by the **Arts & Crafts Movement**, Utility furniture was typified by simple constructions with unadorned surfaces and was essentially modern. In 1948, some materials restrictions were lifted but high taxes continued to be levied until 1951 on furniture that did not comply with the Utility Scheme.

Utility furniture
1943–1952
Great Britain

▲ Page from the "Utility Furniture Catalogue", 1943

**Henry van
de Velde**

*1863 Antwerp
1957 Zurich*

Henry van de Velde studied painting at the Académie des Beaux-Arts in
Antwerp from 1881 to 1884, and trained for one year under Carolus Duran
in Paris. In 1886, he joined Als ik Kan and co-founded L'Art Indépendent –
both Antwerp-based art societies, and two years later became a member of
the progressive Post-Impressionist art group, Les Vingt. Around this period,
he came into contact with Georges Seurat (1859–1891) and Paul Signac
(1863–1935) and his work was strongly influenced by the paintings of
Vincent van Gogh (1853–1890). In 1892, van de Velde abandoned painting
in favour of design, having been inspired by the reforming ideas of John
Ruskin (1819–1900) and **William Morris**, and the same year he exhibited
an embroidery at the Le Vingt salon and designed various ornaments for
books and journals. In 1894, he published *Déblaiements d'art*, in which he
pleaded for a unification of the arts, and began teaching "Arts d'Industrie et
d'Ornamentation" at the University of Brussels – although later in his career
he opposed the notion of industrial design. His first architectural project
was the Bloemenwerf House, which he built for himself in Uccle near
Brussels in 1895. Both Julius Meier-Graefe (1867–1935), who founded the

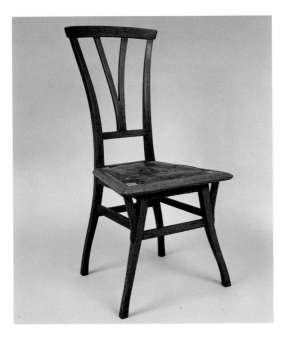

◄ *Bloemenwerf* chair
for Société Henry
van de Velde, Ixelles,
1894–1895

► Dining room of
the Bloemenwerf
House in Uccle, near
Brussels, c. 1895

journal *Dekorative Kunst* in 1897, and **Siegfried Bing** visited the house, and van de Velde later designed four rooms for Bing's gallery, Maison L'Art Nouveau, in Paris. He also exhibited a room at the Salon de la Libre Esthétique in 1896 and the following year, the Société de Henry van de Velde workshop was founded in Ixelles, near Brussels, to produce his furniture designs that were shown at the 1897 "Internationale Kunstausstellung" in Dresden. In 1899, he designed the interior and façade of Meier-Graefe's Parisian shop, La Maison Moderne. Van de Velde's designs were more "anglicized" than those of his compatriot **Victor Horta**, whose work in the Continental **Art Nouveau** style was more suited to Belgian taste. Eventually, van de Velde moved to Berlin where his less decorative and more functional designs, manufactured by Wilhelm Hirschwald's Hohenzollern Kunstgewerbehaus, were highly appreciated. While there, he designed interiors for the Havana Tobacco Company (1900) and for the imperial barber, François Haby's salon (1901) – each remarkable for the balancing of expressive form with functional requirements. In 1902, van de Velde moved to Weimar, where he became artistic adviser to the Grand Duke Wilhelm Ernst, re-designed the entrance and reading-room of the Nietzsche library (1903) and designed the Weimar Kunstgewerbeschule (1906). As the leading exponent of **Jugendstil** in Weimar, van der Velde was made director of this new school

▼ Stoneware vase with salt-glaze for Steingutfabrik & Kunsttöpferei Reinhold Hanke, 1902

▼▶ Silver and tortoiseshell snail fork, caviar knife and oyster fork manufactured by Koch & Bergfeld for Theodor Müller, 1902

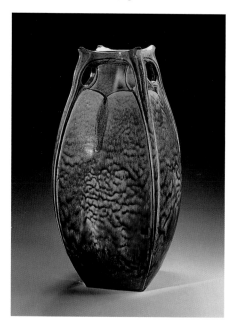

of applied arts when it opened in 1908. He also collaborated with several local craftsmen and workshops, notably the Scheidemantel cabinet-making
firm and the jeweller, Theodor Müller, who produced his remarkably fluid
silverware designs. In 1903, van de Velde designed an elegant yet functional
dinner service for the Staatliche Porzellanmanufaktur Meißen that also incorporated abstracted organic forms and motifs. He was a founder member
of the **Deutscher Werkbund** but could not accept Hermann Muthesius'
(1861–1927) adherence to industrial **standardization** and left the Werkbund
in 1914. A year later, he was forced to give up his teaching position in
Weimar and eventually emigrated to Switzerland in 1917, where he worked
as an independent architect. Between 1926 and 1936, he founded and directed the Institut Supérieur d'Architecture (ISAD) in Brussels, but in 1947 he
returned to Switzerland, where he published his memoirs in 1956. Van de
Velde was an early and highly influential propagandist of modernism and his
Jugendstil designs anticipated **functionalism** and abstraction – two key features of modern design.

▲ Porcelain sauce-
boat for the Staatliche
Porzellanmanufaktur
Meißen, c. 1903

Theo van Doesburg

1883 *Utrecht*
1931 *Davos, Switzerland*

Born Emil Marie Küpper, van Doesburg later took the name of his step-father, Theodorus Doesburg. He first studied drama at Cateau Esser's School of Dramatic Arts, Amsterdam, and then in 1912 began to teach himself painting and started publishing art reviews. From 1914 to 1916, he was called up for national service, and around this time he met the philosopher Evert Rinsema and the poet Anthony Kok and established contacts with **Vilmos Huszár**, Bart Anthony van der Leck (1876–1958), Piet Mondrian (1872–1944) and **Jacobus Johannes Pieter Oud**. In 1916, he co-founded the De Sphinx art group, collaborating on the design of Burgomaster de Broek's house in Waterland, and the following year, after moving to Leiden, he joined Huszár, van der Leck, Kok, Oud and Jan Wils (1891–1972) in founding the influential journal *De Stijl* for which he acted as editor-in-chief. The journal was central to the development of **De Stijl** – a movement involving architects, designers and artists. From 1917 to 1921, van Doesburg also worked on several architectural projects with Oud, Wils, **Gerrit Rietveld** and Cees Rinks de Boer (1881–1966), designing murals and stained-glass panels with strong geometric forms and primary colours. From 1920, he travelled frequently to Belgium, Italy, France and Germany to promote De Stijl concepts, and in 1921 established links with the **Bauhaus**. A year later, he attempted, unsuccessfully, to become a lecturer at the Weimar Bauhaus but did teach a De Stijl course at Karl-Peter Röhl's atelier in Weimar, and in 1923, having moved to Paris, exhibited his work with other De Stijl members at Léonce Rosenberg's Galerie l'Effort Moderne. Opposed to the increasing internationalism that van Doesburg was advocating, Mondrian left De Stijl in 1925, and van Doesburg subsequently published his own manifesto on "Elementarism" – a concept he had developed in 1924. Five years later, he established the magazine *L'Art Concret*, and in 1931 co-founded the Abstraction-Création art group in Paris. Van Doesburg was the leading spokesman for the De Stijl movement, and when he died the last issue of *De Stijl* was published as a posthumous tribute to him.

▼ **Theo van Doesburg & Kurt Schwitters**, "Kleine Dada Soirée" lithographic poster, 1923

Harold van Doren studied languages and subsequently moved to Paris, where he worked at the Louvre. He translated Ambrose Vollard's biographies, *Paul Cézanne* (1923) and *Jean Renoir* (1934), and played a role in Renoir's film, *La Fille d'eau*. After returning to the United States, he worked as an assistant to the director of the Minneapolis Institute of Arts but resigned from this position when given the chance to work in the fledgling field of industrial design. One of his first commissions came from Hugh Bennett, the president of the Toledo Scale Company, for commercial weighing scales. This lightweight and innovative design employed a newly developed plastic, Plaskon, and was one of the first products to incorporate

Harold van Doren

1895 *Chicago*
1957 *Philadelphia*

a large-scale plastic moulding. Van Doren went on to design many streamlined products for Maytag, Goodyear, Ergy, Philco, Swartzbaugh and DeVilbiss, and together with J. G. Rideout designed the widely published green skyscraper-shaped plastic radio for Air-King Products (1930–1931) and a patented child's scooter (1936). A pioneer of industrial design consulting and **streamlining**, van Doren published *Industrial Design: A Practical Guide to Product Design and Development* in 1940.

▶ Photograph showing Harold van Doren (left) and Hubert Bennett (right) with van Doren's re-designed scales for the Toledo Scale Company, 1930s

► Hammered
copper lamp with
mica shade for the
Copper Shop, c. 1915

Dirk Van Erp

1859 *Leeuwarden,
Netherlands*
1933 *San Francisco*

Dirk Van Erp emigrated from Holland to America in 1886, and four years later began working at the US Navy shipyard on Mare Island near San Francisco, making vases out of spent brass shell casings, which by 1906 were being successfully retailed by the fashionable Vickery Atkins & Torrey store in San Francisco. In 1908, Van Erp established his Copper Shop in Oakland so as to devote his time to the production of "art" metalwork, which included his famous copper lamps with mica shades, and during this period he was assisted by Harry Dixon (1890–1967) and his daughter, Agatha. The business moved to San Francisco in 1910, and Van Erp briefly went into partnership with the designer Miss D'Arcy Gaw, who designed several of the firm's early mica lamps. By 1915, the flourishing workshop was producing not only lamps and vases but also bowls, smoking accessories and planters, which sometimes incorporated **Grueby** tiles. The hammered surfaces of these objects and their exposed rivets were manifestations of the **Arts & Crafts Movement**'s credo of "revealed construction". In 1916, Van Erp returned to the shipyards to assist in the war effort and the workshop was taken over by his son William. He retired in 1929, but continued to design metalware sporadically until his death in 1933.

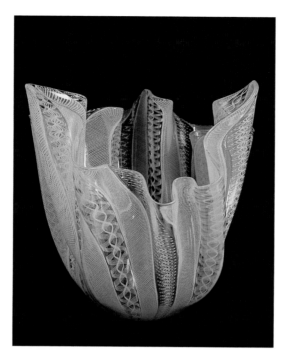

◄ **Fulvio Bianconi &
Paolo Venini**,
*Fazzoletto
(Handkerchief)* vase
for Venini, c. 1949

Paolo Venini trained as a lawyer in Milan, where he met Giacomo Cappellin (1887–1968) who owned a glass shop there. In 1921, together with Andrea Rioda (1878–1921), a former director of the Compagnia di Venezia e Murano, and Vittorio Zecchin (1878–1947), who had designed glassware for the Artisti Barovier glassworks, they founded a glassworks in Venice known as the Vetri Soffiati Muranesi Cappellin, Venini & C. Vittorio Zecchin was the technical and artistic director of this venture until 1925, when Paolo Venini set up his own factory on Murano with the sculptor Napoleone Martinuzzi (1892–1977) and the engineer Francesco Zecchin (1894–1986). Initially, they produced glassware based on the earlier neo-classical designs of Vittorio Zecchin and on new designs by Martinuzzi, which included "lively" glass sculptures and archaic-style wares. Then, from 1927 to 1928, Venini launched three innovations, *pasta vitrea opaca* (an opaque glass), *vetro incamiciato* (double-walled glass) and *vetro pulegoso* (bubbled glass), with an eye to the production of more sculptural vessels, and together with **Gio Ponti**, **Pietro Chiesa** and Tommaso Buzzi (1900–1981) he founded the Il Labirinto group to encourage collaboration between manufacturers and to promote the decorative arts. In 1932, Buzzi became Venini's artistic director and introduced the *vetro*

Paolo Venini
1895 *Milan*
1959 *Venice*

laguna technique in which gold leaf was used to obtain a speckled surface. In the 1930s, Paolo Venini and **Carlo Scarpa** collaborated closely on reproduction of Roman *murrine* glass in which small glass pieces were fused together to make a "wall". The Venini glassworks produced colourful designs by **Fulvio Bianconi** and **Massimo Vignelli** throughout the 1950s and realized the designs of **Tobia Scarpa** and **Tapio Wirkkala** in the 1960s.

▼ *Incalmo* bottles with stoppers for Venini, 1950

◄ **Robert Venturi &
Denise Scott-Brown**,
Queen Anne chair
from the *Venturi*
Collection for Knoll
International, 1984

Robert Venturi studied architecture at Princeton University from 1943 to 1950 and later worked in the offices of **Eero Saarinen** and Louis Kahn (1901–1974). He subsequently won a two-year scholarship to the American Academy in Rome, and after returning to America taught architecture at the University of Pennsylvania from 1957 to 1965. A series of lectures he delivered at the **Museum of Modern Art**, New York in 1966 formed the basis of his hugely influential book, *Complexity and Contradiction in Modern Architecture* (1966), in which he attacked the cultural poverty and visual banality of modern buildings and heralded **Post-Modernism**. This publication was followed by another seminal work *Learning from Las Vegas* (1972), co-written with Denise Scott-Brown (b. 1932) and Steven Izenour and influenced by Roland Barthes' writings on **Semiotics**, which argued for a more symbolic form of architecture that ordinary people would readily identify with. Venturi put his theories into practice and designed many "hybrid" buildings, borrowing visual quotations from historic styles as well as contemporary popular culture. His product designs, such as the *Venturi* Collection for **Knoll** (1984) and his *Tea & Coffee Piazza* for **Alessi** (1983), were similarly symbolic and quintessentially post-modern in style.

Robert Venturi
b. 1925 *Philadelphia*

Vereinigte Werkstätten für Kunst im Handwerk

Founded 1897
Munich

▲ Richard Riemerschmid,
Musicroom,
exhibited at
the "Deutsche
Kunstausstellung",
Dresden, 1899

The founding of the Vereinigte Werkstätten für Kunst im Handwerk (the United Workshops for Art in Handiwork) was prompted by the success of the decorative arts section at the 1897 "Glaspalast" exhibition in Munich. Its participants, including **Berhard Pankok**, **Hermann Obrist** and **Bruno Paul**, decided to establish an applied arts group that would manufacture and retail their reformed designs. Inspired by the guilds of the British **Arts & Crafts Movement**, the Vereinigte Werkstätten für Kunst im Handwerk was the first of many such enterprises to be established in Germany, with the aim of producing high-quality "artistic" designs. Both **Richard Riemerschmid** and **Peter Behrens** were associated with the workshops, and designed practical everyday objects for them. The workshops' commitment to handcraft, however, meant that their **Jugendstil** wares were relatively expensive to produce. The Werkstätten first displayed their work at the 1898 "Glaspalast" exhibition, Munich and later exhibited designs at the 1900 Paris "Exposition Universelle", the 1904 St. Louis "Louisiana Purchase Exposition" and the 1910 Brussels "Exposition Universelle et Internationale".

The Victoria & Albert Museum was the first museum to be dedicated to the applied arts. Its origins can be traced to a report drafted by a Parliamentary Select Committee in 1836, which pressed for the founding of an instructive collection of exemplary manufactured goods. The following year, the Government School of Design was established and a collection of objects was obtained for teaching purposes. The "Great Exhibition" of 1851 acted as a catalyst to the foundation of a Museum of Manufactures at Marlborough House in 1852 that initially displayed the Government School's collection and items purchased at the Great Exhibition. The design reformer, Henry Cole (1808–1882) was appointed the museum's first director and oversaw its move to South Kensington in 1857, but it was the first superintendent, John Charles Robinson (1824–1913) who was primarily responsible for forming the wide ranging collection that exists today. It was re-christened the Victoria & Albert Museum in 1899, when Queen Victoria laid the foundation stone for the existing building, designed by Aston Webb (1849–1930). Today, the V&A continues to house the world's greatest study collection of designed artefacts.

Victoria & Albert Museum
Founded 1899
London

▲ The Glass Gallery at the Victoria & Albert Museum showing Danny Lane's glass balustrade, opened April 1994

► *Fungo (Mushroom)*
lamp for Venini,
c. 1955

Massimo Vignelli

b. 1931 *Milan*

Massimo Vignelli studied architecture at the Politecnico di Milano from
1950 to 1953 and later trained at the Università di Architecttura, Venice.
From 1953, he designed glassware for **Venini**, and from 1958 to 1960 taught
at the **Institute of Design**, Chicago, while his wife, Lella Vignelli (b. 1934),
worked for the architects Skidmore, Owings and Merrill. In 1960, the couple
returned to Italy and founded a Milan-based studio – the Lella and Massimo
Vignelli Office for Design and Architecture. Four years later, Massimo
Vignelli began working for the Container Corporation of America, Chicago,
and designed its new logo. In 1965, together with Bob Noorda (b. 1927) and
Jay Doblin (b. 1920), he founded the Milanese design consultancy, Unimark
International. The same year, the Vignelli's moved permanently to America,
and in 1966 Unimark established a New York office, specializing in **corporate identity** work. In 1971, the couple established Vignelli Associates and
subsequently designed corporate identity programmes for **Knoll**, American
Airlines, Bloomingdales, Xerox, Lancia, Cinzano and Ford; furniture for
Poltronova, Sunar, Rosenthal and Morphos; glassware for Venini, Steuben
and Sasaki; and showrooms for Artemide and Hauserman. The Vignellis'
work is distinguished by their use of clean lines and pure colour.

◄ Antonio Citterio &
Glen Oliver Löw,
T-chair for Vitra,
1990

Willy Fehlbaum founded the Vitra furniture company in Weil am Rhein in
1950 and subsequently obtained a European licensing agreement from
Herman Miller. In 1957, Vitra launched a range of licensed furniture designed by **Charles and Ray Eames** and **George Nelson**, and later undertook
the production development of **Verner Panton**'s *Panton* chair (1959–1960),
which was introduced in 1967. Rolf Fehlbaum took over from his father as
the firm's chairman in 1977, and selected Nicholas Grimshaw (b. 1939) to
design a new factory in 1981 after the earlier production facility had been destroyed by fire. Further buildings for the Vitra factory complex were designed
by high profile architects such as **Frank O. Gehry**, Tadao Ando (b. 1941),
Zaha M. Hadid (b. 1950) and Alvaro Siza (b. 1933). The *Vitra Edition* – a collection of limited edition experimental chairs by **Ettore Sottsass**, **Gaetano
Pesce**, **Shiro Kuramata** and **Ron Arad** – was launched in 1987 to supplement
the firm's office furniture designed by **Mario Bellini** and **Antonio Cittero**. The
same year, Rolf Fehlbaum, who had an existing collection of "classic" post-
war chairs, acquired many others dating from 1880 to 1945 and combined
them to form the basis of the collection now housed in the Vitra Design
Museum, designed by Frank O. Gehry and opened in 1989.

Vitra
Founded 1950
Basel

Vkhutemas
Founded 1920
Moscow

▲ Alexander
Rodchenko,
Furnishing for
the workers' club
reading-room for
the Russian pavilion
at the 1925 Paris
"Exposition des Arts
Décoratifs"

The Vkhutemas (Higher State Artistic and Technical Workshops) evolved from the earlier Svomas (Free State Art Studios), founded in 1918. This progressive Soviet design workshop-cum-school numbered many leading Constructivists among its instructors, including **Alexander Rodchenko**, **Varvara Stepanova**, **Vladimir Tatlin**, Naum Gabo (1890–1977), Antoine Pevsner (1886–1962), Liubov Popova (1889–1924) and Alexander Vesnin (1883–1959). The institution promoted the concept of "production art" and established contacts with industry. It also developed progressive teaching techniques and had close links with the Bauhaus through **El Lissitzky**, **Kasimir Malevich** and Wassily Kandinsky (1866–1944). Like other Soviet art institutions, such as Inkhuk (Institute of Artistic Culture) and Izo (fine arts department of Narkompros), the Vkhutemas played a crucial role in forming artistic ideology in the Soviet Union. Although the Russian **avant-garde** were initially supported by the Bolshevik regime, they were eventually persecuted by the Soviet Central Committee. In 1932, all architectural and design organizations, including the Vhutein (Higher State Artistic and Technical Institute), which had replaced the Vkhutemas in 1927, were abolished in favour of Party controlled unions.

Charles F. A. Voysey was the son of an unorthodox Anglican clergyman who founded the Theistic Church. Like his father, Voysey held strong moral views that would later inform his work. Although he was influenced by **A. W. N. Pugin**, he rejected historicism in favour of vernacularism. From 1874 to 1882, he was apprenticed to a number of progressive Gothic Revival architects, including John Pollard Seddon (1827–1906), Henry Saxon Snell (1830–1904) and George Devey (1820–1886). He set up his own office in 1882 and produced work in the Arts & Crafts tradition established by **William Morris** and **A. H. Mackmurdo**. From around 1888 until 1914, he designed a large number of residences that were the antithesis of "grand statements": low-built, gabled, informal **Gesamtkunstwerk** houses that blended perfectly with the surrounding countryside. The light, comfortable, cottage-style interiors of these buildings were decorated with plain oak furniture and "flat" textiles. Voysey's ahistorical and informal designs exemplified the second phase of the **Arts & Crafts Movement** and stylistically bridged the 19th and 20th centuries. His work was quintessentially English, and through his adoption of vernacular forms and motifs Voysey pioneered a simple domestic style that had a powerful influence, especially on Edwardian suburban architecture.

Charles F. A. Voysey
1857 Hessle/Yorkshire
1941 Winchester

▶ Door fittings, probably made by William Bainbridge Reynolds, 1895

◀ *The Huntsman* design for a machine-woven textile, c. 1919

Wilhelm Wagenfeld was apprenticed to the silverware manufacturer Koch & Bergfeld, and studied at the Kunstgewerbeschule, Bremen from 1914 to 1919. He then attended the Zeichenakademie (Drawing Academy), Hanau for three years and finished his training at the **Bauhaus**, Weimar, where he took the preliminary course and completed a metalwork apprenticeship under **László Moholy-Nagy**. At the Bauhaus, Wagenfeld designed his famous *MT8* table lamp (1923–1924), which was put into serial production by the workshop. After completing his journeyman's exam, he became an assistant to Richard Winkelmayer at the metal workshop of the Bauhochschule in Weimar, taking over the running of this workshop in 1928. The functional objects he made there, such as the *M15* tea caddy (c. 1929), incorporated geometric forms that were less severe than those of his earlier Bauhaus designs. During this period, he also designed door handles for S. A. Loevy, Berlin, and a number of household items for Walther & Wagner, Schleiz. Wagenfeld worked as a freelance designer for the Jenaer Glaswerke Schott & Gen. and re-designed their domestic glassware range, which included his *Sintrax* coffee maker (1931) and his famous glass tea set (1930). During the late 1930s, Wagenfeld's designs became increasingly industrial, as shown by his *Kubus* stacking storage jars that were mass-produced by the Vereinigte Lausitzer Glaswerke, for whom he also devised a trademark and promo-

Wilhelm
Wagenfeld

1900 *Bremen, Germany*
1990 *Stuttgart, Germany*

▲ *Kubus* moulded glass storage jars for Vereinigte Lausitzer Glaswerke, 1938

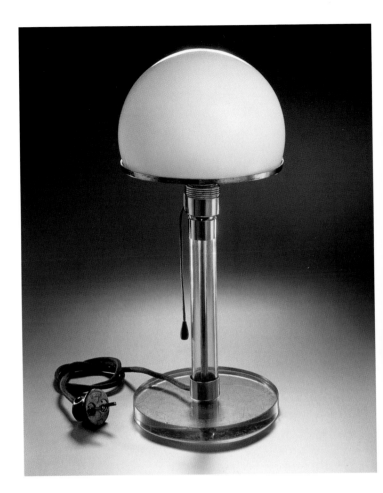

► *MT9/ME1* table lamp for Bauhaus Dessau, 1923–1924

tional material. Wagenfeld designed ceramics for the Fürstenberg and Rosenthal porcelain factories in the 1930s, and outlined his functionalist approach to design in articles for journals such as *Die Form*. He taught in Berlin at the Staatliche Kunsthochschule Grunewaldstraße from 1931 to 1935 and at the Hochschule für Bildende Künste from 1947 to 1949, and in 1954 he established the Wagenfeld Workshop in Stuttgart to develop products for industrial production, including a melamine in-flight meal tray for Lufthansa (1955). As a celebrated Bauhaus designer, Wagenfeld stressed the moral, social and political obligations of designers and focused on the design of inexpensive, functional and democratic products.

Otto Wagner studied at the Technische Hochschule in Vienna and the Bau-akademie in Berlin, and later trained under Eduard van der Nüll and August Siccard von Siccardsburg at the Akademie der Bildenden Künste in Vienna. In 1862, he joined the office of the Viennese architect Ludwig von Förster, which he subsequently took over and operated under his own name. His early architecture – mainly apartment and office buildings – had historicist elements and was influenced by the classicizing style of Karl Friedrich Schinkel (1781–1841). He was commissioned to devise an urban develop-ment plan for Vienna (1892–1893) and re-designed the city's Stadtbahn rail-way system (1893), which included viaducts, bridges and over thirty stations. From 1894 to 1916, Wagner was a professor of architecture at the Akademie der Bildenden Künste in Vienna, with students including **Adolf Loos**, **Josef Hoffmann** and **Josef Maria Olbrich**. In 1894, Wagner published a book en-titled *Moderne Architektur*, which marked a turning point in his architectural career, after which his work became gradually less ornamented. He became a member of the Vienna **Secession** in 1899, and while not completely forsak-

Otto Wagner
1841 *Vienna-Penzing*
1918 *Vienna*

ing classicism, began working in the **Art Nouveau** idiom. By 1900, his office employed a staff of seventy including Olbrich, Hoffmann, Leopold Bauer (1872–1938), Max Fabiani (1865–1962) and Jože Plečnik (1872–1957), and was executing design work as well as architectural schemes. Wagner's masterwork, the Österreichische Postsparkasse (Austrian Post Office Savings Bank) in Vienna (1904–1906), was conceived as a **Gesamtkunstwerk** project and was decorated with specially designed aluminium fittings and bentwood furniture, which revealed an early Functionalist tendency. Variations on the Postsparkasse furniture were later manufactured by Gebrüder **Thonet** and **J.&J. Kohn**. Wagner also designed silverware for J.C. Klinkosch, which was exhibited in the Austrian section at the 1902 "Esposizione Internazionale d'Arte Decorativa Moderna" in Turin. He contributed to the periodical *Hohe Warte* from 1904 to 1907, and later became a member of the **Deutscher Werkbund**. Wagner was one of the most progressive Viennese architects working around the turn-of-the-century, and through his teaching at the Akademie der Bildenden Künste in Vienna and his advocacy of the "Nutzstil" (functional style) he influenced an entire generation of architects and designers.

The son of an engineer and amateur painter, George Walton attended evening classes at the Glasgow School of Art and founded his own decorating business in 1888. His elder brother, E. A. Walton (1860–1922), was one of The Glasgow Boys – a group of Post-Impressionist painters – and his contacts helped his younger brother gain commissions. George Walton exhibited with the Arts & Crafts Society in 1890 and decorated Catherine Cranston's Buchanan Street (1896) and Argyle Street Tea Rooms (1897) in conjunction with **Charles Rennie Mackintosh**. In 1896, his successful firm became a limited company. The following year, Walton moved to London and was commissioned to design furniture and shop-fronts for the Kodak showrooms in London, Glasgow, Dublin, Milan, Brussels, Vienna and Moscow. He opened another office in Scarborough in 1898, and three years later received the first of several architectural commissions for private residences. From 1916 to 1921, he designed public houses for the Central Liquor Traffic Board, and in the 1920s designed textiles for Morton Sundour. While Walton was the of the most successful **Glasgow School** designers, his work was more closely aligned with the English **Arts & Crafts Movement**.

George Walton
1867 *Glasgow*
1933

▲ *Brussels* sideboard for George Walton & Company, c. 1900

Karl Emanuel Martin – or "Kem" – Weber trained under Eduard Schultz, a royal cabinet-maker based in Potsdam. He later studied under **Bruno Paul** at the Kunstgewerbeschule, Berlin, and assisted his tutor with the design and construction of the German pavilion at the 1910 "Exposition Universelle" in Brussels. After graduating in 1912, he worked in Paul's office on the design of the German section at the "Panama-Pacific International Exhibition" held in San Francisco in 1915. He was sent to America to oversee the construction of the exhibit but the work was suspended owing to the worsening political climate. The imminent outbreak of war prevented Weber from returning home, and he found himself stranded in California. After the First World War, he moved to Santa Barbara and established a studio, specializing in the design of Spanish Colonial interiors. During this period, Weber also designed several buildings inspired by Mayan, Egyptian and Minoan structures as well as Cubism. He settled in Los Angeles in 1921, and began designing

▼ *Airline* chair for
Airline Chair Co.,
c. 1934–1935

▲ Model No. 305-P40
The Zephyr digital
clock for Lawson
Time Inc., 1934

modernistic furniture, interiors and packaging for the large furniture and
decorating store, Barker Brothers. He became an American citizen in 1924,
and was appointed art director of Barker Brothers, a position he held until
1927. He then founded an industrial design office in Hollywood, and his
Moderne style designs were shown at the second "International Exposition
of Art in Industry" held by Macy's of New York in 1928, which established
his reputation as one of the most progressive designers working in America
at the time. During the 1930s, Weber produced designs for various Grand
Rapids furniture manufacturers including Widdicomb, Baker, Berkey & Gay
and Mueller, and also designed silverware for Friedman Silver, New York,
and clocks for Lawson Time, Alhambra. He frequently employed **streamlining**, as demonstrated in his *Airline* chair (1934–1935) designed for the Walt
Disney Studios. During the Second World War, Weber designed a pre-fabricated housing system for the Douglas Fir Plywood Association, Tacoma,
and after 1945 he concentrated on architectural commissions that incorporated traditional and natural materials. Although these projects were in
the modern idiom, they were distanced from his earlier **International Style**
buildings; Weber's work typifying the less austere West Coast approach to
modernism.

Hans J. Wegner

b. 1914 *Tønder, Denmark*

▼ *Model No. JH 250*
Valet chair for
Johannes Hansen,
1953 (reissued by PP
Møbler)

Hans J. Wegner, the son of a master cobbler, grew up with a deep appreciation of handcraftsmanship. He undertook a carpentry apprenticeship in H. F. Stahlberg's workshop, and after serving in the military studied in Copenhagen at the Teknologisk Institut from 1936 to 1938. He later trained under the furniture designer Orla Mølegaard Nielsen (b. 1907) at the Kunsthandvaerkerskolen. In 1938, Wegner worked in Arhus for the architects, Erik Møller and Flemming Lassen, and in 1940 began working with Møller and **Arne Jacobsen** on the design of Arhus Town Hall, contributing designs for simple yet well-crafted furniture. From 1943 to 1946, Wegner ran his own Arhus-based design studio, and between 1946 and 1948 worked in partnership with the architect Palle Suenson in Copenhagen prior to establishing an office in Copenhagen. From 1940, Wegner also worked with the furniture-maker and chairman of the Cabinet-maker's Guild, Johannes

Hansen and designed numerous chairs for his manufacturing company, including the *Round* chair (1949), which became known as *The Chair* or the *Classic Chair*. By the 1950s, Wegner was one of the leading exponents of Scandinavian design and was internationally celebrated for his exquisitely balanced and beautifully crafted chairs that were, for the most part, constructed of solid wood. These were manufactured by Johannes Hansen, Fritz Hansen, Andreas Tuck, Getama. A. P. Stolen, Carl Hansen & Søn and PP Møbler. Wegner's characteristically Scandinavian organic approach to design, as exemplified by his *Chinese* chair (1943), *Peacock* chair (1947), *Y*-chair (1950) and *Valet* chair (1953), countered the geometric formalism of the **Modern Movement**. As a gifted designer and craftsman, Wegner simplified form and construction to create beautiful modern re-workings of traditional furniture types.

▲▲ *Model No. JH 50 Peacock* chair for Johannes
Hansen, 1947 (reissued by PP Møbler)

▲ *Model No. JH 512* folding chair for Johannes
Hansen, 1949 (reissued by PP Møbler)

▲▲ *Model No. JH 501 Round* chair for Johannes Hansen, 1949
(also known as *The Chair* or *Classic Chair* – reissued by PP
Møbler)

▲ *Model No. 24 Y*-chair for Carl Hansen, 1950

Bruno Weil

Dates unknown
Austria

Bruno Weil trained as an architect before becoming director of Thonet
Frères, Paris. During his tenure there from 1928 to 1933, he designed under
the pseudonym Béwé derived from the German pronunciation of his initials.
His tubular metal furniture included the *B290* office cabinet (1928–1929),
the *B256* stacking chair (1932), the *B143/144* tables (1932), the *B267* daybed
(1935) and the innovative *B287* modular desk system (1935). Under his
direction, Thonet Frères not only manufactured furniture by German designers such as **Ludwig Mies van der Rohe** and **Marcel Breuer**, but also
produced designs by progressive French architects including André Lurçat
(1894–1970), **Le Corbusier**, **Pierre Jeanneret** and **Charlotte Perriand**. In 1939,
Weil emigrated to the United States where he designed his *Bentply* seating
programme (1943), which was inspired by **Charles Eames** and **Eero
Saarinen**'s earlier prototype plywood chairs.

Daniel Weil studied architecture at the University of Buenos Aires, graduating in 1977, and then trained as an industrial designer at the **Royal College of Art**, London from 1978 to 1981. He subsequently designed a range of radios, lights and digital clocks that were encased in screen-printed plastic envelopes, in an attempt to develop a "new imagery for electronics to escape from the mechanical imagery of the box". These deconstructed designs, including *Bag Radio* (1981–1983), which revealed their wiring and electronic components, were produced by his own manufacturing company Parenthesis Limited from 1982 to 1990. Between 1985 and 1991, Weil worked in partnership with Gerard Taylor (b. 1955), designing products, furniture and interiors for **Alessi**, **Knoll** and Esprit among others. He became a partner of the multi-disciplinary design consultancy **Pentagram** in 1992, and in this capacity he worked for many corporate clients including EMI Records, Swatch, Granada Hospitality and the Crafts Council of Great Britain. Weil was also a "Unit Master" at the Architectural Association, London from 1983 to 1986, and in 1991 he became professor and course director of industrial and vehicle design at the Royal College of Art.

Daniel Weil
b. 1953 *Buenos Aires*

▲ *Bag Radio* for Parenthesis, 1981–1983

► **Josef Hoffmann**,
Cut-glass vase
produced by Ludwig
Moser & Söhne
for the Wiener
Werkstätte, c. 1920

▼ **Dagobert Peche**,
Poster for the
fashion division of
the Wiener
Werkstätte, 1920

The Wiener Werkstätte were officially founded in June 1903 in Vienna by the Secessionist designers **Josef Hoffmann** and **Koloman Moser** and the wealthy banker, Fritz Wärndorfer (1869–1939). The cooperative was based on pioneering British organizations, most notably **Charles Ashbee**'s **Guild of Handicraft** and was similarly dedicated to the pursuit of artistic endeavour through craftsmanship. By October 1903, various workshops had been established for silver and goldsmithing, metalwork, bookbinding, leatherwork and cabinet-making as well as an architectural office (previously Hoffmann's) and a design studio. The Wiener Werkstätte were remarkable for their cleanliness, lightness and exemplary treatment of workers – workmen in the cabinet-making workshop, for instance, received a virtually unheard of one to two weeks' paid leave. The designs produced by the Werkstätte bore not only the monograms of the designers but also those of

the craftsmen who executed them, reflecting the organization's endeavour to promote equality between artist and artisan. Its members, especially Hoffmann, refused to compromise quality for affordablity and insisted on using the best available materials. Although this approach ensured excellence, it also hindered financial success and meant that the Werkstätte's democratizing influence was not as widespread as it might have been. By 1905, however, the Wiener Werkstätte had taken over from the **Secession** as the leading Viennese arts and crafts organization and was employing over a hundred workers. Its work was published in journals such as *Deutsche Kunst und Dekoration* and *The Studio,* and reached a wider audience through the staging of Wiener Werkstätte exhibitions (Berlin 1904, Vienna & Brünn 1905, Hagen 1906) and through participation in various international exhibitions such as the

1914 Cologne "Werkbund-Ausstellung" and the 1925 Paris "Exposition Internationale des Arts Décoratifs". Between 1903 and 1932, the Werkstätte produced furniture, glassware, metalware, textiles, jewellery, clothing, wallpapers, ceramics and graphics by over two hundred designers (many of whom had studied at the Kunstgewerbeschule in Vienna), including **Otto Prutscher**, **Jutta Sika**, Michael Powolny (1871–1954), Carl Otto Czeschka (1878–1960), Berthold Löffler (1874–1960) and Emmanuel Josef Margold (1889–1962). The Werkstätte also undertook three notable **Gesamtkunstwerk** projects: their own theatre, the Cabaret Fledermaus (1907), Josef Hoffmann's Purkersdorf Sanatorium (1904–1906) and the Palais Stoclet (1905–1911). This latter building in Brussels exemplified the Werkstätte's early Secessionist style, which was characterized by severe rectilinearism, elaborate constructions and luxury materials. After Fritz Wärndorfer's emigration to America in 1914, the Werkstätte, managed by their new sponsor Otto Primavesi, began to produce less exclusive products that were more curvilinear and stylistically eclectic and were typified by the work by **Dagobert Peche**. Although branches were established in New York and Berlin in 1921 and 1929 respectively, the Wiener Werkstätte was forced into liquidation in 1932.

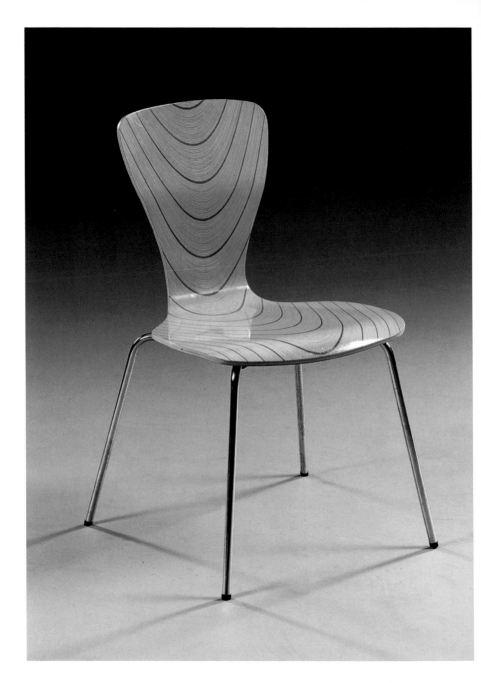

Tapio Wirkkala studied sculpture at the Taideteollinen Korkeakoulu (Central School of Industrial Design), Helsinki from 1933 to 1936, and later worked as a sculptor and graphic designer. In 1947, he shared first prize with **Kaj Frank** in a glassware competition organized by Iittala, and subsequently produced designs for the glassworks on a freelance basis. His blown-glass *Kantarelli* vases (1946), the forms of which were inspired by chanterelle mushrooms, captured the abstract essence of nature and exemplified Scandinavian Modernism – expressive organic forms combined with traditional craftsmanship. This series of vases, produced between 1947 and 1960, helped to establish his international reputation. Wirkkala was also widely celebrated for his laminated wood leaf-shaped bowls and furniture, which possessed an intrinsic natural beauty. The multicoloured plywood laminations were made up by him and then cut and scooped to reveal a remarkable streaked effect. His designs were exhibited at the 1951 and 1954 Milan Triennales where they were awarded six Grand Prix. Wirkkala was artistic director of Taideteollinen Korkeakoulu, Helsinki from 1951 to 1954, and worked in **Raymond Loewy**'s New York office from 1955 to 1956. He also designed glass for Venini, ceramics for Rosenthal, knives for Hackman and lighting for Airam. Wirkkala skillfully balanced craftsmanship with industrial techniques to create beautiful functional objects for the home.

Tapio Wirkkala
1915 Hanko, Finland
1985 Esbo, Finland

▲ *Kantarelli* vases for Iittala, 1946

◄ Laminated wood chair for Asko, c. 1955

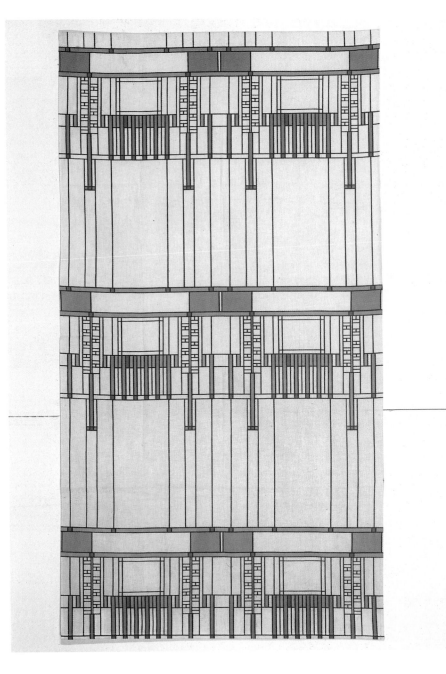

Frank Lloyd Wright studied engineering at the University of Wisconsin from 1885 to 1887, and then moved to Chicago, where he worked briefly in the architectural offices of Joseph L. Silsbee before joining the Adler & Sullivan practice. In 1889, he built his own home in Oak Park, Illinois, and the following year was assigned to oversee all residential commissions received by Adler & Sullivan. However, he left the firm in 1892 after a disagreement about some clandestine architectural work he had undertaken, and in 1893 established his own practice in Chicago, focusing chiefly on the design of private houses in the Oak Park area and other suburbs of the city. From 1900 to 1911, Wright designed some fifty residences that became known as "Prairie Houses". These structures were built mainly from natural materials – stone, brick and wood – and were designed to accentuate the natural beauty of the surrounding Mid-West prairie, with their low elevations and gently sloping roof lines emphasizing the horizontal. Their innovative open-plan interiors – similarly in tune with nature – employed screening walls and soft-toned natural colours that maximized the sense of light. Many of these

Frank Lloyd Wright
1867 *Richland Center, Wisconsin*
1959 *Phoenix, Arizona*

◄ Textile for
F. Schumacher &
Co., 1955

◄ Chairs designed
for the Isabel
Roberts House and
the Francis W. Little
House, 1908 & 1902

residences, as well as later buildings by Wright, were conceived as **Gesamt-kunstwerk** schemes and incorporated site-specific fittings and furniture, that was partly built-in. Wright intended these unified projects to possess a "naturalness" and a spiritual transcendence. Like the Prairie Houses, his later office and public buildings such as the Larkin Company Administration Building in Buffalo (1903–1905) were integrated schemes that were innovatively planned so as to provide as pleasant an environment as possible. The revolutionary layout of the Larkin Building, for example, was not only functionally efficient but, with its open galleries and light-filled central court, promoted a sense of "family" with all the employees working together rather than separately in private offices. His rectilinear steel office furniture was specially designed for this project and was both functionally and visually unified with its surroundings. Like the Larkin Building, the Unity Temple in Oak Park (1904–1907) had geometric external massing that belied the remarkable sense of space and light inside. The innovative cantilevered construction of this building and its non-supporting screen walls – of masonry, wood, concrete or glaz-ing – marked a turning point in Wright's career towards what he called, the "destruction of the box". Wright's work became increasingly distanced from its **Arts & Crafts Movement** origins as he began exploring the structural and decorative potential of "industrial" concrete blocks, which he used to great effect in the design of the Imperial Hotel in Tokyo (1915–1922) and four houses in Los Angeles (early 1920s). During the Depression of the 1930s, when commissions were scarce, Wright founded an educational community known as the Taliesin Fellowship, and in 1932 published an autobiography. His flagging career was then revived by two important commissions – the Johnson Wax Administration Building (1936–1939) and Edgar J. Kaufmann's residence, Fallingwater

◄ Coffee and dinner service for the Imperial Hotel in Tokyo and manufactured by Noritake of Japan, c. 1922

▼ *Peacock* chair designed for the Imperial Hotel in Tokyo, c. 1921–1922

(1935–1939). These projects, like his later Guggenheim Museum (1943–1946
& 1955–1959), incorporated reinforced concrete cantilevered constructions
and heralded an entirely new and liberated style of architecture. All of
Wright's projects, whether they used natural or man-made materials, curved
or rectilinear forms, expressed his reverence for nature and his overwhelming belief in the importance of human values or as he put it, "humanity".
Wright stated that "beauty is but the shining of man's light (soul)", and his
pioneering **Organic Design** attempted to symbolize and capture the spiritual
essence of both man and nature. Neither a historicist nor a modernist,
Wright was first and foremost a humanist. The astonishing breadth and vision of his work continues to impress and influence the world of design.

▼ Workstation designed for the S. C. Johnson & Son Administration Building, c. 1937 (produced by Metal Office Furniture Company)

◄ *American Modern* dinnerware for Steubenville Pottery, c. 1937

Russel Wright

1904 *Lebanon, Ohio*
1976 *New York*

Russel Wright studied painting at the Cincinnati Art Academy and sculpture at the Art Students' League, New York. In 1924, **Norman Bel Geddes** and the playwright Thornton Wilder offered him a job designing theatrical sets, and he began producing sculptural caricature masks that brought him both publicity and an income. He also designed a range of spun aluminium bar accessories that were equally successful and effectively launched his career as an industrial designer. In 1930, he established his own workshop in New York and began producing metalwares, including cocktail shakers, tea sets and pitchers. Wright's **Moderne** products, which combined **Functionalism**, **Art Deco** styling and mission-style vernacularism, were exhibited at the **Museum of Modern Art**'s "Machine Age" exhibition in 1934. Designs, such as his blonde maplewood *Modern Living* furniture for Conant-Ball (1935), were extremely popular, not least because they were less expensive than modern products imported from Europe and were better suited to American taste. His casual yet modern "American Way" approach to design was typified by his well-known *American Modern* dinnerware (1937). Highly celebrated during his career, Wright was the first designer of domestic products to have his name included in manufacturers' advertising copy.

▸ *Butterfly* stool for
Tendo Mokko, 1954

Sori Yanagi
b. 1915 *Tokyo*

Sori Yanagi studied painting and architecture at the Tokyo School of Fine Arts, graduating in 1940. He worked as an assistant in **Charlotte Perriand**'s Tokyo design office from 1940 to 1942 while she was working as an adviser on arts and crafts to the Japanese Ministry of Commerce. In 1951, he won first prize at the inaugural "Japanese Competition for Industrial Design", and a year later founded the Yanagi Industrial Design Institute. His designs, such as the moulded plywood *Butterfly* stool (1954) manufactured by Tendo Mokko, elegantly and harmoniously combined Eastern and Western cultures – traditional craftsmanship and industrial technology. Yanagi's almost spiritual approach to the design process was very oriental, and he declared that "basic concepts and beautiful forms do not come from the drawing board alone". In 1977, Yanagi became director of the Japan Folk Crafts Museum in Tokyo, and in 1982 he participated in the "Contemporary Vessels: How to Pour" exhibition held at the Tokyo National Museum of Modern Art.

Marco Zanini

b. 1954 *Trento, Italy*

Marco Zanini studied architecture under Adolfo Natalini (b. 1941) at the Università di Firenze, and while in Florence met **Ettore Sottsass** at a workshop organized by **Global Tools** in 1975. Between 1975 and 1977, he worked for the Argonaut Company in Los Angeles and as a freelance designer in San Francisco. After graduating in 1978, Zanini began working as an assistant in Sottsass' Milan-based office, and two years later joined the newly established design consultancy, Sottsass Associati. Later that year, he became a founding member of **Memphis**, and subsequently designed furniture for the group including his *Dublin* sofa (1981) and *Union* bookcase (1983). Zanini also designed glassware for Memphis, such as the *Rigel* covered bowl (1982) and the *Arturo* and *Vega* drinking glasses (1982), as well as bizarrely formed and colourful ceramics, including the *Colorado* and *Mississippi* teapots (1983) and the *Victoria*, *Baykal* and *Tanganyka* vases (1983). He and Sottsass co-designed a room installation shown at the "Italian Design Exhibition" in Tokyo in 1984, which was notable for its use of bold geometric forms and colourful screen-printed laminates, and also collaborated on the design of consumer electronics for Enorme.

▲ *Colorado, Sepik* & *Mississippi* teapots produced by Ceramiche Flavia for Memphis, 1983

► *Antropus* chair for
Arflex, 1949

Marco Zanuso Sr. studied architecture at the Politecnico di Milano, graduating in 1939. He established his own Milan-based office in 1945, which undertook product and furniture design commissions as well as architectural and town-planning projects. As one of the leading Italian designers of the post-war years, Zanuso co-edited the journal *Domus* with Ernesto Rogers (1909–1969) from 1946 to 1947 and edited *Casabella* magazine from 1947 to 1949. He was commissioned by the Pirelli company in 1948 to explore the potential of latex foam as an upholstering material, and his subsequent *Antropus* chair (1949) was the first chair to be produced by Arflex – a manufacturing company set up by Pirelli. This was followed by several other latex foam upholstered seating designs, including the *Lady* chair (1951) and the *Triennale* sofa (1951), which were first exhibited at the IX Milan Triennale where Zanuso won a Grand Prix and two gold medals. He was also awarded a **Compasso d'Oro** in 1956 for his *Model 1100/2* sewing machine for Borletti – a design that epitomized his work through its rational yet sculptural form. In addition, he undertook several architectural commissions – the **Olivetti** manufacturing plants in Sao Paulo (1955) and Buenos Aires (1955–1957) and the Necchi factory in Pavia (1961–1962), which revealed his interest in

Marco Zanuso Sr.
b. 1916 *Milan*

"product architecture" and pre-fabricated structures. From 1958 to 1977, Zanuso collaborated on numerous landmark product and furniture designs with **Richard Sapper**. These included the enamelled, lightweight, stamped steel *Lambda* chair for Gavina (1959–1964); the *No. 4999/5* stacking child's chair for **Kartell** (1961–1964), which was the first seating design to be produced in injection-moulded polyethylene; the *Doney 14* (1964) and *Black 12* (1969) televisions for BrionVega that were remarkable for their miniaturized electrical components of technology; the *Grillo* telephone for Siemens (1966) with its innovative folding form; and the *2000* kitchen scales for Terraillon (1970). In 1956, Zanuso became a member of the CIAM (Congrès Internationaux d'Architecture Moderne) and the INU (Istituto Nazionale Urbanista). That same year, he also co-founded the Associazione di Disegno Industriale (ADI) and was its president from 1966 to 1969. He was a town councillor in Milan between 1956 to 1960 and became a member of the planning commission for the city in 1961. Throughout his career, Zanuso experimented with new materials and technologies and designed sleek yet functional products for industrial manufacture that often re-defined the formal potential of existing types.

▲ **Marco Zanuso & Richard Sapper**, *TS502* radio for Brionvega, 1964

◄ *Lady* armchairs for Arflex, 1951

▲ **Marco Zanuso &
Richard Sapper**,
Black 201 television
for Brionvega, 1969

◄ Corrected draft of
the *Melior* typeface
(1949), 1966

In 1938, Hermann Zapf began working at Paul Koch's foundry in Frankfurt, and in 1941 the Stempel foundry published a limited edition of his calligraphic alphabet book, *Feder und Stichel* (Pen and Gouge). After military service, Zapf worked for Stempel, and was their art director from 1947 to 1956. His most notable typefaces for Stempel were *Palatino* (1950), based on a Renaissance antecedent, and the graceful *Optima* (1952–1955), described by him as the "serif-less roman" that was inspired by Roman inscriptions. During this period, he wrote *Das Blumen ABC* (1948) and the *Manuale Typographicum* (1954). He acted as a consultant to the Mergenthaler Linotype Company, New York from 1957 to 1974 and to Hallmark International, Kansas City from 1966 to 1973. In the 1960s, Zapf wrote two further typographic manuals and taught typography from 1972 to 1981 at the Technische Hochschule in Darmstadt. From 1977 to 1987, he was professor of typographic computer programs at the Rochester Institute of Technology, New York, where he pioneered digital typefaces, including the italic *Zapf Chancery* (1979), and adapted many existing faces for use on computers. Zapf re-introduced calligraphic beauty to the design of typefaces and is one of the 20th-century's most influential typographers.

Hermann Zapf
b. 1918 *Nuremberg*

Eva Zeisel
1906 *Budapest*

Eva Zeisel studied painting at the Royal Academy of Art in Budapest from 1923 to 1924. Then, after a pottery apprenticeship, she set up a workshop at the Kispest ceramics factory in Budapest where she developed prototypes intended for industrial production. From 1927, she worked for the Hamburg firm, Hansa Kunstkeramik, and between 1928 and 1930 designed Constructivist-style wares for the Majolika-Fabrik Schramberg, which were characterized by simple geometric forms and polychromatic hand-painted decoration. From 1930 to 1932, Zeisel lived in Berlin and executed ceramic designs for Christian Carstens. She later resided in the Soviet Union and designed ceramics for the state-run Lomonosov and Dulevo porcelain factories. She was appointed artistic director of the porcelain industry of the Russian Republic in 1935, but a year later was imprisoned on political grounds. After her release in 1937, Zeisel returned to Budapest, and the following year fled to the United States via Switzerland and England so as to escape the Nazi occupation. In America, Zeisel continued to design practical modern tableware, including the *Museum White* range (1942–1945) developed in collaboration with the **Museum of Modern Art, New York**, and taught at the Pratt Institute, New York, and the Rhode Island School of Design, Providence.

▲ Stoneware tureen
for Majolika-Fabrik
Schramberg, c. 1930

The Zsolnay pottery in Pécs, Hungary was founded in 1862 by Ignaz Zsolnay. In 1865, Vilmos Zsolnay (1828–1900) became the pottery's director, and in the 1870s the firm grew rapidly, becoming the largest producer of ceramics in the Austro-Hungarian Empire. In 1883, the Zsolnay ceramics factory was employing four hundred and fifty workers and by 1900, this number had risen to one thousand. The firm's early stoneware designs with folk-style decoration, were replaced in the 1870s by highly glazed lustrewares that were inspired by Renaissance ceramics and Iznik-style polychromatic pieces known as Ivoir-Fayence. The factory commissioned several well-known designers and artists to design ceramics, including the painter József Rippl-Rónai (1861–1930) who was aligned to the **Arts and Crafts Movement** in Hungary and who submitted numerous designs for painted wares in the **Art Nouveau** style. Lajos Makk (1876–1916) also designed lustre ceramics for the factory that were remarkably forward-looking. Besides domestic wares, Zsolnay manufactured industrial and architectural ceramics, such as porcelain electrical fittings and tiles that became a distinctive feature of Secessionist buildings designed by architects such as Ödon Lechner in Hungary. Vilmos Zsolnay's son, Mikløs (1857–1925) took over the company's directorship from his father, but after the First World War the factory went into decline, and although the firm is still active today, it is best remembered for its pioneering artistic wares produced around the turn-of-the-century.

▼ **Vilmos Zsolnay & Lajos Makk**, Lustre stoneware vase for Zsolnay pottery, c. 1900

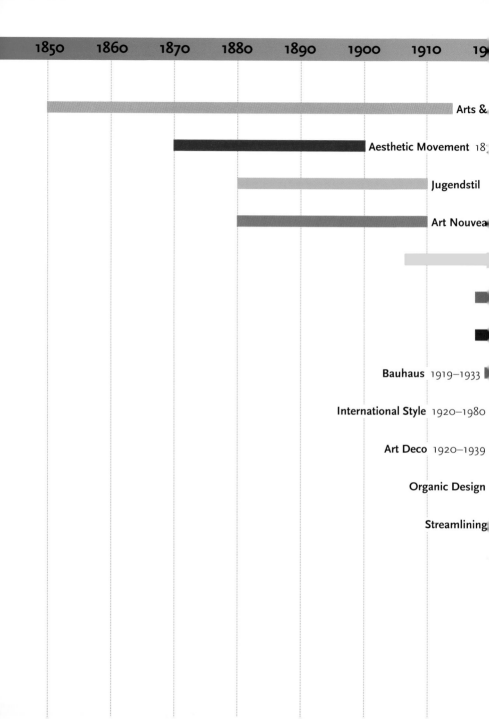

| 1850 | 1860 | 1870 | 1880 | 1890 | 1900 | 1910 | 19 |

Arts &

Aesthetic Movement 18

Jugendstil

Art Nouvea

Bauhaus 1919–1933

International Style 1920–1980

Art Deco 1920–1939

Organic Design

Streamlining

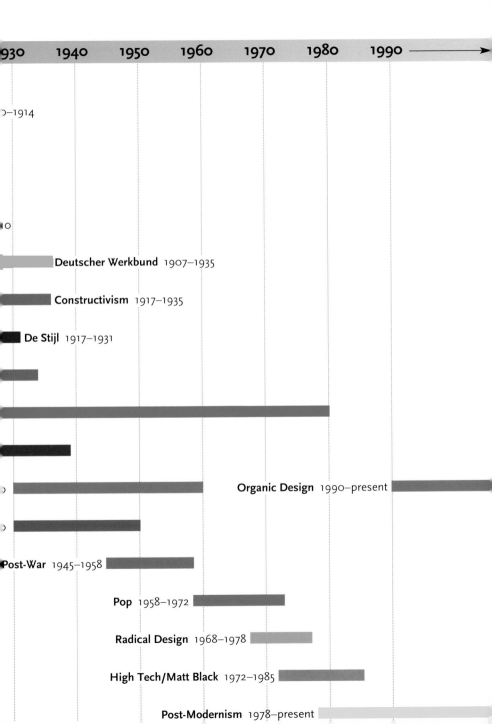

930   1940   1950   1960   1970   1980   1990

⊃–1914

Deutscher Werkbund 1907–1935

Constructivism 1917–1935

De Stijl 1917–1931

Organic Design 1990–present

Post-War 1945–1958

Pop 1958–1972

Radical Design 1968–1978

High Tech/Matt Black 1972–1985

Post-Modernism 1978–present

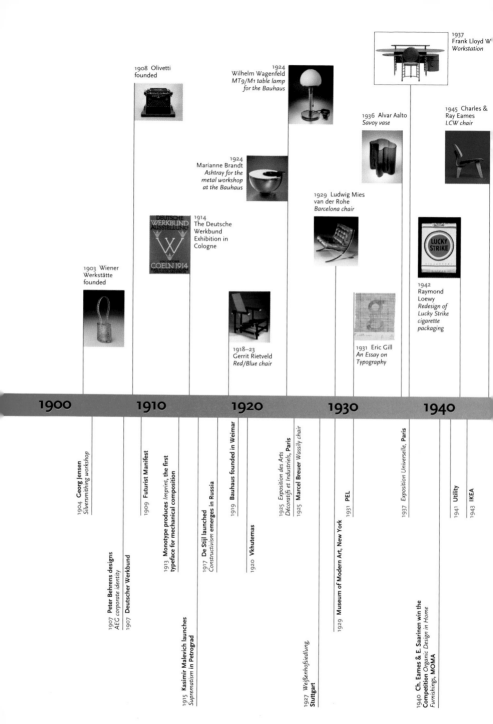

1937
Frank Lloyd W
Workstation

1908 Olivetti
founded

1924
Wilhelm Wagenfeld
*MT9/M1 table lamp
for the Bauhaus*

1936 Alvar Aalto
Savoy vase

1945 Charles &
Ray Eames
LCW chair

1924
Marianne Brandt
*Ashtray for the
metal workshop
at the Bauhaus*

1929 Ludwig Mies
van der Rohe
Barcelona chair

1914
The Deutsche
Werkbund
Exhibition in
Cologne

1903 Wiener
Werkstätte
founded

1942
Raymond
Loewy
*Redesign of
Lucky Strike
cigarette
packaging*

1918–23
Gerrit Rietveld
Red/Blue chair

1931 Eric Gill
*An Essay on
Typography*

| 1900 | 1910 | 1920 | 1930 | 1940 |

1904 **Georg Jensen**
Silversmithing workshop

1909 **Futurist Manifest**

1913 **Monotype produces** *Imprint,* **the first
typeface for mechanical composition**

1907 **Peter Behrens designs**
AEG corporate identity

1907 **Deutscher Werkbund**

1917 **De Stijl launched**
Constructivism emerges in Russia

1919 **Bauhaus founded in Weimar**

1925 *Exposition des Arts
Décoratifs et Industriels,* Paris

1925 **Marcel Breuer** *Wassily chair*

1915 **Kasimir Malevich launches**
Suprematism in Petrograd

1920 **Vkhutemas**

1937 *Exposition Universelle,* Paris

1941 **Utility**

1943 **IKEA**

1927 *Weißenhofsiedlung,*
Stuttgart

1929 **Museum of Modern Art, New York**

1931 **PEL**

1940 **Ch. Eames & E. Saarinen win the
Competition** *Organic Design in Home
Furnishing,* **MOMA**

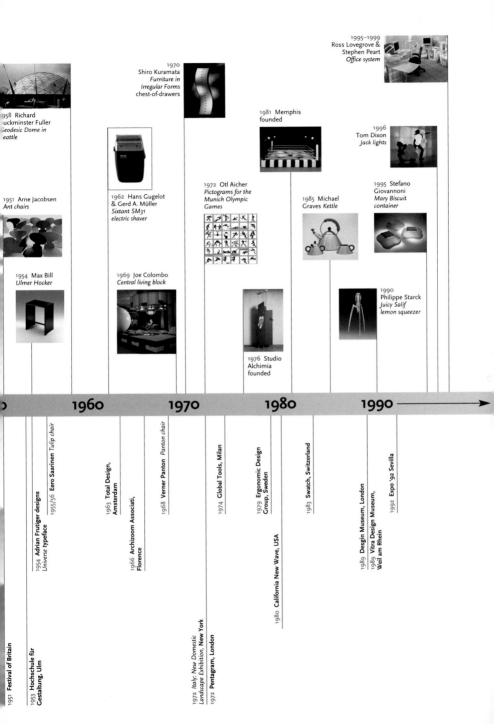

1995–1999 Ross Lovegrove & Stephen Peart *Office system*

1970 Shiro Kuramata *Furniture in Irregular Forms* chest-of-drawers

1981 Memphis founded

1996 Tom Dixon *Jack lights*

1958 Richard Buckminster Fuller *Geodesic Dome in Seattle*

1951 Arne Jacobsen *Ant chairs*

1962 Hans Gugelot & Gerd A. Müller *Sixtant SM31* electric shaver

1972 Otl Aicher *Pictograms for the Munich Olympic Games*

1985 Michael Graves *Kettle*

1995 Stefano Giovannoni *Mary Biscuit* container

1954 Max Bill *Ulmer Hocker*

1969 Joe Colombo *Central living block*

1990 Philippe Starck *Juicy Salif* lemon squeezer

1976 Studio Alchimia founded

1960   **1970**   **1980**   **1990**

1951 **Festival of Britain**

1953 **Hochschule für Gestaltung, Ulm**

1954 **Adrian Frutiger designs** *Universe typeface*

1955/56 Eero Saarinen *Tulip chair*

1963 **Total Design, Amsterdam**

1966 **Archizoom Associati, Florence**

1968 Verner Panton *Panton chair*

1972 *Italy: New Domestic Landscape Exhibition,* **New York**

1972 **Pentagram, London**

1974 **Global Tools, Milan**

1979 **Ergonomic Design Group, Sweden**

1980 **California New Wave, USA**

1983 **Swatch, Switzerland**

1989 **Desgin Museum, London**

1989 **Vitra Design Museum, Weil am Rhein**

1992 *Expo '92 Sevilla*

Appendix

Bibliography
Acknowledgements
Photographic Credits

Selected Bibliography

Abercrombie, S., *George Nelson, The Design of Modern Design*, MIT Press, Cambridge, Massachusetts 1995

Anscombe, I., *Arts & Crafts Style*, Phaidon Press, Oxford 1991

Anscombe, I. & Gere, C., *Arts & Crafts in Britain & America*, Academy Editions, London 1978

Arwas, V., *Glass, Art Nouveau to Art Deco*, Academy Editions, London 1987

Bangert, A., *Italian Furniture Design*, Bangert Verlag, Munich 1988

Banham, R., *Theory and Design in the First Machine Age*, Architectural Press, London/ New York 1960

Bayley, S., *The Conran Directory of Design*, Conran Octopus, London 1985

Bernsen, J., *Hans J. Wegner*, Dansk Design Centre, Copenhagen 1994

Blackwell, L., *20th Century Type*, Laurence King, London 1992

Börnsen-Holtmann, N., *Italian Design*, Benedikt Taschen Verlag, Cologne 1994

Branzi, A., *Il Design Italiano, 1964–1990*, Electa, Milan 1996

Branzi, A., *The Hot House: Italian New Wave Design*, Thames & Hudson, London 1984

Brino, G., *Carlo Mollino, Architecture as Autobiography*, Thames & Hudson, London 1987

Bröhan, T. & Berg, T., *Avantgarde Design 1880–1930*, Benedikt Taschen Verlag, Cologne 1994

Bruchhäuser, A., *Der Kragstuhl*, Stuhlmuseum Burg Beverungen, Berlin 1986

Brunhammer, Y., *André Arbus, Architecte-Décorateur des Années 40*, Éditions Norma, Paris 1996

Brunhammer, Y., *Les Styles des Années 30 à 50*, Baschet & Cie, Paris 1987

Byars, M. (ed.), *The Design Encyclopedia*, Laurence King, London 1994

Carruthers, A. & Greensted, M., *Good Citizens Furniture: The Arts and Crafts Collection at Cheltenham*, Lund Humphries, London 1994

Collins, M. & Papadakis, A., *Post-Modern Design*, Academy Editions, London 1989

Conway, H., *Ernest Race*, Design Council, London 1982

Cumming, E. & Kaplan, W., *The Arts & Crafts Movement*, Thames & Hudson, London 1991

De Bonneville, F., *Jean Puiforcat*, Éditions du Regard, Paris 1986

Dietz, M. & Mönninger, M., *Japanese Design*, Benedikt Taschen Verlag, Cologne 1994

Dietz, M. & Mönninger, M., *Lights. Leuchten. Lampes*, Benedikt Taschen Verlag, Cologne 1993

Droste, M. & Bauhaus Archiv, *Bauhaus 1919–1933*, Benedikt Taschen Verlag, Cologne 1990

Droste, M., Ludewig, M. & Bauhaus Archiv, *Marcel Breuer*, Benedikt Taschen Verlag, Cologne 1992

Du Pree, H., *Business as Unusual, The People and Principles at Herman Miller*, Herman Miller Inc., Zeeland 1986

Duncan, A., *Louis Majorelle, Master of Art Nouveau Design*, Thames & Hudson, London 1991

Eidelberg, M. (ed.), *Design 1935–1960: What Modern Was*, Le Musée des Arts Décoratifs de Montreal/Harry N. Abrams, New York 1991

Eidelberg, M. (ed.), *Designed for Delight, Alternative Aspects of Twentieth-Century Decorative Arts*, Le Musée des Arts Décoratifs de Montreal/Flammarion, Paris/New York 1997

Fahr-Becker, G., *Wiener Werkstätte 1903–1932*, Benedikt Taschen Verlag, Cologne 1994

Favata, I., *Joe Colombo*, Thames & Hudson, London 1988

Fehrman, C. & K., *Postwar Interior Design: 1945–1960*, Van Nostrand Reinhold, New York 1987

Ferrari, F., *Carlo Mollino Cronaca*, Stamperia Artistica Nazionale Editrice, Turin 1985

Fiell, C. & P., *Charles Rennie Mackintosh*, Benedikt Taschen Verlag, Cologne 1995

Fiell, C. & P., *Modern Chairs*, Benedikt Taschen Verlag, Cologne 1993

Fiell, C. & P., *Modern Furniture Classics since 1945*, Thames & Hudson, London 1991

Fiell, C. & P., *1000 Chairs*, Benedikt Taschen Verlag, Cologne 1997

Fiell, C. & P., *William Morris*, Benedikt Taschen Verlag, Cologne 1999

Fleming, J., Honour, H. & Pevsner, N., *The Penguin Dictionary of Architecture*, Penguin Books, London 1966

Forty, A., *Objects of Desire, Design and Society 1750–1980*, Thames & Hudson, London 1986

Friedman, M., *De Stijl, 1917–1931: Visions of Utopia*, Phaidon, Oxford 1982

Garner, P., *Eileen Gray, Designer and Architect*, Benedikt Taschen Verlag, Cologne 1993

Garner, P., *Sixties Design*, Benedikt Taschen Verlag, Cologne 1996

Geddes, N. B., *Horizons*, Little Brown, Boston 1932

Gere, C. & Whiteway, M., *Nineteenth-Century Design: From Pugin to Mackintosh*, Weidenfeld & Nicolson, London 1993

Giedion, S., *Mechanization Takes Command: A Contribution to Anonymous History*, Oxford University Press, New York 1948

Gössel, P. & Leuthäuser, G., *Architecture in the Twentieth Century*, Benedikt Taschen Verlag, Cologne 1991

Greenhalgh, P. (ed.), *Modernism in Design*, Reaktion Books, London 1990

Greenhalgh, P. (ed.), *Quotations and Sources, On Design and the Decorative Arts*, Manchester University Press, Manchester 1993

Hall, G. & Snowman, M. R., *Avant Premiere, Contemporary French Furniture*, VIA/ Editions Eprouve, Paris/London 1988

Heskett, J., *Industrial Design*, Thames & Hudson, London 1980

Hiesinger, K. & Marcus, G., *Design Since 1945*, Thames & Hudson, London 1983

Hiesinger, K. & Marcus, G., *Landmarks of Twentieth-Century Design*, Abbeville Press, New York 1993

Hollis, Richard, *Graphic Design – A Concise History*, Thames & Hudson, London 1994

Hufnagl, F. (ed.), *Einblicke – Ausblicke: Für ein Museum von morgen*, Die Neue Sammlung, Staatliches Museum für angewandte Kunst, Arnoldsche, Stuttgart 1996

Jervis, S., *The Penguin Dictionary of Design and Designers*, Penguin Books, London 1984

Jodidio, P., *Richard Meier*, Benedikt Taschen Verlag, Cologne 1995

Jodidio, P., *Sir Norman Foster*, Benedikt Taschen Verlag, Cologne 1997

Katz, S., *Plastics, Designs and Materials*, Studio Vista, London 1978

Kras, R., *Gerrit Rietveld Centenary Exhibition*, Barry Friedman Ltd., New York 1988

Larrabee, E. & Vignelli, M., *Knoll Design*, Harry N. Abrams, New York 1981

Le Corbusier, *L'Art Décoratif d'Aujourd'hui*, G. Crès, Paris 1925

Le Corbusier, *Towards a New Architecture*, Praeger, New York 1959

Loos, A., *Ins Leere Gesprochen 1897–1900*, Brenner-Verlag, Innsbruck 1931

Loos, A., *Trotzdem 1900–1930*, Brenner-Verlag, Innsbruck 1931

Los, S., *Carlo Scarpa*, Benedikt Taschen Verlag, Cologne 1994

Margolin, V. (ed.), *Design Discourse, History, Theory, Criticism*, University of Chicago Press, Chicago 1989

Margolin, V. & Buchanan, R. (ed.), *Discovering Design, Explorations in Design Studies*, University of Chicago Press, Chicago 1995

Margolin, V. & Buchanan, R. (ed.), *The Idea of Design*, MIT Press, Cambridge Mass. 1995

Mastropietro, M., *An Industry for Design; The Research, Designers & Corporate Image of B&B Italia*, Edizioni Lybra Immagine snc., Milan 1982

Mauriès, P., *Fornasetti, Designer of Dreams*, Thames & Hudson, London 1991

McDermott, C., *Design Museum Book of 20th Century Design*, Carlton Books, London 1997

McDermott, C., *Essential Design*, Bloomsbury, London 1992

Morgan, A. L. (ed.), *Contemporary Designers*, St. James Press, London 1985

Mumford, L., *Technics and Civilization*, Harcourt Brace, New York 1934

Myerson, J., *Gordon Russell, Designer of Furniture*, Design Council/Gordon Russell Ltd., London 1992

Myerson, J., *Makepeace, A Spirit of Adventure in Craft & Design*, Conran Octopus Ltd., London 1995

Nelson, G., *George Nelson on Design*, The Architectural Press, London 1979

Neuhart, J. & M. & Eames, R., *Eames Design: The Work of the Office of Charles & Ray Eames*, Harry N. Abrams, New York 1989

Ostergard, D., *Bent Wood and Metal Furniture: 1850–1946*, The American Federation of Arts, New York 1987

Pevsner, N., *Pioneers of the Modern Movement*, Faber & Faber, London 1936

Pevsner, N., *The Sources of Modern Architecture and Design*, Thames & Hudson, London 1968

Pfeiffer, B. B., *Frank Lloyd Wright*, Benedikt Taschen Verlag, Cologne 1991

Ponti, L. L., *Gio Ponti, The Complete Works*, Thames & Hudson, London 1990

Radice, B., *Memphis – Research, Experiences, Results, Failures and Successes of New Design*, Thames & Hudson, London 1985

Rieman, T., *Shaker, The Art of Craftsmanship*, Art Services International, Alexandria, Virginia 1995

Schaefer, H., *The Roots of Modern Design*, Studio Vista, London 1970

Schweiger, W., *Wiener Werkstätte, Design in Vienna 1903–1932*, Thames & Hudson, London 1984

Sembach, K.-J., *Art Nouveau*, Benedikt Taschen Verlag, Cologne 1991

Sembach, K.-J., Leuthäuser, G. & Gössel, P., *Twentieth Century Furniture Design*, Benedikt Taschen Verlag, Cologne 1991

Sottsass Associati, Rizzoli, New York 1988

Sparke, P., *Italian Design, 1870 to Present*, Thames & Hudson, London 1988

Sparke, P. (ed.), *The Plastics Age, From Modernity to Post-Modernity*, Victoria & Albert Museum, London 1990

Starck, Benedikt Taschen Verlag, Cologne 1996

Taylor, B. B., *Pierre Chareau*, Benedikt Taschen Verlag, Cologne 1998

Triggs, T. (ed.), *Communicating Design, Essay in Visual Communication*, B. T. Batsford Ltd., London 1995

Van Geest, J., *Jean Prouvé*, Benedikt Taschen Verlag, Cologne 1991

Vanlaethem, F., *Gaetano Pesce*, Thames & Hudson, London 1989

Vegesack, A. von, *Deutsche Stahlrohr-Möbel: 650 Modelle aus Katalogen*, Bangert Verlag, Munich 1986

Vercelloni, V., *The Adventure of Design: Gavina*, Jaca Book, Milan 1987

Walker, J., *Design History and the History of Design*, Pluto Press, London 1989

Warncke, C.-P., *De Stijl 1917–1931*, Benedikt Taschen Verlag, Cologne 1994

Whiteley, N., *Design for Society*, Reaktion Books, London 1993

Whiteley, N., *Pop Design; Modernism to Mod*, Design Council, London 1987

Wichmann, S., *Jugendstil Art Nouveau, Floral and Functional Forms*, Little, Brown & Co., Boston 1984

Woodham, J., *Twentieth-Century Design*, Oxford University Press, Oxford 1997

Zerbst, R., *Antoni Gaudi*, Benedikt Taschen Verlag, Cologne 1993

Exhibition Catalogues:

Arts Council of Great Britain, *Thirties, British Art & Design before the War*, Arts Council of Great Britain, London 1979

Centre Georges Pompidou, *Design Français 1960–1990 Trois Décennes*, A. P. C. I. / Centre Georges Pompidou, Paris 1988

Centre Georges Pompidou, *Ettore Sottsass*, Centre Georges Pompidou, Paris 1994

Centrokappa, *Il Design Italiano Degli Anni '50*, Ricerche Design Editrice, Milan 1985

The Detroit Institute of Arts & The Metropolitan Museum of Art, *Design in America, The Cranbrook Vision*, Harry N. Abrams, New York 1983

Fischer Fine Art, *Pioneers of Modern Furniture*, Lund Humphries, London 1991

Library of Congress and Vitra Design Museum, *The Work of Charles and Ray Eames: A Legacy of Invention*, Harry N. Abrams, New York 1997

Museum of Modern Art, *Italy: The New Domestic Landscape*, Museum of Modern Art, New York 1972

Museum of Modern Art, *The Modern Poster*, Museum of Modern Art, New York 1988

Museum of Modern Art, *Mutant Materials in Contemporary Design*, Museum of Modern Art, New York 1995

Singer Museum, *Jan Eisenloeffel 1876–1957*, Waanders Drukkers, Zwolle 1996

Tada Architectural Studio, *Finn Juhl Memorial Exhibition*, Tada Architectural Studio, Osaka 1990

Victoria & Albert Museum, *Art & Design in Europe and America 1800–1900*, The Herbert Press, London 1987
Victoria & Albert Museum, *British Art & Design 1900–1960*, Victoria & Albert Museum, 1983
Vitra Design Museum, *100 Masterpieces from the Vitra Design Collection*, Vitra Design Museum, Weil am Rhein 1996

The Whitechapel Art Gallery, *Modern Chairs 1918–1970*, Lund Humphries, London 1970

We would like to acknowledge the hard work and team effort of those at Taschen involved in this project, especially the Editing, Production and Design Departments.
We are also most grateful to the numerous manufacturers, distributors and design
consultancies and the many auction houses and public institutions who have lent their
assistance. Special thanks must go to Barry Friedman for allowing access to his photographic archive and for his ensuing patience, and lastly, we would like to thank our
families for their help and encouragement and our daughters, Emelia and Clementine,
for their good humour and understanding.

**Acknowledge-
ments**

Special thanks to:

Bauhaus-Archiv, Berlin
Thomas Berg, Bonn
Christina and Bruno Bischofsberger, Zurich
Torsten Bröhan GmbH, Düsseldorf – Torsten Bröhan
Bonhams, London – Alex Payne
Bridgeman Art Library, London
Christies Images, London – Camilla Young
Fine Art Society, London
Fischer Fine Art, Vienna
Barry Friedman Ltd., New York
Haslam & Whiteway, London – Michael Whiteway
Hunterian Art Gallery, Glasgow
International Design Press Agency, Barcelona
Knoll International, New York – Carl Magnusson
Herman Miller, Zeeland – Bob Viol
Mithra Neuman, Exeter
Musée des Arts Décoratifs, Montreal
Museum of Modern Art, New York
Die Neue Sammlung, Munich – Dr. Josef Strasser
The Daniel Ostroff Agency, Los Angeles – Daniel Ostroff
Sotheby's, London – Philippe Garner
Studio X, London – Ross and Miska Lovegrove
Stuhlmuseum Burg Beverungen, Beverungen
John Toomey Gallery, Oak Park – John Toomey
Victoria & Albert Museum, London
Vitra Design Museum, Weil am Rhein

Photographic Credits

We are immensely grateful to those individuals and institutions that have allowed us to reproduce images. We regret that in some cases it has not been possible to trace the original copyright holders of photographs from earlier publications. We would also like to thank the numerous designers, manufacturers and institutions that have kindly supplied portrait images. The publisher has endeavoured to respect the rights of third parties and if any such rights have been overlooked in individual cases, the mistake will be correspondingly amended where possible. The majority of historic images were sourced from the design archives of Thomas Berg Kunsthandel, Bonn; Fiell International Ltd., London and Benedikt Taschen Verlag, Cologne.

Adelta, Dinslaken: 19
Airbourne International, Montreuil-sous-Bois: 496
Studio Alchimia, Milan: 32, 33, 40, 194
Alessi, Crusinallo: 36, 153, 168, 283, 295 (photo: William Taylor), 360, 448, 459, 573, 576, 613 (left), 613 (right), 626, 666, 667 (left), 667 (right)
Alias, Grumello del Monte: 124
AMX Studio, London: 274
Karl Andersson & Söhner, Huskvarna: 484
Arflex, Milan: 30, 96 (left), 96 (right), 121, 745, 746
Artek, Helsinki: 16 (top), 16 (bottom), 17, 531
Artemide, Milan: 627
Artery, New York: 743
B&B Italia, Novedrate: 565, 634
Fred Baier, UK: 183
Bang & Olufsen, London: 365
Ch. Bastin & J. Evrard, Brussels: 57
Bauhaus Archiv, Berlin: 353 (photo: Atelier Schneider), 443
Bayer, Leverkusen: 170–171, 545
Bernini, Milan: 633
Galerie Bischofsberger, Zurich: 563
Bonhams, London: 42, 43, 179, 373, 415, 543, 547, 556, 557, 575
Braun, Frankfurt: 131, 132, 133
BRF, Siena: 349
Bridgeman Art Library, London: 146
Neville Brody, London: 140, 141
Torsten Bröhan, Düsseldorf: 15, 22, 23, 26, 29, 92, 99, 101, 102, 107, 122, 126, 176, 177, 206, 213, 257, 264, 346, 447, 492, 523, 605, 696, 704 (left), 704 (right), 719, 720, 732, 737
Buckminster Fuller Archives, USA: 262
Cappellini, Milan: 399, 491
Casabella, Milan: 288
Cassina, Milan: 104, 205, 347, 382, 411, 412, 562
Cathers & Dembrosky, New York: 67, 241, 612, 708
Chermayeff & Geismar, New York: 159, 181
Christies Images, London: 47, 50 (bottom), 60, 69, 81, 189, 190, 256, 270, 275, 306, 323, 416, 455, 468 (top), 475, 502, 521, 616, 642, 669, 670, 700, 740

Luigi Colani, Cologne: 166

The Corning Museum of Glass, Corning: 54

Riccardo Dalisi, Italy: 289

Michele De Lucchi, Milan: 195 (all images)

Fortunato Depero Museum, Rovereto: 266, 267

Design Council/DHRC, University of Sussex: 120, 292

Design Gallery Milano, Milan: 656, 657

Di Palma – Arteluce, Bovezzo: 379, 380

Draenert Studio, Frankfurt: 572, 574

Driade, Milan: 662, 663

Ecart, Paris: 254

Erco, London: 27

Ergonomi Design Gruppen, Stockholm: 244

L. M. Ericsson, Stockholm: 245

Eurolounge, London: 217

Fiell International, London: (photos: Paul Chave): 154, 192, 228, 355, 384, 398, 401, 410, 438, 559, 588, 620, 682,(photos: Peter Hodsoll): 110, 225, 337, 501, 506, 509, (photo: James Barlow): 172, 689, (Mithra Neuman Collection): 226, 233, 505, (Archive): 272, 463

Fifty/50, New York: 366

Fine Arts Society, London: 71

Fischer Fine Art, Vienna: 14, 452, 728

Flos, Bovezzo: 148, 149, 664

Fontana Arte, Corsico: 75, 160

Frederica Stolefabrik, Frederica: 216

Barry Friedman, New York: 13, 50 (top), 51, 52, 53, 56, 70, 84, 85, 90, 91, 95, 118, 119, 127, 136, 142, 156, 157, 201, 202, 203 (top), 203 (bottom), 206, 208, 209, 221, 237, 240, 269, 271, 313, 314, 315, 335, 345 (top), 371, 391, 394, 409 (top), 418, 419, 429, 433, 435, 440, 472, 474, 476, 487, 493 (bottom), 494, 546, 548, 560, 584, 585 (top), 599, 602, 604, 606, 607, 608, 639, 643, 648, 671, 676, 677, 703 (top), 705, 719, 739

Frogdesign, Altensteig: 258, 259

Fusital, Italy: 302

Studio Gavina, Savena: 79

April Greiman, Los Angeles: 77, 143, 303

Gufram, Balangero: 38, 39, 307

Habitat, London: 175

Carl Hansen, Odense: 727 (bottom right)

Fritz Hansen, Allerød: 4–5, 354

Zaha Hadid, London: 204

Haslam & Whiteway, London: 25, 62, 63, 65, 78, 197, 220, 234, 281, 312, 317, 489, 524, 583, 614, 718 (top), 718 (bottom), 723, (The Birkenhead Collection): 24, 64, 196

H. D., USA: 425, 594

Michael Hopkins & Partners, London: 330 (photo: Tim Street-Porter)

Hunterian Art Gallery – University of Glasgow, Glasgow: 434 (photo: Antony Oliver)

IDPA, Barcelona: 424, 697

Iittala, Helsinki: 253, 628, 629, 735

Italiana Luce, Milan: 570

Georg Jensen, Copenhagen: 357, 361, 362, 363 (left), 363 (right), 364

Kartell, Milan: 147, 167, 375, 376, 665

Lillian Kiesler, New York: 378

Klikki, Helsinki: 519 (photo: Ilmari Kostianinen)

Knoll International, New York: 31, 215, 350, 387, 388, 622

Michael Koetzle, Munich: 247

Kunstgewerbemuseum, Berlin: 174 (photo: Saturia Linke)

Kreo, Boulogne: 681 (four images)

Krueger, Greenbay: 37

Kunsthalle, Tübingen: 342 (Sammlung G. F. Zundel)

Landor Associates, New York: 181

Ligne Roset, Paris: 516

Pearson Lloyd, London: 389 (top), 389 (bottom)

Raymond Loewy Associates, London: 181, 426

London Transport Museum, London: 98

Luceplan, Milan: 458

B. Lux, Berrut Bizkaia: 551

Luxo Italiana, Presezzo: 358, 577 (bottom)

John Makepeace, Beaminster: 182, 442

Institut Mathildenhöhe, Darmstadt: 187

Ingo Mauer, Munich: 457

David Mellor, London: 460

Memphis, Milan: 461, 462, 466, 652, 655, 698

Alessandro Mendini, Milan: 467

MetaDesign, Berlin: 470

Metz & Co. Archive, Amsterdam: 537

Herman Miller, Zeeland, Michigan: 155, 227, 229, 230, 232, 324, 325, 326 (bottom), 327, 328, 508, 578, 611, 675

P. P. Møbler, Allerød: 726 (photo: Schakenburg & Brahl), 727 (top left – photo: Schakenburg & Brahl), 727 (top right – photo: Schakenburg & Brahl), 727 (bottom left – photo: Schakenburg & Brahl)

Museé des Arts Décoratifs de Montreal, Montreal: The Liliane and David M. Stewart Collection: 12, 222, 397, 486 (photos: Schecter Lee): 34, 44, 46, 112, 152, 249, 374, 402, 422, 449, 539 (photos: Giles Rivest): 351, 428, 485, 507, 742 (photos: Richard P. Goodbody); gift of Susan A. Chalom: 566 (photo: Giles Rivest); Anonymous gift: 73, 420, 585 bottom (photos: Giles Rivest); Gift of Dr. Luc Martin: 111 (photo: Richard P. Goodbody); Gift of Artemide S. p. A.: 125 (photo: Giles Rivest); Gift of Paul Leblanc: 129 (photo: Giles Rivest), 377 (photo: Richard P. Goodbody); Gift of Geoffrey N. Bradfield: 223, 609 (photos: Giles Rivest), 587 (photo: Richard P. Goodbody), 724 (photo: Schecter Lee); Gift of Geoffrey N. Bradfield/©Eames Office: 231 (photo: Richard P. Goodbody); Gift of the Société des Décorateurs Emsembliers du Québec: 224 (photo: Giles Rivest); Gift of Herman Miller Inc.: 283 (photo: Richard P. Goodbody); Gift of Mr. and Mrs. Roger Labbé: 334 (photo: Giles Rivest); Gift of Jack Lenor Larsen: 406 (photo: Giles Rivest); Gift of Louise Armstrong in memory of Harris Armstrong: 453 (photo: Giles Rivest); Gift of Dr. Arthur Cooperberg: 507 (photo: Richard P. Goodbody); Gift of Fifty/50 Gallery, New York: 507 (photo: Giles Rivest), Gift of Warner & Sons Limited: 672 (photo: Richard P. Goodbody); Gift of Maurice Forget: 699 (photo: Giles Rivest); Gift of Knoll International: 711 (photo: Giles Rivest); Gift of Massimo Vignelli: 714 (photo:

Giles Rivest); Gift of David A. Hanks in memory of David M. Stewart: 725 (photo: Richard P. Goodbody)

The Museum of Modern Art, New York: 108 (Gift of The Lauder Foundation/ Leonard & Evelyn Lauder Fund. Photograph ©1998 The Museum of Modern Art, New York), 109 (Photograph © 1998 The Museum of Modern Art, New York), 115 (Philip Johnson Fund. Photograph © 1998 The Museum of Modern Art, New York), 503 (Photograph by Leo Trachtenberg. Courtesy The Museum of Modern Art, New York), 610 (Gift of Jay Leyda. Photograph ©1998 The Museum of Modern Art, New York), 680 (Photograph ©1998 The Museum of Modern Art, New York), 695 (Gift of the designer. Photograph © 1998 The Museum of Modern Art, New York), 706 (Gift of Philip Johnson, Jan Tschichold Collection. Photograph © 1998 The Museum of Modern Art, New York), 748 (Gift of the manufacturer. Photograph © 1998 The Museum of Modern Art, New York)

Necchi, Pavia: 286

Néotu, Paris: 273, 641, 650

Die Neue Sammlung – Staatliches Museum für angewandte Kunst, Munich: 18, 28, 61, 82, 93, 103, 113, 130 (photo: S. Gnamm), 145, 165, 219, 246, 284, 285, 287, 290, 308, 319, 333, 396, 414, 423, 427, 439, 445 (top), 445 (bottom), 446, 456, 479, 495, 513, 514, 515, 520, 522, 534 (photo: A. Bröhan), 544 (photo: A. Bröhan), 555, 561, 567 (photo: A. Bröhan), 592 (Photo: Hummel), 593, 595, 603, 631, 632, 644, 668, 673, 683 (photo: A. Bröhan), 685 (photo: A. Bröhan), 686, 693, 709 (photo: Hansmann), 721 (photo: A. Bröhan), 738, 747 (photo: Koller)

O-Luce, Milan: 169, 173, 437

Olivetti, Milan: 512, 526, 527, 528 (four images), 529, 635, 654

OMK, London: 381

One-Off, London: 571

Robert Opie Collection, London & Gloucester: 106, 236

Stuart Parr Gallery, New York: 483

Pentagram Design, London: 293, 294, 552, 553 (four images), 729

Gaetano Pesce, New York: 558

Poltronova, Montale: 338, 653

Polygram International, London: 569 (bottom)

Louis Poulsen, Copenhagen: 320, 321

Swid Powell, USA: 296

Private Collection, London: 97, 191, 498, 499, 630

Prospettive, Pisa: 510

Quasar, Paris: 586

Rud. Rasmussen Snedkerier, Copenhagen: 385 (photo: Ole Woldbye), 392

Leah Roland, New York: 248, 731, 733

Bill Rothschild, New York: 207

Royal College of Art, London: 615

Gordon Russell, London: 619

Sabattini Argentaria, Bregnano: 625

SCP, London: 163, 331

Science & Society Picture Library/Science Museum, London: 517

Silver Studio Collection – Middlesex Polytechnic, Middlesex: 649

Sotheby's, London: 35, 66, 80, 162, 164, 297, 298, 299, 304, 311, 316, 352, 386, 390,

403, 404, 417, 454, 464-465, 468 (bottom), 481, 504, 511, 517, 530 (right), 582, 589, 590, 598, 600, 617, 618, 624, 646, 658, 679, 691, 692, 702, 717, 734, 736, 744

St. Bride's Print Library, London: 260, 280, 318

Steelcase Strafor, Colnbrook: 742

Stelton, Hellerup: 356

Stiletto Studios, Berlin: 577 (top)

Tim Street-Porter, New York: 278–279, 301

Studio X, London: 329 (top), 329 (bottom), 430 (photo: José Lasheras), 431 (photo: John Ross), 432, 535 (top), 535 (bottom), 536

Stuhlmuseum Burg Beverungen, Beverungen: 596, 659

Olive Sullivan, London: 569

Svenskt Tenn, Stockholm: 255

Benedikt Taschen Verlag Archiv, Cologne: 55, 58, 59, 74, 77 (top), 83, 86, 87, 88, 89 (photo: Lepkowski), 94, 134 (photo: Lepkowski), 135 (photo: Lepkowski), 137, 138 (photo: Lepkowski), 139 (photo: Lepkowski), 151, 210, 211, 212, 214, 239, 265 (photo: Lepkowski), 305, 309, 332, 369, 372, 383, 395, 407, 421, 450, 451, 477, 478, 493, 540, 579, 580, 581, 590 (photo: Clarissa Bruce) 601 (left), 601 (right), 749, 751

Walter Dorwin Teague Associates, New York: 482

Tecno, Milan: 123, 252

Tecta, Lauenförde: 144, 651

Thonet, Frankenberg: 405

TWA, USA: 621 (top), 621 (bottom)

UPI/Bettmann Archive, London: 343

Venini, Venice: 564, 710

Victoria & Albert Museum, London (Picture Library): 322, 436

Victoria & Albert Museum, London (Press Office): 300, 490, 713

Vitra, Weil am Rhein: 161, 178, 277, 400, 542, 712 (photo: Hans Hansen)

Vitra Design Museum, Weil am Rhein: 326 (top), 532

Westvaco, New York: 291

Wolfsonian Foundation, Miami: 244

Frank Lloyd Wright Foundation, Scottsdale: 741

Zanotta, Milan: 41, 114, 128, 150 (left), 150 (right), 180, 186, 199, 469 (photo: Ramazzotti), 497, 500, 538, 568 (photo: Masera), 607, 678, 687 (photo: Masera)